Phili

# A HISTORY OF THE CHURCH

## To the Eve of the Reformation
### *Philip Hughes*

## *VOLUME III*

Edited by
Paul A. Böer, Sr.

# Veritatis Splendor Publications
*et cognoscetis veritatem et veritas liberabit vos*

A History of the Church to the Eve of the Reformation:  Vol III

The contents of A History of the Church to the Eve of the
Reformation by Philip Hughes is in the public domain.
However, this version is copyrighted.

Philip Hughes

## DEDICATION
# AD MAJOREM DEI GLORIAM
For Lynne, Paul, Margaret, Michael, Juan, and Lily

# CONTENTS

Philip Hughes

# CHAPTER 1: GESTA PER FRANCOS, 1270-1314

## 1. BL. GREGORY X AND THE GENERAL COUNCIL OF LYONS, 1270-1276

IN the summer of the year 1270, terrible news came to France from Africa, and to all Christian Europe. The King of France, St. Louis, had died of fever in the camp before Tunis, and the crusade was over. A world of effort, of sacrifice, and of suffering had gone for just nothing; and something unique had passed from a singularly troubled world. The one leader whom, for his righteousness, all Christendom might have trusted was dead.

In that summer of 1270 the figure of the great French king stood out with especial significance. It was now sixteen years since the last of the emperors had died, vanquished by that papacy which his house had striven to enthrall. In those sixteen years Germany had been given over to anarchy, while the popes, with very varied success, had worked to consolidate their new, precarious, hold on independence. In the end no way had offered itself to them but the old way, the protection of some Christian sovereign's defensive arm. To find some such prince, and install him in southern Italy as king of their vassal state of Sicily, was, then, a first obvious aim of papal policy. No less obviously, St. Louis IX was the ideal champion. Years of negotiation, however, had failed to persuade him to become a partner in any such scheme. The saint was by no means accustomed to accept unquestioningly the papal solutions for political problems. But, in the end, ten years' experience convinced him that, so long as the chaos in southern Italy continued. the popes must be wholly absorbed by the single problem of how to remain independent amid the ceaseless war of political factions. On the other hand, the general affairs of Christendom stood in too urgent need of the papacy's constructive direction for any such papal absorption in Italian politics to be tolerable: the Italian disorder must be ended; and so St. Louis had not only assented to the papal policy but had allowed his youngest brother, Charles of Anjou, to become the pope's man, and to lead a French army into Italy for the defeat of the last remnants of the Hohenstaufen kings of Sicily. [ ]

The pope's chosen champion had now destroyed the pope's enemies -- but the papal problem remained. Already, by the time Charles had to fight his second battle, it was becoming evident to the pope who crowned him and blessed his arms -- Clement IV -- that the victorious champion threatened to be as dangerous to the papal freedom as ever the Hohenstaufen had been. Strong protests against the new king's cruelty and tyranny began to be heard from the apostolic see. This pope, French by birth and for the greater part of his life a highly trusted counsellor of Louis IX, bound closely to the king by similarity of ideals and mutual esteem, was ideally equipped for the difficult task of guiding the new French venture through its first critical years. His sudden death, in November 1268, only two months after Tagliacozzo, was an immense loss; and this swelled into a catastrophe; first of all when the cardinals left the Holy See vacant for as long as three years, [ ] and then when, while the Church still lacked a pope, death claimed St. Louis too. For long there had been no emperor, there was no pope, and now the King of France had died. The last sure hope of checking the ambitions of Charles of Anjou had gone. In St. Louis's place there would reign the rash simplicity of his son, Philip III. Charles would have an open field, every chance he could desire to build up a situation which the future popes would have to accept -- unless they were prepared to start a new war to destroy him, as he had destroyed for them the heirs of Frederick II.

Of the two deaths the more important by far was that of St. Louis. Sanctity is rare in rulers, and rarest of all is the sanctity that shows itself in the perfection of the ruler's characteristic virtue of prudent practical ability. The pope's death found the Church in crisis -- it did not create the crisis; but the French king alone could have brought the papacy and Christendom safely through the crisis. One thing alone could have saved it, and he alone could have done that one thing -- namely, maintain the tradition, now two centuries old, of French support for the popes in the difficulties which arose out of their office as guardians of political morality, while yet refusing to be a mere instrument for the execution of the popes' political judgments. The papacy needed the French -- but it needed also to be independent of them; and Christendom needed that the French should retain their independence too, and not become mere tools of popes who happened to be politicians as well as popes. This difficult and delicate part St. Louis managed to fit to perfection -- as none, before or since, has fitted it. And never was the lack of a prince to fit the part productive of greater mischief than in the twenty-five years that followed his death. For one main event of those years was the reversal of the traditional Franco-Papal entente that had been a source of so much good to both powers and, indeed, a main source of the peace of Christendom.

The Holy See, when Clement IV's death in 1268 delivered it over to the unprecedented calamity of a three years, vacancy, was already gravely embarrassed by the opposition of various Catholic powers to its leading policies. The popes were, for example, determined on a renewal of the crusade; but the great maritime republics of Genoa and Venice were all for peace with the Turks: war would mean the loss of valuable trade, defeat be the end of their commercial empire. The popes, again, had been favourably impressed by the Byzantine emperor's moves to end the schism between Constantinople and Rome that had gone on now for two hundred years; but Charles of Anjou wanted nothing so little as peace with Michael VIII, whom he was planning to supplant as emperor. The Lombard towns were the scenes of continual strife, the feuds bred by generations of civil war still active. The anti-papal forces in these cities found a curious ally in that wing of the great Franciscan movement which demanded a return to the most primitive form of the Franciscan life, and saw in this the kind of life all Church dignitaries ought to lead.

The anarchic element in this movement, which threatened the existence of all ecclesiastical authority, was naturally welcome to rulers who, in every city of Italy, and beyond Italy too, aspired to restore the arbitrary omnipotence of the emperors of ancient Rome and secure thereby the exclusive triumph of material interests. [ ] This active unnatural alliance of Franciscan Spirituals and totalitarian capitalists of one kind and another, the popes were bound to fight; and here they were gravely hampered by a legacy from the papacy's own recent past. In the long struggle against the last great Hohenstaufen emperor, Frederick II, the central authority in the Church, under the popes Gregory IX (1227-1241) and Innocent IV (1243-1254) "saw itself compelled to turn all its activity towards those resources and influences of a temporal kind that were necessary for its defence, and to expand the whole system of its temporal activity in order to secure itself against the attacks of its tireless foe." [ ]

This use, by the Vicar of Christ, of fleets and armies to maintain his independence -- and the chronic need for this use in the "Ages of Faith" -- this willing acceptance by the popes of suzerain status in the feudal world over more or less reluctant royal vassals, John of England in one generation, Charles of Sicily in another; this raising of huge sums of money by loans from bankers and by levies on all the sees of Christendom in turn; this use of the crusade ideal and formulae to describe and characterise wars against European princes who remained the popes' children in the Faith despite their disobedience; all this, to the modern reader, seems often to need a great deal of explanation. And the popes who defended, in this particular way, those rights and that independent status which, undeniably, were the bases of the general recovery of Europe from barbarism, had to meet, as we shall see, much criticism of a similar kind from their own Catholic contemporaries.

Naturally enough the first form the criticism took was resentment, well-nigh universal, at the financial levies. From the moment when, in 1261, the newly elected French pope, Urban IV, began the great move to haul the papacy out of the political slough where he found it, the popes' need of money never ceases. Both the bad effect on those who collected the money, and the resentment of those from whom it was extorted, are henceforth permanent active elements of the state-of-the-Church problem. Already by the time Charles of Anjou had established himself in the kingdom of Sicily (1266) there was -- we can now see -- cause for anxiety on this score.

At the other pole of the main axis of European affairs the French State, too, had its serious chronic problems. The traditional policy which had, by 1270, secured the Capetian kings' uniquely strong hold as rulers of a great nation, has been well described as "the slow collaboration of interests and public opinion." [ ] In a century when popes are to be counted by the dozen, France had been so lucky as to have but two kings and both of them really great rulers. [ ] Their achievement was very great, but it was not complete; and a modern French historian [ ] has well described some elements of the problem St. Louis left to his son, Philip III, and which, aggravated by the fifteen years of this king's weak rule, faced the next king, one of the most enigmatic figures of medieval history. This was Philip the Fair, whose reign (1285-1314) was a turning point in the history of the papacy and the Church. " France was falling to pieces. One after another the institutions upon which the whole fabric rested were breaking up and giving way. . . . Some of the feudatories were as powerful as the king himself, the Duke of Aquitaine, for example, who was also King of England; others, such as the Duke of Brittany or the Count of Flanders, ruled provinces that were really foreign countries in their way of life; in Languedoc the people detested the French. From one end of the country to the other, a myriad contradictory uses, customs, traditions, jurisdictions, privileges contended and struggled; none of them subject to royal regulation. The great mass of the nation was set against the classes that ruled. . . everywhere the national life was disorganised; anarchy seemed imminent, and it seemed only too likely that several important provinces would become independent states or fall under foreign rule."

Philip the Fair would meet his problems with new resources and a wholly new combination of strength and ruse. In his bid to be really master of every element of French life, not only would he come into violent conflict with the papacy -- as other French kings had done in their time -- but he would inaugurate a new tradition in the relations of the principal monarchy in Europe with the Holy See. He would not be the partner of the pope, but his master. In his grandfather, St. Louis, there had been seen the perfection of the older conception, the French king allied with the papacy in an implicit pact of mutual assistance, a true defender of the independence of religion and at the same time just as truly defender of the rights of the French clergy-rights to property -- against the papacy itself. This devotion of St. Louis to the cause of the papacy did not ever entail any blind following of every detail of the papal policies. The king refused to allow Frederick II to capture Lyons while the General Council assembled there that was to condemn him; he even assembled an army in case Frederick should move. But, on the other hand, he did not, once Frederick was condemned and excommunicated and deposed by the pope, offer the pope his aid to carry out the sentence. St. Louis remained carefully neutral. Again "In his relations with the French episcopate, whether it was a matter of fiefs or even of applying disciplinary power, Louis IX showed a care to exercise control, and a susceptibility about his rights which conflicted only in appearance with his zeal for the interests of religion. It was his conviction that the prerogatives of the crown were necessary to the good order of the community, and thus the saint made it as much a matter of conscience to defend them well as to use them rightly; the prestige of those to whom religious jurisdiction was confided did not obscure the saint's clear vision of what was right, and in all matters he paid less attention to the noisy demands of the representatives of the clergy than to the canonical rules which ought to be the inspiration of their conduct." [ ]

Such was the delicate situation and such the prince lost to the Church, to Christendom no less than to France, on August 25, 1270. Charles of Anjou, supreme for the moment, took charge of the crusade. He made a pact with the Sultan which brought the whole affair to an end (October 20) and, a month later, re-embarked the armies and sailed back to Europe.

Meanwhile, at Viterbo, the papal election continued to drag on. Holy men appeared to harangue and to warn the sixteen cardinals. The General of the new Servite Friars, St. Philip Benizi, fled from the offer of the honour. The kings of France and Sicily tried what a personal visit might effect. Then the people of Viterbo, in desperation with the cardinals' indifference to the scandal caused by their incompetence, took a hand and stripped of its roof the palace where the electors met. At last, on September 1, 1271, the cardinals gave power to a commission of six of their number to elect a pope, and that same day the six found their man. He was Theobaldo Visconti, not a cardinal, nor a bishop, nor even a priest, but the Archdeacon of Liege; and at this moment away in the Holy Land, encouraging the heir to the English crown in the forlorn hours of the last of the crusades. It was weeks before the archdeacon heard of his election, and months before he landed in Italy to be ordained, consecrated and crowned as Pope Gregory X (March 27, 1272).

The new pope, a man perhaps sixty years of age, was one of those figures whose unexpected entry into the historical scene seems as evident a sign of God's care for mankind as was ever the appearance of a prophet to Israel of old. He was largehearted, he was disinterested, a model of charity in his public life no less than in private, free from any taint of old political associations, simple, energetic, apostolic. His first anxiety was the restoration of Christian rule in the East: to this the European situation was secondary. But for the sake of the Crusade, the European complications must be speedily resolved, despite all the vested interests of long-standing feuds. In this work of reconciliation Gregory X's apostolic simplicity, and his aloofness from all the quarrels of the previous thirty years, gave to the papal action a new strength. A vision now inspired it that transcended local and personal expediency.

There was, the pope saw, no hope for the future of Catholicism in the Holy Land, no hope of holding off the Saracen from fresh conquests, so long as Rome and Constantinople remained enemies; and it was the first action of his reign to take up, and bring to a speedy conclusion, those negotiations to end the schism which had trailed between the two courts for now many years. That this policy of reunion, an alliance with the Greek emperor, Michael VIII, cut clean across the plans of Charles of Anjou to renew the Latin empire at Constantinople, with himself as emperor, and across his pact with Venice to divide up the Christian East between them, did not for a moment daunt the pope. Nor did the claims of Alfonso X of Castile to be emperor in the West hinder the pope from a vigorous intervention in Germany which resulted in the unchallenged election of Rudolf of Habsburg, and a close to nineteen years of civil war and chaos. A Germany united and at peace with itself was a fundamental condition of a peaceful Christendom.

This admirable pope knew the problems of Franco-German Europe by personal experience, from the vantage point of life in the middle lands that lay between the rival cultures. His direct diplomacy had thwarted the plan of Charles of Anjou to force the election of his nephew, the King of France, as emperor, and now the pope so managed the diplomatic sequence to the election of Rudolf of Habsburg that it brought these rivals into friendly collaboration. And he managed, also, in a personal interview at Beaucaire, to soothe the disappointed Alfonso of Castile.

Nowhere, at any time, did Gregory X's action leave behind it resentment or bitterness.

The Crusade, reunion of the separated churches of the East, and the reform of Catholic life, thrown back everywhere by the fury of the long war with the Hohenstaufen, were Gregory X's sole, and wholly spiritual, anxieties. Christendom must be organised anew, refitted throughout for the apostolic work that lay ahead. The first, most obvious step, was to survey its resources, to study its weaknesses and then find suitable remedies. This would best be done in a General Council, and only four days after Gregory's coronation the letters went out to kings and prelates, convoking a council to meet at Lyons in the summer of 1274.

Gregory X is, above all else, the pope of this second General Council of Lyons. Nowhere in his well-filled reign is his largehearted trust in the better side of human nature more evident, his confidence that charity and a right intention in the pope would call out the same virtues in others. And certainly the greatest charity was needed in whoever hoped to heal the long, poisoned dissension that kept the churches of the East estranged from Rome. The schism, in its causes, went back centuries. Latin despised Greek as shifty and treacherous: Greek despised Latin as barbarous and uncivilised. The association of the two during the various crusades had steadily sharpened the antagonism. Finally there was the memory of the Latin conquest of Constantinople in 1204, the sack of the great city, the massacres, the expulsion of the Greek ruler and his replacement by a Latin, with a Latin bishop enthroned as patriarch in the see of Photius and Cerularios. That Latin regime had endured for less than sixty years. On July 25, 1261, the Greeks had returned under Michael VIII. Constantinople fell to him with scarcely a struggle, and with the Latin empire there crashed the Latin ecclesiastical establishment. That the immediate reaction of the then pope -- Urban IV -- himself a one-time Latin patriarch of Jerusalem, was to plan a great crusade of recovery, was most natural. That never before in their history were the Greeks so hostile to the Latins, was natural no less. And if this was the moment when Michael VIII proposed to the pope to bring the schism to an end, the observer might see in his action no more than the clearest of signs that the Greek emperor realised how slender was his hold on the new conquest. The King of France -- St. Louis -- had taken the cross in response to Pope Urban's appeal; and Venice, the real author of the piratical conquest of 1204, was also actively preparing. No pope, however, would hesitate between a restoration of obedience forced at the sword's point and a general return to obedience on the part of Constantinople and all its dependent churches. Michael's shrewd move held up the military expedition. From the day when Urban IV sent his Franciscan envoys to discuss Michael's proposal (28 July, 1263) the emperor knew his immediate danger was past.

Urban IV died (October 2, 1264) before much more had been done than to make clearer than clear how diverse were the intentions of emperor and pope. Michael had proposed first of all to complete the work of national unity; to drive out of the imperial territories, that is to say, what Latin rulers still remained. Urban thought that the religious reunion should come first.

Once a new pope was elected, Clement IV (February 5, 1265), Michael was able to begin all over again. It was a great advantage that Clement's plans for a crusade were directed to an expedition against the Holy Land itself. Constantinople now seemed secure against any western attack, and the emperor could safely begin the theological hedging and jousting. The Greeks, seemingly, proposed a council in which the differences of belief should be discussed. The pope replied, in the traditional Roman way, that the Faith being a thing that was settled, such discussionwas impossible. The pope's ambassadors could indeed go into the questions raised by the Greeks and, once the union was a fact, there could be a council to ratify it. And Clement sent a declaration of faith to the emperor (March 1267).

Constantinople was, however, at this moment in the throes of an ecclesiastical upheaval, which produced three successive patriarchs in eighteen months. Politics had the main share in this and now, unfortunately, although the patriarch in possession was a strong supporter of Michael as emperor, he had the disadvantage of being violently anti-Latin. Michael, perforce, must go slowly; and then, while he was considering Clement's reply, the pope died (29 November, 1268) and there began one of the longest vacancies the Holy See has ever known. [ ]

If the long vacancy solved, for Michael, the immediate problem how to frame a submission to Rome that would be palatable also to his patriarch, it raised once more the problem of the security of his empire from western attacks. His chief danger in the West lay in the King of Sicily, Charles of Anjou. For this leading Guelf had no sooner overcome the Sicilian Ghibelline (1266), than he began to show himself, in the East, a most faithful follower of Ghibelline policy. To all the kings of Sicily-Norman, Hohenstaufen, and now Angevin -- the emperor at Constantinople was the traditional enemy. It was an antagonism that went back before the crusades, dating from those days when the Normans first conquered from the Greek emperor these Italian lands. And when the Sicilian kingdom fell to kings who were also German emperors, the traditional Mediterranean policy they inherited cut across the simplicities of the papally planned crusade. For these imperialists were enemies, first, of Byzantium. They might conquer the Turk ultimately, but their present thought was rather the Eastern Empire. An assault of this kind had been in the mind of the Emperor Henry VI when death so prematurely carried him off (1197). Seven years later, with the active assistance of his brother, the Emperor Philip, the plan was realised and Constantinople torn from the Greeks -- though not to the profit of Sicily. In the next generation Frederick II, Henry's son was the champion of the imperialistic idea and, surrendering the whole substance of the crusade, he negotiated a settlement with the Turks without any pretence of destroying their power. And now the conqueror of Frederick II's heirs was showing himself just as hostile to Byzantium, just as openly averse to any war against the Turks.

In 1267, while Clement IV and Michael VIII were seemingly planning a reunion of Latin west and Greek east, Charles began to style himself King of Jerusalem, and made the claim that he was heir to the last Latin emperor of the East. He was carefully building up a strong position for the future, gathering in claims and rights which, once Michael VIII was conquered, would become political realities. Clement out of the way, what should stay him? By the spring of 1270 his plans were completed, and to Michael VIII the end seemed very near. In his desperation he appealed to the cardinals and also to St. Louis. The saint, sympathetic to the scheme for reunion, and ever the enemy of such schemes of realpolitik as Charles of Anjou was promoting, halted his brother most effectively by summoning him to take his place in the crusade then preparing against Tunis.

St. Louis' tragic death (25 August, 1270) set Charles free to renew his efforts against Michael VIII, and he had already done much by negotiations with the Latin princes in Achaia and the Peloponnesus, when he met the greatest check of all, the election as pope of one resolved, before all else, to bring together Greek and Latin to defend Christendom against their common foe the Turk. Charles might now style himself King of Albania, and ally himself with Michael's Greek rivals (1272), and even send Angevin forces and some of his own Saracen archers to attack Michael in Greece (1273): the new pope had passed too speedily from desires to action, the work of the Council of Lyons was a political fact, and on May 1, 1275 the King of Sicily was compelled to sign a truce with Michael.

The motives of the Greek emperor in offering his submission to the various popes and so proposing to bring to an end the schism that had endured for two hundred and twenty years were, then, evidently no more than political. Such practical statesmen as Urban IV and Clement IV would no doubt have grasped this, and acted accordingly, long before any formal act of reunion was completed. Gregory X was more optimistic than such papal realists. He readily listened to Michael VIII's new offers and sent a distinguished commission of theological experts and diplomatists to Constantinople to initiate the good work.

The four envoys [ ] -- Friars Minor -- took with them the creed or profession of faith, drafted by Clement IV. This the emperor, the bishops, and the people were to accept, and thereupon emperor and prelates were to take their places at the coming council. The arrival of this commission at Constantinople was the beginning of an immense theological excitement. It was immediately evident that the bishops would by no means obey mechanically any order from the emperor to submit themselves.

The leading theological question was the Latin doctrine that the Holy Ghost proceeds from the Father and the Son, or rather whether the Latins had any right to express this doctrine by adding to the so-called creed of the Council of Nicaea the words "and from the Son". [ ] The Greek bishops began by denying their right to do so, and gave the Latins an ultimatum to end the scandal by withdrawing the phrase. The emperor then took charge, and explained to his bishops, in private, that if this proposed arrangement with the Latins fell through, the empire was lost. As to the Latin formulae, no one could object to them as a matter of conscience, for the doctrines they expounded were perfectly orthodox. And he brought theological authority, and also earlier declarations of the Greek episcopate, to support the statement. The most learned man of the day was John Beccos, the chartophylax, [ ] and to him the bishops now looked for the reply that would non-suit the emperor's plea. Beccos, however, contented neither party. He did not refute the emperor; but he declared the Latins to be heretics. Whereupon Michael ordered his imprisonment. The patriarch, for his part, organised his bishops to refute the emperor's case and all swore an oath to resist the proposed union.

The prospects of reunion seemed slight indeed. But the emperor could not afford not to buy off the danger that threatened from Sicily and Venice. He was helped by the conversion of Beccos to his views. In prison the chartophylax had set himself to study in the Greek Fathers the doctrine of the processions in the Blessed Trinity. St. Athanasius, St. Cyril and St. Maximus attested that the Latin teaching was the Catholic faith. Beccos, thereupon, revoked his judgment that the Latins were heretics and became the emperor's most enthusiastic aid. While the convert argued with the bishops for the orthodoxy of the Latin position, Michael tried a mixture of diplomacy and pressure. All that would be asked of them, he asserted, was a recognition of the primacy of the Roman see, of Rome's right to judge all cases in final appeal, and that they should pray for the pope publicly in the liturgy. It was in this last point that the final difficulty lay. The popes had tampered with the sacred wording of the creed: how could an orthodox bishop give them any countenance? Michael retorted by threatening the opposition with the penalties of high treason; at the same time he pledged himself that the bishops would not be asked to add so much as an iota to the creed. Reassured, the bishops consented now to accept the emperor's three points; also to make a joint protestation of obedience to the pope.

When the Greek deputation reached Lyons (24 June, 1274) the council had been in session for seven weeks. It had opened on May 7 with elaborate ceremonial and a sermon from the pope. Then, on May 18, it had passed the decree establishing the point of faith about the Filioque, [ ] and on June 7 twelve decrees regulating the procedure to be followed in elections of bishops and abbots.

The arrival of the Greeks interrupted these legislative proceedings. The ambassadors were received with solemn ceremony; they presented the letters from the emperor and the Greek bishops; they declared they had come to show their obedience to the Roman Church and to learn from it the true faith. Five days later was the feast of SS. Peter and Paul. At the mass, sung by the pope, the epistle and gospel were chanted in Greek as well as Latin, and the credo likewise (with the Filioque clause repeated three times by the Greeks). St. Bonaventure preached a great sermon. On the octave day, July 6, the formal act of reunion and reconciliation took place. The letters from Constantinople were read; in the emperor's, he repeated the creed sent to him by the pope and declared it to be the true faith, accepted as such by him because it came from the Roman church. He pledged his eternal fidelity to this doctrine, his obedience to the papal primacy. In return he asked that the Greeks be allowed to keep the creed unaltered by any reference to the procession of the Holy Ghost from God the Son, and also that their ancient rite be left untouched. And the emperor's ambassador confirmed all this by an oath made in his master's name.

The General Council which met at Lyons in 1274 was summoned as a great assize to find means for the restoration of Catholic life no less than for the recovery of the Holy Land. With this in view, Gregory X had asked bishops in various countries to send in statements setting out the main reasons for the spiritual decay which he deplored, and to propose remedies.

By far the greater part of the reforms enacted in the thirty decrees of the Council [ ] have reference to evils in the life of the clergy. . The pope, indeed, was to bring the council to a close with a sermon in which he declared that bad bishops were the principal cause of all that was wrong. [ ] In the council he made no scruple about a direct attack on scandal in the highest place of all, the negligence of the cardinals in allowing vacancies of the Holy See to drag on for months and for years. On more than one occasion already, the faithful people had intervened to coerce the indifference of the cardinals by locking them up until they came to a decision, and a decree of the council [ ] now authorised and regularised these extreme measures, imposing the conclave as the rule henceforward. On the death of the pope the cardinals present in the city where he died were to await ten days, but no more, for their absent brethren. Then, with but a single servant each, they were to take up their residence in the palace, living together in a single locked room without any curtains or screens to shut off any part of it. This conclave [ ] was to be so arranged that none might enter or leave it unseen by the rest, that there would be no means of access to the electors or of secret communications with them; no cardinal must admit any visitor except such as were allowed in by the whole body to treat of the arrangement of the conclave. The new pope -- so Gregory X seems to have intended -- would thus be speedily elected, for his law next provides that should the election be delayed beyond three days "which God forbid', the cardinals' food was to be restricted to a single dish at each of their two daily meals; after five days more they were to be given only bread with wine and water. There are regulations for the admission of latecomers, for the care of sick cardinals who may leave and then wish to return. The cardinals are forbidden to occupy themselves with any other business than the election, and all pacts or conventions made between them are declared null, even though they be confirmed with an oath. Nor is any cardinal to receive anything of his ecclesiastical revenues as long as the vacancy of the Holy See endures; these are sequestrated and at the disposal of the future pope. Finally, in order that these provisions may not become a dead letter, the responsibility for providing the conclave and guarding it is laid on the civic authority of the town where it takes place; heavy penalties being provided for those who over-act the rigour towards the cardinals which the new law demands.

The cardinals objected strongly to the proposed law, and for a time there was a brisk duel between them and the pope, each striving to enlist supporters from among the bishops. And it would seem that the general sense of the council was against the reform as proposed, for it was not promulgated until some months after the council had dispersed.

The most usual way of appointing bishops or abbots was still, in 1274, by an election, where the canons or monks had each a vote. A whole series of decrees enacted in this council shows the many serious abuses which affected the system, and how thoroughly, in these last years before something was devised in its place, the Holy See strove to reform them. Appeals against elections (or provisions) to churches are to be made in writing and to be countersigned by witnesses who swear their own belief in the truth of the objections made and that they can prove this: penalties are provided for those who fail to make good their charges. [ ] The elect must await confirmation before entering upon his charge. [ ] He is to be informed of his election as soon as possible, to signify his acceptance within a month, and, under penalty of losing the place, seek confirmation within three months. [ ] Voters who knowingly vote for one who is unworthy sin mortally, and are liable to severe punishment. [ ] No voter is allowed to appeal against the one for whom he has voted -- certain special cases apart. [ ] Far too many appeals are sent to Rome where the motive is not really serious. This practice is to cease [ ] and in cases where a double election has been made no objection will be allowed for the future against the majority on the score of lack of zeal, of worth, or of authority, where the majority numbers two-thirds of the voters. [ ] If objection be made that there is an evident defect, whether of due knowledge or otherwise, there must be an immediate enquiry into this. Should the objection be shown devoid of foundation, those who made it lose all right to pursue any further objection they have raised, and they are to be punished as though they had failed to prove the whole of their objections. [ ] Finally, to protect the successful against the malice of the disappointed, it is laid down that those who revenge themselves on electors for not supporting them by pillaging the electors' property or that of the Church or of the electors' relatives, or who molest the electors or their families are by the very fact excommunicated. [ ]

The elective system was already beginning to raise problems almost as serious as those it solved. In another hundred years it would have disappeared in the greater part of the Church, and bishops be directly appointed or "provided" by the pope. The foundation of the new system was the decree Licet (1268) of Gregory X's immediate predecessor Clement IV, a lawyer pope who had come to the service of the Church after a great career as jurist and administrator in the service of St. Louis IX. By that decree Clement IV had reserved to the Holy See the appointment to all benefices vacated by death, if the holder at the time he died had been a member of the Roman curia or had died in the city where the curia then was. [ ] This new law had caused much dissatisfaction among the bishops, no less than among other patrons of benefices. At the General Council they strove to have it revoked. But though Gregory X was not, apparently, unsympathetic, he would do no more than modify it slightly, [ ] and allow that vacancies falling under the reservation might be filled by the patron if the pope had failed to fill them within a month from the holder's death. [ ]

What of the man appointed? and especially of the man who was the foundation of the whole system, the parish priest? It had already been laid down, a hundred years before this time, [ ] that no one must be appointed to a parish who was younger than twenty-five. But this law had too often been disregarded, and so the Council now declared [ ] that all appointments which violated the law were null and of no effect. It also reminded the nominee that he was bound to live in his parish and, if he were not a priest already, that he must seek ordination within a year or else ipso facto lose his benefice. Non-residence of beneficiaries -- of bishops and of parish priests especially -- was one of the chronic weaknesses of the seemingly powerful structure of medieval Catholicism. The popes never succeeded in their war against it, nor against the related mischief that the same man held more than one benefice: only too often, indeed, policy led the different popes to connive at these evils, and in the end, more almost than anything else, it was these that brought the imposing structure down to the dust. At Lyons, in 1274, laws were made to control the pluralist. No parish was to be given in commendam [ ] unless to a priest; he must be of the canonical age of twenty-five and not already provided with a parish in commendam, and the necessity (on the part of the Church) must be evident; furthermore such appointments are good for six months only. Any Contravention of these conditions invalidates the appointment ipso iure. [ ] As to pluralists -- clerics who hold more than one benefice -- bishops are to make a general enquiry and if one of the benefices held entails a cure of souls, the holder is to produce the dispensation authorising this. If this is not forthcoming, all but the first received of his benefices are to be taken as vacant and given to others. If, however, he is lawfully authorised he may retain all he lawfully holds, but it is put upon the bishop's conscience to see that the cure of souls is not neglected. Bishops are specifically warned to make certain, when they confer a benefice that entails a cure of souls, that if the beneficiary already holds such a benefice he is dispensed to hold the second with a dispensation which explicitly mentions his possession of the first cura animarum. [ ]

Episcopal control of the clergy is strengthened by a canon which forbids bishops to ordain another bishop's subjects without his leave: bishops who transgress, lose automatically the right to ordain at all for twelve months. [ ] The clergy are given a useful protection against the bishop in a new rule [ ] about visitation expenses. Bishops were already allowed to exact a certain support in kind when they made the official visitation of a parish. The custom was, however, developing of asking money or gifts;

another abuse was to exact procurations -- the payments in kind -
without making the visitations. The council deals with these
abuses (already noted and condemned by Innocent IV) by
decreeing that all who have exacted these unlawful presents must
restore double their amount to the victims. If the restitution is not
made within a month, the bishop loses all right to enter a church
until payment is made; his officials, if they are guilty, are
suspended from office and benefice. Nor is any willingness of
the injured party to remit the amount due, or part of it, to affect
the automatic operation of the law.

Clerical immunity from the jurisdiction of the lay ruler was an
ancient institution more and more contested in the last centuries
of the Middle Ages. Gregory X at Lyons made a concession to
the princes, enacting [ ] that the cleric in minor orders who
contracted a second marriage lost all his clerical privileges and
was henceforth wholly their subject. On the other hand, another
canon [ ] denouncing yet again [ ] the barbarous custom called
'reprisals', -- by which, if the guilty party were beyond the law's
power, the nearest innocent members of the community were
made to suffer in his stead -- fixed a special penalty of
excommunication and interdict for those who subjected
ecclesiastics to this abuse.

There are two new laws to safeguard Church property, whether
from lay rapacity or from cowardly negligence on the part of the
clergy who should be its special defenders. Excommunication is
henceforward to fall automatically on anyone -- whatever his
rank -- who, unauthorised, takes upon himself the occupation and
administration of the property of a vacant see or abbey, and also
upon the clerics or monks who abet this usurpation. Those who
enjoy such right of administration are warned not to go beyond
their right, and that they are bound not to neglect the properties
entrusted to their care. [ ] The second law [ ] forbids prelates --
without the leave of their chapter and the Holy See -- to make
over their lands to the lay lord as the price of his protection,

retaining for the Church a mere use of the property. All contracts of this kind hitherto made without leave are now annulled, even though confirmed with an oath. Offending prelates are to suffer a three years suspension from their office and their revenues, and the lords who force such contracts upon them, or who have not restored what they obtained through past contracts of this sort, are excommunicated.

The reform legislation of the Council did not only touch the layman in his relations with the clergy. In two canons, on usury and usurers, it strove to halt a mischief that lay at the very roots of social life. Already, by a law of 1179, as the Council recalls, the notorious usurer [ ] was barred from the sacraments, and if he died he was forbidden Christian burial, and the clergy were not allowed to take offerings from him. These prohibitions had been largely ignored, and now, not only are they renewed, but it is forbidden [ ] to states and rulers to allow usurers to take up residence within their territories, or to allow those already there to remain. Within three months they must be expelled. If the lord is an ecclesiastic, disregard of this new law entails automatically suspension from his office, a lay lord incurs excommunication, and a community or corporation interdict. As for the usurer himself, [ ] he is not to have Christian burial, even though his will directs that restitution be made, until this has actually been done or substantial pledges given according to forms now provided. Members of religious orders -- and others too -- who bury usurers in disregard of this law are themselves to be punished as usurers. Unless a usurer first make restitution, or give a real guarantee that he will do so, no one is to witness his will or hear his confession, or absolve him. If his will does not provide for restitution it is, by the fact, null and void.

There is also a canon [ ] about conduct in church and abuses of the church fabric from which much may be gleaned about the day to day religious life of the time. Churches are places built for prayer, places where silence should reign, and this especially during the time of mass. All are to bow their heads in reverence whenever the holy name of Jesus Christ is pronounced, especially during the mass. The church is not to be used for secular purposes, such as meetings, or parliaments, nor as a court of law; if trials are held there the sentences rendered are, ipso facto, null and void. Churchyards are not to be used for fairs. It is a terrible thing, says the canon, if places set apart for man to ask forgiveness for his sins become to him occasions of further sin. This canon inaugurated the popular devotion to the Holy Name, and the great confraternity still so flourishing, founded by the Dominicans at the command of Gregory X [ ] to further the devotion.

Five of the remaining canons are directed to the reform of legal procedure; most of them relate to the law governing the punishment of excommunication. Excommunication is not incurred by those who hold intercourse with the excommunicated unless these have been excommunicated by name. This is a clarification of a canon of the last General Council. [ ] Absolution, from any censure, which has been extorted by violence or threats is not only null and void absolutely, but also involves those using such threats in a further excommunication. [ ] Those who give permission to their servants or subjects to murder, imprison or injure in any way, whether it be the officials responsible for a sentence of excommunication against them, or relatives of the officials, or those who refuse all intercourse with them since the excommunication, are by the fact excommunicated a second time; so too are those who carry out these orders. If within two months they have not sought absolution from this second excommunication, they can only be absolved from it by the Holy See. [ ] Another new law [ ] is directed to check the hastiness of ecclesiastics in issuing penalties whose effects are general. Canons who, as a punishment, propose to suspend the church services, must now give notice of this in writing, with their reasons, to the person or persons against whom this action is directed. If the canons fail to do this, or if the reasons assigned are insufficient, they lose all right to their revenues for the time the services were suspended and must moreover make satisfaction for any losses thereby incurred to those they meant to punish. Also, and here is a reference to a superstitious instinct not yet wholly departed from our midst, it is most strictly forbidden to emphasise the fact of the divine displeasure, to which the suspension of offices supposedly testifies, by such detestable practices as treating the sacred images irreverently -- for example, throwing them to the ground and covering them with nettles and thorns. This the bishops are to punish with the utmost severity.

To check the growing tendency to drag out law suits by maliciously contrived delays, and thereby to fleece the litigant, the council now enacted a most stringent canon. All advocates and proctors are henceforward to declare on oath, not only that they will do their utmost for their client, but also that should anything transpire in the course of the trial to convince them that his cause is not just, they will immediately withdraw from the case. This oath is to be taken at the opening of every judicial year, and heavy penalties are provided for neglect to do so or for any breach of the oath. Also, the canon fixes maximum fees for both advocates and proctors and puts upon them the obligation to restore anything accepted in excess of these amounts -- again under heavy penalties. [ ]

Perhaps the Council's most important piece of legislation, after the law establishing the conclave, was the twenty-third canon Religionum diversitatem nimiam, on the new religious orders. From the moment when religious -- men formed by the discipline of the monastic vows and life -- had first begun to give themselves to the apostolic work of preaching the gospel and reconciling sinners to God, there had been trouble with the parochial clergy whose peculiar business and charge this work had always been. It was from among the religious that the missionaries had come who had converted the West from heathendom. On their labours was built the greater part of the present fabric of parishes and sees. It was the religious who was the trained man, in the early Middle Ages, the parochial priest the more or less well-gifted amateur; and as with habits of life so was it with professional learning. The vast mass of the parochial clergy had nothing like the chances of study which were open to the monk. The revival of learning which produced the universities no doubt improved their chances enormously, and indeed it was the chief function of the universities to educate the clergy. But, even so, universities were never so many that the whole body of the clergy passed through them. And long before the medieval universities reached the peak of their achievement as seminaries for the education of the parochial clergy, St. Dominic first and then St. Bonaventure had provided the church with a new kind of religious who was primarily a missionary priest, and the last word in the professional clerical sciences and arts, theologian, preacher and confessor. By the time of the Council of Lyons in 1274 Dominican and Franciscan priests were to be numbered by tens of thousands, and almost as numerous again were the priests of other new orders that had sprung up in imitation. Some of the new orders were as admirable as the models which had inspired them. Others were less so. For very different reasons the appearance of both types ruffled the peace of the clerical mind.

Already sixty years before the Council of Lyons, the Church had shown itself anxious and troubled by the task of controlling the new spiritual enthusiasm as it showed itself in the new missionary brotherhoods. These were almost always lay movements in origin; rarely was it to a priest that the inspiration to) lead this kind of life seemed to come. If there was zeal in plenty in these movements there was rarely any theological learning, or any appreciation that this was at all necessary for the preacher. Very often there was a definite anti-clerical spirit; sometimes there was heresy too. For very many reasons, then, the first rumours that a new brotherhood had been formed to preach penance and the remission of sins, and that it was sweeping all before it in some city of Languedoc or Umbria, can hardly have brought anything but deep anxiety to the Roman curia or to its head.

When the bishops poured into Rome for the General Council of 1215 they brought with them from every see of Christendom the tale of disputes between clergy and religious. Sixty years later, with the new mendicant missionary orders at the flood of their first fervent activity, they took similar tales to Lyons. From Olmuc in Bohemia, for example, came complaints that the Dominicans and Franciscans had gradually ousted the parochial clergy from all contact with their people. Baptism was the only sacrament for which the parish priest was ever approached. And where the people went, there they took their offerings. The bishop's suggestions, in this instance, were drastic indeed. These mendicant orders should lose their general power to hear confessions, or to preach except in the parish churches. Only those should preach or hear confessions whom the local bishop chose and authorised. Nor should any new friary be founded without the local bishop's leave.

The mendicants no doubt put forward once again the solid reason for their admittedly wide privileges; once they lost their exemption from all jurisdiction but that of the pope, how long would they survive in a world where there were bishops? In France, in the early days, the Dominicans, for example, found themselves treated just as layfolk, bidden to attend mass on Sundays, with the rest, in the parish church, and to confess to the parish priest as other parishioners were bound. [ ] Twenty years nearly before this time (1274) the differences between clergy and mendicants had blown into a great conflagration at Paris, where the university had demanded from the pope all but the suppression of the orders and, at the pope's bidding, St. Thomas and St. Bonaventure had stated the orders' case. Now, at Lyons, the question was raised again: it had already become, what it was to remain for centuries, one of the chronic problems of the Church, and one of the chronic evidences how harsh a soil human nature is to divine charity.

The decree now enacted deals drastically with all abuses, with institutes inaugurated in despite of existing law, and with lawfully founded institutes which have degenerated or seem to be tending that way. But it goes out of its way to protect and to praise the two great orders of St. Dominic and St. Francis.

The Council of 1215 -- says the new law -- had forbidden [ ] the foundation of any new orders. This prohibition was now renewed, because, despite that law, rashness and presumption had brought into existence an unbridled mob of new orders -- of new mendicants especially -- who did not deserve approbation. Therefore, for the future, no one is to found any new order, or to enter one if such be founded. All orders and mendicant orders founded since 1215 and not approved by the Holy See are abolished, Those founded since and approved by the Holy See, and which live by alms collected from the general public and whose rule forbids them any rents or possessions, and to whom an insecure mendicity through public begging affords a living, must now follow this rule, namely members already professed may continue to live this life, but no more novices are to be received; no new houses are to be opened; no properties may be alienated without leave of the Holy See, for these properties the Holy See intends to use in aid of the Holy Land, or the poor and for other pious purposes. Any violation of this rule entails excommunication, and acts done in violation of it are legally void. Moreover, members of these orders are forbidden to preach to those outside their ranks, or to hear their confessions, or to undertake their funeral services. This 23rd canon, it is expressly declared, does not however extend to the Dominicans and Franciscans whose usefulness to the Church in general (it is explicitly said) is evident. As for the Carmelites, and the Hermits of St. Augustine, whose foundation dates back beyond the

Lateran Council of 1215, they may continue as they now are until further decision about them is taken. A general scheme, says the canon, is in preparation that will affect them and indeed all the orders, non-mendicants included. Meanwhile members of the orders to whom this new rule now made applies, are given generally a permit to enter other approved orders. But no order or convent is to transfer itself as a whole without special leave of the Holy See.

## 2. THE SHADOW OF ANJOU, 1276-1285

Gregory X died at Arezzo. January 10. 1276, on his way back from France to Rome. Only eleven days later the cardinals, putting into execution for the first time the new law of the conclave, unanimously elected the Friar Preacher, Peter of Tarentaise. This first Dominican pope was a Frenchman. He took the name of Innocent V and reigned for just five months. There was a short interval of three weeks and the cardinal deacon Ottoboni Fieschi, a nephew of Innocent IV was elected -- Adrian V (11 July). His reign was one of the shortest of all: he was dead in seven weeks, before he had even been ordained priest. For the third time that year the cardinals assembled, and elected now a Portuguese, the one-time Archbishop of Braga, Peter Juliani, who has his place in the history of scholastic philosophy as Peter of Spain. He took the name of John XXI but, scarcely more fortunate than the other two popes, he reigned only eight months. On May 20, 1277 the ceiling of his library fell in and the pope was killed.

These short pontificates wrought much harm to the still fragile restoration of Gregory X. In all the elections of that fateful year, Charles of Anjou was active. Both the French pope and the Portuguese showed themselves much more sympathetic to his policy than Gregory had been; Innocent V favouring him in Italy and John XXI, apparently, willing to forward his designs on the Eastern empire. But nowhere was the change in the personality of the pope more to be deplored than in the most delicate matter of all, Rome's relations with the newly reconciled Eastern churches. Here John XXI showed himself heavy handed and perhaps made inevitable the action of his successors that was to wreck the whole work within the next five years.

A more certain -- but accidental -- effect of John's short reign was to revive the abuse of over-long vacancies in the Holy See. The cardinals' opposition to Gregory X's conclave regulation had been strong. Their criticism now brought John XXI to suspend it, meaning to provide a new rule. His sudden death found the cardinals without any rules at all to bind them and the Holy See was thereupon vacant six months (20 May-25 November, 1277).

The pope ultimately elected was John Gaetani Orsini, one of the most experienced diplomatists in the curia, a cardinal for more than thirty years, who took the name of Nicholas III. None since Innocent IV (1243-1254) had come to the high office with such -- extensive knowledge of the curial routine, of the major problems of the time and the personalities around whom they turned. Nicholas had been Innocent IV's close companion in his exile, [ ] and in 1258 had played a great part, as legate, in the national histories of France and of England at the time of Simon de Montfort's first triumph. Since the death of Clement IV (1268) he had been the strong man of the curia, a force to be reckoned with in all the subsequent elections. He is credited with the election of John XXI and in that pope's short reign was, indeed, the power behind the throne. Through all the years that followed Charles of Anjou's introduction into the politics of church defence Nicholas III had been his warm supporter. But events during the several vacancies of 1276 had chilled his enthusiasm. He was now critical, if not hostile, and certainly awakened from the simplicity he had shared with the scholarly French and Portuguese popes, whose inexperience of politics failed to read beneath the surface of Charles's courtesy and seeming submissiveness. The facts were that the King of Sicily's diplomacy had begun definitely to check Rudolf of Habsburg in Germany; that he was once again menacing the Greek emperor and that his power overshadowed all Italy. Charles now took the style of King of Jerusalem, Hugh III having abandoned the mainland and retired to Cyprus, and sent to Acre as his vicar, Roger de St. Severin. The Templars of Venice supported him and the barons of the kingdom had no choice but to do him homage. Of the two great questions of the day, not the crusade seemed now the more urgent but the freedom of the Papal State, and the indefinitely more important thing bound up with this, namely, the freedom of the papal action and so of religion everywhere. It was to be the main aim of Nicholas III to check this new advance of the King of Sicily.

Presently immense plans for the future organisation of Europe began to take shape. New papal agents of proved character and high diplomatic ability -- the future popes Martin IV and Nicholas IV, the Dominican Master -- General John of Vercelli -- began to knit together the medley of jealousies and rivalries in which the ambition of such magnificent men as Charles of Anjou found its perennial opportunity. It was a great pontificate, though all too short for the task before it. Nicholas III was already an old man at his election (25 November, 1271) and in less than three years he was dead (22 August, 1280) Nevertheless he had notably lessened King Charles's hold on central Italy by refusing to allow his re-appointment as Senator of Rome and imperial vicar in Tuscany. More, by a special constitution Nicholas III made it impossible for the future for any reigning prince to be senator. The new senator, in 1278, was the pope himself, and he appointed his nephew to act in his place. Charles, knowing himself for the moment outmanoeuvred, submitted gracefully. In Germany the pope continued Gregory X's policy of support to the new emperor-elect. He won from Rudolf -- and from all the German princes -- an explicit renunciation of all the old claims over any of the territories now counted as States of the Church.

Had Nicholas III still greater plans in mind to establish permanent friendliness between the Habsburgs and Capetians? Did his too speedy death put an end to one of the best of all chances of preventing the coming long centuries of Franco-German warfare and its sequelae of world destruction? Opinions differ, but the pope is credited with the desire to make the empire hereditary in the Habsburg family, and to make the German kingship a reality beyond the Rhine and the Danube. The kingdom of Arles would be detached from the empire and, united with Lombardy, form an independent realm under a French prince. A second Italian kingdom would be created in the lands between the Papal State and Lombardy. Italy, like Germany, would experience a new, peaceful political order. The Papal State would enjoy a new security. Charles of Anjou would be satisfied -- and yet controlled. The major causes of Franco-German rivalry would be forestalled.

But Nicholas died before his liquidation of the political debts of 1276 had been so successful as to allow such major schemes any chance of success. He was the first pope for a hundred years to make Rome his regular dwelling place and all but the last pope to do so for another hundred; he has his place in history as the real founder of the Vatican. The new orders of St. Francis and St. Dominic found in him a constant friend, and his registers show how constantly he turned to them to provide bishops for sees all over Europe. The one real blemish was his over-fondness for his own family. It has won him a most unenviable mark as a pioneer in the vicious business of papal nepotism, and a blistering memorial in the Inferno of Dante.

Among the things which Nicholas III did not find time to do, was to provide the much-needed regulations about the papal election, and after his death the Holy See again remained vacant for six months -- time enough and to spare for Charles of Anjou to turn to his own profit the reaction which usually follows the disappearance of a strong ruler. The new pope, Martin IV

37

(elected 22 February, 1281) Simon de Brion -- was a Frenchman and, from the beginning, he showed himself a most willing collaborator in all the King of Sicily's schemes. It would not be correct to describe him as, in any sense, the king's tool. All goes to show a long-standing identity of views between himself and Charles, and the cardinal's long career in the service of the Holy See had shown him to be a skilful diplomatist and administrator. Like very many of the popes since Innocent III, he was a product of the University of Paris. Like Clement IV, he had been high in the service of St. Louis IX. With many more he had left that service for the Roman curia at the invitation of the newly-elected French pope Urban IV (1261), who had created him cardinal. Much of his life continued to be spent in France as legate, and it was he who had negotiated, for Urban IV, the treaty which made Charles of Anjou the papal champion and set him on the way to become King of Sicily. It is not surprising that in the years between Charles's victories and his own election (1268-1281), Simon de Brion was the king's chief advocate and supporter in the curia. He was, it is said, most unwilling to be elected. No doubt he foresaw the stormy years that awaited him, the difficulties that must follow on any reversal of the cautious policy of the last nine years, and he was an old man. He was to reign just over four years and to initiate a series of political disasters that would leave the prestige of the papacy lower than at any time since the coming of Innocent III (1198).

To Charles of Anjou the election supplied the one thing so far lacking. In the fifteen years since his conquest of Sicily, the king had made more than one attempt to extend his power at the expense of the Byzantine emperor at Constantinople. St. Louis IX had checked him in 1270, Gregory X in 1275, Nicholas III in 1278. Now, with a pope of like mind with himself, his ambition was to be given free reign.

First of all, Martin IV, within two months of his election, reversed the vital decision of Nicholas III that the civil government of Rome should never be given into the hands of a sovereign prince, by appointing the King of Sicily Senator for life. [ ] The immediate result was a miniature civil war in Rome that lasted throughout the reign, with all the customary sequelae of excommunication and interdict. Martin himself never lived nearer to Rome than Orvieto and Perugia.

Next, Martin IV definitely broke with the Eastern churches. It was seven years all but two months since the solemn ratification at Constantinople, [ ] by the Greek bishops, of the reconciliation made at the Council of Lyons. Never, during all that time, had the popes felt happy about the reality of the Greek submission to their authority; and never had the great mass of the Greeks seen in the act of their emperor, Michael VIII, anything more than a base surrender to the despised and hated Latins. From the very beginning, very many of them, courtiers even, and members of the emperor's own family, had refused all relations with the clergy who accepted the union. But, so long as Gregory X lived, Michael was confident that the schemes of the King of Sicily, to restore, in his own person, the Latin empire at Constantinople, would be effectively checked. This pope's personal experience of the gravity of the crisis of Christianity in the East, and his determination, in the interest of the projected crusade, to forestall any warfare between rival Christian claimants to Eastern principalities, were solid advantages that far outweighed, with the ruler at Constantinople, the popular and the clerical hostility to the union.

But the unlooked-for death, in January 1276, of this rarely experienced pope, patient, understanding, the reverse of doctrinaire in his handling of delicate practical problems, changed all. Moreover, Gregory X had three successors in less than twelve months, and the upset in the curia caused by the rapid appearance and disappearance of these popes was, inevitably, a great opportunity both for those who wished to see the union destroyed, and for those who had never thought it could be a reality. The first of these popes, Innocent V, showed himself much cooler towards Michael VIII than his predecessor had been. For Innocent was a Frenchman, [ ] such another man of God as his predecessor, it is true, and no more of a politician. But he was a supporter of Charles of Anjou. When Michael demanded that the pope, for the protection of the Byzantine empire in the approaching crusade, should strengthen the emperor's authority by excommunicating the Latin princes already in arms against him, Innocent, in his perplexity, could only reply by a general exhortation about the need for unity. Before anything more could be asked of him, or a new Eastern crisis develop, his five months' reign was over (June 22, 1276). Adrian V, who followed him, lasted only seven weeks. Then came a third pope favourable to Charles, the scholarly Portuguese, John XXI. It was this pope who despatched to Constantinople the embassy planned by Innocent V, charged to obtain from Michael his own personal oath that he accepted the faith of the Roman See as set out at the General Council, and to absolve the Greeks from what censures they might have incurred through their adherence to the schism now terminated. The nuncios were also to excommunicate, and to put under interdict, all who opposed the union. [ ] At first all went well. The emperor made no difficulties; his son and heir, Andronicus, wrote a most dutiful letter of submission, professing his enthusiasm for the union; and the Greek bishops, at a synod in April 1277, reaffirmed their acceptance of the primacy of the Roman See and of the orthodoxy of its teaching about the procession of the Holy Ghost. But in reaffirming this, the bishops somewhat altered the terminology of the statement adopted at Lyons.

John XXI was dead before this last, disconcerting detail of the Byzantine situation reached the curia. It was five months before the vacancy was filled, and another twelve before Nicholas III took up the question. From now on we can note a new stiffness in the Roman attitude. For example, the Greeks are now told that they must add the Filioque clause to the creed. This was, of course, more than the General Council had asked; but there was now every reason why Rome should be doubtful whether Greek opposition to the use of the clause was not the outward sign of a refusal to accept the Roman terminology as orthodox, of a clinging to the old contention that, on this point, the Latins were heretics. The use of the clause was become a touchstone of orthodoxy, as the use of the word homoousion had been, nine hundred years before, in these same lands. The pope also, it would seem, proposed to pass in review the whole Greek liturgy and rite, for he bade his envoys to allow only those parts which were not contrary to the faith. The nuncios were to travel through the chief cities of the empire and to see that all these various orders were really obeyed, and the emperor was to be persuaded to ask for the appointment at Constantinople of a permanent cardinal-legate; so only could Rome be assured that the Greeks really meant what they had professed.

Already there had been riots against the union, and now the emperor and his bishops came to an understanding. They would not break openly with the new papal commission (since only the pope's intervention could preserve the empire from the designs of Charles of Anjou), and the emperor pledged himself, whatever the consequences, not to consent to add the Filioque to the creed. It was now only a matter of time before the purely political intentions of the chief supporters of the union became so evident that a breach with Rome must follow. While, at Constantinople, the emperor stifled all opposition, and punished with terrible cruelty those who stirred up the ever recurring anti-papal riots, to the pope he perjured himself lavishly. The Greek bishops, subtly contriving neither to refuse the pope's demands nor to satisfy them, sent to Rome a reply that was little more than a mass of texts from the Greek fathers, where any and every word but the "proceed" of the Lyons definition was used to express the relation of the divine Word to the Holy Ghost. Only the sudden death of Nicholas III (August 22, 1280) and the six months' interregnum which followed, delayed, it would seem, the rupture that was now all but inevitable.

Then a final certitude came with the election, as Pope Martin IV, [ ] of the King of Sicily's staunchest partisan in the curia. Charles had now every encouragement to prepare the type of crusade which the kings of Sicily traditionally favoured, the plan whose basic idea was to install themselves at Constantinople as emperors and make war on the Turks from this new vantage point. Venice -- also traditionally hostile to the Greeks, and already responsible for the crime that had transformed Innocent III's crusade into an immense act of piracy -- became his ally (July 3, 1281) and the pope, this time, joined the anti-Byzantine coalition. [ ] The date was fixed for April 1283.

But Michael VIII had not, for a moment, failed to understand that tne bright prospects which the election of Gregory X had opened to him were now gone, perhaps for ever. While he carefully maintained diplomatic relations with Martin IV in the state befitting a loyal Catholic prince, Michael, too, made his preparations. But long before they were complete, only four months after the pact with Venice, Martin IV took the final step. On November 18, 1281, he excommunicated Michael as a patron and protector of heretics, of schismatics and Or heresy.

The emperor did not, however, reverse his religious policy. As long as he lived, another thirteen months only, there was no repudiation of the work of Lyons. It was only after his death (December 11, 1282) that the anti-Roman reaction began. It was extremely thorough. The new emperor, Andronicus, publicly confessed his submission to the pope as a grave sin and begged to be given suitable penance. The patriarch favourable to the Latins -- John Beccos, almost the only sincere convert among the higher clergy -- was deposed, and his successor (the anti-Roman whose place Beccos had taken in 1275) had all the churches of the capital purified with solemn rites, while a sentence of three months' suspension was laid upon the whole body of bishops and priests. The emperor obliged his mother, Michael's widow, to abjure her allegiance to tile pope, and he even refused a religious funeral to his dead father. So Michael, after twenty years of religious trimming, in the interests of Byzantine independence, was found, at the last, rejected and cast out both by the Catholics and by the Orthodox. Although it is extremely doubtful whether, inaugurated in such circumstances, any reunion would have long endured, Martin IV, when he excommunicated its main support, the Emperor Michael, sealed its fate in an instant. Also, in excommunicating the emperor he was excommunicating the prince whom Charles of Anjou was planning to supplant -- excommunicating him at the very moment when the Sicilian king's plans were ripe. It is little wonder that the pope's contemporaries judged his act severely, nor that some were very ready to see, in the disasters to the papal arms which followed, the manifest chastening hand of God.

For chastisement -- if such it were! -- arrived with speed. Far away from Constantinople, at the very opposite end of the Mediterranean Sea, was a prince who, for years, now, had nourished a bitter hatred of the French, the King of Aragon, Peter III. Peter had seen his father make over to St. Louis IX Aragonese rights in Languedoc, and also, in the interests of this settlement, break up the unity of Aragon by creating the new kingdom of Majorca. He had seen St. Louis' son, Philip III, intervene powerfully to the south of the Pyrenees in the neighbouring kingdom of Castile -- and in a succession dispute that concerned Aragon very intimately. The French King of Sicily, Charles of Anjou, was especially an enemy; for Peter's wife was the daughter of that King Manfred of Sicily whom Charles had routed and slain at Benevento in 1266, the granddaughter of the last great Hohenstaufen, Frederick II. She was therefore, since Charles of Anjou's execution in 1268 of Conradin the last male of the line a personage of the greatest interest to all the remnants of the Ghibelline party which, suppressed these sixteen years but by no means destroyed, still swarmed in every state and town of Italy. Peter's court was the last refuge of the party, and there, biding his time in exile, was Manfred's capable Sicilian minister, John of Procida.

It was this political genius who planned the great coup. While Charles was busy with his plans to capture the empire of the East, binding to himself the great commercial states of Genoa and Venice, and securing the assistance of the new pope, John of Procida linked together Peter III and the Emperor Michael, the native Sicilians who had already learnt to detest their French rulers, and the Italian Ghibellines everywhere. A great conspiracy against Charles and his suzerain the pope was already afoot, when Martin IV threw over Michael VIII. The rising at Palermo on Palm Sunday, 1282, [ ] and the massacre of the French which followed -- the Sicilian Vespers -- was the Ghibelline reply. Before Charles was able to put down the insurrection, Peter III had landed in Sicily. The French were out, and out for all time. Only the mainland territory remained to them and a war had begun, in which the pope was directly involved, that was to last for twenty years. [ ]

The pope was involved because Charles was his vassal, the vassal indeed of St. Peter. The pope had no choice but to intervene and, in the name of St. Peter, with all means spiritual as well as temporal, defend his vassal against the Aragonese invader. He excommunicated the King of Aragon -- who, also, was his vassal -- and gave him three months in which to submit; should he obstinately hold out, the pope would depose him. [ ] Peter III ignored the excommunication. He had present victory on his side and, in a war that was to be chiefly decided by sea power, he had also the genius of the great admiral of his day, the Sicilian Roger de Loria. The pope then deposed Peter. [ ] He offered the crown of Aragon to yet another French prince, Charles of Valois, a younger son of the King of France, and, when the offer was accepted, [ ] the pope, to assist the

Frenchman, proclaimed a real crusade against Peter. [ ] Peter's subjects were released from their oaths of allegiance, forbidden to acknowledge him as king, to pay him taxes or other dues. The kingdom was laid under an interdict. To finance his papally-appointed rival, immense sums of money were advanced by the pope from the moneys collected for the war against the Saracens, and special tithes were levied on ecclesiastical property in France, Provence and Navarre, in Aragon, Majorca, Sicily and in all Italy; and also in the dioceses of Liege, Metz, Verdun and Basle. To all who helped the good work of installing Charles and expelling the Aragonese King of Aragon, all the favours, temporal and spiritual, were granted which might be had by going out to the Holy Land to fight the Saracens. The popes had been unable for years to reorganise the holy war. Now it had reappeared, in Spain, and directed against a Christian prince whose crime it was to have made war on a papal vassal.

The King of France took up his son's opportunity [ ] and soon a great French army was preparing to invade Aragon, with a fleet moving in support along the coasts of the Mediterranean. Sicily, since Roger de Loria's destruction of the Neapolitan fleet, was impregnably Aragonese. A direct attack on Peter's homeland, if successful, would be the simplest way to loosen his hold on the island.

At first all went well. The French invaded Rousillon in May 1285, and on September 7 took the Aragonese city of Gerona. But now a double disaster fell upon them. Fever took hold of the army and slew more troops than the enemy. And de Loria, in a great battle off Palamos, destroying the French fleet, cut the main line of the army's communications, the chief means of its reinforcement and supply (September 4). Among those struck down by the fever was the King of France himself, and he was carried back, amid his retreating troops, to die at Perpignan (October 5). For the first time in history French policy had sent a conquering army beyond the natural frontiers of France. The venture had ended in a great disaster.

Charles of Anjou had been spared, at any rate, this crowning humiliation [ ] he had died in January 1285, while the expedition was still in preparation, and its chances seemed excellent. [ ] Pope Martin, too, died before he saw how his collaboration with the Angevin was ending (28 March, 1285). All that the collaboration had in fact achieved was to end the chances of the reunion scheme of Gregory X, and to involve the papacy in a new war where the stake was not, any longer, the pope's independence -- the one real danger to this, anywhere in Europe, was in fact that very vassal of the pope in whose interest the pope was at war. And the papacy was faced now with the fact, surely full of omen, that in two important territories, Aragon and Sicily, the bulk of the people and clergy were standing fast by the ruler whom the pope had declared to be no ruler, ignoring the excommunication, the deposition and the interdict laid upon them. If, despite such lavish use of the spiritual arm, despite this all but official identification of the temporal with the spiritual, the popes should lose in the conflict, what would be the reaction in the sphere of the people's devotion to papal authority as the centre and source of religious life? Again, all over Italy the Ghibelline factions were busy. Lombardy, the Romagna, Tuscany were filled with insurrection and riot, and there too this same intermingling of spiritual and temporal was a leading, and inevitable, feature of the struggle. Those on the one side were, by the fact, bad Catholics: their opponents were engaged in war that was holy. And from Germany, untouched by the actual struggle, came loud complaints about the taxes levied on ecclesiastical revenues to finance the papal diplomacy and arms. Martin IV's successors were scarcely to be envied.

Philip Hughes

## 3. FRANCE AND THE SICILIAN WAR, 1285-1294

The next pope was a very old man, Honorius IV (1285-1287).
The ill-fated French expedition to Aragon had not, indeed, yet
begun its march when he was elected (2 April, 1285); but
although Edward I of England intervened immediately, [ ]
suggesting to the new pope that he persuade Philip III to halt the
military preparations and that negotiations be opened with Peter
of Aragon, the die was cast. Honorius, a noble of ancient Roman
stock, [ ] might well intend -- it would seem he did so intend -- to
reverse his predecessor's policy, and to follow the ways of
Nicholas III and Gregory X, working for peace by removing the
causes of wars before these became impossible to control. He
would hold in check the new powerful French combination, now
master of France and southern Italy, by a constant support of the
Habsburg emperor in Germany; and also, while, as a good
suzerain, he supported the King of Sicily, he would carefully
supervise his whole political activity. But the pope could hardly
condone, out of hand, the Aragonese occupation of Sicily: it was
by all the standards of his time, no more than a successful act of
international piracy; nor could he, humanly speaking, have
expected the King of France to abandon the profitable holy war
against the pirates, now, upon the instant, and at his sole word.
The mischief done by the alliance of Pope Martin with King
Charles must, perforce, work itself out.

Had Honorius IV enjoyed anything beyond one of the shortest of
papal reigns he might, however, really have achieved the aims of
his peace-inspired diplomacy. For within nine months of his
election the whole international situation altered very
remarkably. Charles of Anjou had died and his successor,
Charles II -- a feeble king indeed by comparison with his
formidable father -- was a prisoner of war in Aragon; Philip III
of France had met his tragic death at Perpignan, and the new
king, Philip IV, had tacitly abandoned the crusade against Peter
III; Peter III himself had also died, of his wounds (November 10,

47

1285), and had divided up his lands: [ ] Aragon and the new conquest, Sicily, were no longer united under the one ruler.

Honorius made good use of his opportunity in southern Italy. Taking over, as suzerain, the actual administration, he decreed a general restoration of law and government such as these had been before the first Hohenstaufen kings had built there the centralised, despotic state that was a model of its kind. And the pope even began to show himself willing to negotiate with Aragon about Sicily. At the same time, in Germany, Honorius IV arranged to crown Rudolf of Habsburg as emperor, to set thereby a seal upon Gregory X's restoration of the Empire. Since Rudolf had refused to join the crusade against Aragon, and had protested against German church revenues being used for it, this great gesture would fix firmly before the mind of the time the papal determination not to be the tool of French ambitions.

But Honorius IV was already in his seventy-seventh year, and long before the date appointed for the coronation (2 February, 1288) he was dead (13 April, 1287); his diplomacy had scarcely begun to put the new situation to good use. With Honorius there disappeared the last authentic representative of the skilful diplomatic tradition that went back to Innocent III, the tradition in which the popes had managed the rival chiefs of the respublica christiana while yet contriving never themselves to descend into the arena of inter-state competition, and always to give to their action the authentic note of an intervention from outside all conflict. Martin IV had dealt that tradition a terrible blow; his immediate successor had not been given the time to repair it; now would follow two long weakening vacancies of the Holy See [ ] and two weak pontificates; and when, ten years after the death of Honorius IV, there would come once more a strong pope, moved to remould his universe after the best thirteenth century tradition, the moment had gone by. Nor was that strong pope, Boniface VIII, gifted with the wholly impersonal zeal, and detachment from all but the good cause, which had been the essence of the success he so needed to renew.

The best papal interpretation of the pope's role as chief of the respublica christiana called for action that never passed beyond diplomatic practice backed by sanctions that were spiritual. But in a world where every temporal thing could be regarded as help or hindrance to spiritual well-being, and where, by universal consent, the temporal was subordinate in excellence to the spiritual, it had only been a matter of time before the temporal -- blessed and consecrated for the purpose -- was, in a score of ways, pressed into the service of the spiritual. With Gregory IX (1227-1241) and Innocent IV (1243-1254) especially, [ ] the Holy See's use of such temporal things as armies, fleets, systems of taxation, banking and loans, had expanded enormously; its whole conception of its own authority and jurisdiction over temporal affairs had expanded too. By the time of Martin IV and Honorius IV the papacy had become a kind of supranational European kingship, and to quote as a description, if not justification, of their authority the text of Jeremias about planting and uprooting [ ] was now a commonplace of the stylus curiae. So long as the papal policies were victorious, what criticism there was of these new developments remained, for the most part, underground. But the succession of disasters in the reigns of these two last popes was an opportunity the critics could not resist. All over Italy the Ghibelline tradition was flourishing anew after a generation of eclipse; and alongside it there flourished a lively revival of the spiritual teachings associated with the great name of Joachim of Fiore. [ ]   *crazy teachings*

The Incarnation and the Passion of Our Lord were not, according to this new evangel, the high point of the divine mercy to man, and the foundation of all that would follow. The reign of Christ was but a preparation for a more perfect dispensation, the reign of the Holy Ghost. This was now about to begin. There would no longer be a church; the pope would joyfully resign his power to a new order of contemplatives; the active life would cease, and all Christendom become a vast monastery of contemplatives, vowed to absolute poverty; the law of spiritual effort would cease and, the Holy Ghost being poured out in a new and perfect effusion of gifts and graces, the law of spiritual joy would reign unhindered. Pope, cardinals, hierarchy, systematic theology, canon law -- these would not only disappear but their very presence and survival were, at this moment, hindrances that delayed the coming of the new age. The first duty of the faithful soul, then, was to abandon them, to abandon the reign of Christ, to leave the bark of Peter for the bark of John, and so prepare the way for the coming reign of the Holy Ghost. [ ]

These theories are destructive, evidently, of all that Catholicism has ever claimed to be, and destructive also of the whole civilisation which, then, was very evidently bound up with traditional Catholicism. For many years, however, the theories had found enthusiastic support in one section of the great order of mendicant preachers, vowed to live in poverty, that was the great legacy to the Church of St. Francis of Assisi. To those elements in the order who had looked askance at the new detailed regulations called for by the very expansion of the order, and to those who fought the introduction of systematic theological study for the preachers, and to all those -- and they exist in every generation -- who had joined the brethren to satisfy and achieve their own spiritual ideals (and after their own way) these anarchical doctrines were most welcome. Already, in 1257, the pope had had to intervene to save the order from developments that would have dissolved it into a chaos of spiritual factions. Under the general then elected to govern it -- St. Bonaventure [ ] -- who was maintained in office for seventeen years, unity was slowly and peacefully restored and the "Joachimite" tendencies disappeared. But they had never been destroyed. Always there had been friars who remained attached to them, and the tradition of devotion to them had been carefully handed down through thirty years in more than one convent of Languedoc and central

Italy. The obvious preoccupation of the popes during all this time with the paraphernalia of courts and governments was fuel on which the fire of these "Spirituals" fed greedily. For years they watched these developments and denounced them. In the present disasters to the causes favoured by the Holy See, they saw the manifest chastisement of God's hand, proof that their own theories were true, and the best of all encouragement to press on the attack and destroy the present church.

The "Spirituals" possessed at this time (1287) a leader of great intellectual power, personal charm, and known austerity of life, Peter John Olivi. He was still a young man, [ ] and had been a pupil at Paris of Peckham and of Matthew of Acquasparta, the two greatest of St. Bonaventure's own pupils. Olivi was an unusually complex kind of Franciscan, for he was an "intellectual," a scholastic philosopher and theologian indeed of very high power, a "Spiritual" also, and, lastly, a subtle commentator of the gospel according to Abbot Joachim. From a very early age he was regarded as a force in his order; Nicholas III had consulted him when the great decretal Exiit Qui Seminat was in preparation. And then, four years later, in 1282, at the General Chapter of his order at Strasburg, Olivi was accused of teaching false doctrine. His Franciscan judges condemned several of his philosophical and theological theories and Olivi accepted their verdict, under protest that the Holy See had not condemned them. For four years thereafter he was under a cloud, but now, in 1287, his old master, Matthew of Acquasparta, had been elected Minister General, and Olivi was given a lectorship in the great Franciscan school of Santa Croce at Florence. One result of this promotion was a great revival of "Spiritual" ideals in Tuscany.

Still more important to the Spiritual movement than Olivi's personality was, seemingly, the sympathy professed for these friars by one of the leading figures of the curia, the Cardinal James Colonna. He was the lifelong friend and confidant of the pope, Honorius IV, and his contact with the Franciscan Spirituals came through his affection for his very remarkable sister, herself a Franciscan nun of the strict observance and known to us as Blessed Margaret Colonna.

All the old controversies about the real meaning of the rule of St. Francis now revived. Were the "Spirituals" the only real Franciscans? Had the pope any right to lay down rules which -- so the "Spirituals" maintained -- contradicted the will of St. Francis? And with these controversies, and the controversies and fantasies about Abbot Joachim's theories, there went a medley of speculation, preached and rhymed about everywhere, as to the approaching end of the world, the coming of antichrist, the manner of man he would be, and where he was to be looked for. A great internal crisis was evidently threatening. Unusual wisdom, and sanctity too, would be needed in the popes if these restless elements were to be converted to a re-acceptance of the traditional way to perfection, namely dependence on the supernatural forces which the Church of Christ was founded to dispense. Toxins long latent -- whatever their origin -- in the mystical body were increasingly active in the blood stream. How could they best be rendered harmless, and the members they affected be made healthy?

It was against this background of threatening chaos and revolt that the cardinals debated the election of a successor to Honorius IV. After eleven months they came to a choice, the cardinal Jerome of Ascoli, Pope Nicholas IV: the new pope was a Franciscan.

But Jerome of Ascoli's election promised little to such of his brethren as were tainted with the apocalyptic theories of Abbot Joachim. The new pope had indeed, for a generation, been a leading influence in Franciscan life, but not in the circles where Olivi was a master. After a brilliant early career, as teacher in the University of Paris and administrator, Jerome had been sent to

Constantinople in 1272 as the envoy of Gregory X, charged with the delicate business of bringing the Greeks to take part in the forthcoming General Council. At Lyons he had appeared with the Byzantine ambassadors as a kind of liaison officer and when, during the council, St. Bonaventure, now a cardinal, resigned his charge as Minister-General of the Franciscans, Jerome of Ascoli had been unanimously elected in his place (20 May, 1274). Very suddenly, only seven weeks later, the saint died, and from that time onward Jerome had been the determining force of orthodox development within the order. It was he who, as Minister-General, had summoned Olivi to deliver up certain of his manuscripts and on reading them had ordered them to be burnt for the harmful theories they contained. Another friar to feel the weight of his severity was Roger Bacon who also, amongst other things, showed a passionate credulity about the Joachimite prophecies. It was, seemingly, by Jerome of Ascoli's orders that this now aged Franciscan suffered his last monastic condemnation and imprisonment.

Nicholas III (1277-1280) had made use of Jerome as a diplomatist and, in 1278, had given him the red hat. The new cardinal had, at the pope's command, retained for a time the general direction of the order and he had been the chief influence in the promulgation of Nicholas' great decretal Exiit Qui Seminat (14 August, 1279) which gave an authoritative decision about the real meaning of the Franciscan ideal of religious poverty, in the hope of ending finally the long disputes of fifty years. The next pope, Martin IV, made him cardinal-bishop of Palestrina, the city that was the chief centre of the Colonna influence; and from now on Jerome of Ascoli gave himself to the care of his diocese. History knows little more of him, in fact, until his unanimous election as pope eight years later.

The death of his predecessor, Honorius IV, in April 1287, had not, of course, halted the war or the wartime diplomacy. The long conclave which followed was a golden opportunity for all parties to develop new positions and advantages. The most striking success had fallen to the King of Aragon. It was his especial good fortune that he still held prisoner Charles II of Sicily, and the special opportunity for exploiting this was the proffered mediation of the English king. Edward I (1272-1307). If Charles II -- religious, conscientious, timorous -- is the one lamb-like figure in all this long contest, our own Edward I, caught between the rival duplicities of the Aragonese king and Philip the Fair of France, [ ] shows an inability to appreciate the realities of the case which, in another, might also be taken for lamb-like innocence of the ways of wolves. Time and again Edward's political anxieties made him the tool of the astute Alfonso and so, ultimately, destroyed all belief in the bona fides of his arbitration and played the French king's game, giving the pope whatever justification he needed for favouring France rather than England.

The first fruit of England's intervention was the Treaty of Oloron (25 July, 1287). Aragon consented to release the captive Charles II -- who had already renounced his rights to Sicily -- on the hard conditions of an immense money payment, the surrender of sixty-three noble hostages (among them his three eldest sons), and the pledge to negotiate a peace between the two Aragonese kings [ ] on the one hand, and the chiefs of the Franco-Papal alliance on the other, within three years: should a peace satisfactory to Aragon not be concluded King Charles was to return to his captivity or surrender his lands in Provence. The Papal legates, present at the conference, allowed the treaty to be signed without any protest. It was a quasi-surrender of all that the popes had been fighting for in the last five years.

The King of France, however, refused the offer of a truce, refused the hostages a safe conduct through his territory, refused all facilities for the payment of the indemnity. The college of cardinals, also, showed themselves hostile to the treaty, and when, seven months after it was signed, they elected Nicholas

IV, one of the pope's first actions was to quash and annul it absolutely, to cite the King of Aragon to appear at Rome within six months for judgment, and to order Edward I to negotiate the liberation of King Charles on terms that the Holy See could accept (15 March, 1288).

[genealogy page 39]
Louis VIII + Blanche of Castile => Charles of Anjou K. of Sicily 1266-1285 & St. Louis IX 1226-1270
St. Louis IX 1226-1270 + Margaret of Provence => Philip III 1270-1285

James I of Aragaon => Isabella & Peter III
Philip III + Isabella => Philip the Fair 1285-1314
Peter III => Alfonso III & James II

NB. Margaret, the wife of St. Louis, was also largely Spanish by blood

The vigour of the papal reply was promising. It was followed up by the negotiation, under papal auspices, of a treaty between France and Castile (13 July, 1288) in which the two kings pledged themselves to a new attack on Aragon in alliance with the Holy See, and, after some delay from the pope, by new concessions to Philip IV of Church revenues to finance the offensive (25 September, 1288). The Ghibellines had been too active throughout the summer for the pope to be able to maintain his first independent attitude to France. Pisa had opened its harbours to the fleet of de Loria. At Arezzo the bishop had gone over to the same cause. At Perugia there were like activities, and at Rome itself the city was preparing to welcome the anti-papal forces as it had welcomed Conradin twenty years earlier. The pope was at the end of his funds. The only way to wring a loan out of the French was by more concessions.

Meanwhile Edward I had renewed his diplomatic work with the Aragonese and, for total result, he had achieved a treaty [ ] still more favourable to Aragon than the treaty the pope had annulled. But the English king had, this time, made himself responsible for the indemnity and the hostages, and Charles II had at last been set free.

A sad dilemma awaited him, for the pledged negotiator of peace walked into a world of friends determined on war in his support. The pope ordered him peremptorily to resume the style and title of King of Sicily. The King of France refused to listen to his argument, and sent him on to Rome with a protective escort of French knights. The pope, knowing now that France was really behind him, felt stronger than ever before. He excommunicated the Ghibelline bishops of Pisa and Perugia, and ordered the King of Aragon to give back the money paid over in accordance with the new treaty; also to surrender the hostages and to come to Rome by October 1 (7 April, 1289). Whereupon the Ghibellines in Rome rose, and after bloody street fighting drove out the pope. He fled to Rieti, forty miles to the northeast of Rome, on the very frontier of King Charles' realm and, undismayed by this local defeat, on Whit Sunday (May 29) in the cathedral there, he crowned Charles as King of Sicily with all possible pomp. Just a fortnight later the Florentine victory of Campaldino (11 June) broke the Ghibellines of central Italy. Success, it would seem, had justified Nicholas IV's bold initiative. This was the high-water mark of his reign. The full flood of papal favours was loosed for the King of France, praise for his devotion in resuming the task taken up by his father in 1285, still more financial concessions (to be wrung in specie from the clergy of France), the preaching once more of the holy war against Aragon.

In reality it was the French who had triumphed; and this aspects of events was by no means lost upon the chief hindrance to their domination in western European politics, Edward I. The King of

England was necessarily interested in Franco-Spanish relations because he was Duke of Aquitaine. The fact that he was also, as Duke of Aquitaine, the vassal of the French king made his interest -- and above all his present intervention as mediator -- highly unwelcome to the French, an irritant that came near indeed to being a casus belli. Philip the Fair had not been able to prevent the arbitration, but the award had been so patently anti-French and anti-papal that it had crashed almost of itself.

Edward now approached his problem from a wholly different angle. To divert the pope from the approaching offensive against Aragon, he proposed a new expedition to the Holy Land. He had, months before this, taken the cross and sworn his crusader's oath (December 1288) and now he besought Nicholas IV to rally all the princes of Christendom and to fix a date for the armies to set forth. No demand, publicly made by a special embassy, could have been more embarrassing, at the moment, for the pope. But, as if to prove him right in his preoccupation with the problem of Sicily, de Loria chose this moment to land a Sicilian army on the Italian coast not ten miles from the papal frontier and to lay siege to Gaeta (June-July 1289).

Edward was, for the moment, most effectively answered; and a Neapolitan army moved out to besiege in turn the Sicilian army besieging Naples. And now came two astonishing reversals for the Franco-Papal plans. First a terrible thunderbolt from the East, the news that the Sultan of Egypt had suddenly moved on Tripoli, the second greatest stronghold still in Christian hands, and had taken it. To the English ambassadors' demand that, in the interest of the Holy Places, they should be allowed to negotiate a peace or a truce between the armies around Gaeta the pope could not now say no. And then Charles II -- just as his son Charles Martel had the Sicilians at the point of surrender -- took command of his army, not, however, to fight but to reinforce the pleas of the English. In the conferences which followed he renewed to de Loria his old renunciation of all claims on Sicily, barely three months after the pope had solemnly crowned him as its king. But Charles II was now well away from the pope, and had outdistanced the legates sent to watch his conduct of the negotiations. By the time they arrived de Loria was celebrating his triumph.

All this was a great defeat for the pope, for the new treaty set free the Sicilian fleet to aid the Aragonese. The chances of a successful war against Aragon had suddenly shrunk, with Naples out of the war and de Loria set free to repeat the feats of 1285. With the aid of Charles II the papal diplomacy turned to consider how most easily to make peace with Aragon. The plan finally decided on was ingenious. Charles of Valois, titular King of Aragon since Pope Martin IV's grant in 1285, to enforce whose right the popes had been waging this holy war, would surrender his claims. Alfonso of Aragon -- styled by the popes a usurper, but the actual sovereign, descendant and heir of the long line of Aragonese kings -- would, in return for this recognition, surrender all rights and claims to Sicily. Finally, Charles of Valois, as compensation for surrendering his rights to Aragon, would receive in marriage a daughter of Charles II of Naples who would bring him as dowry her father's hereditary lands of Anjou and Maine. Charles II was willing. It only remained to win the consent of Alfonso, and of Philip IV of France; and in the first months of the new year (1290) an embassy especially strong in personnel left Italy for France. The legates were the two cardinals who had been sent to Gaeta, Gerard of Parma, cardinal bishop of Tusculum, and Benedict Gaetani, the future pope Boniface VIII.

It was now, at all costs, most important that the brother kings of Aragon and Sicily should realise that the King of France actively supported the pope's plan. No one understood this more clearly than the king and, yet once again, he prepared to turn to the permanent advancement of the royal power in France the pope's present need of his support. Philip the Fair's opportunity lay in a dispute that had, for some time now, been raging in France between different bishops and the royal officials.

It was, once more, the bitterly fought question -- never finally decided with any finality in these centuries when all Europe was Catholic -- of the power of the king over ecclesiastics in temporal matters, and the question of the power in temporals of ecclesiastical lords over their vassals; but the conflict was, this time, to prove the greatest opportunity so far given to a new force in the public life of Christendom, to the lay jurist trained in the law of ancient Rome, the man whose political ideal was to create anew, in the person of the medieval king, the emperor of Roman legal theory.

It has already been noted [ ] how one very important feature of the reform of Christian life associated with St. Gregory VII (1073-1085), a turning point in the history of civilisation, was his care to recover, by learned researches, the half-forgotten tradition of the ancient Church law. The development, from these ancient sources, of the new scientific canon law, which, by the time of Boniface VIII, was an almost essential instrument of Church government, was contemporary with a great revival of the study of the law of ancient Rome, as this is set out in the corpus of law books published and imposed by the authority of the Emperor Justinian (527-565). [ ] How the two systems developed side by side, each influencing the other, so that from the schools of Bologna in the twelfth century came the first great canonists and the first great civilians too, is one of the commonplaces of medieval history. [ ] One, most important, result of this renaissance of legal study was the civilians' discovery and development of the Roman conception of sovereignty, as Justinian's books set this forth.

The authority of the ruler, in the early Middle Ages, over his subject who was a free man was considered to derive from a personal relation between the two. It was a relation symbolised in the act of homage, by which the vassal swore to be true to his lord, and by which the lord was considered bound to protect the vassal. What authority over the subject thence accrued to the lord was limited by known and mutually acknowledged conventions. Nor could the lord, rightfully, extend that authority outside the acknowledged field -- say in the matter of exacting financial aids -- without the previous consent of the inferior.

But the civilian legist discovered in the Roman Law an authority that was a different kind of thing altogether -- the res publica, public authority. For the Roman jurist sees not only the thousand, or the million, men living together under the rule of the one prince, but, as a thing distinct from any of them, or all of them, he sees also their collectivity, a something superior to them all, and for the sake of which, and in the name of which, they are ruled -- the State (if we may, by many centuries, anticipate the modern term). It is this res publica that is the real lord: and even the imperator is its servant, even when he is using those extraordinary, final, absolute, sovereign rights that are the very substance of his imperium.

As the centuries go by, the delegation of X or Y to be imperator, and so to wield lawfully these sovereign powers, becomes but a memory, a formality; and then less than that, until, long before the time of Justinian, the emperor has become indeed, what a medieval jurist describes him, lex animata in terris. The State is already a postulate of political order, to which all else is subject; from which all rights derive; owing its authority to none, but itself the source of whatever authority there is; and now the emperor has become the State incarnate. Nowhere do restrictions limit him that derive from any contract with his subjects. Whether he make new laws, or impose new burdens, his right is, of its nature, not subject to their discussion. [ ]

That the splendour of this sovereign omnipotence -- impersonal, imprescriptible, indivisible, inalienable -- dazzled those on whom it first shone forth from the long neglected texts of the ancient Roman jurists, is understandable. And for a time they all clung faithfully to the primitive faith that, upon this earth, there could be but one such source of rights. Princes might be many, but there could only be one incarnation of such sovereignty as this. To the one emperor all other kings must then, in some way, by the nature of the case, be subject.

But gradually, during the thirteenth century, legists in lands where the new emperors of these later times -- the anointed chiefs of the Holy Roman Empire of the German Nation -- possessed not a title of real authority, in the bitterly anti-imperial city states of northern Italy, for example, and in France, developed an accommodation of the theory of sovereignty, that would make, say, the power of the King of France over the French the same kind of splendid, impersonal, all-powerful sovereignty. The new maxim began to have legal force that all kings were emperors, in respect of their own subjects; [ ] and of them too was Justinian's dictum held to be true that the prince's decision has force of law. [ ] No sovereign prince needs to seek assent or confirmation, from any source, in order that his will may truly bind his subjects.

There are many more implications -- of very great importance for the history of the legal, political, and social development of medieval Europe -- in these principles as they are now being developed. But the interest of these developments for this chapter is in a type of mind which they produced, the mind of the lay jurist who was now to win the Catholic prince's first victory over the papacy and always, henceforward, to fight the princes' battles against the claims of the Church. [ ] These developments produced, also, the new "climate" in which, more and more, the fight was from now on to be waged. Against the "common good" which the theologians preached as the criterion of just laws, the legist would now set his own criterion of the "public welfare";

and it would be roundly stated that, given so good a system of law, theology ceased to be necessary for jurists. [ ]

This new conception of royal authority which the study of Roman Law began to produce, would, in the end, alter the whole relationship between king and subject. It also threatened to alter the whole relationship between king and pope. [ ] Whatever its importance, helpful or harmful, for the civil life of a nation, it is yet, by its very nature, a conception inimical to such an institution as the Catholic religion. From its first appearance, therefore, it is an idea which the popes never cease to fight; and the papal preoccupation with this struggle is, henceforward, a main topic of Church history in every century; for no theory about the nature of their power is more welcome to ruling princes than this that their rights are absolute, once the ingenuity of the jurists has really adapted it to their use.

The reign of Philip the Fair is the time when the jurisdiction of the French monarchy makes its first notable advances on the jurisdiction of the vassal lord's courts, advances based on a principle of political theory -- that all institutions in the kingdom are subject to the king's jurisdiction -- and the campaign is conducted systematically by the professional, civilian, jurists in the king's service. When such advances met the jurisdiction of a lord who was an ecclesiastic they encountered opposition that was due, not to something merely local, but to the Canon Law, to a reality more universal even than the king's jurisdiction, a system of law that was likewise based on principle. There had been, in recent years, fights of more than usual importance on this matter between the royal officials and the bishops of Chartres and Poitiers. When, in the late autumn of 1289, after the Truce of Gaeta, the King of France took up again the question of subsidies for the war, he pressed for a settlement of these dangerous disputes about the rival jurisdictions. If the pope wished for effective aid from France he must not hinder the king's plans to preserve the monarchy and keep the nation united.

Philip the Fair is using the pope's extremity to strengthen his position at the expense of ecclesiastical immunities that are centuries old. He twice, within three months, sent to the pope a formidable list of his grievances against the clergy and signified to him that these complaints came in the name of "the counts, barons, universities and communes of the realm." [ ] It is not merely the king, the pope is warned, but the whole nation that demands a settlement favourable to France.

Also, it appeared, Philip was disturbed at the pope's apparent partiality for England. In England, too, the last few years had seen trouble between the king and the Church on similar matters of jurisdiction, but the English king had managed to enforce his will without unfavourable comment from Rome. Moreover, in this very summer when Edward's intervention had, at Gaeta, for a third time in two years, cut across the papal policy, Nicholas had appointed one of Edward's subjects and chaplains, Berard de Got, to be Archbishop of Lyons. Here there was indeed a powder-mine, and under the circumstances the nomination was, on the pope's part, an incredibly imprudent move. For Lyons, on the very borders of France, was nevertheless a free city within the jurisdiction of the emperor, and the sovereign in Lyons itself was the archbishop with his chapter. Of late, the Emperor, Rudolf of Habsburg, had shown a new kind of interest in the affairs of these Burgundian lands, and at Besancon he had intervened with an army. Never had it been so important for France that the Archbishop of Lyons should be friendly; and the pope's nomination of Berard de Got gave Philip the opportunity of claiming to be himself the sovereign of Lyons, and of stating, under a new set of circumstances, the case he was already building up in the disputes at Chartres and Poitiers. That royal case went to the very heart of things, the fundamental relation between pope and king, between Church and State; and it is a foreshadowing of the great storm which, in another ten years, was to rock to its very base the good relations between the two. The king's advisers make no secret that their aim is a strong, centralised, singly-governed state, nor of their enthusiasm for this ideal. And, something never before heard of in France, they now flatly deny that the pope has any jurisdiction in temporal matters outside the lands granted him by Constantine. For the king, they declare, within his own realm is sovereign everywhere. Here indeed was grave matter, threats veiled perhaps, but threats without a doubt, and from the papacy's sole effective supporter in its struggle with Aragon and Sicily; threats of such a kind that, by comparison, the revolt of Sicily was but a trifle.

Nicholas IV's first reply to Philip was to increase his favours; and in order to prove how impartial past severities on the question of jurisdiction had been, a special embassy was sent to England to lecture Edward I on his shortcomings and bid him make himself more pleasing to God in this matter before offering himself as God's champion in the Holy Land. But this did not suffice. Philip the Fair returned to the matter with a further list of grievances and stiffened his terms to Charles II very considerably. Little wonder then that Nicholas IV, stirred mightily, sent his two best diplomatists and legists to France, nor that they were absent on their mission for a good twelve months.

The French king agreed to the arrangement proposed for the reconciliation of Aragon. [ ] At Tarascon, in the following April, Alfonso III too, after some hesitation, accepted the pope's offer, pledging himself to come to Rome and make his submission.

Between the dates of the two political negotiations, the legates had settled with Philip the Fair the dispute about ecclesiastical jurisdiction, after more than one stormy scene with the clergy in a national synod that sat at St. Genevieve in Paris for fourteen days in the November of 1290. A royal ordonnance announced the terms of the agreement. The king's contention that he was, for all his lay subjects, supreme in matters of temporal jurisdiction was accepted; and clerics who no longer lived a clerical life were recognised to be subject to him as though they were laymen. .

On the other hand the king expressly reproved, and condemned as excesses, certain procedures of his officials that cut across the exercise of the bishops' jurisdiction in temporals. The old immunity of the clergy from lay jurisdiction, outside cases that concerned fiefs as fiefs, was confirmed, and also their traditional immunity from lay taxation. It was a treaty where compromises seemed equal or. both sides, fair and reasonable. But the concessions made by the king are, too often, qualified by captious clauses, and the rights recognised to the clergy are set out in language that is vague. There is nowhere mention of any penalty for the king's officials should they return to their old practices; and the important question who shall decide and how, if king and clergy disagree about the meaning of the pact, is left without any means of solution.

For the moment, however, all seemed well, and with a year of busy and apparently successful diplomacy behind them the legates returned to Rome (February 1291). The King of France had been reconciled with the pope and was making ready for the new, and no doubt final, assault on the Aragonese usurper in Sicily. The King of Aragon had abandoned his brother to his fate, and was preparing his own submission and the reconciliation of his kingdom with the Church.

And then, once again, came news from the East that wrecked in an instant all that the pope may have thought he had achieved. (On May 18, 1291, the Sultan of Egypt captured Acre, after a three-weeks' siege; the last stronghold the Christians possessed in the Holy Land had fallen, the most luxurious and civilised city of the Christian world. [ ]

Close upon this catastrophe came another unexpected blow. The King of Aragon died, on June 18. His successor was his next eldest brother, the King of Sicily, late so skilfully isolated from all help from the Spanish homeland. Sicily and Aragon had now a single ruler. And finally, to complete the tale of losses, within another month the papacy's one disinterested supporter in Germany was dead, the Emperor Rudolf (15 July). Nicholas IV had treated him shamefully enough. He had put off the promised coronation, at the very time when he was preparing to crown Charles of Naples, the tool of Rudolf's rival, Philip the Fair; and he had intervened in Hungary to annul Rudolf's grant of the kingdom to his son Albert, preferring to the German yet another French prince, Charles Martel, the King of Naples' younger son. [ ] Rudolf had nevertheless remained loyal to the role of peace-bringer assigned him by Gregory X in the restoration of the empire. Now he was gone, and in a Germany which ignored the pope rival candidates battled for the succession.

By the summer of 1291 the whole policy of Nicholas IV lay in ruins, and from all the malcontents of Italy a great sound of reprobation arose. Ghibellines, "Joachimites" and the dyscoli among the Franciscans all joined in a single cry. The true cause of the loss of the Holy Land was the pope's preoccupation with the war against Sicily; not the Aragonese kings but the Sultan was the pope's real enemy. What these critics, as bitter and as vociferous as they professed to be pious, did not know was that the Aragonese kings had been well informed about the Sultan's expedition before ever it marched. More, they had helped him to prepare it, for they were his secret allies, [ ] sworn to recognise whatever "conquests, castles, fortresses, countries and provinces God should allow the Sultan and his sons to make in Syria, Laodicea and Tripoli." The Aragonese kings had also pledged themselves to disclose to the Sultan any plans made between the pope, the Christian princes or the Mongols for a renewal of the Crusade. Should the pope, or any Christian prince or religious order, attack the Sultan they were pledged to make war on him, and they bound themselves, finally, not to give any aid to the Christian forces in the Holy Land should the Sultan declare that these had committed any breach of the truce arranged at the time of the capture of Tripoli (1289). In return, the Sultan had guaranteed to the brother kings Sicily, the Balearic Isles and whatever conquests they might make from the French. The ink was still fresh on this infamous transaction while Alfonso was negotiating with the legates of Nicholas IV the pact of Tarascon, and pledging his dutiful submission to the pope. And now his successor, the new sovereign of the united kingdoms, James II, had the pope but known it, was the pledged and devoted ally of the Turk: as his father, the hero of the Sicilian Vespers, had been before him, in that very enterprise.

[genealogy page 49]
LOUIS VIII 1223-1226 => St. LOUIS IX => Philip III 1270-1285 => Philip the Fair => 1285-1314
Philip III 1270-1285 => Charles of Valois K. of Aragon (by Martin IV, 1284)

LOUIS VIII 1223-1226 => Charles of Anjou K. of Sicily (by Clement IV, 1226) => Charles II => Charles Martel K. Of Hungary (by Nicholas IV, 1289)

But Nicholas IV, ignorant of this supreme treachery, rose manfully to the task of rallying Christian Europe to the needed new assault on Islam. A council was summoned to devise plans and gather resources; a provisional date was fixed when the expedition would sail, March 1293; ambassadors were despatched to negotiate a peace between the great maritime states of Venice and Genoa, to Byzantium also, and to the Mongols, to knit together an alliance on a Dew grand scale.

Among the first to give a wholehearted adhesion was Edward I of England. But from France came a cold and cautious refusal. Philip the Fair was bidden to take the cross, or make over to those who would the crusade moneys which already, for years now, had been accumulating in France, and to consider a marriage between his sister and Edward I which, healing the new antagonism, would be the basis of the new holy war. But the French king noted how the new King of Aragon, reversing the policy of a generation, had made peace with Castile -- an anti-French peace; and he saw a strong movement in Germany to elect an anti-French emperor in succession to Rudolf. Once more Philip took up his old policy towards Rome, playing now through the Florentine bankers on the pope's fears and needs. He promised nothing about the coming crusade, but instead demanded a new crusade against Aragon and the concession of yet more tithes to finance it.

Nicholas IV gave him the only answer possible. The disaster in the Holy Land had changed the whole situation. Palestine must now be every Christian's first care. All else must wait until the council met and made its decisions (13 December, 1291). And yet, even in this extremity, the pope did not dare to show himself over-generous in reply to Edward I's offer of service. The English envoys also were told they must await the council's decisions and meanwhile the pope repeated his list of grievances against the king (12, 18 February, 1 March, 1292).

The time for the council was now drawing near and gradually there began to come in to Rome the opinions of the various provincial councils, summoned by the pope's order to sound the sentiments of Christendom. More than one of them, especially of course in France, supported Philip's schemes. The Sicilian question should first be resolved by the expulsion of the Aragonese; an emperor should be elected who would be favourable to France. What would have been the opinion and projects of the Church as a whole we shall never know, for the General Council never met. On Good Friday, 1292 (4 April), suddenly, unexpectedly, Nicholas IV died: and in this great crisis of Christian history the cardinals left the Holy See vacant for two and a quarter years.

The death of the pope brought the whole crusade movement to a standstill. Whatever the latent enthusiasm of the general body of the Christian people, the pope was the only sovereign really anxious about the disaster; and once it became evident that the twelve cardinals [ ] would be unable to make a speedy election, the various princes turned their attention to questions nearer home.

The real centre of interest for the Christian princes was the activities of Philip the Fair. The moment was now at last come when the long antagonism between France and England must break into open war. The diplomatic duels of the last few years in which each had fought the other, over Aragon, over Sicily, over the affairs of the Empire and the middle states of the Lotharingian lands had, naturally, sharpened tempers on both sides. But this long fight had been, after all, secondary; a mere struggle for position preliminary to a definite settlement about two most important matters where interests vital both to France and to England were violently opposed. These matters were the clash of jurisdiction in the immense territories of France where Edward I ruled as Duke of Aquitaine, Philip the Fair's vassal; and next the war of semi-legalised piracy between the mercantile fleets of both kings that had gone on now for some years.

It is doubtful whether, by the year 1293, any human power could have averted the coming conflict. Certainly none but the pope could have delayed it any longer; the continuing vacancy of the Holy See made war inevitable.

Both sides looked round for allies and made settlements with their other foes. Philip the Fair now completely reversed his policy towards Aragon. In a war against England he could not afford to be simultaneously at war with a power whose fleet was master of the western Mediterranean, and he made peace with James of Aragon; [ ] at the same time he patched up some of his differences with princes on his eastern border.

Moreover he intervened to create a French party in Rome. He found ready support in the Colonna -- that clan of Roman nobles who, for centuries now, had played a leading part in the politics of the papal state, lords of a score of towns and fortresses in the mountain country between Rome and Naples, [ ] and masters thereby of the communications between Rome and the South; wealthy, ambitious and turbulent. Their present head was that James Colonna whom we have already seen as the patron of the Franciscan spirituals, a cardinal since the time of Nicholas III. In the late pope's reign he had been all powerful, and Nicholas IV, amongst other favours to the family, had created a second Colonna cardinal, Peter, the elder man's nephew. John Colonna, the older cardinal's brother had, in the same pontificate, ruled Rome for a time as senator.

James Colonna was, at this moment, one of six cardinals who remained in Rome, divided against their colleagues who had fled to Rieti from the plague, and divided still more bitterly among themselves into equal groups of pro-Colonna and pro-Orsini. The Colonna were the more powerful and had recently driven out the Orsini and it was to the Colonna cardinals that the French diplomacy now addressed itself, with offers of lands (September 1293).

In return the Colonna cardinals prepared to elect the kind of pope France wanted, and first they notified the absent majority of the Sacred College that they -- the three who alone had remained in Rome -- were the only real electors and that within a certain date they proposed to elect a pope. But this manoeuvre failed completely. All the train of canonists, Roman and foreign, whom the day to day business of the curia drew to Rome, was now at Rieti with the majority of the cardinals. The Colonna manifesto was put to them as a case in law. Unanimously they rejected the claim, and by five votes to two the Rieti cardinals made the decision their own, and fixed the coming feast of St. Luke (18 October, 1293) for the opening day of the conclave, the cardinals to assemble at Perugia. The Colonna had lost the first move, and the appointed day found them reunited with their colleagues at Perugia.

The election, however, still continued to drag, and the factions remained deadlocked for yet another ten months. In March 1294, the King of Naples paid the conclave a state visit. Beyond the fact that he was allotted a seat among the cardinal-deacons, and that he had a lively altercation with one of them, Benedict Gaetani, we know nothing of what he accomplished. In the papal state Orvieto was now at war with Bolsena; the Romans had overturned the government of their city, and called in as senator one of the last surviving officials of the Ghibelline regime of thirty years before. Affairs had gone from bad to worse and seemed about to touch the worst itself, when, in the first week of July, the news arrived that the cardinals had elected a pope.

For the task of reconstructing the badly-damaged fabric of Christendom they had chosen an old man of eighty-five, Peter of Murrone, a hermit who, for many years now, had lived in the inaccessible solitudes of the Abruzzi. The newly elected had begun life as a Benedictine monk. After governing his monastery for a year as abbot, he had sought leave to live as a hermit. Soon the spiritual want of the peasantry around forced him into new activity as a kind of wandering preacher, and he became to this mountainous countryside very much what St. Francis had been, fifty years earlier, to Umbria. Disciples gathered round him and presently Peter had founded a new religious order which followed a way of life based on the rule of St. Benedict. And next, once the various houses of the order were established, the founder had given up his place in it, and had gone back to the life of solitude that had been his ideal throughout. What brought him to the notice of the cardinals in July 1294, was a letter one of them had received from him, violently denouncing their incapacity to provide the Church with a head, and threatening them all with the wrath of God unless they found a pope within four months. The indignation of the letter seems to have been due to a meeting with the King of Naples (whose subject Peter was) after Charles II's fruitless visit to the cardinals at Perugia; the king had explained to the hermit what an immensity of harm the long vacancy had wrought. The effect of the letter was instantaneous. That same day the cardinals chose Peter for pope (July 5, 1294).

Their choice, of course, struck the popular imagination immediately, as it has held it ever since. And yet the brief reign of Peter di Murrone was, as might have been expected, little short of disastrous. No one, in the end, realised this more clearly than Peter himself. There was only one way out of the situation, and being a saint he took it, abdicating his high office as simply as he had accepted it.

Peter was not enthroned as pope -- and did not assume his papal name, Celestine V -- until August 29, nine weeks after his election. The interval was filled with the beginnings of the great scandal that marked the reign, the acts by which the King of Naples laid hold on the whole machinery of church government, while the eleven cardinals -- still at Perugia, still divided -- could think of nothing more helpful than to beg the man they had elected to leave Neapolitan territory for his own Papal State, and to refuse all his demands that they leave the Papal State and come to him at Aquila.

While this deadlock endured (July-August) the Neapolitans and some of the cardinals, and a host of adventurers, clerical and lay, made the most of their splendid opportunity. The basis of this was, of course, the new pope's utter and absolute inexperience of anything beyond the guidance of a small community of peasant monks, his excessively delicate conscience, his simple belief in the goodness of man, and his never-ending desire to put all his authority and power into the hands of others while he retired to solitude and prayer. "His entire and dangerous simplicity" one chronicler of the time remarks as a cause of troubles, while another writes of his unawareness of frauds and of that human trickery in which courtiers excel. [ ] In these brief weeks the papacy fell into the most complete servitude which, perhaps, it has ever endured; and it did so with the pope's entire good will, utterly unaware as he was of the consequences of his acts.

The King of Naples was at Celestine's side almost as soon as the official messengers sent with the news of his election. Two high officials of the Neapolitan kingdom -- laymen both -- were given key posts in the administration of the universal church; another subject of King Charles was put in command of the papal armies; and a fourth, who as Archbishop of Benevento had already betrayed Celestine's predecessor, was given the highest post in the curia after the pope. Next the king suggested to Celestine that the number of cardinals was dangerously small -- there were but ten of them. Celestine agreed to create more, and accepted a list of twelve, all proposed by Charles. Five were Frenchmen, like the king himself. Of the others, six were clerics very much at Charles's service (and all Neapolitans) -- one of them the chancellor of the kingdom -- while the seventh was really promoted in order that the king's son, Louis, [ ] could be given the vacated see of Lyons. Thus was the number of cardinals more than doubled in a day, and a permanent majority secured for Neapolitan interests.

The king's next move was to persuade the pope to leave the little town of Aquila, that had been the scene of these unusual events, for Naples, his capital. This proposal was strongly opposed by the cardinal Benedict Gaetani who, after holding aloof long after the others, had now joined Celestine. But the king's will prevailed and Celestine, with Charles alone beside him, and carefully segregated from the independent cardinals, set out for Naples. The journey saw still more surrenders to the king. He was freed from the oath he had sworn not to detain the cardinals on Neapolitan territory should Celestine chance to die; the

Archbishop of Benevento was created a cardinal, privately and without any ceremony, or notification to the rest of the Sacred College; and the important law of Nicholas III that forbade any sovereign prince to accept the office of Roman Senator was repealed. Also, as the pope passed by Monte Cassino, he changed the rule (substituting that of his own order) and appointed one of his own monks as abbot.

Meanwhile, the papal resources had been shamefully exploited for the private profit of all who could get at the machinery; appointments, pensions, grants of land, of jurisdiction, of dispensations fell in showers. The pope was even induced to set his signature to blank bulls, which the recipient filled up as he chose.

And now the King of Naples overreached himself. It had been a lifelong practice with Celestine to pass the whole of Lent and of Advent in absolute solitude and prayer, making ready for the great feasts of Easter and Our Lord's Nativity. Towards the end of November 1294, as Celestine began to speak of his coming retreat, the king suggested to him that, for the conduct of church affairs during these four weeks, it would be well to name a commission of three cardinals with full power to act in his name. Celestine agreed, but a cardinal (not one of the three) came across this extraordinary document as it awaited a final accrediting formality. He urged upon the pope that here was something beyond his powers. The Church, he said, could not have three husbands. And with this, Celestine's scruples began to master him. Quite evidently he was not the man for the office; ought he not to give it up? and after days of prayer and consultation with friends and with the canonists, he finally resolved the two questions that tormented his conscience. Could the lawfully-elected pope lawfully resign the office? How ought this to be done? The first point Celestine appears to have decided for himself on the general principles of resignation to be found in the manuals of Canon Law. The cardinals whom he consulted agreed that his view of the law was correct. In the delicate technical question about the best way to carry out his plan, Celestine had the expert assistance of Gerard Bianchi, cardinal-bishop of Sabina, and of Benedict Gaetani. Finally, he issued a bull declaring the pope's right to resign and then, in accordance with this, before the assembly of the cardinals, he gave up his great office, laying aside his mitre, his sandals and his ring (December 13, 1294).

## 4. BONIFACE VIII, 1294-1303 ⌒

Celestine V had renewed the law of the conclave. [ ] This excellent measure brought it about that the vacancy was soon filled, for the election was over in a single day. At the first ballot Matteo Orsini was elected. He refused the office. The second ballot was inconclusive. At the third, the cardinals chose Benedict Gaetani, December 24, 1294. He took the name Boniface VIII.

Not the least of the difficulties that awaited whoever succeeded Celestine was the primary duty of neutralising the harm produced by the scandalous exploitation of the hermit pope's inexperience. And whatever the personal character and disposition of that successor, it would be only too easy to distort, for the generality of men, his restoration of the ordinary routine of a pope's life after the idyllic episode of Celestine -- the pope who rode upon an ass to Aquila for his coronation, and who had lived in a hut of rough planking set up in the splendid hall of the royal palace at Naples.

Boniface VIII was not the man to be turned, for a moment, from his obvious duty by any such anxieties as these. Indeed -- and this is one of the weaknesses in his character -- it is doubtful if they would occur to him as causes for anxiety. He had a firstrate intelligence, highly trained, and a first-hand acquaintance with every aspect of the complex problem before him, and with most of the leading personalities whom any attempt to solve it must involve. His own speciality was Law, and as a papal jurist Boniface was to close, not unworthily, the great series of popes that began with Alexander III, just over a hundred years before him. He was himself the nephew of Alexander IV, and was thereby kin to the great Conti family whence had also come Innocent III and Gregory IX. For many years the various popes had made use of him in diplomatic missions, and one of these, in 1268, had brought him, in the suite of Cardinal Ottoboni, [ ] to the London of Henry III, in the turbulent years that followed the Barons' War. The French pope, Martin IV, had created him a cardinal, and Boniface, in the Sacred College, seems to have been what, as pope, he described himself, always a strong friend to the interests of France and of Charles of Anjou. Certainly in his great mission to France in 1290 -- the peak of his diplomatic career -- he had not given signs of anything like a militant independence of the lay power as such. Indeed he had been all that was tactful and conciliatory towards Philip the Fair. In the conclave at Perugia he had shown himself amused and sceptical about the move to elect Celestine V, [ ] and for some time had kept aloof from the regime which followed. When finally he had rejoined his colleagues it had been to watch, somewhat disgusted, the uncontrolled plunder of rights and property that was the order of the day, and then, with his firm advice -- once this was asked -- to point the only way out of the scandal.

The nine-years reign of Boniface VIII was to be one of the most momentous in all Church history; it is, indeed, generally regarded as marking the end of an epoch, and the beginning of the new age when the popes and religion gradually cease to be taken into account as factors in the public life of the Christian nations. And from its very beginning the reign was one long crisis for the pope -- a crisis which, for by far the greater part, was not of his making and which arose from the convergence, brought about by a master adversary, of forces which had plagued the Holy See for years. The chronic problem of the

Sicilian revolt; the active Ghibellinism of central and northern Italy; the anti-papal hostility among the Spiritual Franciscans; the determination of the French to maintain and increase their hold upon the Holy See; the renaissance of the wild theories associated with the prophecies of Abbot Joachim; the prevailing talk about the speedy coming of anti-Christ -- these were elements of trouble for which Boniface VIII was in no way responsible. Nor were the new elements his invention; the carefully fostered rumours, for example, that he was not lawfully elected, the jealous hatred of the Colonna cardinals, the libel that he was a heretic (this derived from Charles II's anger at his influence with Celestine and was heard from the very outset of his reign), the associated libel that he had first procured the invalid resignation of Celestine and then his murder -- all these elements were rapidly combined and used in the business of making the pope a tool of French policy.

On the other hand, Benedict Gaetani continued to be his old, violent self, too well aware of his own splendid talent, of the great successes of his public career. He was jealous of his authority, impatient of contradiction, his self-control easily shaken by evidences of malevolent opposition, of treachery, of blackmail -- and these were all to come in plenty. As a cardinal he had had the opportunity of improving his family's fortunes, [ ] and he had used it to build up a really considerable feudal lordship in the countryside whence he came, the Lepini mountains and the valley of the Sacco, the neighbourhood of Anagni and Segni. He had not succeeded without making bitter enemies of those he had managed to dispossess. From among them the great clan of the Colonna, whose rivalry he had thereby challenged, would one day recruit willing assistants for the great raid on Anagni that brought the pope's life to an end. It had been a great career for thirty years or so, and it had brought Boniface many, many enemies. He knew well the general duty that lay before him, to deliver the Holy See from the toils in which the events of the last twenty-five years had enmeshed it. Once free of these it would resume its natural place, and lead Christendom as in the great days of Urban II, of Alexander III and Innocent III.

The new pope was confident, and a new strong tone would be evident from his first acts, but there would not be anywhere that reality of strength which only comes from new, generously conceived solutions; from solutions devised by the rare mind which, at a turning point of history, has divined that the actions of men in a long-drawn crisis have ceased to be merely the fruit of political expediency, and that they are now the signs and proof of fundamental change in their whole view of life. It was to be the pope's greatest misfortune -- and the misfortune of religion -- that he remained unaware of the nature of what was now happening, and hence had no more resource with which to meet a real revolution of the spirit than those political and legal combinations in which his genius excelled. The time needed a saint who was also a political genius: it was given no more than an extremely competent, experienced official. [ ]

The new pope, immediately, so acted as to prove the freedom of his see from all royal influence. He solemnly rebuked and degraded the senior cardinal who had been Charles II's first and principal instrument in the enslavement of Peter of Murrone; he instantly (as requested by Celestine) [ ] revoked all dispensations, grants, appointments, pensions, exemptions, incorporations, the whole mass, indeed, of what were now described as varia minus digne inordinata et insolita, made by his predecessor; also all promissory grants of benefices made since the death of Nicholas IV, Celestine's predecessor; he suspended all bishops and archbishops nominated by Celestine without the advice of the cardinals; he dismissed the laymen whom Celestine had appointed to curial posts; he dismissed from his household all the officials and chaplains appointed under Celestine; and he ordered the papal court to leave for Rome, forbidding any official business to be transacted as from Naples, or any letters to be issued until he had been crowned in Rome and had established the curia there in manifest independence. It was the height of the winter for that fearful journey over the mountains, the last days of the old year, but Boniface forced the pace, and Charles II was forced to accompany the caravan: the king, this time, in the suite of the pope. On January 23, 1295, Boniface was crowned, with all possible pomp, as though to drive home the lesson that the Church by no means refuses, in its mission, to make use of that world it is appointed to save by ruling it.

The first task was to bring together the kings of France and England, now furiously at war. For his legate to France Boniface chose his one-time adversary, the cardinal Simon de Beaulieu. It was misplaced generosity. Simon's rancour had survived, and his mission to the court of Philip the Fair (May 1295) was one starting-point of the schismatical manoeuvres that were the French king's most ingenious instrument to lever the pope into submission. Cardinal Simon laid bare to the French all the weaknesses in the pope's position: the discontent of some of the cardinals at this would-be Innocent III's ambition for his own family, the theories that he was not lawfully elected, the possibilities of the Colonna coming out in opposition to him, the latent menace of the innumerable followers of Abbot Joachim; in brief, the welcome news that at Rome all the material for a control of the pope lay to hand for whoever could organise it. Philip's response was to despatch to Rome the Prior of Chezy, to sound the disaffected and weld them into a party.

While the Prior of Chezy was busy at Rome undermining the new pope's position, reports and complaints were beginning to come in from France of taxes levied on the clergy without their consent, and of sequestration of Church property when payment was not made. The war with England had already drained the meagre resources of the crown, and knowing well the uselessness of asking Rome to grant Church moneys for a merely national war against another Christian prince, Philip the Fair defied immemorial custom, and his own pledge given in 1290, and imposed one tax after another upon Church properties. The like necessity was, at this very time, forcing Edward I of England to adopt similar measures, and the English king also was meeting with opposition from the clergy. [ ] The bishops of France, indeed, made no protest, but from the clergy and the religious orders bitter complaints now went to Rome that evil counsellors were misleading the king, but "no royal judgment," it was urged, "can destroy canonical rights." The bishops were showing themselves dumb dogs that had forgotten how to bark, and "no one any longer dares freely to defend the Church against the powers of this world." Will not the pope come to their aid?

As in England and in France, so also was it in Italy, and the petition from France found Boniface already considering the problem. His interest was not lessened by a new turn of events in Sicily, [ ] and the certainty of an active renewal of the war and therefore of the Holy See's needing all the ecclesiastical revenues it could gather in.

To levy taxes on all the inhabitants of a country has been, for generations now, one of the most obvious rights of all states; and taxation is a permanent feature of public life everywhere. There is never a time when every citizen is not paying taxes regularly, and as a matter of course, to the government of his country. It is only with an effort that we can realise that this is a comparatively recent institution, that for our ancestors the normal thing was that governments paid their way without need of such permanent assistance from the general body of the people, and that taxes were only lawfully levied when some extraordinary crisis -- a just war, for example -- arose. Moreover, taxes were the outward sign of servitude. Nobles were in many cases immune from them; so too were the clergy. A new theory of taxation was indeed beginning to be heard at this very time, namely that equity demands that all shall contribute to the cost of what profited all [ ]. But, as yet, this was a new and novel idea. the pope only followed the then classic opinion that related taxes to servitude when, in answer to the complaints of the clergy of France and elsewhere, he published his new law. This is the bull Clericis Laicos (February 24, 1296). It is written in challenging confident style, without any attempt to argue the reasonableness of the now violated clerical immunity, or to make allowance for the possibility that this was at times abused. The laity -- so it opens -- it is well known, have always hated the clergy. Here is a new proof of this, in the extraordinary new financial oppression of the Church. So the pope, to protect the Church against royal rapacity, enacts the new law. Unless the Holy See had authorised the king to levy it no cleric must pay any state tax levied on church revenues or property. Those who pay such unlawful taxes are to be punished by suspension and, if they are bishops, by being deposed. Rulers who levy such taxes without leave of the pope, are to be excommunicated and their kingdoms placed under interdict. [ ]

The law appears all the more severe when it is studied through the storm of conflict which it provoked. But there is every reason to think that the opposition was a surprise to Boniface, and that nothing gave him more genuine and painful surprise than that the opposition came from Philip the Fair. It was a general law, and Boniface had not in mind a particular attack on any prince -- least of all on the King of France. For what now occupied the pope, almost to the exclusion of all else, was the war in Sicily. No prince was at this moment more necessary to him than Philip, and throughout the following months favours continued to descend upon the French king from Rome, while the papal diplomacy was active in restraining the emperor from joining in the French war as Edward I's ally.

Nor did Philip the Fair, for months, give any sign of displeasure at the bull. He first learned of the bull when the Archbishop of Narbonne begged not to be pressed for taxes due, since a new law made by the pope forbade him to pay them (April 1296). The king was in no condition to begin a campaign against Boniface;

the war with England was going against him. So, for the moment, he merely noted the fact and was content not to force the archbishop to pay. Later on, in that same year, he came to an arrangement with the emperor which saved him any need of papal protection on his eastern frontier and he now began to work upon the French bishops to petition the pope to withdraw the bull. The king's anger was such, they wrote to Rome, that the most terrible things would happen to the Church in France if he were not appeased.

And then (August 17, 1296) as part of the emergency regulations called for by the war, Philip did something that touched the pope vitally. This was to enact a law forbidding the export of munitions of war, horses, gold and foreign exchange, and expelling all the foreign bankers from France. This was done at the very moment when certain funds belonging to the Holy See, but actually in France, were about to be transferred to Spain, to pay the expenses of the King of Aragon's at last arranged visit to Rome. This, of course, was no ceremonial journey but a highly important move in the papal diplomacy. For the king was going to Rome in order to persuade, or force, his brother, the King of Sicily, to come to an arrangement with the pope. And much diplomacy, it may be understood, had had to be used to bring the King of Aragon to consent. Now, at this crucial moment -- and not without knowledge that the moment was crucial -- the King of France had given his answer to the pope's new law about clerical taxation. It is one of the oddest coincidences that so far was Boniface, even yet, from suspecting this enmity that, on the very day almost of Philip's edict, he wrote to France ordering the legate now to publish the bull. And he wrote on the same day the like instructions to the legate in England. The benevolence to France still continued. This last act was part of it. To publish the bull in France and in England, simultaneously, would be to cut off supplies from both the contending parties, and thereby end a war that was running against Philip. On the same day the pope wrote a third letter to support his pro-French intervention, to the emperor this time, warning him not to attack the French.

The whole action of Boniface during all these months does indeed prove "the confidence with which the alliance with France inspired him." [ ] His bitterness when the news of the French edict undeceived him was all the greater. It took shape in the letter Ineffabilis Amoris, [ ] a menacing if fatherly lecture addressed to the king, telling him that Clericis Laicos is a law which Philip, as a good Catholic, must obey. How foolish of him to choose such a moment as this to quarrel with Rome, when everywhere in Europe the French are hated ! The pope is the king's one friend. Let him dismiss his evil counsellors, the real authors of that aggressive policy that has antagonised all the Christian princes. Will he now, in a final blunder, force the pope to become their ally, or make the Holy See his principal enemy? Let him disregard the lie that the pope's new law is meant to forbid the clergy to help the state in its necessities. This was not ever the pope's meaning, as the pope has already made clear to the king's ambassadors.

This letter was known in France by the November, and in the next two weeks two very noteworthy commentaries on it began to circulate, the Dialogue between a Knight and a Clergyman and the tract which begins Antequam essent clerici. Both were anti-papal, shrewdly conceived, [ ] well written, the work of the lay scholars in the king's entourage. To make his reply to the pope, Philip sent to Rome once more the Prior of Chezy; part of that "reply" was to work up the Colonna and "soften" the pope's defences in preparation for a new French aggression.

The winter months of 1296-7 were, in fact, a critical time for Boniface. The King of Naples -- a principal ally in the Sicilian business -- had taken up the case which the Colonna were preparing. These last were not the only cardinals dissatisfied with the pope's Italian policy, and the great rival of the Colonna,

Napoleone Orsini, was hoping, through the King of Naples, to persuade Philip the Fair to undertake the salvation of the Church from the pope ! Then the King of Aragon's visit was a failure. He agreed to the plans proposed, but his ideas about the money that would be needed seemed to Boniface astronomical. The pope had not anything like such sums -- unless he could recover his money from France and also what the Cistercians and Templars (also in France) were willing to give.

And then gradually, slowly, the pope began to yield to the King of France. A new letter went to Philip [ ] that was a milder version of the Ineffabilis Amoris and still more explicit in its statement that Boniface had in no way meant to control the king's right to take all necessary measures for the safety of the realm. But Philip should be more careful and precise in the terms of his edicts, lest he chance to infringe on the rights of others. The lines of the compromise are already evident, the formula to be devised to save face on both sides when both return to the status quo ante. A second, private, letter of the same date promised Philip a continuance of the old favours, and new ones also. The cause of Louis IX's canonisation was now complete -- the ceremony would be a pleasant ending to the contest. And a third bull, Romana Mater, also of the same date, practically suspended the Clericis Laicos so far as it concerned France. The principle of that bull, indeed, remained untouched; but a system of general exceptions to the law was announced. Its most important feature was that it was now left to the king to define what was a national necessity, and so a lawful occasion for imposing taxes on the Church without consulting the Holy See.

At the same time the legates in France were notified that, should Philip not allow the transfer of the pope's moneys out of France for the Sicilian war, they were publicly to declare him excommunicated. Boniface had not, by any means, wholly surrendered. And he gave signs of this in another, public, declaration only a few weeks later. This was a letter to the bishops of France allowing them to vote subsidies from Church moneys to the king, now in the first crisis of the revolt of Flanders. The pope is lavish in expressions of sympathy for France. He is most willing that the bishops should aid the king, and he gladly allows them to do so. But it is evident, from the letter, that the pope interprets the petition from France as an acceptance of the principle behind the Clericis Laicos, the right of the Holy See to decide whether church revenues shall be used to aid the state.

The French king was, however, very far from any such surrender as this and, as if to show it, he now worked upon the University of Paris to debate the question, already so much canvassed wherever Boniface had enemies in Italy, whether a pope could lawfully resign; and to publish its decision that he could not do so. As Celestine V was dead it followed that there was now no pope, and this declaration from what was the most influential centre of Christian learning, was an immense encouragement to the various enemies of Boniface.

The chief of these were, by now, the Colonna, and the pope's policy of checking them by increasing the power of his own kinsfolk drove the Colonna, in May 1297, to open rebellion. One of the clan attacked a convoy and captured papal treasure en route for Rome. The pope gave the cardinals of the family four days in which to restore the money, to surrender all the family fortresses and submit themselves. They ignored the command and were thereupon deposed from their rank. Whereupon, a day later, from their stronghold of Longhezza, they issued a manifesto denouncing the crimes of "Benedict Gaetani who styles himself the Roman Pontiff". Celestine V had no power to resign, they declared, and the election of Boniface was no election; a council must meet to put things right, and meanwhile the pope should be considered as suspended from his office. To this they added the accusation that Boniface had murdered his predecessor.

The pope was by no means to be intimidated. He excommunicated the whole faction of the Colonna as schismatic, and made a solemn declaration of the validity of his own election which, for three years nearly, the Colonna cardinals (who had voted for him) had fully and freely recognised. This was a telling blow; and it gained force when all the other cardinals set their signatures to a special statement which told the story of the conclave that elected Boniface, and declared that they wholly concurred in the excommunication of the rebels. The answer of the Colonna was to appeal to their allies in the University of Paris (15 June). Again they demanded a General Council, and denounced Boniface as a man whose sole aim was to amass a fortune. Bishops everywhere, they said, were appointed for a price, and the idea behind this centralisation of power was a hierarchy so dependent on Boniface that they would not dare to question his legitimacy.

It was with Italian affairs in this critical state that Philip the Fair now sent to the pope a mission headed by the chief of his professional lay counsellors, the legist Pierre Flotte. The Colonna had appealed to Philip to keep the promises of support made through the Prior of Chezy and now, on his way to Orvieto, Flotte assured them that his business there was to denounce the pope's crimes and solemnly publish the appeal to the General Council that should judge him: in which, as will be seen, Flotte lied -- but successfully, for, because of his assurance, the Colonna remained in the field and, prolonging the crisis, secured for the French that atmosphere of anxiety and alarm at the papal court in which they could best wring from Boniface the new concessions they had in mind.

In the diplomatic duel now engaged, the Frenchman, from the beginning, had the upper hand. For Boniface was in a weak position; the Colonna were still active and evidently confident, the French possibly willing to aid them, and, what was infinitely more serious, threatening to support a movement that denied him to be pope at all, and so initiate a schism. The danger here was deadly, and under the threat of it the pope gave in at point after point. The surrender was set out in a series of bulls -- sixteen in all. It amounted to a wholesale withdrawal of Clericis Laicos, a very serious modification of the clergy's immunity from arrest and trial in the king's courts, and grants of church money; and a well-timed threat of excommunication to the King of Aragon should he fail in his word to France. "In exchange for the imaginary document which had kept the Colonna in rebellion and Boniface in a crisis of anxiety, the ambition of Philip had won immensely important advantages, positions for future development." [ ] From now on, for the best part of four years, Boniface VIII would be no longer the independent chief of Christendom but "an obliging agent for the schemes of Philip the Fair". [ ] It was at the conclusion of these negotiations, and as a final gesture of good will to Philip, that the pope published the already decided canonisation of the king's grandfather, Louis IX. Through what a world of revolution had not French -- and papal -- policy passed since the saint's death, twenty-seven years before.

The history of the three years that followed the pope's capitulation at Orvieto to Pierre Flotte, makes the least pleasant reading of the reign. During the rest of that summer of 1297, and the autumn, the war continued to go well for the French in Gascony, in Brittany and in Flanders; while Edward had to face a new leader in Scotland, William Wallace, to suffer defeat from him and then find his own barons resolutely opposed to the whole war policy. It was as one result of a constitutional crisis at home that Edward, in the closing weeks of the year, sought a truce, and when it was made a condition that he should agree with Philip to submit the whole difference to the pope's arbitration he gladly agreed (18 February, 1298).

The French king knew well what he was about, and that he could count on having the pope, by the time the peace talks began, in such a position that France would control the decision The months that had seen the French position grow so strong while Edward's so weakened, saw Boniface VIII ever more feeble in face of the Colonna rebels and Sicily. The rebels still flouted his demands for unconditional surrender, and with the aid of such brilliant lampoonists as Jacopone da Todi they kept up a very successful anti-papal propaganda among the many friends of the Franciscan Spirituals, the visionaries, and the Ghibelline politicians of the towns. When they proposed a league with the King of Sicily, the pope was at the end of all his resources. His only hope lay in the Kings of Naples and Aragon; these would not move without a certainty of money supplies, and Boniface was all but bankrupt.

As a last alternative to surrendering to rebels and schismatics Boniface now proclaimed a crusade against the Colonna (27 November, 1297). To fight against them was as good an action -- and as munificently rewarded in spiritual favours -- as to travel to Jerusalem and fight the Turk. Everywhere legates were sent out to preach the crusade and to gather in alms. But response was slow, and the pope's anxiety had hardly lessened when, towards the end of March 1298, the Flemings and the English came into Rome for the arbitration.

The French followed some weeks later, and from the moment they arrived they had it all their own way. First they refused to take for arbitrator the pope as such: he must judge the case as Benedict Gaetani merely. And the pope agreed to this. Then they hinted to the pope that the English and the Flemings stood to them as the Colonna stood to Boniface -- they were rebellious feudatories. And Boniface, only a few weeks ago so grateful to the Flemings for their wholehearted support, now deserted them. And when the Flemings consulted their English allies-pledged not to make terms without them -- these advised them heartily to accept whatever the pope had in store for them. The English indeed had not much more to expect. The arbitrator's sentence was published on June 30, 1298. It carefully refrained from any decisions on the matters that had caused the war; it established a peace between the two kings, to be confirmed by a double marriage, and it provided for a mutual restoration of captured goods; the territorial questions were postponed. The whole decision had been inspired by one thing only, the pope's desire to please the King of France.

The papal arbitration of 1298 seems a singular mockery of the high claim to supervise the affairs of princes in the interests of justice. It marks the very nadir of the international action of the medieval papacy. But the same months which saw Benedict Gaetani so lend himself to the French king's game, were also those in which Boniface VIII, in the tradition of the greatest of the canonist popes, promulgated a great measure of law reform, completing and bringing up to date the first official code published in 1234 by Gregory IX.

The sixty years since that great event had seen the two General Councils of Lyons, both of them notable for a mass of new legislation. They had seen the reigns of a dozen popes, among them Innocent IV, "the greatest lawyer that ever sat upon the chair of St. Peter", [ ] and Clement IV, one of the great jurists of his day. Boniface himself was no unworthy successor to such popes in professional competence as a lawyer. A host of new laws had been made, some to meet special emergencies, others for permanent needs. Until some official collection and arrangement was made of all this mass the law must, in very many matters, remain doubtful and uncertain. Nowhere was the harm of this state of things better understood than at Bologna, the university which was, for Law, what Paris was for Theology. Boniface was no sooner crowned than Bologna besought him to remedy the disorder.

The pope immediately set himself to the task in masterly professional fashion. Four canonists [ ] were named and given extensive powers to review the whole mass of legislation since

1234, to suppress what was temporary or superfluous, to resolve contradictions, to abridge, to modify, to correct and to make whatever additions were needed to make the law's meaning clear beyond doubt. Their work was not to be incorporated in the five existing books of Gregory IX's arrangement; but to form a separate, sixth book of decretals -- hence its name, the Sext. In its own framework the Sext -- in its divisions and subdivisions, and in the headings for all these -- is a replica of Gregory IX's book. Thus the Sext is first divided into five "books", each corresponding to and bearing the same name as the several books of the larger collection. In each "book" of the new work, in the same order and under the same headings, are the chapters (capita) which represent the laws of the intervening sixty years. In all the Sext contains 359 chapters arranged under 76 titles, the greater part of these new laws (251) taken from the decretals of Boniface himself. As an appendix there are the Regulae Iuris, 88 in number. The commission took three years to complete its task, and on March 3, 1298, it was officially despatched to Bologna, with the bull promulgating it, as law for the schools and for the courts. This, and this alone, of the legislation enacted between 1234 and 1294 was henceforth law. In its opening words the bull declares once more the traditional divinely-given primacy of the Roman See over the whole Church of Christ, and it does so with that easy serenity that never deserts the bishops of that see whenever they refer to this fundamental truth: Sacrosanctae Romanae Ecclesiae quam imperscrutabilis divinae providentiae altitudo universis, dispositione incommutabili, praetulit ecclesiis, et totius orbis praecipuum obtinere voluit magistratum regimini praesidentes. . .: [ ] it also makes an unmistakable reference to the pope's claim to be really, on earth, King of Kings.

At last the tide of war began to turn in Boniface's favour. In October (1298) the Colonna lost their last stronghold, their own "home-town" of Palestrina, to the papal army. And then the rebels gave themselves up. The two cardinals appeared before the pope; kneeling before him, they abjured their wicked manifesto of Longhezza, and acknowledged him as the lawful pope. "Father I have sinned against heaven and before thee," said the older cardinal to Boniface, "I am not now worthy to be called thy son."

It was at Rieti that Boniface received their submission, and he was still resident there when the famous earthquakes of Advent Sunday, 1298, shook the little town to its foundations, and set the whole population in flight to the fields and hills around. The pope had been about to begin a solemn pontifical mass, surrounded by all his court, when the shock occurred. He seems to have behaved with the coolness which all stories of him indicate as a leading characteristic and, with the impatience that was no less characteristic, he snubbed the suggestion of a pious cleric standing by, that perhaps this was the beginning of the end of all.

There were, however, hundreds of pious folk for whom the earthquake was a special revelation of the divine opinion about Boniface and his policies. Rieti lay in a district where every valley had its hermitage of Franciscan Spirituals. Not so far away was Greccio, hallowed for all time by its memories of the great Christmas night when St. Francis set up there the first crib. Down to this time it had continued to be a chief centre of the Spiritual movement. There, for more than thirty years, almost to the time of Boniface's election, had been the refuge of John of Parma, the great Spiritual who had been general of the order until St. Bonaventure displaced him (1257), and who, at the very end of his life, [ ] barely ten years ago, had been summoned out of his retirement to advise the cardinal James Colonna. In no part of Italy was there more pious resentment against Boniface, and the coincidence that the pope was sojourning in the midst of it when a thing so unheard of as the earthquake happened, was the clear judgment of God on the surrender of the protectors of the Spirituals to the false pope who had persecuted these holy men.

To the Spirituals Boniface was no pope at all, for he had been elected in the lifetime of the last lawful pope, and the only pope to befriend their movement, Celestine V: and, his succession to Celestine apart, the party had known Boniface for years as a leading enemy. The election of Celestine had, in fact, followed very closely upon the return to Italy of a group of leading Spirituals, allowed by a rare Minister-General of the order who favoured the party to go as missionaries to Armenia. They presented themselves to the hermit pope, explained that they were the only true followers of St. Francis, that they desired only to live according to his rule and spirit (which they alone interpreted faithfully) and to be freed from persecution by the Franciscans now living a bogus Franciscan life according to a caricature of his rule. Celestine saw in them nothing more than men whose way of life recalled his own ideal. He seems not to have realised that, impliedly, to accept this version of the complicated disputes was to call in doubt a whole chapter of his predecessors' legislation; nor to have been aware of the heretical, Joachimite, strain that affected the whole of the Spiritual movement. Without any investigation, or qualifications, he accepted their story and allowed them to form themselves into a new order with Peter of Macerata at its head. They would, however, not be called Friars Minor but "The poor Hermits of Celestine V". [ ]

Never had the hopes of this exalte revolutionary party been so high as at this pontifical decision. Peter of Macerata marked well how it could be interpreted when he changed now his religious name and called himself Fra Liberato. From all parts the zealots flocked in to join his order. And it was, seemingly, the realisation what an immense service Celestine had unwittingly rendered to the prestige of the heretical fantasies of these poor fanatics, that brought Benedict Gaetani to abandon his isolation at Perugia and join the pope at Aquila in the September of 1294.

For Benedict Gaetani knew all that was to be known about the great Franciscan question. He was an expert authority on all its phases since the time when, in 1279, Nicholas III had called him to take part in the long discussions out of which came the bull Exiit qui Seminat that gave an authoritative ruling about the Franciscan way of life; it was Benedict Gaetani, indeed, who had written the text of that famous decretal. In those weeks during which Nicholas III and his experts, and the leading Franciscans, had set aside all other business to find a solution for these troubles, the future Boniface VIII learned what he never thenceforward forgot, the invariable tendency in those who clung to the Spirituals' interpretation of the Franciscan ideal to cling no less firmly to the mad theories of Joachim of Flora. [ ]

It is not surprising that, once elected pope, he revoked Celestine's rash concession to the Spirituals, nor that he removed from his high office Raymond Gaufredi, the Minister-General of the Minorites who had favoured them, and imposed on the order a superior of his own choice who would resolutely track down these zealots. A last touch to this unpleasant work of correction was a bull [ ] that denounced the Spirituals as heretics and listed their several errors and offences. Henceforward it would be for the Inquisition to deal with them.

Nothing was, then, more natural than that the story of the earthquakes at Rieti, as the Spirituals interpreted it, should spread rapidly throughout Italy. The pope was soon threatened with a new crisis. [ ] His reaction was to set the Inquisition to work, and soon there was a steady exodus of the Spirituals towards the Adriatic coast and across the sea to Greece and to that church of Constantinople which Joachimite prophecy pointed out as the last refuge of true spirituality. One tiny group -- five men and thirteen women -- passing through Rome, and finding themselves conveniently in St. Peter's, elected one of their number pope.

There was one leading centre of this anarchic religiosity where for years the pope's writ had ceased to run, namely the island of Sicily; and one effect of this latest revival was to stiffen Boniface still further in his determination to expel the Aragonese and to re-establish normal relations with this most important fief of the Holy See. The pope's latest ally, the King of Aragon, had for five months been vainly besieging his brother Frederick in Syracuse, and in his demands for money he outdid even Philip the Fair. Boniface, driven to the last extremity, had to put himself into the hands of the Florentine bankers and the Jews; and as he descended to these humiliations, his rage against the Colonna, to whose patronage he attributed the latest Franciscan ebullition, poisoned his judgment. They were still at Rieti, interned, with all the misery of an indeterminate fate hanging over them, and when the pope now (June 1299) ordered the total destruction of their town of Palestrina as a warning to all future time, and commanded the very site to be ploughed up and sown with salt, despair seized on the Colonna, and breaking out of prison, they fled across the frontiers, to be active centres of opposition as long as Boniface lived, and to nurse a revengeful hatred that would afflict his memory for many years after he was dead. The King of Aragon chose this moment to desert (I September, 1299) and the pope's sole support now was Florence.

It was now that the complicated manoeuvres of papal and anti-papal factions in the Tuscan capital brought into conflict with Boniface the greatest man of all this generation, one of the world's supreme poets, Dante Alighieri. In his verse, Boniface was to live for ever, the object of undying hate as a man and as a ruler, and, then for his last broken hours, the object of Dante's pity as a symbol of that defeat of the spiritual by its own which is the eternal tragedy of the history of the Church. The great poem still lay in the distant future, but in this crisis of papal history Dante set his talents as scholastic and legist to a vigorous attack on that theory of the supremacy of the spiritual power in temporal affairs which had long been current in official ecclesiastical circles, the theory of which Boniface was about to show himself a most uncompromising exponent. [ ]

While Pierre Flotte had been successfully exploiting his hold on the pope to the advantage of France abroad, he had used these same years of what we may perhaps call the pope's servitude to consolidate at home the royal victory over ecclesiastical jurisdiction. There was not any attempt to enact anti-clerical laws: the crude mistake of our own Henry II enforcing the Constitutions of Clarendon was carefully avoided. But the exercise of ecclesiastical jurisdiction over the layman was fettered as much as possible, hindered by every restraint which administrative genius could devise; and everywhere the lay lord was encouraged when he came into conflict with an episcopal suzerain. Soon there were bitter fights in many French sees. And Flotte was planning a new attempt to restore the Latin empire in the East, with a French prince reigning at Constantinople, with Venice and Genoa (reconciled at last and in alliance) supporting him. Italy too would be remodelled, after the plan accredited to Nicholas III, but this time with French princes on both the new thrones of Lombardy and Arles. It was to be a French dominated Christendom, of the kind Pierre Dubois was about to describe in his famous memorandum and, the pope playing his part, Tuscany and Florence would be added to the papal state.

The year which followed the pope's arbitration between the kings of France and England was hardly a time when Boniface VIII could flatter himself that it was principally his ideas and will that regulated the public life of Christendom. The year was to end, however, with a great demonstration of the role of the papacy in the interior life of its subjects, in the system of the believer's relations with God; a demonstration at once of the pope's understanding of his spiritual power and of the Church's faith in it and eagerness to see it exercised.

As the new year 1300 approached there was, to a very unusual degree, all that popular interest which greets the coming of a new century, the usual vague expectation of coming good fortune, but this time heightened -- no doubt very largely through the recent revival and popularisation of the prophecies of Abbot Joachim.

The numbers of the pilgrims bound for Rome began to increase, and when they arrived they showed themselves clamorous for the expected, extraordinary, spiritual favours. Once every hundred years, some of them were saying, by a special act of the divine mercy, not only were a contrite man's sins forgiven, but (upon appropriate penance done) the punishment his guilt deserved was also remitted. Boniface VIII does not, by any means, seem either to have created this spirit of expectation or to have exploited it at all in the service of his public policy. [ ] Apparently he did little more than fulfil what, spontaneously, Christian piety was expecting of the Roman See when, by the bull of February 22, 1300, he instituted the Holy Year of Jubilee. It is, in effect, a grant "to all who, being truly penitent, and confessing their sins, shall reverently visit these Basilicas [of St. Peter and St. Paul] in the present year 1300. . . and in each succeeding hundredth year, not only a full and copious, but the most full pardon of all their sins." [ ]

The news of the great concession brought pilgrims to Rome by the hundred thousand, and from every part of Christendom, as a mass of contemporary literature testifies; [ ] and this novel and unmistakable evidence of what the papacy's spiritual power meant to the Christian millions seems greatly to have affected Boniface VIII.

To the pope too, it has been argued, the Jubilee was a year of special graces. The spring of this Jubilee year saw a joint embassy to Boniface from Philip the Fair and the new emperor Albert of Habsburg, and it saw also an anti-papal revolution at Florence: events that were the occasion, and the opportunity, for a reawakening in Boniface of his natural spirit of independence. But the enthusiasm of the hundreds of thousands of pilgrims did more than put new heart into the pope mall now approaching his seventieth year. This concrete demonstration of universal faith in his supernatural office recalled to him in overwhelming force his first duty to be the father and shepherd of all Christian souls -- so it is argued. [ ] The whole burden of Benedict Gaetani's case against Celestine V had been that the pope was too weak to defend the Church's freedom against the princes. But what else had Boniface VIII done, for years now, but surrender to princes? [ ]

At the audiences given now to the French ambassador, the pope made no secret of his suspicions of Flotte's designs. Tuscany, he declared, was the pope's by right. The very empire itself was the creation of the Holy See, "All the Empire's honour, pre-eminence, dignity, rights" being, as he wrote at this time to the Duke of Saxony, "derived from the liberality, the benevolence and gift of this see." As popes have set up, so they can tear down. Tuscany is a centre of discontent and hate, and so "for the honour of God, peace of Christendom, of the Church, of his vassals and subjects," the pope has determined to bring it once more under the rule of the Church. The authority of the apostolic see suffices for this. The Florentines were reminded of the same truths. The pope is the divinely appointed physician of all men's souls and sinners must accept his prescriptions. To hold any other theory is folly, for any other theory would mean that there are those in this world whom no law binds, whose crimes may go unpunished and unchecked.

Full of this new strength, Boniface brushed aside now the attempt of the French ambassadors to bully him with tales of what his enemies were saying about his private life and his faith, and taking up the complaints that came in from France about the attacks on the jurisdiction of the bishops, he sent to the king the letter Recordare Rex Inclyte (July 18, 1300). [ ] This is a remonstrance after the style of the letter -- Ineffabilis Amoris -- which had so roused the king in 1296. Boniface, as though that storm -- and the defeat it brought -- had never been, now told the king roundly that his usurpation of jurisdiction was seriously sinful, and that God would surely punish him for it did he not amend. The pope had, indeed, shown himself patient, but he could not be dumb for ever. In the end he must, in conscience, punish the king if the wrongdoing continued; and the tale of that wrong -- doing is mounting up in the files. As for Philip's advisers, these are false prophets: it is from God's grace alone that his eternal salvation will come.

From the stand taken in this letter Boniface never retreated, though it was to bring him within an ace of violent death.

Philip was too busy with the last preparations for the conquest of Flanders to make any retort, but when Flotte went to Rome in the following November (1300), the atmosphere of the court was very different from what it had been at Orvieto three years earlier. "We hold both the swords," Boniface is reported as saying, and Flotte as replying, "Truly, Holy Father: but your swords are but a phrase, and ours a reality." But there was no break of relations, and the French sent Charles of Valois into Italy to help in the double task of subduing Florence and Sicily. What brought the break was Philip's arrest of the Bishop of Pamiers in the summer of 1301. Serious charges were of course made against the prelate; he was lodged in the common prison, then taken under guard to Paris to stand his trial before the king's court. But his innocence or guilt was a detail beside the real issue, the right of the king to try him, and the fact that the king could trample down with impunity the most sacred of all clerical rights in public law. There is no doubt that this was a deliberately engineered cause celebre, whose success would mark a new era for the expanding royal jurisdiction, and greatly discredit the ecclesiastical world before the nation. [ ] And mixed up with the charges against the bishop there was a quarrel about the jurisdiction of the Inquisition, in which prominent Franciscan Spirituals attacked the Dominican inquisitors, and in which it was made very evident that in Languedoc the Albigensian movement was still a power under the surface of life. It is one of the several ways in which Philip the Fair recalls our own Henry VIII that now, while leading a life of blameless Catholic orthodoxy, he was secretly patronising and encouraging these heretics and rebels against the Church as an obvious move in the business of bringing pressure to bear on the pope.

Dom Leclercq, also, notes how "the analogy between the methods employed in the trials of Boniface, of the Bishop of Pamiers, of the Templars and of Guichard de Troyes, reveals a single manoeuvring mind at work. . . [features that] give a family likeness to a set of trials which, actually, are very individual things. Another trait in which they are alike is that, in all cases, it is difficult to bring legal proof that the charges are false. The crimes faked in Nogaret's imagination are all crimes done in secret." H.-L., VI, pt. i (1914), p. 578.

It was late October (1301) before the trial of the Bishop of Pamiers came on. It went well for the king until, in November, the Archbishop of Rheims made a strong, formal protest, in a Provincial Council, held at Compiegne, against the whole business of the bishop's arrest. The council, indeed, laid an interdict on all who, in contravention of the canon law, arrested a cleric. If a cleric so arrested should be transported to another diocese, the diocese in which he was arrested was "interdicted", and the domains of the authority responsible for the arrest. A certain amount of skilful juggling by the king's legists and the more subservient of the French bishops did indeed soon find a way through this law. But the moral effect of the declaration of Compiegne was very great, and nowhere was it more welcome than at Rome. It was indeed the first real check to the king from the French bishops for many years, the first unmistakable sign to the pope that there were bishops in France on whom he could rely.

But Boniface had not waited for this sign before taking the offensive. Flotte had written him a lying account of the trial, [ ] but it crossed a packet from the pope with a whole batch of strong, decisive letters for France. The revelations in the Pamiers case that the king was backing the Spirituals and the Albigenses, attacking the Inquisition, and that the mass of the French bishops were looking on indifferently at a most spectacular attack on the rights of their order, lifted the pope above the mere diplomatic game. From now on his action has the grave, apostolic quality of Hildebrand himself.

In these letters, written in the first week of December 1301, the pope demands that the Bishop of Pamiers be set free and allowed freely to make his way to Rome. [ ] He suspends all those privileges granted to Philip in the matter of clerical taxation and church property. [ ] He summons all the bishops of France to a council, to be held in Rome (in November 1302) where the whole question of the state of religion in France, and of the king's government of the country, will be examined; to this council the king is also invited, either to come in person or be represented there. [ ] Finally there is a letter, a confidential letter, for the king. This is the bull Ausculta Fili, 5 December, 1301, [ ] which as handled by the French, played a most important part in the events of the next eighteen months.

In many ways this letter hardly differs from the remonstrances which Boniface had already sent to the king. It tells him that his sins, as a Catholic ruler oppressing the rights of the Church, are notorious and a bad example to all Christendom. It lists these acts of usurpation and adds the crime of debasing the coinage. It again warns the king against his advisers, and points out that the whole of France is restive under their harsh, oppressive rule. The king cannot make the ministers an excuse for his sins: and the pope urges him to take part in the coming council. If he does not appear, its business will go forward without him. But all this somewhat familiar lecture acquires a new gravity from the opening passage of the letter, in which there is an extremely clear statement of the king's subject-status in relation to the pope, a statement in which we may read yet a further contribution to the controversy now engaged in which Dante, Pierre Dubois and the two great Augustinian theologians, Giles of Rome and James of Viterbo, are playing leading parts. The Church has but a single head, Boniface reminds the king, and this head is divinely appointed as a shepherd for the whole flock of Christ. To suggest, then, that the King of France has no earthly superior, that he is not in any way subject to the pope is madness, is indeed, the prelude to infidelity. This doctrinal note is to appear again, and still more strikingly, in the controversy.

Ausculta Fili was not a manifesto nor a public state paper, but a confidential letter sent privately to the king: and therein lay Flotte's opportunity. The bull was no sooner read than destroyed, and a tendentious summary of it drawn up, to be the basis of a most effective, national, anti-papal campaign. This summary -- called Deum Time from its opening words -- Flotte first submitted to a conference of theologians and legists. It adapted the teaching and claims of the first part of Boniface's letter to cover power and jurisdiction in the temporal sphere. The pope is now skilfully made to appear as claiming to be, because pope, the king's feudal overlord; the pope's consent is needed, then, for the validity of all such acts as sub-infeudation, and all the grants made so far for centuries must be invalid; also the king, as vassal to the pope, is liable for aids to the pope in all his wars.

This preparatory work done, it now remained to ask the nation's opinion on the papal claim as thus stated. The setting for this was the famous church of Notre Dame in the capital where, on April 10, 1302, representatives of the clergy, the nobles and the towns came together in the presence of the king. Flotte made a great speech, in the king's name, expounding the thesis of Deum Time, adding that the pope's citing the king to appear before him at Rome was a sample of what all had now to expect, the crown of all those usurpations of the Church of Rome on the Church of France under which, for years now, true religion had been withering away. The King of France had no superior as a temporal ruler; he stood out as the real champion of religion. And Flotte ended with an appeal to the nation to support Philip.

In the debate which followed, the suggestion was made that Boniface was a heretic and the nobles set their seals to a letter which, ignoring the pope, recounted to the college of cardinals all the charges made against Boniface, to whom they only referred as "he who at the moment occupies the seat of government in the church"; and, an incendiary statement surely, they say that "never were such things thought of except in connection with anti-Christ." Unanimously the laity pledged their support to the king.

The clergy were not so ready. They first asked for time to think it all over. It was refused them; they were told that opposition would only prove them the king's enemies. So they promised obedience to the king as vassals and asked leave to obey the pope, as they were bound, and to go to the Roman council. This also was refused them. And then they wrote to the pope, an anxious letter telling him that never had there been such a storm in France, never had the Church been in such danger, and begging the pope to abandon the plan for a council.

It was not until ten weeks later (24 June, 1302) that the delegates from the national assembly reached the pope with these letters. They were received in full consistory at Anagni, and two addresses were made to them, one by the Cardinal Matthew of Acquasparta and the other by the pope himself. The cardinal explained that the Ausculta Fili was the outcome of many weeks' deliberation between the pope and the cardinals, and he denied absolutely the interpretation put upon it in France. It was a purely pastoral act of the pope who makes no claim in it to be the king's superior judge in temporal matters but who, all men must allow, is the judge whether those whose office it is to exercise temporal power do so in accordance with morality or not.

The pope spoke most vigorously. He reprobated the chicanery which, evidently, had falsified for the public his message to Philip. He denounced Flotte by name as the real author of the mischief and with him Robert of Artois and the Count of St. Pol; they would, he prophesied, come to a bad end. Once again he gave warning that the French were hated everywhere; all Europe would rejoice when the hour of their defeat arrived. The king seemed not to realise it, but the facts were that he was on the brink of disaster. As for the council -- this to the clergy -- it must take place and, severely rebuking the cowardice of the bishops, the pope threatened the defaulters with deposition from their sees. [ ]

The cardinals sent a written reply to the letter from the nobles and in it they severely reproved their neglect to give the pope his proper style, and their reference to him by "an unwonted and insolent circumlocution".

Drama was never lacking at any stage of this long-drawn-out controversy, but now it touched the heights. While all France was being rallied to the support of the king against the pope, the French invasion of Flanders had begun. Philip had now to meet, however, not merely the feudal levies of his rebellious vassal the Count, but the enraged craftsmen of the towns. And before the envoys to Boniface had returned with the news of the pope's lurid warnings, barely a fortnight after the scene in the consistory, the French army suffered one of the greatest defeats Or its history, outside the walls of Courtrai, at the hands of Peter de Koninck and his weavers (Battle of the Golden Spurs, 11 July, 1302). And among those slain were the three men whom the pope had singled out by name, Flotte, Robert of Artois, and the Count of St. Pol.

Philip the Fair was now in full retreat, and not alone from Flanders, now lost to the French crown for ever. He no longer sounded defiance to the pope, but allowed the bishops to explain, apologetically, that they could not leave their sees at such a national crisis; and he sent an embassy to represent him at the council, an embassy which made full recognition of Boniface as pope (October 7, 1302).

Of what passed at the council we have no knowledge, but nearly half of the French bishops took part in it (39 out of 79). The pope had so far softened towards the beaten king that there was no repetition of the events at Lyons, sixty years before, when a council had tried and deposed the emperor Frederick II. There was no trial of Philip the Fair in 1303, nor sentence or declaration against him. The solitary outcome of the proceedings was a general declaration to the whole Church, the most famous act of Boniface's career, the bull Unam Sanctam (November 18, 1302). But there was not, in this, any reference to the points at issue with France, such as the list in the Ausculta Fili a twelve month before; these difficulties were now to be dealt with privately, through diplomatic channels, and as his envoy to Philip the pope chose a French cardinal, Jean Lemoine

"The dramatic context" of the bull Unam Sanctam [ ] says Boase, [ ] "gave it pre-eminence over all statements of papal power," and, we may think, has been largely responsible for the extraordinary interest in the bull ever since. For the more that is known of the detailed history of the struggle between Boniface and the French king, the less dramatic does the famous bull really appear. Two distinct -- though related questions have been in hot dispute for now nearly two centuries, namely the canonist's question about the pope's authority as pope over the temporal affairs of the world, and the theologian's question of his authority as pope to correct what is morally wrong in a ruler's conduct of temporal affairs. The bull deals chiefly with the second of these, but it also touches on the other. Throughout the dispute with Philip the Fair, Boniface VIII has denied that he is putting into force any claim to interfere with the king as a temporal ruler, ill the way for example that the king's suzerain (were there such) would have had the right to interfere. One thing alone has moved the pope throughout -- it is Boniface's constant assertion -- namely his duty to warn the king of sins he has committed in the exercise of his kingly office.

From this point of view Unam Sanctam does but continue the series in which Ineffabilis Amoris and Ausculta Fili have their place. But, unlike these, this last declaration is not addressed to the French king at all. It makes no mention of any particular ruler, but exposes the pope's case in general terms, reminding the Church in general of the nature of the pope's authority over all its members, and of the superiority which an authority of this kind must inevitably possess over every other kind of authority. And, after a certain amount of citation from Holy Writ -- none of it new -- and from Christian writing, to confirm the theory as it is explained, the document ends with the solemn definition, that for every human being it is part of the scheme of salvation that he be subject to the authority of the pope.

The general theme of the bull is that there is but one Church of Christ, a single body with but one head, Christ and his own vicar, Peter first and then Peter's successor. This scheme of things is not a human invention. It was God Himself who so arranged, when He commissioned Peter to feed God's sheep -- not these sheep, or those sheep, but all the sheep. It is by God's will that over His flock there is but a single shepherd. As for those who say they are not placed under the rule of Peter and his successor, they only confess thereby that they are not of Christ's flock, for there is but this one flock of Christ.

At the disposition of this one Church of Christ there are two kinds of power -- two swords, as the Gospel teaches us -- spiritual power and material; and the pope explains, following traditional lines, how the Church herself wields the spiritual authority, and when necessary calls upon kings and soldiers to wield on her behalf the material power. Of these two powers, the spiritual is the superior, in this sense that it is the business of the spiritual to call the material authority into existence, and to sit in judgment upon it should it go astray. Whereas the spiritual power -- in its fullness, that is to say (i.e. as realised in the papacy) -- is not subject to any judge but God. For although those who wield this spiritual power are but men, the power itself is divine, and whoever resists it strives against God. Whence it follows that to be subject to the Roman Pontiff is, for every human being, an absolutely necessary condition of his salvation: which last words -- the sole defining clause of the bull -- do but state again, in a practical kind of way, its opening phrases, "We are compelled by the promptings of faith to believe and to hold that there is one holy Catholic Church, and that the apostolic church; and this we do firmly believe and, unambiguously, profess, outside which church there is no salvation, nor any remission of sins. . . "

The bull Unam Sanctam then is a document which contains a definition of the pope's primacy as head of the Church of Christ; it is a reply to the claim, made by all parties to the anti-papal coalition, that their opposition is religious and Christian; it is a re-statement of the reality of the Church's divinely-given right to correct the sins which kings commit as kings; but the bull does not set out this right in detail, nor, though it states the right in the forms common to similar papal documents for now a hundred years and more, does it define this right in those forms, or indeed define it at all, except in so far as it is included in the general definition with which the bull ends.

The ultimatum sent through the legate to Philip -- for it was nothing short of this -- was dated November 24, 1302. It appears to have been delivered during the national assembly called for February-March of the new year. Philip's reply is embodied in his edict of March 18, 1303. The pope had noted that, seemingly, Philip was already excommunicated and the legate was given power to absolve him if he made amends. The misdeeds noted in Ausculta Fili were recalled once more. Should the king disregard this last admonition, the worst would certainly follow. The king was too shrewd to ignore the message; nor, though diplomacy had greatly improved his position since the disaster of Courtrai, did he make any sign of open defiance. He preferred to say now that his actions had been misinterpreted; and where he did not deny the charges he was evasive. If the pope was not satisfied with the answer, the king would willingly re-examine the case. It was hardly the kind of reply that would suit the pope in his new mood, nor did it at all convey the king's real mind. This public ordonnance, indeed, masked the greatest scheme yet of violence and blackmail.

While the king was playing before the assembly the part of the misunderstood champion of right, William de Nogaret, who since Flotte's death seems to have been the chief of his counsellors, was given a vague and all-embracing commission for some secret work in Italy (7 March, 1303). On March 12 he appeared before the king and his council and made a striking protestation. Boniface VIII was no pope but a usurper; he was a heretic and a simonist; he was an incorrigible criminal. Nogaret formally demanded that the king call upon the cardinals and bishops to assemble a council which, after condemning this villain, should elect a pope. Meanwhile Boniface, being no pope at all, should be put under guard, and this should be the king's care and duty; and the cardinals should appoint a vicar to rule the Church until it had once more a real pope. The king listened to this impassioned harangue with all due attention, and then solemnly consented to take on himself this serious duty. And Nogaret left to play his part in the scheme in Italy!

While he was busy there, knitting together all the forces and interests that hated Boniface, the public duel between pope and king went forward. For the pope did not leave unnoticed Philip's reply to the ultimatum. He wrote to his legate that it was equivocal, evasive, insulting, contrary to truth and equity, and sent a new summons to Rome to the regalist bishops. On both sides the decks were being cleared for action. Boniface at last recognised Albert of Habsburg as King of the Romans and emperor-elect and authorised the princes of the middle kingdom to do him homage. Most significantly of all, the pope brought to an end the long twenty-years-old Sicilian war by confirming the peace, made nine months before, [ ] between Charles of Naples and his Aragonese rival, in which the Aragonese conquest of the island was recognised. And Philip made peace with England.

When Boniface's letters and instructions to the legate reached France, the king held them up and, once again, summoned the whole nation to hear his case against the pope. It was at the Louvre that they met, bishops, nobles, commons (13 June, 1303) and the scenes of the Easter meeting of the previous year were repeated. This time the mask was fairly off and the language more violent. The pope, it was said, was a heretic, an idolator, a man who worshipped the devil. There was something to suit each of the many interests represented, and the assembly called out for a council which should judge Boniface and demanded that the king see to its summoning. And Philip, with a great protestation of love and respect for the Holy See, accepted the task. Of the twenty-six bishops present all but one set their names to the protestation and appeal. Just a week later the doctors of the University of Paris came together in the king's presence and made common cause with him, and on June 24 there was yet a third meeting, for the whole populace of Paris, in the gardens of the king's palace. The king was present, and his sons, the ministers, the bishops, the clergy. There was a harangue by the Bishop of Orleans, another by a Dominican and a third by a Franciscan; and with enthusiastic shouting and cheering, the people acclaimed the royal policy of emancipating religion from the rule of Boniface. There followed a purge of the foreign religious who stood firm for the pope, and commissioners were presently touring the whole of France, summoning everywhere meetings after the model of Paris, where the king's case was put and signatures gathered in support of it. Everywhere this organised propaganda of schism succeeded; nowhere did anyone oppose it.

In all these three months no news had come from Nogaret and on August 15 the Prior of Chezy was despatched on the last of his sinister missions to Italy. He was to find Nogaret and commission him to publish, to the pope's face if possible, the charge of heresy and the appeal to a General Council. But, by the time he reached his man, all was over.

The news of all the exciting events in Paris had leaked through the king's censorship and, on the very day the Prior of Chezy received his instructions, the pope replied to the king's attack in five letters which suspended, until Philip had submitted, all elections to vacant sees, all nominations to benefices, and the conferring of all degrees by any university. The Archbishop of Nicosia, the chief of the ecclesiastical traitors, was put under interdict, and finally there was a blistering manifesto that at last exposed the king, and defended to the world the reasonableness of the pope's action.

The French king, Boniface noted, [ ] had never questioned the pope's orthodoxy while papal favours were lavished on him. His present criticisms arose from resentment that the pope had dared to remind him of his sins. This is the whole reason for his charges against the pope. The king makes them in bad faith, hoping to escape the need of amendment by blackmailing the superior whose duty it is to correct him. The pope cannot submit to this. "What will become of the Church, what value will remain to the authority of the popes, if kings, princes and other powerful personages are allowed such a way out as this? No sooner will the pope, successor of St. Peter and charged with the care of all the flock, propose to correct some prince or magnate, than he will be accused of heresy or taxed with notorious, scandalous crime. Redress of wrong will be altogether impossible, the supreme power will be wholly overthrown." How could the pope possibly grant this French demand that he summon a General Council and submit himself to its judgment? How could a pope lend himself to the spread of such a demand? Far from assenting to it, says Boniface, the pope will, in his own time, and despite any such disingenuous appeal, proceed against the king, and his supporters too, unless they repent their now notorious crimes.

Boniface immediately proceeded to that further action he threatened, and began to draft the bull solemnly excommunicating Philip and threatening his deposition if, within a fixed time, he had not submitted and sought absolution. It was arranged that the bull should be promulgated in the cathedral at Anagni, where Boniface then was, on September 8. Nogaret learnt of what was in preparation. He realised that, at all costs, the publication of the sentence must be prevented. With a mixed troop of soldiery, gathered from half-a-dozen neighbouring towns hostile to the pope, with one of the Colonna at his side, and the standard of Philip the Fair in the van, he made for Anagni. On the eve of the appointed day he arrived before the little hillside city. Treason opened a gate for his force and after a short, sharp battle, he and his men, to the shouts of "Colonna! Colonna!" were in the papal palace and presently in the papal presence. They found the old pope prepared for them, robed and clasping his crucifix. Nogaret demanded that he withdraw the excommunication and surrender himself for judgment. He replied that he would rather die. Sciarra Colonna offered to kill the pope. The cooler-headed Frenchman held him back. Then Colonna struck the old man in the face.

The outrage was the end of Nogaret's success, however. While he parleyed with the pope, and while the Italian soldiery plundered the palace -- all they wanted and were fit for, Nogaret noted -- the fighting began again in the town, and shouts of "Death to the French!" filled the streets. It would have ruined the French monarchy to kill the pope; it was not practicable to carry him a prisoner to France through an aroused Italy. Indeed, unless Nogaret speedily fought his own way out of Anagni, he would hardly survive to tell France what he had accomplished. Within twenty-four hours he and his band were well away on the road to the north.

But the shock of this terrible Sunday was more than the pope could endure. His rescuers found a broken old man, muttering desires and threats, incapable now of thought or decision. The cardinals persuaded him to return to Rome, and within three weeks he was dead (October 20, 1303).

## 5. PHILIP THE FAIR'S LAST VICTORY, 1303-1314

Ten days after the death of Boniface VIII the cardinals went into conclave. They chose one of the late pope's most loyal supporters, the one-time Master-General of the Order of Preachers, Nicholas Boccasini; and they chose him on the first ballot. This pope was no Roman of noble family, but a poor man's son from the Venetian provinces. He was not a canonist but a theologian; and if a skilled and experienced ruler of men, he was, first of all, an excellent religious, a priest with a pastoral mind. As Master-General, Boccasini had kept his order obedient to the pope in the crisis of 1297, and he had been at Boniface's side in the hour of his last ordeal. But he had had no part in the struggle that opened with Ausculta Fili. During the last two critical years of Boniface's reign he had been away from Rome, serving as legate at the court of Albert of Habsburg. It was possibly because he was the one cardinal whom the late struggle had not touched that he was so speedily elected. Here was a man

whom none hated because of any share he had had in that
struggle, and a pope who would be able to devise policies free
from the strain and fury of the late crisis. And his first gesture as
pope gave a clear sign, that, while he would be loyal to the past,
he would be loyal in his own way. The disciple of Benedict
Gaetani did not call himself Boniface IX; with a nuance that only
emphasised his substantial loyalty, he announced himself as
Benedict XI.

Benedict XI was in a strong position, able to be generous,
therefore, towards Philip the Fair, and so resolved. The policy he
proposed to adopt was simple, delicate and firm. Nogaret, still in
Italy and faced with the perplexing problem of a new pope who
was, too, a saintly man, with whom worldly motives would be of
no avail, was again meditating the threat of schism -- the
Colonna cardinals had had no share in the conclave, therefore the
election was not valid. But Benedict XI passed over this new
intrigue for the moment; making, from the beginning, a careful
distinction between the various personalities responsible for the
outrage of Anagni. The case of each should be separately decided
according to the past mind and future intention of each. The chief
culprit, the one most culpable from his rank, was of course the
King of France. If he made a movement of submission Benedict
would take it as sincerely meant, and would show himself the
representative of Him who called himself the Good Shepherd.
And when the pope forgave he would save the position his
predecessors had declared themselves bound to defend, and the
reality of the forgiveness, by saying outright in what spirit he
was acting. But Philip must first of all make his move towards
the pope. Benedict was no "appeaser", diplomatically angling for
submission by a timely announcement that the terms would be
easy and the gesture nominal.

No official notice, therefore, of the new pope's election was sent
to Philip, nor any copy of his first inaugural letter. The pope
treated the king for the excommunicate he was, and was careful

to remind the world of this by a renewal of the sentences of his predecessors, that all those are excommunicated who hinder free communication between the Holy See and the bishops. The deadlock did not last long. It was conveyed to Philip that the pope did not desire revenge; that forgiveness awaited him if he would submit; that the pope would only be inflexible about the principle of free communication with the Church in France: in this matter satisfaction would certainly be demanded, liberation also of all the clerics imprisoned, and revocation of the royal edicts.

Meanwhile, the Colonna cardinals had come out from their hiding places, to throw themselves at Benedict's feet and beg for mercy. He showed himself generous, although "for the moment" he did not restore them to their dignity or their benefices and possessions. The same determination to make peace in a truly priestly spirit moved Benedict to send a legate to Florence, in the first weeks of 1304, with very extensive powers to settle differences and to reconcile the forces so hostile to the Holy See since the "pacification" of the town by the pope's champion, Charles of Valois.

The embassy from Philip the Fair reached Rome in March 1304. It was, by the fact, a submission; and yet a submission craftily prepared, by accepting which the pope would give the French a basis to argue in the years to come that Benedict's pardon was an implicit condemnation of Boniface. Nogaret, returned now to the French court, was as influential as ever and no less dangerous. But Benedict cut through the snares by pardoning the king without any discussion of conditions, and stating that he did so as a loving father will always forgive a repentant child. The bargaining which Nogaret had planned, and which would have made the resultant absolution from excommunication seem an act in a kind of treaty or compromise, did not take place. The pope's simple directness turned the diplomatist's schemes with ease. Philip was absolved because he had repented, and because to forgive the repentant is the pope's first duty -- and all Europe would know this from the bulls. And when the King of France, his position as a Catholic prince restored, raised the question of Pope Boniface's actions towards him, renewing the demand for a council to judge this, Benedict put him off without discussion or comment of any kind.

A few weeks later, from Perugia, whither the pope had now moved, further bulls took up the detail of the settlement, and firstly the problems raised by the law Clericis Laicos. The pope did not retreat from the principles then laid down, but he did the cause of the monarchy a great favour and, very skilfully, he did this by virtue of those very principles. The penalties of Clericis Laicos against lay oppressors of Church revenues were maintained, but those which awaited the clerics who submitted to such oppression were modified, so that they no longer fell automatically on such transgressors. And to help France in the desperate state to which debasement of the coinage had reduced the country, the pope allowed the clergy to pay a tithe for two years and the first fruits of all benefices coming vacant during the next three years, the moneys to be used for the restoration of the coinage (13 May, 1304). About the same time a series of decisions proclaimed what was in fact a general amnesty for all those who had fallen under excommunication in the more recent crisis following the bulls Ausculta Fili and Unam Sanctam. Whoever would repent, the pope would forgive, because he was the pope, and on terms fixed by himself -- namely the sincere repentance of the culprit.

One group was however excepted, and by name, from this generous act of reconciliation. Not even Benedict XI's charity could presume that Nogaret had repented his share in these acts, or that he was likely to do so. At this very moment he was still actively manoeuvring for the council that should degrade the memory of Pope Boniface, and striving to form a party among the cardinals. Nogaret was still, in fact, the principal force at the court of France, influential, determined, ruthless; and the new pope, in the action he now took, showed unmistakably that it was not any fear to strike or any lack of strength that had prompted his willingness to be reconciled with the enemy. A special bull -- Flagitiosum Scelus -- denounced by name Nogaret, Sciarra Colonna and fifteen others for their share in the outrage at Anagni. They were summoned to appear, in person, by the coming feast of St. Peter, June 29, to receive the sentence their crime had merited. To this citation they paid no attention; but before the pope could proceed to the next act against them, he was no more. Benedict XI died, very suddenly, at Perugia on July 7, 1304.

The sudden disappearance of Benedict XI was such good fortune for the policies of Nogaret that, not unnaturally, the rumour spread that the Frenchman had had him poisoned. The Church had lost that rarity, a pope who was a saint, [ ] and a saint who had in perfection the ruler's gift of prudence; and how real the tragedy was now brought home to all as, for a long eleven months, the factions in the conclave wrangled and fought.

The majority of the cardinals -- ten of them -- were strong for a pope who would resist the French, and exact some reparation for the outrage on Boniface VIII. But there was a pro-French minority of six, the party which Nogaret had influenced during the last pope's brief reign. Eleven votes were needed to elect, and as both sides held firm the deadlock was complete. On the French side there were threats of schism unless someone friendly to Philip the Fair were chosen. "If any anti-Christ usurped the Holy See," said Nogaret ominously, he must be resisted. On both sides the cardinals began to consider candidates outside the Sacred College. Finally, the intrigues of Cardinal Napoleone Orsini gathered a bare two-thirds majority for the Archbishop of Bordeaux, Bertrand de Got, and on June 5, 1305, he was elected, [ ] Pope Clement V.

From many points of view it must have seemed an admirable choice. Clement V was well on the young side of fifty; he was by birth a subject of the English king, and yet on friendly terms with Philip the Fair. He was brother to that Cardinal Berard de Got who had been one of Boniface VIII's chief diplomatists, [ ] and had himself been employed by that pope in important diplomatic work in England. In the furious months that followed the Ausculta Fili the Archbishop of Bordeaux had been loyal to the pope, and he had gone to Rome for the great council which preceded the Unam Sanctam. His technical qualifications were high, for he was an accomplished canonist, a competent administrator and a skilled negotiator. The most serious drawback, perhaps, was his health; for, although this was not yet known, he was ravaged by a terrible cancer of the stomach. Again and again during his reign, for weeks and months at a time, his sufferings were to withdraw him entirely from all contact with affairs, and finally, after nine years, to bring his life to a premature end. He is spoken of as a man naturally kind and goodhearted, but vacillating, lacking the energy to make final decisions in policy, or to stand by them when made, increasingly at the mercy of his fears, and bound to be the tool, or the victim, of that pitiless cunning and determination which, for years now, had characterised the action of Philip the Fair.

Clement V, as pope, never left the soil of France. He is the first of a series of French popes who lived out their reigns in France, the so-called Avignon popes. But with Clement this novelty of ruling the Church from outside the Papal State and Italy seems to have been the outcome of a series of accidents rather than of settled policy. He hoped to arrange a final definitive peace between France and England and, inviting both the kings to his coronation, fixed this for the (then) imperial city of Vienne on the Rhone. Later, to please Philip, he decided on Lyons and there, in Philip's presence and that of the ambassadors of Edward I, he was crowned, five months after his election, 14 November, 1305.

It was no doubt one of the misfortunes of history that Edward I was not present at Lyons, for in a critical hour the French king carried all before him. It was, in fact, after this first famous interview with Philip that the pope gave up his idea of an immediate journey to Rome and, in the consistory of December 15, he gave a sign of what was to come by creating ten new cardinals, of whom nine were Frenchmen.

The leading motive of the French king's policy was, of course, to win from Rome a formal renunciation of all that Boniface VIII had claimed, and a revocation of that pope's anti-regal acts. These hindrances to the establishment of a real royal control of the Church were to be removed by the only power that could remove them -- the papacy itself; and to bring this about the methods once employed so successfully with Boniface were once more to be put into operation. Pressure would be more easily applied if the pope were established nearer to Paris than Orvieto, or Anagni. And to detain the pope yet awhile in France -- and at the same time to excite such real alarm that he would yield more easily to the demand for a condemnation of his predecessor -- the king had ready a prepared scandal of the first magnitude. This was the question of the religious and moral condition of the great military order of the Knights of the Temple. To the newly-crowned pope, Philip the Fair, in the talks between them at Lyons, made known that for some time complaints of a most serious kind had been made about the Knights. They were, it was said, secret infidels who, on the day of their reception and profession as knights, explicitly and formally denied Christ and ceremonially spat upon the crucifix; the centre of their religious life was an idol, worshipped in all their houses; their priests were always careful to omit the words of consecration in the masses celebrated within the order; the knights practised unnatural vice as a kind of ritual and by prescription. An enquiry was urgently necessary.

The pope was sceptical. The malevolent gossip about an order hated and envied by many rivals left him unmoved, as it had left unmoved the King of Aragon to whom the "revelations" had first been made. But the French king, and Nogaret, set themselves to produce yet more evidence. They found witnesses in ex-Templars languishing, for one crime or another, in the king's prisons. They introduced spies into the order itself. And then, in the spring of 1307, at a second meeting with the pope at Poitiers, the king repeated his demands.

Clement, at first, refused. Philip then raised anew the question of the condemnation of Boniface VIII. Already, twelve months earlier, the pope had, with certain reservations on the principles, withdrawn the two great bulls of his predecessor, Clericis Laicos and Unam Sanctam (1 February, 1306) [ ] and the king had, thereupon, ceased his demand for the dead pope's trial. Now, as Clement showed fight about the Templars, the ghost of Pope Boniface was made to walk once more -- and effectively. For the curia proposed a compromise: the pope should quash all the anti-regalist acts of Boniface VIII, and the king should leave the question of the condemnation of Boniface entirely in the pope's hands. But the king refused all compromise. And then, August 24, 1307, Clement gave way and signed the order for a canonical enquiry into the accusations against the Templars. It was to be an enquiry according to the Canon Law -- as was only right where it was a religious order that was accused; and, also, the enquiry was ordered at the petition of the Templars themselves, eager to disprove the calumnies.

This, of course, was not the kind of enquiry the French king had looked for, with the accused condemned beforehand. He took his own line and suddenly, in the early morning of October 13, all the Knights Templars of France were arrested by the royal order. Next, amid the consternation caused on all sides, Nogaret launched a campaign of anti-Templar "publicity"; France was flooded with proclamations and speeches that explained what criminals the Templars were, and how the pious king, on the advice of his confessor, careful of his duty as champion of the Catholic religion, had ordered their arrest, after consulting his barons, and the pope.

The next few weeks were filled with the examination of the Knights -- examinations by the king's officials and, of course, under torture, whose object was to induce the accused to admit their guilt. Everywhere the unhappy men broke under the strain, and soon the king had, from the lips of the Templars themselves, all the evidence he needed that the order merited suppression and that its wealth should be confiscated -- if such avowals, and known to be obtained by such means, are indeed evidence. It sufficed to bring conviction to the pope that, at any rate, there was something seriously wrong in the order, and he ordered all the princes of Christendom to arrest the Templars and to place their property under sequestration (November 22, 1307).

This hideous business of torturing men accused of crime was, by the time of Clement V, part and parcel of the routine of trials wherever the Roman Law influenced criminal jurisprudence. From the spheres influenced by that law it had passed, nearly a hundred years before this, into the procedure of the Inquisition. The canon lawyer was as familiar with the use of torture as his civilian brother, and as little likely to question its morality. Short of being a few hundred years before his time -- or a few hundred years behind it -- no canonist of Clement V's generation would have seen any objection to using the hostile "evidence" procured by Philip the Fair's torturers from the accused Templars.

The pope had not indeed let Philip's vigorous coup succeed without a strong protest (27 October, 1307). The king had violated the immunity of clerics from the lay power of arrest, and this despite his knowledge that the pope had reserved the whole affair to himself. The pope had demanded, therefore, that Philip surrender his prisoners and their property to two cardinals named as the pope's commissioners. [ ] But Clement had done no more than this, and when the "confessions" were placed before him had admitted them juridically.

The Templars now passed into the care of the Church and immediately, fancying themselves free of the royal torturers, solemnly revoked all their confessions. Whereupon the pope took the whole affair out of the hands of all lower tribunals and reserved it to himself. [ ]

Philip the Fair's reply was to call up once more the ghost of Boniface VIII, and to launch a campaign of slander against Clement. All that had ever been said against Boniface, against his administration of the Church and against his private life, was now laid to the charge of Clement. [ ] The scenes of 1302 began to be repeated; there were declarations that if the pope neglected his obvious duty, the king would have to see to it, and, for the sake cf. the Church, act in its name; there was a great meeting of the States-General at Tours (11-20 May, 1308) and the assembly declared the Templars worthy of death. And, finally, Philip descended with an army on Poitiers. Once more, Clement -- who had attempted to escape out of Philip's dominions, but, discovered, been forced to return -- was lectured and threatened to his face, and bidden to act quickly, or the nation, whose indignation no king nor baron could restrain, would take the law into its own hands, and make an end of these enemies of Christ. And the pope was told that prelates who covered up crime were as guilty as those who committed it.

This moral siege of the pope at Poitiers, where the king met him with an immense array of nobles, bishops, legists, soldiers, lasted for a month (26 May-27 June). But the pope's courage did not yet fail. He did not believe the Templars' guilt proved, and he refused to condemn the order. The king thereupon made an official surrender of the whole case to the pope and shipped off to the Papal Court a picked band of seventy-two Templars, ready to swear to anything as the price of future royal favour or of pardon for past crimes. It was the testimony of these men, many of whom Clement himself examined, that finally broke through the pope's scepticism, and for the trial of the order throughout the Church he entirely remodelled the whole Inquisition system [ ] (July 1308). In these same weeks of the conferences at Poitiers, the pope was again summoned to condemn Pope Boniface. Celestine V -- so the French king urged -- must be canonised, the victim of Boniface VIII; and Boniface's corpse dug up and burnt (6 July, 1308). This time Clement had to make some show of acquiescence, and as he had consented to put the Order of Templars on trial, so he now set up a commission to judge his predecessor (August 12, 1308), and fixed a date for the first hearing, a fairly distant date, February 2, 1309.

The pope's scheme for the trial of the religious was elaborate. Two enquiries were to function simultaneously throughout Europe. The one, a pontifical commission, its members nominated by the pope, was to examine the charges against the order as such: the other, an episcopal enquiry, to judge the individual knights, was to be held in each diocese where the Templars had a foundation, and in this tribunal the judges would be the bishop with two delegates of his chapter, two Dominicans and two Franciscans. These diocesan findings would be reviewed by a council of all the bishops of the province, who would decide the fate of the individual Templars. As to the order, the findings of the pontifical commissions would be laid before a General Council, summoned to meet at Vienne for October 1, 1310, and the council would decide what was to be done with the order.

The pontifical commission in France was far from hasty. [ ] It did not hold its first session until August 1309, and the real work did not begin until the following November. The prelates who sat as judges were, all of them, devoted to the policies of the French king; its president, the Archbishop of Narbonne, was one of the Templars' chief foes. And, contrary to the law by which they judged, the commissioners allowed the royal officials to assist at the trials, and to have access to the depositions confidentially made to the court by the accused. This paved the way for some of the most tragic scenes in this terrible story. For when the Templars appeared before the pontifical tribunal, many of them immediately revoked the confessions of guilt they had made. Publicly they now described the tortures which had been used to make them admit their guilt. "If the like torture is now used on me again," said one, "I will deny all that I am now affirming: I will say anything you want me to say." Something like 573 knights stood firm in this repudiation and in testimony that the charges against the order were calumnies. But the chiefs of the order wavered: they understood, better than the rest, the peril in which such retractation would involve them. The immense scale of the retractations, and the contrast presented by the miserable character of the outside witnesses produced by the royal officers against the order, were building up a popular feeling that it was innocent. And, lest he should lose the day, the king again intervened with force. The order as such might be winning its case before the pontifical commission: the king's opportunity lay with the machinery set up to judge these men as individuals. His instruments were the bishops of the provincial council of Sens, to which, in those days, the see of Paris [ ] was subject; upon whose judgment, by Clement V's decision, the fate of these knights as individuals depended. Their retractation, before the pontifical commission, of their confession of heresy was a relapse into heresy, and the punishment for this was death.

So the Archbishop of Sens summoned his council -- he was Philippe de Marigny, brother of Enguerrand de Marigny, one of the king's chief ministers -- and without any further hearing the council condemned to death fifty-four of the Templars who had retracted their confession (11 May, 1310). The next day they were taken in batches to the place of execution and all of them burned alive, protesting to the last their innocence of any crime. Four days later there was another execution, of nine, at Senlis.

This atrocious deed had the effect hoped for. The condemned men, still under the jurisdiction of the pontifical commission, had begged its intervention. The only answer given by the president was that he was too busy, he had to hear mass, he said, or to say mass. Nothing, it was evident, could save a Templar who did not admit all the crimes laid against him, and so provide evidence to justify the destruction of his order. Henceforth the courts had all the admissions they could desire. The speech of one of the knights to the papal commissioners, made the day after Philippe de Marigny's holocaust, has come down to us. "I admitted several charges because of the tortures inflicted on me by the king's knights, Guillaume de Marcilly and Hugues de la Celle. But they were all false. Yesterday, when I saw fifty-four of my brethren going in the tumbrils to the stake because they refused to admit our so-called errors, I thought I can never resist the terror of the fire. I would, I feel, admit anything. I would admit that I had killed God if I were asked to admit it."

The pontifical enquiry in France now speedily came to the end of its business. It had henceforward no more exacting work than to take down confessions, and by June 5, 1311, it had finished.

When we turn from the bloody scenes which took place wherever Philip the Fair had power, the contrast in what the trials of the Templars produced is striking indeed. In these islands, councils were held, as the pope had ordered, at London and York, in Ireland and in Scotland. But nowhere was there found any conclusive evidence against the order. So it was in Spain also. No torture was used in England until the pope insisted on it; [ ] but torture was used in Germany, and despite the torture the pontifical commissioners found the order in good repute and publicly declared this. All tended to show that, when the General Council met, the order would find defenders everywhere except among the bishops subject to Philip the Fair. That the council would vote the destruction of the order was by no means a foregone conclusion.

While the Templars were going through their ordeal at Paris before the pope's commissioners, the pope himself, at Avignon, was also suffering duress. For on March 16, 1310, the trial -- if the word be allowed -- of Boniface VIII had at last begun in his presence. To accuse and revile the dead man's memory, all the cohort of Philip the Fair's legists had appeared, Nogaret leading them. Boniface had been a heretic; he had been a man of immoral life, in his youth (sixty years ago now) and through all his later years. He had been an infidel, an atheist, an idolator. He had never been lawfully elected, he had murdered his predecessor after tricking him into a resignation that was void in law. All the malevolence amid which Boniface had pursued his difficult way was now given free reign; and Clement, fearful of provoking yet new savageries from the French king, knowing, nevertheless, that he could never deny the principles for which Boniface had fought, could do no more than delay the proceedings by every expedient which practised finesse could suggest to him.

At last the international situation played into his hands. The emperor, Henry VII, had just received at Milan the iron crown of Lombardy (6 January, 1311) and, with Robert of Naples, he was planning the reconstitution of the kingdom of Arles. The possibility of the whole of the lands east of the Rhone passing for ever beyond the influence of his house was more than Philip the Fair could allow. He was driven to seek the pope's good offices, but Clement, realising that this was his hour, received him coldly. The French cardinals advised the king that the cause of Boniface VIII was about to cost France more than it could ever be worth. And so, while the Templar commission at Paris was slowly coming to an end, pope and king came to an understanding. The king agreed that the accusers of Boniface should withdraw, and that the fate of the Templars should be left to the council: the pope, in a series of bulls, without condemning Boniface, or adverting at all to the vile charges made about his faith or his character, quashed all the papal acts against the king made from November 1, 1300, by Boniface or by his immediate successor, Benedict XI. He ordered, moreover, that all record of these various bulls should be erased from the papal registers. Nogaret was absolved, and with him Sciarra Colonna and others of the conspirators of Anagni. Finally, Philip the Fair was publicly praised for the zeal he had shown, and his good intentions in his anti-papal strife were officially recognised (27 April, 1311). [ ] It was a heavy price to pay for the cessation of the king's attack on Pope Boniface and, through him, on the reality of the pope's jurisdiction. And, like all similar surrenders, it did not really succeed. For the king was to threaten to renew the attack at a critical moment of the coming council, and so once more gain his way. Two years after this "settlement", Clement canonised the pope who had abdicated, the "victim" of Boniface VIII. But he was careful to canonise the saint not as Celestine V but as Peter di Murrone, and in the bull of canonisation to attest the validity of Celestine's act of abdication (May 5, 1313). [ ]

The Council of Vienne, summoned for October 1310, actually met just a year later, October 16, 1311. Its principal business was the settlement of the affairs of the Order of Templars; and to consider the report of the various commissions a special committee of the bishops was appointed. To the pope's embarrassment -- with the ink hardly dry on his recent arrangement with Philip the Fair -- the committee, by a great majority, reported that the Templars ought to be heard before the council in their own defence (December 1311). The pope, characteristically, set the report aside, and offered for consideration schemes -- much needed schemes -- of Church reform, and plans for a new crusade. And the French king, raising the memory of his "injuries" at the hands of Pope Boniface, came himself to Vienne, to try all that blandishment and threats could do with the obstinate majority. He was, horrible to relate, entirely successful, and on March 22, 1312, the committee reversed its decision of the previous December and, furthermore, by a majority of 4 to 1 recommended that the Order of Templars be suppressed.

The next solemn session of the whole council was fixed for April 3, twelve days later. Would the bishops have accepted this recommendation had they been free to discuss it? It is an interesting question; but the pope forestalled all possibility of trouble by imposing silence under pain of excommunication, and instead of deciding the fate of the order the assembled bishops had read to them the pope's own sentence and decision. Without judging the order, or condemning it, Clement simply suppressed it as an administrative action [ ] and not as a punishment for any crime. And next, despite enormous efforts on the part of Philip and some of the bishops, the pope transferred the possessions of the order to the kindred military order of the Hospitallers, except in Spain where the new possessors were the military orders who fought the Moors. The individual knights the pope left to the judgment of the provincial councils.

The trial of the Grand Master and the chief superiors Clement reserved to himself, and eighteen months after the closing of the council he named a commission of three French cardinals to judge them (22 December, 1313). They were found guilty, on their own previous admissions, and on March 18, 1314, before the main door of Notre Dame, in the presence of an enormous crowd, they were sentenced to life imprisonment. And now, once again, tragedy crowned the proceedings in very terrible fashion. The Grand Master and one of his brethren, free of the prospect of a death sentence, their lot definitely settled at last, renounced their confessions and protested that the order had been gravely calumniated. "We are not guilty of the crimes alleged against us," they said. "Where we are guilty is that to save our own lives we basely betrayed the order. The order is pure, it is holy. The accusations are absurd, our confessions a tissue of lies." Here was an unexpected problem for the three cardinals, and while they debated, uncertainly, how to deal with it, Philip the Fair acted. That very day he decided with his council that here was yet another case of relapse into heresy. The two knights, without more ado, were hurried to the stake and that same evening given to the flames, proclaiming to the last their innocence and the innocence of the order.

Was the order indeed innocent? The controversy has raged ever since it was brought to so cruel an end. It is safe to say that the controversy is now over, and that it has ended in agreement to acquit the knights. [ ] The order was the victim of Philip the Fair's cupidity, and the pope was, in very large measure, the king's conscious tool in the wicked work.

The suppression of the Templars, and the associate villainy of the "trial" of Boniface VIII, are events so monstrous in scale that all else in the nine years of Pope Clement's unhappy reign is dwarfed beside them. Certainly these events were, for seven of those years, his chief anxiety and his almost daily care; and they were the chief obstacle to the realisation of his never wholly abandoned intention to live, like his predecessors, the normal life of a pope within the Italian Papal State. For the papal establishment at Avignon, that was to last for some seventy years, was not -- it seems certain -- due to any one definite act of policy, based on a Frenchman's preference for life in his own country. Clement V had been pope for nearly four years before he so much as saw Avignon. It was only when he realised, in the summer of 1308, after the second Poitiers meeting with the French king, the gravity of the imminent crisis, that the pope determined on Avignon as a more or less permanent place of residence (August 1308). To return to Italy while such menace hung over Catholic affairs in France would have been unthinkable. Avignon was on the French frontier and yet no part of Philip's dominions; the surrounding territory -- the County of Venaissin -- had been papal territory for now thirty years. In the circumstances, to set up the curia at Avignon was an ideal solution; and it is simple matter of fact that during the seventy years of what has been called, too easily, the Babylonian captivity, the papal action was far less hindered by civil disturbance not only than in the seventy years that followed the return to Rome of Gregory XI (in 1377) but than it was hindered in the seventy years that preceded the election of the first Avignon pope.

It was in March 1309 that the pope took up his residence at Avignon -- a very modest establishment in the priory of the Dominicans -- and had sent to him from Rome the registers of letters for the two last pontificates, and a certain amount -- not by any means the greater part -- of the papal treasure. There is no reason to doubt that Clement, had he lived, would, once the General Council had settled the double crisis in France, have passed into Italy. But he was already a man marked for death by the time that council ended. Once more he left Provence and, in the desperate hope of improvement, set out for his native country of the Bordelais. But he had gone no farther than Roquemaure, on the Rhone, when just a month after the terrible end of the Grand Master of the Templars, death claimed him too (April 20, 1314). Six months later Philip the Fair, still on the young side of fifty, followed him into the next world. The Church had lost one of the weakest popes who has ever ruled it, and religion had been delivered from the menace of one of its most insidious foes.

In two respects Clement V set a new and a thoroughly bad example which was to become a papal fashion through all the next two hundred years. He found places for a host of relatives in the high offices of the Church; and he spent the treasure of the Church lavishly for their enrichment. No fewer than six of his family he made cardinals -- at a time when the total number of the Sacred College rarely exceeded twenty. Others he named to well-endowed sees, while for those who were not clerics he created well-paid posts and sinecures in the temporal administration. It was now that there began what must be judged the most evil part of the Avignon tradition, the excessive preoccupation of the curia with fees. And with the new interest in lawful fees there developed, inevitably, a regime of graft and jobbery where all, from the highest to the lowest, expected bribes and demanded them, a regime which the popes in the end became powerless to change. Cardinal Ehrle has calculated, from the papal accounts of the time, that Clement V was able to save nearly one half of his immense annual revenue. The treasury at his death amounted to over a million florins. Of this he left to friends and relations 200,000 florins, and to a nephew, pledged to equip a troop of knights for the crusade, half as much again. Clement V also inaugurated the Avignon tradition of filling the Sacred College with Frenchmen. He created twenty-four cardinals in all; one was English, one Spanish; the rest were all Frenchmen, and of the twenty-two, six, as has been said, were closely related to him by blood. [ ]

Return to Index

129

# CHAPTER 2: 'THE AVIGNON CAPTIVITY', 1314-1362

## 1. CRISIS IN THE WORLD OF THOUGHT
### i. The Problem of Church and State

WITH the death of Philip the Fair, in the autumn of 1314, the assault of the French monarchy on the papal claims came to a sudden end. The regime of co-operation between the two powers was resumed, if not in all the friendliness of former days, at any rate with an equal practical effectiveness; the peace, such as it was, would not be broken until the very eve of the Reformation, two hundred years later. "Such as it was", for not only had the issue between Boniface VIII and Philip not been decided, despite the surrenders of Clement V -- so that it remained a possible source of further disaster through all those two centuries -- but there was a permanent memorial of the controversy in the literature circulated by both parties during the fatal years. The issue was practical, it was important, it was urgent -- and it has never ceased to be so. "The pope's imperative intervention in French affairs was not anything merely arbitrary and suddenly thought up, that can be explained by the pope's ambition, or excused by the king's tyranny. It was bound up with a body of teaching, with the supremacy of the spiritual power as the Middle Ages had known and practised it, a supremacy in which the Church still saw a lawful and necessary function of the mission she held from God." [ ]

Both king and pope realised fully that the fight was no mere clash of personal temperaments. That the temperamental weaknesses -- and worse -- of the contending potentates had their influence on the course of the struggle is evidently true, but these were not its most important elements; they can, by comparison, be disregarded in a study of the fight and its consequences, as we can disregard the slander and invective of the controversialists. But the controversialists dealt also with other things than slanders: on both sides, theories were set out and defended, and the best writing of this sort was carefully preserved, armament for future like conflicts, and -- this is true of the anti-papal works at least -- carefully translated into French, so that others besides the priest and the legist could see how right it was for the king to challenge the pope. [ ] As this literature remained and grew, in the course of two hundred years, to become a formidable menace to Catholic unity, something more must be said of it and of how the "grand differand" between Boniface and Philip continued to poison Catholic life for generations after them. [ ]

With this in mind we may go on to note the attitude of the writers on the papal side as an affirmative answer to the question "Did Our Lord mean the Pope to be the Lord of the World?" This answer meant, in practice, that the Church's mission towards the state included "not only the consecration of kings, but also the verification of their title, and the control of their administration. . . the right and power to judge and correct their conduct [i.e. as rulers], to invalidate their acts and, in extreme cases, to pronounce their deposition." [ ]

Kings, of course, did their best to escape the exercise of such powers and, as they grew more literate, they began to raise doubts whether they were indeed lawful powers. So Frederick II, in 1245, had denounced his excommunication as "a misuse of priestly authority"; and he had gone on to declare to the princes of Europe that "nowhere do we read that by any law, divine or human, has power been given to the pope to punish kings by depriving them of their kingdoms, or to pass judgment on princes." Such a situation would be ridiculous, said Frederick, "the claim that he who as emperor is loosed from all laws is yet himself subject to law." [ ]

The emperor here is evidently setting up the law of ancient Rome against what the pope claims of him as a disciple of Christ; but his contention is also a reminder of another factor of the struggle that must be ever before the mind of those who perhaps stand amazed at the immensity of the papal claim. This is the fact that nowhere, in these centuries, is it a question of conflict between the papal claims and some royal scheme of a balanced distribution of royal and ecclesiastical jurisdiction. From the moment when these fights first began in the time of St. Gregory VII (1073-1085) was always between two claims tobe absolute. These popes who, reforming the Church, slowly drew Christendom back from the depths, found their greatest obstacle in the actually existing, all-embracing, imperial and royal absolutism which had all but merged the Church in the state. If the pope was not to be all, [ ] then the king would be all; the pope must be all, or the Church would be nothing. The alternative before Christendom was the supremacy of the Church over the state, or else Caesar, to all intents and purposes, the pope. The popes, with remarkable faith -- and courage -- did not shrink from choosing; they dutifully climbed the heights and thence proceeded to judge the world.

Did our Lord mean the pope to be the Lord of the World in this sense? Canonists, by the time of Boniface VIII, had been saying so for a long time, and saying it in such a way that they seemed to claim still more. Hostiensis [ ] for example who died in 1271, one of the greatest of all the eyes of his contemporaries, declared that it is the pope who is the true source of all the state's authority; and that the state, indeed, in all its actions, is really deputising for the pope; the emperor is no more than the pope's vicar for temporal affairs. For there can only be one Lord of the World, namely Christ, Our Lord; and the pope alone is Christ's vicar, Who "committed all things to Peter", giving him not a key, but the keys; "two keys" says the cardinal, by which are signified the two fields of papal supremacy, to wit, the spiritual and the temporal. And this strong doctrine is no more than a reflection of what an equally eminent master in the law had proclaimed to all Christendom when, having become pope, he was engaged in a life and death struggle against the absolutist schemes of

Frederick II. This was Innocent IV (1243-1254) [ ] and against the emperor's claim to incorporate the Church into the State, this canonist pope set up his own, "We exercise the general authority in this world of Him who is the King of Kings, who has granted to the prince of the apostles and to us a plenitude of power to bind as well as to loose upon earth, not only all persons, but all things whatsoever." We have seen Frederick's scornful comment on this language. But the emperor's rejoinder was as barren, apparently, as his military genius or political power. The pope, in this particular conflict, was victorious and his high conception of papal duties and powers seemed more firmly established than ever.

When, fifty years later, the papacy, in the person of Boniface VIII, next called up for judgment a powerful ruler, the spirit and tone of the intervention was, if possible, more "Innocentian" than Innocent IV himself ! but this time the royal rejoinder was far indeed from fruitless. And Christendom saw the popes suddenly compelled to lower their tone: the contrast between the actions (and the language) of Boniface VIII and Clement V, less than ten years later, was something to marvel at. Phaethon, it would seem, had fallen from his car. And, whatever the rights of the question, the rebel responsible for the catastrophe had not only gone unpunished, but had been lauded by the victim for his good intentions. Here, surely, was mischief indeed, grave scandal in the most literal sense. The crisis had produced a stumbling block for Catholics over which many would continue to trip until the Catholic state disappeared from the political world.

For Philip the Fair's challenge, whether the popes really possessed such authority, was now set before the mind of Catholic Europe so forcibly and so clearly, that the debate about it never really ceased thereafter. In the two hundred years and more during which that authority had been claimed, exercised and generally acknowledged, it had come to be one of the fundamentals of the Christian political system, of the Christian-religion-inspired civilisation of Western Europe. Revolt here was revolt indeed, and when, from such a revolt, the Church failed to emerge victorious and able to punish the rebel, its prestige suffered a defeat that was irreparable. Never again does the Church dominate the conflict from above; henceforth the popes too, are in the arena, and if the high papal tone persists (as naturally it does, for the popes do not immediately understand that the former things have passed away) it serves as an additional aggravation to the world. Gradually the popes came to abandon this position so long defended by the great medieval canonists, this theory which had been the Church's defence against the all-invading state; and it may be well if, to avoid confusion, and the better to understand the tragedy which accompanied the slow changeover, we remind ourselves what was really -- in the mind of the popes -- the nature of the power they had claimed, and the kind of arguments by which they had defended it. " It was in its source an authority that was spiritual, and it made no claim, therefore, to absorb the authority of the state; but it was a power that extended to the furthest boundaries of the moral order, and which, as an inevitable consequence of this, included the right to survey the conduct of rulers and to call them to account for their behaviour as such, to correct them, to pass sentence on them if they were at fault, and even to depose those who prove recalcitrant." [ ] The popes never claim that they may administer France or Spain as though it were their own Italian Papal State. But they do claim authority to correct the rulers of these lands for sins committed in ruling, as they correct all other delinquencies in the flock placed under their charge; and they claim the right to correct rulers in a particular way, by excommunicating them and declaring them to have forfeited the right to rule. Boniface VIII's bull Unam Sanctam is nothing more than an official statement of this theory and claim.

What of the standing of this papal claim to punish kings by deposition? Whether it be true or not it " has never, in any way, been proposed as a doctrine of the Church; but, nevertheless, it certainly won the assent of many popes, and, in an especially grave moment of history, it coloured the traditional background of the papal claims, namely in the solemn document that expresses the distinctive views of Boniface VIII." [ ] Perhaps it is here, in the association of a theory peculiar to a particular age with a definition of general Catholic duty, that we must look for the source of the most serious part of the ensuing and mischievous misunderstanding. What was really defeated may indeed have been no more than a "personal system", that is to say, a theory and policy really " personal " to a succession of popes, but hitherto everywhere taken for granted. But this "personal system" had now been defeated and defied at a moment when it was set out in the closest association with a solemn definition of essential Catholic duty. If the one was defied the other could not but appear compromised. Henceforth the first was always on the defensive and acceptance of the second might suffer accordingly.

The debate between the canonists and legists had, then, revealed the whole deep chasm that separated these antagonistic views of public life. It had also produced that third theory from which the ultimate true solution was one day to be developed, and had thereby thrown into high relief the deficiencies in the canonists' argumentation and the exaggerations in the claims they made. These exaggerations produced, naturally enough, an exaggerated reaction that carried the canonists' lay opponents to a denial of papal prerogatives and rights (in spiritual matters).that were beyond all question. It is, for example, from this time that the appeals from the pope to a General Council first begin to appear with anything like frequency, a new tendency that grows steadily through the next sixty years, and which the opportune disaster of the Schism [ ] then so fosters that, at the Council of Constance, an effort is actually made to give this abuse force of law. [ ] Again, the canonists have quoted Scripture in support of their assertions, but Scripture understood metaphorically. For example, two actual swords had once been brought to Our Lord by the Apostles for his defence: [ ] the canonists had read the act allegorically, and used that allegory to justify a theory. Now, a critical attack was made on this method of using Scripture -- an attack which could be supported by the new, clear, strong teaching of St. Thomas Aquinas, that arguments about doctrine can only be based on the literal sense of the sacred text. [ ] Once this mentality developed, a whole host of arguments, classic with the canonists for two centuries and more, would simply disappear overnight. [ ] And much else would disappear too -- the prestige of the theological scholar, for example, with that new educated lay world which is the peculiar distinction of this fourteenth century, the age where the greatest figures among orthodox scholars are Dante and Petrarch, and where no cleric writing theology attains to eminence and yet manages to keep entirely orthodox.

The latest historian to study the conflict of ideas that underlay the crisis, analyses the works of some seventeen polemists. [ ] There are, first of all, the antagonists who set out and defend the rival theories: on the papal side two Augustinian friars, Giles of Rome [ ] and James of Viterbo [ ]; on the king's side the authors of the treatises called A Dialogue between a Cleric and a Knight and Rex Pacificus. Next there is a group of nine writers whose aim is to find some middle way in which to reconcile the rival jurisdictions. Working from the papal side towards this are the Dominican John of Paris and the authors of the gloss on the bull Unam Sanctam, and the treatise called Quaestio in Utramque Partem: on the other side are six writers the best known of whom is Dante? whose De Monarchia here comes under consideration. Finally, there are considered four "practical" schemes. It is hardly possible in a work of this kind to attempt anything more than to list all these, and to refer those interested to the long analysis of them (180 pages) in Riviere's authoritative work. But something must be said of John of Paris -- as a critic of the papal apologists -- for it was with his theory that the future lay; nor can Dante be merely mentioned.

What the canonists held about the relation of the pope to Catholic princes, considered as princes, has already been described. In the controversies of 1296-1303 the two great theologians, Giles of Rome and James of Viterbo, Augustinian friars both, strove to give these theories a still greater prestige. The temporal ruler, they held, was strictly subjected to the spiritual ruler; the pope, because the vicar of Christ, was the source of all law and of all earthly power and authority; the governmental action of pnnces was subject to the pope's control; and these themes were, for Giles of Rome and James of Viterbo [ ], part and parcel of the Catholic faith. It is the first merit of John of Paris that, in the very hour when this inconveniently favourable apologetic was born, he provided the needed theological criticism.

The work in which the Dominican thus corrects the Augustinian -- Kingly Power and Papal Power [ ] -- was written apparently in 1302, just before the publication of the Unam Sanctam. Its author is not a partisan, but well aware of the controversy -- as a lecturer in the University of Paris could not but be aware of it; but he explicitly detaches himself from the rival schools of thought, and sets himself to the search for a via media. With all due submission he makes his own analysis and he sets out his ideas as a hypothesis.

In his view there is not -- as the Waldenses continue to say -- any inconsistency between the true Idea of the Church of Christ and a concern with power in temporal matters. Nor -- as the theologians he criticises assert -- is the Church's power in temporal matters a consequence of its spiritual authority. It does not follow that because the Church possesses authority over men in spiritual matters that it also possesses authority over them in temporal matters -- an authority which it allows the state to exercise as its vicar. Wherever the Church does in fact enjoy authority in temporal matters, this is the outcome of some grant made by the State "out of devotion". The two entities Church and State -- though unequal in dignity -- are co-ordinate in the exercise of authority. Both originate in the divine plan. The State derives its authority from God no less really than does the Church. The spiritual power is indeed the superior of the two, but it is not superior in everything. The pope, though truly Vicar of Christ by Christ's appointment, is not in fact heir to the totality of Our Lord's universal royalty over men and kings. In its own order the State is, under God, sovereign.

Has the spiritual power, then, no authority to regulate the temporal? It has indeed; for the purpose of the spiritual power is a higher thing than the purpose of the temporal, and the lower purpose is subordinate to, and for the sake of, the higher. But -- and here again lies the really great importance of John of Paris -- the Dominican insists that the pope is to exercise this control by instructing the conscience of the prince, and, if the prince fails, by administering correction that is spiritual. The pope instructs the prince, he says, de fide and not de regimine; [ ] the only instrument of the Church's empire over the prince is its charisma to instruct the Christian mind in things of faith and morals, and its moral authority over the Christian conscience. [ ]

The presence of the great name of Dante among the parties to this discussion, is a useful reminder that the quarrel's importance was by no means merely French. [ ] Again, while Dante is a layman, he is a layman who is not a legist; and, like John of Paris, he has no official locus standi in the quarrel. He is moreover a layman who, in refuting the papal thesis as the canonists propound it, makes use of their own chosen method of argument, and uses this to deny the validity of their use of Scripture. All this is extremely interesting; we have here one of the first appearances of the private lay citizen in the public life of the Church. And he appears as not only a most orthodox believer, an undoubted "good Catholic", but as the author of a theologico-political treatise directed against currently accepted ecclesiastical theories, and written to promote the revolution that will save the Church's soul.

Nevertheless Dante is to be classed with John of Paris; for he, too, is looking for the via media. This has not, indeed, always been clear to the readers of his treatise De Monarchia. [ ] The general theme of that well-known book is that a universal monarchy is essential if civilisation is to survive and humanity to make lasting progress. Dante's arguments in proof of this build up a conception of monarchy so high that only when a saint was the monarch would the system really work: or so we might think as we read. But for Dante that ideal monarchy was actually in existence. It was the Holy Roman Empire of the German nation, and all that was needed for the millennium to arrive was to convince the world of the duty of all princes to accept the emperor's superiority. The greatest hindrance was nationalism, and for nationalism -- "the nations that so furiously rage together, the peoples that imagine a vain thing" [ ] -- Dante has strong, religiously-phrased condemnation. How shall the universal monarch accord with the universal pope? In the first place, he is politically independent of the pope; and Dante, attacking, not indeed the papacy, but the canonists who have devised the theory of the papacy's supreme political authority, systematically reviews -- and denies -- all the " spiritual" proofs these are wont to adduce: proofs from the sun and moon, the two swords, Saul's deposition by Samuel, Our Lord's promise to St. Peter, all this is rejected as beside the point.

So far there is nothing to distinguish Dante's thought from that of other contemporary writers -- not even the almost religious tone of his language about the empire is personal to him. It is in the closing chapter of the third book that he makes his own contribution, and that very briefly. If the empire is independent of the Church -- and since it existed before the Church this must be so -- and if the Church's power is wholly spiritual, then the emperor's authority derives immediately from God. The electors merely indicate the man who shall lawfully wield this power. But the emperor yet remains in some way subject to the pope "since mortal happiness is in some way established with a view to immortal happiness." [ ] What is this way? and what, in hard detail, does this relation involve, for both pope and emperor? Dante does not tell us. But he says that the emperor receives from the pope "that light of grace by which he may rule more virtuously"; and he lays it down that the emperor shall act towards the pope "as a first-born towards his father, so that radiating the light of the father's grace, he may the more virtuously shine in all that world over which he has been set by Him Who alone is governor of all things spiritual and temporal."

This, it may be thought, is little enough and disappointing in its generality. Yet it is a statement of principle. Dante conceives the State as politically independent of the Church, and yet the temporal power as subordinate to the spiritual; and he conceives it as possible that these two realities -- independent, and yet the one subordinate to the other -- can so co-exist. And it is on this note that the treatise ends.

This, it is true, is not the aspect of Dante's political thought that has chiefly attracted attention. What has been chiefly regarded is his idealistic exaltation of the empire and his protest against the medieval claim that the popes enjoyed, as popes, a primacy in political matters; and his championship of the State's independence of such ecclesiastical tutelage. In his own time also it was this which made the great impression and Dante's De Monarchia suffered the reception which received opinion inevitably gives to the pioneer! When, after his death, during the war between the popes and the schismatic emperor Lewis of Bavaria, these themes again became practical politics, there was even for a moment the danger that Dante's bones would be digged up and burnt as those of a heretic! [ ]

It cannot but be reckoned as a great misfortune -- even if perhaps an inevitable misfortune, given that human nature influences scholars too -- that, despite these artificers of the via media between the contending absolutisms, it was the extreme theories of the canonists, given theological form by the genius of Giles of Rome, which continued to shape the mind of the papal champions; and that these theories maintained their hold all through the next most difficult centuries, through the time of the Schism and the Conciliar controversies, and the Reformation, until the great spirit of St. Robert Bellarmine restated and determined the issue. The great Jesuit doctor recognised John of Paris as a distant ancestor of his own thought; and a modern, somewhat disgusted, commentator -- a very great scholar indeed -- has presented Dante as being not much better than Bellarmine. It is always a loss to base a good case on poor argument -- and that was the loss which champions of the papacy, often enough, suffered in those centuries. It was an additional loss that, by their proscription of the theorists of the middle way, the writings of this school passed into the armoury of the enemy, and the obiter dicta of John of Paris (for example) became the foundation of more than one useful plaidoyer for Gallicanism. [ ]

ii. The Problem of Faith and Reason

One of the most serious consequences of the duel between Pope Boniface and the French king was, then, something quite unpredictable; namely, that a considerable body of Catholic thought was now permanently roused, not indeed, as yet, against any Catholic doctrine about the papacy, but against a principle of administration which, for generations, had been almost as sacred as doctrine, a principle with which the prestige of the papacy was most intimately linked. Here, for the future, there was a great division in Catholic thought. And, unfortunately, it was not the only division. Already, only fifty years after the death of St. Thomas Aquinas, Christendom was beginning to suffer from the failure of its thinkers to rally to his thought, and most of all from their failure to accept its supreme practical achievement, the harmony he discerned between the spheres of knowledge naturally known and of that which we know supernaturally, the true character of the relations between reason and faith. The story of philosophy among Catholics in these fifty years is, in that

*decline in Catholic thought*

respect, one of steady deterioration. Already, by the time John XXII canonised St. Thomas (1323), the work was well begun that was to sterilise the movement which was the glory of the previous century, to dislocate the teaching in the theological schools (not the faith of the theologians indeed, as yet, but their scientific exposition of it), to destroy the theologians' confidence in philosophy and the pious man's confidence in the theologians, and to leave the ordinary man, in the end, "'fed up' with the whole business" [ ] of speculative theology.

What is the end of a society that ceases to have any use for thought, or any confidence that thought can produce certitude? Pessimism surely and despair, a flight to the material in compensation, or else to a wrong -- because unintelligent -- cultivation of the mystical life of devotion, to superstition thereby and to worse. For to this must devotion come once it disinterests itself from that explanation of revealed truth which true theology is, and once the mystic is tainted with the fatal error that considers theology as mere scholarship, the professional occupation of the theologian, whereas it is an essential condition of healthy Catholic life; and for the mystic, especially, is it important that theology should flourish and good theologians abound, for in the guidance which objective theology supplies lies the mystic's sole certainty of escaping self-illusion.

All of these calamities were to develop in time. Not all of them came at once, nor within a few years. But it is now that the seeds of much lasting disaster are sown, through the new philosophical theories of leading Catholic thinkers. The two greatest names associated with this movement away from the positions of St. Thomas Aquinas are John Duns Scotus and William of Ockham, Franciscans both of them, and teachers of theology at Oxford.

Before we consider how they came to build up their new critical theories of knowledge, let us note, what we cannot too much insist upon, namely, that the problem which all these thinkers were trying to solve, about the nature of faith and of reason, and about the relations between the two, is one of the permanent practical anxieties of mankind. Upon all men, sooner or later, the hard experiences of life force the issue. Are the relations between faith and reason such that a reasonable man can continue to have faith without suppressing, or ignoring, the activities of his reason? Here is the difficulty from the side of the philosopher. Is theology -- the body of knowledge whose first principles are truths known by God's revelation -- really a science? i.e. is it a matter fit for, and capable of, scientific treatment? Is it really a field for the exercise of the reason? Or is not philosophy (where the reason has the field to itself), the exercise of the natural reason, a thing to be feared by theology, the sphere of the natural reason being so separated from the sphere of revealed truths that the introduction of reason into this last cannot but be as harmful as it is, scientifically, illegitimate? Here is the dilemma from the side of the theologian.

St. Thomas had so understood faith and reason that he was able to explain how, of their own nature, they are harmonious; they are means of knowledge independent, indeed, the one of the other, but not antagonistic; they are productive of distinct spheres of knowledge, but spheres which are yet in contact, so that man's intelligence can thereby be satisfied that to believe is reasonable, and be satisfied also that faith is not a mere vicious circle in the mind.

This teaching of St. Thomas left man's mind at peace with itself. Man was delivered from doubts about his power to know with certitude natural reality external to himself; he was certain that he could know with certainty, by the use of his reasoning intelligence, not only facts but also general truths of the natural order. Beyond this sphere of the natural truths lay that other sphere of truths, about God as man's final destiny, unattainable by the merely finite, reasonable intelligence. Many of these other truths had been made known to man -- revealed -- by God, and these truths man also could know with certainty, through his belief in the divine veracity and his knowledge that God had revealed them. Between these two ways of knowing -- by reasoning out the truth from truths already known, and by acceptance of the word of God revealing truths -- there was no conflict; nor was there any conflict between what was known in the one sphere and in the other; there could not, from the nature of things, be any such conflict. And the two spheres were connected and interrelated, so that man's reasoning intelligence could make with the sphere of faith that contact without which man could never be satisfied, and at rest, about the reality of belief, in that intellectual part of his soul whose activity is the very foundation of all his life and happiness. The means of this contact, the delicate all-important nexus, the medium of the thinker's hold on the fact of that higher sphere's existence, was reason's power to arrive, by its own natural operations, at the sure knowledge that there is a God Who is the cause of all else that exists, and at an equally sure knowledge about several of the divine attributes.

Such a theory as this, about faith and reason and their interrelation, is an evident aid for philosopher and theologian alike. It is even a necessity, if philosophy is not to degenerate into scepticism or if theology is not to become a mere psittacism. It guarantees the integrity of both the sciences and the right of each to use the methodology natural to it. The philosopher is saved from the temptation to infidelity, and the theologian from reliance on rhetoric and emotion. Now it was the unfortunate effect of the great thinkers who followed St. Thomas that their theories of knowledge destroyed the all-important nexus between the spheres of reason and faith, when they denied the power of reason really to prove the existence of God.

John Duns Scotus and William of Ockham were, both of them, Franciscan friars; they were Englishmen, and they taught theology, the one after the other, in the university of Oxford. We are now assisting at the very early appearance of what has been a recurring phenomenon of history -- the confection in England of revolutionary doctrines fated to pass across the Channel and to be productive, in the different mental climate of the Continent, of really significant upheavals. The University of Oxford had, from the beginning, very marked particular characteristics. While Paris was, and continued to be, the first home of pure speculation, the philosophers at Oxford, from the beginning, were particularly attracted to the study of the physical universe. To one of the earliest of these Oxford teachers, Robert Grosstete. we owe a whole corpus of thought related to the theory of light. With another, Adam Marsh, it is mathematics that colour his speculation. And the pupil of these two doctors was the still greater physicist Roger Bacon. [ ]

Roger Bacon, too, was a Franciscan, and, like all the thinkers of his time, he was first of all a theologian. It is theology which is the mistress-science, but philosophy is needed if theology is to be explained. Bacon -- like his great contemporary, and superior, St. Bonaventure, Minister-General of the Franciscan order -- holds that a divine illumination of the mind is the beginning of all knowledge. He explains how all knowledge, of natural things as well as of what is sacred, has descended to us through the ages from a first divine revelation. The Hebrew prophets and the Greek philosophers played similar roles in the divine plan. The philosophers were the successors of the prophets, they were themselves prophets. Nay, Roger Bacon is a prophet too, and conducts himself as such, whence doubtless not a little of the sufferings he had to endure from his brethren. He is a fierce critic of all his contemporaries of the university world, and no less fiercely he contests the prestige allowed the teachings of the great men of the past. Aristotle, unexamined, is a superstition; the only way to certain progress in knowledge is to return to the actual sources, and to make experiments. [ ] Knowledge of the ancient languages then -- no one should rely on translations -- of mathematics [ ] and physics, and the capacity and habit of experiments; these are the first things necessary in the formation of the true philosopher. There is no natural certainty to equal the certainty produced by experiment; indeed, by all internal and spiritual experiment we may come to the highest flights of the mystical life. The use of experimental method will reveal in time all the secrets of the world's natural forces. The Church ought to foster such researches. Their fruits will be invaluable to the Crusaders, for example, and also in the approaching struggle with Antichrist that is at hand: for this hard-headed critic of the superstition of Aristotle-worship was, in many things, a fiercely faithful believer in the fantasies of Abbot Joachim.

By the time Duns Scotus came to Oxford as a student [ ] his confrere, Roger Bacon, was nearing the end of his very long life. The university was still filled with the disputes caused by the Franciscan criticism that the differences which characterised St. Thomas's philosophy were not orthodox. [ ] The Dominican criticism of that philosophy, of which also Oxford had seen a great deal, had been ended, in 1287, by the instruction of the General Chapter of the order that the brethren were to follow St. Thomas's teaching. But with the saint's chief Franciscan opponent, the passionate John Peckham, still Archbishop of Canterbury, his teaching was hardly likely to be favourably regarded at the English university.

John Duns Scotus, indeed, was well acquainted with it, and in two ways he shows himself a kind of product of the Thomist revolution. For Scotus is an Aristotelian, breaking away and taking the schools of his order with him, from the Augustinian theories dear to St. Bonaventure; and he is so preoccupied with St. Thomas that his own major work is a kind of critical commentary on the saint's achievement.

It is an erroneous and very superficial view that sees in Scotus a conscious revolutionary, a turbulent Franciscan set on to vindicate the intellectual superiority of his order against the

Dominican rivals. Duns Scotus has all the calm and the modesty and the detachment of the theologian who daily lives the great truths of which he treats. Always it is to the judgment of the Church that he submits his proferred solutions; the spirit in which he presents his teaching could not be more Catholic, more traditional. But it is not with the great Franciscan as a theologian that we are now concerned, but with his philosophical teaching, more particularly with his theories of knowledge and what follows from them.

More than any other of the scholastics Scotus is preoccupied with the problems of logic. It is not surprising that so studying logic in the scientific and mathematical-minded university of Oxford, and in the order that was the especial home of these studies, Scotus was most exigent in his idea of what is needed to make a proof that is really conclusive. We can argue to the existence of things either from their causes, or from their effects. The first kind of proof is the better, St. Thomas would say -- when we can get it; the second kind, though inferior, is yet conclusive and so useful. But for Scotus, only the first kind is really a proof.

And so there disappears a whole celebrated series of proofs from reason of the existence of God: and with them go the rational proofs of the providence of God, and of the immortality of the human soul. The human reason cannot, by its own powers -- it is now said -- arrive at certitude here. These are truths indeed, but truths only to be known by faith. Theology is their true home, the learning which deals with truths rationally unprovable. So, then, there disappears that middle ground where philosophy and theology meet, the all-important nexus between natural and supernatural know] edge; and there disappears with it the notion that philosophy and theology have it in common to give to man speculative knowledge: for theology is now rather a source of practical direction for life than a science. Philosophy and theology are no longer in contact. The day will come when they are conceived as necessarily opposed. [ ]

Duns Scotus also moves away from St. Thomas, and again by what at first sight may seem only a nuance of method, in that his philosophy makes its first contact with God not in answering the question, Whether God exists? but this, Whether there exists a Being who is infinite? The truth of God's infinity is, in fact, central for Scotus: it is for him God's "essential" attribute. [ ] And in association with this characteristic approach there is to be noted the place the Franciscan gives to the divine will. It is here, so he teaches, and not in the divine intelligence, that the cause of things being what they are is to be sought. A thing is good because God has willed it as it is. Had God willed it to be otherwise, then it would equally have been good. Law is right in so far as law is acceptable to God. From the point of view of St. Thomas, this is a topsy-turvy way of regarding the matter: and in its ultimate logical consequences it is, of course, far more serious than that. Those consequences will in the next two hundred years be worked out to the full.

Scotus, it may be thought, had a different kind of mind from that of the great Dominican. His tendency to develop his thought through an analysis of ideas already known, and to rely on such analysis as the only way, are in great contrast to the versatility of St. Thomas. But in this chapter we are merely considering the Franciscan doctor as the first in time of the thinkers whose critique of the philosophico-theological synthesis of St. Thomas did so much to prevent the general acceptance in the Catholic schools of that metaphysical teaching which later generations of Catholics have seen as a conditio sine qua non of sound theology. [ ] To know Scotus in this role alone is, of course, to know him barely at all. His theological teaching was to form the piety of his order for centuries, under the active patronage of many popes, and especially was it to be the inspiration of the three great saints who revived the order in the dark days that followed the Schism, St. Bernadine of Siena, St. John Capistran and St. James of the March. The teaching of Duns Scotus on the Incarnation, and the spirituality which flowers everywhere in it, are one of the permanent treasures of Catholic thought. Most famously of all, Scotus is the first great doctor to set out, as we know it to-day, the mystery of Our Lady's Immaculate Conception and in one office for the feast Duns Scotus is described as another St. Cyril, raised up to defend this doctrine as St. Cyril was raised up to defend that of the divine maternity.

John Duns Scotus was a holy man, venerated as a saint. and perhaps one day to be officially recognised as such. Canonisation is a distinction that no one has, so far, proposed for William of Ockham. Of Ockham's early life we really know very little. He was younger by a generation than Scotus, [ ] born somewhere about 1285. [ ] He joined the Franciscan order and he studied theology at Oxford, where, however, he never proceeded to a higher degree than the lectorate, i.e. the apprentice stage where the graduate taught under the doctor's supervision It was at Oxford that Ockham's career as a teacher began. He never, it would seem, taught at Paris, and he was still busy with his lectures at Oxford on the Liber Sententiarum of Peter Lombard (the classic occupation at this stage of the theologian's career) when, in 1324, on the eve of his doctorate he was summoned to the papal court to defend the orthodoxy of his views. He had, in fact, been denounced to the pope as a heretic by the chancellor of the university, John Luttrell,

Ockham's many writings are all extant, and the most of them have been in print since the end of the fifteenth century. [ ] And, since 1922, we possess the report of the Avignon Commission appointed by the pope to enquire into his orthodoxy. [ ] Ockham's influence was undoubtedly as mischievous as it was extensive. It is the mind of Ockham which, more than all else, is to dominate the university world from now on to the very eve of the Reformation, but it would be rash, [ ] in the present state of our knowledge, to attempt to trace the pedigree of his ideas. But Ockham was certainly anti-Scotist, in full reaction, that is to say, against the super-subtlety and multitude of the new distinctions which mark that system.

Perhaps the readiest way to make clear the nature of the harm Ockham did, is to review the Avignon report, and to note [ ] how Ockham's misunderstanding of the nature and limitations of the science in which he excelled -- logic -- led him to deny the possibility of metaphysics, to divorce completely the world of natural reasoning from that of supernatural knowledge, and to colour even theology with the baneful theory that all our knowledge that is not of singular observable facts is but a knowledge of names and terms. In a curious subtle way the reality of theological truth is thus dissolved, while the appearances (and the terminology) remain the same. Ockham's nominalist theory about the nature of our intellectual knowledge is far more radical than that of Abelard; for him "general ideas cannot correspond to anything in reality," [ ] a philosophical position which is not consistent with the Faith. And he revealed himself as a philosophical revolutionary of the first degree in the new classification of knowledge which he proposed. There is a kind of knowledge which is self-evident, intuitive knowledge Ockham calls it; this alone is certain knowledge, and this alone enables us to say whether things exist or not. This alone can be the foundation of scientific knowledge. All other knowledge -- of images, of memories, of ideas -- abstractive knowledge, he names it, is not really knowledge at all. [ ] It is not the business of this book to demonstrate where Ockham's mistake lay -- this is not a treatise of philosophy. But if Ockham were right, our knowledge would be no more than a mere system of useful mental conventions with no objective justification. We should, necessarily, from the nature of things, be complete sceptics about everything except our own physical sensations.

150

Given such a conception of knowledge, there can hardly be any common ground between reason and faith; and the two spheres are indeed, for Ockham, entirely out of contact. So little can what goes on in the one be related to the activity within the other, that faith may even assure us of the existence of what reason tells us is impossibly absurd. This separation of faith and reason was the greatest mischief of all. [ ]

Ockham, like Scotus, is fascinated by the truths of God's omnipotence and of the divine infinity. For him, too, it is the will which in God is all important. And he is thence led into developments that far surpass the novelties of Duns Scotus. Even the divine command to love God could, thinks Ockham, equally well have been the command to hate Him; and God could, if He chose, damn the innocent and save the guilty. The whole of our knowledge could be an illusion, God causing us systematically to see and feel as existent things which actually do not exist, and this without any reflection on the divine veracity, or trustworthiness: our sole certitude that God does not so act lies, not in any belief that God is Truth itself but in this that miracles are not part of the ordinary machinery of the divine ruling of creation. One day, what these subtly argued theses posit as possibilities will, without any of Ockham's delicate argumentation, be crudely stated as the fact, and God be hailed as an arbitrary tyrant who must therefore, paradoxically, be merciful to man his victim. From Ockham to Luther is indeed a long road, and the Franciscan's thought doubtless suffers many losses as it makes the journey along it. But it is a road whose trace is unmistakable, and the beginning of that road needs to be noticed. From one point of view Luther has a claim to be regarded as the last in the long line of Catholic theologians of the scholastic decadence. It is not an unimportant point of view.

From this time onwards -- from the middle of the fourteenth century -- it is Ockham's system that dominates the minds of Catholic thinkers. And this, strangely enough, despite the

151

discovery of all its latent mischievousness by the officials first appointed to judge it, and despite the still more evident fact of Ockham's open rebellion against the pope, and the subversive literature of propaganda in which he justified this to all Europe.

The Avignon Commissioners noted in Ockham's philosophy the opinions which might lead to errors in theology -- especially his theory that the object of our knowledge is not reality but an idea of reality only -- with special reprobation and alarm. They condemned his agnostic notion that we cannot know anything more of God than the concept which we form of God: this they declared was manifest heresy. His special dialectical method they found to be " subversive of philosophy and of theology alike." They had faults to find with his criticism -- as he applied it to the doctrine of the Blessed Trinity -- of the current philosophical teaching about relation. And, finally, they signaled for condemnation a number of theological errors that were to have a great fortune in the future, for they were to appear prominently in the theological foundations of the new Protestant religion. For example, Ockham's notion that, after justification, sin and grace can coexist in the soul; his theory that the merit which a soul has in God's sight is really wholly due to God's acceptance of man's actions as meritorious, and in no way to any worth possessed by the act itself; moral guilt, again, for him, is not so much a reality that inheres to the soul, as a blameworthiness that cries out for punishment; [ ] and although Ockham does not deny the defined teaching that Our Lord is present in the Blessed Sacrament by transubstantiation, he declares that "consubstantiation" -- the theory that the bread and the wine remain after the consecration -- would be a more suitable theory.

Why, it may be asked, did there not follow upon this report a strong, and even violent, condemnation of the English friar? Perhaps his sudden flight to the schismatic emperor, and the new crisis that followed upon this, first delayed that condemnation; and then, later, the need for it was obscured by the resounding excommunication of Ockham for other heresies. Certainly the pope, John XXII, had no doubts about the quality of Ockham's Oxford work when he described him in a letter to the King of Bohemia (July 27, 1330) as "a heresiarch who publicly taught many heresies, and had composed writings full of errors and heresies." On the other hand, Ockham does not always set out his ideas as proven true, but often puts them forward as suggestions and hypotheses. And he had, of course, a master mind, and the competence that goes with such, in his special gift of dialectic. No doubt, in the long four years he debated with the commissioners, he put up a good defence. Even so, whatever be the reason for it, the escape of this system in 1326 from the needed condemnation is something that still surprises the historian. Certainly the alleged tyranny of the clerical system over the mind of the medieval thinker seems at the moment to have been functioning badly. [ ]

But Ockham's philosophical novelties did not by any means go entirely uncondemned. If the papacy had other aspects of his career to occupy its energies, the university of Paris, the capital of theological studies, was immediately active against these. Ockhamism was gaining a hold on the younger masters and a decree of November 25, 1339, forbade the use of his books and the teaching of his theses in the faculty of arts. The next year saw a still stronger condemnation of that teaching, as definitely erroneous, and a ban on the use of the new dialectic in argumentation in the schools. Then, in 1346, came the papal condemnation of Nicholas of Autrecourt [ ] for teaching which is distinctly Ockhamist, and the university's condemnation of two others of the sect, Richard of Lincoln in 1346 and John of Mirecourt, a Cistercian, in 1347. But, in the end, it was Ockhamism that prevailed at Paris. More and more the great names are, all of them, his disciples, Buridan, Marsiglio of Inghen, Peter d'Ailly and John Gerson. By the end of the fourteenth century Paris is, indeed, the chief stronghold of what is now called the via moderna, of its logic, its metaphysics and its theology.

It may be asked why the antiqui proved so powerless against the novelties? -- the followers of St. Thomas and Duns Scotus. So far the answer to this natural question is not fully known. One part of it, perhaps, is that the two schools were, increasingly, more interested in fighting about their mutual differences than in continuing to study reality. They contracted something of that fatal preoccupation with mental processes for their own sake which is the characteristic vice of the fourteenth century, and began to "philosophise about philosophies." [ ] Had they, in truer imitation of their first begetters, given their attention to the new problems of the new age, dealing less with St. Thomas and Duns Scotus as antagonists, and more with what had been the cause of their activities as thinkers, they would have discovered, amongst other things, that they had more in common than they supposed. [ ] Had they realised how, very often indeed, St. Thomas and Duns Scotus complement and complete each other, the easy victory of the followers of Ockham would scarcely have been possible.

But while Thomists and Scotists were thus locked in a chronic state of sterile warfare, it was the new Nominalism that took up the new problems raised by the new developments in the knowledge of nature. These new truths could not, of course, cure the radical ills of the nominalist philosophy; but in the association of those who discovered these truths with the adherents of a philosophy more and more at odds with Catholic theology, we may already see signs of the great characteristic of later ages, the assumed necessary antagonism between religion and science. St. Thomas had indicated the true starting point for the harmonious development of natural knowledge and theology; and with this he had exemplified the spirit in which the philosopher and the theologian should work. Neither was to be regarded as the lucky possessor of an armoury of solutions and recipes for all possible problems that the future might throw up; but as a thinker, ready to investigate everything, with a first hope always of assimilating novelties, that derived from a passionate conviction of the unity of all truth. Once that true starting point was lost, and that spirit fled, there was no future for thought.

And this is what had happened round about the middle of the fourteenth century. Henceforth there was stagnation in orthodox circles, and elsewhere a steadily increasing disruption in the life of the spirit. Once the Catholic mind had ceased to think, the faith of the multitude, deprived of its natural protection, would be a prey for every vagary of idea or sentiment. [ ]

## 2. THE TROUBLED TIMES OF JOHN XXII
### i. The Friars Minor

Twelve days after the death of Clement V, the twenty-three cardinals met to choose the new pope in the palace of the bishop at Carpentras, [ ] the temporary seat of the curia (May 1, 1314). To elect the pope sixteen votes were needed, according to the law of Alexander III, [ ] but the college was so divided that no party commanded this needed two-thirds of the whole: there was a Gascon party -- the friends, relatives and fellow-countrymen of the late pope -- ten in all; there was a "Provencal" party of six, that included two Normans; and there were seven Italians, by no means united but continuing in France the hereditary feuds of unhappy Italian memory. For twelve weeks these groups steadily maintained a deadlock, Italians and "Provencaux" supporting an admirable candidate, Cardinal Guillaume de Mandagout, the Gascons resolved to have none but a Gascon. Presently there were quarrels, riots next, and then, July 24, armed bands of free soldiers, under the command of the late pope's nephew, raided the town, massacring what Italians they found, clerics and bankers, and pillaging the goods of the Italian cardinals. A blockade of the conclave seemed likely, and the Italian cardinals, with the troops clamouring for their lives, fled from the city. For the Gascon party this was their chance to remove to Avignon, and thence to declare themselves the conclave and to announce that whoever they elected would be the lawful pope. But a timely manifesto from the Italians checked this manoeuvre; and then, for nearly two years, the two groups, refusing to meet, gave themselves to endless and sterile negotiations.

It was the future Philip V of France who, in the end, induced them to come together, at Lyons in March 1316. He had sworn not to use any violence against them, and to leave them free to enter into conclave when they chose. But when, in June, his brother the King of France (Louis X) died, and Philip left Lyons for Paris, his lieutenants disregarded the sworn engagement, and forced the cardinals into conclave, telling them that locked up they should remain until they found a pope (June 28, 1316). For six weeks there was again a deadlock, until three Italians joined with some of the "Provencaux" and the whole Gascon party to elect the Cardinal-Bishop of Porto, Jacques Duese (August 7). He took the name John XXII.

The choice was singular, for Jacques Duese, a man of conspicuous administrative ability, and long episcopal experience, of exceptional legal talent, and sternly upright character, was a frail old man of seventy-two. He was, however, destined to last out another eighteen years of vigorous life, after escaping in the first months of his pontificate an attempt to get rid of him by arsenic and witchcraft, in which two bishops and one of the Gascon cardinals had a share. Whenever the constitutional history of the Church comes to be written, John XXII will be one of its greatest figures, for he is one of the chief architects of that centralised administrative and legal system through which, for centuries now, the popes have exercised their divinely instituted primacy. But " incomparable administrator " as he was, John XXII was no less a vigorous ruler, dealing as strongly as subtly with the host of problems that awaited him; and he was, above all else, a most militant defender of the traditional rights of the papacy. With this election the initiative in the affairs of Christendom passed once more to the pope, and to one of the strongest of all his long line. The first problem to which he set his hand was how to bring peace to the much troubled order of the Friars Minor.

It has been told [ ] how as the companions of St. Francis grew, within a few years, to be numbered by the thousand, the simple informal "rule" that had served for the saint and his score of friends inevitably proved to be insufficient. If a movement that now extended half across Europe was to survive, and with it the special approach to the service of God that was the personal gift of St. Francis of Assisi, the ideal would need a carefully-devised protective code of legislation; and it has been told how the imposition of the new rule in 1223 left many sore hearts among those whose Franciscan life went back to the first early days. Such tragedies as these, when idealism has to face the cold air of reality and either develop a protective covering or die, are not infrequent in human history. Only an infinity of charity can, when they occur, save the ordinary idealist from ruin.

But with the Franciscans there was one change especially which, from the moment it was made, caused very much dissatisfaction indeed among this little group of "primitives," for it seemed to them to affect the most characteristic of the new order's virtues, poverty. Religious poverty -- the renouncement of ownership, of the right to own property and the right to acquire it henceforward -- had been part and parcel of the monastic life from the beginning. From those first days in the deserts of Egypt, the religious who owned -- or who wanted to own -- anything had been regarded as highly unfaithful to the life to which he had consecrated himself. But when this first fashion, of solitary religious life in deserts, had given place to that of a common life lived in monasteries, although the individual monk -- whatever his rank -- continued to be a monk through religious poverty as well as through religious obedience, some proprietor there had to be for the monastic buildings, the lands which the monks worked, the woods, the farms and the like. That proprietor was the abbey or the order.

It was the desire of St. Francis -- and the special characteristic of his religious ideal -- that not even the community of his brotherhood should own. The order as an order should profess, and practise, religious poverty. This was an ideal easily realised while the order was no more than a few groups of friars, making their way through the Umbrian countrysides that were their native home, preaching their simple exhortation to penance, begging the elements of sustenance at the first door to which they came, sleeping under hedges and in barns; beggar-men who were apostles, apostles who cheerfully lived the life of beggars. But as the numbers grew, the mission of the brotherhood expanded. Soon it had before it a much more complex work than this simple apostolate. And as a code of rules was called for, and courses of study, so too were stable centres where the brethren would live. There had to be buildings, no matter how simple, and land on which they were built. Who was to own all this?

One important complication was the appearance, within the very lifetime of St. Francis, of Brother Elias, a friar with a genius for making the order "a going concern" and a "real success"; here was the practical man, who knew how to gather in the money, and how to spend it, and who rose indeed to the highest place in the order. His sad spiritual end strengthened the hands of the party called "the Spirituals" -- who wished for the impossible restoration of the order's first days. The Spirituals had much to say of the inevitable effect of deserting the first rule, and, no doubt truly, they could point to many friars, in these later days of elaborate organisation, who reminded men of nothing so little as St. Francis. But the zeal of the Spirituals did not stop here. They could see no good at all in any way but their own way, and they bitterly denounced, along with such friars who really were disgracefully unfaithful, the great mass of the order, the brethren who had settled down to live according to the popes' official interpretation of the mind of St. Francis. It is sad, but not surprising, to record that the poverty of these militant Spirituals was often only surpassed by their lack of charity in judging their fellows, and by their determined insubordination towards those very superiors to whom, for the love of God, they had vowed away their wills in religious obedience.

The first great organiser, charged by the popes with finding a way out of this chaos, and so preserving the great ideal, was the seventh Minister-General, John of Fidanza, whom we know as St. Bonaventure (1221-1274). He served the order, humbly and patiently, as its head for seventeen years (1257-1274) and for his success in devising a way of life, faithful to the ideal of St. Francis, accessible to the man of average good will, and suited to the extended mission of the order, he has merited to be called its second founder. [ ] The solution which his long experience devised is set out -- often in St. Bonaventure's own words -- in the decretal bull published five years after the saint's death by Nicholas III. [ ]

The problem how an order was to continue to exist that had no right to own, and of how religious pledged to so rigorous a view of poverty were to be faithful to it, and yet be able to accept from the faithful all that was needed to keep the community alive, the decretal solved by the device that the Holy See became the owner of whatever was given to the Friars Minor. In all their use of whatever was given for their use, the Franciscans were not their own masters; they were dependent on the good will of the Holy See. Nor need this have been the mere legal fiction which it has, very superficially, been made to seem. A truly conscientious man uses in a very different spirit and way the things that are his own and those which he has borrowed. The friars were still forbidden even to handle what St. Francis -- the wealthy merchant's son -- held in peculiar abhorrence, money. Not even through a third person, was any friar to use money for his own profit. But he was not bound to refuse, of what was given him, all beyond what sufficed for his own immediate personal necessity. It was lawful, for example, for the monastery to lay in a store of food. But always, and in all things, the friar was supposed, and commanded, to make such a use of this power of using as would accord with the high ideal of St. Francis. Martin IV, in 1283, added a practical detail to this system by appointing an official (called syndic) to act for the Holy See as a protector of the temporalities in every town where there was a Franciscan house.

These were the years when the war of the Sicilian Vespers was bringing upon the Holy See the succession of disasters already described, and it has been noted how a revival of Joachimite fantasies now developed and how, as in an earlier generation, the Franciscan Spirituals were again prominent in that revival. [ ] The system set up by the decretal of Nicholas III was, in Italy and in southern France, rudely shaken before it could well settle. Next came the advent of the hermit pope, Celestine V, in whom the Spirituals saw, not only a holy man who had led their own kind of life for sixty years and more, but the papa angelicus foretold by Joachim, as they were the new religious order which the prophet had seen. One of the few personal actions of this hermit pope's short pontificate was the permission granted to the Italian Spirituals to form themselves into a new order, on the model of Celestine's own institution, a kind of Benedictine foundation, and with the Celestinian rule. This solution Boniface VIII had revoked. Moreover, Celestine's scheme had left untouched the problem of the Spirituals outside the mountain lands of central Italy. And the stormy reigns of Boniface VIII and Clement V went by to the accompaniment of violent anti-papal agitation from this turbulent Franciscan minority.

The division in the order was by this time (1311) one of the papacy's chronic troubles, a perpetual menace to the general peace, and, given the vast expansion of the order, a potential

Franciscan battle within the order on total poverty vs ownership things threat to the general unity of the Church. [ ] And side by side with this fresh trouble within the order, there was a steadily developing trouble from without, the complaints -- true or false -- from every part of Christendom about the friars' abuse of their privilege of exemption from the authority of the local bishop and the parochial system. Hence Clement V, once the meeting of the General Council of Vienne was decided, appointed a commission to review the whole Franciscan problem. Its findings could be studied at the council and a lasting decision then be taken.

But that decision -- given in Clement's bull Exivi de Paradiso [ ] -- was so even and so nuanced that both Spirituals and Conventuals -- so their opponents were coming to be called (the common party, the party of the conventus) claimed a victory. The trouble was thus barely appeased and when, after Clement's death two years later, the Holy See remained vacant for two and a quarter years, it had ample time to break out in all its old fury. In more than one city of Tuscany and Provence feeling ran so high that the Spirituals, throwing off their obedience, drove out the Conventuals after riots and fighting. To add to the trouble the Minister-General now died, and by the time the long vacancy of the Holy See was ended these provinces of the order were in a state of anarchy. To reduce that anarchy was one of the first of the tasks to which the new pope, John XXII, set his hand.

The new pope was a professional legist, a trained and experienced administrator. His sense of order, his well-earned name as a strong and capable administrator, his acute legal mind can have left no one doubting how he would solve the problem. But long before John XXII had finished with the troubles of the Friars Minor, even his tenacity and native toughness must have felt the strain. In a bull [ ] of 1317 he excommunicated and summoned to an unconditional surrender, the rebellious Spirituals from Tuscany who had now made Sicily their headquarters, and he gave characteristically strong support to the new Minister-General, Michael of Cesena, [ ] who offered the

161

same terms to the insubordinate friars of Provence. After a hearing in his own presence, where both parties were represented, the pope ordered the Spirituals, under pain of excommunication, to abandon their claim to wear a different kind of habit, and to accept it as good Franciscan doctrine that it was lawful for the convent to take the normal measures to secure that there was food enough for the brethren.

But the sequel had its tragic side. All but twenty-five of the Spirituals gave in; these twenty-five were handed to the Inquisition. They were not only disobedient in a grave matter, defying even excommunication, but, it was ruled, heretics also, for they had expressly declared that the ground on which they refused obedience was that the pope had no authority to alter the rule of the order. Of the commission of theologians responsible for this example of "constructive heresy," the Minister-General was one. The "heretics" were condemned to the stake, and four of them who held out to the end were actually burnt at Marseilles (May 1318). Thereupon an uneasy peace settled upon the friaries of Provence.

Four years later the affairs of the Friars Minor again troubled the pope. It was not now the small band of Spirituals whom he had to bring to heel, but the whole order; and this in a matter of such importance that, by the time the dispute was over, John XXII had made the order into a different kind of thing.

In the bull [ ] which marked the final defeat of the Spirituals the pope had warned them that great as is the virtue of poverty, it is not the greatest of virtues. The new dispute turned precisely on this point, namely the theoretical or doctrinal point of the exact value of religious poverty as the Friars Minor conceived this. A Franciscan had been denounced to the Inquisition in Provence for stating in a sermon that, like the Franciscans, Our Lord and the Apostles had neither owned anything as individuals nor as a body. Among the judges was another Franciscan, and he declared that so far from this being heresy, it was the Church's own teaching. This was towards the end of 1321, and within a few months the dispute was occupying the whole attention of the papal court. From the beginning the Franciscans made much of the fact that in the decretal which was the Magna Carta of the order's ideals, Exiit qui Seminat, [ ] Nicholas III had not only declared that the friars in giving up all things were showing themselves true followers of Our Lord, but had forbidden, under pain of excommunication, any further reopening of this question. John XXII now suspended this prohibition, and soon a tremendous theological tourney was in full swing.

The Franciscans argued for the consecration as Catholic doctrine of the theory that their own way of life was exactly that of Our Lord and the Apostles; that Our Lord was, as one of them actually said, a Franciscan in all but the habit. The other orders, resentful of the suggestion that the Franciscan way was a more perfect following of Our Lord than any other, joined with the secular clergy to oppose them. The air was filled with the extravagances of the rival parties, and all the charges ever made against the Friars Minor were now vindictively renewed. Then, while the question was still sub iudice, the General Chapter of the order, meeting at Perugia, declared, in a public manifesto, that it had been for many years part of the Catholic faith that Our Lord had lived in the utter poverty of St. Francis, and they appealed to the pope to support them and to renew the law, and the prohibition, of his predecessor Nicholas III.

The rash public action of the General Chapter raised a second question that went beyond the simple question of fact (i.e. whether Our Lord had indeed lived in this way), the question namely whether it had ever been declared that all Catholics must believe this as a part of their faith.

The pope proceeded, in orderly fashion, to answer both questions, in two decisions given 8 December, 1322, [ ] and 12 November, 1323. [ ]

The first decision does not touch the question of doctrine at all. It is a practical ruling as to how the ideal of poverty must be carried out by the Friars Minor, and it is an argued reply to the contentions of their agent at Avignon, Bonagratia of Bergamo. This friar, a highly-skilled theologian and lawyer, had examined the question, What is ownership? from all points of view, seeking to show that no matter what theory of it one adopted, the Franciscan contention was right. The pope followed him point by point in careful refutation; [ ] and, developing the point he had made against the Spirituals six years earlier, he laid it down that religious poverty does not of itself constitute perfection, using here that teaching of St. Thomas Aquinas, on charity as the essence of perfection, which had preserved the other great medieval order from disputes of this sort. The pope noted -- a good fighting jab that Bonagratia had not looked for -- the singular fact that the Franciscan order, so anxious to bear this distinction of a peculiarly absolute poverty, was, as a matter of fact, more anxious to acquire property than any of the other orders. The plan of Nicholas III, that made the friars users only and the Holy See the owner, had worked out badly. It was to be abolished and henceforth the Franciscan order would be, as an order, on a footing similar to the others. [ ] All the subtle argumentation by which Bonagratia had endeavoured to show that the friars did not only not own even the food they put to their lips -- an ownership which would have sufficed to disprove the absoluteness of poverty they claimed -- but could so use (and thereby destroy) it without having that right to destroy which is a mark of ownership, the equally argumentative pope routed with ease. Henceforth the Franciscans must be content to be poor, [ ] in the same way that the other orders were poor, however much they might continue to make poverty their speciality.

The chiefs of the order did not take this decree calmly. Bonagratia replied to the pope with a violence and contempt that earned him imprisonment. He no doubt saw that the revolution now commanded in the practical way Franciscan poverty was lived, foreshadowed a judgment no less drastic on the doctrinal question.

This matter seems to have been most carefully considered during the ensuing months, and all parties were heard. Then came the decision, [ ] 12 November, 1323. To declare that Our Lord and the Apostles were not owners (i.e. had not a right to use the things they used, a right to sell them, to give them away, to use them in order to acquire other things) is heresy.

The order, before this solemn and serious adverse judgment, was silent and submissive; but a few months later the condemned ideals found an unlooked-for champion in the emperor, Lewis of Bavaria. He had, for a long time now, been openly at war with the pope, and recently -- 23 March, 1321 had been excommunicated. And he found it a useful thing, in the new defiance that was his reply to the pope, to cry out to all Europe that John XXII was a heretic, whose wickedness spared not Christ nor His mother nor the saints. Seven popes, said the emperor, have approved the rule of St. Francis, and Christ by the stigmata of the saint has sealed it with His own seal. And now this enemy of God, and so forth.

But still the order as a whole did not move against the pope: it remained obedient and loyal. The pope, however, replying to the emperor, undertook [ ] to reconcile his direction for the Franciscan way of life with that of Nicholas III, and thence sprang a new controversy, for here the pope was dealing with something less privileged than dogmas and heresies. At the General Chapter of 1325 [ ] Michael of Cesena had to remind the brethren not to speak disrespectfully of the pope. And then Michael himself fell.

The pope had summoned him to Avignon. There were rumours (August 28, 1327) [ ] that he had come to an understanding with the emperor, and that he was to be the expected imperial anti-pope. Michael arrived at Avignon in December of that year, and spent some months making certain changes in the administrative staff of the order at the pope's command. Then, on April 9, 1328, there was a tremendous scene in open consistory when the pope's anger at the Minister-General's dissimulation broke all bounds and overwhelmed him, John blaming him for the declaration at Perugia in 1323 that had been the source of so much trouble. Michael did not deny his responsibility and now, so he tells us, resisted Peter to his face. He was placed under open arrest, and a few weeks later, with Friar Bonagratia, he escaped from Avignon. Outside the city a guard was waiting, sent by the emperor for their protection, and at Aigues Mortes there was a ship to take them to Lewis at Pisa.

At Avignon Michael had found one of his subjects who was also in difficulties with the pope. This was Ockham, so far indifferent to these public questions that were rending his order. But Michael now showed him how John XXII was a heretic, contradicting the "faith" as Nicholas III had taught it. And when the General fled to Pisa, William of Ockham accompanied him. It is at this moment that the Englishman passes into the history of European politics, and its literature; and the Franciscan problem ceases to be a major problem troubling the harmony of Catholic life. A few faithful followers went out with Michael into the wilderness, as the remnants of the Spirituals had already done, to form yet another element in that underworld of religious rebels which everywhere seethed below the surface of medieval life, devoted, narrow, fanatical, apocalyptic, and ineffective as all tiny groups must be which are wholly cut off from the life of their time.

ii. The Last War with the Empire, 1314-1356

At the moment when the Franciscan chiefs, and their English brother with them, threw in their lot with Lewis of Bavaria, the emperor's fortunes in his war with Pope John XXII were mounting to their highest point.

It was now nearly four years since Lewis had first defied the pope; in all that time -- the same years that saw John XXII's troubles with the order of the Friars Minor -- the war had never slackened. From the emperor's point of view it was a war of independence; to the pope it was a crusade. The question that divided them was the old, old question yet once again, what rights had the pope, as pope, over the empire. Although the protagonists did not know it, this was to be the last of these great conflicts. Lewis was indeed to end broken and defeated, like many an emperor before him, but the cause he defended was, this time, to win through, and in less than ten years from his death be tacitly given droit de cite by the papacy.

The wisdom of John XXII's successor -- Innocent VI -- tacitly granting that right when he ignored a new "provocation" by the successor of Lewis in 1356, no doubt neutralised much of the mischief to religion which such struggles as these inevitably caused. But, like that earlier fight, between Boniface VIII and Philip the Fair, this contest too had its literary side; and the two chief writers who supported Lewis, Marsiglio of Padua and William of Ockham, were not only publicists but, as political thinkers, adversaries of far greater weight, and more permanently dangerous, than any the popes had yet had to face. Against them the popes might publish condemnations and sentences of excommunication, but, on the Catholic side, there was no thinker equal to them. Their anti-papal, anti-clerical, anti-religious writings survived the condemnations, to be studied more and more, in university circles, slowly infecting Catholic life everywhere, to become indeed the first great literary source and reasoned justification of that "laicism" which the modern popes never cease to denounce as the deadliest foe of religion. In these centuries between St. Thomas and Luther there is no more powerful agent of disintegration than the work of Marsiglio and Ockham.

To understand something of the German situation as the newly-elected John XXII faced it, [ ] the history of papal-imperial relations during the previous eight years must be recalled, the results of the election as emperor, in 1308, of the Count of Luxembourg, Henry VII.

His short reign (1308-1313) was almost wholly taken up with an active military intervention in the complicated politics of Italy. The then pope -- Clement V -- suspicious of imperial schemes that would give new life to the anti-papal party in every Italian state and city, sought an ally in his vassal the King of Naples -- Robert the Wise. Henry strove to form a league against Naples, incurred excommunication by the attack he made, and then, as he marched south from Siena, he was suddenly carried off by fever (August 24, 1313).

Clement V understood to the full the opportunity that had now fallen to him. The late emperor had ignored his formal commands about Naples, and had disregarded the conditions set by the pope for his coronation at Rome. The pope now announced that, during the vacancy, the Holy See would administer the empire. He explained that the oaths sworn by Henry VII (at his coronation) were real oaths of fidelity to a suzerain, [ ] and acting as suzerain he quashed [ ] the sentence of deposition passed by Henry (April 26, 1313) on Robert of Naples. The terms of this papal declaration are all one might expect from a pope so versed in the traditions of the canon law: it is "In virtue of the undoubted supremacy which the Holy See enjoys over the empire, of the right which the head of the Church possesses to administer the empire when there is no emperor, and by that plenitude of jurisdiction which the successor of St. Peter has received from Jesus Christ, the King of Kings and Lord of Lords" that he annuls the emperor's sentence.

Clement V soon followed the emperor out of this world (April 20, 1314) and it was not until six months after the pope's death, and while the Holy See was still vacant, that the German princes met to elect Henry VII's successor. They made a double election: five of them voting for Lewis, the Duke of Bavaria, and two for Frederick of Habsburg (October 19, 1314). Each was acknowledged as emperor by his own partisans and both were crowned, and on the same day, though in different cities. As the cardinals continued to keep the Holy See vacant for the best part of another two years, the situation in Germany had time to harden. By the time John XXII was elected (August 7, 1316), a miniature civil war was in progress, and the Italian princes (the papal or Guelf part of them) were suggesting that here was the pope's opportunity to end the noxious institution which the empire continued to prove itself, to Italy, to France, and to the Church.

But John XXII refused to be drawn into this plan. He was inclined to a policy that would protect the independence of religion by balancing the forces of the contending princes; the central point of the policy was the idea that there should be no prince in Italy so powerful that he dominated the whole peninsula. So of the rivals in Germany he supported neither, calling on both to submit their claims to a peaceful arbitration. Then, in 1317, he announced that he considered the empire as vacant; and acting as its administrator, he appointed Robert of Naples imperial vicar in Italy.

For the next five years there was no change in the situation, until, at the battle of Muhldorf (September 28, 1322), Lewis overwhelmed his rival, and took him prisoner. Then the pope, after an interval of some months, in which Lewis asked for recognition, stated his terms, in the spirit of Clement V's intervention in 1313. Lewis refused to ask the empire as a gift from the pope and thereupon the new war began.

It may be asked how far this new war was necessary, a war -- as it proved -- singularly disastrous for religion. Had John XXII not been the fiery-tempered old man he was; had he shown the awareness of, say, Innocent VI, that a new world had come into being since the fall of the Hohenstaufen, a world in which the empire was so little more than a shadow dignity that it was folly to fight a war about one's rights over it, and still more mischievous to link up the cause of religion with those rights; had the pope been something younger than a man of eighty, could this catastrophe not have been averted? John XXII's temperament cannot, it is true, be discharged of much heavy responsibility for many of the troubles of his reign and their long-lasting consequences.

But, it must also be considered, Lewis of Bavaria was, at this moment, and had been for a considerable time, a most helpful ally to those Ghibelline foes in Italy with whom, for the last five years, the pope had been at war; a war intended to make Italy really safe for the papacy by destroying the Ghibelline power wherever found. [ ] The pope, in the spring before Muhldorf was fought, had called in, against the anti-papal party in Italy, the aid of Lewis's rival. Now that Lewis was victorious in Germany there was every reason to believe he would pass into Italy as the Ghibelline leader. That he brushed aside the condition by which the pope designed to protect the papal interests against him, confirmed this suspicion. In April 1323 Lewis's envoys in Italy demanded the withdrawal of the papal armies from before Milan; in May they won over to Lewis, Mantua and Verona, at the very hour these were making their submission to the pope. In July Lewis sent a force to assist the Ghibellines of Milan, a small force it is true, but sufficient to relieve the city. The whole situation in northern Italy, lately so favourable to the pope, was in six months, and by the emperor's action, wholly reversed.

These are the very months, it will be remembered, in which the pope has remodelled the order of Friars Minor; [ ] he is about to destroy a cherished Franciscan opinion about the peculiar relation of their order to Our Lord; [ ] and Lewis, in the Declaration of Sachsenhausen (May 22, 1324), will denounce the pope as a heretic for these actions, and take the order under his protection in the hope that throughout Germany, and especially throughout Italy, he will now be possessed of a whole army of enthusiastic propagandists.

On October 8 of that same year, 1323, then, the pope warned Lewis to cease to act as emperor within three months, or excommunication would follow. Lewis, playing for time, secured a delay of another two months; but finally the blow fell (March 23, 1324); just eighteen months after the victory of Muhldorf had made him master, in name, of the German world.

The next event in the war belongs to the history of political science; it was the appearance on June 24, 1324, of Marsiglio of Padua's great book The Defender of Peace. [ ] The empire, it was here argued, was something wholly independent of the Holy See; the prerogatives invoked by a succession of popes were mere usurpation. There was much other revolutionary doctrine in the work, as will be seen, and presently its authors [ ] fled from what awaited them in Paris to the court of the emperor.

Lewis, on July 11, was once more excommunicated and deprived now of all right ever to be elected emperor. Against him the Habsburg party in Germany now combined with the King of France (Charles IV, 1322-1328) to elect, with the favourable support of the pope, a more suitable kind of emperor. But Lewis countered this by freeing his old rival Frederick of Austria, also a Habsburg, and coming to an arrangement by which Frederick should rule in Germany while Lewis would remain emperor and be master of Italy. And now Lewis, with the aid of Marsiglio's advice, began to prepare for the Italian expedition.

The great affair opened with a kind of congress at Trent (January-March 1327), where the purpose of the expedition was announced, a war for religion against "the priest John" who is a heretic; it was a procedure very reminiscent of Philip the Fair's national assemblies against Boniface VIII. [ ] In March Lewis marched out of Trent. He was crowned King of Lombardy at Milan (March 31) and then slowly made his way from one city of northern Italy to another. The misfortunes of Henry VII, and the military mistakes that had caused them, were carefully avoided. By October Lewis had gained Pisa and in the first week of the new year (January 7, 1328) he was at Rome and in possession of St. Peter's, where enthusiastic services of thanksgiving marked this first fruits of triumph.

And now began a series of highly-spectacular happenings. The emperor, reconciled by their apparent usefulness to the most revolutionary of all Marsiglio's political theories, and as though he had never opposed to the papal claims his own theory that he was emperor by God's direct institution, now consented to appear before the world as the elect of the populus romanus. On January 11, 1328, at a great assembly, "the People" voted him the imperial crown; and, moreover, chose four proctors to invest him with it. Six days later Lewis was anointed as emperor, with the usual ritual, by two bishops, and then crowned by one of the proctors: this proctor was no less a personage than Sciarra Colonna, the assailant of Boniface VIII at Anagni a quarter of a century before.

John XXII had not, of course, looked on idly at the invasion of Italy. While the crown of Lombardy was still a fresh joy to Lewis the pope declared him deprived of his hereditary states, [ ] and about the time that Lewis entered Pisa the pope condemned him as a heretic for his patronage of the Franciscan Spirituals and also of Marsiglio. [ ] In that same bull the Defensor Pacis was also condemned. Then, in January 1328, the month of Lewis's new "election" as emperor, the pope had declared the war against him to be a crusade, and had ordered it to be preached everywhere as such; and in Germany, brushing aside the Habsburg claim because the party would not submit it to his judgment, the pope, acting as the vacant empire's overlord, had summoned the electors to a new election. They obeyed, and met: but were not able to come to any agreement.

To all this papal activity Lewis replied by allowing Marsiglio to persecute those who, in Rome, dared to stand by the pope. But as the weeks went by, shows still more bizarre were prepared. Three times within a month, "the People" were summoned to exercise, in full assembly, their sovereign rights. On April 14 they solemnly presented John XXII for the emperor's judgment, accusing the pope of heresy; four days later, at another assembly, Lewis, crowned and bearing the imperial insignia, delivered sentence on the pope for his "heretical" declaration about the nature of Our Lord's poverty, and for the treason of his attack on the emperor; the sentence was, of course, deposition. Then on May 12, Ascension Day, a new pope was presented for "the People's" approval. He was, of course, a Friar Minor, Brother Peter of Corvara. The assembly approved him with acclamations, three times in all, and Lewis thereupon invested him with the fisherman's ring. On Whit Sunday following Peter was consecrated and crowned in St. Peter's as Nicholas V. [ ] There is about all this that note of naive comedy which never, somehow, fails to be absent from solemn anti-clerical incursions into the realms of liturgy and ecclesiastical ceremonial.

It was just six days after Peter's coronation that the Minister-General of the Friars Minor made his escape from Avignon, bringing out with him, for the emperor's service, that still greater power -- as yet unsuspected -- William of Ockham.

At this very moment of triumph, however, Lewis of Bavaria's good fortune left him, never to return. He was to live for another nineteen years, in all that time to claim to be emperor, and to attempt to enforce his claims by what arms he could gather, and by diplomacy with a succession of popes. But never again was he to achieve a victory of any kind, and only the failure of his many enemies to combine saved him, as he drifted helplessly through these years. Only three months after the grandiose installation of "Nicholas V" the emperor was forced out of Rome; his army shrank to little more than a bodyguard; every city in Italy closed its gates against him; by the close of 1329 Lewis was once more in Germany.

The anti-pope, of course, fared no better than his master. Never had he exercised any power except in those rare districts of Italy where Lewis could command obedience, and nine months after his coronation "Nicholas V" issued his last bull (March 4, 1329). He had left Rome with the emperor, hissed and booed by the most treacherous populace of all the Middle Ages, and thereafter, for some time, he had followed in the imperial suite. But to Lewis he was not worth the trouble of transporting into Germany and, left behind, he disappeared from sight, until John XXII's agents discovered him. A public confession of his follies might be serviceable to the papal cause, and a generous pardon was offered to induce him to submit. So, clad in his friar's habit, with a halter round his neck, Brother Peter at last made his ceremonial submission to the pope (Avignon, July 25, 1330), to disappear thereafter from history. [ ]

For the short remnant of John XXII's long reign, it was the policy of Lewis to seek reconciliation. But John was inflexible in his demand for an unconditional surrender: whatever happened Lewis was never to be acknowledged as emperor, a new election should choose in his stead someone more suitable. In 1333 [ ] all the parties came to a complicated agreement, one part of which was the emperor's resignation. But this plan, so it seemed to the King of Naples, would make France too powerful in Italy, and he combined with the schismatic Franciscans at the Bavarian court to persuade Lewis to withdraw his assent. [ ]

Five months later John XXII died. [ ] From the new pope,
Benedict XII -- a theologian where John had been a canonist, a
man of peace where John had been a fighter, conciliatory and not
intransigent -- Lewis had, seeming] y, much to hope. The seven
and a half years of Benedict's short reign were filled with
negotiations between the two. Benedict never repelled the
emperor, he was not over-exacting; Lewis continued to be his
weak and vacillating self. But the negotiations never came to
anything. Always the King of France, unwilling to see pope and
emperor reconciled, managed to influence the pope and to delay
the settlement that ever seemed so near. Benedict XII knew well
what the French were at, though he seems not to have known
how to defeat their diplomatic finesse: he had none of the
political gifts. Edward III of England was, in these years,
preparing to open the long Hundred Years' War with France, and
looking for allies on the Continent. Benedict foresaw what would
happen. " The Germans," he said, " will understand, in the end,
where the real cause of all these delays lies, and they will make
common cause with the English." Which, of course, came to
pass; [ ] and with the beginning of the war all communication
between Lewis and Avignon ceased.

But in the next few years two things happened in Germany that
foreshadowed the new age, which, all unsuspected as yet, was
surely approaching. All these wars between pope and emperor,
that had gone on with so little interruption for now nearly two
centuries, had necessarily had a most brutal effect upon the daily
religious life of the unhappy peoples of Germany. Sooner or
later, in all these wars, the emperor was excommunicated, and
thereupon all who sided with him would share the terrible
sentence which deprived a man of all right to receive sacraments
and which cut him off from the divine life that enlivens the
members of the mystical body of Christ. And, as often as not,
there would follow upon this excommunication the sentence of
interdict, local or general, which closed all the churches, often
for years at a time., depriving the whole people of the mass and

indeed of all sacraments but those for the newly born and the dying. [ ]

Would the generality of mankind, understanding the policy behind the interdict, co-operate with the pope by accepting it in a spirit of religious humility, and, associating themselves with it penitentially, offer up these grave spiritual inconveniences in a kind of reparation, embracing the very interdict as an opportunity to deepen their own private spiritual life? Such expectations could only be nourished by those whose optimism could see in the average man and woman a soul obviously called to serve God in the high perfection of some strict religious order. The enforcement of the interdict meant in practice -- not necessarily, of course, but as things usually are -- a grave falling off in the liveliness of faith and in morality: while to disobey it entailed, of course, sacrilege each time the forbidden religious rite was performed.

And to add to the chaos there was, very frequently indeed, what amounted to a kind of schism, the activity of the two factions, pro-pope and pro-emperor, which everywhere divided sees and parishes, monasteries and religious orders. While the scholar was hesitating (in another matter) between Thomas and Scotus and Ockham, the ordinary man -- if he really cared about religion -- was wondering which of the rival clergy he knew was telling the truth, or knew what the truth was.

Here, in part, are some of the causes of that decline in religion which the contemporary preachers and mystics describe so luridly, and against which councils are forever legislating, and which has its reflection in the tales and poems of the new vernacular literatures, where -- very significantly -- it is not so much matter for reprobation, or shocked surprise, as it is unconsciously supplied as part of the natural background of the story's action.

Germany, by the year 1338, had suffered nearly fifteen years of spiritual chaos, and the prelates and princes now besought Lewis to be reconciled with the pope, and petitioned the pope in the same sense. To this appeal the pope appears not to have made any reply; and in the July of that year, the prince-electors, meeting at Rense, made a joint declaration on oath that they would defend the rights and freedom of the imperial dignity, which they declared was not the creation of the pope but derived directly from God; the man whom they elected was, they asserted, emperor by the very fact; no papal confirmation or approval was in any way necessary for the lawfulness of his acts. They declared, moreover, that John XXII's various sentences of excommunication passed on Lewis were unjust, and they threatened the pope to his face that they would provide remedies of their own should the Holy See not withdraw these sentences.

Was it the genius of Marsiglio of Padua that shaped such declarations? He certainly had a share in the next innovation, a very foolish intervention by the emperor in the discipline of the sacraments. For Lewis, in 1342, of his own imperial authority, declared null (on the ground of the man's impotence) the marriage between John of Bohemia and Margaret, the heiress of the Tyrol. He wanted Margaret (and the Tyrol) for his own son, another Lewis, and since these two were doubly related within the forbidden degrees, the emperor now issued dispensations from the impediment of consanguinity. And Marsiglio wrote a treatise to justify him.

When the austere, but somewhat unpractical, Benedict XII died (April 25, 1342) the cardinals chose [ ] in his place the Cardinal Archbishop of Rouen, Pierre Roger, as near an approach to Aristotle's magnificent man as the order of St. Benedict has ever known. Clement VI -- so he chose to be called -- was a personage far too experienced in public life to waste any time over the debris of the emperor's hopes and chances. Lewis was bidden, somewhat in the manner of John XXII, to cease to style himself emperor; and his position in Germany, where his incompetence was now regarded as the main hindrance to peace, was by this time so desperate that he made a very humble submission to the pope and offered to abdicate (September 18, 1343).

The pope's first inclination was to accept this surrender. But once again, while he debated, other influences prevailed, the combination of the emperor's many foes in France, in Italy and in Germany. Clement stiffened the terms of submission -- only to find that he had now roused all Germany against him. [ ] But it was not in favour of Lewis that the German princes moved, for a few days later they decided on the man whom they would like to see in his place, Charles of Moravia, the son and heir of the blind King of Bohemia who had been Lewis's great enemy in Germany. [ ] Lewis had all but ruined Germany, they thought, and "No more Bavarians" was their answer when he ventured to plead for his own line.

And now, at last, the pope shook himself free of his political tutors. The French king preferred to see Lewis acknowledged rather than Charles elected. But Clement VI, this time, ignored the French. He again declared Lewis no emperor (April 13, 1346), and called upon the prince electors to fill the vacancy. This they did, two months later, electing Charles: three of his five electors were prelates, the pope supported him, and so Charles IV has come down as "the priests' emperor." The gibe was no more than a last flicker from the party of Lewis. He died of apoplexy (October 11, 1347), and when his successor died soon after (June 14, 1349) Charles IV's troubles from the house of Wittelsbach were at an end.

" The priests' emperor " had succeeded in great measure because of the pope's powerful aid; and the pope had first used every care to make sure that Charles was really his man. The emperor-to-be, French by his upbringing and Clement's one-time pupil, had appeared at Avignon and had sworn cheerfully to accept all manner of restrictions on his authority. Once securely elected he did not even trouble to ask the pope's confirmation. He did not, indeed, break his promise not to enter Italy until the pope had confirmed the election. But so long as he would not ask such confirmation, Clement would not give the desired permission for his coronation at Rome. The peace was never broken, but the deadlock endured as long as Clement VI reigned.

Charles found the next pope -- Innocent VI [ ] easier: leave was given for the expedition into Italy and Charles was crowned, by the papal legate, in St. Peter's, on April 5, 1355. And now, secure of his position, and certain that there would be no resistance from the pope, he published on January 13, 1356, the famous "Golden Bull" which regulated anew the constitution of the Holy Roman Empire. In this it is declared that the election of the emperor is a matter for the prince-electors alone, and that during vacancies the Elector of Saxony is to act as imperial vicar for the north and the Count Palatine for the south. Of all the great papal claims, so resoundingly set forth (and exercised) for centuries, and were, so recently, the occasion of a twenty years' war, there is not a single word. They are not denied, but simply ignored, treated as though they had never been.

Here truly is a sign that a new age has begun; and this, not only in the definitive secularisation of the imperial dignity by the unilateral act of the emperor, but, even more, in the tacit acceptance of this act by the pope. For Innocent VI, who had known, for months beforehand, what was in preparation, remained silent. He could not approve, but he did not condemn. True enough, there was in the bull substantial compensation for the papacy. The empire as such is, henceforth, to mean Germany only. The fatal ambition to realise imperial rights through an actual domination of Italy was thereby cut out forever from the imagination of the German imperial mind. When next a Holy Roman Emperor plays any part in Italian affairs it is because he happens to be, at the same time, the hereditary King of Naples. [ ] But that claims so great were allowed by the papacy to fall so silently [ ] -- this was surely a great event, and it marks a real turning point in history.

iii. Marsiglio of Padua

The surrender of Innocent VI to the fait accompli of the Golden Bull of the Emperor Charles IV is still more striking when it is set beside the contemporary theories of Marsiglio of Padua, as to the proper place of the Church in the Christian State, set out in the Defensor Pacis; [ ] theories which, as yet, were mainly important by reason of Marsiglio's position among the counsellors of Lewis of Bavaria. Lewis had indeed been badly beaten where "the priests' emperor" was now, in 1356, victorious; but it was, none the less, the patronage and protection of Lewis that had preserved Marsiglio, and his book, despite the massy condemnation of John XXII. The Defensor Pacis, so preserved, was now to take on a new lease of life; its doctrines to become yearly more "actual," and more and more infect the world of Catholic thought, and to influence the political advisers of Catholic princes until the book became, in fact, what its author intended it to be, " one of the strongest implements of war ever imagined against the social action of the Church." [ ]

For in Christendom, as Marsiglio proposed to reorganise it, the pope was not merely fettered in his function, as the legists would have fettered him: he was not to function at all. It is the peculiar and lasting mischief of Marsiglio that he creates, for the controversy, an entirely new politico-religious atmosphere, where the problem of Church and State is treated in all its generality. No longer is it any particular right or claim of the Church which is called in question; what is now attacked is the very idea of the Church as an institution. And the layman's desire to throw off the cleric's control of social life is now itself made the basis of a kind of religious teaching.

About the life of Marsiglio we know very little. One of the rare facts is that in 1312-1313 he was rector of the University of Paris. We do not know at what university his student days were passed, nor what he studied. He is, not impossibly, the Marsiglio de Maynandrino to whom John XXII, in 1316, provided a canonry at Padua; and the " Italian named Marcillo " of whom the same pope complained, three years later, that he had gone to the future Charles IV of France (1322-1328) as an envoy of the Italian Ghibellines. We meet him again, seemingly, as a witness to the profession of faith, made, at the demand of ecclesiastical authority, by the Averroist philosopher of Padua, Peter of Abano; and a set of verses by another fellow citizen, Albertino Mussato, describes Marsiglio as hesitating between a career in the law and medicine, and also as seduced from his medical studies by the lure of a military life in the service of two of the great condottieri of the day, Matteo Visconti and Can Grande della Scala.

Marsiglio was, very evidently, a man of parts, and in his great book the student will find, turn by turn, the influence of very varied tastes and accomplishments. He is the passionate Italian patriot; he is religiously anti-Catholic; but he is never the legist, never the philosopher. Aristotle is indeed his master, Aristotle idolised as the Averroist tradition did idolise him; [ ] but Marsiglio's interest in the Philosopher was scientific, not philosophical. He was, very evidently, not of that elect company possessed of the metaphysical intuition of being and this, inevitably, vitiates his understanding of that part of Aristotle's work upon which he concentrated his vigorous militant mind, the social philosophy of the Politics. As the strongest part of the Defensor Pacis is its main section, that which deals with the nature and role of the Church, so the weakest is the political introduction where Aristotle's theories are discussed, and his formulae used, by a mind that is not metaphysical but positivist, not interested really in natures and causalities, and which therefore is prone to overlook the profound ideas that lie behind simple and seemingly obvious terminology. Marsiglio is not a philosopher, in the strict sense of the term. [ ] Nor is he a jurist, although he is familiar (as an educated man might be who has frequented the company of jurists) with the legal aspect of the social questions that interest him. Nor is Marsiglio at all a theologian, and what religious ideas he has are akin to those of the Waldenses. Finally, there is every probability that Marsiglio knew, and had been in personal contact with, the group of French legists who, led by Nogaret, had waged the last stages of Philip the Fair's war on Boniface VIII; and he was an active Ghibelline. Considering all these elements in his formation one by one, it may be thought there could hardly be a better recipe from which to prepare the genius who was to devise the most mischievously anti-Christian work of the whole Middle Ages. [ ]

Marsiglio's objective was nothing less than the social influence of the Catholic religion, exercised through popes and bishops and clerics generally upon the whole life of the time. This he proposed to destroy by explaining to the Catholic world what the State really is, and what is the true place of the true religion of Christ within the State rationally constructed. It is, then, necessary to say something about each part of his elaborate argument; and first, about his theory of the State and its powers.

Marsiglio's master, Aristotle, sees man as an animal which is social and political by its nature; and Aristotle's great commentator St. Thomas, understanding that problems about natures are metaphysical problems, and being himself no mean metaphysician, draws from Aristotle's principle a whole corpus of sociological teaching. But always St. Thomas relates his ideas to this first idea of what man's nature is. So, for example in discussing the great questions, What exactly are States? What kind of authority is it that they exercise? How does the citizen stand, relative to the State? What are the right and duties of each? it is to a truth about human nature that St. Thomas, each time, returns. It is by a theory built on a consideration of what natures are, that he answers such questions. How do there come to be

States? Why, because it is the nature of men to live in a multitude, "and so there must be in men something by which the multitude is ruled": [ ] and the saint speaks of the natural impulse [ ] of men towards the State, which State came into being through human action originating in that urge of human nature.

The importance of seeking the beginnings of any understanding of human political action in such a fundamental as a nature, quite escapes the non-metaphysical Marsiglio. His thought remains on the surface; and he interprets the Aristotelian teaching in the light of a conjectured historical beginning, where the gathering of men in a community is due to circumstance alone, physical or economic. What ultimately, in his view, decides the new move to live in ordered groups is the fact that to form such a group is the choice of the majority. The State is, essentially, nothing more than this "collection" of individuals; and its only unity is that which comes from the imposition upon this multitude of a single will, to which all their individual wills now conform.

In the State -- as Marsiglio conceives it -- force is thus not merely an instrument by which the ideal of Social Justice overcomes whatever hinders its accomplishment, but it is an essential constituent of Law. Law is the imposition of the State's will upon the citizen; [ ] where there is no force there is no legal obligation, and wherever, in that will, there is force, there is force of Law. Law that does not conform to the objective standard of justice, St. Thomas roundly says, is not Law at all; rather it is mere wickedness. [ ] But Marsiglio explicitly contradicts this -- wickedness too is Law, if only it is commanded under legal penalties.

This same defect, that makes the goodness and badness of actions derive from something outside the act -- from laws, for example -- vitiates Marsiglio's theory of public authority. For the ruler's authority, in his view, originates in the expressed intention of these who make him the ruler. Whatever he does in accordance with that intention is good, whatever he does against it is bad; and the ruler so acting in accordance is the pattern for all his subjects' acts, their rule indeed and their measure.

Whence comes this designation of any particular individual to be ruler? Who is it that confers on him this extraordinary kind of power? Here we come to the best known feature of Marsiglio's theory, namely, his teaching about the sovereignty of the people. The source of all authority in the State is the will of the people. The proof of this, apparently, does not lie in any truth about the nature of man, but in the practical consideration that such "consultation" of the people must make for future harmony in the government of the State; and a wise ruler will also "prepare" the people, before he submits any matter to their judgment. Also, a most important consideration, it is the whole body of the people, assenting to the sanctions that accompany laws, which gives to laws that which really makes them
laws: it is the whole people that can alone impose what obliges universally. "Sanctions: in this consists the whole being of law, and the people alone has the power needed for the imposition of sanctions. In this is summed up the whole theory of Marsiglio." [ ]

This is, of course, no more than a very general summary of an elaborate discussion that runs to far more pages than there are here lines. And the discussion may seem remote enough from Church history, whose business is to record the fortunes of the Gospel. But some familiarity with Marsiglio's leading notions is necessary in order to understand what is by no means remote, the character and scale, that is to say, of his attack on the traditional Catholic theory of the Church. For it is with the aim of producing an ecclesiastical revolution that Marsiglio has constructed his version of Aristotle's Politics.

The great source of all the evils that afflict the age, he says, is the hold which the clergy have secured on religious life. One main instrument of their power is the false notion of the Church which they have devised. For the Church, like any other " society, " is really no more than the aggregation of the individuals who compose it; it is "the ensemble of faithful believers who invoke the name of Christ." All such believers are equally "of the Church"; the distinctions which now obtain between, for example, clergy and laity are secondary, not essential, and produced by human authority merely. The Church, in the traditional sense, has no real existence, nor ever had any.

In Marsiglio's sense the Church has only one divinely instituted function, the administration of sacraments. The power to say mass, to forgive sins, to ordain priests is indeed of divine origin, and belongs only to priests themselves duly ordained. But with these essential liturgical functions clerical activity ceases. It is not for any clergy to decide who it is shall be ordained, nor in what part of the Church and in what capacity, and under what conditions the priest shall exercise his priesthood. Everywhere in the primitive history of the Church -- as Marsiglio reads it -- the determining factor at every stage of the evolution of Catholicism has been the action of the generality of the faithful. Here is still the true source of religious authority, the guarantee of fidelity to Christ's teaching. It is from this source that general councils derive what authority they possess, from here that the right to designate to particular offices derives, and also the right to inflict the supreme sanction of excommunication. In such a scheme there is obviously no place for episcopal authority, nor for the universal primacy of the pope. This last, particularly, is a flagrant usurpation

We never go far in studying such schemes before we are halted by inconsistencies, and by unresolved, and unresolvable, contradictions. For example, the question soon suggests itself whether these faithful, collected together in the Church, are an authority, a religious sovereign, distinct from themselves as the sovereign people of the State. Is this -- seemingly -- democratic

Church independent of the -- seemingly -- democratic State? We would hardly expect it to be so; and indeed, by carefully thought out distinctions, Marsiglio shows how all the powers of ruling the Church which he denies to the clergy really belong to, and should lawfully be exercised by, the civil ruler. The Church is, indeed, no more than the religious aspect of civil society, the reflection of what that society feels, at any given moment, about religion.

Not only, then, may the civil ruler lawfully exercise all authority in the Church: to do so is, for him, a primary duty. For example, nothing is more fatal to the State, as Marsiglio conceives it, than the clear distinction between the legality of what it ordains and the intrinsic goodness (or badness) of these acts. It is therefore highly important, in practice, that there should never be any moral criticism of legislation. But, for centuries now, the Church of the popes has had the inconvenient habit of making such criticism; it is indeed one of the popes' chief activities. Laws have been denounced as tyranny because contrary to justice; rulers have been lectured, warned and punished for enacting laws declared to be unjust; subjects have been told that they need not, indeed must not, obey such laws. The State of the future must, then, see to it that no pope or bishop or other cleric is ever suffered to put into action a doctrine so treasonable, destructive indeed of the very basis of civil authority. The spheres of conscience and of obedience to civil authority are distinct, separate, and independent. Activities proper to the first must never be allowed to overflow into the second, or the most terrible confusion will follow and the peace and unity of the State be forever endangered.

" Unity within the State" -- here is an ideal very close to Marsiglio's heart. Therefore, within the State let there be one single authority, one single jurisdiction, no privileged bodies, no immunities. To introduce a second jurisdiction, to seek immunities for a particular section of the citizens (judicial

immunities, legislative immunities, fiscal immunities) is treason
to the State in the highest degree. The ruler must then, in simple
duty to the peace of the State, destroy the privileges of the
clergy. Also, in those matters where the divine law needs human
agents for its execution, it is the State which must be that agent;
for there cannot be two coercive jurisdictions operating over one
and the same people. Only thus will the State become, what it
needs to be, the real ruler of all its citizens. Law is, as it were, the
atmosphere of a particular country -- all who live in that country
must breathe the same air. Nothing, Marsiglio argues, with
undisguised bitter passion, has been more noxious to the peace of
states than that immunity of the clergy from the prince's
jurisdiction which the popes have championed for so long; and in
a kind of parody of the concluding phrases of Boniface VIII's
Unam Sanctam [ ] he declares his own gospel, that for its own
well-being the Church, all the faithful people of Christ, must be
subjected to the civil ruler, his laws and his judges.

The needed subjection of the Church to the State will not,
however, be achieved by such merely negative acts as the
destruction of clerical privilege. A more continuous, positive,
action upon the Church is needed, and this is in fact vital to the
welfare of the State. Here Marsiglio -- like all his followers ever
since, down to our very contemporaries -- flings consistency to
the winds, and having first divorced morality from the business
of ruling, he now proclaims that to foster morality is one of the
State's gravest duties; the State, undoubtedly, has moral and even
spiritual functions. The secularist patriarch enlarges on them with
evident and conscious unction.

There is, for example, the State's duty to promote among its
citizens the practice of virtue and of all the duties which God's
revelation has made known to us, which last (we note) is not only
necessary if man is to save his soul, says Marsiglio, "but is also
useful for the needs of this present life"; and so the state must
appoint learned men to teach religion and to organise divine

worship. There is nothing spiritual, he says, that does not somehow affect the welfare of the body politic. Therefore the State must control the spiritual. It ought, for example, to regulate the lives of the clergy, determining the standards of their conduct, their fasts, prayers, mortifications and so forth. It must decide the nice question whether they will not be better clergy if they do not possess property, but if, instead, surrendering all right to be owners, they throw themselves -- for maintenance -- on the generosity of the State, as God's agent, once they have committed all their care to Him: evangelical poverty imposed by the State on all the clergy will be yet another means of control. Finally it is the State's duty to take into its own hands the whole vast business of education, of forming, controlling, directing the literate class of the future, and of so shaping it that it will be yet another willing instrument of State policy.

The Defensor Pacis was completed on the feast of St. John the Baptist, 24 June, 1324. While its author was planning the new venture of setting up as a lecturer in theology, his book was denounced to the Church authorities. Marsiglio and his ally, the notorious Averroist, John of Jandun, saved themselves by flight (1326). They joined Lewis of Bavaria at Nuremberg and thenceforward their history is one with his; their influence upon his action alternating curiously with that of the emperor's other anti-papal allies, the Franciscans Michael of Cesena and Ockham. The first papal condemnation of the book, which does not, seemingly, name its author, is a bull of 1326 which has not survived. [ ] The next year, April 3, 1327, a second bull, [ ] addressed to Lewis, upbraids him for his patronage of these two "sons of perdition," but even yet the full text of the book does not seem to have reached the papal court. But by the date of the next bull, October 23 [ ] of the same year, the pope is more fully informed, through the bishops of Germany. In this bull five of the six propositions which the bishops sent on as resuming Marsiglio's leading ideas, are condemned after a most understanding criticism. The pope went directly to the heart of the subversive doctrine, and set in the broad light of day the mischievous principles that underlay the mass of subtle argumentation, satire and bitter, passionate rhetoric. The condemnation was, indeed, one of the most characteristic and masterly acts of John XXII's long, eventful reign.

The Defensor Pacis -- appearing in the midst of a war between pope and emperor -- naturally made a sensation. It was translated into French (1330) and into Italian (1363). In Germany especially it was a success. Nevertheless, it seems certain that there were but a few copies of the original in circulation before the time of the Schism (1378). It is not without interest to note that the so-called "democratic" theories of Marsiglio appear to have caused no comment at all. What, everywhere, roused attention was his application of them to the Church. How ruinous this was to traditional belief was immediately understood on all sides. Lewis of Bavaria himself cuts a somewhat comical figure, earnestly striving to dissociate himself from such scandalous ideas and explaining, in 1336, to Benedict XII that he has no head for these matters and has never really understood what Marsiglio had in mind.

But whatever the scandal caused by the Defensor Pacis to the mind of Catholic Europe, it remained unanswered, save for the papal condemnation. [ ] Was it indifference, on the part of theologians, to a work which, in its new "positivist" approach to a theological problem, was an offence to current scholastic good form, and which, thereby, classed itself with all the rest of the new scientific knowledge of the fourteenth century? It is surely strange, and disconcerting, that Marsiglio's attack did not stimulate some Catholic to produce, not merely a controversial rejoinder, but a new constructive statement of traditional doctrine. Be that as it may, when the ideas of Marsiglio came alive again, in the last years of the fourteenth century, they met no contradiction from Catholic learning. His influence is evident now in France, in John Wvcliff, and in the heresies that from this time begin to dominate Bohemia. We find no less a person than Gerson recommending the book, and it undoubtedly played a part at the General Council of Constance. [ ] It was more and more copied in the fifteenth century, more and more eagerly read, as the breakdown of Christendom drew nearer. The first printed edition appeared in 1517, the year of Luther's first appearance as an innovator, and the publication of an English translation, in 1535, was one of the earliest moves of Thomas Cromwell, then busy with the publicist strategy that accompanied the creation of the Church of England as we know it to-day. [ ]

iv. The End of John XXII

Marsiglio's adversary, John XXII, was harassed by trouble and crisis literally to the very end of his life. For his last hours, ere he passed from this world, at ninety years of age, were given to a theological controversy, and one which his own act had begun. In this controversy, about the state of souls in the interval between death and the General Judgment of mankind at the end of the world, the pope took a line that went against the general body of received opinion and tradition. The peculiar ideas which he championed were set forth in three sermons, preached at Avignon on All Saints' Day, 1331, on December 15 of the same year and on the following January 5. In these sermons John XXII declared that the souls of the just do not enjoy the intuitive vision of God (in which consists their eternal heavenly reward) until, after the last day, they are again united with their bodies; and also that neither the souls of the lost nor the devils are as yet in hell. but will only be there from after the last day.

These sermons of the aged pope astonished the theological world, at Avignon and elsewhere. The startling news of this papal innovation, in a matter belonging to the sphere of doctrine, was speedily conveyed into Bavaria by the cardinal Napoleone Orsini, who had long been secretly planning and hoping for John's deposition. There, Ockham and his associates gladly fashioned it into a new weapon against the pope. He had already, they said, repudiated one point of the Christian faith, to wit the belief in the absolute poverty of Our Lord and the Apostles: now, he was repudiating a second. It was the very way heretics had always acted; little by little they came to deny the whole body of traditional belief. John, now obviously heretical to all the world, could not any longer be regarded as pope.

The pope's own attitude to the controversy he had occasioned is of the greatest interest. Significantly, he made no attempt to use his pontifical authority to support what he had said in his sermons. Quite the contrary: as one who had been doing no more than express an opinion which he considered to be as good as any other, and who, quite evidently, is surprised at the chorus of dissent, he now set theologians of various schools to examine the whole question and to report. Notable among them was the Cistercian cardinal, James Fournier, one day to succeed John as Benedict XII. He was an extremely competent professional theologian, and without difficulty he clearly showed that the opinion of John XXII had scarcely any support and that the body of tradition was firm against him; on the other hand, in the controversy against those who, like Ockham, were beginning to denounce the pope as a heretic, Fournier noted first of all that, so far, the Church had never expressed its mind on the question by a definition, and next that in these three sermons John XXII had made no claim or pretence whatever to be doing anything more than preach a sermon to the particular congregation which at the moment filled the church; the pope had spoken simply as any bishop or priest might have spoken, as a private theologian, and not as the pope laying down a definition of doctrine for the assent of the whole Christian Church.

But the controversy continued to rage for all the short remainder of John's life. The new head of the Friars Minor, the successor of the excommunicated Michael of Cesena, with sycophantic misunderstanding of the situation, became a most enthusiastic advocate of the pope's unusual views; and, unfortunately for himself, declaimed them at Paris, where he immediately fell foul of the greatest body of theologians in the Church. The university discussed the theory, found it contrary to the general teaching, and as such reported it to the pope. Then John XXII fell into his last illness. On December 3, 1334, from his sick bed, he made a public explanation, and a submission of what he had said to the teaching of the Church. He believed, he said to the assembled cardinals, that "the souls of the just, separated from their bodies, but fully purified from sin, are in heaven, in paradise, with Jesus Christ, in the company of the angels, and that, according to the common law, they see God and the divine essence face to face, clearly, as far as the state and condition of a soul separated from the body allows this." But this qualified retraction the pope explicitly submitted to the Church's decision. And the next day he died.

Benedict XII closed the controversy by the bull Benedictus Deus, of January 29, 1336, in which he defined, as the teaching of the Catholic Church, that the souls of the just (i.e. the souls of those who leave this world with no stain upon them that needs purifying, and those souls also which, after death, have been purified in purgatory) immediately after death (or on the completion of such purification) see the divine essence by an intuitive and even facial vision, and this before they are reunited with their bodies, before the general judgment. Moreover the souls of the lost are in hell from the moment of death. [ ]

## 3. THE AVIGNON REGIME
## i. The Centralised Administration

The seven Avignon popes were a singularly competent line. Rarely indeed has there been, in the papacy, such a continuous succession of administrative ability. No less unusual -- in its medieval history -- was another feature of the regime, namely, that for as long as seventy years the papacy was established in the one place. Nowhere, in fact, had the popes -- from the time of

St. Gregory VII (1073-1085) at least -- been less at home than in Rome; and for three-quarters of the century that divides the reign of Innocent III from the establishment at Avignon, the curia had wandered from one town to another of the papal state, settled anywhere rather than at Rome. Now, from 1309, that vast establishment was for seventy years stably fixed; and three successive generations of Catholics saw, as a new thing, what has, ever since, been so much the rule that it appears to us in the very nature of things, namely the pope and the great administrative machine through which he works permanently, and as it were immovably, placed.

To say this of the Avignon papacy is to say that conditions then favoured, as never before, all that conscious development of a centralised papal government of the universal Church, which had been so notable a part of the papal policy ever since St. Gregory VII had discerned in it a mighty means of reform and a strong defence of reforms accomplished. More than ever, then, this is a period which sees the translation of rights and law into the fact of a regular bureaucratic administration; the fixing into hard tradition of tile ways of administrators, financiers, judges. The Corpus Iuris Canonici is now, at last, really to begin to come into its full supremacy, not merely as an instrument which men use, but as that greater thing than any of these individuals, a law which they all serve; and it is to produce the most competent, completely centralised system of government -- i.e. on a very great scale -- which the Middle Ages knew. [ ] Perhaps more than any individual pope of the next two hundred years it is this system which is to matter. In an age when theology declines, the canon law flourishes -- as does its twin sister, the Roman law as the Middle Ages knew it; it is now that the Roman law receives a new birth in the genius of Bartolo. It was but the justice of history that, when the great catastrophe of the sixteenth century arrived, the canonists should come in for some of the blame. "Holy Father, it is the teaching of the canonists," so the report begins of the cardinals whom Paul III, in 1537, commissioned to examine the causes of the new revolt. [ ]

The pope's chief agents in the ruling and administration of the affairs of the Church universal continued to be the college of cardinals. Its numbers were still restricted, by comparison, that is, with the standards of the last four hundred years: [ ] in the conclaves of this period (1305-1378) the number of electors fluctuates between eighteen and twenty-six. But never, after Boniface VIII, did the college shrink to the dozen and less, which was all that it counted in the great thirteenth century. [ ]

The importance of these high dignitaries in the life of the universal Church -- in origin they are but the more prominent cf. the clergy of the local Roman Church -- goes back, of course, to the decree of Nicholas II in 1059, which constituted the cardinals the sole electors of the pope. The Avignon period is most important in their history as a college because they now, very definitely, begin, as a college, to aim at influencing, and even controlling, the action of the pope. Here, and not in the universal episcopate, is the beginning of the dangerous movement to reduce the traditional administrative supremacy of the pope. The cardinals are few, they are wealthy, they all reside in the curia -- for, as yet, in the rare event of the hat being conferred on a diocesan bishop, he leaves his see to live in the curia -- and they are organised. Their pressure on the papacy is constant. At every vacancy, from the end of this century, they make election pacts to ensure their own enrichment and to fetter the action of the future pope. It is the bad will of the cardinals -- if not their bad faith -- that is primarily responsible for the Schism of 1378. They play the traitor to Urban VI in 1378, and -- so general by now is the idea of their independence -- in 1408 both sets of cardinals betray their masters, the rival pontiffs Gregory XII and Benedict XIII. At every crisis throughout the fifteenth century, and down to the very eve of Luther's revolt, the pope's first anxiety is how the cardinals will behave. Not until e coup d'etat of Leo X, who, in 1517, swamps the opposition. by creating thirty-one cardinals in one act, are the popes really free of their factious collegiate interference.

Meanwhile their importance could not be greater. It is in the consistory that the main acts of Church government take place, where each cardinal has rights of speech and of opposition. The pope needs their consent for many acts and, very notably, before creating additional cardinals -- and to new creations the college is, almost by instinct, habitually opposed.

In the consistory there is also transacted much political and international business. This makes the cardinals objects of great interest to the different Catholic princes -- an interest that increases steadily as the great states of modern times, and the new permanent international rivalries, take shape in the fifteenth century. But already, at Avignon, it is beginning to pay the princes to be on good terms with the cardinals, to attach particular cardinals to their interests, to make them handsome presents, to dower them with pensions.

Not that the cardinals are necessarily poor men otherwise. Far from this, they are in the fourteenth century a byword for wealth, pomp and luxurious living; Petrarch in Italy and Langland in England speak here a common tongue. By law they have a right -- that is to say the college -- to divide equally with the pope the taxes called servitia comunia. [ ] In the eighteen years of John XXII, pope and cardinals thus shared more than a million gold florins. They enjoyed the revenues of the numerous benefices which it was now common form should be heaped on each of them, parishes, canonries, abbeys and diocesan sees -- benefices they never saw, where the work was done by a deputy at a fixed salary, while agents farmed the revenues for the absentee cardinal titular. Then there were the gifts made by the popes at fixed occasions, on their election for example, and on its succeeding anniversaries. So John XXII, in 1316, and Benedict

XII, in 1334, divided up 100,000 florins between the cardinals. Clement VI, in 1342, gave them 108,000; Innocent VI, 75,000 in 1352; Urban V, ten years later, only 40,000.

The princely style in which the cardinals lived brought them bitter words from Petrarch -- somewhat ungratefully, for he had his share of it in his time. And it brought, also, frequent reproof from the popes. Cardinals began to be most unpopular figures in the Church. The feud between them and the bishops deadlocked, and nearly wrecked, the Council of Constance. Continually, for the next hundred-and-fifty years, whenever projects of reform take practical shape the first item is usually that the cardinals shall diminish their households, dismiss the horsemen, the jesters, the actors, and all the varied paraphernalia of their courts, that they shall take for their service only clerics, and that these shall be dressed as clerics and live as clerics, and so forth. But all will be in vain, for all that time, until the day comes when the Dutch reforming pope, entering his States on his election, will need to have it explained to him that the gaily-caparisoned princes who salute him are indeed the cardinals of the Holy Roman Church.

One last word about the college under the Avignon popes -- it is almost wholly French. The seven French popes of this time created between them 134 cardinals; 111 of them were French, there were sixteen Italians, five Spaniards, two Englishmen. It will be noted there was none from Germany, the perpetually unsolved problem of the papal administration But this was not merely because these popes were French. There had been no German cardinal in the sixty years before the "Captivity" began. Nicholas of Cusa, created cardinal in 1448 by Nicholas V, was well-nigh the first German cardinal for two hundred years.

Like every other system of government, the papacy had had to create a highly-organised department where all state documents were prepared, and whence they were despatched: grants, licences, monitions, and appointments of various kinds; this was the Chancery and at its head was the vice-chancellor. In its archives copies were preserved of all the documents despatched, and also the original petitions from which so many had originated. Here was a vast secretariat which put into writing, in the appropriate form, the day-to-day decisions of the pope and saw to their transmission to the interested parties. But for matters of conscience which touched the private lives of individuals there was a special office called the Penitentiary. [ ] Here, under the direction of the cardinal grand penitentiary, a host of experts in theology, and canon law, dealt with such matters as requests for dispensation from the innumerable impediments to marriage; or for the removal of excommunications, interdicts and suspensions; or for power to absolve from sins reserved to the pope. This department had its own staff of clerks, and also a staff of eighteen penitentiaries who sat in the churches of the city to hear the confessions of all comers, with special faculties to absolve from sins reserved and also from reserved censures.

Another feature, common alike to the government of the Church and of states, was a system of law courts. Here the Avignon popes were great innovators. Their predecessors had devised the practice of naming judge-delegates who did all that was necessary in a lawsuit save to give the sentence -- this being reserved to the pope and, generally, his personal act. But the number of cases which came in to the pope for decision increased so enormously, from the beginning of the fourteenth century, that the popes now began to grant, to the judge-delegates whom they appointed, power to give a definitive sentence. Alongside these new methods the old permanent tribunals continued to function: the consistory, and the court that came to be called the Rota.

The consistory was the whole body of cardinals present in curia, with the pope in person presiding. it was the primitive, omni-competent, engine of the ecclesiastical system; the pope's cabinet, his council, his tribunal for any case it cared to hear; where all kinds of business was transacted, spiritual, political, administrative, international; where ambassadors were heard and treaties signed. And during the Avignon period it remained the principal instrument of government as before.

The origin of the court which, about this time (1336), came to be called the Rota is obscure. It is really the "court of audience for causes of the Apostolic Palace, " and its competence extends to all cases sent to it for judgment by the pope or the vice-chancellor. [ ] But its principal, and indeed usual, employment is to hear and decide suits arising out of presentations to benefices. This is the period, as will shortly be explained, when the papal centralisation reaches to such a height that almost every clerical appointment may come within reach of the papal curia. What hordes of petitions, and cross-petitions, pour in to Avignon from now on can easily be guessed. The judges of the Rota-the auditors, there are eight of them ill 1323 -- hear and decide these disputes. From their sentence there is no appeal. But the elaborate law of procedure gives the litigant a rich variety of means to delay the sentence, or to hold up the trial. When the canons of Hamburg and the citizens of the town brought their disagreements before this court, the ingenuity, first of one side and then of the other, dragged out the case for as long as sixteen years. [ ] So many were the pleas for delay, and so great an opportunity was thereby offered to legal chicanery, that the popes set up a special court to examine the expedients brought in to delay discussions. This was the court of "audience of disputed letters" (audientia litterarum contradictarum), more usually called "the public audience. " [ ] It seems not to have been notably successful, and, in the end, only added yet another complication to the already complicated system.

There were also courts where the various cardinals were judges. But these were courts that only functioned when commissioned by the pope to judge a particular case. For the most part, they undertook the preliminary enquiries needed to bring out, for the pope or the consistory, the real facts at issue in the suit. Clement V greatly simplified their procedure; but there were two serious inconveniences? always, for those who made use of these courts. The one was that, since cardinals were liable, at any time, to be despatched on missions abroad, there was great uncertainty when the case before them would finish; and the other was the extent in these courts of what is best and most expressively described as "graft, " if not for the cardinal's services, then for those of his household and his officials.

The law administered in all these courts, [ ] to which suitors came from every diocese in Christendom -- they were indeed the only courts that could hear suits between sees in different ecclesiastical provinces [ ] -- was the canon law as this was promulgated in the great compendium of 1234, [ ] to which Boniface VIII had, in 1296, added a sixth book [ ] and John XXII, in 1317 [ ], the laws of his predecessor, Clement V -- the Clementines. It was a law made up of the decrees of councils, and decrees and decisions of earlier popes; some of these had been enacted for the generality of the Church, and others were decisions given in particular cases but establishing a general doctrine of law, and henceforward given force of law universally.

The first legal foundation of this massive, and -- by this time-scientifically organised, instrument of government was the collection of disciplinary canons of the earliest councils of the Church, as far as these were known, and of what rules of discipline could be found in the history of the earliest popes. Much of the more ancient part of this lore -- whatever its legal usefulness, or its intrinsic truth -- was, historically, mere apocrypha, the -- as yet unsuspected -- invention of ingenious ninth-century forgers, anxious to produce new and most convincing evidence in support of beliefs and practices long traditional.

These forgeries, which we know as "the False Decretals, " [ ] added nothing to the substantial foundation of the corpus of the canon law. Much more important was the influence upon that corpus, in its critical nascent years, of the contemporary revival of the study of Roman law. Like all the other early medievals, the first professional practitioners of the canon law (whether they functioned as legislators or in the ecclesiastical tribunals) could not have escaped -- even had they so wished -- the far-reaching influence of this great creation of legal thought. It is not so much that here is a code of laws ready made for a variety of occasions; but here is law as a body of coherent thought; here are legal principles and doctrines, laws seen as the fruit of law; and also a most remarkable, technical, legal language. [ ] The first founders of the canon law, as this appears from 1234 in the papal books, were no less skilled in the Roman law, the civil law, as it is also called; and in the legal procedure thence onwards built up by papal legislation, the influence of the Roman procedure in law is everywhere apparent. Roman influence is apparent elsewhere too, in more than one canon-law doctrine, and also in the spirit in which the canonists develop the administrative machinery by which the popes rule the Church divinely committed to their supreme authority. [ ]

It was not, however, the canonist who was the leading figure at the Avignon curia. The pope's most confidential adviser, the official whose word was necessarily most weighty, was the cardinal placed at the head of the finances, the Camerarius. [ ]

And here something must be said of a new practice -- not the invention of the Avignon popes indeed, but one which' they developed enormously, namely the reservation to the Holy See, and its use in practice, of the right to present to benefices throughout the universal Church. Here is the most striking act of the centralised papacy of the Middle Ages. It began forty years before the "Captivity" when Clement IV, in 1268, by the famous decretal Licet, declared that for the future the popes would keep in their own hands the nomination to all benefices vacant by the death of their holder while at the Roman curia. The principle set forth was speedily developed by succeeding popes. Boniface VIII, in 1296, extended "at the Roman curia" to mean within two days' march of the Roman curia. Clement V's extensions, and those of John XXII, as codified in the constitution Ex debito, bring within the papal reserve all benefices vacant through the deposition or privation of the last incumbent, or through his election not being' confirmed, or by his resignation made to the pope, or vacant by the incumbent's acceptance of a new benefice through papal provision or papal translation, and a host of other ingenuities. Further extensions followed until, by the end of Gregory XI's reign, almost every benefice in the Church was at the pope's disposal.

This new development inevitably increased the work and importance of the Camerarius. At every nomination, or concession of a provision, there were fees to be paid. At every death of a beneficiary nominated by the pope there were certain rights due to the pope. The Camerarius needed to have agents in every diocese of Christendom, and, because of the wide range of his department, no officer of the curia was so much in touch with the universality of the papacy's problems. By his office, too, it was the business of the Camerarius to know all about the rights and privileges of the Holy See everywhere. In political crises he was, for this reason, an extremely important person; and, financial transactions on his imperial scale necessarily involving contacts with governments, the Camerarius was, at all times, the pope's chief agent for the day-to-day business with the Christian princes; the political correspondence of the Holy See was done through his clerks; and his collectors -- who are already by this time the regular source of the Holy See's information about the state of Europe -- will one day develop into the nuncios who, with the Secretariat of State, to-day make up the papal diplomatic service.

The Camerarius had also his own system of courts -- with a special bar -- to hear and decide the inevitable, and innumerable, disputes about assessments and payments. He had a special prison at his disposal, and he controlled the papal mint.

The vast engine of collectors which the Camerarius controlled is, perhaps, to students of the vernacular literature of these times, to readers of Chaucer say, or of Langland, the best known, indeed the most notorious, feature of the "Avignon Captivity." It was, from the papal exchequer's point of view, a most admirably devised machine. Never before had so much milk been got from the cow. The system of taxes and charges was twofold; one series was payable at the curia itself, while the other was collected in the taxpayer's own diocese. In all cases it was a taxation of Church property and of Church revenues only.

All bishops and abbots paid, on appointment, one third of the annual assessed income of their see or abbey, and also a second tax which varied in amount from one twelfth to one twenty-fourth of this income; the receipts from the first tax (servitia communia) were divided between the treasuries of the pope and the sacred college, those from the second went to officials and to the officers of the cardinals. If the prelate was an archbishop he had pallium fees also; and if he were actually consecrated at the curia (or blessed) there were additional fees amounting to a sixth of what he paid as servitia communia. From these fees only those were exempted whose revenue was less than, say, £500 a year, present (1946) value. [ ] At fixed intervals bishops were bound to make, personally or through an agent, a pilgrimage "to the threshold of the Apostles" to report on the state of their dioceses, and to pay a special ad limina tax. There were of course, as in all governments, taxes and fees at every stage of the concession of privileges, licences, appointments; another source of revenue lay in the money payments to which vows and penances were at times "commuted." And there was also the tribute, paid annually by the vassal kings of Naples, Sicily, Aragon and England. [ ]

More familiar to the generality of Christians, however, were the taxes gathered by the small army of officials sent from the curia into every part of the Church. These taxes were of two kinds. First of all there were taxes levied for special occasions; the tithe for example, that is to say one tenth of the income of all benefices as this had been officially assessed, and the "loving aid" (subsidia caritativa). [ ] This last was, originally, a voluntary contribution made by a benefice holder in response to an urgent general appeal from the Holy See. But by the time of the Avignon popes it had ceased to be voluntary; the collector fixed the amount due, and delay was punished (as everywhere in the system) by excommunication.

The permanent taxes were, of course, a much more serious matter. The most profitable was that called Annates, the first year's revenue of every benefice after the appointment of a new incumbent. It was Clement V who devised this system, first of all for England only, in 1306, and for benefices vacant by the death of their holder while at the curia (apud curiam Romanam). Twenty years later this tax was extended to the whole Church for all benefices to which the Holy See had nominated. The number of benefices where the Holy See reserved to itself the right to nominate grew steadily all through the fourteenth century, and by 1376 hardly any see was exempted from this extremely heavy tax.

A second principal permanent means by which the popes drew on the resources of the clergy anywhere and everywhere was the right called "spoils." From the custom of pillaging the household goods of a dead bishop or abbot, there arose the retaliatory practice of the bishop or the abbot pillaging in the same way when beneficiaries died who were under their jurisdiction. As the Holy See became, more and more, the universal collator to all benefices of any value, it took over this right of spoils, and under Urban V it was extended to the property of all benefice holders whatsoever, regular or secular, wherever they died. The local representative of the papal collector entered into possession. He paid all debts due for work that had profited the Church or the benefice, and he paid off the servants. The dead man's heirs were given his books and all else that had been bought either with his private fortune or from the fruits of his own industry. The church ornaments and plate the collector left undisturbed (unless he could prove these had been bought out of benefice revenues in order to defraud the pope) and he did not take the food, wine, cattle and tools. But the rest he sold up. These sales of the moveables of dead bishops often brought in vast sums. Their best vestments and church plate the popes often kept for the papal treasury; and they also kept the valuable books. So, between 1343 and 1350, their library at Avignon was the richer by no fewer than 1,200 valuable works. [ ]

As the popes now claimed the first year's revenue of the newly-appointed holder of a benefice, so they also began to demand all the revenue for the time the benefice had lain vacant. A final, general, permanent charge on sees was that levied for dispensations for procurations. A "procuration" was the amount of money which a bishop had a right to receive when he made the visitation of a benefice. Originally this was no more than hospitality for himself and his suite. But, gradually, it had become a money payment and in 1336 the maximum amount was fixed by a law of Benedict XII. The practice now began that bishops begged the Holy See for the right to exact the procuration even though they had not made the visitation, and the popes began to grant such petitions, on the understanding that the bishop paid to them a fee that varied from a half to two-thirds of the sum he himself received. The bishops next endeavoured to recoup, by a diocesan tax, the sums they had been compelled to disgorge to the curia, but here the popes intervened and a law of Urban V, in 1369, forbade the practice.

How far did the system really work? What sums of money did it bring in? The accounts of the central exchequer, and of the collectors dispersed through the different sees of Christendom, survive in very large part and they have been extensively studied. [ ] From them we can trace the financial history of the Avignon popes through fifty years of fluctuating solvency to a final state that borders on chronic bankruptcy. For expenses always outran receipts, and it was upon a papacy that had exhausted its own resources, that had scarcely any effective hold on its own territories, and that had severely tried the patience of Catholics everywhere, that the terrible crisis of the Great Schism fell.

On the death of Clement V (1313), there was a sum of something more than 1,000,000 golden florins in the treasury. But the dead pope's generosity to his heirs left his successor, John XXII, little more than 70,000 of them. It is this pope who was the chief architect of the system just described. The new taxes which he devised, and the system of collecting them, raised the revenue to an annual sum of 228,000 florins. Expenses, however chiefly due to the wars in Italy -- topped receipts throughout his long reign, and John XXII would have died insolvent but for loans and timely legacies. As it was, he left to the new pope, Benedict XII, a fortune of 750,000 florins. Under this Cistercian pope drastic economy ruled, and the Italian wars slackened; Benedict was even able to remit taxes (including the highly profitable first fruits) and to manage on a revenue of less than a fourth of what his predecessor had enjoyed. At his death (1342) the treasure, nevertheless, amounted to more than 1,100,000 florins. But Clement VI, to whom all this came, was the most princely of all these popes in his way of life, a pale but sinister forerunner of the Medici and della Rovere of the next age. As his expenses mounted, the taxes mounted too. Soon the revenue was 188,000 florins, threefold what it had been under Benedict XII. But, even so, it did not nearly suffice, and the pope was forced to borrow. To Innocent VI, who succeeded him in 1352, Clement VI yet managed to leave 300,000 florins. The next ten years are the last in which the financial situation is even tolerable. Taxes contrive to mount indeed, and the annual revenue rises to a quarter of a million florins, but the war in Italy is once more raging violently and it eats up all this and more. The Holy See falls now into a chronic state of debt; and under the last two of the Avignon popes, Urban V (1362-1370) and Gregory XI (1370-1378), though the hold on benefices is pushed to the extreme limit and the taxes are crushing, the financial history of the Apostolic See is one long misery.

The discontent which the system caused was general and it was immense. Where did the money go? To judge from the discontent, as the new popular literature expresses it, the complainants, naturally enough, saw it as the life blood of the princely style in which the Avignon popes lived, the means by which they maintained one of the most splendid courts of the time. But modern study of the accounts has made it clear beyond all doubt that the amount spent on the court was small indeed compared with the sums swallowed up by the endless wars waged in Italy for the recovery and defence of the papal states. The total revenue received by John XXII, for example, in the eighteen years of his reign, amounted to 4,200,000 florins. [ ] The household expenses for one year that we know (1329-30) were 48,600 florins [ ]; if this were an average year the total on this account would be in the neighbourhood of 875,000 florins; but the Italian wars cost this pope no less than 4,191,446 florins. [ ] Nothing so sweals away the riches of a government as war.

We do not, however, need to turn to the poets, the novelists and the satirists of the time for evidence of the immense discontent, nor to the papacy's foes. We can find it in the outspoken comment of such personages as St. Bridget of Sweden and St. Catherine of Siena, and, even, in the very account books of the collectors. And were there no evidence at all, given the facts of human nature, we could surely take it for granted; at no time would men ever have continued to suffer such a yoke in silence. In France the royal officials systematically did all they could to hinder the functioning of the system -- and it was in France that the business was best organised, for there were as many collectors for France as for all the rest of Christendom together. In Germany the collectors were frequently attacked and imprisoned, and at times the clergy banded together in non-payment leagues, taking oath to stand by one another if penalties were inflicted. In England the joint business of the taxation of benefices [ ] and the extension of the papal right to collate, raised a very great storm indeed.

England, since King John's surrender in 1213 to Innocent III, had been subject to the Holy See in temporal matters too, that is to say as a vassal to its suzerain. But this had never hindered the English bishops from protesting strongly against the popes' provision of foreign clerics to English benefices; and the barons -- speaking for the lay patrons whose rights were thus, at times, curtailed -- were more vehement still. The one personage in England whose action was always uncertain, and ever seemingly inconsistent, was the chief patron of all, the king. Whatever the king's personal resentment at new extensions of the papal claims to collate and to levy taxes, he had usually too great a need of the pope's aid in the complexities of international diplomacy to allow his resentment free play. From the time of Edward I (1272-1307) onward England offers the interesting picture of laity eager to protest against this papal policy and to check it, of clergy willing to connive at the protest, and of the crown seeking to use this situation as a means whereby to coax, or coerce, the pope in other policies.

The first anti-papal, parliamentary event to have any lasting effect was the debate in the Parliament of Carlisle in January 1307, the last parliament of Edward I's reign. Here all the grievances of the time were set out in a petition to the king: complaints about papal provisions as an injury to the rights of patrons, about papal claims to first fruits. The king listened to the petition but it was not allowed to mature into a law. The one law certainly made in this parliament [ ] is a prohibition against monasteries which owe obedience to foreign superiors paying taxes and tributes to them or lending them money.

Edward I died within six months of the Parliament of Carlisle, and in the twenty years' anarchy of his successor's reign -- Edward II -- there is more than one protest from the clergy against the double taxation to which they were now beginning to be continually subjected: the popes taxed them for papal purposes, and the kings taxed them -- with the popes' permission -- for national purposes. Edward II, like his father before him, seized the priories subject to alien superiors and confiscated their revenues for a time; and in 1325 a royal writ ordered the bishops to ignore all papal bulls unless the king had given leave for their introduction into the realm. [ ]

But the events of 1307 bore no real fruit until the reign of the next king, Edward III (1327-1377). Once Edward III had begun the great war with France (1338) it could not be long before the English kicked hard against the French popes. Not only were the French legates these popes employed unpopular, but by the papal hold on appointments, and their taxation of English clerics, good English money was now flowing, via the papal treasury, into the war fund of the national enemy. [ ] In 1343 a bill was introduced into parliament to make it a penal offence to bring into the country any bulls from the pope, any provisions to benefices, or reservations, and forbidding the acceptance of such provisions; also, clergy who, on the basis of such provisions, brought suit, either against the patron of a benefice or against the incumbent whom the patron had presented, were also to be punished. In 1344 the penalty of outlawry, perpetual imprisonment or exile was proposed against those violating this law; also, a most significant addition, the same penalties were to be enacted for those who appealed in these matters from the royal courts to the Holy See. Neither of these projects passed into law. For the moment the king held back the indignation of his subjects. The barons, in May 1344, sent a petition of grievances to Clement VI, but the pope answered evasively. In 1347 the barons made a new attempt to enact the bills proposed in 1343 and 1344. They were again not successful. These hints to the papal officials, threats of what might be done, were wholly without effect at Avignon, and the king at last consented to allow the enactment of a statute. So there was passed, in 1351, the first Statute of Provisors. [ ] This famous law begins by telling the story of the Carlisle petition of 1307, and makes its own the complaint of that document that the papal policy of granting English benefices to foreign clerics -- who are always absentees -- is doing serious harm to every kind of religious activity. Now, in 1351, the mischief is worse than ever. English kings are bound, by law and by their oaths, to provide remedies for it. So, with a statement that the legislation of 1307 has never been repealed, it is now enacted that all elections of bishops and abbots are to continue to be freely made by the various chapters, and that all ecclesiastical patrons are freely to present to the benefices in their gift, and that where the Roman curia "in disturbance of the free elections, collations or presentations aforenamed" has made provision of a benefice, the presentation is, for that occasion, to fall to the king. Anyone who, fortified with a papal provision, presumes to disturb the person presented by the king or by an ecclesiastical patron, [ ] is to be arrested and, on conviction, imprisoned until he pays a fine left to the king's discretion, makes satisfaction to the party aggrieved and also gives security that he renounces his claim and that he will not prosecute his suit or make any appeal in the pope's court. If the provisor cannot be found he is to be outlawed.

Two further acts of parliament supplement the Statute of Provisors and, thereby, perfect this new instrument of royal control of Church affairs; they are the Statute of Treasons (1352) [ ] and the Statute of Praemunire (1353). [ ] The first of these was enacted in order to state with precision what those offences were which amounted to high treason, and one clause of the statute declares that all who procure from the papal curia any provison to a benefice fall outside the king's protection; they are outlaws and whoever finds them may do as he wills with them. This is only incidental to the main purpose of the act, but the papal jurisdiction in matters of benefices is the very subject of the second statute. This first Statute of Praemunire does not indeed make any mention of the pope or his courts. It declares that many of the king's subjects complain that they are cited abroad to answer in a foreign court for things cognizable in the king's court, [ ] and also that appeal is made to "another court" from decisions in the king's court. This is a manifest injury to the king's authority and to the common law. So it is now enacted that whoever, bearing allegiance to the king, thus draws another out of the realm, or who sues in another court to defeat a judgment given in the king's court, shall be given two months and a day to answer personally in the king's court for this contempt. If he comes not -- and here follows the penalty known henceforward as a Praemunire, and still good law for various offences -- he is from that day outside the king's protection, the whole of his property is forfeited to the king, and when found he is to be imprisoned for as long as the king chooses.

Papal presentations to benefices in England are, from this time onward, by English law, null. It is a crime to procure them, and a crime to make any appeal to the pope's courts to bring about the execution of the pope's provision -- and indeed a crime to make any use of the pope's court for matters where the king's court claims jurisdiction. Here is the most ingenious instrument so far devised by which a nation can check the pope's universal power of control over the Church. The interesting thing is that the kings made almost no direct use of this instrument. The next forty years saw many conflicts between the English and the popes; in 1364 the penalties of Praemunire were renewed in an act of finer mesh that brought in all those accessory to the offence of using the pope's courts; in 1366 the whole nation repudiated for ever the papal suzerainty; in 1369 the alien priories were seized once more, and their monks finally banished in 1377; strong complaints were made in parliament in 1376 about the heavy papal taxation of English benefices and the luxury in which the collectors of these taxes lived -- and also of the way in which the best of the benefices went to absentee cardinals of the papal curia. The Statute of Provisors was evidently not in operation -- even as a threat it was hardly effective; and there was thus no occasion for the Statute of Praemunire to be put into force. The fact was that the king continued to find the pope useful, and had no desire to begin a major quarrel on such a general issue as underlay these English statutes. In the Concordat of Bruges, of 1375, neither side raised the issue of principle; and both agreed to annul actions which contravened the legal arrangements made by the other, and to remit the penalties incurred. But in 1390 the Statute of Provisors was re-enacted, [ ] and in 1393 the Statute of Praemunire. [ ]

To accept a benefice in contravention of the law entailed, from now on, banishment for ever; and the same penalty was decreed against whoever harboured those so exiled. Also all who brought into the realm any summons, sentence or excommunication affecting those who put the Statute of Provisors into execution were liable to capital punishment. The new Praemunire law declares its motive to be the recent acts of the pope. [ ] He has excommunicated English bishops who, in accordance with English practice, have instituted to benefices the presentee declared to be such by a decision of the king's court; and he has planned to translate bishops from one see to another, without their consent and without the king's consent -- which translations go against English law, and to acquiesce in this policy would be to submit the crown of England to the pope. At the suggestion of the Commons the king has put the matter to the Lords temporal and spiritual. The barons, like the Commons, agree to stand by the king. The bishops and abbots will neither deny nor affirm that the pope can so excommunicate or translate bishops, but they agree that such excommunications and translations are against the king and his crown. And it is thereupon enacted that all who have any share in such excommunications or translations "or any other things whatsoever which touch our lord the king, against him, his crown, and his royalty or his realm" incur from now on the penalties of Praemunire.

The effect of all this legislation -- against which, in 1426, Martin V protested strongly but in vain -- was to make the king so far master in his own house that, although the popes continued to name and provide to benefices, and Englishmen to accept the provision, in contravention of the law, none was named to whom the king had any objection; and to bishoprics the popes always provided the man the king named to them. Not until the closing years of the fifteenth century was any foreign absentee cleric named to an English see, and then it was done at the king's request, the cleric provided being the king's ambassador at the papal court. [ ] The laws brought about a tacit understanding between the papacy and the crown -- so long as pope and king continued to be friendly the laws might as well not have existed. But the instrument lay by, ready for service whenever crisis came. Thanks to these laws, long before Henry VIII's new invention of the Royal Supremacy the English were well habituated to a very great measure of royal control in religious affairs. It is no more than the bare truth to say that Henry's Catholic ancestors had furnished him, not only with an armoury of useful precedents, but with more than one of the main instruments his policy called for. [ ]

In the end, the curia broke down these alliances of princes and people against its claims, by the simple policy of offering to the prince a share of the tax; and by a system of agreement as to the candidate to be provided to the vacant sees, it gained the princes as allies against the discontented chapters now deprived of their right to elect.

But to the last the papacy remained powerless, comparatively speaking, in Germany, where the bishops were themselves sovereign princes. Here the chapters -- close corporations with their membership reserved to aristocratic and princely families -- steadily ignored the system of papal provision and elected their own candidates. There are stories of the canons, arms in hand, driving out the papal nominees; and one Bishop of Wurzburg even forbade, under pain of death, that anyone should bring into his jurisdiction a papal provision. To assert their rights, in the face of such opposition, and to avoid at every vacancy conflicts which would never end, the popes were reduced to the miserable expedient of first quashing the election (as invalid) and then themselves nominating to the see the man whom the chapter had elected.

Gradually, however, the system of papal provision established its hold almost everywhere, and it is one mark of the new state of things that prelates now begin to style themselves, "Bishop of X by the Grace of God and the favour of the Apostolic See."

It was once a thesis largely taken as proved that one thing alone had produced this system of papal provision, to wit papal greed for power and money, libido dominandi. Certainly abuses now began to flourish as never before; and it was perhaps the immense fact of the abuses that distracted the attention of scholars from the question why the popes came to construct and to extend this system of reserving benefices to their own appointment. There is a world of evidence [ ] that the elective system had, by the fourteenth century, so broken down that, in one see after another, it led to double elections, to doubtful elections, to disputes, riots, feuds, and even to schisms. It is also becoming certain that the popes were really alarmed at the fact that, in Germany, religious life was passing into the control of a laicised clerical aristocracy, whose power they were resolved to break by destroying their right to co-opt others of their kind as their successors. A very high proportion of the opposition to the system of papal provisions -- as distinct from the opposition to abuses in the system -- came from that lay aristocracy whose hold on religion the popes had been steadily fighting ever since the days of Gregory VII. It is only in recent years that a study of the actual process of Provisions as a working system has begun to reveal these all-important elements of the question. [ ]

They are, indeed, all-important elements, because the terrible abuses which, in the end, accompanied the system everywhere did more than anything else to bring about that indifference of Catholics to the cause of the Church as such, which is, perhaps, the chief single cause of the collapse of Catholicism in the sixteenth century. For with papal reservations the systematic practice grew of giving papal dispensations for the same man to hold more than one benefice -- the grave abuse called pluralities; an easy way for popes to reward (or to maintain) high officials to whom they could not pay a sufficient salary. [ ] With the appearance of pluralities as an ordinary feature of high ecclesiastical life, there came simultaneously the inevitable, related abuse of absentee pastors -- bishops or parish priests -- who drew the revenues while some deputy did the work (in his fashion) for what stipend the titular could be compelled to pay. Here are the seeds of incredible scandals, of sees left for generations without a resident bishop, and of bishops appointed to sees solely for the sake of the revenue they will draw from them, bishops who do not so much as trouble to seek consecration, nor even ordination as a priest. It is now that the hideous ulcers begin to form which disfigure the Church of those later years in which were born such iron reformers as St. Ignatius Loyola and St. Charles Borromeo. And over it all there begins to be noticeable the stench of accretions of immense ecclesiastical wealth, [ ] of wealth acquired or wealth desired; wealth that comes according to law and by lawful dispensation; wealth that comes against all law, in ways no dispensation can legitimate -- by simony. It is one of the greatest sources of all these evils that the benefice -- an ecclesiastical office that carries with it a right to a sure, ascertained income -- comes more and more to be discussed as a property (which of course, in part, it is) and that considerations of Canon Law rather than Pastoral Theology inspire the discussions.

The main problem of the Church in this century of the Avignon popes is, of course, the eternal problem, how to keep men good, how to keep them up to their obligations and their professions. It was one great, and inexplicable, weakness of these popes of the later Middle Ages that they never devised a system of training adequately the parochial clergy. Laws of clerical behaviour there were in plenty; on every possible occasion they were proclaimed anew, and when opportunity offered they were stiffened up enthusiastically. But none of these popes seems ever to have taken stock of the problem as a whole, to have proposed or considered such a reconstruction as, for example, John XXII introduced as a solution for the disorders that for so long had vexed the Friars Minor. Denunciation of sins there is indeed in plenty, but nowhere a constructive policy that will affect, as well as the causes of sin, the circumstances that serve to assist these causes. The "State of the Church" problem begins now to be chronic, and to the official ecclesiastical world it is in danger of becoming an inevitable element of Christian life. Officialdom never ceases to protest against abuses, nor to call for amendment; but it never effects any substantial lasting improvement. The day comes, at last, when the whole framework begins to fall apart. By that time the papal control of the whole initiative of Christian life has been, for centuries, a fact known to every Christian man; it is not possible so to take on the burden of a universal administration and to remain untouched in the hour of disaster. The papacy was to feel the full force of the storm, and nowhere more than in the collapse of men's faith in the divinity of its origins; and in that same day it would be seriously suggested as a necessary measure of reform, that the totality of the religious orders be abolished.

ii. The Popes, 1334-1362

John XXII had survived to the great age of ninety. He was active and mentally vigorous to the end, and in some respects his death seems to bring to a close a whole age. It was not merely that the pope was so old that he could recall the momentous pact between the great French pope, Urban IV, and the crown of France from which had come the destruction of the Hohenstaufen (and also the new menace of the Angevin princes); nor that, in him, there had been active a personality formed as long ago as the age of St. Louis IX. But John XXII was the last of the series of popes whose genius created the canon law; with him there was finally brought to completion the work that had begun with Gratian's own pupil, Alexander III. For a hundred and seventy-five years now the genius of that first great papal jurist had dominated the public action of the papacy. In all that time the great popes -- with scarcely an exception -- had been great canonists, churchmen who had viewed their world, and worked for its betterment, through the medium of this new great instrument. It was then a striking reversal of history that John XXII was succeeded by a pope who was a theologian and a monk, and that in this pope, Benedict XII, there reappeared for the moment the kind of pope who had characterised not so much Gratian's age, but rather the age that had produced Gratian, the golden age of those monastic popes who, from the time of St. Gregory VII, had pulled the Church free of the slough of the Dark Ages.

Benedict XII was still, at the time of his election, a faithfully observant Cistercian, after nearly twenty years spent in public life. Inevitably he was a reformer. There was already much to reform; it is now indeed that we first begin to meet, as an acknowledged feature of Christian life, the "State of the Church" problem. Benedict XII -- it is his great glory -- gave himself wholeheartedly to its solution. Though he was still some months short of fifty when he was elected, he reigned for little more than seven years, but in that time he laboured to restore or remodel every one of the greater religious orders. To this fruitful activity the Bullarium is a simple and striking witness, where Benedict's decrees occupy three times the space taken by the acts of the longest-lived pope of all this period. [ ]

The Cistercian pope came to the supreme charge with an enviable record as a good, competent and hard-working bishop in the two poor country sees he had occupied. [ ] He seems to have been especially successful in his work against the heretics -- Vaudois and Cathars -- who still lingered in those mountainous regions. This was, however, hardly the career to train a man for the first place in the government of Christendom. The monkpope's inexperience of diplomatic business, and of general politics, was to cost him many a reverse, and a certain narrowness of outlook was to give some of his monastic legislation a rigidity of detail that would not stand the strain of practice. But Benedict has the great merit that he recognised the nature and the scale of the evil of monastic decay, and much of what he did remained until the Council of Trent -- and has remained even to our own day -- the basis of the organisation of the great religious orders. [ ]

The pope began early, sending home from Avignon, only a month after his election, the innumerable bishops who had deserted their sees to live there in expectation of favours to come. In May 1335 he abolished the iniquitous system of granting abbeys to non-resident abbots (who, often, were not even monks) to be held in commendam, and in December of that same year he revoked all grants made of the next appointment to benefices. The system of papal provisions he maintained, but showed himself most conscientious about the qualifications of those to whom they were granted -- so conscientious, in fact, and so personally concerned, that the system began to break down, the pope keeping places vacant for months until he found a man thought really suitable. He was a striking exception to almost all the popes of this and the following century in his horror of nepotism, and he was almost as exceptional in his disregard of the wishes of ruling princes about appointments.

Something has already been said about Benedict XII's share in the remodelling of the Curia Romana. He showed himself a deadly enemy to the systematic jobbery that disgraced it, and in the first month of his reign there was a general flight from Avignon of guilty officials anticipating discovery and punishment. The history of the papal finances during this century shows how Benedict XII was able to carry through the work of building the great palace of the popes at Avignon, and yet leave the treasury in good condition, despite a generous surrender of fruitful sources of revenue. This was due in part to the pope's careful administration, but also to his resolute abandonment of the war policy of his predecessor. At the very outset of the reign Benedict XII declared explicitly that he would not resort to war even for the defence of the territories of the Church. The Church, he declared, could in the long run only lose by using such a means. [ ]

Benedict XII secured peace also in the heart of the curia, in the delicate business of the pope's relations with the Sacred College. For he habitually worked with his cardinals, discussing all matters fully with them, and labouring to win their consent to his plans. He was sparing in his creations, adding only seven to the college, in the consistory of 1338, of whom all but one were French, and four were religious. In the next conclave there would be eighteen cardinals, fourteen of them Frenchmen.

The work of Benedict XII as a restorer of the life of the religious orders began with an attempt in the bull Pastor Bonus, [ ] to check an evil from which none of them was free, the presence all over Europe of monks and friars who, on one pretext or another, had taken to live outside their cloisters. Superiors were urged to find out where their missing subjects had gone, and were given new powers to compel their return. They were also to work for the return of those who, without proper authorisation, had made their way into other orders, and to make provision for the return of those who had abandoned the monastic state altogether -- the apostates in the technical language of the canon law. To make the path of these last unfortunates smooth, the superiors were authorised to lighten the penances due for this offence, and indeed Benedict urged upon them that clemency was a duty.

Next the pope took up the reform of the several orders, Cistercians, Benedictines, Franciscans, Dominicans and Augustinian Canons-Regular. In every case he took the superiors of the order into his confidence, and -- with the exception of the Dominicans -- they all agreed to, and accepted, the reforms he proposed.

Two abuses, the Bull Fulgens, 12 July, 1335, suggests, lie at the root of the Cistercian decay, namely the abbots' disregard of the monks in their administration of the monastic properties, and the growth of new customs which have destroyed all real community life. The pope, in great detail, now forbids abbots to alienate property, to grant leases, or to contract loans without the consent of their monks. Abbots are to take an oath to observe this law, and their officials also. The bursars of the monastery, who are to be appointed by the abbot and the senior monks, are to render a quarterly account. Abbots are henceforth to be fined who refuse, or neglect, to attend the general chapter of the order -- that mechanism whose good functioning is the condition sine qua non of Cistercian well-being; and new powers are given to the superiors of the order to punish those abbots who neglect to pay their quota to the order's general fund, which fund is to be collected and administered according to rules put beyond the chapter's power to alter. The order is sternly recalled to its first austere ideals, by decrees that forbid all use of silver plate, and that limit to a single companion the train of abbots en voyage. There are to be no more dispensations from the rule of perpetual abstinence from flesh meat, and those hitherto granted are revoked. Breaches of this rule are to be punished by three days of bread and water, and a flogging. [ ] Abbots and monks alike are to wear the same simple habit. All are to eat the same food, in the one common refectory, and all are to sleep in a common dormitory -- where cells have been built they are to be destroyed within three months, under pain of excommunication. There are to be no more arrangements to divide revenues as between the abbot and the community, and concessions of this sort are revoked. Abbots who break this law are to be deposed, and the monks imprisoned. A long section which forbids the abuses by which monks have, in fact, become owners, says much, in its carefully detailed prohibition, of the general decay that has come upon the fundamental monastic ideal of voluntary poverty. Finally, there is a careful provision for monastic studies. In every abbey a master is to be engaged who shall teach grammar, logic and philosophy to the young monks; and every year monks are to be sent -- in the proportion of one for every twenty monks in the monastery -- to the various universities, Paris, Oxford, Toulouse, Montpellier, Salamanca, Bologna and Metz. Monks found suitable for university degrees in theology are to be left to complete their course, but none are to study canon law, the science which is the high road to ecclesiastical preferment and a standing temptation to the monastic vocation.

The bull in which Benedict XII sets his hand to the restoration of the classic monachism of St. Benedict is one of the longest of all. [ ] It repeats very largely the provisions in the Cistercian reform about care for monastic property, for a revival of the life in common, and for study. It recalls the famous decree of 1215 which imposed on the Benedictines the Cistercian invention of provincial chapters, and it went a step further in the same direction by now grouping the Benedictine houses of the various countries into provinces, thirty-one provinces in all. [ ]

The same defects in the community life are legislated against, yet once again, in the long bull that remodels the Augustinian Canons. [ ] The abbeys and priories of this rule were, seemingly, establishments on a very much smaller scale than the Benedictine or Cistercian monasteries. Special reminders are given that the canons are not to go hunting, nor to carry arms without the leave of their superiors; and again that conspiracies, and sworn pacts amongst the brethren, are to be sternly put down.

Benedict XII did not wait to be crowned before he publicly expressed his opinion on the state of the order of the Friars Minor -- still, it may be supposed, unsettled by the late tragedy of Michael of Cesena and Ockham. In the Advent Consistory of 1334 the pope reproached the Franciscans with their tendency to heresy, their scorn for the hierarchy, their relaxed discipline and their revolutionary turbulence. Two years later the bull Redemptor Noster [ ] prescribed appropriate remedies. The tone of the bull is extremely severe. Yet once again, all tendencies towards the "Spiritual" movement are condemned; the friars are bidden to take more seriously the duty of the choral recitation of the Divine Office, all are to be present at it, and there is to be no levity in carrying it out. Once again there are special laws to restore a common table, with silence and reading during meals. The brethren are to be given sufficient food; and all are to have the same food, clothing and sleeping quarters -- superiors and subjects alike -- so that none may have excuse to live lives of their own outside the community. The greatest care is to be taken as to what friars shall preach outside the convents. None is to be sent unless of mature years and formed character; and even so, he is not to go unless with a kind of passport that states exactly what his mission is, and until what date he is lawfully outside his friary. [ ] One very necessary condition of good preaching is theological knowledge, and Benedict XII is here most insistent In addition to the studies made in the convents of the order; he decrees that every year three friars are to be sent for theological studies to the university of Paris, three to Oxford and three more to Cambridge -- all of whom must first have read the four books of Peter Lombard with the commentary of approved doctors. [ ] The pope goes out of his way to insist that all friars thus engaged in studies are to be treated with special care and respect by their brethren, and lays down that each convent shall be plentifully supplied with books of grammar, logic, philosophy and theology. Also, there is to be a careful censorship of new publications.

The Minister-General of the order is to visit personally, within ten years of his election, all the provinces -- except Ireland, Greece and the Holy Land, to which remote territories he is allowed to send a deputy. Finally -- a most important innovation -- novices are to be sent for their training to a special house, under the care of a special "master of novices"; and until they reach the age of twenty-five the professed friars also are to be under the rule of a "master of the professed."

When Benedict XII publicly lectured the Franciscans in 1334, he held up to them as a pattern of life their great rivals, the Friars-Preachers, even saying that St. Dominic headed all the orders. It is a curious irony that with the Dominicans alone the pope's efforts at reform failed, and even produced a violent struggle, that only ended with the pope's death.

Benedict XII died, all too soon, after a short seven years and a half, before he had had time to do more than promulgate his many schemes of reform. His austerity and his reforms gained him enemies everywhere, and especially among the courtiers and humanists. He died one of the most reviled of all the popes. Yet if there is any other of the long line whom this great Cistercian brings to mind, it is the Dominican, St. Pius V, the one undoubted glory of the Counter Reformation. So great then was the effect of a saint upon the papal throne, when a saint did finally appear there, that even his naturally easy-going successor was compelled to a faithful continuation of his work. Benedict XII was less fortunate. Those who had chafed at the new rigour had their way in the conclave which followed his death. [ ] His successor, Clement VI, was also, it is true, a monk; he was a brilliant man of affairs, and an experienced administrator, but one who, by the prodigality with which he scattered dispensations of all kinds, ruined much of his predecessor's work. The next ten years' reign was indeed a time "du laisser-aller et des largesses." [ ]

The crowd of needy clerics that had lately fled Avignon now returned, at the new pope's express invitation to send in their petitions within two months. To satisfy them, and as a means to put into execution his own express declarations that "no one should leave a prince's presence discontented," and that "a pope ought to make his subjects happy," Clement extended the reservations of appointments to cover the whole field of benefices. When complaints were made of this prodigal use of his authority, he had but one word, "My predecessors did not know how to be popes." Whether these sayings are really authentic, they undoubtedly describe the spirit which reigned at Avignon for the next six years -- when the Black Death suddenly descended and carried off half the population. [ ]

Clement was liberality itself to his own innumerable relations and to the French kings, [ ] and to his princely neighbours, lending them huge sums of money. He completed the great palace that Benedict XII had begun, and it was he who, in 1348, finally bought from its lord the city of Avignon. Upon Clement VI there lies the main responsibility for the chronic bankruptcy in which the popes henceforth laboured. In many respects Clement VI is an unique figure among the Avignon popes, and it is of him alone that the conventional picture of an Avignon pope is true. The fourteenth century was a time when ways of life were rapidly growing more luxurious, and that clerical life -- the life of the clerical aristocracy -- reflected this is, of course, yet another evidence of religious decay. "The pope," says M. Mollat, examining critically the charges brought against the Avignon popes, "regarded himself as a king, and as a king he surrounded himself with a magnificent court where the cardinals took the position of princes of the blood-royal. . . . In the fourteenth century no power, not even one essentially spiritual in kind, could dominate the world, if its means of action were not based on territorial property, on moneyed wealth, and above all on that pomp and circumstance which simple folk have always looked on as the characteristic evidence of wealth and authority. . . . The example given by the pope became contagious. . . . The clergy began to dress sumptuously, wearing the check silks and long-toed shoes which were then the height of fashion and, what went contrary to all ecclesiastical custom, with their hair allowed to grow its length." [ ] That a pope who chose to live in such a style -- a pope who was still in the prime of life -- should be accused of grave moral offences is not surprising. Petrarch, especially, has piled up against the memory of Clement VI "un requisitoire accablant." [ ] But Petrarch is far from being a disinterested witness, and a very different kind of testimony must be adduced before Clement VI can be condemned for this also.

Clement VI's reign was marked by two great catastrophes, the effective opening of the Hundred Years' War between England and France, and the Black Death. The immense upheaval caused by the war in the social life of both countries is a commonplace of general history. In that general deterioration -- and from that deterioration -- the religious life suffered too, as it must, when such calamities come upon a generation where religion is already failing and lacking zealous and competent leaders. [ ]

The Black Death is the special name given to the great plague which, between 1348 and 1350, visited every country of Europe in turn, carrying off from all of them between a third and a half of the population. The witness of the contemporary writers in all these various countries is roughly concordant. In the proportion of dead to survivors which they give their accounts tally, as they do in the description of the symptoms and course of the disease. What the effect -- the immediate effect, first of all -- was of this sudden appalling catastrophe on the general spirit of the age, on its religious organisation and life, on its social and economic history, no one has yet worked out in detail, with the full contemporary documentation which the proof of any thesis about the matter must call for. The old theory that the Black Death wrought an immediate revolution in modes of land tenure, and was the cause of an immediate social upheaval, no longer has the universal approval of the historians. And the readiness of apologists to lay to the score of this great plague all the ills which manifestly afflicted religion a hundred and fifty years later, has bred an equally unscientific tendency -- in people who are not apologists -- to speak as though it were impossible that the unprecedented calamity could have had any really important lasting effects. [ ]

It was in the early weeks of 1348 that the disease first appeared in the West, at Genoa, brought thither by a ship from the Genoese colony of Caffa in the Crimea. Thence it rapidly spread to Venice, where 100,000 died, and down through central Italy, to Florence, where again 100,000 is given as the number of the dead, and to Siena, where 80,000 died, four-fifths of the population. Sicily was especially its victim. At Marseilles, where the disease began to show itself in the same month it arrived at Genoa, 57,000 died in a month -- two-thirds of the population -- with the bishop, all his canons, nearly all of the friars. The ravages at Narbonne and Arles and at Montpellier -- the seat of the great medical university of the Middle Ages -- were just as severe. Avignon suffered still more severely, losing more than half its population in the seven months the plague raged. As the year wore on the contagion gained the north of France, 80,000 falling victims at Paris, and in July it reached the south coast of England, whence it spread, during the next eighteen months, over the whole of the country.

No part of northern and western Europe escaped. The plague ravaged Spain in 1349 and, crossing the Alps from Italy, it passed through Switzerland and the valley of the Rhine to Germany and to the Low Countries, and by Denmark to Sweden and Norway. The ease with which the infection was taken, the speed with which death followed, the seeming hopelessness of the case once the disease took, caused everywhere the most terrible panic and, with the general fear, a general feeling of despair that showed itself in wild outbreaks of licentiousness.

At Avignon the luxury-loving Clement VI rose to the occasion, organising what scientific knowledge was at his command, sanitary services and medical aid; and, when the horror and the terror found an outlet in a furious burst of anti-Semitism -- the Jews had caused it all by poisoning the streams and wells -- especially in the Rhineland cities, the pope intervened to denounce the calumny, and threw open his own state to the persecuted fugitives.

Gradually, in the winter of 1349-1350, the plague wore itself out, and the survivors slowly took up the task of reconstructing their social and political life. Ten years later the disease appeared again (1361), to ravage France and England once more, and more severely than any plague, except that of 1348. Who shall reckon the extent of the moral disaster of these visitations? Did they indeed, coming at a time when spiritual resistance was already low, take the heart out of the Middle Ages?

Certainly the Black Death was not the sole begetter of the complication of spiritual evils under which the medieval organisation of religion ultimately went down. But in many respects life was never the same. The population seems never to have climbed back to its earlier density, the elan of the earlier time was never recovered, the note of despondency, of pessimism. in religious writers is now hardly relieved, the spring has indeed been taken out of the year. One particularly heavy loss ought to be mentioned. The Church, considered as a great organisation of human beings, finds itself henceforward faced with the insoluble problem of staffing its innumerable conventual institutions from the depleted and less generously-spirited population. The thousands of its great abbeys depend, ultimately, for their spiritual effectiveness on the diligent performance of the

Opus Dei, the daily round of solemn liturgical prayer. If in an abbey, over a long period, there are not monks or nuns enough to ensure this as a matter of course, its end as a spiritual power-house is inevitable; and not only does the semi-derelict abbey cease to be useful to religion, it is a parasite, an active source of new serious weakness. And more and more this now came to pass. Very few indeed were the abbeys which, after the plagues of the fourteenth century, ever regained the full number of religious needed for the fullness of healthy community life. From such a situation there was but one way out -- the suppression and amalgamation of the depleted houses, retrenchment until better times should come. It was not taken. The great monastic reforms of Benedict XII were thus, at the outset, seriously checked by the social catastrophe that fell so soon after they were decreed, and then by the ensuing development, within the world of monasticism, of an entirely new situation.

Innocent VI, who succeeded Clement VI in 1352, was, in ideals and intention, another Benedict XII. But he was already a very old man, vacillating and despondent, and from the outset depressed by the immensity of the task his lighthearted and prodigal predecessor had bequeathed to him.

The conclave which elected him lasted little more than a day, but the cardinals found time to draft the first of those election pacts -- called capitulations -- which are an eloquent sign of new anti-papal tendencies, even in the Sacred College, and which were from now on to be the bane of pontifical activity. This pact, to which all the electors swore, bound the future pope in such a way that he would be little better than the chairman of a board of governors. There were, for example, never to be more than twenty cardinals, and no more cardinals were to be created until the present numbers had fallen to sixteen, nor should anyone be made a cardinal without the consent of the cardinals. Similarly, without their consent the pope would not depose a cardinal, lay censures upon him, or deprive him of any rights or properties.

Again, before alienating, or granting in fief, any province, city or castle of the dominions of the Church, the consent of two-thirds of the cardinals would be required; and the consent of the same majority must be sought for any appointments to the chief places in the curia. The future pope would not make grants of money to princes without the consent of the cardinals, and for the future the papal exchequer would pay over to the treasury of the Sacred College one half of all the revenues. As though somewhat doubtful of their right to make these conditions, the cardinals had attached to the pact a restrictive clause, "If and in so far as this is according to law." [ ]

Innocent VI, for all his age and his weaknesses, was still too much the famous lawyer he once had been [ ] not to find a way out of the pact. Six months after his election he declared it null, as being contrary to the conclave laws of Gregory X and Clement V, which forbade the cardinals to busy themselves in the conclave with anything else than the choice of a new pope.

Once again a more rigorous spirit informed the curia, the legal qualifications for benefice holders ceased to be a matter of form, and there was an exodus of idle clerics from Avignon. Innocent VI had his troubles with the Franciscans, and his severity towards the remnants of the old "Spiritual" group drew down on his memory terrible words from St. Bridget of Sweden. [ ] It was before this pope that so much of the enmity of the secular clergy against the friars found vent in the famous speech of the Archbishop of Armagh, Richard Fitz Ralph (November 8, 1357), a new quarrel which the pope stifled by imposing silence on all parties. The condition of the Friars-Preachers, that Benedict XII had vainly endeavoured to improve, had, in places, been seriously worsened by the Black Death, and now the Master-General of the order had no choice but to call in the pope to aid him in his work of reform. Once more the proposed reforms seemed likely to split the order; by a majority of four the definitors voted the deposition of the Master-General; but, after a papal enquiry into the charges against him, Innocent restored him to office.

Innocent VI's reign ended miserably -- not through any fault of the pope. He was never able to make good the financial disasters of his predecessor, and finally he was compelled to sell off paintings and other art treasures, jewels and church plate. To add to his distress the truce of 1357 between France and England, and the definitive peace of Bretigny three years later, set free thousands of hardened mercenary troops, and these descended on the helpless Papal State. Only at the last moment was the pope saved, by a general rally of new crusaders from Aragon and southern France, and even so it cost him thousands to bribe the mercenaries to leave his territories and betake themselves to the wars in Italy. Then, in 1361, came a renewal of the plague, and in three months 17,000 people died of it at Avignon, including a third of the cardinals. By the time Innocent himself came to die, September 12, 1362, all the glory of the Avignon papacy had gone, never to return.

Return to Index

# CHAPTER 3: THE RETURN OF ST. PETER TO ROME, 1362-1420

## 1. INFELIX ITALIA, 1305--1367

WITH the death of Innocent VI in 1362 and the election of Urban V to succeed him, a new stage begins in the history of the "Avignon Captivity." There now comes to an end the only time when the papacy can really be said to have seemed stably fixed there. At no time was it any part of the policy of these Avignon popes to establish the papacy permanently outside of Italy. What had kept the first of them -- Clement V -- in France throughout his short reign was a succession of political accidents and crises. His successor, John XXII, strove for nearly twenty years -- as will be shown -- to make Italy a safe place for popes to return to and to dwell in. But he failed disastrously. And it was upon that failure that there followed the long central period of the Avignon residence -- the reigns of Benedict XII, Clement VI and Innocent VI -- when for the popes to return to Italy was something altogether outside the range of practical politics. It is this period, [ ] of enforced stable acquiescence in the exile, which the election of Urban V brings to an end. For with this pope the idea of the return to Rome now begins once again to inspire papal policy, and in 1367 Urban V actually realised the idea.

Now, whatever the personal preference of any of these popes for residence in his own country, and whatever the pressure exercised over their choice by the various French kings, there was another, permanent, factor, beyond any power of the popes to control, which, throughout the period, was, time and again, a final deciding consideration against any movement to return. This factor was the political condition of Italy. The anxious dilemma which these popes had to face was not of the* making, although -- it can hardly be denied -- by every year of the* absence from Italy they increased the difficulties that stood in the way of the* return. It was, in essence, the dilemma as old as the

Papal State itself, and indeed older still. How was the central organ of the Christian religion -- the papacy -- to be securely independent of every other power in the exercise of its authority as teacher and spiritual ruler of the Christian Church? The papacy would not be regarded as free in its action ii the popes were subjects of any particular prince. Therefore the popes must themselves be sovereigns. But once the popes are sovereigns, there is not only created a state where the ruler is elected but -- because of that state's geographical situation -- an elective sovereignty whose policies have a vital effect on all that international Mediterranean life which, in those days, is the Western world's very centre. Control of the papacy, once the pope is sovereign, is indeed a prize; and inevitably, with the establishment of the Papal State, the competition begins among the noblesse of the Papal State to capture the prize for their own families. Inevitably, too, one extra-Italian power, the emperor, is never indifferent to this competition. Constantly he intervenes -- to protect the papacy from its barons, and to seize the prize for himself, in order to make the papacy an organ of his own government. Never, for nearly three hundred years after the first establishment of the Papal State (754), are the popes so strong as temporal rulers that they can control their own barons without that assistance from the emperor for which they, yet, must pay by some new surrender of freedom.

Then the great series of monk -- popes, of whom Hildebrand -- St. Gregory VII -- is the most famous, finds a way out of the dilemma. In a spirit of wholly unworldly zeal for the restoration of the spiritual, these popes denounce the protecting emperor's encroachment on their spiritual jurisdiction as a sin; they reject it, and defy him to do his worst. Thence come the first of the mighty wars between empire and papacy that fill the next two centuries (1074-1254).

These popes of the Hildebrandine restoration are first of all monks and apostles; and, because they are men of holy life, moved to action by horror at the universal degradation of Christian life, they manage to use the temporal arm without prejudice to the wholeness of their own spirituality, and without any such scandal emerging as the encouragement of clerical ambition disguised as zeal for the gospel. [ ] Their successors, if good men and fighting for the best of causes, are yet not saints. They are not sufficiently careful about the purification of the means they needs must use -- law, diplomacy, the military arts, their financial system, their own characters, the characters of all their subordinates, and of their allies. And by the time when they too achieve victory over the would-be temporal lord of the world of religion, the ecclesiastical character shows evident signs of grave deterioration.

The most serious sign of this in the papal action would seem to be that, as though the Church were a great temporal state, it is in the natural, political and military arts that the popes now chiefly put their trust. There is a difference in kind between the spirit at work in the wars of St. Gregory VII against Henry IV, and in those of Boniface VIII against Philip the Fair, or those of John XXII against Lewis of Bavaria. The golden key to the eternal dilemma, found by St. Gregory VII, has indeed, by these later successors, been dropped in the dust; and once more the Church suffers because the popes are victims of the dilemma. Are they to go back into Italy and to Rome? Then they must be certain that they can live there safe from the rebellion of their own barons and the Roman mob, and so be strong that no foreign prince will think of assailing them. There must be security that Anagni will not be repeated. The Papal State must, for the future, be something like what all states are from now on to be, a strong kingdom, in every part of which the prince really rules. Before the pope can go back to Rome a whole world of anti-papal Italian turbulence must first be conquered. There is now no other way in, but by a victorious war.

At the time when the election of Clement V began the series of Avignon popes (1305), it was more than eight hundred years since Italy had been effectively united under a single political authority. The name was, quite truly, no more than a geographical expression. The island of Sicily formed, since 1302, the kingdom officially styled Trinacria; the southern half of the peninsula was the kingdom called, now and henceforth, Naples; an irregular central Italian territory formed the Papal State, over the greater part of which the papal rule had never been much more than a name; the rest -- Tuscany, Lombardy, Liguria, the ancient March of Verona -- was, for the most part, still the territory of a multitude of city states. Some of these communes were still republics, the great trading and maritime states of Venice, Genoa and Pisa for example, Florence again and Lucca; others had already become the prize of those great families whose names are household words, at Verona the della Scala, at Milan the Visconti, at Ferrara the Este, at Mantua the Gonzaga; and these last states were despotisms, where the princes' whims were indeed law. In the north-west corner a group of states survived of the kind more general in western Europe, feudal in their organisation, the marquisate of Montferrat, the marquisate of Saluzzo and a border state -- as much French as Italian -- the county of Savoy.

The history of the relations of the exiled papacy to the seething political life of an Italy so divided is far too complex to be intelligible, unless the story is told in a detail which the scale of this book altogether forbids. Briefly it may be said that Sicily and Naples play very little part in that history; the King of Naples is, usually, the pope's more or less inactive ally throughout. The main problem for the popes is, first, to recover control of the Papal State that has, in effect, fallen into a score of fragments, each the possession now of the local strong man, or of some lucky adventurer; and then, simultaneously with this, to regain the old papal influence in the leading small states to the north of the Papal State, most of which are now dominated by the anti-papal, Ghibelline faction. So long as the papal faction is not dominant in these city states (whether they are still republics or, like Milan, ruled by a "tyrant") the popes can never hope for peace in their own restless frontier provinces, and especially in Bologna, the most important of all their cities after Rome.

The turning point of the story that begins with Clement V, in 1305, is the despatch to Italy, as legate, of the Spanish cardinal Gil Albornoz in 1353. Until that great man's appearance on the Italian scene, the story is one long tale of incompetence and disaster. It is Albornoz who makes all the difference. It is the ten years of his military campaigns, and of his most statesmanlike moderation as ruler, which at last make it possible for the popes to return to Rome as sovereigns.

The tale of disaster is simple enough to tell, in its essentials. The first chapter is the military action of Clement V in defence of his rights over the city of Ferrara and its surrounding hinterland. When his vassal, Azzo d'Este, died in 1308, it was found that the dead man had bequeathed the succession to his natural son. But Azzo had two brothers, and they disputed this son's right. Whence came a civil war and an appeal, by both sides, to "the foreigner": to Padua by the brothers, to Venice by the son. The son was victorious and Padua, deserting the brothers, went over to him. The brothers appealed to their overlord the pope. Clement thought he saw his chance to recover the old direct hold over Ferrara, always a highly important strategic point in Italian affairs, and now not unlikely to become more a Venetian possession than papal. Venice had, in fact, already won a concession of territory from her Ferrarese protege and ally. So, in August 1308, a war began between the pope and Venice which was to last for a good five years. The pope was finally victorious, and, it is important to note, in the war he used the spiritual arm at least as effectively as the temporal. For he excommunicated the Venetians, put their lands under interdict, and declared the war against them to be a crusade; all who joined in against Venice were, by the fact, enriched (supposing, of course, true contrition for their sins and reception of the necessary sacraments) with all those spiritual favours once only to be had by the toilsome business of fighting the Saracens in the Holy Land. The small states that for years had hated and feared the great republic eagerly joined the alliance. Soon Venetian commerce began to feel the effect of the boycott, and a peace movement began. But the pope inexorably demanded unconditional surrender, and at last Venice had to yield. The republic gave up all the rights it had acquired over Ferrara, agreed to pay the costs of the war, and to surrender many of the commercial advantages and treaty rights which had been one great source of its power in the north.

The pope had won -- and now he had to provide for the government of a singularly turbulent city. The chronic weakness of these French popes showed itself immediately. Clement would trust none but the French -- until, after four years of bloodily inefficient rule under French administrators, the state of affairs at Ferrara compelled him to withdraw them and to offer the rule of the city to the King of Naples. This semi-French administration fared no better than the other; and in three years the Ferrarese had driven out the Neapolitans and recalled the Este. Except for the huge cost of the war to the papal finances, and the huge mass of anti-papal hatred in Ferrara, things were now, in 1317, where they had been before the war started.

Clement V was as ill-advised in beginning the war of Ferrara as he was ill-starred in his victory. But at least he had for a reason the solid fact that a valuable possession of the Church was threatened -- something that was actually his, and valuable from the point of view of the independence of the Papal State. The next war, however -- of John XXII in Lombardy and Emilia -- originated in a claim of the pope that since there was no emperor he had the rights of the emperor, and so the right to interfere in the internal affairs of Milan (that was never a papal city at all), and to demand of its anti-papal ruler, Matteo Visconti, that he surrender to the pope the one-time pro-papal ruler of Milan whom he had long ago displaced and since held in prison. The demand was refused, and there followed eighteen years of war.

The pope looked round for allies but, this time, they were not forthcoming. Then he declared the war against the Visconti a crusade (1322), and presently Milan -- which the pope had laid under an interdict [ ] -- forced out its excommunicated leader. Next, when John seemed on the point of victory, Lewis of Bavaria intervened on the Visconti side (1324), as has been told already. [ ] In 1327, however, the pope was once more master of Bologna, and he planned to make this his headquarters, and to transfer the curia from Avignon. But first the Ghibelline hold upon northern Italy must be really destroyed. The King of Bohemia [ ] now, in 1330, came to the pope's aid, and John XXII, taking up a great scheme that went back to the days of Nicholas III, [ ] proposed to carve out for him in Lombardy a new hereditary kingdom, to be held in fief of the Holy See. The Sicilian experiment was now to be renewed in the north, Italians again to be ruled by a foreigner under the papal suzerainty, for the benefit of the Papal States and the freedom of the Church (1331). But upon the news of this new combination, all parties, Guelfs and Ghibellines in all the cities, came together. Twice in the one year (1333) the papal armies were defeated; the King of Bohemia abandoned the enterprise; Bologna revolted and drove out the papal government and then, in March 1334, John's legate, at the end of his resources after these many years of struggle, fled the country. With his return to Avignon, in the spring of 1334, the last hope for John XXII's great scheme disappeared. "The return of the Holy See to Italy, bound up so closely with the annihilation of the Ghibellines, remained, for the time, all but impossible." [ ] And the war had absorbed the totality of the very high papal revenue of John's long reign. [ ]

Pope John did not long survive this last of his Italian catastrophes. His Cistercian successor, Benedict XII, was wholly a man of peace. There was no attempt to reinforce the papal armies, nor to renew the war. The pope explicitly declared that not even to recover his states would he go to war. Peace -- of a sort -- was indeed achieved; but it was the local tyrants who, everywhere, really reaped its fruits and now consolidated their usurpations. The rot continued all through the next reign also, city after city in Romagna and the Marches falling into the hands of such powerful -- and notorious -- families as the Malatesta.

Then, at the eleventh hour, Clement VI intervened (1350), and once more a papal army marched across Italy to assert the papal rule over the last of what remained to the pope of the Romagna. The expedition failed, as badly as such expeditions had ever failed. The Visconti, from Milan, took a hand and, in October 1350, Bologna received them as its masters. Next the pope's general, failing to receive from Clement the money to pay his troops, disbanded the army. Whereupon the Visconti immediately hired it. As of old, excommunications and interdict were decreed against the Milanese ruler, but this time they were totally ignored. Clement applied to Florence for aid, but Florence was not to be moved. Whereupon the pope reversed the policy of generations of popes, and, in a mood of anger against Florence, admitted the Visconti claims, acknowledged him as the lord of Bologna and planned with him a league against Florence, September 1352. Where this terrible series of blunders would have led no man can say, but luckily the death of the pope (December 6, 1352) ended the crisis.

The next pope, Innocent VI, had this great advantage over his predecessors, that his own personal glory was in no way bound up with the fortunes of the Italian War. Also the Visconti was, first of all, alarmed by the possibility that the Emperor Charles IV might enter the field, and he was eager to make peace with Florence to leave his hands free for a projected attack on Venice. It was not difficult for the papal diplomacy to reconcile Florence and Milan, and Florence and the Holy See. Within four months of his election Innocent VI, by the Treaty of Sarzana (March 31, 1353), had skilfully extricated his cause from a really dangerous entanglement. And, for the task that still remained, of recovering his hold upon the states of the Church, the pope found to hand, at Avignon, the ideal agent -- churchman, statesman, and soldier at once -- the Spanish cardinal Albornoz.

Gil Alvarez Carillo Albornoz, the greatest ecclesiastical figure of his generation, was at this time a man in the early fifties. He was a Castilian, and descended from the two royal families of Leon and Aragon. From an early age he had been destined for a career in the Church and, his university studies ended, he was named to a post at the court of Alfonso XI of Castile (1312-1350). In 1338, while still on the young side of forty, Albornoz became Archbishop of Toledo, Primate of Spain, and Chancellor of Castile. He showed himself, as archbishop, a capable and intelligent reformer of Christian life. When the war against the Saracens of Andalusia was renewed he was appointed papal legate to organise the crusade, and in a critical moment of the great battle of Tarifa (1340) it was Albornoz who rallied the wavering army of crusaders and turned defeat into victory. This was the beginning of a new career. He played a great part in the siege of Algeciras in 1342, and in the siege of Gibraltar seven years later. Then, in 1350, Alfonso XI died. His son, Peter the Cruel, promptly disgraced all his father's friends and Albornoz left Castile for Avignon. Clement VI received him generously, and at the consistory of December 1350 created him cardinal.

Albornoz was commissioned as legate just three months after the Treaty of Sarzana was signed, and on August 13, 1353, he left Avignon for Italy. For the next ten years all turns on his action; and the result of that long activity -- though compromised more than once by the weakness of the sovereign he served -- was to make the popes' authority over their state more of a reality than it had ever been before. It was at last possible for the popes to feel secure from violence within their own frontiers. Not even the long crisis of the Schism that was to come, so shook the work of Albornoz that it needed to be done anew. To few of its servants has the papacy been more indebted than to this great Spaniard, who, very truly, was the second founder of its temporal power. [ ]

Albornoz entered Italy with the design of recovering territories long lost, in hard fact, to the popes. His first care was to secure that no Visconti hostility should either block his communications with Avignon or sow fresh trouble by knitting alliances between the defiant usurpers of papal territory and the host of petty tyrants along the neighbouring frontiers. His diplomacy at Milan was entirely successful, and in 1354 he passed on to the first part of his task, the recovery of Rome and the province called the Patrimony, [ ] the centre and first nucleus of the popes' state. Here conditions were worse -- politically -- than in any other part of Italy. The French officials whom the French popes had obstinately continued to send as their agents, had been tyrannous, corrupt, and incompetent. Civil war between the various cities was continual, a Ghibelline was master of Rome and busy with the conquest of the rest of the province. The war went on until June 1354, when the Ghibelline, Giovanni di Vico, yielded and by the Treaty of Montefiascone (June 5, 1354) accepted the legate's terms. The Patrimony was henceforward undisputed papal territory. Albornoz proceeded to reclaim the Duchy of Spoleto, and by the end of the year, here too he had been successful.

In 1355 he crossed the Apennines to face the more difficult work of subduing the ever-restless cities of the Marches and Romagna. There was a victory in the field in April at Paderno, and a great siege of Rimini. Fermo too was taken, and Ancona. The chief of the tyrants -- Galeotto Malatesta -- made his submission and the Parliament of Fermo, June 24, 1355, marked the definitive pacification of the Marches.

But now Albornoz came up against the greatest difficulty so far -- Ordolaffi, the tyrant of Forli in the Romagna. Here, in July, the papal army was beaten in a pitched battle. A crusade was proclaimed against Ordolaffi, and in the first months of 1356 reinforcements of supplies and men came in to Albornoz. Nevertheless, he still failed to take his enemy's stronghold of Cesena, and through the rest of 1356 Ordolaffi successfully held his own.

And now the cardinal began to suffer something worse than checks from the enemy. The great successes of these last two years had roused the fears of the Visconti. The hold they had established, in Clement VI's time, on Bologna was in danger; and soon, at the papal court, they were busy undermining the pope's confidence in his greatest man. Already there had been serious differences between Innocent VI and his lieutenant. The pope thought Albornoz dealt too leniently with the rebels he overcame. For the cardinal -- far more of a statesman than the pope, a realist who knew men where the pope remained in many respects what he had been most of his life, a professor of canon law -- strove always to ensure that his late enemy should become his ally, and the faithful servant of the papacy. Never did he utterly crush any of them. When they surrendered, and abandoned all their claims, Albornoz appointed them to govern, as papal officials, a part at least of the territories they had once claimed for their own.

The intrigues of the Visconti were, in the end, only too successful. Albornoz received orders to negotiate with the rebel in Bologna the cession of the city to the Visconti. This, giving his reasons, he refused to do, and in March 1357 the Abbot of Cluny was sent out to supersede him. The abbot's diplomatic manoeuvres at Bologna failed, as Albornoz had known they must fail, and when it was clear that the pope's policy was to reinstate the Visconti in this key city, the cardinal asked to be recalled. Innocent was sufficiently disturbed to beg him to remain until

Ordolaffl -- now besieged in Forli -- had been subdued. In June
Cesena was taken at last, but Ordolaffi still held out, and in
August Albornoz handed over his powers and sailed for
Avignon. The last great act of his administration was the
promulgation, at the Parliament of Fano (29 April-1 May, 1357),
of the Constitutiones Aegidienses which were to remain for
nearly five hundred years [ ] the law of the Papal State.

Twelve months of disaster under the incompetent Abbot of
Cluny determined the pope to reappoint Albornoz, and in the last
days of 1358 the cardinal once more made his appearance in the
Marches. Within six months he had overcome the formidable
Ordolaffi, whom he treated with his habitual generosity. He
visited the Patrimony to arrest the beginnings of new trouble, and
then, in 1360, he approached once again the problem of
regaining Bologna. Again the Visconti marched to its assistance,
and for a good four years the steady duel was maintained.
Albornoz took it; the Visconti besieged his conquest (1360); at
the approach of an army of Hungarian crusaders they raised the
siege, only to renew it the next year (1361). In June 1361 the
Visconti forces were heavily defeated at Ponte Rosillo, and what
was left of their army fled to Milan. But Albornoz realised that
this was an enemy altogether too strong for his resources. He
therefore negotiated an anti-Visconti league, in which the della
Scala, Este, Gonzaga, and Carrara joined forces with him, and
1362 saw the war renewed more hopefully.

And then, September 12, 1362, came the death of Innocent VI, to
throw the alliance into momentary confusion and uncertainty. No
one could tell which of the cardinals would be elected -- it so
happened that none of them were, for the new pope was chosen
from outside the Sacred College -- nor what a new pope's policy
would be. The Visconti, naturally, were ready at Avignon to
persuade whoever was elected, that peace, at any price, was a
pope's first duty. But Innocent's successor -- Urban V -- resisted
the intrigues, and, for the first year of his reign, gave Albornoz

strong support. A new crusade was preached against the Visconti; they were once more defeated in battle at Solaro (April 6, 1363); and when the vanquished sought again to win by intrigue what they had failed to hold by force, the pope again stood firm. But this holy pope was no match for the wily Visconti leader. Urban V's great ideal was the renewal of the Holy War against the Turks, masters, by this, of all the Christian lands in Asia Minor and now, for the first time, possessed of a territory in Europe also. [ ] The pope dreamed of uniting against them the hordes of savage mercenaries -- the free companies -- who, no longer employed in the Hundred Years' War, were now ravaging at will through France and Italy.

It was easy to persuade such a man that the needed first condition for the crusade was peace in Italy, and that it could not be bought too dearly. Albornoz was superseded (November 26, 1363) at the very moment when such strong forces from Germany, Poland and Hungary were coming in to him that the final victory seemed certain. Three months later -- March 3, 1364 -- the Visconti restored to the pope all the cities and fortresses they had occupied in his states, and the pope, in return, agreed to pay them the immense indemnity of half a million florins.

The treaty was a signal victory for the wily Visconti over the political simplicity of Urban V. All the fruits of Albornoz's diplomacy and military skill through four hard years were thrown away. The pope had more confidence in the word of his treacherous enemy than in his own legate and general. Once more the incompetent Abbot of Cluny was named legate for the north of Italy, and Albornoz -- who had asked to be recalled -- was urgently begged to remain in Italy as legate to the Queen of Naples. Cut to the heart by the pope's disastrous failure to support the real interests of the Holy See in his own dominions, Albornoz yet continued his work for the suppression of the free companies. He fell seriously ill at the end of 1365 and then Urban, accepting as true charges of corrupt handling of public moneys, without hearing the cardinal, deprived him of his authority in the Romagna. Again Albornoz demanded his recall; accusations of this sort, the multitudinous hates amid which he was living, he said, were too much for him in his old age (he was now well over sixty) and he had a strong desire for more leisure for the care of his soul.

But he was much too useful to the papacy in Italy for the pope to be willing to agree. Publicly, in the consistory of January 30, 1365, Urban declared him innocent of all these calumnious charges, and he besought the cardinal to continue as legate in Naples. Luckily for the pope, and for the papacy, the great cardinal rose above the immense disappointment of seeing his work scrapped for the profit of the Church's enemies. He remained at his post, and it was his continued skilful diplomacy, and military success against the companies, which, by the end of 1366, made at least the Patrimony of St. Peter and Rome a territory to which the pope and the curia might safely return.

## 2. THE POPES LEAVE AVIGNON, 1362-1378

The conclave of 1362 that followed the death of Innocent VI [ ] was one that produced many surprises. There were twenty cardinals to take part in it and the strongest group was that of the Limousins, compatriots of the last two popes. They were not indeed a majority, but the remainder had nothing to unite them except their determination that there should not be a third Limousin pope. The first vote was taken before there had been time for any prearrangement; and, in the hope of delaying the election until some profitable combination had been devised, each cardinal followed his own instinct to vote for the least likely man. But these chance-inspired votes happened to fall, in the required two-thirds majority, on the same cardinal; he was a Limousin; and the brother of the last pope but one, Clement VI. The disappointment of the cardinals was general, and unconcealed. But the pope-elect, the cardinal Hugues Roger, preferred to decline the high office, and thence onwards, in the ballots that followed, the cardinals were so careful about their votes that it soon became evident that no one of them stood any chance of gaining the votes of as many as two-thirds of his colleagues.

It was, then, upon the name of an outsider that agreement was at last reached (September 28, 1362), and the cardinals elected the Benedictine monk Guillaume de Grimoard, Abbot of St. Victor at Marseilles; a man fifty-two years of age, and at the moment papal nuncio in the kingdom of Naples. He was a man of very holy life, whose monastic spirit high offices, and years of external employment as nuncio, had never in any way diminished. He reached Avignon a month after his election, chose the name Urban V, and was crowned on November 6, privately, in a purely religious ceremony, within the walls of his palace, resolutely putting aside all the apparatus of secular magnificence that was now the rule. As pope he contrived to lead the life of a monk, never wearing any dress but his religious habit, and keeping faithfully all the monastic fasts and austerities.

Urban V was a most industrious worker, and scholarship owes him many acknowledgments. Like all these Avignon popes, he was a very real patron of learning. He founded new universities at Orange, at Cracow and at Vienna, and a school of music at the existing university of Toulouse. He restored his own university of Montpellier, and he found the means to support as many as fourteen hundred students in different universities. It was made a reproach to him at the time, and it has been held against him since, that his liberality and charities were a serious burden on the papal resources. For, as has been said, [ ] the finances had now settled down into something like chronic bankruptcy. But, it will be admitted, there have been less deserving reasons for financial embarrassment, and it was ever Urban V's own justification to his critics that to promote true learning -- whether the student persevered in his clerical calling or returned to secular life -- was the best investment any pope could make who regarded the Church's future. [ ]

It has also been laid against Urban V that he had little skill in the arts of ruling, and was too easily the victim of political roguery, and that he failed as a religious reformer. But all these defects -- very real, of course -- shrink beside the double glory that he continued to live his own holy life in surroundings of which St. Catherine of Siena could say that they stank like hell, [ ] and that, at the first opportunity, he left Avignon, and, despite all the opposition, took the papacy back to Rome.

It was in September 1366 that Urban V made known his intention. Immediately, and from all sides, good reasons to the contrary rained upon the pope. The King of France sent special embassies to explain that nothing but the presence of the pope could heal the feuds that were destroying his kingdom. Was the pope to show himself a hireling, by flight? The cardinals, all but unanimously, opposed him. Albornoz, of course -- still in Italy -- welcomed the decision. He considered that the return of the pope, at this moment, when in Rome and the Patrimony his authority was secure and order re-established, would consolidate the work of restoration.

Urban held firmly to his resolution. He disregarded a last threat from his cardinals that they would leave him to make the voyage alone, and on April 30, 1367, left Avignon. By May 6 he had reached Marseilles; there was a long wait for favourable weather, and then the great fleet, the papal galleys and an escort provided by all the maritime states of Italy, made its leisurely way along the coasts of Provence and Liguria. Toulon, Genoa, Pisa and Piombino in succession saw the convoy that bore such precious auguries. On June 3 the pope landed, in his own states, at Corneto. Albornoz was there to meet him. Thence he passed to Viterbo, where he remained for four months, and here he had the great misfortune to lose Albornoz, for the great cardinal died on

August 22. [ ] And at Viterbo the old rioting now broke out again. For three days the city was in the hands of the mob, and there were cries of "Death to the Church, long live the people. " But the pope remained unmoved, and on October 16 he at last entered Rome.

For a time all went well. The return of the papal court was a beginning of new prosperity for the city. There were visits from reigning princes -- the Queen of Naples and the Emperor Charles IV -- that brought crowds of visitors, and once again new trade and wealth. The ruined churches began to be restored, and the old permanent traffic between Christendom and its natural centre took up its wonted course. For the hot Roman summer the pope went to live at Montefiascone, forty miles to the north, on the shores of Lake Bolsena. It was during his stay there, in 1370, that the papal city of Perugia rose in rebellion, and the Romans came to its aid. Urban took refuge at Viterbo and there he was presently besieged by the rebels, who had now hired one of the most notorious of the "free companies" led by the Englishman Sir John Hawkwood. The pope had no choice but to surrender the town. And now the forces of the Visconti crossed into Tuscany, making for the Patrimony. Urban appealed for help to the emperor, and to the King of Hungary. But they were deaf to his needs, and, finally, he decided to return to Avignon. Though the Romans outdid all former shows of loyalty, and though St. Bridget of Sweden prophesied to the pope's face that his return would be followed by a speedy death, Urban was now as resolute to depart from Italy as he had previously been resolute to leave Avignon. On September 5, 1370, he sailed for France. He arrived at Avignon on the 27th and there, three months later, as had been foretold to him, he died (December 19, 1370). [ ]

But the unfortunate ending of the great venture attempted by Urban V did not -- as might have been expected -- sterilise, for yet another generation or so, the ideal which inspired it. His successor, Gregory XI, made it clear, from the beginning of his reign, that it was his intention also to take the papacy back to Rome.

Gregory XI was one of those rare popes elected unanimously by a conclave that lasted only a matter of hours (December 30, 1370). This last Frenchman among the popes -- Pierre Roger de Beaufort -- was a Limousin, the nephew of Hugues Roger, who had been elected eight years before but had declined, and of Clement VI, elected in 1342. It was this papal uncle who had made Pierre Roger a cardinal, at the age of nineteen. The young prelate had shown immediately the manner of man he was, when he deserted the splendid opportunity of worldly fortune and enjoyment thus opened to him, and returned to his study of law at Perugia, then the centre of a real transformation of legal learning, with the great Bartolo teaching Roman law as the development of principles and thereby founding a new science, and with his pupil Baldo de Ubaldis infusing a like new life into the understanding of the canon law. Under such masters the youthful cardinal became an accomplished canonist, with a really deep knowledge of law and with great gifts of judgment. And he grew up to be a man of prayer. Gregory XI was not yet forty-two when he was elected pope, but his health was frail, and he was already tending to be a permanent invalid.

From the first winter of his reign the new pope had determined that, with him, the papacy would return to Rome. And from Rome itself there now came, to urge this upon him as his first duty, the voice of that veteran admonitrix of the popes, St. Bridget. Through her, so she now declared to the pope, Our Lady sent him a message that was at once a command, a promise and a warning. Gregory was to go to Rome by April 1372, and if he obeyed, his soul would be filled with spiritual joy. Should he fail, he would assuredly feel the rod of chastisement; and his young life would be cut short. The pope, who had stood at his predecessor's side when, only twelve months before this, St. Bridget had prophesied to Urban V that his return to Avignon would be followed by a speedy death, was sufficiently moved to order his legate in Italy to ask further explanations of her. What the saint told the legate is not recorded, but we do know the message she sent for the pope's own ear. "Unless the pope comes to Italy at the time and in the year appointed, the lands of the Church, which are now united under his sway and obedience, will be divided in the hands of his enemies. To augment the tribulations of the pope, he will not only hear, but will also see with his own eyes that what I say is true, nor will he be able with all the might of his power to reduce the said lands of the Church to their former state of obedience and peace. " [ ]

This message was apparently sent to the pope in the first months of his reign. Nearly two years later, on January 26, 1373, the saint had a second vision that she was bidden transmit to him. This time it was Our Lord who appeared to her, and told her that the pope was held back by excessive attachment to his own kinsfolk, and coldness of mind towards Himself. Our Lady's prayers for the pope would, in the end, the saint was told, overcome these obstacles and Gregory would, one day, return to Rome.

Then, in February of that same year (1373), came a new vision, in which St. Bridget beheld the pope standing before Christ in judgment, and heard the Lord's terrifying speech to his vicar. "Gregory, why dost thou hate me?. . . Thy worldly court is plundering My heavenly court. Thou, in thy pride, dost take My sheep from Me. . . . Thou dost rob My poor for the sake of thy rich. . . . What have I done to thee, Gregory? I, in my patience, allowed thee to ascend to the supreme pontificate, and foretold to thee My will, and promised thee a great reward. How dost thou repay Me?. . . Thou dost rob Me of innumerable souls; for almost all who come to thy court dost thou cast into the hell of fire, in that thou dost not attend to the things that pertain to My court, albeit thou art prelate and pastor of My sheep. . . . I still admonish thee, for the salvation of thy soul, that thou come to

Rome, to thy see, as quickly as thou canst. . . . Rise up manfully, [ ] put on thy strength, and begin to renovate My Church which I acquired with My own blood. . . . If thou dost not obey My will, I will cast thee down from the Court of Heaven, and all the devils of hell shall divide thy soul, and for benediction thou shalt be filled with malediction -- eternally. . . . If thou dost obey me in this way, I will be merciful to thee, and will bless thee, and will clothe thee with Myself, so that thou wilt be in Me and I in thee, and thou shalt possess eternal glory. [ ]

Gregory was sufficiently shaken to send his legate yet once again to ask the saint for some definite sign. In July 1373, a few days only before her death, [ ] St. Bridget sent her last word to him, and it was a word of practical counsel about the latest difficulty that had arisen to hinder Gregory's departure -- the new war with the Visconti. The pope is bidden to make peace at all costs "rather than so many souls perish in eternal damnation. " He is to place his trust in God alone and, heedless of the opposition, to come to Rome for the establishment of peace and the reformation of the Church; and he is to come by the following autumn. [ ]

And now, soon after the death of the Swedish saint, Gregory XI made his first contact with a still more wonderful woman, Catherine Benincasa, the child of a dyer of Siena, sister of penance in the third order of St. Dominic. St. Catherine of Siena -- for it was she -- was at this time in her twenty-seventh year, and since her very babyhood not only had she been, manifestly, a child of special graces and divine attentions, but one around whom the marvellous and the miraculous flowered as though part of her natural course through life. Prayer; a life of charitable activity; corporal austerity; solitude without churlishness in the midst of a busy family life -- a family where she was the twenty-fourth child; a refusal of marriage, but no desire for the life of a nun; the direction of the friars of the neighbouring Dominican church; visions; colloquies with the saints, the Blessed Virgin and Our Lord; the great wonder of her mystical marriage in sign of which He set on her finger the ring she thenceforward never ceased to see there; the stigmata; and the great vision in which -- so she always believed she had really died, and been sent back to life for the purpose then divinely made known to her; such was the saint's life through all these years, in which she had never left her native town and hardly even her father's house, or her own little room in it. But never was any saint to fulfil more exactly in the Catholic Church the role assigned to the prophets of old, to appear suddenly in the public life of the time, to correct rulers -- the highest ruler of all, the very pope -- and, divinely commissioned, to offer them guidance back to God; and never did any saint offer better illustration of the doctrine traditional in her order since St. Thomas Aquinas, that in the highest form of contemplation the activity flows over into a charitable apostolate and care for all mankind. Already, in Siena, Catherine was a power, and the radiance of her unearthly personality had gathered around her a most extraordinary band of followers, men and women, friars, tertiaries, poets, artists, noble and plebeian, married and single, the most of whom she had converted, all of whom she instructed, and who were one great means of the apostolate of peace that was now her life.

It was, of course, in the midst of war that St. Catherine of Siena's life was passed; of the bitterest wars of all, the bloody feuds that were the life of all the fourteenth-century city states in Italy. In Siena, as in Florence and in a host of lesser towns, there was blood everywhere, as the never-ceasing cycle turned of revolution and counter-revolution; oppression, conspiracy, arrests, torture, executions, revolts, a new regime and then oppression and the rest yet once again; an age of horrible cruelties, of which the terrible savagery that accompanied our own Wars of the Roses is only a pale reflection. And in St. Catherine's many letters, and in her great mystical book of Christian teaching, the Dialogue, -- it is not surprising -- the thought of the Blood, and the word is rarely absent from a single page, of the Blood of Christ shed in love to save sinful man.

St. Catherine had already, early in 1372, written to Gregory's legate at Bologna, Cardinal d'Estaing, bidding him make charity the foundation of all his acts, "Peace, peace, peace! Dearest father, make the Holy Father consider the loss of souls more than that of cities; for God demands souls more than cities. " [ ] This was to be the keynote of her apostolate to the popes. When Gregory himself sent to ask her advice, the saint had no other message but that he should turn from his nepotism, his tolerance of bishops who were "wolves and sellers of the divine grace, " and reform the Church: "Alas, that what Christ won upon the hard wood of the Cross is spent upon harlots. " [ ]

The pope, however, continued in his own way, pressing the Visconti hardly in the field, diplomatically waiting for the opportune moment to do the will of God as he saw it, and especially waiting for the Visconti to be conquered before finally defying the universal opposition at Avignon and setting his course towards Italy and Rome. It is a nice question -- hardly a historian's question -- what ought Gregory XI to have done, or, better, what did he think God wanted him to do? The messages from St. Bridget had clearly left him uneasy. But, so far, his neglect of them and his use of the natural means, of arms and diplomacy, and his preoccupation with the affairs of France and England, had not brought upon him the judgments which St. Bridge. had seemed to foretell. On the contrary, the pope's good offices, for which the two kings had begged, and for the sake of which they had both besought him to delay his journey to Rome, had resulted in the Truce of Bmges (June 27, 1375)
and a year's truce with the Visconti, made in that same month, seemed about to bring peace to Italy too. All was now ready for the voyage to Rome, but the pope's innumerable relatives won new delays from him. Twice within a month the decision to sail was countermanded, and then, on July 28, the expedition was put off until the spring of the next year (1376).

But, in the autumn of 1375, the storm broke in central Italy. and all that St. Bridget had foretold was speedily fulfilled to the letter. At the heart of the storm was Florence's fear of what a papal-Visconti alliance, with a French pope again at Rome, French legates and governors through all the papal cities along her frontiers, might hold in store for her. The summer was busy with efforts to knit together an anti-papal league. A general rebellion was successfully engineered in the pope's own territory. By the end of the year (1375) eighty of his cities had gone over to the league. In March 1376 Bologna, too, joined it. This was about the time that Gregory had finally hit upon for his journey to Rome. Instead, he was once more caught up in the full business of war, and on March 31, putting aside all Catherine's counsel to rely on love, to work for peace alone, and her pleas for leniency, the pope put Florence to the ban. Interdict, excommunication, and a general command to Catholics everywhere to join in the war against her -- if only by confiscating Florentine property wherever found. So began the most bitter struggle of the pontificate.

" Sweet Christ on earth," St. Catherine now wrote to Gregory, "let us think no more of friends and kinsmen, nor of temporal needs, but only of virtue and of the exaltation of spiritual things." And in June the saint made her appearance at the pope's court, envoy of the Florentines, driven near to desperation by the losses to their commerce and the ruin that seemed at hand. But a change of government in Florence destroyed the saint's usefulness as an intercessor. "Believe me, Catherine," the pope said to her, "the Florentines have deceived and will deceive thee. . . if they send a mission it will be such that it will amount to nothing." [ ] In part he was right; but it was also true that the pope's own excessively harsh terms held up the negotiations. It was hard for the saint to ask mercy for the Florentines, now, as repentant children, when they had disowned her in order the better to prepare a new campaign.

Catherine turned to the greater matter of the pope's return to Rome. In one of her first audiences she spoke openly of the wickedness in the curia, and of Gregory's tolerance of it, and when the pope asked for her advice about the matter of Rome the saint finally convinced him that she spoke in God's name, for she told him what none but himself knew, how, in the conclave of 1370, he had secretly vowed to God that, if elected, he would return to Rome.

From about this time (July 17, 1376) preparations really began to be made for the voyage, and then for two months the saint fought the cardinals for the soul of the pope, one only of them all -- d'Estaing -- supporting her. They used all weapons against her, among them the very subtle one of a "revelation" through a holy man that contradicted Catherine's own message. But this time there were no further delays, and on September 13,

1376, the last of the French popes left the great palace by the Rhone, stepping manfully over the last obstacle of all, his old father, who threw himself down at the threshold in a last desperate argument.

The voyage was stormy and disastrous. At Genoa there was even a consistory to discuss whether it was not now obviously God's will that Gregory should stay at Avignon. But Catherine also was at Genoa; and the pope, too fearful of his cardinals to receive her publicly, went to her by night, in disguise, to be strengthened in his purpose. On October 29 he sailed from Genoa and, at long last, on January 17, 1377, the pope landed from his galley in the Tiber before the great basilica where lies the body of St. Paul.

"Come like a virile man, and without any fear. But take heed, as you value your life," the saint had once written to Gregory XI, " not to come with armed men, but with the Cross in your hand, like a meek lamb. If you do so, you will fulfil the will of God; but if you come in another wise, you would not fulfil but transgress it." [ ] Side by side with the preparations for the great return, however, preparations had also gone forward for the renewal of the war against Florence. A papal army -- mercenaries from Brittany and England in part -- was raised, and set under the command of the cardinal Robert of Geneva. As part of the campaign against the great key city of Bologna they ravaged and burnt right up to the city walls. Then (July 1376) they were defeated at Panaro. Bologna still held firm. Next -- a fortnight only after Gregory's arrival in Rome, and a week after his refusal to lower his terms to Florence -- there took place the horrible massacre of the civilian population at Faenza, for which Robert of Geneva must bear the blame. All through the summer of 1377 the negotiations for peace dragged on, and the war of skirmishes continued. The pope rejected St. Catherine's plans "useful for the Church if they had been understood," [ ] -- but, at his wits' end for money to pay his troops, he again sent the saint to Florence in the hope of inducing a surrender. Florence too was desperate, and presently a congress had been assembled at Sarzana to discuss a settlement. It had hardly begun its work when the news came of Gregory's death, March 27, 1378. He was still two years short of fifty.

Twelve days later the cardinals chose to succeed him an Italian, Bartolomeo Prignani, Archbishop of Bari, who took the name of Urban VI (April 8, 1378). Six months later these same cardinals, who had been steadily drifting away from Urban since a fortnight or so after his election, declared him no pope, and in a new conclave, at Fondi, elected Robert of Geneva. He took the name of Clement VII. The division of Christendom into two allegiances, to the popes of rival lines at Rome and at Avignon, which then began, lasted for close on forty years.

## 3. CHRISTIAN LIFE, MYSTICS, THINKERS

The names of St. Bridget of Sweden and of St. Catherine of Siena, coming upon every page of the critical story of the last two popes, are a reminder -- should we need one -- that, beneath that history of the Church which we see as a dramatic pageant, there lies another history, the real and truly vital history of the Church, the history of the inner life of each of the millions of Christian souls. To the actuality, and to the paramount importance indeed, of this other history the saints are, at all times, the standing witness, and it is never an idle criticism of any account of Christian history to ask "Where are the saints?" The presence of saints in the public life of the Church, and the reception given to them, is indeed a kind of touchstone by which we may judge the tone of that life in any particular age.

In this interior history of the Church -- in its fullness known only to God -- there is no distinction or rank, save that which comes from the use of opportunities accorded. Here all are equal. Popes, bishops; religious, clergy; kings, nobles; scholars, merchants; peasants, townsfolk, beggars -- what more are any of these but souls equal in their need of salvation, equal in their utter inability to achieve salvation by any power of their own? And all the vast apparatus, at once as simple and as complex as man himself, of theology, of ritual, the divinely-founded Church, nay the sacred humanity itself of God the Saviour, what are all these but means to that single end, the salvation of man, the return of the rational creature to his Creator for the Creator's greater glory?

Although we cannot ever know more than mere fragments of such a history as here is hinted, this history is a fact never to be lost count of as the more obvious maze of visible activity is explored and all that it holds assessed. For example, the one sole business for which popes and bishops and clergy exist is to lead man back to God Who is man's sole happiness. All popes have known this, all bishops, all clergy; and therein lies, not only the basis of the most terrible judgment that can ever be passed upon them, but the reason for the horror which failure on the grand scale in this primary pastoral duty caused to the serious-minded among the contemporaries of such sinners, and also the source of our own incredulity, as, to-day, reading much of their history, we remind ourselves with an effort that these men were indeed popes, bishops, religious, priests.

What has chiefly occupied this history, so far, is the story of the ruling of religion, of the administration of the bona spiritualia, and the care of the ruling authority to defend the greatest of these, the freedom of religion, from forces that would destroy it in the interest of civil government; it has been, also, a history Or thinkers, of priests and of religious. Something has been told of the success of all these eminent personages; of their mistakes also; of their failings and their sins; and of their never-ceasing struggles. It has been very largely the history of the Church teaching and ruling, rather than of the Church taught and ruled, the story of the shepherds rather than of the flock; and when the flock has been glimpsed it has been, very often, at a moment when in hostile reaction against its shepherds. For with whom else, in this constant battle, are the popes ever engaged but with Catholics, their own spiritual children? It is important to see history from the point of view of these also at whose expense history is made. Quidquid delirant reges, plectuntur Achivi, and Church History, too, has its Greeks; of whose lives we do not by any means, as yet, know nearly enough to be able to call our story complete. What of their spiritual history in these years of continual warfare between the sacerdotium and the imperium? Much of it is written -- sometimes indeed between the lines -- in the lives of the contemporary saints.

It must already be evident, even from the summary account which is all that a general history can attempt, that during the hundred years between Gregory X and Gregory XI (1276-1370) the pastoral sense in high ecclesiastical authority had suffered grievously. From the point of view of that internal history of which we have been speaking this might seem the most important fact of all. But it is not the only fact; and against it we need to set all that can be reconstructed of that inner history. "It is the spirit that giveth life" and, lest we falsify by omission, something needs to be said of those for whom attendance on the Spirit is the main business even of earthly life. For this century, that saw in the public life of the Church so many victories of the world over the gospel, is also the century of the first great attempt to popularise the mystical life by a literary propaganda that describes its joys and analyses its processes; it is the century of Eckhart and Tauler and Suso, of Ruysbroeck and Gerard Groote, of St. Luitgarde and St. Lydwine, of Angela of Foligno as well as of Angelo Clareno, of St. Catherine of Siena and St. Bridget of Sweden, of our own Richard Rolle, of "The Cloud of Unknowing" and of Mother Julian of Norwich; it is the century also of the "Theologia Germanica", of heretical mystical Beghards, Beguines, and others innumerable; and it is the century in which one of the greatest of English poets set out in his Vision of Piers Plowman the whole theory of the life with God as St. Thomas Aquinas had elaborated it, an achievement complementary to that of Dante, and comparable with it. [ ]

What then of the saints of the time? Who were they, and in what corps of the militant Church did they come to sanctity? What of the role of these many celebrated pioneers of the literature of mysticism? And what other new manifestation of the spirit does the century offer, whether in religious orders, or devotional practice? [ ]

Dunng the hundred and four years which this book has so far covered (1274-1378) there appeared, in one part of Christendom and another, some 130 of those holy personages whom the popes have, in later times, found worthy of public veneration, 27 as saints and 103 as beati. [ ] Sixteen of the 130 were bishops, (four of these popes); fourteen came from the old monastic orders; five were secular priests; twenty-one were laymen; and seventy-four belonged to the new orders founded since the time of Innocent III. The share of the new orders is really greater still, for of the sixteen bishops eleven were friars, and of the twenty-one layfolk sixteen were members of the various third orders. It would, no doubt, be rash to say that the number of canonised, and recognisably canonisable, personages alive at any given epoch is an index of the general tone of the life of the Church. There are, it may be supposed, many more souls, whose holiness is known to God alone, than there are those whose repute brings them to the ultimate testimony of canonisation. On the other hand, sanctity, in the technical sense, involves the practice of all the virtues in the heroic degree and this is not only a marvel so rare that it can hardly long escape recognition, but it is the fruit of such extraordinary supernatural action in the soul that it may almost be taken for granted that the subject of that action is meant by God to be recognised as such. Without, then, any desire to propose a few comparative statistics as a new, rapid and infallible guide by which to assess in any given age the force of the mysterious tides of grace given to man, we can perhaps agree that there are times when saints abound and times when they are rare, and examine with something more than curiosity the distribution of these 130 personages over the century or so in which they "flourished. "

The richest period of all is the first third of this century, the last generation to be born in what has been called, with some excuse, "the greatest of the centuries. " [ ] Between the second Council of Lyons (1274) and the election of the first Avignon pope (1305) we can note as many as eighty-eight "saints. " [ ] In the next generation (1305-1342) they are fewer; thirty-seven of these eighty-eight have died, and only seventeen new " saints " appear to fill the gap. In the thirty years that follow next the lifetime of St. Catherine of Siena -- the "saints" are fewer still; of the sixty-eight "saints" active between 1305 and 1342, forty-five have died and only twelve new " saints" appear. These thirty years, from just before the Black Death to the Schism of 1378, are, in fact, the most barren age of all. The actual period of the Schism -- the forty years 1378-1418 -- reveals itself however, as a time of revival; twenty-three of the thirty-five "saints" of the previous generation have died by 1378, but they are replaced by no fewer than thirty-five new "saints"; more new "saints, " in fact, in forty years than in the previous seventy.

If we examine the list of those new " saints " whose appearance relieves the sombre history of the disastrous fourteenth century so far as we have traced it -- they are twenty-nine in all -- we notice among them three bishops (one a Benedictine, [ ] two Carmelite friars [ ] ); there are two others from the older orders, namely the canon regular, John Ruysbroeck and a second Benedictine; [ ] and there are eleven more friars [ ] and the founder of a new order, the Jesuati. There are, also, six nuns (who came, all of them, from the new orders), one layman and five laywomen. The high direction of ecclesiastical affairs is, evidently, no longer a nursing ground for saints, nor do saints any longer appear among the princes of Christian thought. The most striking changes, by comparison with the figures for the thirteenth and twelfth centuries, are the greatly lowered number of saints among the bishops, [ ] and the reduction to vanishing point of the saints from the old monastic orders, from the Benedictines and the Cistercians especially.

It is the spirituality of the new orders of friars that gives to the sanctity of this period its special characteristics; and the special character of the vocation of the friars, and the new way of religious life which they have constructed in order to carry out their special work, are far-reaching indeed in their effect upon the whole interior life of the Church. The friar is, almost by definition, a religious who lives in a town. The life of the vows, with its foundation of the divine office chorally celebrated, its discipline of fasts, vigils, enclosure and other austerities, was now brought before the daily notice of every Catholic. And as with the friars -- whose foundations ran easily into tens of thousands by the beginning of the fourteenth century -- so was it with the new orders of women associated with the friars from the very beginning; their convents, too, were in the towns. And around these numerous new town churches -- Dominican, Franciscan, Augustinian, Carmelite and Servite churches -- whose very raison d'etre was the sermon, churches of a new architectural type, great preaching -- halls in fact, [ ] there speedily grew up the great militia of the orders of penance: associations of layfolk who really formed part of the new religious order, who continued to live their ordinary life in the world, but in the spirit of the order, according to a definite rule and under the guidance of the order's priests. St. Dominic's new invention of the priest-religious who was an active missionary, and for whom the monastic life was but the designed means to this apostolic end, transformed the whole business of the management r of a Christian life; and in nothing did this show so powerfully as in the sudden appearance of a whole new literature treating | of this matter, a literature in which, for the first time, the most I learned of theologians and the most mystical of contemplatives said their say in the vulgar tongue. The life of devotion -- la vie devote -- now became the main business of thousands and thousands of lay men and women also, and the immediate consequence was a great multiplication of pious books. The Bible especially -- in translations -- was the popular devout reading, book of this multitude, such classics too as St. Augustine's City of God, St. Bernard's sermons, St. Gregory's collection of the marvellous lives of the saints of old, and the meditations on the ' Life of Our Lord still -- and for centuries yet to come -- ascribed to St. Bonaventure, meditations in which the imaginative art of the writer developed, above all else, the terrible reality of the human agony of the divine Redeemer. Such a book -- well in the new, Franciscan tradition and the kindred works of the Dominican Ludolf of Saxony, [ ] gave new life (and a new direction) to the popular devotion to the sacred Humanity; and these books were among the main sources of those many forms of prayer to Our Lord in His passion which are the best-known feature of the last two centuries of medieval piety. In the statues and the painted windows and the pictures of the time there is, from now on, no subject more frequent, nor any more lovingly wrought. The same influence is to be seen in the countless brotherhoods spontaneously formed to foster and to practise these devotions, and it received a powerful aid in the Book of Revelations written by St. Bridget of Sweden about the detail of the sacred passion, and in the sermons and writings of the German Dominican, B. Henry Suso.

Of new religious orders there is but one of any importance, that founded by St. Bridget. This was an order for men and women, consecrated to devotion to the passion of Our Lord. The nuns were strictly enclosed, but the monks were preachers, itinerant missionaries. The monasteries were subject to the bishop of the diocese where they were founded, and, in honour of the Blessed Virgin, they were ruled by an abbess. The first foundation was at Vadstena, in Sweden, in 1371. The order grew slowly. By 1515 there were twenty-seven houses, thirteen of them in Scandinavia. [ ] But everywhere the spirit of Christian charity is seen active in foundations, now, of hospitals and refuges of various kinds, in the organisation of companies of nursing sisters and brothers, a movement that is summed up in the great figure of St. Roch, the patron of the poor and needy sick, whose cult, from the day of his death in 1350, has never ceased.

The outstanding feature of all this new birth of the spirit is the avidity for news about the life with God -- unmistakable everywhere, in all ranks of society -- and the literature which this need created. From this literature we may gather some notion of the perfect life as it was presented to the Catholics of these last generations before the catastrophe of the Schism unchained the forces of anarchy; and we may also read there signs of future development and, alas, of future disintegration. For the life of devotion is not a thing antithetical to the life of Christian thought, but, rather, closely dependent on it. Mysticism and scholasticism are not alternative ways of arriving at the one goal; [ ] and in some of the new spiritual exercises now devised, and proposed to Christians as the way to union with God, we meet the last, and the most ruinous consequence, so far, of the failure of the Catholics of this century to rally to the thought of St. Thomas Aquinas.

To-day the word "mystic" is used for so many purposes that it has almost ceased to have any recognisably definite meaning beyond that of emotional sensitiveness to the non-material. But for our purpose the mystic is the man whose main interest and care in life is to unite himself in mind and will with God. It is for men and women of this kind that the monastic life was devised, as providing the ideal setting for those activities to which they had chosen to devote themselves. And now, in the fourteenth century, the kind of people we thus call mystics had, largely through the activity of the various orders of friars, come to be a very notable element of the public life of the Church. The new literature of mysticism had developed in order to provide this new mystical public with matter for its prayerful meditation, and with advice about the pitfalls of this high adventure; but it also studied the happenings of the mystical life so as to offer the mystic some means of checking his course, and from this it was an obvious next step to discuss the nature of mysticism, and especially the nature of the mystic's union with God, and the role and importance of the unusual happenings with which the lives of the mystics were, from time to time, studded. The mystics whose needs called forth this new literature were, as has been said, very largely the spiritual children of those new religious orders, and it was these orders which also had created the new scientific theology we call scholastic. That these corps of professional theologians should be attracted to the study of mysticism for its own sake, as one of the normal features of Christian life, was inevitable. Soon, the discussions about the nature of the mystical fact became a commonplace in theological literature. The solutions -- like the advice offered to mystics and the practical recipes -- varied as the theological colour of the different orders varied. There were to be controversies between the different schools about mystical questions, as there were controversies about so many other questions.

There are then, from this time, two kinds of mystical writing, that written for the use and help of the mystics themselves, and that written to analyse and explain what mysticism is and how it all comes about. Among the writers of both types of book not only theologians are to be found, but others too, with minds not trained perhaps to orderly thought, or the saving niceties of technical correctness, but with a tale to tell of experiences that have transformed their lives, and driven by an apostolic charity to convey the glad news to whoever will hear it.

Who these first pioneers of popular mystical literature were, what story they had to tell, the different points of view from which they told it, the variety of explanations they offered, and the sources which -- often enough unconsciously -- influenced their mystical outlook, may be read in the well-known book of M. Pourrat, who has collected a list of some sixty or more writers active between the time of St. Thomas and Luther's revolt. [ ] What a general history, it would seem, needs to signalise as especially important in all this development, is the emergence of a really new school, after nearly a century and a half of the influence of the Friars; a school whose influence continued and developed until the very end of the period this volume studies. This is the school which produced the so-called Devotio Moderna and, as cautiously as may be, [ ] something needs to be said of the way in which some of its leading adepts regarded, not so much the theologians of their time, as the role of the theologian and the place of theology in the life of the spirit. And something must be said, too, of the way in which, ever since Ockham, theologians had been moving still further away from St. Thomas's conception that there is necessarily a harmony between faith and reason. For these two contemporary developments have the effect, ultimately, of converging forces.

The simplest way in which to understand what is meant by the Devotio Moderna is to take up again, and devoutly read, the Imitation of Christ: for this is the classic production of the school. What is there modern about it? how is it new? and who were the men that made up the school whence came the Imitation and many other works, now perhaps forgotten, of like character?

The Devotio Moderna was a product of the country we to-day call Holland, and the pioneer in the movement was a native of Deventer, Gerard Groote (1340-1384). He was a man of considerable education, bred in the schools of his native town, of Aachen and in the universities of Cologne and Paris. He never seems to have proceeded beyond his mastership in arts, nor was he a priest; and for some years he led an ordinary worldly kind of life until, when he was about thirty-five, he was converted through his friendship with the greatest of all the Flemish mystics, B. Jan Ruysbroeck.

In the last few years of his life Gerard, [ ] who died an early death in 1384, gathered round him, in his native town, a group of like-minded associates and together they formed the " Brotherhood of the Common Life" (1381). The associates were not bound by any vows, but they met for regular exercises of prayer, and they gave their lives to copying pious books -- forming the equivalent, in that age, of a religious press association. [ ] A later development was the foundation and direction of schools for poor boys; the most famous of these, that at Zwolle, came to number 1,200 scholars. In their youth Thomas a Kempis, Nicholas of Cusa, Erasmus, and Luther too, came under the influence of the brothers in their schools. From Deventer some of the brethren passed to make a new foundation at Windesheim, but this group definitely went over to the religious life in the technical sense of the word, becoming canons-regular of the Augustinian type. The congregation of Windesheim flourished, and next eighty years (1384-1464) it came to number eighty-two priories. At Windesheim, and in the other priories, the spirit of Gerard Groote inspired all, and the priories also continued to be centres for the spread of spiritual books. The best known of all these Windesheim canons is the German, Thomas of Kempen, [ ] the most likely candidate for the signal honour of being the author of the Imitation; and known to his contemporaries as a calligrapher of unusual skill.

It was not in the minds of the pioneers of this movement that the brethren should themselves be authors. But gradually books began to grow out of the little addresses with which, within the seclusion of these Dutch cloisters, they exhorted one another to perseverance in virtue and prayer and recollection, and in fidelity to the life of withdrawal from the world and its occasions of sin. And all these books -- collections of sayings, or sermons, or set treatises on special topics -- bear an extremely close resemblance to each other. There is little sign anywhere of the diversity of personalities among the authors. But what is everywhere evident -- and immediately evident -- to the reader is that the author is a man in whose life the loving communion with God is scarcely ever interrupted. And the reader can always understand what is written directly he reads. For the treatment of the great theme is concrete, and practical. With a most finished, albeit unconscious, artistry the writers set out their instructions in maxims, simply stated, with all the finality of proverbs or axioms; [ ] and always, the guidance offered is so perfectly related to what every man knows the better side of himself craves for, that as he reads, it seems rather as though he were actually listening to his own better self. From time to time the flow of the maxims in which the reader sees the better things, and once again professes them, is broken by touching colloquies between the soul and Christ Our Lord.

Once these books composed by the new religious began to appear, they made headway rapidly -- there was, of course, at work here, besides the quality of what was offered, the new immense advantage that to propagate such literature was the congregation's main activity. The earliest manuscript of the complete Imitation that has survived is of 1427; in another forty years the book was known, and used, and loved, all over Europe.

Criticism is always an ungracious task, and never more so, surely, than when the critic is set to examine coldly the elements of a work inspired by the love of God, and stamped in every line with generous dedication of self to God's service. The Imitation of Christ, for example, is a work that all humanity has agreed to call golden. This makes the historian's task hard, but nonetheless necessary. For this Devotio Moderna was not all-sufficient; and once it had passed beyond the cloisters where it was born, and had begun to flourish in a different setting, its insufficiency might, and did indeed, tell increasingly.

The most notable insufficiency was that almost nowhere, in the literature of this school, was piety related to doctrine, [ ] which is as much as to say that about much of it there is nothing specifically, necessarily, Catholic. It is a piety which, taken by itself, is, in the modern phrase, very largely undenominational; and, as everyone knows, the chef d'oevre of the school [ ] has for centuries been used as extensively by those outside the Church as by those within. The absence of any care to relate piety to those revealed doctrines which the Church was divinely founded to set forth, is the more serious because it was deliberate. Not, of course, that these writers were indifferent to Catholic doctrine or hostile to it. They were, all of them, excellent Catholics, as whole in faith as in charity or in zeal; they would presuppose a dogmatic foundation, known and accepted. But they were Catholics in violent reaction against the fashionable spirituality of their time -- or rather, against its excesses -- and this had been a learned spirituality, very much occupied with theories about the mystical life, concerned to elaborate systems based on its theories, and interested, in some cases perhaps over-interested, in theological subtleties.

The great figure of this earlier movement had been the German Dominican Eckhart; and the Dominican priories and the convents of Dominican nuns in the Rhine provinces were the centres where it chiefly flourished. John Tauler and Blessed Henry Suso, also Dominicans, masterly theologians and great mystics, preachers and writers too, were the leading figures in the world of mysticism during the generation in which Gerard Groote grew up. Eckhart -- who had taught theology at Paris during the years when Scotus taught there, and who was involved in the controversies around the Franciscan's teaching -- was indeed a theologian of the very first class. [ ] But over the end of his long and active life there lies the shadow of the condemnation of many of his doctrines -- after his death -- as heretical. [ ] About the exact meaning of that condemnation scholars are now divided. The texts of Eckhart's work, as they have been known for the last three centuries, are far from trustworthy. It is only in the last few years, indeed, that any critical work has been done on his Latin writings. But whether Eckhart, the real Eckhart, was orthodox or not -- the gravest charge is that he was, in fact, a pantheist -- he is in these texts extremely obscure. This is by no means true of Tauler and Suso. Tauler was a master of spiritual direction, as learned in the workings of the human personality as in the ways of the Spirit, who had the rare gift of bringing home to the most workaday congregation the real importance of ideas. Henry Suso, no less learned in theology, and no less faithful, like a true Dominican, to the duty of associating piety with what can only be apprehended by the intelligence, namely truth divinely revealed, was a more passionate soul. In burning words he preached to all comers devotion to the divine intelligence, to the eternal wisdom of God. It was around this love for the second Person of the Blessed Trinity that all spiritual life turned for Suso; and to the propagation of this devotion he brought -- what obviously the task requires -- deep and sure theological learning. Above all others his master is St. Thomas Aquinas, whose calmly-argued ideas break into flame once they make contact with Suso's ardent mind.

The effect of Christian doctrine preached in this fashion had been to produce a host of mystics of rare quality in the Rhineland, and especially among the nuns of the order from which these preachers chiefly came. The movement was not, however, confined to friars and nuns; for it was one of the special characteristics of this Dominican school to teach that the life of the mystic is open to every Christian; that it is not, in kind, a new life which is the special privilege of contemplative monks or nuns, but a simple extension of, and an intensification of, that Christian life inaugurated in every soul by baptism. Hence the care of these German Dominicans, as of Ruysbroeck, to preach -- and also to write -- in their native tongues; and hence also, what has often caused surprise, their preaching about these high themes to the ordinary congregations who filled their churches.

It is not hard to understand that, once out of the hands of men really masters of their task, really theologians as well as holy men, such an apostolate could easily go astray. The subtle explanations of the soul's mystical union with God could, and did, give rise to idle and mischievous debates among the less learned and the half-learned; the delicate business of the practical relation of the workaday moral virtues to the high theological virtues could be neglected, and men and women, who visibly reeked of pride, insubordination, injustice and intemperance of every sort, could ignore their sins while they busied themselves with the higher prayer. And, of course, the movement will not have been spared its host of camp followers, many times larger than the army of disciples -- infinitely noisier and much more in evidence -- whose main occupation was to exchange gossip masked in the phrases of high theological learning, to turn these into party slogans, and, in the devil's eternal way, accomplish to perfection all the complicated manoeuvres of the religious life while their hearts were wholly unconverted, their wills obstinately unrepentant.

The reaction of the brethren of Deventer and Windesheim against what has been called [ ] the speculative school of spiritual teaching, was, no doubt, very largely a reaction against the dangerous humbug into which this particular way of the interior life had tended to degenerate. But it was a reaction that went much further than a protest against abuses. For example, it was not merely the abuse of learning that was now decried in many sayings of the Devotio Moderna, but the idea that learning had any necessary part to play in the interior life: "Henceforward," wrote Gerard de Groote in his rule of life, [ ] "no more benefices, no more learned titles, no more public disputations. . . . The learning of learning is to know that one knows nothing. . . the one research that matters is not to be sought out oneself." " Do not spend thy time," he also said, [ ] " in the study of geometry, arithmetic, rhetoric, dialectic, grammar, songs, poetry, legal matters or astrology; for all these things are reproved by Seneca, and a good man should withdraw his mind's eye therefrom and despise them; how much more, therefore, should they be eschewed by a spiritually-minded man and a Christian. . . the purpose of a degree is either gain or preferment, or vain glorification and worldly honour, which latter things if they lead not to the former are simply useless, empty and most foolish, being contrary to godliness and all freedom and purity." Only the carnal-minded could, he thought, be happy in a university.

Nearly a hundred years later than Gerard Groote the same spirit can be seen in one of the greatest teachers associated with the movement, [ ] John Wessel Gansfort (1420-1489), a friend of Thomas a Kempis and a pioneer in the business of systematic meditation. [ ] "There is a strong and weighty argument against universities to be drawn from the fact that Paul secured but little fruit at Athens, accomplishing more in the neighbouring city of Corinth and in Thessaly, which was then almost barbarous, than in the Attic city, at that time the fountain of Greek philosophy. It goes to show that liberal studies are not very pleasing to God." [ ]

269

There is a sense in which the Imitation, too, can be called "a late medieval protest against the vanity of all philosophy," [ ] and indeed the best known of such, and the most influential. All the world knows the passages in the opening pages of the Imitation, "What doth it profit thee to discuss the deep mystery of the Trinity, if thou art from thy lack of humility displeasing to the Trinity. . . . I would rather choose to feel compunction than to know its definition. . . . Vanity of vanities, all is vanity save to love God and serve Him only. . . . Have no wish to know the depths of things, but rather to acknowledge thy own lack of knowledge. . . ." That goodness matters more than learning, that it is the mistake of mistakes " to prefer intellectual excellence to moral" [ ] no one will ever contest; nor that the learned may need, even frequently, to be reminded of this. But of all forms of goodness truth is the most fundamental, and yet, while learning is the pursuit of truth, it is hardly deniable that the author of the Imitation -- and others of this school with him -- do continually suggest, at least, an opposition between advance in virtue and devotion to learning, even to sacred learning; and certainly the tone of such admonitions is far removed from the teaching of St. Thomas that learning -- even the study of letters -- is a most suitable ascetic discipline for religious. [ ] With these authors, however, learning, it is suggested, is for most men the highroad to pride and vanity -- "the greater part in knowledge than in virtuous living" -- and he who gives himself to the pursuit of holiness is in better case if he is not handicapped by any desire to know. "Quieten thy too great desire for learning, for in learning there is discovered great distraction and much deception." As for the learned generally: "those who are learned gladly choose to be regarded, and to be hailed as wise men. . . . Would that their life were in accordance with their learning, then would they have read and studied well." Again: "Happy is the man whom Truth instructs through itself, not through passing images and words, but as itself exists. . . . And wherefore should we be anxious about genera and species? He to whom the Eternal Word speaks, is set free from the multitude of opinions." Learning -- this is definitely said -- is not, in itself, blameworthy, that is to say "simple notions about things": it is indeed good, and part of God's scheme of things, but a good conscience and virtuous living is always to be preferred to it.

The facts are, however, that to all but a very select few, knowledge, even of truths about supernatural reality, only comes through the ordinary natural channels -- faith is by hearing. It is the natural human intelligence [ ] that must lay hold of the truths of faith and make the judgment that these are things it must believe. [ ] It is no part of Christian perfection to neglect the ordinary means of making contact with these truths -- namely the teaching of those already learned in them -- and to trust for a knowledge of them to the possibility of the extraordinary favour of a special personal revelation. And although it is most certainly true that theological learning is by no means a prerequisite for sanctity, such learning remains, nevertheless, a necessary instrument for those whose lot it is to journey towards sanctity by guiding others thither. Hence when good men begin to suggest that the world of piety can manage very well -- if not, indeed, very much better -- without the presence of theologians acting upon it, there is surely something wrong; and when priests write books about holy living which suggest that the theologians are more likely to go to the bad through learned vanity than to save their souls through the deeper knowledge of divine truth that is theirs, there is something very wrong indeed. Once more we are brought up against the all-important role of theological learning as the salt that keeps Christian life healthy. And what theology is to piety, metaphysical truth is to theology; for it is the natural condition, the sine qua non of healthy intellectual certitude in the mind of the theologian. [ ] Once the direction of so delicate a thing as the Devotio Moderna passes into the hands of those unlearned in theology, all manner of deviation is possible. It can become a cult of what is merely naturally good, a thing no worse -- but no more spiritual -- than, say, the cult of kindness, courtesy, tidiness and the like. And what the master, unwittingly, is soon really teaching is himself; he is the hero his disciples are worshipping; there are, in the end, as many Christianities as there are masters, and chaos begins its reign.

Once it ceases to be recognised that there must exist an objective rule by which to judge the whole business -- theory and practice, maxims, counsels, exhortations, ideals, and criticism of other ways -- of the inner life and the business of the director with the directed, and that this objective rule is the science of the theologian, substitute rules will be devised to fill the absent place, rules which, there is every chance, will be no more than the rationalisation of a man's chosen and preferred activities. Someone, somewhere, must be interested in compunction's definition, or it will soon cease to be understood that there can be, and is, a certainty about what compunction is and what it is not; and if that certainty goes, very strange things indeed will begin to wander about, claiming the name of compunction in the lost land that once was Christendom. [ ]

Let us turn from the defects, now so easy to be seen, in the Devotio Moderna, recalling only -- what will occupy us more hereafter -- how it is into one of the priories of the Windesheim congregation that, some eighty years ahead of the date our survey has reached, a pupil of the Brothers of the Common Life, and now an unhappy lad of eighteen, will be thrust to become, in spite of himself, a canon-regular, Erasmus Or Rotter (lam: in his career we shall surely see the shortcomings of the system hampering the greatest Catholic scholar of his generation, at a time when Catholicism is fighting for its very life. Let us leave the thought that Erasmus is the greatest witness to what the Devotio Moderna lacked, and consider now another group of pious men who, in this same late fourteenth century, are diligently sapping the foundations of men's intellectual certitude about the saving faith -- though of this they are utterly unconscious. These are the new theologians, products of the Via moderna, and they are, professedly, defending the faith. But their faith has gone awry; in this fact -- that they are wrongheaded and are fashionable -- as in the deficiencies of the spirituality of the pious Hollanders, we can read signs that are ominous. At the moment when certain mystics were beginning to hint that those who wished to advance in virtue had best leave theological problems alone, since ability to discuss them would lead inevitably to pride and vainglory, certain theologians were beginning to say that these same problems were insoluble, since no one could know anything at all with certainty, and that the only safe thing, for a Christian, was to cease to think about divine truths and to content himself with a faithful acceptance of them and a life of prayer. The influence of the mysticism that despaired of the theologian's salvation, was to be reinforced by that of theologians who now despaired of theology, and this because they had come to despair of reason itself.

There is, for instance, the revealing story of Nicholas of Autrecourt, a Parisian theologian, who has been called the Hume of the fourteenth century, [ ] in whose work Ockham's principles reach their last extreme consequences. Nicholas used the new dialectic to examine Aristotle, and he finds thereby that Aristotle did not really know -- that is to say possess certitude about -- any one of the basic metaphysical truths on which his thought is built: for these truths -- if truths, and they may be truths -- are not things that can be known. We do not know, and it can't be known, that there are such things as substances, causes, ends, and the like. There is, says Nicholas, no "evidence" for their existence. "Evidence" is one of his favourite terms; "probable" is another, and this word "probable" sums up increasingly the mentality of the fourteenth-century thinkers. No philosophical truth is any longer certain: probability is all that human reason can attain. For example, Nicholas asks whether matter is eternal, and he answers that we cannot say with certainty that it is; but that it is eternal is more likely than not; it is probable. It is of course now, at this moment, that this is probable; what it will be, hath not yet appeared, and Nicholas, a devout ecclesiastic, conscious that thought (if this is all that thought really is) cannot offer itself as a way to truth, whether to Christians or to others, can only warn Christians of this and exhort them to stick more closely to the teachings of faith. He has, of course, if only by implication, suggested thereby to the Christian that reason and faith tend to contradict each other, that they can be in permanent opposition, [ ] after which it seems a poor way out, indeed, to advise the Christian to stick to the one rather than the other. For what is faith but an assent of the reason? and with what other reason can the Christian give his assent but with that which has already been described by Nicholas as necessarily incapable of certitude?

To study Aristotle is also, therefore, pure waste of time; and Nicholas says so, expressly. Then what of the great doctors whose minds fed so largely on him? St. Thomas, for example, and Duns Scotus. It is barely thirty years since Scotus died, and not yet twenty since John XXII canonised St. Thomas with the most resounding eulogy of his work; but for Nicholas (and the many whom he will influence) the mass of all this writing is but so much lumber. Advancing a stage from his great discovery, "scared," says Gilson, "by the conclusions to which his logic has brought him," this philosopher who is a good Catholic looks for a remedy, and finds it; and here his solo voice anticipates what a whole chorus of superficial simpletons [ ] will presently be bawling. What is needed, he tells us, are "spiritual men who will not waste their whole time in logical argument or the analysis of Aristotle's obscure propositions, but who will give to their people an understanding of God's law." [ ] It is the old final-wisdom-seeming sophistry of the "practical" minded that is still with us. And this first of such prophets is a man whose theories of knowledge "cut us off from the only ways by which we can come to God." [ ]

Nicholas of Autrecourt was a good man [ ] who proposed to make the world a safe place for Faith by showing the utter impossibility of thought. It was not long before this tragic aberration brought him to the notice of the authorities, and after Clement VI had condemned eighteen of his leading theses, [ ] he made a humble submission. [ ] Nicholas may seem an obscure personage, but the most astonishing part of the story is this, that forty years later a personage who was by no means obscure, a chancellor of the university of Paris, and one of the two brightest ornaments of the world of Christian thought in that day, was explaining that the real reason for the condemnation of 1346 was jealousy, and offering as proof of this the fact that these theses were now publicly taught in the universities. Such is Peter d'Ailly's superficial comment on this grave affair. [ ] The other glory of Paris, and of France and of Christendom, in this generation was d'Ailly's pupil and successor as chancellor, Jean Gerson, one of the holiest men of his time (1363-1429). He too was an Ockhamist, and he too sought in the cult of the interior life an escape from these difficult and urgent intellectual anxieties. " Lorsque la foi desespere de la raison, c'est toujours vers l'intuition mystique et la vie interieure qu'elle se retourne pour s'y chercher un plus solide fondement." [ ]

The Christian mind, then, unable to think itself out of the impasse to which "thought" brought it, and mortally uneasy at the now unresolved fundamental contradiction that the teachings of Faith and the findings of reason may be incompatible, is bidden for its salvation resolutely to ignore the contradiction, to stifle reason, and to seek God in the interior life; again, to seek Him with what? With a mind accepting on Faith what it knows may be impossible? The eternal lesson recurs, that we cannot manage our religious affairs without true philosophy, however elemental; that true religion does not survive healthily unless philosophy flourishes. For without philosophy, or with a philosophy that is false, the educated mind [ ] turns to scepticism -- theoretical or practical; and assents to religious truth made by a mind that is sceptical about natural truth, produce in the end superstition: and from the educated mind the poison seeps down, until in time it corrupts the faith of the whole community. [ ]

For the popular and fashionable philosophers and theologians Aristotle was now, at the end of the fourteenth century, finished; and the famous Thomistic alliance of thought and faith at an end. A further blow was dealt to the prestige of that older school -- a prestige bound up inevitably with the prestige of Aristotle -- by the appearance in these same years of the first non-Aristotelian physicists, of the critical work of Jean Marbres [ ] and, especially, of Nicholas of Oresme, [ ] Bishop of Lisieux. It was theological speculation that set these clerics to their radical reconstruction of Aristotle the physicist, Oresme writing, perhaps all the more damagingly, in his native French -- yet another of the many signs that a new age is at hand. From the Bishop of Lisieux' work came ultimately three great discoveries linked to three better known names, Copernicus' hypothesis of the movement of the earth, Galileo's theory of the law of falling bodies, and Descartes' invention of analytical geometry. Here are far-off medieval origins of important elements in our modern scientific knowledge; in the circumstances in which they appeared they served to give the coup de grace to Aristotle as a force to be reckoned with in the university world. And that world, in the fourteenth century, was in process of a remarkable extension. Nine new universities were founded in northern Europe between the years 1348 and 1426, [ ] and another nine [ ] between 1456 and 1506. In the better part of these it was the Via moderna that dominated the philosophical outlook.

And now it is that there befalls the Church one of the most fearful calamities of all its long history, the so-called Great Schism of the West -- a forty years wandering in a wilderness when no one knew with certainty who was the head of the Church, a forty years in which the unity of belief was indeed marvellously preserved, but in which administrative chaos reigned and in which there sprang up an abundance of new anarchical theories about the nature of the papacy and its role. That catastrophe came at the end of a century when the whole strength of the politicians had been exerted to compel the Church to retire from all concern with temporal affairs; in an age when thinkers would have had it retire from the field of thought, and mystics would divorce its piety from the pursuit of truth; the trader, too, will be pleased if religion will now abandon its claim to regulate the morality of exchanges, and Marsiglio's ideal is only slumbering that will satisfy all of these by making religion a matter of rites alone and of activities within a man's own soul. [ ]

## 4. THE SCHISM OF THE WEST, 1378-1409
### i. The Two Conclaves of 1378.

"This is milk and honey compared with what is to come, " St. Catherine had said, [ ] when the news reached her, in 1376, of the general rebellion of the Papal State against Gregory XI. Already the saint foresaw the Schism, the forty years during which two -- and even three -- "popes" simultaneously claimed the allegiance of Catholicism, which thereupon split -- geographically -- into several "obediences. "

Gregory XI died on March 27, 1378. Twelve days later the cardinals elected in his place Bartholomew Prignani, Archbishop of Bari -- Urban VI. Four months went by and then, on August 2, these same cardinals publicly declared that this election of Urban VI was no election; and on September 20 they proceeded to fill the alleged vacancy by electing as pope the cardinal Robert of Geneva -- Clement VII. Urban VI reigned until 1389; he was followed by Boniface IX (1389-1404), Innocent VII (1404-1406) and Gregory XII (1406-1415). Clement VII, meanwhile, reigned until 1394; and Benedict XIII, elected to succeed him, lasted for twenty-eight years more. Of these two lines, which were the real popes? To decide this we should first have to decide a question of historical fact; was Bartholomew Prignani, on April 8, 1378, really elected pope? or did the election take place in such a manner that it cannot be held a true election?

It is all-important, if the history of the Church in the next forty years is to be understood at all, to realise not only the fact of the ensuing division in Christendom, but the sincerity of the doubts and hesitations on both sides, and also the apparent practical impossibility -- especially once the generation passed away of those who, by their double election, had made the division -- of determining by any investigation of facts where the truth of the matter lay, the truth, that is to say, about the election of Urban VI. [ ]

There exists an immense mass of information about that election from contemporaries, many of whom were eye-witnesses and participants in the great event. But the greater part of this evidence was set down after the second election, that is, after the dispute had begun. Party spirit is already evidently active, and in these accounts flat contradiction about simple matters of fact is frequent. Nevertheless, despite the unsatisfactory nature of much of the material, it is possible to reconstruct with certainty [ ] the main events of the forty hours of crisis that began with the entry into the Vatican, for the conclave, of the sixteen cardinals [ ] then in Rome, on Wednesday, April 7, at about five in the afternoon.

From the moment when Rome learnt of Gregory XI's death, one thought alone, seemingly, possessed the whole city; at all costs the cardinals must be brought to elect a pope who would not return to Avignon, a pope, therefore, who was Italian and not French. All through the next eleven days the excitement grew, and very soon Rome was wholly in the hands of those who could rouse and manoeuvre the mob of the city. The nobles were driven out; guards were set at the gates to prevent any electors from escaping while the see remained vacant; the shipping in the Tiber was stripped of sails and rudders. Thousands of peasants and brigands were brought in from the surrounding countryside, and armed bands paraded the streets, escorting the cardinals wherever they went, advising them of the best choice they could make, Romano lo volemo, o almanco Italiano. . And when the day at last arrived for the conclave to begin the cardinals had to make their way to the Vatican through a crowd as numerous as the very population of the city. [ ]

The guardians of the conclave had been careless in their preparations, and they showed themselves weak and ineffective once the cardinals had arrived. Some of the mob, armed, to the number of seventy, made their way in with the cardinals, impressing upon them to the last, with coarse familiarity, the importance of making a right choice. When these were got rid of, there arrived the heads of the thirteen regions into which Rome at that time was divided (the Caporioni), with their escorts, demanding audience. They too were admitted, and once more the cardinals had to hear what, throughout the night, the mob continued to shout and chant, Romano lo volemo and the rest. The cardinals managed to be rid of the Caporioni without any definite answer, and after pillaging what they could they too left.

The night was noisy. The mob had settled down to a kind of kermess, its revelling helped on by the feat of those who had broken into the wine cellars of the palace. Just before dawn the cardinals were summoned to the first of two masses they were to hear, and while the second was in progress the mob wakened up to fresh activity. Presently the tocsin was heard to ring, and the bells of St. Peter's to answer it. While the senior cardinal was formally opening the proceedings the governor of the conclave sent in an urgent message. " Haste, for God's sake; elect an Italian or a Roman, or you will be massacred." Stones were indeed beginning to come through the windows, and axes to be plied against the doors.

Excitement flared high within the chapel where the cardinals, still isolated, were gathered. After half an hour they agreed to tell the mob that they would elect an Italian, and this was announced by the junior among them, James Orsini. On his return to the chapel this cardinal now suggested a mock election, of some Friar Minor who could be persuaded to play the part, be dressed in papal robes and presented to the mob -- what time the cardinals got away, to hold a real election elsewhere, later. But to this none would agree. And now it was that, within the conclave, the name of Bartholomew Prignani was first mentioned, [ ] by the Aragonese cardinal Pedro de Luna. A rapid consultation among the little group showed that two-thirds of them would vote accept him. The voting then began, by word of mouth, the Cardinal of Limoges casting the first vote for the future Urban VI. Three alone, of the sixteen, demurred; of whom, two, in the end, came to agree with the rest. Orsini alone held out to the last, declaring that in his opinion there was not sufficient freedom for the election to be valid.

Thus was Urban VI elected, towards nine in the morning of Friday, April 8, 1378. But not only was the elect not a cardinal: he was not, at this moment, within the palace, and between him and the news of his destiny was a city at the mercy of an armed and hostile mob. Until the archbishop accepted the election it could not be announced; and the first hint to the mob outside that the election had been made was the command from the cardinals to half a dozen Italian prelates -- of whom Prignani was one -- to come immediately to the Vatican.

It was, however, some hours before they came, and meanwhile the mob grew ever more violent and began to find its way into the palace. The six Italians arrived while the cardinals were at their midday meal. They, too, were given a meal by the guardians of the conclave, [ ] who joked with them about the probability that one of the six had been elected, and made mock petitions for favours; and then, before Prignani could be summoned to hear of his destiny, the strangest scene of all took place.

Fear had now really invaded the minds of some of the electors -- fear that because Prignani was not a Roman the savages outside would resent the choice, and put the palace to the sack. When, after their meal, the cardinals met in the chapel, someone proposed that, since the mob now seemed less active, they should take advantage of the lull and re-elect Prignani. But "We all agree to him, don't we?" said a cardinal, and all present assented (thirteen of the sixteen who had taken part in the morning election). But by now the mob was at the end of its patience. It was the afternoon of Friday, almost twenty-four hours since the election had begun. This time nothing could halt the Romans, and by all manner of ways they poured into the palace and into the conclave itself, whose terrified guardians surrendered the keys. Some of the cardinals, the better placed, fled; others were arrested as they tried to leave. And to appease the mob -- supposedly enraged because a Roman had not been chosen -- other cardinals went through the farce of dressing up in papal robes the solitary Roman in the Sacred College, the aged Cardinal Tebaldeschi, hoisting him, despite his threats and curses, on to the altar and intoning the Te Deum. This exhibition lasted for some hours, and it was, seemingly, from the old man's protestations against this mockery -- "I am not the pope; it is the Archbishop of Bari " -- that Prignani, somewhere in the palace, and by this time hiding from a mob to whom all that savoured of prelacy was spoil, learnt that he had been elected.

The palace was, indeed, thoroughly pillaged, and at last the mob went off elsewhere. Night fell, and in the Vatican there remained two only of the cardinals, and the man whom they had all, twice, agreed upon as the pope, but found no time to notify of the fact.

Gradually, on the next day, Friday, April 9, the cardinals began to come in from their hiding-places in the city. It took the best part of the day to persuade the six who had gone to St. Angelo that they could safely emerge. By the evening there were twelve cardinals in the Vatican. They first met, themselves alone, in the chapel of the election, and immediately sent for the Archbishop of Bari. They announced to him his election. Me accepted it; and chose the name of Urban VI. Whereupon he was robed in the papal mantle, enthroned, and homage was done to him as pope by all, while the Te Deum was sung.

Two days later was Palm Sunday. Urban presided at the great liturgy of the day, and all the cardinals received their palm at his hands. They took their traditional places by his side at all the Holy Week ritual. On Easter Sunday he was crowned in St. Peter's (April 18) and took possession as pope of his cathedral church of St. John Lateran.

Urban VI at this moment was, to all appearances, as much the lawful pope in the eyes of the cardinals as ever his predecessor, Gregory XI, had been. How then did they come to abandon him, to denounce their own electoral act as invalid? and when did this movement begin? It is not easy fully to answer either of those questions.

What does seem certain and beyond all doubt is that from the very first day of his reign -- the Monday after his coronation -- Urban began to act so wildly, to show himself so extravagant in speech, that historians of all schools have seriously maintained that the unexpected promotion had disturbed the balance of his mind. He had evidently made up his mind that his first duty was to cleanse the augean stable of the curia, to banish clerical worldliness and impropriety, and to begin this good work by reforming the cardinals and the other major prelates. The first signs of the new policy given to the world were violent general denunciations of whoever appeared before the pope to transact ecclesiastical business. When, for example, all the bishops present in Rome came to pay their homage, Urban rounded on them for hirelings who had deserted their flocks. An official of the Treasury came in to make some payments of moneys due and was met by an imprecation from Holy Writ, "Keep thy money to thyself, to perish with thee." [ ] The cardinals were rated in consistory as a body, for their way of life, and singled out for individual reprobation; one was told he was a liar, another was a fool, others were bidden hold their tongues when they offered an opinion. When the Cardinal of Limoges appeared, the pope had to be held down or he would have done him violence, and the noise of the brawl when the Cardinal of Amiens came to pay his first homage, filled the palace. Urban boasted that he could now depose kings and emperors, and he told the cardinals that he would soon add so many Italians to their body that the French would cease to count for ever.

This extravagance of manner was the more disturbing because it was utterly at odds with the habits of a man who was by no means a stranger to any one of his electors. Urban VI was, at this time, a man close on sixty, and he had been one of the leading figures in the curia at Avignon for nearly twenty years. Urban V had, long ago, made him assistant to the vice-chancellor, perhaps the highest post that could be held by one who was not a cardinal; then, in 1364, the same pope had given him the see of Acerenza and when Gregory XI returned to Rome he had brought Bartholomew Prignani back with him to be, in all but name, his vice-chancellor. Urban VI, then, had been for the fourteen months preceding his election the chief personage of the curia after the pope himself; and among the cardinals he had enjoyed, very deservedly, the reputation of an extremely competent and serviceable official. He was learned, modest, devout; and, from his long life at Avignon, he was, so they thought, if not a Frenchman, as near to it as any mere foreigner could hope to be. This pope whom the cardinals now beheld, daily "breathing out threats and slaughter," was not the same man at all as the peaceable Archbishop of Bari. They were consternated; and so was all the curia with them. And whether Urban had indeed gone somewhat out of his mind, or whether this was merely the excessive noise of the explosion of a good man's disgust too long repressed, it seems certain that it is in these extravagances -- now the order of the day -- that the beginnings of the general breakaway are to be found. Had Urban shown ordinary tact and prudence there would never -- it seems certain -- have been the second conclave and election of 1378, whatever the doubts about the legality of his election that may have existed in the minds of some of his electors; or, at any rate, that second election would never have so impressed the world outside -- for its impressiveness, when it came, lay in the fact that it was the act of the whole college of cardinals.

The chief architect of the Schism, so Urban VI declared, [ ] was the one-time Bishop of Amiens, Cardinal Jean de la Grange. This cardinal had not taken part in the momentous conclave; diplomatic business kept him at Sarzana during Gregory XI's last illness, and long before he could reach Rome Urban had been elected. When he arrived -- already enraged that his colleagues had chosen an Italian -- he had a violent, unfriendly reception from the new pope, who publicly called him a traitor to the Holy See for his activities at Sarzana. This was somewhere about April 25, and from now on the palace of Jean de la Grange was a kind of headquarters where all whom the pope's methods antagonised could meet and plot. One of the cardinal's first associates was his colleague Robert of Geneva, the cardinal whom Gregory XI had made commander-in-chief, and who was responsible for the massacre of Cesena. Between them these two did much to encourage the French commander in St. Angelo not to hand over the fortress to Urban, and with it the papal treasure taken there, on the day of the election, by the camerlengo the Archbishop of Arles.

One by one the cardinals now began to leave Rome for Anagni, the reason first alleged being the increasing heat of the Roman summer. The first two left on May 6, and by June 15 all the French cardinals were there together. On June 24 Peter de Luna, the Aragonese, and the ablest man in the whole college, joined them. From Anagni they called to their aid the Free Company of

Gascons that had served Gregory XI. At Ponte Salario a body of Roman troops barred the way. There was a fight, but the Gascons won through, killing two hundred of the Romans (July 16, 1378). The cardinals, all the world could see it, were now a power beyond Urban's reach.

The pope was seriously alarmed. He had already sent three [ ] of the Italian cardinals to offer terms, promising better treatment in the future. But the only result of this was to enable the whole college to meet away from any influence the pope might exercise. At that meeting momentous decisions were taken; the cardinals agreed that the election made on April 8, was void, and means were discussed to rid the Church of the "usurper." For a time these three Italian cardinals, indeed, strove to be neutral, but in the end they made common cause with their brethren, who, on August 2, had issued a manifesto stating that the election made in April was void by reason of the pressure exerted upon the electors, that Urban, therefore, was not pope, and inviting him to recognise the fact and to cease to exercise the papal office. One week later than this, after a mass of the Holy Ghost and a sermon, an encyclical letter of the cardinals was read aloud in which they solemnly anathematised Bartholomew Prignani as an usurper. From Anagni the cardinals moved, on August 27, to a refuge safer still at Fondi, just beyond the papal frontier, in the kingdom of Naples. Here the sovereign -- Queen Giovanna -- supported them, and it was now that their Italian colleagues, abandoning their neutrality, joined them. The address of the cardinals to the Christian world had gone out already, and their embassy to the King of France -- Charles V -- had won him to their view that the election made in April was null and void. The king's reply reached them on September 18. Two days later they went into conclave, and at the first ballot they chose as pope Robert of Geneva. He called himself Clement VII. [ ] The three Italian cardinals, although present in the conclave, did not vote; but they acknowledged Clement and did him homage at his coronation on October 31.

For the next nine months the rival popes confronted each other in Italy, separated by a mere sixty miles and their own armed forces. Urban, on November 29, excommunicated Clement and some of his chief supporters; and Clement, in December, held his first consistory, creating six new cardinals and appointing legates to the various Christian princes.

Clement's cause, indeed, at the beginning of the new year 1379, seemed the more promising of the two. If England stood by Urban, and most of Germany too, France was decidedly for the Frenchman, and the Spanish kingdoms had at any rate refused to accept Urban, while in Italy Clement had Sicily on his side and also the Queen of Naples. But the situation changed greatly once Urban managed to hire the army of the best Italian captain of the day, Alberigo di Barbiano. On April 27, 1379, the French garrison that still held out in Castel S. Angelo at last surrendered to Urban, and three days later Alberigo routed and destroyed Clement's army at the battle or Marino. Clement now made for Naples, where the Queen received him with great pomp (May 10). But the populace rose in indignation that, in Naples, a Frenchman should be preferred to a pope who was a Neapolitan, and three days only after his arrival Clement had to flee to save his life. If he was not safe in Naples he could be safe nowhere in Italy; his first -- and, as it happened, his main -- attempt to drive Urban from Rome had failed indeed; nine months to the day after his election Clement sailed for Avignon (June 20, 1379).
ii. Discord in each 'Obedience,' 1379-1394.

These tremendous events had not gone by without comment from St. Catherine. At the moment of Urban VI's election the saint was at Florence -- whither Gregory XI had sent her -- and she was still there when, in July 1378, she wrote her first letter to Urban. It was a strong plea that his first care should be to reform the Church, and a reminder that for such a task "You have the greatest need of being founded in perfect Charity, with the pearl of justice. . . letting the pearl of justice glow forth from you united with mercy," and so to correct "those who are made ministers of the blood." [ ] The cardinals were, by this time, already leaving Rome, and the next letter of the saint to the pope which we possess is dated September 18 -- the very day, had St. Catherine known it, when the cardinals went into the conclave that was to make Robert of Geneva Clement VII.

When this news reached her the saint straightway wrote to Urban the warning that, more than ever, must he now be " robed in the strong garment of most ardent charity"; she also wrote to the Queen of Naples, and to the cardinals who had elected Clement. Already, when first the division between them and Urban was becoming known, St. Catherine had written to Pedro de Luna, then considered as Urban's main supporter and the principal cause of his election, reminding him above all "never to sever yourself from virtue and from your head. All other things -- external war and other tribulations -- would seem to us less than a straw or a shadow in comparison with this." How the saint wrote to the schismatic electors can be guessed, "men, not men but rather demons visible." It is not true, St. Catherine tells them, that it was through fear of death that they had elected Urban "and, if it had been, you were worthy of death for having elected the pope through fear of men and not with fear of God." Briefly, in a couple of sentences, the "case" of the cardinals is exposed and the real motives declared which had driven them to this new sin. "I know what moves you to denounce him. . . your self love which can brook no correction. For, before he began to bite you with words, and wished to draw the thorns out of the sweet garden, you confessed and announced to us, the little sheep, that Pope Urban VI was true pope." [ ] The saint was, likewise, under no illusion about Urban's own character as it was now showing itself. "Even if he were so cruel a father as to hurt us with reproaches and with every torment from one end of the world to the other, we are still bound not to forget nor persecute the truth." To the Count of Fondi, under whose protection Clement's election had taken place, the saint wrote of the cardinals, "Now they have contaminated the faith and denied the truth; they have raised such a schism in Holy Church that they are worthy of a thousand deaths." [ ]

At the beginning of November 1378, in obedience to Urban VI's command, the saint came to Rome -- with her usual accompanying escort of disciples -- and for the short remainder of her life gave herself ardently to the tasks assigned to her, to mobilise "the servants of God" in the cause of the true pope and to write ceaselessly, burning and passionate letters, to all whom it was thought she could influence. When St. Catherine passed from this world, April 30, 1380, the cause of the Roman pope lost the one saint it had enlisted, and the pope's own vices the only human check they were ever to know.

Once the great figure of St. Catherine disappears from the story of the Schism, it becomes, indeed, for many years no more, to all appearances, than the dreary, material strife of politicians, clerical and lay. Nowhere is the deterioration more marked, at this time, than in the character of the pope whom the saint had supported. Now that Clement had been forced away from Italy, it was an obvious move for Urban to strengthen his hold on the Holy See's vassal state of Naples, where alone in Italy his rival had found a sovereign to support him. So, in April 1380, Urban VI deposed the treacherous Queen Giovanna, and offered the crown to her kinsman, Charles, Duke of Durazzo. Charles -- flushed with recent victories in the service of his cousin, the Angevin -- descended King of Hungary, Lewis the Great -- came to Rome with his army in the August of that same year. Giovanna, anticipating the pope's move, had previously named as her heir a French prince, Louis, Duke of Anjou, a brother of Charles V of France (June 29, 1380). But her papal suzerain gave the crown to Charles of Durazzo (June 1, 1381), and, the following day, himself crowned the new king. [ ]

To provide supplies and pay for Charles III's army, Urban strained every nerve, selling church plate and jewels and levying new taxes upon what clergy acknowledged and obeyed him as pope. The new king marched south and met with little opposition. His French rival was detained in France by the death of his brother, Charles V, whose heir, Charles VI, was a child of twelve. The Urbanist king took Naples in August 1381, and captured Giovanna also, whom, ten months later, he seemingly had murdered (or executed). He was then, already well established when Louis of Anjou crossed into Italy at the head of one of the finest armies the century had seen. Louis also had been crowned King of Naples, by the pope at Avignon (May 30, 1382). The fate of the rival obediences was once more, it seemed, to be determined by the conflict of armed forces. But Louis, if a good soldier, was a poor general. He made no attempt to capture Rome, but marched on the kingdom that was his objective by the circuitous route of Ravenna and the Adriatic coast. When at last (October 8) he arrived before Naples disease had already begun to destroy his army. His rival had no need to do more than harass Louis in a war of skirmishes. Long before Louis' own death, two years later at Bari (September 20, 1384), he had ceased to be a danger; and then the broken remnant of his troops made their way back to France.

And also, long before this, Urban had fallen foul of his own chosen champion. History was repeating itself; the prince called in to protect the papacy by force of arms had no sooner conquered its foe than he openly gave all his energy to consolidate his own new position as king and, therefore, inevitably, to ward off any interference from his suzerain the pope. Indeed, by this time, the suzerain-vassal relation -- where the vassal was sovereign prince at least -- had become no more than a formality; and a suzerain so little experienced as to wish to make it a reality, risked, every time, the chance of serious war. Nor would the fact that this particular suzerain, being also the vassal's spiritual ruler, was able to use against him such spiritual weapons as excommunication and interdict, ever again be a serious consideration in the politics of a prince politically strong.

It was another grave weakness for the papacy that Urban VI did not go into this conflict with Charles III of Naples with an entire purity of intention. The pope had a nephew -- a worthless blackguard of a man -- for whom he was anxious to provide. Part of the price which Charles III had agreed to pay was to carve out a great principality for this nephew, to be held in fief of the King of Naples. In the summer of 1383 Urban, partly in order to press these claims of his nephew, set out with his court for Naples Six of his cardinals -- of the new cardinals, that is to say, created since the debacle of 1378 -- had, it seems, already opposed this scandalous piece of nepotism. Urban was careful to take his critics with him. When, in October, he arrived at Aversa, in Charles's dominions, the king greeted him with all conventional respect, but Urban found himself in fact a prisoner; and it was in a kind of extremely honourable captivity that, in great pomp, he entered Naples shortly afterwards.

The war with the French claimant presently absorbed Charles III's energy, and Urban was allowed to go to Nocera. Here new trouble arose, with Charles's wife Margaret -- now acting as regent -- when Urban began to interfere with the government of the kingdom, alleging his rights as suzerain. Soon the pope found himself besieged in the castle of Nocera (summer of 1384). But the career of Louis of Anjou was now nearing its end, and Charles was free to give all his attention to the troublesome pope. He found willing allies in the six cardinals. They conspired, apparently, to hand over Urban to the king, or to have him placed under restraint, as incapable of ruling. But a traitor betrayed them. The pope had them horribly tortured to extract confessions of guilt, a Genoese pirate known for his hatred of priests being called in to organise the enquiry. And outside the torture-chamber Urban walked up and down reading his breviary and listening to their shrieks and cries. Amongst other things, the torture produced statements that the King and Queen of Naples were partners in the plot, whereupon Urban made the fatal mistake of citing Charles to appear for judgment. An unusually savage sentence of excommunication followed. But the king's only reply was to send an army to besiege the pope, upon whose head he set a price of 11,000 golden florins (January 31, 1385). The command of this army was given to one of Urban's bitterest enemies, and it is a comment on the hold which the world now had upon monasticism that this general was the Abbot of Monte Cassino. Urban held out, in the citadel, for five months after the town had fallen, going to the ramparts four times a day, with full liturgical attendance, to excommunicate anew Charles and all his supporters.

In July 1385, however, at the approach of a new Angevin army, the abbot abandoned the siege, and Urban put the sea between himself and his dangerous vassal, sailing to Genoa on August 19. He took his unhappy prisoners with him. One, the Bishop of Aquila, he appears to have had killed on the road when he was no longer able to stand the pace of the journey. The six cardinals -- all but the Englishman, Adam Easton -- no one ever saw again. Officially they had " disappeared, " and Urban so spoke of them. Historians seem agreed that the pope had them thrown into the sea.

Was Urban VI wicked or merely insane? We shall never know. He stayed at Genoa for over a year (September 23, 1385- December 16, 1386) and when the murder of Charles III, in Hungary, relieved him of his most dangerous enemy, he slowly made his way south once more. He was at Lucca for nine months and thence, in September 1387, he went to Perugia to prepare an expedition against Naples, now, since June, in the hands of Clement VII's party. But Urban's soldiers deserted because he had no money for their wages, and the pope got no further than Rome. Here, too, his life was not safe; and here, on October 15, 1389, death ended his unhappy career.

During this first stage of the Schism (1379-1389) the observer has the impression of Christendom as made up of two spheres between which there is no contact save an occasional collision; and in each of the two spheres Catholicism, as all the fourteenth century had known it, continues in its habitual way. Such collisions were, for example, the Italian expedition of Louis of Anjou, while the struggle between Charles III and Urban was but a new instance of the troubles which any pope of the Middle Ages might expect at any time during his reign. And in the sphere from which Louis of Anjou's expedition set out, the sphere ruled from Avignon by the French pope Clement VII, the most prominent feature of the Church's public life was a renewal of the long-standing conflict in which the kings strove to subject the Church and make it an instrument of State policy, while the popes strove to resist them and to maintain the freedom of religion from State control. Sometimes -- as before now -- the popes were indeed ill advised in the methods they chose, and more than unfortunate in the spirit in which they waged the fight, but to fight against the stifling control of the State they never ceased. And this is as true of the French popes during the Schism -- whose legitimacy has never been more than doubtful -- as it was of the earlier popes whom all agreed were really popes; it is true, especially, of the second of these popes, Pedro de Luna (Benedict XIII), but it is true also of Clement VII. Whether Clement VII and his successor were popes or anti-popes, their public action -- in the principles that inspired it, in the forms it took, and even in its errors and its blunders -- has always about it, curiously enough, the authentic papal note: interesting and significant testimony that this division of opinion about who was pope did not affect the unity of faith about the authority of the papacy, nor occasion any revolutionary novelty in papal practice.

Legend relates that when Charles V of France heard of the election of Clement VII he exclaimed, "Now, I am pope." If ever any such idea had possessed the mind of any of the princes who ruled France during the next forty years, they were surely soon disillusioned. This French papacy of the years of Schism was as much -- and as little -- under their control as had been the French papacy of 1305-1378, or the Italian papacy of the forty years before that. And not only did the Avignon popes of the Schism period act, always, with the traditional papal independence towards the king in all matters of principle, but from the very beginning of the Schism there was also active in France a strong and organised body of educated clerical opinion that was always independent of the crown and often in conflict with it. The consistent aim of these scholars and doctors, was not, ever, to establish successfully the claims of the Avignon line; but rather to bring to an end the terrible spiritual evil which the Schism was. The centre of this great body of opinion was the University of Paris, and its endeavours were ceaseless through all these forty years. No praise is too high for the long fidelity of these men. In very great measure they were the instruments of the subsequent reunion. But it is also the fact, unfortunately, that their theology was not equal to their good will; their zeal, because ill-instructed, produced new complications, and a legacy of new theories about the place of the papacy in the Church destined to harass religion for the next four hundred years, and to be, during the century that followed the Schism, a most useful arm for the Christian prince who wished to wring concessions from the Holy See.

No one doubts that, as a matter of historical fact, it was the determination of France to support Robert of Geneva's claim to be the true pope which gave his party, at the critical moment, whatever chance of survival it ever possessed. Did Charles V support the cardinals against Urban VI, and pledge himself to whichever pope they should elect, because he really believed in their case, or was it mere State policy, the hope of power, which moved him? The question is still debated.

When the first envoys of the cardinals came to his court (September 1378) [ ] Charles V called a meeting of ecclesiastics before whom they stated their case. There were present to hear them thirty-six archbishops and bishops, a number of abbots, doctors of theology and of canon law, with representatives of the universities of Paris, Angers and Orleans; and, at a second session, lawyers also from the parlement. Their advice to Charles was to wait for more information before coming to any decision. But Charles privately wrote [ ] the letter to the cardinals at Fondi which encouraged them to go forward with their plan. They elected their pope on September 20 and in October the six cardinals whom Gregory XI had left in charge at Avignon went over to Clement [ ] and proclaimed his election. On November 16 the king called a second meeting to discuss the matter. This was a very different affair from that of September; it was much smaller, and was made up largely of the king's own "household" clerics; nor was the University of Paris represented. The result of this meeting was the king's public recognition of Clement as pope, and a royal order that he should be proclaimed as pope in all the parish churches of the kingdom. And Charles now strove, through special embassies to the various states, to win over other princes to recognise Clement.

The University of Paris was still not so sure. Two "nations," [ ] the English and the Picard, refused to recognise Clement, and the rector asked for more time. Six months after this, in April 1379, Clement sent as his legate, to win over the university, the Cardinal of Limoges, Jean de Cros, and it was now that the university definitely deserted Urban, the English and Picards still resisting. [ ] But they were not the only independent spirits. Charles V died in September 1380, and the university now approached the court to ask support for what it already thought to be the only way out of the impasse -- the calling of a General Council. But the court was hostile to the plan; the doctors who appeared before it were thrown into prison, and only released when the university agreed to recognise Clement VII as really pope. [ ] Four years later the university again approached the court, this time to beg the king to protect the clergy from the ruinous taxes levied by Clement VII to pay for the armies of Louis of Anjou.

When Urban VI died (October 15, 1389), Clement VII immediately proposed to Charles VI that he should try, through diplomatic channels, to persuade the Roman cardinals to end the Schism by electing him, Clement VII. But the fourteen cardinals Urban had left behind moved too quickly for the Avignon pope. On November 2 they elected their pope, Pietro Tomacelli, a young man of thirty-three -- Boniface IX. Clement promptly excommunicated him; and Boniface excommunicated Clement. And Boniface also declared [ ] that the plan to end the division through a General Council was sinful.

But from this moment the political aspect of the Schism changed, and contacts began once more to be made between the two "obediences." Boniface IX was tactful and kindly; he soon won back the Italian states which Urban VI had estranged politically (though they had remained faithful to the cause of the Roman pope); and he gradually conquered the last few strongholds that held out for Clement in the Papal State.

In France, meanwhile, great plans were being worked out to bring down the cause of the Roman pope. Clement VII's plan centred round the heir of the ill-starred Louis of Anjou, a boy of twelve, another Louis. To finance a new expedition to Naples that should establish Louis II as king, Clement gathered the immense sum of 60,000 golden florins. On August 13, 1390, the little king and his army landed at Naples and for three years all went well, victory in the field, and town after town falling to the Angevins. Expenses of course mounted, as the months and years went by, and Clement tightened the financial screw. Boniface IX did the same on behalf of his own protege, Ladislas, the son of Charles of Durazzo. The King of France planned to lead a new expedition against Rome itself and so re-establish the unity of the Church by force of arms. Clement VII was to go with him, and the date for the assembly was already fixed (March 1391), when the diplomacy of Richard II of England was set in movement by Boniface, and it effectively halted the scheme.

This was a serious blow to Clement. A second soon followed, a royal scheme for such a reorganisation of Italy that the French would control the whole country; Boniface IX would indeed be crushed, but the papacy installed at Rome with Clement would be more openly dependent on the lay power than at any time since the days of St. Gregory VII. One of the chief elements in this scheme had Clement himself for its unwitting first author.

In the critical days of 1379, when there were still hopes of driving Urban VI from Rome, Clement, as a reward to Louis I of Anjou for his spontaneous offer of support, had carved out for him a kingdom in central Italy, that included almost the whole of the Papal State save Rome itself and the Patrimony, and to which he gave the name Adria. [ ] This kingdom was to be held in fief of the Holy See, and was never to be held by the ruler of the other papal fief to the south, the kingdom of Naples. Only a fortnight after this rash offer the battle of Marino put an end for years to Clement's chances of effectively shaping Italian kingdoms. And now, in 1393, the heir of the "King of Adria" was actually King of Naples. But the French court, none the less, now revived the scheme.

It was proposed to Clement that he should confer Adria -- on the same conditions -- upon another French prince, a younger brother of the King of France, Louis of Orleans; this Louis was also the son-in-law of Galeazzo Visconti, the ruler of Milan. If Louis of Anjou maintained his hold on Naples, and the new scheme also went through, the French thus would dominate all Italy. To induce Clement to consent, the French pointed out how the task of maintaining order within the Papal State, and of keeping it independent of the neighbouring states, had been for centuries a burden far too heavy for the papacy to bear; and how this crushing burden permanently hampered the popes in their real work of promoting the interests of religion throughout the Catholic Church. All of which, however true, did not alter the fact that in an Italy so reorganised the papacy would, more than ever before, be the sport of the Catholic princes. Clement VII -- a much wiser man after fifteen years of responsibility -- fenced off the offer. For reply he submitted his own terms, and then the negotiations began to drag.

And while, in the last months of Clement's life, he had thus to fight his less than disinterested protectors, the University of Paris, persisting in its view that the division of obedience was a scandal to be ended at all costs, began to renew its agitation; and in the statements it now put out [ ] the anxious Clement saw clearly, and was dismayed to see, the first signs of the university's unorthodox theories about the place of the pope in the Church, theories which it adopted in order to justify its determination to end the Schism even though, to do this, it had to bring to an end the careers of both the rivals, of the lawful and the unlawful pope alike. [ ]

Clement VII's reign ended, then, just as a new movement was beginning which, without being in any way more favourable to his rival, threatened him even more seriously than did his rival; for its first principles were a denial of the fundamental tradition Prima sedes a nullo iudicetur. The only way out of the scandal, the university was now saying, was for both popes to resign, and whichever of them did not do so was to be judged by the very fact as obstinately schismatical and a heretic, and therefore no pope. To gather the opinion of the university world, a locked coffer was set in one of the churches of Paris; whoever among the graduates had a plan was invited to set it down in writing and place it in the chest. When the box was opened it was found that 10,000 graduates had submitted their views (January 1394). Fifty-four professors were set to read and classify the suggestions. For the most part, so it appeared, they came to this that there were only three ways to solve the problem -- the popes should both resign, or they should appoint a joint commission whose verdict they would accept as final, or they should summon a General Council and leave it to this to decide. Meanwhile there were great religious demonstrations in Paris, processions to ask the blessing of God on the movement for reunion, and in these the king and all the court and a small army of clerics took part. Clement VII was so far carried along by this new enthusiasm that processions were ordered at Avignon too, and he had a special mass composed for the peace of the Church.

But the pope did his best to check the movement of new ideas before it could spread further. He invited some of its chiefs-Peter d'Ailly very notably -- to Avignon to put their case, an invitation they were careful not to accept; and he sent a special envoy to Paris to work the court and university away from these dangerous schemes. The university indeed held firm, but Clement won over the court. When the university next appeared to plead before the king, the atmosphere had changed, and the university found itself forbidden for the future to busy itself with the dispute between the popes (August 10, 1394).

But, barely a month before this prohibition, the university had said its last word to Clement, a letter (July 17) that urged him to punish his legate at Paris, Peter de Luna, whose diplomacy, said the university, was wrecking the movement for reunion. The university also wrote to the cardinals, and the cardinals did not hide their sympathy with the doctors of Paris. Worst of all the cardinals began now to meet together, without the pope's leave, in order to discuss the new developments. No doubt Clement's mind went back sixteen years to the meetings at Anagni that had so speedily led to the conclave of Fondi. When the cardinals openly told him that the only thing to do was to adopt one of the schemes recommended at Paris, the pope fell into a kind of melancholy. Sometimes he spoke of resigning and then, as news reached him of the breach between the court and the university, he talked of a new expedition into Italy. The last weeks of his life were given up to this idea. But, on September 16, 1394, a fit of apoplexy carried him off.

iii. Benedict XIII's Quarrels with the French, 1394-1403

The interregnum at Avignon was extremely short. Ten days only after the death of Clement VII his twenty-one cardinals unanimously elected Peter de Luna to succeed him; he chose to be called Benedict XIII. With the election of this Spaniard the conduct of the Schism rises at once from the misery of petty expediencies in which it had for so long been caught. Peter de Luna had been a cardinal since 1375, and he was now an old man of sixty-six. He was universally esteemed as a scholarly and experienced jurist, and a practised diplomatist; he was learned, eloquent, pious; a man of principle, indeed, and soon to show himself the most obstinate of mankind -- and the most unscrupulously ingenious -- in defence of the principle which he considered to matter most of all, namely that the pope has no master in this world and is answerable to God alone for his rule of the Church. The election of Benedict XIII was a most definite turning point in the long involved story of the Schism; from now on there is added to the conflict between the rivals who claim to be pope, a second conflict between Benedict and the crown of France in which the principles at stake, the rights and the claims, are manifestly fundamental.

The action of the popes of the Avignon line, in the history of the Schism, as this is usually told, quite eclipses that of the Roman popes. It is no doubt inevitable that the towering ability of Benedict XIII plays all his rivals off the stage for years. It is also the fact that the records of the Avignon line are far more complete than those of the Roman popes. [ ] But, quite apart from these two very real considerations, the dramatic struggle between Benedict XIII and the French is of the very highest importance because it is now that the theories, the methods, and the spirit are developed which will one day produce the Councils of Pisa and of Constance, the "conciliar" theory and the baleful myth of the "liberties" of the Gallican Church.

It is in Peter de Luna's relations with France -- with the court, the hierarchy and the university world -- that the chief interest lies of his long thirty years' career as Benedict XIII. For, very soon after his election a conflict began of practical policy, about the best way to end the Schism. It ended -- after nearly four years -- by the French "withdrawing" their "obedience" (July 5, 1398). This schism within a schism lasted for five years and two months -- until May 30, 1403; the French then "restored" their "obedience" to Benedict and they continued in it for another five years nearly -- until May 21, 1408; when they again withdrew it, absolutely this time, and for ever.

The occasion of the breach between this second pope of the Avignon line and its royal French protector, was the oath by which each cardinal, in the short conclave of 1394, had bound himself, should he be elected, to resign if the Roman pope agreed to resign simultaneously, and also to be guided in this by the advice of the majority of his cardinals. All Benedict XIII's troubles arose from this oath. He had been extremely unwilling to take it, as he had been unwilling to accept elections as pope -- and as he had been extremely unwilling, sixteen years earlier, to take part in the conclave of Fondi. Once elected he declined to be bound by the oath, while the cardinals, and the French generally, endeavoured to hold him to it. Peter de Luna, however, did not begin by any explicit renunciation of his promise, by any declaration that promises of this kind were unlawful in themselves, and therefore could not bind, such as Innocent VI had published after his election in 1352. But with a patient, persistent wiliness unmatched in history, he raised objection after objection; he contrived endless delays, and he devised all manner of distinctions; ever careful on occasion to make private protest, in legal form, that he would not necessarily consider himself bound by the public engagement he was now about to contract, he so extended, for the peace of his own conscience, the principle that promises made through fear are not binding, that in the end he wore out the patience of all concerned and all men's belief in his own truthfulness. [ ] Benedict XIII has gone down to history as a prodigy of conscientious double-dealing and elaborate self-deception -- the inevitable penalty of such genius.

The contest began when the King of France, in May 1395, begged the Avignon pope to communicate the actual text of the oath he had sworn in the conclave. Benedict kept the royal ambassadors dancing attendance on him for 120 days, and even then, though he did not hand over the text, he contrived not to express any disagreement with the scheme for a double resignation which Charles VI was urging on him. The king next turned to look for allies among the princes of Christendom in his effort to heal the division. His diplomacy produced, in June 1397, a joint Anglo-French mission which visited both Benedict and Boniface IX. But it won no concessions from either.

Twelve months later Charles had induced the emperor, Wenzel, to plead with Benedict; and now, in May 1398, to the emperor's ambassadors, the Avignon pope spoke out his mind, denouncing the resignation scheme as sinful and utterly repudiating it. Whereupon the French court resolved to force the old man to consent to it.

This new determination to try what force could do against Aragonese obstinacy was not due merely to zeal for religion. For a whole generation now -- since 1368 -- the kings of France had enjoyed, from the different popes, a permission to levy taxes on Church property for the nation's ordinary needs. This permission Benedict XIII had renewed, at first for two years only, and then for one. Latterly he had refused any further renewal. The crown urgently needed the money; the pope would not grant it; and if the clergy still acknowledged him as pope they could not be persuaded to defy him and vote the money without his leave.

And so the crown came round to a plan which certain pillars of the University of Paris had devised, that the nation should withdraw its obedience from Benedict, as a kind of threat that he had better look to his election promises and begin to fulfil them. The withdrawal was to be done with the semblance of legal form -- through a council of the clergy, a full debate and a general vote. This council met at Paris, May 22, 1398, and it remained in session until the beginning of August. In some ways it is the most pregnant event in all the religious history of the two hundred years that separate Philip the Fair from Henry VIII -- both for what was done, and the way it was done.

Forty-four archbishops and bishops took part in the council, with two delegates from the various cathedral chapters, two doctors from each university, and a great number of abbots -- some 300 voters in all. The first session was thrown open to the public, and the opening speeches were made before a huge audience of thousands. The presidency of the council was singular: [ ] five royal princes, the brother, [ ] uncles, [ ] and first cousin of the king, [ ] Charles VI, who was now once again out of his mind. The real guiding spirit in the affair was the royal chancellor, Arnauld de Corbie. [ ]

It was explained to the council -- by the king's party -- that Benedict was a perjurer, for he had broken the oath sworn in the conclave; no one, therefore, need henceforth obey him. The Holy See was, in a kind of way, vacant and it was now the duty of the King of France, acting as its protector, to bring about Benedict's formal resignation. While the king could choose for himself how best to do this, he had nevertheless thought well to ask advice. Hence this council. The real source of Benedict's strength was financial. Let him once be deprived of taxes, and of the right to appoint to benefices, and he would presently be starved into surrender.

The policy suggested was subtle. There was no open denial that Benedict was pope; and there was, of course, an abundance of reverential language about his office and the rights of the Holy See. But the pope's acts were for the future to be silently ignored. More than one speaker of the king's party pointed enviously to England where, with such statutes as Provisors and Praemunire, things of this kind at any rate were now so much better ordered than in France. It was also urged upon the prelates and clergy that this was the golden moment to recover the ancient liberties of the Gallican Church, and to force through the much-needed reforms so long held up, it was suggested, by papal indifference.

Against the court prelates it was bluntly pointed out that what they proposed was in reality nothing less than an attack on the bases of the pope's position as pope. The corruption complained of in the papal administration would not come to an end through any mere change in the personnel who ran the machine. And moreover, it was asked, what authority had a merely local council, of one particular country, to sit in judgment on the head of the universal church, and declare him not to be the pope?

The debate went on for days, and then, on June 11, the voting began. The system adopted was highly ingenious. Each member of the council gave his opinion in writing, and he handed it privately to the little group of the royal princes and the chancellor, who thereupon proceeded to argue the opinion if it did not favour their design of immediate total withdrawal of obedience from Benedict. The device avoided all chance of the council as a whole knowing how the voting was going; it also revealed to the government -- and to the government alone -- the exact views of all these leading ecclesiastics; and it gave to the government the best opportunity conceivable of influencing the vote, and of changing it, in the very moment it was to be cast.

About the views of the University of Paris there was no secret whatever. On the day the voting in the council began it publicly declared for the policy that Benedict should be coerced by an immediate, total suspension of obedience.

Then for four weeks there was a curious silence; and when, gradually, the council began to show its anxiety, the government explained that the classification of all these votes was naturally a slow business. However, on July 28, with a public of something like 10,000 looking on, the chancellor announced the result. For the government's plan there were no fewer than 247 votes, for all other schemes 53; a royal decree would "implement" the council's advice. That decree was, of course, already prepared; it was, in fact, dated for the previous day, July 27, 1398. Its effect -- along with a complementary declaration from the prelates [ ] -- was to organise the Church in France after a fashion hitherto unknown among Catholics, as an autonomous body independent of all papal control.

The king, advised by the council, orders by this decree that from now on none of his subjects are to render any obedience to Benedict XIII. Penalties are provided for any breach of the law. The pope's partisans are to be deprived of their benefices by the bishops, and the administration of such benefices is to pass to the king who will, of course, enjoy the profits while they remain vacant. Papal judges and commissaries engaged within the realm on suits against the king's subjects are immediately to terminate such proceedings under penalty of loss of goods and imprisonment. All bulls and letters of any kind from Benedict are to be surrendered to the king, and if they are bulls against this decree, those who have brought them into the kingdom will be imprisoned.

The prelates in the council decreed that, until the end of the schism, [ ] elections of abbots in monasteries exempt from the jurisdiction of the bishops should henceforth be confirmed by the bishop of the diocese -- where, until now, it had been the pope who confirmed them. All promises of appointments made by

Benedict were to be ignored. Marriage dispensations were to be granted by the bishops or the cardinals. Appeals that had once gone to the papal curia were now to be decided by the bishop of the diocese, the metropolitan of the province and, finally, by the annual provincial council. As for cases (whether of ecclesiastical penalties or of sins) where absolution was reserved to the pope, they were for the future to be sent to the penitentiaries of Avignon, if these had abandoned the pope; if they remained loyal to him the bishops were to absolve, under the condition that the penitent sought absolution later from the universally recognised pope, once such a pope was elected. First fruits, procurations, and all the taxes payable to the pope were abolished -- a reform intended by the council to be final and definitive. Any sentences Benedict might pass in reprisal were declared in advance null and void. Notaries were forbidden to style Benedict "pope" in the acts they drew up and finally, to quiet the anxieties of the scrupulous, the government declared that Catholics were bound in conscience to conform in these matters to what the king had decided.

Here, on the face of it, was a great victory for the government of France; and it was the activity of Catholics that was thus victorious over the papacy, the activity of Catholic bishops and clergy -- no less than of Catholic laymen -- against the man whom all of them believed to be the lawful pope. The events of 1398 are important, ultimately, not because they compromised the fortunes of Benedict XIII, but because they laid the axe to the root of the tree and compromised the traditional Catholic teaching about the nature of the pope's authority in the Church of Christ. The material object of all this hostility may indeed be no more than an anti-pope, but formaliter, so to speak, this hostility is Catholic action -- action of the Catholic state, of the hierarchy, of the studium -- upon the papacy, as will be the action of the Council of Pisa, and of the still greater Council of Constance. The schism is now, in 1398, twenty years old. Twenty years of disunion, of discontent and unrest, have produced this collaboration of university and clergy with the crown, and its dire fruit. For yet another twenty years Christendom will more and more feed upon that fruit, and strange maladies thence develop, in more than one of its organs, to trouble the general body for centuries.

Already the spirit is active in the University of Paris which, at Pisa, ten years from now, will sweep away the claims of Roman and Avignon pope alike, and elect a third claimant in their stead; already, in this very council of 1398, this very suggestion has been made. [ ] We can note other things too; how few open defenders there are of the rights of the Holy See among the bishops; how eager the bishops are to strip the Holy See of its power to appoint to ecclesiastical offices, and to tax appointments and the property of the Church; how easily in fact, the government finds, within the hierarchy, quisling prelates ready to betray the Holy See. After a demonstration of this kind, and experience of a regime where such anarchical doctrines are, for years, given every freedom, and even built into a system, how long will it be before France is again normally Catholic in its relations with the papacy? We are assisting, in 1398, at the birth of the notion that there exists a Gallican church with privileges in its own right, sometime ago " usurped " by the papacy, and to recover which rights or liberties all good French clerics will -- in the best interests of religion -- always unite with the crown against the papacy. The proceedings of this council of Paris in 1398 are surely momentous in the general history of the Church.

There was to be, of course, a reaction in favour of Benedict, but before describing this it is important to notice how the French government in 1398 achieved its disconcerting success. For the decision was a carefully manipulated swindle, "a lie that has triumphed even down to our own times." [ ] The slips on which these 300 or more members of the council recorded their votes or views were not destroyed at the end of the month of arrangement and classification. Still in the canvas bags where the chancellor had then stored them after the event, they remained forgotten and unexamined down to recent years. M. Noel Valois set himself to study them and his conclusions are startling. The government did indeed win a majority of the council to its plan, but a majority of about 180 to 120 rather than 247 to 53; and of the episcopate and the greater prelates a half, at least, voted against the government. "So slender was the majority of those in favour of the suspension of entire obedience that we may ask whether the result of the council would not have been entirely different, had it not been for the pressure that the government brought to bear from the very first day." [ ]

With parties so nicely balanced, reaction was bound to develop soon.

On September 1, 1398, the French ambassadors arrived at Avignon with the official news of the royal decree. The immediate effect was a general flight to the king's side of all the Frenchmen in Benedict's service, led by eighteen of his cardinals. The townspeople, too, deserted the pope. Nothing was left him but five cardinals, a few personal friends and his troops, in the great fortress palace that Benedict XII had built sixty years before. To capture this, the eighteen cardinals now called in one of the local lords and his band of mercenaries, and a seven months' siege began. After four weeks of fruitless assaults, in which, more than once, storming parties were led by the military-minded cardinal, Jean de Neufchatel, the besiegers turned to the less costly tactic of starving out the garrison.

While the siege continued, French diplomacy was busy in the courts of Benedict's supporters. The French claimant to Naples -- Louis II -- was won over to desert him, and the kings of Navarre and Castile also. But Martin I of Aragon, Benedict's own sovereign, remained his friend; [ ] and it was through Martin's good offices that, in the spring of 1399, the King of France came to the pope's aid. In return for a declaration by Benedict that he accepted the resignation scheme, and that he would discharge the troops of his garrison, the king undertook to protect the pope, and to compel the cardinals to raise the siege. It will be noted that no "restitution of obedience" was promised. The French merely pledged themselves that no harm should come to the pope or to his property (10 April, 1399); and the better to survey the activities of the pope (whom they did not trust in the least degree), as well as to ensure his protection, a commission of prelates and royal officials was now sent to Avignon. For the next four years Benedict was, to all intents and purposes, the French king's prisoner, and during all this time the Church in France was governed according to the decrees of 1398.

It was not, of course, a happy time, either for the churchmen or for the cause of religion. The new freedom of chapters to elect the various bishops and abbots was never a reality. The king, the great nobles, the womenfolk of the king and great nobles, all had their candidates, and ample means to influence the electors. The university world complained bitterly that far less attention was paid to clerical learning and talent than under the oppressive papal regime, and in 1400, as a protest against the systematic appointment of ignorant and illiterate clerics to high places, the University of Paris suspended all lectures and examinations. It was a more general cause of complaint among the clergy that the burthensome papal taxes abolished by the council of 1398, continued to be levied -- but now by the king, in order (so it was explained), to pay the immense expenses of the royal action in liberating the Church; also, these taxes were now collected by the royal officials, and much more efficiently than of old. "The old truth was being proved yet once again that no church frees itself from the pope without falling under the heavier yoke of lay control." [ ]

But the harsh treatment of the man whom all France believed to be the pope, was alienating the common people; the exploitation of church property and patronage was alienating the clergy and the universities; in the king's council there was a serious personal conflict about the treatment of Benedict between the king's brother, Louis of Orleans and his uncle the Duke of Burgundy; Benedict himself remained resolute on the vital point, he would not consent that any other mind than the pope's should decide for the pope how he ought to act in the matter of ending the Schism. Discontent in France, then, was steadily growing, and the government already greatly embarrassed, when, on March 12, 1403, the old pope [ ] broke the tension by escaping from his captivity. With seven attendants he got through a hole in the wall of his palace, and, in the night, made his way past sentinels and guards. By morning he was in safety, in the territory of the Count of Provence. [ ]

And now the reaction in Benedict's favour was immediate. The leading personages of the tiny papal state came in to make their submission, and the eighteen cardinals sent a delegation begging to be received into the pope's favour. They came back on the pope's terms -- unconditional surrender indeed -- Benedict refusing to the last to pledge himself by oath even to show them ordinary good will, the cardinals kneeling before him and tearfully promising all manner of devotion for the rest of their lives (April 29). And just one month later, the negotiations for the restitution of obedience ended with Benedict's triumph over France too. An assembly of bishops at Paris (May 28), declared for the restitution, the king -- now for the moment lucid -- was eagerly of the same opinion. Benedict, without any new commitment -- except what might be inferred from promises made to the Duke of Orleans -- was, for the moment, victorious over all his foes. There was a great ceremony of thanksgiving at Notre Dame (May 30, 1403), at which Peter d'Ailly, now Bishop of Cambrai, preached and at the end of his sermon he read out the pledges Benedict had given to the trusting duke.
iv. The Roman Popes, 1389-1406

These first nine years of the reign of the second pope of the
Avignon obedience (1394-1403) were taken up almost entirely
with the fight to maintain his independence against the French
crown and the University of Paris. Benedict XIII had been left
little leisure so far in which to plan any attack on the position of
his Roman adversary, Boniface IX. But the Roman, too, had had
his difficulties during these years, difficulties often of a like
nature. There was not, indeed, among the princes loyal to Rome
any one power so strong and so well placed, should it turn to
oppress Boniface, as the French monarchy and its great academic
ally. But all the princes of Christendom realised the weakness of
the papal position, and there was scarcely one that did not, in his
turn, make use of it to wring concessions from the Roman pope
too. Boniface IX was never really free to profit from the
embarrassments of Benedict XIII. And within less than eighteen
months of Benedict's temporary victory over the French in 1403,
Boniface had died; and with the election of Innocent VII in his
place, the whole relation of the rival popes takes on a new
colour.

Throughout his reign of fifteen years (1389-1404), the double
anxiety had never ceased to worry Boniface IX, where to find
money and how to keep the different princes faithful to him. He
had to suffer serious losses of territory in Italy, when Genoa went
over to his adversary, and Sicily too. Then, in 1398, the emperor
Wenzel -- whose support had brought to the Roman line a
prestige that neutralised the French support of the Avignon
obedience -- was won over by the French to declare himself
neutral; and England, also influenced by France, began to show
herself less partisan than before. From the danger of the empire's
adherence to Benedict XIII the Roman pope was delivered by the
revolutionary act of four of the prince electors who, in 1399,
declared Wenzel deposed and elected in his place Rupert of
Bavaria. But although Rupert declared for the Roman line,
Boniface was for the moment too wary to recognise him as
emperor-elect. It was doubtful whether the deposition of Wenzel

was good in law, and Rupert was only acknowledged in the west of Germany. Moreover, warned by the fate of Benedict XIII, and by the beginnings of the like trouble among his own supporters, Boniface would not recognise Rupert unless he swore to leave entirely to the pope the business of bringing the schism to an end; and this pledge Rupert refused to give.

Meanwhile, there were the beginnings of civil war in Germany between the partisans of Wenzel and Rupert. In 1401 Florence called Rupert into Italy to help in the war against pro-French Milan. But the emperor-elect was badly defeated (October 21, 1401), and in April 1402, he returned to Germany with barely enough troops for an escort. He still, however, steadfastly refused the pope's terms, and when, after his defeat, Boniface had made them stiffer still, Rupert's refusal had stiffened too. The princes of Germany supported his refusal, and in the autumn of 1402 Rupert began to negotiate with France and with England for united action to force both Boniface and Benedict to resign. Boniface IX was finding that the new emperor was no more his subject than the old. Then, in August 1403, the pope recognised the king who was his one real supporter, Ladislas of Naples, as King of Hungary also, to the great offence of a rival claimant -- Sigismund -- who was the emperor Wenzel's brother. Whereupon Sigismund openly deserted the Roman cause, and Boniface, pushed by necessity, was driven to recognise Rupert as emperorelect without any of the special conditions upon which he had been insisting for the previous two years.

This was in October 1403. Boniface's reign had, to the very day, just a year to run. His hold on the states that acknowledged him as pope could hardly have been feebler, and had Benedict XIII now been free to intervene in Italy the political fortunes of the Roman pope might have been brought crashing to the ground. But Benedict was once more involved in the old conflict with the French crown and with the University of Paris. Mission after mission was arriving at Avignon to remind him of his promises;

but all in vain. The wily old man eluded the most practised of the diplomatists, and showed himself in his speeches more pious than the most pious of the bishops who bade him think only of the cause of religion. He steadily refused to recognise any of the ecclesiastical appointments made during the five years of the withdrawal of obedience; and he sent out collectors to demand the arrears of moneys due to him for that period. As the clergy had already paid their dues, but to the crown, they now turned to the king for protection against the pope, and this was solemnly guaranteed to them by a royal edict of January 10, 1404. [ ]

Six months after this, Benedict re-opened negotiations with Boniface, interrupted now for nearly seven years. His ambassadors arrived at Rome in late September 1404, and Boniface IX granted them audience. But there were stormy scenes, the pope calling Peter de Luna a liar and a dissembler, and the ambassadors retorting that Boniface was a simonist. The pope was already failing in health, and this interchange ended fatally. On October 1, 1404, two days after the interview, the pope collapsed and died.

Was Boniface IX indeed a simonist? For his latest biographer [ ] the charge is proved beyond all doubt, and the blistering phrase " the crooked days of Boniface IX " [ ] seems only too true a description. Like Urban VI -- the pope who made him a cardinal when scarcely out of his teens -- Boniface was a Neapolitan. He was a practical man, ignorant indeed in matters of professional clerical learning, but a realist, able to manage men, and to get things done, "the man the crisis called for," and he was young, little more than thirty when elected pope. Throughout the reign which followed -- fifteen years -- the pope was far too busy with the urgent political problem before him to have any leisure for religious affairs properly so called. His own life was, seemingly, correct; the immense sums he raised were not spent on pleasures, nor on his own personal artistic fancies. But the young pope's superficial mind misread the nature of the evil he confronted.

That his view of the division of Christendom ruled out all possibility of seriously negotiating with Avignon, cannot indeed be held against him. But the pope stands charged with the dreadful error of treating this religious tragedy as a matter of politics, and in his anxiety to raise the money he needed, Boniface sank to the lowest levels. [ ] The papal collation of benefices now became a matter of simple marketing. Provisions and expectatives were given for cash down, and for prices which only the rich could afford, and without any guarantee that they would not be sold a second time to anyone who offered a higher price. Then, in 1402, Boniface annulled all grants made hitherto, unless the holders had them renewed within twelve months. Also the tax of annates was extended to all benefices worth more than twenty-four gold florins annual revenue. But the most mischievous wickedness of all was in the matter of indulgences. The pope multiplied, beyond all wisdom, the grants of indulgences ad instar -- indulgences, that is to say, whereby, in general terms, there was granted such a remission as might have been gained by doing other (and immensely more laborious) penances and good works, pilgrimage to the Holy Land for example or enlisting as a soldier in the crusades. For the jubilee of 1390, Boniface called in the bankers to organise the collection and despatch of the moneys to Rome. This jubilee was liberally extended to other cities outside Rome, but to gain it an offering of money was one condition needed, and the amount was fixed at the cost of a journey to Rome from the place where the indulgence was gained, plus the amount that would have been offered by the pilgrim at the different Roman shrines. Of the total taken, a half was to go to the banker as commission. "It seemed as though one could get the indulgence for cash down. It even happened that confessors gave absolution in exchange for money, without exacting any true repentance or reparation of the injustices done to others. Boniface, more concerned to demand that the preachers of the indulgence should send in accounts that were in good order than that they should explain the doctrine of indulgences correctly, assuredly bears the responsibility of the deformation of religious sense among the masses which was to result from such imprudences and from abuses on such a scale." [ ] In Germany especially there was great indignation, strong, violent and organised opposition indeed; and the German clergy made the reformation of this system a main point in the programme which they presented to the Council of Constance and Martin V a few years later. [ ]

Sixteen days after the death of Boniface IX, the cardinals elected in his place the Bishop of Bologna, Cosmo Megliorati; he took the name of Innocent VII. As in 1389, all the electors had sworn that, if elected, they would do their utmost to bring the division to an end, even resigning the Holy See if necessary, and that immediately after the election they would call a General Council. This last pledge Innocent was prompt to fulfil and the council was summoned for 1 November, 1405. [ ]

The envoys Benedict XIII had sent to Boniface returned to their master -- now at Genoa -- with a very strange tale (April 11, 1405). The Romans, they said, had looked on them as the murderers of Boniface IX; they had been imprisoned in Sant' Angelo, and had only been freed on payment of an enormous bribe. They had besought the Roman cardinals not to elect any new pope in a hurry, but to take this opportunity to consult Benedict XIII and so end the schism by an agreed election. The Romans had, however, rejected this offer.

But about the same time that this account of the conclave reached the French court from Benedict, there came in another, very different, version sent by Innocent VII. According to this, the Roman cardinals, before the conclave opened, had offered to delay it until Benedict XIII had been told of their offer not to proceed to an election by themselves if the Avignon pope would now abdicate. To this the Avignon envoys had replied that Benedict would certainly never resign, and also that the resignation scheme was contrary to all law and right.

This revelation, that only Benedict's now notorious determination
to cling to his position had prevented the best chance of a
settlement that had appeared in nearly thirty years, infuriated the
influential parties in France with whom, for so long, he had been
at war. A letter to Innocent from one of the royal princes brought
a reply that strengthened belief in the Roman pope's first letter,
and then, in September 1405, the University of Paris opened
direct negotiations with the Roman pope.

The result was to confirm the French suspicion of Benedict's
good faith, and also to instil in the Roman pope unshakable
mistrust of his rival. Benedict had, for some time now, really
been planning a new assault on Italy. Barely six weeks after the
election of Innocent VII, he had left France, and before Easter
1405, he was established at Genoa. His diplomacy was busy in
Florence too, and at Lucca, and it seemed for the moment as
though his loss of position in France would be balanced by gains
in Italy. Pisa promised him recognition and Florence agreed to
remain neutral. And all this time Benedict never ceased his
demands for money, especially from the clergy of France and
Spain. Even religious orders always exempted hitherto from such
taxation were now subjected to it. Finally, from Castile, there
came in the spring of 1406 a new plan to end the schism; but a
plan which must entail the disappearance of Benedict. To work
against the Castilian ambassadors he sent a special legate to the
French court. All unknowingly he thereby set in motion a new
anti-de-Luna movement that produced a new council of Paris,
and a new withdrawal from his obedience -- a withdrawal that
was, this time, to be permanent, and to meet which there would
be a corresponding withdrawal of the cardinals of the Roman
pope.

When Benedict's legate, the Cardinal de Challant, appeared in
Paris at Easter 1406, he was rudely told, "All that interests your
master is money"; and when the university was admitted to state
its case its orator, Jean Petit, immediately struck a note that was

to be heard in all the debates of the next ten years. Pope
Benedict, he said, has broken his sworn promises, and thereby he
has lost all claim on men's obedience. In the great debate before
the court called the Parlement de Paris (June 7 and 8, 1406), this
was urged more passionately still, and the plight of the French
church, bled white by Benedict, was set forth in detail; prelates
pawning church property to pay the fees due to the curia on their
nomination, the pope keeping benefices vacant in order to make
their revenues his own, the high cost of absolution from censures
to the unfortunate clerics too poor to pay the papal taxes. In the
three years since France came back to Benedict's obedience he
had gathered, it was said, no less than 1,200,000 francs from her
clergy. The crown decided that a new council should meet at
Paris to decide whether to continue in obedience to Benedict.

This council met in November 1406, and its debates went on
until the first weeks of the new year. It was not so much the
creature of the crown as the council of 1398 had been; the
dominating influence now was the University of Paris, to whose
initiative the whole of this new movement against Benedict XIII
was due. Each side selected a panel of speakers to thrash out the
different points in dispute, and the anti-de-Luna party made no
endeavour to hide their feelings. " For the sake of the ship," said
Jean Petit, [ ] "let us throw both these quarrelsome, incompetent
captains into the sea." Another doctor, Pierre Plaoul, set out the
theory of the pope as the servant of the Church and as enjoying,
thereby, an inferior kind of power to that possessed by kings. [ ]
Benedict's supporters asked how, since not even Christendom
itself had any authority to judge the pope, this council could so
presume? No action on its part could possibly deprive him of "la
puissance dez cles". And, in lighter vein, the Archbishop of
Tours, arguing that to attack Benedict was not a practical policy,
reminded the council that he came from a country world-famous
for its mules.

The long debates ended in a compromise. Benedict XIII was to be obeyed as the chief in spiritual matters, but his appointments to benefices were to be ignored and also his taxation of church property. It was these last two points, indeed, which now, as through all the next forty years, chiefly occupied the speakers of the anti-papal party; and when the question was raised how the pope could be brought to accept these restrictions, nine-tenths of the council voted that the king ought to compel his acceptance. Whereupon (January 3, 1407), the clergy petitioned Charles VI to make perpetual the edict of September 11, 1406, that had abolished first fruits, servitia, and procurations, and also to abolish the papal tithes and papal collations to benefices in France; and this the king consented to do, in a new decree of February 18, 1407. But this new decree was, almost immediately, suspended. Since the council of Paris began a new pope had been elected at Rome, and there seemed every hope that the schism was now really to be brought to an end.

The very short, and very stormy, reign of Innocent VII had, in fact, ended just ten days before the council opened in Paris. The fourteen Roman cardinals had, thereupon, bound themselves by a pact more stringent than any yet devised; and after a seven-days' conclave they had chosen, unanimously, the Venetian cardinal, Angelo Corrario. [ ] This new pope Gregory XII -- was an old man of seventy, known for his austere life, and chosen for one reason only, that he seemed to live for nothing else but to work to heal the division. All the circumstances of his election seemed, indeed, to make him "less a pope than a proctor charged to abdicate the papacy in the interests of unity". Gregory XII was, before he finished, to prove the greatest disappointment of all, but the first seven months of his reign seemed the beginning of a new age, and it was in the first flood of these hopes that the King of France held up the decrees that would otherwise have engaged all the ecclesiastical energies of his people in a new war with Benedict XIII. They would now be better employed in negotiations with this unexpectedly helpful pope newly elected at Rome.

The cause of all these hopes was the pact sworn to by Gregory XII before his election, and sworn to again immediately afterwards, and the care which the pope took to give the pact all possible publicity. The pope, in fact, had bound himself to abdicate if Benedict XIII should do the same or should chance to die -- provided that the cardinals of both obediences would agree to join for the election of the new pope; also he had promised that within a month of his election he would notify Benedict and his cardinals, the various Christian princes, and the bishops everywhere of this undertaking; also that he would send ambassadors, within three months, to arrange with Benedict a suitable meeting place for a personal interview; finally, Gregory XII promised not to create any new cardinals while these negotiations were in progress, unless to equalise his college with that of Benedict. [ ] From this pact the new pope swore, moreover, that he would not dispense or absolve himself.
v. Benedict XIII and Gregory XII, 1406-1409

Gregory XII carried out to the letter all that he had promised. His envoys reached Paris in the last days of the council, and on January 21, 1407, a solemn service of thanksgiving took place at Notre Dame for the appearance in the church of such an apostolic spirit. Throughout France and Italy the rejoicing was universal.

Benedict's answer was in much the same tone as the Roman letter, but those experienced in his ways -- the French bishops, for example -- did not fail to detect that his ingenuity had once more devised avenues of escape. And the King of France, on the very day that he suspended the decrees against Benedict, decided to send an embassy both to the Avignon and the Roman courts. About the same time that this embassy was commissioned, Gregory XII also despatched an embassy to his rival, and it was this embassy that reached Benedict first, who was now in residence at Marseilles. The chief business of the mission from Gregory XII was to arrange where the contending principals should meet, and the audience was as stormy as most audiences were in which any of these popes met the envoys of their rivals. But after nearly three weeks an accord was reached, the so-called Treaty of Marseilles (April 20, 1407), and it was agreed that Gregory and Benedict should meet at Savona by the feast of All Saints next following at the latest (November 1).

The embassy from the King of France, a much more elaborate affair, took weeks to gather and to make its way to Marseilles. Long before it could arrive, the Italian embassy had finished its business, and meeting the Frenchmen was able to report what it had achieved. It is of interest that the Italians strongly advised the Frenchmen to handle Benedict gently if they wished for concessions. Finally, on May 10, Benedict received the French king's envoys, and in a most eloquent speech he accepted their point of view wholeheartedly. But when, the next day, the ambassadors begged him to publish his concessions in a bull, all the old trouble began anew. For a week the two parties wrestled, but without any result. Benedict refused absolutely to declare publicly that he, too, was willing to resign if Gregory would resign. We know, now, that he was moreover, at this very time, preparing an elaborate sentence of excommunication for all who had urged this resignation scheme; and the ambassadors knew, then, that, in order to resist any repetition of the siege of 1398, he was gathering men and arms.

So the French embassy, leaving two of its members at Marseilles to keep watch on Benedict, now made its way to Rome. But by the time Rome was reached, July 18, 1407, a great change had come over Gregory XII. His family had worked him round to cling to the papacy -- as the family of Gregory XI had once worked round that pope to cling to Avignon; they had also infected the old man with the idea that Benedict planned to kidnap him when the two met; and, moreover, the Roman pope's chief political supporter, Ladislas, King of Naples, was strongly opposed to the plan of any meeting between the popes. From now on Gregory's court is the scene of intrigues as complicated and as obscure as any of Peter de Luna's feats; one series of these, it seems, was a hidden understanding with Ladislas, in virtue of which the king attacked Rome, and so provided Gregory with the best of reasons for not leaving the Papal State.

Against this new mentality in the old pope, not all the efforts of the French could prevail. When they offered oaths as security, and armies, and hostages, he only reminded them how they had treated Benedict whom they believed to be the lawful pope. Could he, Gregory, really expect to be treated better?

After nearly three weeks of sterile argument the French at last left Rome (August 4, 1407), certain that Gregory would now prove a second Peter de Luna, but certain of this also, that he had lost the confidence of his own cardinals. For the Roman cardinals had privately assured the ambassadors that whatever Gregory did, they at least would go to Savona, and also that should Gregory die they would not give him a successor.

The news of the change in Gregory was, of course, highly welcome to Benedict. Assured in his mind that the Italian would never come to a meeting, Benedict now spoke about the plan with enthusiasm, and setting out with a great escort he was at Savona long before the appointed day. For the next seven months these two ancient men worked to outwit each other with the infinite pertinacity of the senile; with embassies passing constantly between the two; arrangements half-made, suggestions and new suggestions, discussed, accepted, and then questioned; with suggestions first to change the place of the meeting, and next about the conditions; until finally they wore out the patience of all but their own personal attendants. How could they meet, said the wits: the one was a land animal that dared not trust the water, and the other a sea monster that could not live on land. At one moment less than a day's journey separated the two, Gregory at Lucca and Benedict at Porto Venere.

Then, on April 25, 1408, the King of Naples took Rome, without a blow struck in its defence. Gregory's joy -- and the joy of his family -- was undisguised. Ladislas demanded that whenever Gregory and Benedict met, he must be present. All hope of free action by the two was now at an end. The plan to end the schism by a double resignation died a natural death, and at the Roman court it was forbidden henceforth to preach sermons reminding Gregory of his famous oath. The pope also considered himself freed from his pledge not to create new cardinals, and his unusual preparations for the consistory fired the long smouldering discontent of the Sacred College. On May 4, in a palace packed with soldiery, [ ] Gregory -- first forbidding any comment or discussion -- told the cardinals that he proposed to add four to their number. They protested energetically, but the pope silenced them, and sternly forbade them to leave the city, or to meet, together without the pope, or to negotiate with either Benedict's ambassadors or those of the King of France The mild old man had suddenly shown himself terribile. Was he to be another Urban VI? Gregory XII already knew enough about the cardinals' opinion of his change of policy to fear that a repetition of the acts of 1378 was, indeed, in preparation. One week later the consistory was held and the names of the four new cardinals were announced; two of them were nephews of Gregory, Gabriele Condulmaro (the future pope Eugene IV), and Angelo Corrario, Gregory's chief adviser since his election and commonly held to be the chief cause of his apostasy from his election promises.

That same night one of the cardinals fled to Pisa in disguise, and the next day six of the rest followed him [ ] (May 12, 1408). From Pisa the seven cardinals issued manifestos protesting against Gregory's restriction of their liberty, and appealing from the vicar of Christ to Christ Himself. They spoke of the dungeons Gregory had made ready for them, and declared that their conclave oath bound them to seek out the cardinals of Benedict XIII and to make common cause with these to bring the schism to an end. Finally, they appealed to all the Christian princes to support their efforts. They also sent an urgent invitation to Benedict to fulfil his promise and come as near to them as Leghorn.

The Florentines, however, refused Benedict a safe conduct, and he sent to Leghorn four cardinals in his place. The Roman cardinals at Pisa delegated as many again, and the eight soon reached agreement on the principle that a joint council of both "obediences" should be summoned, at which both popes should simultaneously abdicate and a new pope be elected, whom the whole Church would then know to be the true successor of St. Peter. But Benedict's cardinals first explained the pact to their pope as a plan for a joint council where he would preside; and it was in this way that they won from him a kind of general approval of all they were doing to promote the union. He was eventually to be undeceived; but his treacherous legates were, by that time, free from any anxiety which the thought of his anger might bring. For, on June 5, they learned that a great ecclesiastical revolution had, a fortnight earlier, wrested France once more from its obedience to Benedict. The long malaise in the Aragonese pope's relations with Charles VI had ended in a most violent rupture, and in the same weeks when Gregory XII's feeble mismanagement was renewing the disaster of 1378, Benedict XIII was losing for ever the sole source of what real importance he had ever possessed. The French cardinals, now that their king was no longer behind Benedict, could desert him without fear of the future.

Benedict's new misfortune had begun when, in the previous November (1407), the Duke of Orleans, his one really loyal supporter among the French princes, was murdered. [ ] On the 12

January following, Charles VI came to a decision -- unless by the feast of the Ascension next (May 24, 1408) unity of government in the Church had been restored, France would finally withdraw its obedience from the Avignon pope. Benedict was not, of course, to be moved by such threats. He received this declaration on April 18, and immediately sent a warning to the king that, unless he revoked the ultimatum, the bull which he now sent under cover would be published. This bull was a sentence, drawn up in May 1407, excommunicating all who suspended their obedience to the pope, or who appealed from him to a future council. The reaction of the French to this was violent in the extreme. [ ] The decrees of February 1407, abolishing all payments to the pope of first fruits and other taxes -- the decrees hitherto suspended -- were now published; Benedict's leading supporters were arrested, and an order was sent to seize the pope himself. At Paris, all the scenes that had marked the struggle between Philip the Fair and Boniface VIII were renewed. There was a great public demonstration, [ ] where the king and the royal princes were present, with many bishops, the chief figures of the university, the lawyers of the parlement, and the chancellor of the kingdom. Speeches explained once more the king's duty as champion of religion against the schismatical and heretical pope, a perjurer and a persecutor of the Church; and then the bulls were brought out to be ceremonially ripped in pieces by all the notables, king, bishops, state officers and the dignitaries of the university, all lending a hand. On May 25 appeared the royal decree declaring that France, henceforward, was neutral as between Benedict XIII and Gregory XII, and imposing obedience to this policy on all the king's subjects.

It was on June 5 that news of this change in their pope's fortunes reached Benedict's cardinals at Leghorn. He had taken the precaution of sending with them some of his personal friends [ ] to keep watch on their activities, and it was from these -- who remained faithful to him -- that on June 11, at Genoa, he learnt of his own danger. Very speedily he decided to leave for Perpignan, a town then within the frontiers of his native land. But on June 15, immediately before he sailed, Benedict issued a summons calling a General Council to meet at Perpignan on November 1, 1408.

Both popes had now suffered the fate of Urban VI in 1378 -- each was deserted by almost all his cardinals. But the deserters had combined and on June 29, 1408, the feast of SS. Peter and Paul, the fourteen united [ ] cardinals published the agreement to which they had sworn, and appealed to the whole body of the faithful to support them. Each college -- it had been agreed -- would invite the prelates of its own pope's obedience to a council and the two councils would open simultaneously, if possible in the same city. Each college would do all in its power to induce the pope it acknowledged to be present in person at the council and to induce him to offer it his resignation. If the pope refused to abdicate, the council would depose him. Once Benedict and Gregory were out of the way -- whether by abdication or by such deposition -- the two colleges would unite and elect a pope and the councils would become one.

The pact was announced to each of the popes by the cardinals of his own group, to the King of France also and to the University of Paris; and Gregory XII's cardinals now instructed all those who had so far acknowledged him to withdraw their obedience.

The history of the next nine months (June 29, 1408-March 25, 1409) is unusually complicated, for there are now three centres from which instructions and commands go out to the Church. Thus, three days after this declaration by the independent cardinals, Gregory XII convoked a General Council, to meet at Pentecost 1409, in some city of north-eastern Italy, to be named later. Then, leaving Lucca, he made his way by Siena to Rimini, where Carlo Malatesta, one of the best captains of the day, and an admirable Christian, offered him protection. And the cardinals on July 14, twelve days after Gregory's summons, announced that the joint council they had in mind would meet at Pisa, on March 25, 1409.

For the next three months it is in France that the most important events are happening, at the national council summoned by the king to meet in Paris in August. This council was called to organise support for the king's policy of neutrality, to punish those who supported Benedict XIII, to provide for the religious government of France until the schism was ended, and to arrange for the representation of France at the coming Council of Pisa. The council was not very well attended: there were, for example, never more than thirty-five bishops present out of the total of eighty-five. But there was, this time, no opposition to what the crown and the university proposed. The messengers who had brought in Benedict's letters, and the threat of excommunication, were pilloried with the maximum of Gallic contempt; [ ] and in official sermons or harangues, made to the populace in front of Notre Dame, the pope himself was most grossly reviled. [ ] He was declared to be a heretic, and so also were his leading French supporters. As in 1398 the supreme religious authority in France was to be, in each province, the annual provincial council. It is noteworthy that, for all the bitterness against this particular pope, and the drastic act of rebellion against his rule, there is nowhere any movement to destroy the papacy, neither to abolish the office, nor to organise religious life as though it would never reappear. The whole system now set up does indeed "smack of the provisional"; [ ] and there is no attempt to set up for religious affairs any single authority for the whole nation. The several ecclesiastical provinces retain their equal status, and their independence of one another; they are not formed into a new body under some single authority (ecclesiastical or lay), some new "Church of France as by law established." It was also by provinces that this Council of Paris voted; and the council decided that by provinces the Church in France should be represented at Pisa, twelve delegates to be sent from each province in addition to the bishops and other prelates who would, of right, be convoked individually. Also the council, before it separated, on November 6, chose these 130 delegates; and the king issued a decree commanding all those summoned to Pisa not to fail to attend

Meanwhile, Benedict XIII had reached Perpignan in safety, with the three cardinals who remained true to him. On September 22, 1408, he created five new cardinals, and on October 22 he at last received the letters from his cardinals at Leghorn explaining what they had done, and inviting him to ratify it by coming to the Council of Pisa or by sending representatives. He sent, on November 7, the reply which they doubtless expected, denying them any power to call a General Council -- that is the prerogative of the pope alone -- and commanding them to appear at the council which he had summoned and which was now about to begin. Benedict opened his council in person just a fortnight later. [ ] He sang the inaugural high mass, presided at all the sessions -- stormy sessions many of them -- and with wonderful vigour, now an old man turned eighty, he argued and fenced, publicly and privately, with men as stubbornly skilful as himself -- for the vast majority of the fathers were of his own race. There was a small handful of prelates from Lorraine, Provence, and Savoy, but scarcely anyone from France, where Charles VI had closed the frontier. The mass of the council were Spaniards, in all something like 300 clerics of various ranks, [ ] to be argued with or persuaded.

The pope found them unexpectedly independent. They acknowledged him, fully, to be the lawful pope; but they were most critical of his policy and, anxious above all else that the schism should be ended, they urged Benedict not to ignore the council that was to meet at Pisa; he should send a delegation at any rate, and give it the widest powers, powers even to offer the council his abdication; at least -- so the Spanish council thought -- Benedict might pledge himself to abdicate if at Pisa they deposed his rival. On every side Peter de Luna was receiving this

same advice, even here "at the uttermost bounds of the earth."
But he was still Peter de Luna, and he held stubbornly to his plan
never to surrender his right to make decisions, never to commit
himself, and never to give any answer that he could not later
distinguish and sub-distinguish and thereby most veraciously
evade. As the sterile weeks went by, the council grew weary,
bishops, abbots, and delegates began to steal away to their
homes, and by the end of February (1409) there was not a
handful in attendance. It was this remnant who tendered to
Benedict the council's official advice: to be represented at Pisa,
to make a definite pledge that he would abdicate, and to forbid
his cardinals to elect a successor to himself should he chance to
die. Benedict, of course, accepted in principle; and then
adjourned the council for seven weeks, until March 26

Long before that day came -- it was the day following the
triumphant, splendid opening of the council at Pisa -- the cause
of Gregory XII had shrunk to far less even than that of Benedict.

From Rimini, Malatesta had worked earnestly for an
understanding with the cardinals at Pisa, but Gregory was now as
stubborn as Benedict -- he, too, was a very old man, now
seventy-three. Henry IV of England added his plea, but without
any effect. Then, on December 24, 1408, England, too, deserted
the Roman pope. Two days later Wenzel -- who had already
gone over to the cardinals as King of Bohemia -- now gave them
his support as emperor, while his rival Rupert put his miserable
remnant of prestige at the service of Gregory. In the first days of
the new year, 1409, Gregory excommunicated his rebellious
cardinals, depriving them of all their dignities, their cardinalitial
rank and rights. Then, January 26, Florence deserted him. The
Roman pope had now none to acknowledge him but Malatesta,
Venice and Ladislas of Naples. The vast bulk of the princes and
bishops were wholeheartedly neutral, pinning all their hopes on
the united cardinals and the council which they had summoned.

## 5. THE CHURCH UNDER THE COUNCILS, 1409-1418
i. Pisa, 1409

The Council of Pisa opened on the day appointed, March 25, 1409. If judged by the number who came to it, and by the variety of countries from which they came, the council was a huge success, the most splendid gathering certainly that Europe had seen for two hundred years. All its twenty-three sessions were held in the nave of the cathedral, the last of them on August 7 of this same year. It seems not to have been easy for contemporaries to say exactly how many ecclesiastics took part in it. The numbers varied, of course, from one session to another, and seemingly they were at the maximum in the important sessions in which Gregory XII and Benedict XIII were judged and deposed -- when something more than 500 fathers attended. These would include the twenty-two cardinals and eighty-four bishops who came (102 other bishops were present by proxies), the eightyseven abbots (200 more were represented by proxies), the forty-one priors, the four generals of the Dominicans, Franciscans, Carmelites and Augustinians, the three representatives of the military orders (the Hospitallers, the Holy Sepulchre and the Teutonic Knights), the hundred deputies from cathedral chapters, the deputies from thirteen universities, and the 300 or so doctors of theology and law -- these last a new and significant element in a General Council's composition, for they were given a voice in its judgments. Moreover, seventeen foreign princes also sent ambassadors -- the kings of France, England, Bohemia, Poland, Portugal, Sicily and Cyprus; the dukes of Burgundy, Brabant, Holland, Lorraine and Austria; the prince-bishops of Liege, Cologne and Mainz; the rulers of Savoy, Thuringia and Brandenburg: the whole body of Christian princes in fact, save those of Scandinavia and Scotland, of Spain and of Naples.

The council was a marvellously unanimous body. There was little or no discussion in its main sessions. All were agreed on the business that had brought them together, and the council had little to do beyond giving a solemn assent to the decisions as the cardinals and its own officials had shaped them. If any nation was predominant it was the Italian; fifteen of the twenty-two cardinals present were Italian, and so were ten of the fourteen chief officials, though the presidency was given to the French, and first of all to the sole survivor among the cardinals of the college of Gregory XI, the last pope before the schism, sole surviving cardinal, too, of those who had elected Urban VI in April 1378 and then, five months later, elected Clement VII. This was Guy de Malesset.

The key-note speech of the council was made by the Archbishop of Milan -- Peter Philarghi, an ex-cardinal of Gregory XII's obedience -- who on March 26 excoriated Gregory and Benedict alike, for their crimes and their treason to the cause of religion. Meanwhile, before proceeding to any juridical consideration of the position of these rivals, the council solemnly summoned both to appear before it -- a ceremony five times repeated in the first month of its sittings.

While the fathers were awaiting the expiration of the time allowed for the popes' appearance, they had to meet the practical problems set by two embassies that now arrived, the one from the Emperor Rupert [ ] (denying them any right to be considered a General Council) and the other from Gregory XII, inviting them to abandon Pisa and join him at Rimini in a council where he would preside.

It was on April 15 that the imperial ambassadors were received in audience. They presented a lengthy memorandum in which Gregory XII's case against the cardinals who had left him was well set out, and the traditional doctrine that the General Council is subject to the pope in its convocation, its proceedings, and the ratification of its acts, was well argued against the new theories by which the united cardinals had publicly justified their action.

Much of this criticism was unanswerable. Gregory had, at one time, undoubtedly been acknowledged as pope by these cardinals who had elected him. When, asked Rupert's envoys, had he ceased to be pope? The universal Church had not condemned him; he had not been convicted of heresy. To convoke a General Council is a prerogative that belongs to popes alone, and, in point of fact, Gregory XII -- they said -- had long ago actually convoked one, that would meet within a few weeks. Moreover, if the popes of the Roman line were really popes, the popes of the Avignon line were not -- if the cardinals of the Roman line were really cardinals, the Avignon cardinals with whom they were now joined were not cardinals at all. What then was their value as a basic element of this new union? The ambassadors therefore proposed a meeting between the council and Gregory XII. That pope would then carry out his election promises; and if he refused, Rupert would support the cardinals in their move to elect a new single pope -- a curiously illogical conclusion, surely, to the arguments made in his name !

The council heard the lengthy argument, and appointed a day for the answer. But the argument, and the way it was presented, seem thoroughly to have annoyed the council. The ambassadors realised how hopeless were their chances of persuading the fathers, and on April 21, without awaiting the formality of any official refutation, they left Pisa, secretly, leaving behind a public appeal [ ] from this assembly to a true General Council when this should meet.

Gregory XII's own champion -- Carlo Malatesta -- had no better fortune with the council, although he managed to carry on the discussion in a friendly spirit. The cardinals appointed to meet him gave forty reasons why they could not abandon the work begun at Pisa; Gregory XII ought to abdicate and the best service that Malatesta could do the Church was to persuade -- or coerce -- him to come to Pisa and there lay down his authority. There was much discussion about the compensation to be given

Gregory (and his relatives) if he consented; Malatesta seems to have raised a general laugh when he twitted the ambitious Philarghi with his known willingness to bear the terrible burden of the papacy; and the cardinals agreed to meet Gregory at Pistoia or at San Miniato for a conference. On April 26 Malatesta went back to Rimini and reported to Gregory that this was all he had been able to achieve. The old man wept, explained again his dilemma -- that if he went back to his first policy he would be deserting his present supporters, Rupert, for example, and Ladislas -- and finally he refused to meet the cardinals elsewhere than at Rimini.

These embassies had distracted the council for weeks from completing even the preliminaries of organising itself. But now, on May 4, the fathers declared the union of the cardinals lawful, and that this was a lawfully convoked council, a true General Council with sovereign rights to judge Gregory XII and Benedict XIII; and by appointing a commission of nineteen cardinals and prelates to examine witnesses, the council began what, in effect, was a trial of the popes. That Ladislas of Naples was now besieging Siena -- only sixty miles away -- evidently making for Pisa, and that Gregory was subsidising him, no doubt stiffened the council's resolution.

The lengthy enquiry about the rival popes at last came to an end; a sentence was prepared, and the council made it its own. On June 5, 1409, the council solemnly declared that both Angelo Corrario and Peter de Luna, once called Gregory XII and Benedict XIII, were notorious heretics, and perjurers, ipso facto excommunicated and incapable in law of ruling as popes; and as such it deposed and excommunicated them. [ ] All nominations they might make were declared null; all Catholics were forbidden, under pain of excommunication, to obey them or give them any support; if necessary the secular authority would be used against them and their adherents; their censures against members of the council were declared null and void; and the cardinals they had created since the cardinals now legislating deserted them were no cardinals at all.

How contradictory this was of all tradition -- and of tradition explicitly set forth at the very threshold of that Canon Law which so many of the council professed (to say nothing of theology) -- let two texts from Gratian witness: (I) Cunctos iudicaturus, ipse a nemine est iudicandus, nisi deprehenditur a fide devius; [ ] (2) Aliorum hominum causas Deus voluit per homines terminari, sedis autem Romanae praesulem, suo, sine quaestione, reservavit arbitrio. [ ] By what steps had so many, and so famously learned, ecclesiastics come to such a revolutionary position as to vote the mischiefs of the Schism, the opportunity which it provided for strange novelties to develop in the doctrine de Romano pontifice, and indeed to be developed as part of any zealous Christian's duty to restore peace and harmony to the Church.

Since the time of John of Paris, whose De Potestate Regia has been described as part of the contest between Boniface VIII and Philip the Fair, [ ] there had been in circulation two new ideas which appear in that work. First of all, there should function under the pope, an advisory council for the whole Church, of delegates elected by each ecclesiastical province; thus the faithful might have a share in the administration of the Church. Next there is a theory that justifies the deposition of a pope for heresy, on the ground that, besides the supreme papal power there is in the universal Church a latent supremacy exceeding the pope's power, which comes into play in just such an emergency. In that case orbis est maior urbe, says the Dominican. That a pope is answerable to the Church for the orthodoxy of his own belief was no new invention of John of Paris. The quotation from Gratian just given is one earlier evidence of the idea; and John the Teutonic adds two other causes for which popes may be judged, notorious sin and public scandal. This author says explicitly that in matters of faith the Council is superior to the Pope, and that it is for the Council to judge a disputed papal election. A third writer previous to the Schism, the Cardinal Bertrand, also considers that a bad pope -- although not a heretic -- is answerable to the General Council, and that should he refuse to summon it and take his trial, the right to convoke it passes to the cardinals.

These three writers are, all of them, eminently respectable Catholics -- which is more than can be said of the three most revolutionary theorists on the matter which the century produced, Marsiglio of Padua, Michael of Cesena and Ockham. Marsiglio's theory of the General Council has no roots at all in canonist tradition. His idea of the pope as the Church's delegate and servant (to which Pierre de Plaoul was to give dramatic utterance in a famous council at Paris [ ] ) is of Marsiglio's own devising. Ockham is less simple -- more aware of the depths of the problem he is trying to solve. But for him the source of all authority is representation. Sovereignty lies in the Church as a whole, and the council's power comes from this alone that it is the Church's agent. Since the man in whom the divine authority to rule the Church as pope is invested, receives it through an agency that is human -- since only the authority is divine, and not either the mode of its devolution or the detail, why not then, if it should prove convenient, two popes at once, or three, or indeed one for each country?

It was not, however, to the theories of any of these ingenious revolutionaries that the canonists turned, once the election of Robert of Geneva had brought about the state of schism. They went where men ex professo so conservatively minded must go, to the canonists. Prior to the question whether Urban VI's election was valid was that other, who had the power to determine this question juridically? Was it within the competence of a General Council? This was the main pre-occupation of the earliest writers who studied the matter once the Schism was a fact, Conrad of Gelnhausen, for example and Henry of Langenstein. The conclusion to which they came was that it was for the General Council to decide, and this, not because the Council is the pope's superior, but because this is the exceptional case that falls within the Council's special competence.

It is only later on, with the second generation of the Schism, when the feeling grows that the case is desperate, that the desperate remedies appear in the shape of the new conciliar theories. It is now that we have Francis Zabarella, the leading canonist of his generation, declaring plainly that the pope is but the first servant of the Church, that his power derives from the Church and that the Church cannot so delegate its power to him that it retains none itself. Peter d'Ailly is no less extreme, and if Zabarella has read Ockham so too, it would seem, has the Bishop of Cambrai. The Church alone, he says, is infallible. That the General Council is infallible is no more than a pious belief, and that the pope is infallible is wholly erroneous. The papal authority is only a matter of expediency, a practical device to ensure good government. General Councils may judge the pope not only for heresy, and for obstinacy in sin, but also for opposition to the Council. Gerson's famous sermon at Constance [ ] does not say more. The Pope, for Gerson, is merely the executive organ within the Church, the legislative power remains with the General Council.

Such is the intellectual and academic hinterland that has bred the men now to function, not only as reformers of Catholic life, but as the architects of reunion, the saviours of the papacy from schism. [ ]

Nine days after this "crowning mercy" of the council, an embassy arrived from the King of Aragon, escorting the envoys whom Benedict XIII had sent, in fulfilment of his pledge to his own council at Perpignan three months earlier.

Out of respect for the king the council appointed a commission to meet Benedict's legates. The news of their arrival in Pisa had been the signal for a great riot, and noisy crowds, bent on mischief, surrounded the church where they were received by the commissioners. The negotiations never went beyond this first meeting. It was explained to Benedict's party that their safety could not be guaranteed, so violent was the anger of the people against Peter de Luna at this moment when the cardinals were about to enter the conclave and, by electing a pope, bring the schism to an end; and that night the ambassadors left by stealth, happy to escape with their lives. They had previously approached the cardinal legate of Bologna -- Baldassare Cossa -- for a safe conduct which would take them to Rimini and Gregory XII; but he only swore that he would burn alive any of them who came into his hands.

The embassy had indeed arrived at the least lucky moment of all, when the council's creative act was, men believed, about to give the Church the pope of unity. On June 13 a conciliar decree had ordered the cardinals to proceed to the election of a pope, authorising them to unite for this purpose, although they had been created cardinals by rival popes who mutually denied each other to be pope; for this once they would elect the man they chose by an authority deriving from the council. And the cardinals swore only to elect the candidate who gained two-thirds of the vote of each of the two groups. The conclave lasted eleven days, and on June 26 it was announced that Peter Philarghi, Archbishop of Milan, had been chosen unanimously -- Alexander V.

Alexander V -- pope by the authority of the Council of Pisa, was, like Gregory XII and Benedict XIII, a veteran of these ecclesiastical wars, and now seventy years of age at least. He was Greek by birth, a foundling whom the charity of an Italian Franciscan had rescued from the streets of Candia. He had later become a Franciscan, and a theologian of sufficient merit to fill chairs at Paris and at Oxford. One of the Dukes of Milan had found him a valuable counsellor; he had been given -- the see of Piacenza, thence promoted to Novara and, in 1402, to Milan. Innocent VII had created him cardinal and he had taken part in the conclave that elected Gregory XII. When Gregory's first fervour declined, Philarghi had been one of the most active, and effective, of his opponents. His nationality -- not Italian, nor French, nor Spanish -- made him a most "available" candidate in this first conclave for generations in which Italians and French men divided the votes. Guy de Malesset is credited with the proposal to elect him, and Baldassare Cossa -- late the strong man of the Roman obedience -- with the negotiations that won over to Philarghi the partisans of other candidates. It was Cossa who was to be all powerful in the short ten months' pontificate which is all that fate allowed Alexander V.

The first thought of the electors and supporters of Peter Philarghi was the personal profit they could draw from his elevation. Even before his coronation the hunt after spoils was in full cry; and sees, abbeys and benefices were showered on all lucky enough to be near the new pope. [ ] And from Alexander V's willingness to make men happy the whole of his obedience gained. In the twenty-second session of the council -- July 27, 1409 -- a great comprehensive decree validated all manner of appointments and dispensations lately made without due reference to the papal authority, and the pope generously forgave all arrears due, on various accounts, to the papal treasury and lifted all sentences of excommunication and the like that lay upon defaulters. He also surrendered his claim to revenues that had accrued, from the estates of dead bishops and prelates, during the vacancy of the Holy See, and he asked the cardinals to follow his example and give up the half of what payments were due to them. Also, it was decreed that a new General Council should meet in April 1412, at a place to be determined later. Finally, in the closing session, August 7, 1409, the first preparations for this next council -- whose work was to be the reform of Christian life -- were outlined; local councils were to be summoned -- provincial and diocesan synods, chapters of the various monastic orders -- where matters calling for reform were to be discussed and schemes prepared. Then, with Alexander's blessing, and a last sermon, the fathers dispersed.

At Cividale, meanwhile, seventy miles to the north-east of Venice, the council summoned by Gregory XII was all this time still struggling to be born. It had been convoked months before, and the place announced on December 19, 1408. But when it opened, on the Feast of Corpus Christi, 1409 -- the day after Gregory had been sentenced at Pisa -- almost no one had arrived. On June 20 the letters of convocation were renewed, and a second session took place on July 22, Gregory XII presiding. A declaration was then made that this was a true General Council, and also that the popes Urban VI, Boniface IX, Innocent VII and Gregory XII were true popes: Clement VII, Benedict XIII and Alexander V being sacrilegious usurpers. The Emperor Rupert continued to support Gregory, who rewarded him by lavish powers to take over the revenues of all bishops and clerics in the empire who supported the anti-popes. Ladislas of Naples, too, remained faithful to Gregory XII: by now he was master of almost the whole of the Papal States. But Venice -- Gregory XII's own. native state -- upon whose territory the Council of Cividale was held, was wavering. The deed accomplished at Pisa, and the immense support given to it by all the princes, were not without effect upon this most politically-minded of all states. The Pisan council soon opened negotiations with the most serene republic, and on August 22, by sixty-nine votes to forty-eight, Venice went over to Alexander V. Gregory realised his danger, and announced his departure for Rome. But before he left he held a third session of his council (September 5). In this he announced that, as always, he was most anxious to bring the long division to an end. But now that Alexander V had appeared, what would his resignation and that of Benedict avail? However, if both Benedict and Alexander would resign, and their cardinals would promise to join with his to elect a single pope, Gregory XII would resign too. Also he would submit to the wishes of a new council if Benedict and Alexander would do likewise. Next day he left for Latigiana, and dropped down the Tagliamento to the coast where the galleys sent by Ladislas were waiting to take him to Pescara. Thence, with an escort provided by the king, the pope crossed the Abruzzi, and in November 1409 he took up his residence at Gaeta.

There could hardly have been a greater contrast between the splendid position of Alexander V, the elect of this great parliament of the Christian nations, with seventeen princes, bishops innumerable, and thirteen universities supporting him, and the miserable condition of Gregory XII, now reduced to a single faithful supporter, Carlo Malatesta, for Venice had now deserted Gregory for Alexander, and Ladislas of Naples was serving his cause only so long as this served himself. There could hardly have been any greater contrast, except perhaps between the Pisan papacy's prestige now and what it would be in a short two years. All this grandeur was, indeed, of its nature, transient. For it rested on nothing more enduring than the opinions of scholars and the good will of princes, the novel opinions of scholars about the right of the Church to control the papacy, to set up popes and to pluck them down in appropriate season. Here was the source of all its power, and no papacy thus conceived could long continue to hold men's allegiance.

Alexander V reigned for less than a year. [ ] The reign began with a military expedition against Ladislas of Naples -- excommunicated and deposed by Alexander on November 1, 1409 -- in which the French claimant to Naples, Louis of Anjou, and the warlike cardinal-legate of Bologna, Baldassare Cossa, joined forces. On the first day of the new year they recovered Rome. But the pope to whom they restored the shrine of St. Peter did not live to take possession. Before his death he had, once more, solemnly excommunicated Gregory XII and Benedict XIII and by a bull in favour of the mendicant orders [ ] -- Alexander was himself a Friar Minor -- he had managed to rouse the hostility of the University of Paris. This squabble came to nothing, for Alexander's successor rescinded the bull, but it is a squabble of more than passing interest, for the university, as by a habit now become second nature, while speaking of Alexander with the utmost respect, and in no way denying his authority, declared that the bull had been obtained from him by misrepresentations; it could therefore be disregarded, and from the pope misinformed the university would appeal to the pope truly informed; also the king's aid was sought, and Charles VI forbade the parochial clergy to allow any Franciscan or Augustinian to preach or administer the sacraments in the parish churches of France.

The successor of Alexander V was Baldassare Cossa, elected on May 17, 1410, after a short three days' conclave held in the castle of Bologna. He took the name of John XXIII. About the events of that conclave we have no certain knowledge. It is known that Malatesta moved to delay the election, in the hope of reconciling the cardinals with Gregory XII. Cossa replied that this would be tantamount to a surrender of the Pisan position; moreover, were there any delay in providing a successor to Alexander his curia would disperse.

Was the election of John XXIII vitiated by simony? The charge has been made, and very generally believed. Those who hold Gregory XII to have been the true pope in all these years can afford to be impartial about Cossa's character. He has indeed come down in the history books as a finished blackguard. But most of the atrocious stories are from the memories of men who had good cause to hate him, and when John XXIII came to take his trial at the next great council only a very small fraction of the charges made against him figured in the sentence of deposition. The first great patron of his ecclesiastical career had been Boniface IX -- a fellow Neapolitan -- who made him a cardinal in 1402 in reward for his practical service of finding badly-needed sums of money, and appointed him as legate to rule Bologna. For the next six years Cardinal Baldassare Cossa was the strong man on the Roman side, and after the surrender of Gregory XII to his relatives he was that pope's chief opponent, and luridly characterised as such in Gregory's later bulls.

Historians have noted how, as his reign went on, all John XXIII's wonted political sagacity seemed to desert him. The truth is that his position was, from the beginning, simply impossible; and, after a time, every month that went by showed this more clearly. At first, indeed, his cause seemed to prosper. Malatesta and Ladislas of Naples continued the war on behalf of Gregory XII, but John retained Rome and occupied the city in April 1411. Ladislas was next beaten in the field, re-excommunicated by John, and a crusade preached against him; and in June 1412, brought for the moment to his knees, he opened negotiations with John and on October 16 acknowledged him as pope. Whereupon Gregory XII -- who was still at Gaeta -- fled, lest Ladislas should arrest him and hand him over to John. So far all had gone well; and the election as King of the Romans on July 21, 1411, of the ex-emperor Wenzel's brother, Sigismund, had also been a gain to John, for Sigismund had been Gregory XII's enemy ever since that pope had supported Ladislas against him in Hungary. But this was the last of John's good fortune, and Sigismund -- for the moment his greatest support -- was soon to become the chief instrument in the pope's ruin.

This Pisan line of popes was bound, by its pledges to the council of 1409, to summon a new council which would promote reforms, not later than 1412. The place where it should meet had not been determined, and when John XXIII convoked it to come together in Rome there was great dissatisfaction in France and Germany. John however, more confident perhaps since the submission of Ladislas, held firm and in the last days of 1412 the council opened. It was poorly attended; indeed, the delegates from France and Germany did not arrive until all was over, for on March 11, 1413, John prorogued the council until the following December. The solitary permanent achievement of the council was its condemnation of John Wyclif, [ ] but in John XXIII's personal history it figures as the beginning of the movement among his own supporters to make an end of him. .

To some of his own newly -- created cardinals [ ] -- Peter d'Ailly notably -- the council was an opportunity to rebuke John to his face for his evil life, and the chief effect of the meetings between the pope and the various delegations was to spread far and wide the belief that John XXIII was indifferent to the cause of reform, and only interested in the papacy as a means of personal power.

The reformers were, of course, far from being a united party. As always, side by side with the idealists, there were others chiefly interested in changes for the personal profit they might be made to produce. From France and from Germany there came, very generally, loud demands yet once again for the abolition of papal taxes on Church property and revenues. But the University of Paris, fresh from its recent experience of how little bishops were disposed to encourage ecclesiastical learning by promoting learned men to benefices, was now strongly opposed to any movement that would limit the pope's power to collate universally to benefices. The Roman Curia had been much more friendly to learning than the local episcopate; and so now the university expressed itself as shocked and horrified at the anti-papal tendencies [ ] -- although, in its turn, it was bitter with John XXIII when he chose Rome as the meeting place for the council.

Here, then, was a first serious division among the reformers. The action of the King of France produced a second. The only reform in which he was interested was that the pope should give him vast new rights of nomination to benefices of all kinds; and his ambassadors warned the pope that were this refused him the king might make common cause with the university, and champion its theory of the liberties of the Gallican Church -- or perhaps follow the example of the Kings of England and enact, for France also, an anti-papal statute of Provisors. [ ]

These disturbing embassies from France and Germany had scarcely left Rome when Ladislas suddenly broke his treaty with the pope. In May 1413 his armies invaded the Marches, and on June 8 he took Rome -- which made no resistance whatever. John XXIII fled to Florence, and appealed urgently for aid to Sigismund, and the emperor in reply demanded that a new General Council be summoned. John sent two cardinals to him at Como -- the Savoyard diplomatist de Challant and the great canonist Francesco Zabarella. With the emperor they decided on the place and the time for the council, the German city of Constance for November 1, 1414. John XXIII was now at Bologna (November 8, 1413). The prospect of a General Council in a territory where he was not the civil ruler dismayed him. He had no choice, however, but to accept; the initiative had, by his own act, passed to Sigismund. Pope and emperor now came together (November 1413 to January 1414), and on December 9 John published a bull convoking the council for the time and at the place the emperor had chosen.

Ladislas, meanwhile, carried all before him in the Papal State, sacking Rome a second time in March 1414. Then he made for Bologna, and John; but the Florentines turned him back, and on August 6 death brought to an end this last meteoric fifteen months of his career. Their one lasting achievement had been to put John entirely into Sigismund's power. On October 1, 1414, the pope, reluctant to the end, and his plan to return to Rome thwarted by the cardinals, left Bologna for the council and on October 28 he made his solemn entry into Constance, very apprehensive about his own fate, and about that only.
ii. Constance, 1414-1418

The great Council of Constance is the closing, transformation scene of the medieval drama, if the Middle Ages be considered as a time when the mainspring of all public action was western Europe's acceptance of the spiritual supremacy of the pope. Not, indeed, that the moment has arrived when that supremacy is rejected by large parts of Christendom; nor that there are, as yet, signs not to be mistaken of that coming revolution. But after Constance things are never again the same; the ecclesiastical system -- the Catholic Church built on the divine right of the popes to rule it -- has suffered a shock, and there has been a settlement. The intangible has been struck and to the ordinary man it has seemed to stagger if not to crack up. The great scandal of the attack at Anagni has now, a hundred years later, been evidently renewed. Rough hands have again been laid on the ark; and again the assailants have survived their sacrilege -- the harm done is none the smaller for the fact that the assailants are in good faith, invincibly ignorant and unaware of the sacrilege.

The hundred years that lie between Constance and the first movements of the coming revolution, these last hundred years of a united Catholic Christendom, are a transitional period, in which a new order of things is struggling to be born, socially, politically, culturally, philosophically; they are a period in which it is not only the way in which popes exercise their power that is more and more generally questioned, but their very right to exercise it; the very existence, as well as the nature, of their spiritual authority over the Church of Christ. Ideas which are of their nature noxious, and even fatal, to the traditional theories and beliefs about the papacy, had already been given a kind of public recognition at Pisa. Now they were to be recognised again, by a much more imposing kind of council, a council itself recognised -- at one time or another -- by two of the three claimants to the papacy, and a council through whose activity came the pope whose legitimacy the whole Church was to acknowledge. No council ever sat so continuously for so long a time as did this Council of Constance; and no council ever changed so often its character -- if by character we mean its authority as canon law and theology define a council's authority.

In certain of its widely different phases this council enacted decrees that were as contradictory of fundamental Catholic practice as anything any heretic who appeared before it for judgment had ever held. The theologian who to-day studies the acts of the council has no difficulty in distinguishing between the value of the decisions to which it came in one or another of these phases. Nor had the popes of the united Christendom any difficulty at the time. But the new harmony of Christendom achieved in the council -- its great achievement indeed, because of which historians have been loth to speak harshly even of its really serious shortcomings -- was too frail a thing, on the morrow of the council, for all ambiguity to be stripped away from the council's proceedings, the ambiguity which made it possible for the untrained mind of the ordinary observer to see Constance as an authoritative consecration of the revolutionary doctrine of Pisa that the General Council is the supreme authority in the Church of Christ; the ambiguity which, from now on, could be exploited by chauvinistic theologians, everywhere, in the interests of their princes whenever popes were enmeshed in any crisis of political or religious revolt.

The history of the Council of Constance cannot ever be too closely studied. [ ] If it was the occasion of the disappearance of all controversy which of the men who then claimed to be pope was really the pope, controversy that had troubled the Church for forty years, its proceedings were also the cause of a survival of ideas -- materially heretical -- that harassed religion and sorely debilitated it for another four centuries and more. For example, the grave anxiety -- henceforth chronic -- arising from the fact that influential Catholics clung to theories that would make the pope the Church's servant and not its ruler, and that such Catholics only awaited a new chance to put them again into action, was to be not only a good excuse for lazy popes and weak popes and bad popes to ignore the clamant need for a spiritual restoration -- only to be brought about with the aid of a General Council -- but, much more tragically, it became a valid reason whereby good popes too hesitated, really fearing lest with the abundance of tares they would root up the little wheat that remained. These theories did much to bring it about that the popes of the next four hundred years were no longer so much the master in their own household as their medieval predecessors had been -- unless a pope knew that his primatial authority over the whole Church was unquestioned, in practice and in theory, he could hardly proceed to the drastic house-cleaning that was called for. Saints perhaps would have gone ahead, and in the name of God dared all; but the average pope was no more than an average in his own kind, and spiritual mediocrity was unable to surmount the general habitual feebleness which consciousness of divided opinion on this vital matter did so much to produce.

The Council cf. Constance was in continuous session for three years and five months, [ ] and perhaps the most convenient way to study briefly what it accomplished is to disregard the timetable of events, and to set out the problems which it faced and the solutions it found for them. These problems were, in the main, the three matters of the Schism, the new heresies in England and Bohemia, and the reform of Christian life; the second of these will be more conveniently dealt with in the next chapter, where Wyclif's heresy, the work of Wyclif's disciple, John Hus, and the significance of the Hussite wars will be treated together.

But before problems could even be stated, the council must organise its own procedure, and in these preliminary discussions, which went on all through December 1414 and the first weeks of the new year, traditional serious divisions showed immediately. The first to offer an agenda (December 7) were the Italians. To them this new council was but a continuation of the Council of Pisa. It should decree stricter censures than ever on Gregory XII and Benedict XIII and their supporters, and call on the Christian princes to put an end to the dissensions by force of arms; John XXIII's position being thus strengthened, the council could then be dissolved, to be followed by another General Council in ten, or perhaps twenty-five, years. The impudent naivety of this programme provoked a tough reply from the leader of the French delegation, Peter d'Ailly. His main thought, as always, was to heal the divisions of Christendom, and he now proposed that every effort should be made to conciliate the popes deposed at Pisa and to win them over to take part in the new council; and, thanks in great part to his effort, it was agreed that if Gregory and Benedict sent cardinals as envoys these should be received as such, and allowed the insignia of their rank. This was a first defeat for the friends of John XXIII, a clear indication that he was not to be any more the master of the council than was Gregory or Benedict.

The English arrived on January 21, 1415, and some days later the Germans. Both joined the anti-Italian forces; and the Germans, in their plan for the council, made the revolutionary demand that not bishops and mitred abbots alone should have a defining vote, but also the proxies of absent bishops and abbots, the delegates of cathedral chapters also, and of universities; and that masters of theology and doctors, and the envoys of princes should also be allowed a vote. If all this were allowed, the band of supporters which John XXIII had brought from Italy -- in numbers almost half of the bishops so far present -- would be swamped at every vote.

By what succession of controversy and compromise, of offers and of threats, John XXIII and his supporters were brought to surrender does not appear. It was, however, agreed that all these various classes of clerics and laymen should share in the council's work, but not by voting as individuals in the General Sessions where the decrees were solemnly enacted. They should have their vote in the preliminary discussions on the decrees, and for these discussions the council was divided into "nations," after the fashion of the University of Paris. There were four of these nations, the Italian, German, French and English. When, by separate discussions, a solution had been agreed upon in each nation, it was to be adopted in a General Congregation of deputies from all four, and then reported to the General Session of the Council and officially voted. Each nation, whether represented at the council by hundreds or by single units, would thus have equal power whenever there was a conciliar vote.

The political genius behind the scheme is evident; it was an innovation, and it succeeded. But such a system destroyed all possibility of the council's being reckoned one of the General Councils in the traditional sense of the word, for in these the function of the bishops is to speak and vote, not as contributing to the general fund the quota of their own personal learning and wisdom, but as witnesses testifying to the belief of the churches they rule. Peter d'Ailly's argument that learned doctors of theology were of greater importance in a General Council than ignorant bishops, was beside the point altogether. The assembly he had in mind was no more than a congress of Christian learning; it was not a gathering of the teaching Church witnessing to the faith held everywhere by the faithful.

The Council of Constance was well attended, if not by bishops, by doctors of theology and law, by the clergy generally, by princes, by statesmen, by nobles and laity of all ranks and of all degrees of virtue. The numbers varied largely during the three and a half years it was in session. At its maximum attendance there were 29 cardinals, 186 bishops, [ ] more than 100 abbots, 300 and more doctors either of theology or of law, 11 ruling princes -- the Emperor Sigismund at their head, and ambassadors from twelve other Christian princes. With their suites -- the elaborate suites of the princes and the great prelates -- and the huge spontaneous inflow attracted by the chances of profit which such a gathering must offer, the little city of Constance saw its normal population of 6,000 many times multiplied, over the long period of nearly four years.

John XXIII had journeyed to Constance as to a doom that was certain; and, indeed, the immediate question in the minds of most of the prelates making the same journey was how to disembarrass Christendom of its latest scandal, a pope who was notoriously an evil liver. In the ten weeks between the first and second general sessions of the council, the opinion gained ground that John must go. A well-written pamphlet, of anonymous authorship, that set out his misdeeds and called for an enquiry by the council, was brought to John's notice sometime in February 1415. Whatever plans he had made to brazen out his position crumbled; he asked advice of cardinals he could trust, and they all urged him to abdicate, to spare the Church the scandal of a trial where the pope must be proved guilty of crime. John yielded, and at the mass with which the second general session opened (March 2, 1415), his solemn pledge to abdicate was publicly read. The pope was himself the celebrant of the mass, and at the words "I swear and vow" he left his throne to kneel before the altar in sign of submission. But he speedily changed his mind, and while the details of the resignation were being worked out, in the night of March 20, he fled from Constance in disguise, hoping to bring about the dispersal of the council.

For a moment the pope's flight produced its intended effect, and the council seemed about to break up in a general confusion. But the vigorous action of the emperor saved the day, and he won from the cardinals a pledge that they would carry on. There was, naturally, a most violent outbreak of anti-papal feeling and the nations, trusting neither the pope nor the cardinals, forced on the third session, March 26, at which only two cardinals -- d'Ailly and Zabarella -- attended. This session is the turning point of the council's history, the moment when it awakens to the opportunity before it and boldly takes the revolutionary step of decreeing that whether the pope returned or not the council's authority remained sovereign and intact; that it would not dissolve until the Church had been fully reformed, the papacy and the Roman Curia no less than the general body; and that the council could not be transferred elsewhere without its own consent.

To the envoys whom the council sent to him in his refuge at Schaffhausen, John gave a shifty answer, that only provoked at Constance a demand for strong action and for a new general session. In preparation for this, the English, French and Germans combined (March 29) to secure the enactment of four decrees that would officially establish the doctrine that in the Catholic Church the General Council is the pope's superior. But, only a few hours before the council met, the cardinals won over the emperor to support an alternative scheme, and he persuaded the nations to accept it; at the general session (March 30) it was this that was passed. The excitement in the city was, by this time, at its height; the divisions within the council were known, the Italians it seemed were still loyal to John, and also a party among the cardinals, several of whom had gone to join him; the emperor was gathering troops for an attack on the pope's protector, Frederick of Hapsburg, Count of Tyrol. At this moment came the news that the pope had moved still further into Germany, after revoking and annulling all he had conceded. Opinion now hardened rapidly against him, and at the next [ ] general session -- April 6 -- as a legal basis for operations against the pope, the council voted the original four articles of March 29.

These most famous articles [ ] declared that this council, lawfully assembled, was an oecumenical council representing the whole Church Militant and that it derived its authority directly from God; that the whole of the world, therefore, the pope included, owed it obedience in all that concerned the faith, the extinction of the schism, and reform; whoever, then, obstinately refused to obey its decrees, or the decrees of any other General Council lawfully assembled, made with reference to the matters mentioned, was liable to the council's correction and to the punishment it ordered, even were that person the pope himself; the flight of John XXIII was an act of scandal, entailing the suspicion that he was fostering the schism and had fallen into heresy; within the council, it was stated, the pope -- and indeed, all the fathers -- had enjoyed full freedom of action.

As the emperor's troops moved out from Constance, the cardinals who had joined the pope returned to the council and John sent in an offer to abdicate -- at a price. He was to remain a cardinal, to be named legate for life for Italy, to be given the Avignon territories of the Holy See and the sum of 30,000 ducats in cash. All this the council ignored; it was now busy constructing a formula of abdication in which there would be no loopholes. Then, on April 30, John's protector surrendered to the emperor. The crisis was over. The pope could now be rounded up whenever the council needed him.

On May 2 John's trial was officially demanded in the council on six general charges, namely notorious heresy, complacency in schism, simony, dilapidation of Church properties, misconduct and incorrigibility. While he continued, for the next four weeks, to fence with the successive citations to appear and take his trial, a special commission heard the witnesses and sorted out their charges as a preliminary to drawing up a formal indictment. Officials of the curia, bishops, and cardinals too, appeared to tell the story of John's misdeeds, ever since he was a disobedient and incorrigible boy in his own home. On May 17 the pope was arrested at Freiburg-in-Breisgau and brought to the castle of Radolfzell, near Constance. All the fight had now gone out of him; he wept and asked only for mercy, surrendered his seal to the council and wrote that he would, if they chose, abdicate, or accept and ratify any sentence of deposition they chose to pass. When the fifty-four charges, proved to the council's satisfaction in the session of May 25, were read over to him, he had no reply to make save that he put himself in the council's hands; it was holy and could not err, he said. He did not accept the offer to defend himself, but again begged only for mercy. Two days after this, on May 29, in the twelfth general session, sentence of deposition was passed on him and on May 31 John formally accepted it and ratified it and with an oath swore never to call it in question. And then he was taken off to the prison where, under the guard of Lewis of Bavaria, he was to spend the next three years. [ ]

Just five weeks after Baldassare Cossa so meekly accepted the council's sentence, the fathers met to receive the solemn abdication of Gregory XII. He was in fact, and to the end he claimed to be in law, the canonically elected representative of the line that went back to Urban VI, the last pope to be acknowledged as pope by Catholics everywhere. [ ] The abdication was arranged and executed with a care to safeguard all that Gregory claimed to be; and this merits -- and indeed, requires -- much more detailed consideration than it usually receives. [ ]

Gregory XII sent to Constance as his representatives his protector Carlo Malatesta, the Lord of Rimini, and the Dominican cardinal, John Domenici -- to Constance indeed, but not to the General Council assembled there by the authority, and in the name, of John XXIII. The envoys' commission was to the emperor Sigismund, presiding over the various bishops and prelates whom his zeal to restore peace to the Church had brought together. To these envoys -- and to Malatesta in the first place -- Gregory gave authority to convoke as a General Council -- to convoke and not to recognise -- these assembled bishops and prelates; [ ] and by a second bull [ ] he empowered Malatesta to resign to this General Council in his name.

The emperor, the bishops and prelates consented and accepted the role Gregory assigned. And so, on July 4, 1415. Sigismund, clad in the royal robes, left the throne he had occupied in the previous sessions for a throne placed before the altar, as for the president of the assembly. Gregory's two legates sat by his side facing the bishops. The bull was read commissioning Malatesta and Domenici to convoke the council and to authorise whatever it should do for the restoration of unity and the extirpation of the schism -- with Gregory's explicit condition that there should be no mention of Baldassare Cossa, [ ] with his reminder that from his very election he had pledged himself to resign if by so doing he could truly advance the good work of unity, and his assertion that the papal dignity is truly his as the canonically elected successor of Urban VI.

Malatesta then delegated his fellow envoy, the cardinal John Domenici, to pronounce the formal operative words of convocation; [ ] and the assembly -- but in its own way -- accepted to be thus convoked, authorised and confirmed in the name "of that lord who in his own obedience is called Gregory XII". [ ] The council next declared that all canonical censures imposed by reason of the schism were lifted, and the bull was read by which Gregory authorised Malatesta to make the act of abdication [ ] and promised to consider as ratum gratum et firmum, and forever irrevocable, whatever Malatesta, as his proxy, should perform. The envoy asked the council whether they would prefer the resignation immediately, or that it should be delayed until Peter de Luna's decision was known. The council preferred the present moment. It ratified all Gregory XII's acts, received his cardinals as cardinals, promised that his officers should keep their posts and declared that if Gregory was barred from re-election as pope, this was only for the peace of the Church, and not from any personal unworthiness. Then the great renunciation was made, [ ] ". . . renuncio et cedo. . . et resigno. . . in hac sacrosancta synodo et universali concilio, sanctam Romanam et universalem ecclesiam repraesentante"; and the council accepted it, [ ] but again as made "on the part of that lord who in his own obedience was called Gregory XII". The

Te Deum was sung and a new summons drawn up calling upon Peter de Luna to yield to the council's authority.

The work of Pisa was now almost undone, and by this council which, in origin, was a continuation of Pisa. It had suppressed the Pisan pope -- John XXIII. It had recognised as pope the Roman pope whom Pisa, with biting words, had rejected as a schismatic and no pope. One obstacle alone -- the claims of Peter de Luna -- now stood between the council and its aim of giving to the Church a pope who would b., universally accepted. To some of the nations who made up the Council of Constance Benedict XIII had been, for six years now, no more at best than an ex-pope, deposed by a General Council for perjury, schism and heresy; for others he had never been pope at all. Yet the promoters of the council, in their desire to remove all possible causes of future discord, had in 1414, by an agreement that was unanimous, disregarded consistency and invited him to take part in the discussions. Benedict had consented at any rate to send an embassy, and his envoys were received in audience on January 12 and 13, 1415. But the business of the embassy was really with the emperor, whom they were commissioned to invite to a meeting with their master and the King of Aragon in the coming summer, when means to re-establish unity would be discussed. It was nearly two months before they were answered, and then, at the urgent request of all parties, envoys, cardinals and the nations, Sigismund agreed (March 4). By the time he was free to leave Constance, however, the situation had been immeasurably simplified (for the council) by the disappearance of both Benedict's rivals. Benedict alone now stood before Christendom claiming its spiritual allegiance, and if behind him he had only Scotland and the Spaniards, he had also the prestige of twenty-one years' exercise of the papal authority and a long life unstained by any of the vices that stained most of the personages of the high ecclesiastical world, nepotism, simony, and undue regard for the favour of princes.

Emperor and council took leave of each other in the general session of July 14; by the Feast of the Assumption, a month later, Sigismund had reached Narbonne, and on September 18 he entered Perpignan, where the King of Aragon awaited him and Benedict. The negotiations that now began, dragged on until the last day of October. Benedict -- now eighty-nine years of age -- was as ready to resign as ever he had been, but, as always, on carefully thought-out conditions which, somehow, could not but leave him victorious. The latest safeguard he had devised was a proviso that the pope to be elected after his resignation must be canonically elected -- an innocent phrase indeed, but whose inner meaning was that it must be left to Benedict to choose him, for, Benedict explained, he alone was certainly a cardinal, the single surviving cardinal created by a pope whom the whole Church had acknowledged, Gregory XI.

Sigismund wasted no time in rebuttal of such subtleties as this, but simply repeated his demand that Benedict should abdicate; whereupon the conference broke up. But while the emperor was at Narbonne, on his return from Perpignan, the King of Aragon with envoys of the other princes of Benedict's obedience begged him to make yet another attempt on the old man's obstinacy, pledging themselves that if this failed they would renounce him and go over to the council; Benedict was to be asked to abdicate in the same forms that had been used by Gregory XII. The emperor's envoys found the old man in the impregnable rock fortress of his family at Peniscola. Again he refused; he announced the convocation of a new council, and he sent word to the princes at Narbonne that he would deprive them of their kingdoms if they dared to withdraw their obedience. This message put an end to their last doubts, and after a fortnight's discussion the details were settled [ ] of an accord with the council. Benedict's cardinals were to go over to the council, and to be received as colleagues by the other cardinals; the council thus fully representative was next to come to a decision about Benedict (i.e. to depose him) before electing the desired new pope, the sentence of Pisa being tacitly ignored, and the business done over again. All sentences against those obedient until now to Benedict, by whomsoever decreed, were to be declared null by the council, and also all Benedict's sentences against the council and its supporters. Also, the council would confirm all grants and favours and dispensations made by Benedict up to the day of his last refusal to the princes. Should Benedict die, his cardinals would not elect a successor, and if they did so the Spanish kings would give such successor no recognition.

The council ratified this treaty two months after it was signed (February 4, 1416), but it was many more months before it began to go into effect, before the Spaniards arrived at Constance -- where they formed a new, fifth, nation -- and the new trial of Benedict XIII could begin. The first to arrive were the Aragonese, in October 1416, and the preliminaries to the trial began in the twenty-third general session, November 5, when a commission was named to enquire into Benedict's responsibility for prolonging the schism. He was cited on November 28 to appear before the council, and its envoys then had to make the long journey to Spain to deliver the summons. It was March 1417 before they had returned. Then came the consideration of his refusal to appear, a decree that he was contumacious, a new commission to examine the evidence against him, its report May 12, 1417), and finally, on July 26, [ ] sentence of deposition was given. No one had ever sinned more -- the sentence declared -- against the Church of God and the whole Christian people, by fostering and encouraging disunion and schism. Peter de Luna is declared a perjurer, a scandal to the whole Church, schismatical, and a heretic notoriously and manifestly; and thence it is that the council declares him deprived of all right to the papacy and excommunicates him; and Sigismund sent trumpeters through the streets of the little city to proclaim the great news that this ancient nuisance was no more.

The Christian world was now once more united in its acceptance of a single spiritual authority, the council at Constance. It only remained to elect a pope. But the question now became urgent, who should vote in the election? As the law had stood for three hundred and fifty years [ ] none could be pope whom the cardinals did not elect. On the other hand the council did not trust the cardinals. Feeling ran high on both sides, and to serious men it must have seemed that there was again every chance of an election whose legality must be questionable. The problem had been for a long time in the minds of all when it was publicly raised by the Castilian ambassadors to the council in the April of this year 1417. They had then been told that the council would decide the procedure once all the signatories to the Treaty of Narbonne had joined it, and from this moment the election problem became the chief subject of debate among the nations. It was complicated by a second division of opinion as to whether the council should elect a pope now or, first of all, enact a scheme of general reforms. The emperor was anxious that reforms should first be dealt with; the cardinals [ ] and the Latin nations gave priority to the election; the English and German nations supported the emperor.

Various schemes were drafted, and the discussions grew so violent that, in June 1417, it seemed as though the council was about to break up. The deadlock between the cardinals and their party on the one side, and the party in the council whom the emperor supported on the other, lasted until July 13, when it was agreed to allow the council to discuss the reformation of the papacy and curia before proceeding to elect a new pope; and a fortnight later the council, free at last from the incubus of the trial of Benedict XIII, turned to the question of reform.

It was soon evident that there were as many plans for reform as there were sections in the council, and that, without such leadership as a pope alone could provide, the stress of the reform discussions must dissolve the council into a mass of petty factions. The cardinals again raised the question whether it would not be wiser to elect the pope immediately. They had the French on their side, and now only the German nation gave wholehearted support to the emperor's determination that the new pope should inherit an authority reformed and trimmed by the council, that the papacy should be reformed, without consultation or consent, while the Holy See lay vacant. Presently the two parties were in open public conflict and accusations of heresy flew from each side to the other. New quarrels -- equally bitter -- about precedence also developed between Castilians and Aragonese. The cardinals asked for their passports. The emperor spoke of putting their leaders under arrest. They swore an oath to stand firm until death itself.

It was an Englishman who, in the end, brought all parties together, Henry Beaufort, Bishop of Winchester, uncle of the English king, Henry V. He had arrived at Constance less than a month after the death of his fellow countryman the Bishop of Salisbury, Cardinal Hallum, [ ] who had been the emperor's chief supporter in the council, and while the English there were still suffering from this sudden loss of their leader. Beaufort proposed a compromise -- and both sides accepted it; the council would first decree that after the election of a pope the question of reforms was to be seriously undertaken, and then immediately publish decrees for reform in all matters where agreement had already been reached, while, thirdly, a commission would at the same time be set up to decide how the pope was to be elected. This was at the beginning of October 1417, and by the end of the month an agreed procedure for the election had been worked out, which the council adopted in the general session of October 30. [ ] To the twenty-three cardinals there were to be added, for the purpose of this election only, six delegates from each of the five nations; the pope to be elected must secure, not only two-thirds of the cardinals' votes (as the law had required since 1179), but also two-thirds of the votes of each of the five nations; all these

357

electors were to be bound by the conclave laws already in force, and the conclave was to begin within ten days of this decree.

The carpenters and masons of Constance rose to the occasion nobly. By November 2 they had prepared fifty-three cells and accommodation for the electors' attendants in the great merchants' hall of the city. The emperor isolated the building with a cordon of troops -- there was to be no chance of any repetition of the events of 1378 -- and after a solemn session of the council on November 8, at which the names of the chosen electors were published, the conclave began. It was surprisingly short, and on St. Martin's Day, November 11, at 10. 30 in the morning, the announcement was made that the Cardinal Odo Colonna had been chosen by a unanimous vote, and had taken the appropriate name of Martin V. [ ]

The election of Martin V -- the first pope for forty years whom all Catholics acknowledged as pope -- is, no doubt, the high-water mark of the work of the Council of Constance. It was not only an end accomplished but the means to further accomplishment, a means to ensure that reformation of Christian life throughout the Church, which, for many of the fathers, was the most important question of all. A very strong party had, indeed, only consented to give priority to the settlement of the papal question when experience brought it home to them that, without the leadership of a pope, the council would never agree on reforms.

Of many practical matters that called for attention, the first and most important, so it seemed to all, was to bring about a better understanding between the papacy and the local ordinaries everywhere. Until a pope universally recognised had been elected, the council could not seriously hope to reach any agreement on reform that would be effective, and until, under the pope's leadership, the grievances of the episcopate against the Roman Curia had been frankly discussed, it was just as hopeless to expect that immense united action of pope and bishops through which alone could come the wholesale reformation which all openly acknowledged to be everywhere urgently needed. When, during the opening weeks of the council, the different delegates came in to Constance, each had brought its own plan of reforms -- even those Italians who had come in order to support John XXIII through thick and thin, had their proposals for a restoration of virtuous living among clergy and laity.

The council was, from the first, in its own mind and intention, a body assembled largely for the purpose of reform, and its desire for reform is the expressed motive for the revolutionary theory of a General Council's powers set forth in the decrees of its third and fifth sessions. The council here proposes, in fact, to reform the Roman Curia and the papacy, and no papal obstruction, it is stated, can lawfully withstand the council so acting. Until its task is finished it retains its sovereign authority despite all papal declarations to the contrary. Again, its power being from God directly, the pope is bound to obey the council's decrees just as other Catholics are; and if he is disobedient the council can correct and punish him.

Once the council had thus corrected, and punished, the pope who had called it into being (John XXIII), it set up a special commission of thirty-five members to prepare the needed reformation decrees. This commission immediately turned its attention to the highly centralised control of the universal Church which the popes of the last hundred and fifty years especially had so largely develop. d -- that control, through taxation of church property and through appointments, which has already been described in its main lines. [ ] The question was now raised whether the practice of papal provisions should not be entirely abolished. The bishops favoured the proposal but -- a first serious division in the ranks of the reform party -- the universities preferred the new system; the popes, said the delegates from the university of Vienna, repeating what the university of Paris had said already, had more thought for learning than the bishops, in those to whom they gave appointments. About the next great source of general complaint, the taxes payable on appointments of bishops and abbots, there was also a marked division of opinion. To zealots who sought the total abolition of these fees it was objected that the pope and his curia must have some fixed source of revenue in the universal Church in order to pay the expenses of a universal administration.

These discussions occupied the commission for the next seven or eight months, and meanwhile Sunday by Sunday, the best preachers in Europe (many of them bishops) never ceased to tell the assembled council the tale of the sins -- the clerical sins especially -- which afflicted the Church, to point out that episcopal simony and the simony of the Roman Curia were the chief cause of the decay of Christian life, and to exhort the fathers to pass from talking to action. [ ]

But between the appointment of this special commission and the appearance of reform decrees in a session of the council, two years and more were to elapse. There were many reasons for this delay; it was not by any means mere clerical supineness. For one thing, since there was now no pope (for all but the Spaniards and Scotsmen, still faithful to Benedict XIII), there had devolved upon this heterogeneous assembly the all but impossible task of the day-to-day administration of the universal Church. This parliament now had to function as a cabinet, and a general department of state, and this at a time of long drawnout crisis. It had to consider and provide for affairs like the trials of John Hus and of Jerome of Prague for heresy, for the civil war in Bohemia that began after their execution, for nominations to vacant sees, for the arrest of the wicked Bishop of Strasburg, for the trial of the crimes of Frederick of Tyrol against Church jurisdiction; there was the great case of John Petit's defence of tyrannicide and Gerson's great attack on this theory, a case beneath which burned the great question of Burgundy against Armagnac that had set all France ablaze with civil war. Later the collapse of Benedict XIII's hold on Spain slowed down the whole activity of the council, for the Spaniards had been invited to the council in such a way that only after they had come to take part in it could it continue as a General Council; and it was more than a year after the Treaty of Narbonne before the last of the Spaniards had come in. Then, too, in June 1416, the emperor (now in England negotiating an alliance with Henry V, lately victorious at Agincourt) sent an urgent petition that the council would halt its plans for reform until his return; and he did not return to Constance for another seven months. And before he had returned, in November 1416, the trial of Benedict XIII had opened that was to take up the most of the council's time for the next nine months nearly. Nor did this last great event proceed against any background of monastic calm. The English invasion of France, their alliance with the anti-royalist faction in the French civil war, and their victories, were an inevitable cause of the most bitter strife within the council. There were ever-recurring disputes about right and precedence between other nations too; and presently, as has been told, in the summer of 1417, the old question of the relation between the papacy and the council came to life again in the violent discussions about the way the new pope should be elected.

Such were the causes and occasions of the delay in producing and enacting schemes of reform. When the council was at last free to attend to the problem of reform, it set up a new commission to draft decrees, and now the old controversies broke out afresh, and during August, September and October of 1417 they raged most violently. What the fathers were now actually debating was whether the Roman See should continue sovereign in the Church, or whether the Church should for the future be ruled by an aristocracy of its bishops, and university dignitaries. Were the cardinals, it was asked, of any real value to religion,
or would it not be best to abolish the Sacred College as a

permanent hindrance? The cardinals, offering to reform what was amiss in their organisation, stood firm for the traditional rights of the Roman See, and the Italians and Spaniards supported them. It was from France and Germany and England that the proposals came for radical changes; but even here opinion was not unanimous in each nation.

It has been told how the Bishop of Winchester reconciled these warring factions, and there was now sufficient agreement among them for the council to enact five decrees of reform in its public session of October 5, 1417. [ ] The first of these -- the famous decree Frequens -- opens with the statement that General Councils are the chief instrument for the tillage of God's field and that neglect of them is the chief reason for the decay of religion. Therefore, within five years at most of the conclusion of this present council, another General Council shall be summoned, and a third council within seven years from the end of the second, and after that there shall be a General Council every ten years for all time. The pope shall consult each council about the place where its successor is to meet and this shall be announced before the council disperses; if the Holy See happens to fall vacant the council shall choose the place. The Church will, for the future, live from one General Council to the next.

Then there comes a decree which provides a remedy against future schisms, and this decree, apart from the ingeniously minute procedure it enacts, [ ] a is interesting evidence that it was the mind of the council that not only this particular Council of Constance but the General Council as such is the pope's superior. The third decree provides a new profession of faith to be made by future popes the day they are elected. The fourth states that religion has suffered greatly from the practice of translating bishops from see to see, and that the fear of being translated has been used to coerce the freedom of bishops; to protect future popes, ignorant perhaps of the facts, from assenting to translations promoted by crafty and importunate self seekers, and also from any careless use of the papal power, the council decrees that bishops shall not be translated against their will, unless after the case has been heard by the cardinals and their consent obtained. Finally, there is a decree about the burning question of the pope's rights to spolia and procurations. [ ] Papal reservations of these are no longer to hold good, but such procurations and spolia are to belong to those to whom they would have gone had this papal custom never been introduced.

There was, it may be remembered, a second clause about reforms in the Bishop of Winchester's settlement or pact, by which both the cardinals and the nations agreed to vote, in a general session of the council, a pledge that, after the new pope's election, the work of reform would be seriously undertaken. This pledge was given in the first decree of the fortieth general session held on October 30, 1417, three weeks after the voting of the five reform decrees just described. In this decree the council ordains that the pope to be elected must, in union with the council or with deputies chosen by each nation, reform the Church in its head and in its members and the Roman Curia also, before the council is dissolved; and the matters to be reformed are then set out in the decree under eighteen heads. But the commissioners of the five nations still failed to come to any practical measure of agreement about the detail of the reforms, and the Germans then suggested that two schemes should be prepared, the one of general reform, for the whole Church, and the other of reforms to meet the particular needs of the several nations; and that these last should be set out, not in decrees of the council, but in specially drawn agreements between the various nations and the pope -- the so-called first concordats.

The Germans presented to the new pope, in the first days of January 1418, a list of eighteen suggested reforms; the French and Spaniards did likewise; and on January 20, Martin V sent to the nations for their study a draft of eighteen decrees based on the eighteen points of the council's decree of October 30. It is worthy of note that the pope takes up all the topics which the council recommended, save one only: he makes no mention at all of the council's thirteenth point namely, How popes shall be corrected and deposed for crimes other than heresy. It was from the discussions of this draft within the various nations, that there finally emerged the seven decrees of universal reform published ill the forty-third session (March 20, 1418), and also the text of the several concordats.

These seven decrees deal almost entirely with the long-standing conflict between Rome and the bishops about papal taxation of benefices. By the first decree Martin V, with the approval of the council, revokes all privileges of exemption from the jurisdiction of the local ordinaries [ ] granted since the death of Gregory XI (1378), by whatever personages -- says the decree -- who acted as though they were popes; [ ] and he promises that, for the future, no such exemption shall be granted without the bishops' opinions being heard. All unions of benefices and incorporations made since Gregory XI's death are to be revoked if the parties concerned desire this, provided there has not been true and reasonable cause for the amalgamation. The pope surrenders all rights to the revenues of vacant sees, monasteries and benefices. As to simony, no law, says the pope, has yet succeeded in really extirpating this vice, so he now proposes one "with teeth in it". Those ordained simoniacally are ipso facto suspended from the exercise of the order thus received. Elections where simony has intervened are null and void, and they confer no right of any kind. Those who, so elected, make their own any revenues or profits attaching to the office to which they have been elected are bound to restitution. [ ] Both those who give, and those who receive, in simoniacal transactions are by the fact excommunicated, and this even though they be cardinals or the pope himself. The fifth decree abolishes a kind of papal dispensation whose very existence is surely evidence of immense decay in the religious spirit of the high ecclesiastical world, dispensations that is to say, which allow men to hold sees without ever being consecrated, to hold abbeys without receiving the abbatial blessing, to hold parishes without being ordained priest. All such dispensations are now revoked, and those who hold them are, under pain of losing the benefice to which their dispensations refer, to receive the appropriate order or blessing within the time the existing law appoints. The burning grievance of the papal tithe is next reformed, and the sixth decree gave some hope of relief to the sees of Christendom which had for so long been tithed by the popes, systematically, at every crisis of the fortunes of their own state and of the states of their allies among the Christian princes. For Martin V now revived the old law that only the pope could tithe and tax sees and ecclesiastical revenues, and he pledged the Holy See never to tax the whole body of the clergy except for some extraordinary cause that affected the whole Church, and even then only with the written consent of the cardinals and of what bishops could be consulted; nor would special tithes or taxes be levied on any particular country or province without the consent of the majority of its bishops; and such tithes, if levied, would not be collected except by ecclesiastics using only the authority of the Holy See. The last -- seventh -- decree deals with the needed reform of clerical life. It has nothing to complain of but that priests and bishops tend to dress like nobles, and that they even dare to appear thus clad, with only a surplice thrown over the " deformity ", to celebrate the divine office in their churches. The new law provides the new penalty of loss of a month's income for such unseemliness.

These seven decrees, it may be thought, are slender fruit indeed after four years of conference between priests and prelates from every part of Christendom, reputedly zealous for the reform of Christian life. They are not, of course, the whole programme, but even the several concordats [ ] do not contain much more than prohibitions in restraint of the more glaring financial abuses. Nowhere is there any sign of constructive thinking, and it is surely a notable failure that nowhere is there any care to provide for the formation and the better education of the parochial clergy.

The chief subjects, yet once again, are the claims of the bishops against the new papal control of the benefice system, and their complaints about the Roman Curia.

The pope promises -- in all the concordats -- that there will not for the future be so many cardinals that these will be a burden to the Church, or that the dignity will be held cheaply. The maximum number is fixed at twenty-four, and it is promised that the cardinals shall be chosen proportionately from all parts of Christendom. They will be men distinguished for their learning, their way of life and experience, and will be doctors of theology or law -- unless they are of the kin of reigning princes for whom competens litteratura will suffice. None shall be created cardinal who is brother or nephew to a cardinal already created, nor shall more than one cardinal at a time be chosen from any one of the mendicant orders. The cardinals, moreover, are to be consulted as a body about new creations.

Two nations speak for their own special interests in the curia; the German concordat recognises that in the present condition of the affairs of the Roman Church there is no other way to provide subsistence for the pope and cardinals but by the old method of granting them benefices and through the payment of the servitia communia. [ ] But no cardinal, the principle is laid down, is to enjoy a revenue of more than 6,000 florins from church revenues. Rules are made that the cardinals shall provide suitable priests to act for them in benefices which they hold, and that they shall not let out such monasteries or benefices to laymen, and that they shall not cut down the number of monks, and so increase their own profits. If, through the negligence of the cardinal's deputies, the monastery falls into decay, and if the cardinal ignores the injunctions of the monastery's religious superiors, the Holy See is to be approached; and if the pope does not remedy the evil, the superiors are to bring action against the cardinal's deputies as though they were the abbot and monks in whose hands the property once lay. The special concession to the

English was simpler -- that Englishmen too, should be employed in the different posts of the Roman Curia.

In all the concordats, except that with the English, there was also a clause restricting the number of suits to be heard in the Roman Curia. It would no longer, for example, be possible in Germany for suits that in no way touched on Church business to be taken to the pope for judgment simply because the suitor was a crusader; or (in Italy, France and Spain) to take to Rome matrimonial suits for a hearing in first instance. Penalties were also provided for litigants who interjected appeals to Rome that were judged to be frivolous. There are five clauses which reform the law and practice of clerical appointments, three of them applying everywhere but to the English, one applying to the English alone, and one universally. First, by whom are appointments to be made -- the question of Provisions? The pope, henceforth, will not reserve to himself the appointment to any benefices except those vacated apud sedem apostolicam; [ ] or by the deposition, deprivation, papal translation, or defective election of the late holder; or where the late holder was an officer of the Roman Curia. The other benefices to which the popes had been used to appoint would, for the future, be filled alternately by the pope and the proper collator. Secondly, to whom might benefices be given? The concordats restrict the papal practice of giving them in commendam. To no one -- not even to a cardinal -- is any abbey to be given in commendam which has a community of more than ten monks, [ ] nor any major dignity in a cathedral chapter, nor any parish, nor any hospital or hospice, nor any benefice worth less than fifty florins annual net revenue. These last two clauses do not appear in the English concordat, but this contains, like all the others, a clause by which the pope promises certain restrictions in the use of his dispensing power. For the future, no one will be dispensed from the need to be of the canonical age in order to receive the episcopate, [ ] or an abbey or a parish, 9 by more than three years: except in especially rare cases, and here the cardinals will be previously consulted. To the English the pope promises still more. The law already provides that more than one benefice shall never be granted to the same person (unless he is of noble birth or of outstanding learning), and the present custom by which lords (both temporal and spiritual) obtain dispensations from this law is to cease, and the rule be observed. Again, in England, the Holy See has of late years granted an unusual number of dispensations to allow beneficed clerics not to proceed to the needed holy orders and still keep their benefices, to the great scandal of the Church. All these dispensations are now revoked, and those who hold them must obey the common law in this matter and seek ordination, if they are otherwise suitable for ordination. Also, in England, it has been a serious obstacle to the cure of souls, and a cause of contempt for the bishops' administration, that papal dispensations have allowed beneficed clerics to live away from their posts and archdeacons to make their visitations by proxy. For the future such dispensations are not to be granted without reasonable cause which must be expressed in the dispensations; all dispensations granted so far without such cause are revoked, and it is left to the bishop to determine which these are. Likewise the pope revokes all faculties by virtue of which religious in England have obtained benefices, except in cases where the religious has actually been put in possession. For the future no such faculties will be conceded.

The beneficiary, once appointed and installed, pays to the Roman Curia, as a tax, one year's revenue -- annates. This was now fixed as the amount for which the benefice was inscribed in the papal tax books under the heading servitia communia. [ ] If this is not a just amount the beneficiary's case will be heard, and a new assessment made, due account being taken of such special circumstances as a country's poverty at a particular time. Annates, also, will only be asked once in any one year, even though there is more than one change in the incumbency during that time; and an incumbent is no longer to be liable for his predecessor's arrears of annates. To France, then ravaged by the invasion of Henry V and the civil war, Martin V made the special concession that only half the annates would be asked for the next five years. To England the pope made the concession that there should, for the future, be no appropriations of parish churches [ ] unless the bishop of the diocese has satisfied himself that religion will really benefit from them. All appropriations made during the schism are annulled.

The sole remaining changes of general importance are the regulations about indulgences. While in France, Spain and Italy the pope decided to make no changes, to the bishops of Germany he promised to be more careful for the future in granting indulgences, "lest they became cheapened, " and he revoked all those granted since 1378 in imitation of previous indulgences. [ ] To England also he gave a special pledge. Here the numerous indulgences granted by the Holy See to those who visited certain shrines or made offerings to them, and the special faculties enjoyed by those administering to such pilgrims the sacrament of penance -- together with the collectors [of alms for pious objects], of whom, it is stated, there are far too many in England -- are for many people, the concordat states, an occasion of sin. These people scorn their own parish clergy, and desert their parish churches for the shrines where these indulgences and absolutions can be had, and they take thither the tithes and offerings due to their parish churches. The bishops are given power to enquire into these scandals and to suspend the indulgences and the special faculties of confessors, and they are to report the matter to the pope that he may revoke these privileges.

The concordats were only to run for five years -- perhaps because, in accordance with the decree Frequens, the General Council would then reassemble? -- but the English concordat is noted as binding for all time. [ ]

Return to Index

# CHAPTER 4: FIFTY CRITICAL YEARS, 1420-1471

## 1. THE MENACE OF HERESY AND SCHISM, 1420-1449

THE task before Martin V was immense; [ ] his resources were scanty; the greatest of his difficulties were perhaps, as yet, scarcely known. Never was it to be more forcibly brought home to any pope that the pope's real power is a moral power. It was true that the Church was once more united in its acknowledgment of a single head. But bound up with this fact that Martin V was the universally acknowledged single head of the Church, were such other facts as those revolutionary proceedings at the late council in which, as Cardinal Odo Colonna, Martin V too had played his part; and from which council he had emerged as pope. The new pope's prestige was inevitably bound up with the proceedings at Constance. Some of the acts of that council no pope could accept and remain pope; and yet, any immediate blunt repudiation of them would probably have thrown Christendom back into all the chaos of the schism. Here was a first weakness bound to hamper the pope once he faced the task of rebuilding Sion.

A second weakness derived from the inability of the recent reforming councils even to diagnose, much less prescribe for, the main evils that were eating away the vitality of religion. What was to be devised at Trent, a hundred and fifty years later-- whether through drastic reorganisation such as to make the worst abuses simply impossible, or whether, through the invention of such new methods and institutions as the diocesan seminary, to do vital work which in all these centuries had never yet been done -- all this needed to have been done, given the times and the nature of the crisis, at Constance.

But it was with the old machinery, the very machinery to whose defects the disaster of the schism had been largely due, that the popes after Constance had to do their work. Whatever their good intentions, their zeal, and their realisation that a reformation of Christian life was imperative, they were bound, under such conditions, in great part to fail. Things were to be very much worse, before they were ever given a real chance of becoming permanently very much better.

Martin V knew that he must return to Rome and, somehow, bring it about that the Papal State was a stronghold for the security of the freedom of the popes in their government of the Church. He knew too that he must exorcise the new, radically anti-Catholic theory that popes are subordinate to General Councils; and yet he must contrive not to alienate the influential churchmen who had either invented this view, or adopted it as a way out of the long deadlock of the schism. He knew he must reform the general life of all Christians, clerical and lay. He probably did not realise, as yet, that the Turkish conquest of south-eastern Europe was imminent; nor of what immense consequence to Christendom that revival of letters was so soon to prove, the first beginnings of which he was now unconsciously patronising. Problem, then, of the new theories about General Councils; problem of the independence of the Papal States; problem of the reform of Christian life; problem of the Turks; problem of the Renaissance -- here, in rough summary, is the task before the popes in all the hundred years between Constance and Luther.

The Council of Constance assembled for the last time on April 22, 1418, and Martin V, refusing the French suggestion that he should re-establish the papacy at Avignon, and Sigismund's offer of a Germany city, made his way towards Italy. He moved slowly and with the greatest caution, by way of Berne and Geneva and Milan. In five months he had got no further than Mantua, where he wintered, and in February 1419 he moved to Florence. The condition of the pope's own territory offered him little prospect, either of security or real freedom of action; Bologna was an independent republic; various other new "states" had been carved out by the successful condottieri; Benevento, and Rome itself, were held by the Neapolitans. Gradually the pope's diplomacy brought about the restoration of Rome, and also won over the actual ruler of central Italy, Braccio di Montone. Bologna was subdued by July 1420, and on the last day of September Martin V made his solemn entry into Rome a city of ruins, and deserted, grass-grown streets, into which the wolves came, unhindered, by night to ravish from the cemeteries the corpses of the newly-buried dead.

But the recovery of his states was not the only critically urgent problem to harass the pope on the morrow of the great council; Catholicism was now fighting for its life in Bohemia, and the crusade against the new heretics was beginning to be a catastrophic failure. Bohemia, after Constance, was like Egypt after Chalcedon; a heretic had been condemned at the General Council and punished who was, at the same time, a national leader; and the reaction against the council, involving the cause of Czech culture against German imperialism, so shook the hold of the papacy on these lands that never again could the popes take their spiritual allegiance for granted. The event was a first demonstration -- had some gift of prophecy been granted the pope whereby to read the fullness of the sign -- of what could happen, and would henceforth happen repeatedly, when propagation of anti-Catholic doctrine was bound up with a people's ambition to assert itself as a nation or as possessed of a specifically national culture. This first Bohemian war of religion lasted for seventeen years (1419-1436). It ended in a compromise which, nominally, was to the advantage of the Catholics. But the memory of the long succession of national victories over the Catholic crusaders -- brought in from every part of Europe -- never died out; more than once, in the years between the settlement of 1436 and Luther, the war flared up again. Bohemia, for the generation to which Luther spoke, was a watchword, whether of warning or of promise, and down to our own day the memory of the heretic burnt at Constance, John Hus, [ ] has been the constant rallying point of all that is militant and revolutionary in the patriotism of the Czechs.

What made the fortunes of the religious theories which Hus preached was the circumstance that his appearance as a religious leader coincided with the critical hour of a great national renaissance, fruit of the wise and capable rule of Charles IV (1347-1378). In the later fourteenth century, as to-day, the land of the Czechs, the kingdom of Bohemia and the margravate of Moravia, was a country where very varied influences -- national, social, cultural -- fought for mastery. Both the kingdom and the margravate, which were now united under the one ruler, were vassal states to the German king, and part of the Holy Roman Empire. Everywhere there were pockets of German settlers. Many of the native nobility had gladly surrendered to the influence of German culture; many of the traders were German too; and for centuries the sees of the kingdom had been subject to metropolitan sees in Germany. The Czech Catholics had, however, a strong anti-German tradition that went back for hundreds of years. Catholicism had originally come to them through missionaries of the Greek rite, the famous ninth-century saints, Cyril and Methodius. Later they had been "Latinised, " and from resentment of this -- it is said -- there was among them a certain anti-papal tradition, and an especial resentment of two reforms for which the medieval popes were responsible, their revival of the ancient discipline of clerical celibacy and the practice of administering the Holy Eucharist under the form of bread alone.

Fourteenth-century Bohemia had all its share of the chronic ills of late medieval Catholicism, worldliness, simony and evil living among the higher clergy, and general slackness among the parochial clergy and in the monasteries; and the Waldensian heretics were more numerous here than in any other part of Europe outside their native mountain fastnesses. But from the time when the Emperor Charles IV -- Luxemburger by birth,

French by upbringing -- made the development of his hereditary kingdom of Bohemia the central purpose of his life -- and so determined the Czech renaissance -- the country had seen a succession of vigorous and plain-spoken reformers of ecclesiastical life, most of them orthodox Catholics. As a reformer John Hus was, then, only in the tradition of his age. But where others had but talent he had genius, and in addition to all his religious and ascetic qualities he was a great Czech. He was also to prove himself a great heretic, and in the main his heresies were importations from the England of Richard II. The first begetter, indeed, of all these ideas which served to promote the long Bohemian wars was an Oxford theologian, a one-time scholar and Master of Balliol, John Wyclif.

Wyclif belonged to the generation intermediary between Marsiglio and Hus, and his career as a reformer of Christian life and as a heretic was, like that of Marsiglio, bound up with a quarrel between his sovereign and the Holy See. When this dispute -- which involved no point of traditional Christian doctrine -- brought the English theologian for the first time into public life, he was a man just past his fortieth year. Parliament, in 1365, had passed a law protecting, against the pope's jurisdiction, suits about benefices, a matter in which the royal courts had always claimed jurisdiction. The pope, Urban V, retaliated by asking for the payment of the tribute due from England as a vassal kingdom of the Holy See -- but now thirty-three years in arrears -- and threatening, should this not be paid, to sue for the penalties provided in King John's surrender of his kingdom one hundred and fifty years before. The storm which this reply raised may be imagined. The whole country -- king, lords, commons, prelates and barons for once united -- joined to repudiate, and for ever, not only the arrears but the papal suzerainty itself. King John, they said, had acted without the consent of, the nation; his surrender therefore was void in law and fact. It was as a champion of the nation against the pope that Wyclif, on this occasion, entered literature and public life. Five years later, when a "cabinet" made up of ecclesiastics was displaced by a lay ministry, Wyclif was again to the fore, inspiring one of the earliest proposals to disendow the Church for the profit of the State; and when, in 1374, the long dispute with the papacy which had dragged on since the crisis of 1366 was settled by the Concordat of Bruges, Wyclif was one of the royal commissioners appointed to negotiate the treaty.

These were the years when the long reign of Edward III was coming to its end in a misery of incompetence and scandal. The sins of churchmen did not escape the censure of this disillusioned and discontented time, as the bitter language of a petition of the House of Commons "against the pope and the cardinals" remains to show. In language which, to the very words, re-echoes what St. Catherine of Siena was saying at that very moment, it is there said, "The court of Rome should be a source of sanctity to all the nations, but the traffickers in holy things ply their evil trade in the sinful city of Avignon, and the pope shears his flock but does not feed it. " [ ] When the Prince of Wales -- the Black Prince -- died, June 8, 1376, the prospect of better days was indefinitely lessened, for now the chief person in the realm was his younger brother, the weak, blustering intriguer John of Gaunt, Duke of Lancaster. The duke was also the anti-clerical leader, and Wyclif now seemed likely to become a force in the national life. But he overplayed his hand, and his anti-clerical harangues in the London churches gave the Bishop of London an opportunity to cite him for trial (19 February, 1377). Wyclif appeared, with Lancaster to escort him. There was a bitter quarrel between the duke and the bishop and then the mob, friendly to Wyclif but hostile to the duke, broke up the assembly before the trial began. There, for the time, the matter ended.

But in May, that same year, Gregory XI, to whom nineteen propositions taken from Wyclif's works had been delated -- by whom we do not know -- wrote a stern reproof to the Archbishop of Canterbury for his sloth and indifference in this vital matter.

The pope condemned the propositions, and the primate was ordered to arrest Wyclif, to interrogate him about them, and to hold him prisoner until the pope's judgment on his answers was made known. However, by the time these instructions reached the primate, a great change had come over English life. In June 1377 Edward III had died; the new king was a boy of ten, and the new parliament decidedly anti-papal. Lancaster was, for the moment, all-powerful, and Wyclif safe. Then in the following March the pope died, and within a few months his successor, Urban VI, had the problem of the election of Clement VII to distract him from the question of Wyclif's heresies. But the English bishops, once William Courtney had been translated from London to succeed as primate the feeble Simon of Sudbury, [ ] pursued the heresiarch relentlessly. At a great council in May 1382 twenty-four of Wyclif's doctrines were condemned as opposed to Catholic teaching, [ ] he was expelled from the university and forbidden to teach. Whereupon he retired to his rectory of Lutterworth and gave himself to writing what was to be the most popularly effective of all his works, the Trialogus, and at Lutterworth he died of paralysis on the last day of 1384.

It was Wyclif's thought which formed the mind of John Hus, and of a whole generation of Czech theological rebels. That thought had developed in the way the thought of most heretics develops who would, at the same time, be practical reformers of institutions. The new ideas are, in very great part, the product of exasperation at authority's indifference to serious abuses, and there is only a difference of detail between Gregory XI's condemnation of the nascent heresy in 1377 and Martin V's, of the finished heresiarch, forty years later. Gregory XI, in a letter to Edward III, drew special attention to the social mischievousness of the heresy, and to the bishops he noted how Wyclif repeated Marsiglio and John of Jandun. [ ]

In the nineteen propositions condemned by Gregory XI in 1377, Wyclif, like Marsiglio, proposes as the ideal a Church which is no Church at all. Its sacramental jurisdiction is declared to be superfluous, its external jurisdiction is so hedged about that it ceases to be a reality, while all clerics are to be answerable to the lay power for the whole of their conduct; the clergy are to be incapable of ownership and the Church's ownership is to be at the discretion of the prince. Five years later Wyclif is explicitly stating that all sacerdotal sacramental powers disappear once a priest or bishop falls into mortal sin, and that the pope in such circumstances ceases to be pope; the Schism is now four years old and for Wyclif this is, he says so explicitly, the opportunity to abolish the papal office for ever. He has already emancipated the prince from the Church's jurisdiction, and now he does as much for the preachers. Also he declares that the religious orders are manifest and inevitable hindrances to salvation, and that the great saints who founded them are in hell, unless they died repentant of their life's work; for a friar to ask alms, for a layman to give to him, is damnation for both. But what struck Wyclif's contemporaries as the crowning wickedness was his revival of the old heresy of Berengarius, namely that in the Blessed Sacrament of the Eucharist Jesus Christ is not really and corporally present. The Mass, he said, had no warrant in Holy Scripture, and Scripture -- this is a doctrine of his last years -- is the sole source and test of religious truth. All men can understand Scripture, for as they read it the Holy Spirit will make its meaning clear to them; and Wyclif's efforts to bring the Bible to the ordinary man have given him a well-known place in the history of Bible translators. Another doctrine of Wyclif's later years was fatalism -- all things happen as they do because they must so happen; yet another was a revival of the old heresy that oaths are always unlawful. Learning, he said, universities and university degrees were the invention of the devil; and again, that to the devil God must be obedient, for it is God who is the real author of our sins. [ ]

In this year, 1382, which saw the great condemnation of the English heretic, the English king, Richard II, married the sister of the King of Bohemia -- the Emperor Wenzel -- the daughter of the late king and emperor Charles IV. One effect of the marriage was to bring into close contact the universities of Oxford and Prague, and thereby to introduce Wyclif's theories to Bohemia. It was not, however, until the first years of the new century that his main theological work, the Trialogus, reached Prague, [ ] and the man who, already familiar with Wyclif's philosophical writings and won over by his violent condemnation of clerical sins, was from this time on to prove himself Wyclif's second self. John Hus was now thirty-three years of age, rector of the university, and incumbent of the Bethlehem Church lately founded for the preaching of sermons in Czech, and already, through the sermons and lectures of Hus, "a university for the people. " Hus was not a particularly good theologian, but he was a great orator and preacher, a severe critic of the ways of his clerical brethren and a man of extremely austere life. Once he was won over to the English theories all Prague would soon be taking sides for or against them.

The fight opened when, in the next year (1403), the ecclesiastical authority in the Czech capital condemned the twenty-four Wyclifite theses condemned at Oxford in 1382 and another twenty-one also extracted from his works. There was a second condemnation in 1405, at the demand of Innocent VII, and a third in 1408. Hus had accepted the condemnation of 1403, but five years of effort as a reformer had turned him into an extremist. The clergy's attachment to goods, he was now saying, was a heresy, and as for Wyclif -- who had thundered against it in much the same terms -- Hus prayed to be next to him in heaven. Hus was now suspended from preaching, but as the king continued to favour him he disregarded the prohibition. There was a schism in the university -- where the German, anti-Czech element was strongly anti-Wyclif -- and presently a solemn burning of Wyclifite literature. Hus was now excommunicated, first by the Archbishop of Prague and then by Cardinal Colonna [ ] acting for John XXIII, and Prague was laid under an interdict, so long as he remained there. In 1411 he appealed from the pope to a General Council; in 1412 a still heavier excommunication was pronounced against him; he began to organise his following among the Czech nobles, and when, at the king's request, he left Prague, it was to spread his teaching by sermons in the country villages and the fields. Prague, and indeed all Bohemia, were now in great confusion. The king still supported Hus and exiled his Catholic opponents, even putting two of them to death, and the crisis was the first topic to occupy the General Council summoned at Rome by John XXIII in 1413, from which came a fresh condemnation of Wyclifite doctrine. When it was announced by the emperor that a new council was to meet at Constance, Hus declared that he would appear before it, to defend the truth of his teaching, and on October 11, 1414, with a body of associates and an escort of Czech nobles, he set out from Prague. He reached Constance on November 3, two days after the solemn entry of John XXIII. For both of them the city was to prove a prison, but for Hus a prison whence he was to go forth only to his execution.

The story of the trial of John Hus at the Council of Constance is too important in its detail to risk a summary history's distortion of it. His heresy was manifest and the longer the discussions continued the more clearly was it proved. He refused to abandon his beliefs, and, declared a heretic, on July 6, 1415, he was handed over for execution to the town authorities, and burnt at the stake that same day. One year later his associate, Jerome of Prague, a layman, after trial before the council, suffered the like fate.

Death by execution of the capital sentence was, before the Victorian Age, the common lot of the malefactor everywhere. Thieves, forgers, coiners ended at the gallows then, as surely and as inevitably as do murderers with us. Nor was there much ado about the gravity of their fate. And heresy was, by universal consent, a crime of the worst kind. These were by no means the first executions which the fifteenth century saw for this particular offence, nor the last. But they were the first that ever caused, in any community, a general reprobation of the authority by which they were brought about. Their effect in Bohemia was amazing. Four hundred and fifty Czech nobles signed a protestation to the king, and a solemn league and covenant was sworn, by which it was agreed to defy the condemnation of the doctrines Hus had preached, to ignore the proscription of Hussite literature, and to defend against ecclesiastical authority the priests who were of the new way. To one point of ritual -- which, indeed, had never been a great consideration with Hus -- the party gave much importance, namely that Holy Communion should be administered under both forms, and this became with them the badge and the criterion and the shibboleth of Hussite orthodoxy; whence the general names of Calixtines and Utraquists. [ ]

King Wenzel was personally hostile to all this movement, but, as ever, weak and incapable of action; his consort was strongly in its favour. The king had no children. His heir was his brother, the Emperor Sigismund, than whom none was more orthodox, and who would hardly bear it indifferently that his brother's impotence should now lose him a kingdom. But on August 16, 1419, Wenzel died, and in anticipation of Sigismund's repression the Hussites prepared for war. Unfortunately for the new king and for the cause of the Catholics, the Hussites had a general of genius, John Zizka, and Zizka did not wait to be attacked. Presently he was master of the capital. After centuries of foreign rulers the Czech race was master in its own land (1420).

The epic of the Hussite wars must be read elsewhere; the story of how, first under Zizka and after his death under Procop, the Czechs successfully defied the Catholic-Imperialist coalition and brought to nothing the successive crusades organised under the authority of Martin V. After Zizka, in 1420, had compelled Sigismund to raise the siege of Prague (July to November) there was, indeed, an effort to reach agreement, to unite Hussites and

Catholics and also to reconcile the factions into which, already, the Hussites were themselves dividing. The Four Articles of Prague -- proposed by the Hussites as a basis of agreement -- provided that in the Czech lands there should be full liberty of preaching, that all those guilty of mortal sin should receive due punishment, that the clergy should lose all rights of ownership, and that Holy Communion should be administered under both species. But though the papal legates were not to be inveigled into the labyrinth which these vague and ambiguous propositions concealed, the Archbishop of Prague accepted the articles, and a kind of national church was set up. Then a political revolution set a Lithuanian prince on the throne of Bohemia and soon the war was on once more. Within three months (October 1421-January 1422) Zizka had destroyed Sigismund's armies, [ ] and crippled the Catholic effort for the next few years.

It was only the divisions among the Hussites that now kept the party from a permanent mastery of Bohemia. The quarrels between the moderates -- Catholic in all but their attachment [ ] to the use of the chalice in Holy Communion -- and the extremists, the Taborites, [ ] who had adopted the full Wyclifite creed and now showed themselves a species of pre-Calvinian Calvinists, developed into a bloody civil war. In this war the Taborites lost their great commander Zizka, but they found a second, of hardly less genius, the priest known as Procop the Great. In the hope of ending the dissensions, and in order to compel the Catholics to acquiesce in a settlement, Procop in 1426 took the offensive. Once more there were bloody defeats for the crusaders, and the Czechs invaded Hungary and Silesia, wasting and destroying countrysides and towns. Sigismund, to halt the advance, now offered to negotiate, but the Czechs would have none of it, and in December 1429 they invaded Germany itself. The main army ravaged Saxony, while flying columns carried the work of destruction and terror into the north. The imperial commander now accepted their terms, and in return for an indemnity, and the pledge of a settlement based on the Four

Articles of 1420, Procop fell back on Bohemia (February 1430). But Martin V, far from accepting such terms, prepared a new crusade, and to organise it he sent to Germany the most capable man in his service, Giuliano Cesarini. [ ] The question now, it seemed, was not so much when the Czechs would be crushed, but rather whether all Germany would not soon be Hussite. Not since the days when Innocent III made a stand against the Albigenses had Catholicism faced such a possibility of catastrophe.

Cesarini did his work well and presently a new army of crusaders was in the field. It invaded Bohemia in August 1431 and, almost immediately, it suffered one of the bloodiest routs of all, at Taussig, on August 14, when the Czechs again slew the fleeing Germans by the thousand. This was the end of the papal attempt to crush the heretics by force of arms. Orthodoxy, lacking commanders of military genius, will never -- except by a miracle -- triumph over heretics possessed of such commanders and leading troops passionately interested in victory. Cesarini, who had greatly distinguished himself on the battlefield by his brave endeavour to rally the panic-stricken host, seems to have realised to the full how strong the Hussites were, and why. From this time on he turned all his ingenuity to discover a means of arresting and containing their hostility by some scheme of concessions. The instrument he proposed to use was the General Council summoned by Martin V to meet at Basel in the very summer of the great defeat, and to preside over which Cesarini had been appointed at the same time that he was commissioned for the affairs of Bohemia. But Cesarini's plan was immediately complicated by a desperate crisis within this council itself.

The anti-papal spirit that had so largely inspired the debates in the Councils of Pisa and Constance was once again in action at Basel. If Constance had been orthodox enough to burn John Hus, it had been as anti-papal as Hus himself when it decreed that the General Council is the pope's superior, with a right to punish his disobedience to its decrees; and at Basel the pattern and precedent of Constance would now be followed in every jot and tittle. From the beginning the council would show itself, if zealous against the heretics, determined to control the negotiations with them, and at the same time to control the papacy too. The crisis opened by the Hussites was to be turned, now, to something still more threatening, and the popes to be caught between the Wyclifite heresy, militant and successful, without, and the rebels within, sapping and mining the very basis of papal authority and of the unity which is the Church's life. The history of the Council of Basel, which tormented the popes for a good eighteen years (1431-1449), made clear beyond doubt the existence of the most subtle danger of all, namely the persistence of a mentality among theologians and canonists and bishops -- a mentality very welcome to princes -- which would transform the reality of the divinely organised primacy, while it left unchanged and unchallenged the outward appearance and reverence, and the mass of the traditional Catholic beliefs.

The popes of the time -- Martin V and Eugene IV -- were well aware of the danger, and of the weaknesses in their position. To control and arrest the new development, on which the great assembly at Constance had conferred such prestige, was indeed the main anxiety of their reigns, the need urgent beyond all else, and because of which, in a structure that seemed to shake and totter uneasily with every speech, anything so challenging as the needed ruthless destruction of abuses must be indefinitely postponed. Neither of these popes was -- it is true -- a great man in any sense. Neither will, for example, stand comparison not only with such contemporary bishops as St. Antoninus [ ] or St. Laurence Giustiniani, [ ] but even with such contemporaries as the cardinals they created, with Cesarini, let us say, or Capranica or Albergati, the great Carthusian bishop of Bologna. Martin V and Eugene IV were, indeed, mediocre popes, but the ultimate reason for the apparent sterility of the thirty years after Constance, and for the apparent incompetence with which these two popes met the successive councils, was something far deeper than their own personal incapacity.

At Constance, acceptance of the old Catholic idea that the pope was answerable to God alone for his rule of the Church had suffered badly. The relation of Pope and Church, as this gathering had set it out, no pope could accept. [ ] And in less than a month after the dissolution of the council the very pope it had elected made this clear. Martin V had not, while the council was still assembled, confirmed any of its acts except its condemnations of the Wyclifite heresies. This [ ] was his sole reference to the critical activities that had filled the last four years. But, on May 10, 1418, in public consistory, dismissing an appeal from the Polish ambassadors (against the decision that John of Falkenburg had not been condemned by the council), the pope declared, "It is not lawful for anyone to appeal against the judge who is supreme, that is to say, against the judgment of the Holy See, of the Roman Pontiff, the vicar of Jesus Christ, nor to evade his judgments in matters of faith; these last, in fact, because of their superior importance, must be brought for judgment to the pope's tribunal. " [ ]

Yet once again the phenomenon was seen how the most unlikely man, once elected pope, became a man of principle in matters of faith. Odo Colonna, created cardinal by a pope of the Roman line (Innocent VII), had in 1408 deserted the Roman pope Gregory XII and joined with the rebels from the Avignon camp to set up the Council of Pisa. There he had played his part in the " deposition " of Gregory XII, and in the " election " of Alexander V. He had also his share of responsibility for the "election" of John XXIII, and when Constance, five years later, put this pope in the dock, he had been a principal witness for the prosecution. What were the personal opinions of the cardinal Odo Colonna about the powers of General Councils over popes, and about the validity of these successive depositions in which he had played his part? Contemporaries describe him as a simple, amiable man, free from any spirit of intrigue, not at all self-opinionated or obstinate; the last man in the world, one would have said, to hinder the further evolution of the work in which he had played his own important part.

Martin V did not, however, publish to the Church this manifestation of his mind made, publicly enough, in the consistory, at the very outset of his reign. [ ] He would not, he could not, accept the principle on which Constance had founded so much of its actrion. But, on the other hand, he did not refuse to be bound by its prescription that a new council should meet in 1423 and yet another in 1430. It was his policy to lie as low as he was let, and to say as near to nothing as was possible. And so the twelve years of his reign were no more than an uneasy truce.

Martin V duly opened the General Council of Pavia (April 23, 1423), arranged and announced at Constance five years earlier (April 19, 1418). The legates appointed to preside (February 22, 1423) found awaiting them in the city of the council two abbots, from Burgundy. During the next two months four bishops arrived, two of them from England. Then in June the legates transferred the council to Siena -- the plague had broken out in Pavia, and the pope could come to Siena, whereas Pavia was a city in the territory of his enemy, the Duke of Milan. It was November before the first general session was held -- and even then no more than twenty-five bishops had appeared. But decrees were passed against the Hussites, and reprobating slackness in the pursuit and punishment of heretics. Then the handful of bishops came to the practical business of reform, and the storm began in earnest. The pope had given the legates the power to transfer the council from the city where it was convoked, and one party in the council now declared that such a grant was a violation of the law [ ] made at Constance. The French were demanding that the nations should have their say in the nomination of cardinals. The ghost of Benedict XIII (dead at last [ ] in the opening months of the council), appeared when the

King of Aragon recognised his successor "Clement VIII" and intrigued with the Republic of Siena to secure recognition for him in the very city of Pope Martin's council. Then a friar preached before the council a strange sermon in which he explained that, like Our Lady, the Church had two spouses. There had been St. Joseph (who obeyed her) and the Holy Ghost whom Our Lady herself obeyed: so the Church, too, must obey the Holy Ghost but could command her other spouse, the pope. The months were going by without the Church in general showing any interest in the council, and the council was proving itself no more than a debating society on the solitary, but inexhaustible, topic of conciliar supremacy. There were, of course, those whom these debates bored, and presently they began to make their way home. The legates made their plans accordingly and announcing that the next council would meet at Basel in 1431, they dissolved the Council of Siena (March 7, 1424).

The pope promised that he would himself reform the curia, and the decrees he published [ ] have been taken, not unnaturally, as the measure either of his inability to recognise wrongdoing when he saw it, or else of his indifference. For they are little more than pious generalities about the need for cardinals and their suites to set a good example to the rest of mankind, and a repetition, for the hundredth time, of ancient laws about their dress and ornaments. [ ]

"The very word 'council' filled Martin V with horror, " said a contemporary. There was every reason why it should; [ ] and as the time drew near for the council at Basel, to which he was pledged, placards appeared on doors of St. Peter's to remind him of his duty and threaten revolt if he failed in it. On February 1, 1431, he appointed the legate who was to preside, Giuliano Cesarini, and three weeks later Martin V was dead, carried off by apoplexy.

The conclave was short, and its choice (March 3) was unanimous, the Venetian cardinal, Gabriele Condulmaro; he took the name Eugene IV. The new pope was forty-seven years of age, a Canon Regular, and greatly reputed for his austere life. He was a nephew of Gregory XII, and one of those four cardinals whose creation, in 1408, had been the occasion of Gregory's cardinals deserting him and of the subsequent Pisan extension of the schism. As a cardinal Eugene IV had stood loyally by Gregory XII until his abdication. Only then had he taken any part in the council at Constance. The Church had in him a pope whose action would not be hampered by any memories of a past in which he had patronised the new conciliar doctrines and used them as a whip to chastise unworthy popes. But while Eugene IV faced the approaching crisis with this undoubted advantage, he had unhappily inherited something of the vacillation which had ruined the career of his uncle, Gregory XII. And not only had he, like the rest of the cardinals, signed and sworn the pact drawn up in the conclave, [ ] but as pope he publicly renewed his promises, pledging himself thereby to increase the importance of the cardinals, and to give the Sacred College, as such, a real share in the direction of the Church, making it almost an organ of government. [ ] The curia was to be reformed in head and members; cardinals would only be chosen according to the decrees of Constance; the pope would ask their advice about the new General Council and would be guided by it; and, as well as guaranteeing them a half of the main papal revenues, he would not, without their consent, make treaties and alliances nor any declaration of war; finally, all vassals of the Holy See would henceforth, swear allegiance not only to the pope, but to the Sacred College too.

Cesarini, it has been said, [ ] had been given a two-fold commission by Martin V. He was to preside at the council and also to organise, in Germany, the new crusade against the Hussites. The new pope confirmed both the commissions. Actually, the more urgent matter now was the Hussite invasion of Germany, and so while the fathers of the council made their slow way to Basel, and while the pope was beginning to turn his own thoughts to the new offers of reunion from the emperor at Constantinople, the legate to the council was busy preaching the Holy War in Germany and organising supplies for the army. On June 27 Eugene had sent word to him that the opening of the council might wait until the Hussites had been settled, but that settlement proved to be the disastrous defeat of Taussig. [ ] It was with this dreadful catastrophe still very fresh in his mind, and with a certitude about the fact and the nature of the crisis before the Church, that Cesarini, only three weeks after the battle, came to the council (September 9).

The legate's first act was to begin a vigorous campaign to secure a better attendance. So far, in fact, it was the experience of Pavia and Siena all over again, a mere handful of prelates who could not conceivably be taken to represent anything but themselves. However, on December 14, after three months more of publicity, the legate held the first solemn general session.

And now began the long story of misunderstanding and cross purposes, not only between the anti-papal majority at the council and the Holy See, but between the pope and his legate. For, nearly five weeks before this solemn opening, Eugene had despatched to Cesarini a new commission which, reciting with great detail all the hindrances that were making, and must make, this council such another miserable fiasco as Siena had been, gave the legate power to dissolve it, and to announce a new council to be held at Bologna in the summer of 1433, without prejudice to the council which Constance had decreed must meet round about 1440. This new commission did not, however, reach the legate until nine days after the opening session, at which the one piece of business accomplished had been to re-affirm the fundamental decree Frequens of Constance. Had the legate known it, a second, still more drastic, commission was already on its way to him. Even before Cesarini had received the first,

Eugene IV, on December 18, had signed a bull dissolving the council, and giving as the determining reason the invitation which it had sent to the Hussites (on October 30), to attend and state their case. The second bull came to Cesarini's knowledge on January 10, 1432, and although he did not leave Basel he ceased from that date, to preside over the council.

From the moment when Eugene IV, in 1431, decided to bring the council at Basel to an end, and thereby provided the advocates of the new conciliar theory with their opportunity to renew the attack on the traditional practice of the papal supremacy, all other questions sank into comparative insignificance -- even the question of a peace with the victorious, militant Hussites of Bohemia. The story of the council's handling of the Bohemian crisis is, however, closely bound up with the still more involved story of its long duel with the pope; but the history may be more intelligible if the stories are told separately.

The Council of Basel -- as will be told -- decided that it was its duty to ignore the pope's will and to continue in session; and when (February 10, 1432) the Hussites decided to accept its invitation, they were told that, despite the pope's instructions, the council would go on with its work. The next seven months were taken up with diplomatic preliminaries, and especially with the arranging for safe conducts for the Hussites, in which no loophole was left that would allow for their execution as heretics should they fail to convert the council to their way of thinking. In October deputies from Bohemia came to Basel to make the last arrangements, and in January 1433, three hundred Hussites arrived and the discussions began. They continued for more than three months (January 7-April 14), and they settled nothing at all, except the real meaning of the Four Articles of 1420 and the impossibility that any Catholic could accept them. The council proposed ammendments that would make the articles acceptable, and when the Hussites returned to Bohemia a deputation from the council went with them, to urge the council's views at Prague.

This mission -- it was the first of five -- remained in Bohemia for six months (June 1433-January 1434). Its great achievement was the Hussites' acceptance of the articles as the council had amended them -- the so-called Compactata of Prague (November 30, 1433). The Hussites had been divided now for years into mutually hostile sections; and this helped the council's envoys. A further cause for their success -- wholly unconnected with the intrinsic reasonableness of their demands -- was the victory of the Bavarians over the Hussites on September 21, 1433, the first real military disaster which the party had suffered. The Compactata amounted, in the first place, to a treaty of peace. The war was to cease and all ecclesiastical censures on the Hussites to be lifted; they were to have full liberty to administer Holy Communion under both kinds if, in all other respects, they accepted the faith and discipline of the Church and returned to union with it, and it was agreed that priests so administering the Sacrament were to explain to the people that it was equally truly and as well received under the one kind as under both; the demand that those guilty of mortal sin should be punished was allowed, but it was stated explicitly that the power of inflicting punishment on the guilty belonged only to those who possessed jurisdiction over the guilty, and not to private individuals; as for liberty to preach, here again there was a restriction, preachers must first be approved by the appropriate authority; the fourth article, against the cleric's right to own, was also made more precise so that it was now admitted that the clergy could own what came to them by inheritance, or gift, that the Church could own also, and, finally, that while clerics were bound to administer ecclesiastical property like faithful stewards, the property itself could not be taken over by others without the sin of sacrilege.

Obviously the articles so qualified were not the articles for which the enthusiasts had fought in Zizka's armies. They were no sooner signed than a party among the Hussites proposed to re-open the discussion. The envoys went back to Basel to report, and the rival factions among the Hussites began a civil war. On May 30, 1434, the more extreme party were badly defeated, at Lipau, and their great leader Procop was among the slain.

The victors now approached Sigismund with offers of peace and recognition of him as King of Bohemia. The basis of the negotiations was the agreement made at Prague in the previous November, but when the Hussites met the emperor (Diet of Ratisbon, August 22-September 2, 1434), they demanded that the use of the chalice in the administration of Holy Communion should be compulsory. The council's envoys, however, stood firm for liberty, and the Hussites had to yield. When these, however, came to make their report to the Bohemian Diet at Prague (October 23), the Diet put out for Sigismund's acceptance thirteen points, many of them altogether new; such for example, as that bishops in Bohemia should henceforth be elected by their clergy and people, and that the pope should exercise no jurisdiction over criminous Czech clerics.

The council's envoys refused to accept the novelties; war broke out once more between the Hussite factions; and then, when the moderates were again victorious, the council at Sigismund's request, sent yet another commission -- the fourth -- to try and negotiate a peace. The scene of the negotiations this time (July-August 1435) was Brno in Moravia. Here the Hussites stood stubbornly by their demand for the thirteen points, while the Basel legates asked how a party could expect further concessions which had not yet honoured the pledges solemnly given in the Compactata of 1433? The single result of the conference was that Sigismund -- weary after sixteen years' exclusion from his kingdom -- began to lean towards the Hussites, to whom he made, in great secrecy, the promise that he would somehow secure for them recognition of their thirteen points (July 6, 1435). [ ] The final breakdown came when the Hussites asked for a change in the wording of the article about Church property, and on September 16, after eight months' absence, the envoys returned to Basel.

Seven weeks later they were taking the road once more. The peace party -- so Sigismund reported to the council -- had now triumphed at Prague. He was recognised as king, the council was to be accepted, but, the right of the Czechs to elect their bishops must be conceded. The envoys were, then, commissioned to attend the diet about to meet at Stuhlweissenburg, and to obtain first of all a guarantee that the obligations sworn to in the Compactata would be honoured, and also that there would be liberty for all to communicate as they chose; if driven to it the legates could accept the Hussite modification of the articles about Church property. The diet opened on December 20, 1435, and on December 28 the envoys bluntly put it to the emperor that he was playing a double game. The storm that followed raged for days and on January 1, 1436, the envoys demanded a written promise from the emperor that he would not interfere in matters of Church discipline. The Hussites strongly opposed them. A compromise was arranged -- Sigismund was to make the promise to the legates verbally, but there was to be no mention of it in the treaties. All was now ready for the solemn promulgation of the Compactata, but the act was deferred until a new diet should meet at Iglau. Here, in June 1436, the old controversy began all over again, but at long last, on July 5, the Compactata were published, and on August 14 Sigismund was recognised as King of Bohemia.

The war was over at last, and a peace patched up by which the Hussites were recognised -- by the Council of Basel -- as Catholics. But the peace rested on pledges which no real Hussite ever, for a moment, intended to honour. On the very morrow of the great ceremony of reconciliation, the Archbishop of Prague publicly broke the agreement about the manner of administering Holy Communion, in the very city where the ceremony had taken place.

A few weeks later there was another shift in the balance of the Hussite factions, and he fell from power. Once again a delegation left Prague to report the change to the council, but it arrived to find the fathers of Basel facing the most anxious hour of their history. The enforced long-suffering of the pope had at last reached its end. The council was under orders to transfer itself to Ferrara. None of its negotiations with the Hussites had as yet been submitted to the pope for his judgment, nor would they now ever be submitted to him. For the council was about to disobey the bull translating it, and so itself to incur an excommunication as real as any that had ever lain upon the Hussites.

While the last scenes of the tragic farce were being acted at Basel, Sigismund died (December 9, 1437), and the lately pacified kingdom of Bohemia split yet once again into civil war, the prelude to years of anarchy. The danger to Christendom from militant Wyclifism was indeed over; but the Hussites remained, very much alive in Bohemia; and Bohemia was now a frontier province of Christendom, for the Turkish conquest of south-eastern Europe had begun, and the long Turkish occupation of the lands between the Adriatic and the Carpathians.

When, in January 1432, it had come to the knowledge of the council at Basel that Eugene IV had issued a bull dissolving it, the council did not refuse to obey him, nor simply ignore his act, but in a solemn general session (February 15) it re-enacted the decree of Constance which laid it down that it is the pope's duty to obey a General Council, and the council's duty to punish his disobedience, and that without its own consent a General Council cannot be dissolved nor transferred to another place. Eleven days later, the bishops of France came together (under the king's patronage) at Bourges; their meetings continued for six weeks, and they begged and exhorted the pope to continue the good work being done at Basel. The emperor, Sigismund, also intervened strongly on the council's behalf, only to draw from the pope a curt reminder that this was an ecclesiastical affair. And the council pressed on to beg the pope to withdraw his decree of dissolution, and also to cite him to take his place at Basel. The cardinals too, were "invited" and given three months in which to appear. [ ] These citations were nailed to the doors of St. Peter's on June 6, and on June 20 the council made special regulations to provide for an election should the pope chance to die, and it also forbade the pope to create any new cardinals while the present misunderstanding continued.

On August 20, 1432, the council was given the pope's reply. Eugene granted practically everything the council had demanded, but he did not grant it in the way they demanded. The council was allowed to continue its negotiations with the Hussites, and to plan the reformation of clerical life in Germany, and it could choose another city for the coming council instead of Bologna. But the council wanted an explicit withdrawal of the decree dissolving it, and an acknowledgment that without its own consent it could not be dissolved (September 3). General Councils alone, the pope was told, were infallible. At this moment the council consisted of three cardinals and some thirty-two other prelates, though the lower clergy (and especially the doctors) were there in great numbers. England too, however, had joined with France and the emperor to support the council, and -- what must have weighed very heavily indeed with a pope who recalled the crisis of 1408 -- out of the twenty-one cardinals only six were securely on his side. Then, in the last week of 1432, the council gave Eugene sixty days to withdraw his decree, and to approve, without any reservation, all it had enacted; and the council declared null all nominations made by him until he obeyed it.

The sixty days went by, and Eugene did not surrender; but in a bull of December 14, 1432, he explained that the coming council at Bologna would really be a continuation of that at Basel, and that only in this sense did he intend to dissolve the Council of Basel. But this did not relieve the situation at all, and the council grimly persisted that the pope must acknowledge that what had been going on at Basel continuously since the beginning was a General Council, guided by the Holy Spirit. There were, again, long and impassioned discussions between the pope's envoys and the council (March 7-10, 1433), and then, on April 27, the eleventh general session published eight new decrees which completed the fettering of the papacy that Constance had begun.

The pope next appointed new presidents for the council -- a tacit recognition that it still existed -- but the council would not recognise them: the pope must be explicit in his withdrawal of the decree of dissolution. The powers he gave the new legates were too wide for the council's liking; and his act was, in fact, a reassembling of the Council. On July 13 the council took away from the Holy See for ever all right to appoint bishops and abbots, [ ] and decreed that all future popes must swear to obey this law before being installed. Eugene was threatened with punishment, and reminded how patient the council had been so far and he was now ordered to withdraw the decree and to announce solemnly his acceptance of all that the council had done. [ ]

Eugene meanwhile prepared two bulls, the first of which annulled whatever had been done against the rights of his see (July 29), while the second (August 1) accepted the council as a lawful General Council and formally withdrew the decree of December 18, 1431, that had dissolved it. This still did not satisfy the council. It was not enough that the pope recognised it now, and as from now; he must say that his own decree had never any force, could never have had any force. On the very day that the council made this retort, [ ] Eugene, at Rome, was making his formal reply to the acts of July 13, quashing and reprobating this mass of anti-papal legislation.

And now, political necessity cast its shadow over the isolated pope's defiance. The Milanese -- at war with Venice, the pope's homeland, and, because of that, the pope's ally -- invaded the Papal State in force. They won over the pope's own vassals and commanders and he was soon forced out of Rome, a fugitive. What relation there really was between the invaders and the council we do not know -- but they gave out that they came in its name to chastise the pope. Eugene now made a further concession to the council (December 15, 1433). He re-issued the bull of surrender of August 1, 1433, but with the changes which the council had demanded; he admitted now that he had decreed a dissolution in 1431, and that his act had been the cause of grave dissensions; he decreed that the council had been conducted in a canonical way ever since it opened and, as it were, now ordered it to continue its good work, and amongst other things, to reform the papacy. The dissolution then was null, and all sentences against the council are annulled; and the pope no longer demands that the council shall retract its anti-papal decrees. This bull was read in the council on February 5, 1434, and the council declared itself satisfied.

The council now had the ball at its feet. Eugene was presently an exile, [ ] in Florence, and on June 26, 1434, at the eighteenth general session, the declaration of Constance was published once again, that a General Council derives its power immediately from God and that the pope is bound to obey it in all matters of faith and of the general reform of the Church, and that he is subject to its correction should he disobey. From the unhappy pope there came not a sign that he was aware of this dangerous impertinence. [ ]

In silence, and with a newly acquired patience, Eugene IV waited until he could intervene without more loss to his cause than profit. Given a little more rope the council would in the end destroy itself. Month by month, through 1434 and 1435, it assumed to itself one after another of the administrative and executive and juridical functions of the papacy, repeating here the great mistakes made at Constance. Soon there was time for little else. The council occupied itself with the Jewish problem and closed the profession of medicine against the feared and hated race; it decreed a distinctive dress for them; and, with their conversion in view, it ordered that chairs of Hebrew should be founded in all the universities. [ ] Then, in January 1435, it turned to the problem how to reform the lives of Christians. It made a stringent decree against clerical concubinage from the terms of which it would not be unfair to deduce that this was common enough, [ ] and even a notorious feature of ordinary life; there are countries, says the new law, where bishops take bribes from the clergy to connive at misconduct of this kind. Such bishops must make over to charities the double of what they have so received. Bishops must also be less lavish in their sentences of interdict; these have indeed become so frequent as to be a real scandal. There is also a notable mitigation of the law that made excommunication infectious as it were, through communication with the excommunicated; and a fourth law to restrict vexatious appeals from the bishops' tribunals. [ ]

Then, in the summer of that same year, [ ] the council made a clean sweep of all the papal taxes due on appointments to benefices, annates included, and enacted that any further attempt to levy them was simony. Should any pope disobey this canon, he is to be denounced to the next General Council and this will deal with him. All the papal collectors were bidden to send in their accounts to the council for examination, and to pay into the council the moneys they had received. [ ]

It is important here to note to what extent the universal Church was in fact represented at Basel in this, the high noon of the council's power. The legate Ambrogio Traversari, writing about this time, [ ] says that although there are between five and six hundred who take part in the proceedings, there are barely twenty bishops among them, and many of the great mass are not clerics at all. The truth of this is borne out by the recorded attendance at the general session of April 14, 1436 when there were present twenty bishops and thirteen abbots. [ ]

When the council's envoys brought to the pope the decree of June 9 that abolished all his main sources of revenue, they lectured him for his failure to give a good example by obeying the council, and they stiffened their lecture with threats. But Eugene merely acknowledged that he had heard them, and to the council he sent a reply that the pope is its superior, and that the Holy See cannot function without a revenue.

The deadlock -- for such the situation had become -- was destined to be solved by the success of the pope in winning over the Greeks to discuss the proposed reunion with himself rather than with the council. For there had actually been rival embassies negotiating at Constantinople, from the pope and from Basel. As it became evident -- to both parties -- that the Greeks would disregard the council, the pope's defiance of its threats increased. The greater part of 1436 (April to December) went by in mere repetition of these threats, and it was not difficult for the pope to charge the council, before the princes of Christendom, with utter sterility save for its proposal to enlarge the authority of the bishops at the expense of that of the Roman See.

With the new year, 1437, active preparations began for the reception of a host of Greek delegates and their suites. It was necessary to decide, once and for all, where the meeting of pope and emperor should take place. The pope, explaining that the Greeks preferred the convenience of a city in Italy, invited the council's vote. But the council treated the Greeks with as little ceremony as it treated the pope. The Greeks had objected that Basel was too far away, and the council then proposed Avignon.

These debates were the most heated of all. Venerable prelates had to be forcibly held back as their brethren replied to their speeches. Roysterers in a tavern, said a cynically-amused spectator, [ ] would have behaved more peaceably. Troops were brought into the cathedral [ ] to prevent bloodshed, where the Cardinal-Archbishop of Arles, the leader of the anti-papal majority, had been sitting on the throne, fully vested and mitred, since cockcrow, lest another should capture this point of vantage. Each side had its own decree ready, and once the cardinal began the mass they were read out, simultaneously, the rival bishops racing anxiously, each eager that his own side should first begin the Te Deum. The scene is indeed worthy of what the council had been for far too long, and not unrepresentative of all that the so-called "conciliar movement" ever really was. [ ]

But the pope now felt himself master at last, and to yet another summons to appear before the council and answer for his disobedience, he replied by the bull Doctoris Gentium, September 18, 1437, which transferred the council to Ferrara and gave the assembly at Basel thirty days more to wind up its negotiations with the Czechs. When the legates left Basel, in December 1437, many of the bishops went with them. And while the little rump which remained now began the first formalities of the trial of Eugenius, the Greeks arrived at Ferrara, and there, on January 8, 1438, the first general session of the council took place.

There seemed now no longer any real danger to Catholic unity in the West, whatever the lengths to which the handful of clerics at Basel might go; but in truth the crisis was by no means at an end. The Christian princes, even though they did not break with the pope, and probably, never intended to break with him, found the little council too useful an arm against the papacy for them to be willing to see the pope destroy it. For France, and for Germany, this was an opportunity to lay the beginnings of that blackmailing tutelage of the papacy which was not wholly to disappear until our own times.

It is this last important aspect of the Basel activities that alone justifies the seemingly inordinate length at which the story has been told of an assembly so insignificant in numbers; and it is this which makes it necessary to tell the weary tale to the very end with the same detail. Here, in fact, we can observe, for the first time, not so much the new ideas about the royal control of Catholicism, but those ideas given political form, and that form blessed by the approbation of theologians, of canonists and of Catholic bishops, the local episcopate now showing itself quisling to the Holy See, despite the long tradition and despite the consecration oaths of personal fidelity to the pope.

Much has been written about the "conciliar movement, " but does not the phrase itself do the thing too much honour? A general movement there was indeed, for a whole generation, to bring about the restoration of unity by means of a General Council. But when was there any general enthusiasm for the government of the Church through councils? Not even the tiny active minority of bishops, so ready to use the machinery of a council to control the Holy See, proposed to obey the existing laws which subjected them to meet in provincial councils for mutual correction and the good of religion. As for the "democratic" idealists among the lower clergy, who made up the mass of the demonstrators, what more did any of them want but a career?

Again, what did those reforms amount to, of which it has been said so often that had not the papacy blocked them, they would have purified, and given new life to, the Church? What is there new in them beyond the liberation of episcopal incomes from the papal taxation? Nowhere do they provide remedies for the real troubles that were rotting away the bases of men's allegiance to the faith; the lack of any system to form and train a good parochial clergy; the need to reorganise of all the major monastic orders; the reorganisation of sees to make the needed contact of bishops and clergy possible; the de-secularisation of the episcopate -- which would make the bishops really shepherds of men's souls; the correction of what was wrong in the philosophical and theological schools; the relating of the religious life of the common man to the fundamental doctrines of the faith; the needed restoration of the sacrament of the Holy Eucharist (that is, as Holy Communion) [ ] to its proper place in Christian life. Of all these needs our reformers of Basel and Constance seem wholly unaware. Independence of the higher authority of Rome in the administration of their sees, and above all a tighter grasp on their revenues, such were the main considerations that moved the fathers of these assemblies when they turned from their novel speculations about the papal office to the practical work of reform. " It is the spirit which giveth life, " to the clerical reformer as to all other things Christian. The great historian of these times [ ] has, it would seem, said the last word about these men and their constructive work, and he does but re-echo the biting language already quoted from their contemporary Aeneas Sylvius. [ ]

" [These zealous Gallicans] might have been still more persuasive, and more interesting, had they been as keen to promote those useful reforms which would not have put money into their pockets; if they had acknowledged the need for themselves to meet occasionally in provincial councils and synods; [ ] if they had adopted the praiseworthy custom of living in their sees. . . if, in a word, after having (according to the day's current phrase) reformed 'the Church in its Head, ' they had set themselves seriously to reform it 'in its members' -- in other words to reform themselves. "

The miserable history shows, too, in what an anaemic condition the papacy came forth from the long ordeal of the Schism; and of how little support in Christendom it could be certain, when it had to take such notice, and for so long, of the crude impertinencies of such insignificance. Surely none but minds already formed in a tradition of opposition to the very idea of the papal supremacy could, with the facts before them, ever have exalted and glorified the proceedings of this wretched assembly, and seen in them the promise -- blighted, alas ! almost ere it was born -- of a new age when religion would be purified from tyranny and from the abuses which tyranny must breed. The story of the Council of Basel in the last eleven years of its existence (1438-1449), and of the opportunity it proved to the Christian princes, needs to be known well in all its concrete detail (and it is rarely told in more than vague generality) [ ] if the suspicion is to be understood which henceforward attached in the eyes of the Roman Curia to all who, wishing to reform the Church, spoke of a council as the obvious tool for the job. There is need, at any rate, to know exactly what the Council of Basel did, and exactly what it was that the popes reprobated in it, and exactly what those reforms were which the council proposed and whose development the popes arrested. The opportunity now (1438) offered to the Catholic princes -- and the history of the next eleven years is the story of their eager use of it -- lay in this that the Council of Basel reopened the Schism. The consequent crisis between the Roman Curia and these princes was over, in France, in less than two years; in Germany it dragged on for another seven. In both countries the crisis was ended by a compromise that left the princes stronger than before in their control of the Church.

About a fortnight or so after the opening of the council at Ferrara, the assembly at Basel declared Eugene IV suspended from his functions as pope (January 15, 1438). Just a month later, to the day, Eugene replied by excommunicating his judges (February 15); and just a month later again the principle on which Basel had been acting for the last seven years, that no pope could transfer a council against its will, was declared by the little assembly to be an article of the Christian faith (March 15). At Frankfort, in these same weeks, the diet of the empire was assembled for the last formalities of the election of an emperor, and it declared -- what the new emperor, Albert II, [ ] confirmed -- that, as between Eugene and the council at Basel, Germany would be neutral, that a new (third) General Council ought to be called to reconcile the pope and the fathers of Basel, which council should meet in an imperial city, Strasburg, or Constance, or Mainz. The crisis, then, was to be prolonged and the settlement would be a German-influenced settlement.

In France, on May 1, 1438, the king -- Charles VII -- called together a great assembly of prelates and notables at Bourges. Two questions were proposed for their opinion; what ought the king to do in this new conflict between the pope and Basel? what action should be taken about the Basel decrees for a reformation of Christian life? After six weeks of discussion, in which envoys from the pope were heard and envoys from Basel also, the first demanding that Charles withdraw all support from Basel and the second that he should support its condemnation of the pope, the assembly answered that the king ought to work for the reconciliation of Basel with the pope, and that he ought to accept the reform decrees, with some changes of detail. The second opinion was embodied in a royal edict that gave the reform decrees force of law in France -- the so-called Pragmatic Sanction of Bourges, June 7, 1438. [ ] Without any reference to the pope, in defiance indeed of his known will, the Church in France was henceforth to be governed by the decrees of a "council" which the pope had just excommunicated.

The new emperor, Albert II, reigned for only a short eighteen months, but long enough for the Diet of Mainz (March 26, 1439) to adopt the Instrumentum Acceptationis which was substantially the German equivalent of the Pragmatic Sanction of Bourges. [ ] And now the various reforming princes and prelates set themselves, individually, to gather what privileges and favours they could, both from the council at Basel and from the pope; and German Catholicism began to split up; the same city, chapter and see being at times divided for and against the pope, and rival bishops appearing, here and there, to claim the same see. In support of the plan for a new council, an informal league of princes began to form, France, Castile, Portugal, Navarre, Aragon and Milan, in addition to the German princes bound by the decision of Mainz.

Seven weeks after that decision the Basel prelates promulgated a "definition of faith. " It was declared to be a doctrine that all must believe, under pain of heresy, that General Councils are superior to the pope, also that the pope has no power to transfer a General Council against its will (May 16); and a month later the council deposed Eugene IV (June 25, 1439). On this momentous occasion there were present no more than twenty prelates and only seven of these were bishops; and the president had relics brought in from the churches and placed on the waste of vacant seats -- the pope, it should appear, was condemned by the saints as well. The Holy See -- in the eyes of these twenty prelates and their somewhat more numerous following of doctors -- was now vacant, and it remained vacant for another seven months, while the rest of Christendom, with Eugene IV, gave itself, at Ferrara and Florence, to the business of reuniting the Eastern Churches with Rome. But at Basel, throughout the summer, the plague was raging, sweeping away the inhabitants of the little town by the thousand. On September 17, however, the " fathers " defined the doctrine of the Immaculate Conception, [ ] and on October 24 they approached the problem how to form a conclave for the election of the new pope.

They had but one cardinal to support them, [ ] and they decided to add to him thirty-two electors chosen from the council, who must, all of them, at least be deacons ! Of the thirty-two, eleven were bishops, seven abbots, five doctors of theology, and nine doctors of law (canon or civil). Next there was a violent dispute, about who should have the best accommodation in the conclave, that nearly wrecked the whole affair. The bishops demanded first pick of the rooms, but they were persuaded to allow the more usual practice of drawing for them by lots. Then, on October 30, this miserable parody of Constance proceeded to its consummation and the conclave opened. From the beginning the favourite candidate (16 votes out of 33 in the first ballot) was the Duke of Savoy, Amadeus VIII. [ ] As he rose in successive ballots to within one vote of the required two-thirds, the opposition grew violent. He was a layman, it was argued, and a temporal prince; he had been married and four of his children were still alive. Sed contra, this was a time when the Church needed a pope who was rich, [ ] and well-connected. At last, on the fifth ballot (November 5), Amadeus was elected, with 26 votes out of 33. The council (on November 19) confirmed the election and on January 8, 1440, the duke accepted. He proposed to call himself Felix V.

Never surely has there been so odd a choice. Cesarini reassured the council at Florence. Amadeus was so avaricious, he said, that he grudged to pay for food enough to keep himself alive; there would soon be open war between the anti-pope and his council. [ ] Truly enough, his first reply to the council's offer was to ask how was he to live now that the council had abolished the annates? He had to support him his own state and Switzerland generally, Scotland too, and Aragon, with its dependencies Sardinia and Sicily. Eugene IV excommunicated Felix on March 23, 1440; Felix, however, went through with the sacrilegious farce, was ordained, consecrated and crowned on July 24. But the King of France, though not repudiating the act of 1438, protested against the election, and obliged his subjects to continue faithful to Eugene. Brittany followed suit, so did Castile.

The only real additional anxiety which the election brought to Eugene was in Germany, where the Emperor Frederick III, [ ] although he did not acknowledge Felix, maintained the policy of neutrality, and continued to call for a new council in Germany. This was in the spring of 1441, by which time the first disputes between Felix and his council were well under way. They had refused, on principle, to accept the president he gave them; and their scheme for nuncios and legates to enlist the support of the princes had broken down when Felix refused to contribute to the expense. It was yet another grievance that he refused his newly-created Sacred College [ ] the half of the revenues to which they were entitled. In November 1442, and soon after his meeting with Frederick III -- who carefully avoided all dangerous occasions of implicit acknowledgement, and whose main concern was to marry off his widowed daughter to one of the pope's sons -- Felix left Basel, for ever. He had spent as much on the adventure as he proposed to spend, and he settled now at Lausanne. In that year, 1442, the council had held no public session and on May 16, 1443, it held its forty-fifth, and last. In June Alfonso of Aragon had returned to his allegiance, a most important gain to Eugene, for he was king now of Naples too, with a frontier coterminous with the Papal State on its southern and eastern sides; and with Alfonso there also returned his ally, the Duke of Milan.

The whole interest henceforth lay in the fate of the Roman hold on Catholic Germany. Hussite zeal was still hot in the south below the deceptive agreement of 1436. How much of the country would the pope be able to hold to union with his see? In Germany little could be done during the next two years, for war broke out between the Swiss and Austria. The war left the princes of Germany still more divided, and it aggravated the differences between the partisans of the council and those who, with Frederick III, leaned towards Eugene. In January 1445 Eugene began to move against two of these pro-council princes, the Archbishop of Cologne and the Bishop of Munster, who were anti-imperialist also. There was a diplomatic exchange between pope and emperor -- Aeneas Sylvius Piccolomini representing Frederick, and the Spanish canonist Juan Carvajal the pope; and out of this there emerged the foundations of a lasting settlement. But now the pope's habitual impetuosity nearly wrecked all.

Feeling himself secure, Eugene deposed the archbishop-electors of Cologne and Treves (January 24, 1446) [ ] and caused thereby such a storm in Germany that barely a month after his legate had signed with the emperor the accord of Vienna (February 1446), the whole body of the prince-electors had formed a league to resist the pope and to compel the emperor to the same policy (March 21). The electors demanded, in fact, not only that the depositions should be revoked, but that the pope should accept the principles of Constance and Basel about his subordination to General Councils, should accept also the reforms decreed by these councils, as Germany had accepted them at Mainz in 1439, and should convoke a new council to meet in Germany. If Eugene accepted their terms the electors would recognise him provisionally as pope, that is until the council met: if he refused they would -- so they secretly decided -- go over to the Council of Basel.

It was in July 1446 that the envoys of the princes delivered this ultimatum to the pope. Aeneas Sylvius accompanied them, sent by Frederick to warn Eugene of what awaited should he refuse. But the pope, for once, forbore to be rash and merely pledged himself to send a reply to the diet that was to meet at Frankfort on September 1.

At Frankfort the critical discussions went on for three weeks (September 16 to October 5, 1446). The pope sent a strong team of diplomatists and canonists, Parentucelli (the future Nicholas V), Carvajal, Nicholas of Cusa (already the greatest German churchman of the time), and Aeneas Sylvius. Very skilfully they brought it about that what the diet discussed was not any reply of Eugene to their ultimatum, but the pope's acceptance of their terms as the pope had modified them. To the legates Eugene had indeed made very clear the limits beyond which he could not go. [ ] The diet, however, was far from satisfied, and it broke up without reaching any decision. The legates, in fact, had managed to divide the princes, and to form, secretly, and at the slight cost of some 2,000 florins, a bloc favourable to the pope. All parties now made for Rome and in the first days of the new year, 1447, Eugene received the envoys of the princes in public audience (January 12, 1447). Their demands -- the demands of 1446, but now more politely stated -- he referred to a commission of cardinals specially appointed, and a month later, in four documents, he gave his decision. The princes -- the majority of them -- accepted it. The pope was already seriously ill when the envoys arrived. During the next four weeks he rapidly grew worse, and it was actually kneeling round his deathbed that the princes swore their fidelity. Sixteen days later Eugene IV died (23 February, 1447).

What, in the end, had he managed to save of the authority of his see? Against all likelihood he had preserved it intact, and had seen it acknowledged in all its integrity; but he had had to make large concessions. He had had to accept the princes' scheme for a new council to meet in Germany in two years' time; and he had had to make a show of accepting the new, unacceptable theories about the superiority of General Councils. It was, however, no more than a show, for the pope's acceptance did not admit any obligation to call such a council, nor that it was necessary to call councils, nor that it was useful to do so -- he even went out of his way to say that he did not believe it to be useful. Nor did he declare -- as the princes desired -- that it would be for the council to decide the disputed question whether he was really pope. As for recognition of anything done at the Council of Basel, the pope, now, never even referred to it. Moreover, a limiting clause, "in the way our predecessors have done, " destroyed any reality of submission which the clause might at first sight present, and where the princes demanded recognition of the "pre-eminence" of General Councils, the pope only acknowledged their "eminence. " And while the other matters in dispute were settled with the solemn finality of a bull, this, the most important of all, was set down in the comparative informality of a brief. As to the deposed elector-prelates, Eugene indeed promised to reinstate them, but only when they had sworn obedience to him as "true vicar of Christ. "

Here was the main point at issue -- the pope's primatial authority over the whole Church, laity, clergy, episcopate, and over all these, it might be, united. And what the pope conceded here was something substantially different from what had been demanded with such noise and threatening. That the princes accepted without demur this singular and scarcely concealed transformation was due, of course, to the simple fact that they were really interested in something else, and in that alone -- in drawing to themselves as much as they could of the control of Church properties, and of the scores of ecclesiastical principalities that lay within the empire. And in this matter the pope's surrender was very great. He accepted the Basel statement of the German grievances, and the decrees by which that council had hoped to remedy them -- the statement, in fact, adopted by emperor and princes at Mainz in 1439. He ratified and validated all appointments to benefices, all sentences and dispensations granted during the ten years of the "neutrality, " even those made by prelates who had stayed on at Basel after he had transferred the council to Ferrara. There was, in fact, a general and unconditional lifting of all the sentences laid upon the members of the council and their adherents. After ten years the princes -- and especially the ecclesiastical rebels -- had won, in this more material field, all they had fought for; but they had only won it as a grant from the very authority which they had, for all that time and longer, professed to call in doubt, and which they had desired to cut down until it could scarcely exist at all.

Ten days after the death of Eugene IV, Tommaso Parentucelli, the late legate to Frankfort, was elected in his place -- Nicholas V. He, of course, confirmed all that Eugene had sanctioned, and in July 1447 he sent the promised legate to discuss with the princes the indemnity which they had agreed should be paid the Holy See now that annates were abolished. The fruit of these

409

discussions was the concordat of 1448. [ ] This agreement, repeating the concordat of 1418, set permanent limits to the pope's collation to benefices within the empire. Except in the special circumstances which the concordat carefully enumerates, appointments to vacant sees and abbeys are henceforth to be by election, the elect needing from the pope confirmation only. The pact also greatly restricted the pope's power to reserve to himself appointments to benefices in the future; and finally -- the principal object of the concordat -- in place of the tax called first-fruits which the pope has surrendered, it is agreed that the newly appointed bishop or abbot will pay a sum determined separately in each case. [ ] No see will be so taxed more than once in any one year, even though there be several successive bishops in that year; and arrears due on this account to the pope's treasury will, for the future, die with the debtor.

Now that the pope and the princes of Germany were at one, the very days of the council at Basel were surely numbered. The emperor was at last able to bring pressure to bear on the city authorities, and in June 1448 they asked the council to find another meeting-place. On July 24 its members trekked as far as Lausanne, where their pope still abode. Switzerland and Savoy were, in fact, still loyal to him and to them. But the new pope, Nicholas V, had been secretly negotiating a surrender, and Felix now announced, with the consent of the council, that he was ready to resign. On January 18, 1449, Nicholas V lifted all the sentences and censures with which the anti-pope was loaded, and freed the council too, and all its supporters. On April 4 Felix was allowed to do the same for Nicholas V and for the dead Eugene, and to confirm all grants he had made and to announce his coming abdication. The great event took place three days later -- not a penitential submission in forma as "Clement VIII" had made to Martin V in 1429, and as the Franciscan "Nicholas V" had made to John XXII a hundred years earlier, but a formal abdication made to the council for the good of the Church, and ending with a prayer to the princes to take the act in a friendly spirit and to uphold the authority of General Councils. On April 16 the council met once more, to withdraw all the excommunications and deprivations it had decreed and then, on April 19, it solemnly elected as pope "Thomas of Sarzana, known in his obedience as Nicholas V"; the pattern of Constance was faithfully followed to the end. An end only reached five days later when the council, conferring on Felix, as legate and perpetual vicar, ecclesiastical jurisdiction over all the lands that had continued faithful to him to the last, granting him the first place in the Church after the pope, and the privilege of wearing the papal dress, decreed at last its own dissolution.

Nicholas V, a humanist of cultivated wit as well as an admirable Christian, patiently tolerated these last ritualistic antics and then in June, the council now out of the way for ever, he created Felix a cardinal and gave him, for life, authority as legate over his old domain; and, what the ex-pope no doubt appreciated just as much, a handsome pension. [ ] Nicholas was generous also to the cardinal who for all these years had directed the anti-Roman activities at Basel, Louis Aleman. He re-accepted him as a cardinal and as Archbishop of Arles; [ ] and he also gave the red hat to three of the cardinals Felix had created.

The indulgence shown by Nicholas V to the susceptibilities of these trans-alpine rebels, once they gave signs of submission, had gone very far -- farther than, from precedent, might have been expected. But here was a pope with the very unusual experience that he knew Germany personally. He also had at his side a great German ecclesiastic who was a scholar and a theologian and possessed by a truly apostolic zeal -- Nicholas of Cusa. The pope now determined to advance a step further the new reconciliation with Germany, in this hour when all was, presumably, love and joy, by sending Nicholas of Cusa [ ] as legate with full papal powers [ ] to put right all that he found wrong in the ecclesiastical life of the country.

The legate's tour of Germany and the Low Countries lasted a whole twelve months (February 1451 to March 1452). In that time he visited all the chief cities from Brussels to Magdeburg and Vienna, and from the Tyrol to the Zuyder Zee. His own mode of life continued to be that of the scholarly ascetic. Everywhere he went he preached, and nowhere would he accept the magnificent presents offered him. For the ills which troubled religion he had two main cures to propose -- closer relations with the Holy See and a thorough reform of the greatly relaxed religious orders. At Salzburg, Magdeburg, Mainz and Cologne he held provincial councils; at Bamberg a diocesan synod. The commission he appointed at Vienna visited and reformed some fifty Benedictine houses of men and of women, and also the houses of the Canons Regular of St. Augustine. At Wurzburg the legate himself presided over a provincial chapter of seventy Benedictine abbeys, and here each abbot came to the high altar in turn, to bind himself by vow that he would introduce the reforms into his monastery. There was already at work in Germany the great reform associated with the abbey of Bursfeld; the pioneer of this movement was in the closest touch with the legate, and Nicholas of Cusa, at Wurzburg, urged the Bursfeld reform on the assembled abbots.

The legate made a lengthy stay at the university town of Erfurt, and the commissioners he left behind spent seven weeks investigating, and amending, the lives of the monks and friars and nuns of the town. At Magdeburg, where there was a good archbishop, things were in better order, but the provincial synod enacted very rigorous legislation to correct the unreformed religious houses. At Hildesheim the legate deposed the abbot for simony, and at Minden -- where he found the diocese in a deplorable state -- another problem exercised him, the growing tendency for the pious laity to trust in the mere externals of religion for their salvation. The latest source of this danger was the confraternity spirit, and the legate forbade the founding of any more confraternities.

Undoubtedly this missionary year, where the missionary was a cardinal and legate of the pope, brought about many changes for the better. But if the changes were to be permanent, return visits, and by legates of the same character as Nicholas, were called for; by legates, also, who were themselves natives of these countries. This great expedition stands out however, as a thing unique in the history of these last two hundred years before the Reformation -- as Nicholas himself is almost the unique German of these centuries to be given the prestige and the power for good that goes with the coveted honour of the cardinal's hat. [ ]

Another cardinal, Giulio Cesarini, legate in Germany twenty years before this, had written to Eugene IV that unless the German clergy amended the* ways of life their people would massacre them, as the Hussites were massacring the clergy in Bohemia. a The laity were, however, not so interested in the matter as the Italian cardinal seemed to think. Except for sporadic raids -- of which Nicholas of Cusa's expedition is the best example -- the clergy and churches of Germany remained untroubled in their chronic state of disorder, under their impregnable prince prelates, awaiting the ultimate inevitable day of doom, and the saving grace of the Jesuits and St. Peter Canisius.

## 2. THE RETURN OF ISLAM, 1291-1481

The submission of the Council of Basel to Nicholas V in 1449 brings to fulfilment, after nearly ninety years of effort and strife, the determination of the popes to re-establish themselves at Rome. Never again, until the French Revolution, will the pope be forced out of Rome, and never again will there be an anti-pope. In the face of the many evident defeats which the popes sustained during their ninety years of effort, it is well to establish these two facts firmly and in all their high significance. But from that precariously won victory Nicholas V turned to find, confronting the Christian hope, the menace of an imminent Mohammedan conquest of all that remained of the Christian East. The ninety years which had seen the papacy's recovery had also seen the rise of a new power in the world of Islam, the Ottoman Turks.

At the time when the loss of St. Jean d'Acre, the last Latin stronghold on the mainland of Syria, had plunged the West into a stupor of despair (1291), the Ottomans were no more than a petty tribe in the service of the Sultan of Iconium, a Moslem state in central Asia Minor. By the time Clement V had suppressed the Templars (1312), they had acquired a small, strategically placed, territory of their own, that ran from the Sea of Marmora to the Black Sea, behind the strip of Asiatic shore where the Byzantine Empire still held the ancient cities of Nicea and Nicomedia. Then, in the next generation, under their sultan Ourkhan (1326-1359), the organisation began that was to make the Ottomans, for the next two hundred years, an all but unconquerable scourge: the nation turned itself into a drilled and disciplined professional army, the cream of which was the corps of Janissaries recruited from Christian European children, sometimes given as hostages, sometimes kidnapped. From the middle of the fourteenth century everything fell before this new, most formidable engine of conquest. The Ottomans made themselves the first power in the Mohammedan world and they also conquered, without any great difficulty, all that remained to the emperor of his territories in Asia Minor.

In 1356 the rivalry of a Byzantine prince, John Cantacuzene, with the emperor, gave the Turks their first footing in Europe; they became masters of Gallipoli. Nine years later they took Adrianople. And, at last, the Christian princes were roused to action. Peter I of Cyprus, with the active support of Pope Urban V, gathered a fleet which, in 1367, raided several of the Syrian ports, destroying arsenals and stocks of munitions and supplies, and thereby halting the Turks for some years. But the great princes of western Europe held aloof. From Edward III of England and Charles V of France, exhausted both of them by the first long bout of the Hundred Years' War, the pope had a flat refusal; to the maritime states of Italy, Genoa and Venice, their own commercial interests in the East were of greatest importance, and, if these called for it, Genoa and Venice would even side with the Ottomans against the crusaders.

Yet upon these states -- and upon Venice especially -- there already lay a great deal of the responsibility for the weakness of the Christian position in the East, and for the policy of appeasement which was the only defence that the Byzantines could now contrive whenever the Ottomans increased the pressure. Venice had been the inspiration, and the chief director, of the great act of piracy which, in 1204, had virtually destroyed the Eastern empire; and, with Genoa, it had, ever since, clung desperately to the valuable territories which it had then been able to wrest from the empire. Never again, after that fatal date, was there any power in the East capable of holding off a new Mohammedan offensive should such occur. The modern country of Greece was henceforward in the hands of a medley of Latin princes, Dukes of Athens, Princes of Achaia, Counts of Cephalonia and the like; the Serbs rose to found an empire of their own on the ruins of the power of the hated Greeks; the Bulgarians, too, established themselves as independent. The territory of the empire at the time when Michael VIII negotiated with Gregory X the reunion of 1274 was, then, only a tiny fraction of that which the Latins had conquered seventy years earlier. By the time that Michael's successors, in the fifteenth century, were once more planning a union with the West, their power had shrunk to little more than the capital and its immediate hinterland (1423). The Serbs had gone down at the bloody defeat of Kossovo (1389), and the Turks were masters of Greece and Bulgaria too. Constantinople, thirty years before its fall, was already isolated from the West. The last joint crusade to relieve it -- a great host of French, Germans and Hungarians led by Sigismund, King of Hungary [ ] -- had ended in yet another catastrophe at Nicopolis (1396), and it was only the appearance of a rival Mohammedan power, taking away the Ottomans to defend their own capital, which now saved the empire from the coup de grace.

It is very easy to list the causes of the chronic Christian disasters; [ ] they were as evident to the fourteenth and fifteenth centuries as they are to us, and they were as much discussed. An abundance of writers agreed that there was no hope until the Christian princes put aside their own jealousies and vanities; until the crusading armies consented to accept some form of discipline; until there re-appeared, what had been lost for a century and more, the old religious fervour; and until the Italians could be persuaded to forgo their lucrative trade with Islam. The missionaries -- the most practical men of all -- had no hope whatever that the way of war would succeed. The sole solution for the problem of the Turks was, they held, to convert them to Christianity.

As to practical measures, here again there was general agreement about what ought to be done, and almost never was any of it done. Egypt was the vital centre of the Mohammedan world. Egypt lived by its commerce. So let a blockade of Egypt be proclaimed, and an international fleet be formed to enforce it; especially let Venice and Genoa be forbidden the* traitorous trade. Thus it was that, so early as 1291, Nicholas IV put a ban on the trade and raised a small fleet of twenty galleys to enforce it; and Clement V made this blockade the special business of the Knights-Hospitallers.

But these were gestures far too slight to have any permanent effect. The popes were, already, almost alone in their understanding how truly Christendom was a unity, that no one part of it could look on indifferently while an alien civilisation and cult made itself master of another part. They were alone in their anxiety, and the Turks established themselves in Europe, to be for four hundred years and more an unmitigated curse to the

416

millions whom they misgoverned, and, when finally expelled, to leave behind them within the very heart of those peoples, a degrading, if inevitable, legacy of feuds and pride and hate, of cruelty and treachery, the legacy which still threatens to plunge the East back into anarchy and barbarism. From the moment when the Ottomans first established themselves on European soil the popes, unhesitatingly and instinctively, in what was perhaps the most critical hour their own rule had known for a thousand years, set themselves to organise the defence of Europe against Islam. A writer of the time, one day to be pope himself, and to die at Ancona after years of exertion in this business, as the fleet he had painfully assembled sailed into the harbour of that ancient city, has vividly described their impossible and thankless task. "The titles of pope and emperor, " he says, "are now no more than empty words, brilliant images. Each state has its own prince, and each prince his own special interests. Who can speak so eloquently as to persuade to unity under a single flag so many powers, discordant and even hostile? And even should they unite their forces who will be so bold as to undertake to command them? What rules of discipline will he lay down? How will he ensure obedience? Where is the man who can understand so many languages that differ so widely, or who can reconcile characters and customs that so conflict? What mortal power could bring into harmony English and French, Genoese and Aragonese, Germans, Hungarians and Bohemians? If the holy war is undertaken with an army that is small, it will be wiped out by the unbelievers; if the army is of any great size, it will court disaster just as infallibly through the insoluble problems of manoeuvre and the confusion that must follow. To whatever side one turns, one sees the same chaos. Consider only, for example, the present state of Christendom. " [ ]

One effect of the Ottoman conquests after their victory of Nicopolis (1396) was to convince Venice, at last, that her only chance of survival lay in making herself feared. From the beginning of the fifteenth century Venice shows a new spirit of independence in its dealings with the Ottomans; the republic was now all for a crusade, and all for a reunion of the churches which would bring to an end the most bitter of all the differences that hindered joint Christian action against the common foe. It was then by no means coincidence, or accident, that the election of a Venetian as pope -- Eugene IV -- in 1431, brought the possibility of reunion into the sphere of urgent practical affairs, nor that to this pope, from the first weeks of his reign, the Eastern question was the principal question. His plans were simple and grandiose: to reunite Constantinople and Rome and to preach a general crusade that would sweep out the Turks for ever. Here, if anywhere, is the positive intent of the pope who fought the long duel with the assembly at Basel, here is the real Eugene IV. That council was, from the beginning, wholly taken up with its scheme to make the papacy, for the future, the servant of the clerical element in the Church; and that the pope had to spend years fending off this peril was an immense distraction from the no less urgent business of the menace to the Christian East. It was not the only way in which the council hampered his action, for independently of the pope, and in a kind of competition with him, the prelates at Basel also began to negotiate a reunion scheme with the Eastern emperor and his bishops.

These negotiations began with the council's invitation to the Greeks to take part in its proceedings (January 26, 1433). In the end, after nearly four years, they broke down completely, partly because the council was unable to find the money to pay the expenses of the Greek delegation, and unwilling to remove to some Italian city more convenient to the Greeks. But the principal cause of the breakdown was the Greek determination not to recognise any synod as oecumenical unless the pope (as well as the other patriarchs) took part in it. It might be hazardous to negotiate a reunion with the West at all, but to discuss reunion with a council that was permanently at loggerheads with its own patriarch -- and him the pope -- would be an obvious waste of time.

Meanwhile the pope had been extremely active. He had not only begun discussions with the emperor, but with the Christian rulers of Trebizond and Armenia too. His nuncios had penetrated to Jerusalem, and they were, ultimately, to negotiate not only with the Orthodox Churches but with the Monophysites of Syria and Ethiopia, and with the Nestorians also. By the year 1437 Eugene felt himself strong enough to risk all that the enmity of Basel could effect, and, as we have seen, on September 18 of that year he transferred the council -- reunion now its main business -- to Ferrara.

It is interesting to note how completely the precedents of the reunion council of 1274 were now disregarded. This time the theological questions at issue were to be discussed in the council itself, and the reunion was to be the act of a council in which Greeks and Latins sat together, under the presidency of the pope. And the General Council was preceded by a synod at Constantinople in which the Greeks chose the. delegates who were to represent them at Ferrara, bishops and other leading ecclesiastics. It was a small army of some seven hundred which in the end set out, and at its head was the emperor himself, John VIII. The Patriarch of Constantinople -- who, if the reunion were accomplished, would be, by virtue of Innocent III's decree, the first personage in the Church after the pope -- was the only one of the four Eastern patriarchs to attend in person; but the other three -- Antioch, Alexandria and Jerusalem -- were represented by proxies to whom they had given unlimited powers.

The Greeks sailed from Constantinople in November 1437, and after a ten weeks' voyage, on February 8, 1438, they reached Venice. There the Doge and the papal legate received them in a scene of dazzling splendour. On March 4 the emperor entered Ferrara and on April 9 Greeks and Latins assembled in the cathedral for the first joint session, and agreed on a first decree recognising the council as truly oecumenical.

Then the difficulties began to appear. The emperor's one anxiety was that nothing should now mar the prospect of a firm military alliance to drive out the Turks, and since the discussion of theological differences (all alleged by many of his bishops to be differences about the Faith) would be the speediest way to disturb the momentary harmony, he made every possible effort to put off the discussions. Apparently he would have preferred some act of accord in as general terms as could have been devised, to be ratified and consecrated by whatever gestures of reverence the pope cared to ask for; and the Greek bishops showed themselves, in this, the emperor's faithful and obedient subjects. It took all the tact of the Latin diplomatists -- and here, as at Basel, the principal role fell to Cesarini -- and all the good will of the pope, to keep the peace while the Greeks were slowly compelled to come to the point, to say, that is, why they thought the Latins heretics, and to listen to the Latin explanations of the Latin formularies that must -- if understood -- convince them of Latin orthodoxy.

The four main differences were the Latin teaching about the relation of the Holy Ghost to the other two Persons of the Blessed Trinity, the Latin use of unleavened bread in the Mass (the Greeks using ordinary bread), the Latin teaching about Purgatory, and the primacy of the Roman See over the whole Church of Christ. The pope proposed that a preliminary commission -- ten Greeks and ten Latins -- should be set up to discuss these four questions. The emperor, however, would not hear of any discussion except upon the third topic; and it was only after some time that he would agree even to this. But at last the discussions on Purgatory began, and they went on steadily for two months (June-July 1438). On July 17 the Greeks agreed that what the Latins believed was not different from what they, too, believed. And then nothing more was accomplished for another three months.

However, by October, the emperor was brought to allow that the alleged diversities in the doctrine about the Blessed Trinity night be considered, and so there began a long nine months' theological discussion. [ ] It ended, on June 8, 1439, [ ] by the Greeks accepting that the Latin doctrine that the Holy Ghost proceeds from the Father and the Son is not heresy, and that the Latins did not sin in adding to the creed the word Filioque to express this doctrine. Then, after another week of hesitation, the emperor once more showing great reluctance to renew the debates, the most delicate question of all was attacked -- the claim of the pope to a universal primacy in the Church. But the debates, this time, were surprisingly soon over. By June 27 agreement had been reached, and after another week's work the text of the reunion decree had been drafted. It was signed on July 5 by 133 Latins and 33 Greeks and solemnly published in a general session of the council, July 6, 1439. [ ]

The decree is in the form of a bull, Laetentur Coeli, and published both in Latin and in Greek. While, at the earlier reunion council of Lyons in 1274, the only theological difference determined by the council was the controversy about the orthodoxy of the Filioque, now, at Florence, the council reviewed the whole position. The bull is, in form, a definition of faith made by the pope with the approval of the council (hoc sacro universali approbante Florentino concilio diffinimus) The pope, then, explicitly defines, as a truth to be held by all Christians, that the Holy (Ghost proceeds eternally from the Father and the Son, and that the addition of the word Filioque to the creed, made for the sake of greater clearness in expressing this truth, was lawful and reasonable. He defines, also, that it is indifferent to the validity of the consecration in the mass whether the bread used be leavened or unleavened; and that it is Catholic doctrine that all the souls of those who die in charity with God but before they have made satisfaction for their sins by worthy penances, are purged after death by purgatorial pains, from which pains they can be relieved by the pious acts of the faithful still alive, by prayer for example, by almsdeeds and by the offering of masses. Finally there is a detailed definition about the fact and the nature of the Roman primacy. This part of the decree calls for the council's own words, or a translation of them. "We define, in like manner, that the holy Apostolic See and the Bishop of Rome, have a primacy (tenere primatum) throughout the whole world, and that the Bishop of Rome himself is the successor of St. Peter the prince of the Apostles, and that he is the true vicar of Christ, and the head of the whole Church, and the father and teacher of all Christians; and that to him in St. Peter there was committed by Our Lord Jesus Christ full power to pasture, to rule and to guide the whole Church; as is also contained in the acts of the General Councils and in the sacred canons. " Here, without any reference to the new theories of the last sixty years, without any reference to those decrees of the assemblies at Pisa, at Constance and at Basel, which attempted to give the new theories a place in Catholic belief, the tradition is simply and clearly stated anew. And it is also worthy of notice that, although various Greek bishops opposed the definition of Florence in its preliminary stages, for various reasons, no one of them ever urged against the papal claim the theories set forth so explicitly at Constance and at Basel. [ ]

The union of East and West once more established, the Greeks left Florence with their emperor (August 26, 1439). To John VIII it had been a disappointment, which he did nothing to disguise, that the council had been so purely a theological conference, that none of the great princes of the West had appeared, and that it had not, in the manner of the famous council of 1095, been the starting point of a great military effort.

But the Council of Florence did not break up when the Greeks departed. Its later history is indeed not very well known to us; all the acts of the council, the official record of its proceedings, have disappeared, and when the most interesting events were over the contemporary historians lost interest in the council. It continued, in fact, for another six years or so, at Florence until 1442 and in its final stages at Rome. It is not known how or when it actually ended; [ ] But in the years while it was still at Florence the council was the means for other dissident churches of the East -- some of them heretical bodies -- to renew their contact with the Roman See, to renounce their heresy and to accept again its primatial authority. Thus in 1439 the Monophysite churches of Armenia, led by the Patriarch Constantine, made their submission; [ ] in 1441 the Monophysites of Ethiopia (Jacobites) did the same [ ] and the Monophysites of Syria too; in 1445 the Nestorians (Chaldeans) of Cyprus came in, and also the Maronites.

The Council of Florence is perhaps chiefly important to us as the General Council which, of all the long series, was most visibly representative of Greeks and Latins, where the differences which for so many centuries had sundered them were discussed in all possible detail, and at great length, through eighteen successive and eventful months; a council whence there emerged a detailed agreed statement about the supreme earthly authority in the Church, so explicit and so all-embracing that, after five hundred years, it still retains all its practical usefulness. [ ] But to the pope, as well as to the Greeks, the council was an assembly of Christians met to cement a new unity under the menace of imminent catastrophe. The Greeks had come from a city that seemed doomed; it was to a land fighting its last battles against an invader that they went back. The year in which the Greeks appeared at Ferrara, Transylvania was invaded and Belgrade attacked. In 1442 there was a second invasion of Transylvania, and from its bloody scenes there at last appeared a great military commander on the Christian side, the Hungarian nobleman John Hunyadi. For a time the Turkish advance was halted, and their armies defeated. The pope again deputed Cesarini to organise a crusade, and in 1443 the combination of the great cardinal, John Hunyadi and Ladislas of Poland drove the Turks out of Servia and Bulgaria, and forced a ten years' truce on them. The sultan --

Murad II -- was so discouraged that he went into retirement. But
when reinforcements came in to the Christian armies, in 1444,
Cesarini persuaded Hunyadi -- against his better judgment -- to
break the truce and to invade Bulgaria. This brought Murad into
the field once more. There was a bloody battle outside Varna
(November 10, 1444) and the Christian army was destroyed.
Ladislas and Cesarini were among the slain.

The sultan now turned south and made himself master of the
Morea (1446) and two years later, on the already fatal field of
Kossovo, he destroyed yet another Hungarian army which
Hunyadi had managed to raise. In 1451 Murad II died. His
successor was the still greater Mohammed II, who almost
immediately began the long-distance preparations for the capture
of Constantinople. Against him there was nothing but the
personal valour of the emperor -- Constantine XII -- and his
handful of an army. The emperor, like his brother and
predecessor, John VIII, stood by the union with the pope, and his
fidlity cost him the support of the mass of his people. So bitter,
indeed, was the anti-Latin spirit in the capital that even after
thirteen years the emperors had not dared to publish officially the
reunion decrees of the council. In all that time, the prelates who
had accepted the papal authority for political reasons, and against
their own real convictions, and the very much smaller band who
had never, even at Florence, accepted it at all, had made good use
of their unhindered freedom to campaign against the Latins.
Never did the mass of the Greeks hold the Latins in greater
detestation than in these last years and months before the Turk
administered the final blow. It was, indeed, in these very months
that the famous saying (or its equivalent) was first uttered, "
Better the turban of the Prophet than the Pope's tiara. "

By this time the pope of the reunion council was dead, and in his
place there reigned the great humanist and patron of Greek letters
Thomas of Sarzana, Nicholas V. Like his predecessor he did the
little that was possible to help the city, endlessly pleading with

the princes of the West, and gathering what money and ships and men he could. It was a great misfortune that this pope was by nature what we have lately come to call an " appeaser. " The Christian cause had suffered so badly that Nicholas V had almost come to dread the thought of an offensive. Especially did the disaster of Kossovo in 1448 fill him with dismay, and he strongly urged the Hungarians to keep to a war of defence. But to the emperor at Constantinople, who was again appealing piteously in 1451, the pope sent a strong warning that so long as the Greeks trifled with their pledged word and refused in their pride to submit to the divinely founded authority of the pope, they could hardly expect anything but chastisement from the justice of God; [ ] the emperor must make a beginning and, without further delay, proclaim the divine faith to which he has pledged himself. But the pope did not merely lecture the emperor. He sent all the aid he could, money to repair the fortifications, a little fleet, and, as his legate, one of the Greek bishops who had been resolute for reunion at Florence and consistently loyal to it since, Isidore, once the Metropolitan of Kiev, and now a cardinal.

On December 12, 1452, the union of the churches was at last proclaimed, in a great ceremony at Santa Sophia [ ] -- and from that day until the very evening before the city fell, the mass of the people avoided the church as though it were plague stricken.

It was nearly five months later than this that the pope's ships arrived, after fighting their way through the blockading fleet (April 20, 1453). Outside the city, and all around it, was the vast Mohammedan host, 160,000 regular troops. Within the walls perhaps 7,000 men stood by the emperor, nearly two-thirds of them Westerners, Italians chiefly. The population, cursing their emperor and dreading Mohammed, awaited in passive superstition the arrival of a miracle. But after two months of siege the city fell (May 29, 1453). Its capture was the crown of a hundred years of Moslem victories, and immediately it gave to the Ottoman achievement a solidarity, a consistency and an air of permanence it had never hitherto possessed. Their hold on this city which for one thousand five hundred years had been a key point of world strategy, gave to the Turks a kind of prestige as invincible which the race never lost.

Its more immediate effect was to make it certain that the yoke laid upon the Christians of south-east Europe would not be lifted for centuries, and that the tyranny would, in the near future, extend to yet further provinces of what had once been Christendom. The West, Christian Europe, has now before it -- and will continue to have before it down to our own time -- the permanent anxiety of the "Eastern Question"; and the popes, since they at least realise the menace and resist it, are henceforward burdened with a second, [ ] and permanent, major distraction from their duty to attend to the badly-needed reform of Christian life and thought. It is perhaps this last effect of the Turkish conquests which was the most disastrous of all, from the point of view of religion. Even had the popes been able to bring about the impossible, to put new life into the France of Charles VII, to unite in immediate harmony the England of the Wars of the Roses, to banish the Hussite feuds still eating away the vitality of Germany, and then, uniting these mutually antagonistic national interests and combining these princes with those maritime states of Italy whose policy was in its inspiration the least Christian of all, to launch a well-planned, well-organised joint attack at a distance of months of marching from its bases and even had the attack been successful and the Turks, five hundred years ago, been crippled for ever, what could the papacy thereby have gained for religion? Territories where the victorious Latin princes would assuredly have been the rulers, and where populations violently attached to their anti-Latin prejudices would continue to prefer the temporal rule of Islam to the spiritual rule of the pope. Nothing but a succession of miracles -- suspensions of the laws of the nature of things -- in the fields of diplomacy and war could have now brought the Christian cause to triumph over the Turks, and nothing but a new series of miracles could have saved the lands so liberated from the bloody anarchy which had been their fate already for generations wherever Latins ruled Greeks and hellenized Slavs. [ ] It is, however, rarely given to any man to see the problem of his own hour in all its dimensions. What is demanded of him, by posterity, is that he shall have faced the crisis generously, with a total abandonment of self-interest. By this test the popes of this generation must be judged to have succeeded, and in the continuous nine years' effort of the two popes Calixtus III and Pius II, the papacy now reaches to heights unscaled since Gregory X.

When Nicholas V died (March 24-25, 1455), fifteen cardinals met to elect his successor. [ ] Seven were Italians, there were two Frenchmen, two Greeks, and four Spaniards. An Orsini party in the Sacred College favoured a French pope, while a Colonna party aimed at another Italian. The only way out of the deadlock was to elect a cardinal who was neither, and for a brief moment it seemed that the new pope would be the Greek Bessarion, the hero of the reunion party at Florence, a fine scholar, a theologian, and a good administrator; in many ways the most noteworthy churchman of his age. But prejudice was too strong, and jealousy of the neophyte. There was next a movement to elect, from outside the cardinals, the Friar Minor Antonio of Montefalcone; and then, "as it were to postpone the contest, " [ ] on April 8 the cardinals elected an aged Spaniard, Alonso de Borja. [ ]

Calixtus III -- this was the new pope's title -- came of a race for which militant opposition to Islam, still, after seven centuries, in occupation of the south of Spain, was of the essence of Catholicism. He was, moreover, a Catalan, and the kingdom of Aragon, in whose service he had spent the greater part of his life, was the greatest of the Christian maritime powers. The pope began his reign by a solemn public vow to work for one thing only, the expulsion of the Turks from Europe and the liberation of their Christian victims. Then he set himself, with wonderful energy and skill, to reorganise the crusade. Indulgences were announced, tithes decreed, the date of departure fixed and legates sent to all the Christian princes, cardinals to the chief of them, bishops and the new Franciscan Observants [ ] to the smaller states. Calixtus made his own generous personal contribution, sending jewels to the saleroom and his plate to the mint, and even selling off castles. The restoration plans of Nicholas V were abruptly halted. Sculptors were set to cut stone cannon balls, and architects bidden design ships and engines of war. There was to be an expedition by land under the command of the Duke of Burgundy, [ ] while the sea warfare would be the task of the pope's old master the King of Aragon and Naples. [ ] There was already a small papal fleet in existence, and it was now ordered into the Aegean to succour the population of the islands still in Christian hands. During the winter of 1455-1456 the pope set up shipyards along the Tiber, and at an immense cost built a second fleet of twenty-seven ships.

The difficulties which had hampered earlier popes did not disappear. From no one of the Western princes was there any real response to the pope's enthusiasm. Hardly any of the money laboriously collected from the clergy and people ever reached the pope. The Kings of France and Denmark and Aragon, and the Duke of Burgundy himself, simply transferred it to their own use. In France it was even denied that the pope had any right to levy taxes on French Church property, and Calixtus was threatened with a General Council should he not withdraw the tax -- a threat which this tough old man met by excommunicating those who had signed this protest. In the first summer of the reign war broke out in central Italy -- a war in which the King of Naples secretly helped the freebooter Picinnino against the pope, while the papal fleet (commanded by an Aragonese archbishop), instead of sailing to the Aegean, joined itself to the Aragonese fleet in an attack on Genoa. Nor was the new fleet, at first, a more useful instrument. It was not until August 6, 1456, that the cardinal who commanded it -- Scarampo -- could be persuaded to leave the security of Naples. And by that date the one great event of the war was over, the relief of the besieged city of Belgrade.

The conqueror of Constantinople, Mohammed II, who had in 1455 made himself master of Serbia, next planned the conquest of Hungary, the last power between himself and the West. Throughout the winter and spring (1455-1456) he made his careful preparations, and in June 1456 he moved, with a well-equipped force of 150,000 men. In July he laid siege to Belgrade. Against all likelihood the siege was raised, and Mohammed was forced to retire, with heavy losses in men and in material. The heroes of this amazing feat were the nameless thousands whom the sanctity and burning eloquence of the General of the Observant Franciscans, St. John Capistran, had recruited for the new crusade, whom the genius of the Spanish cardinal legate, Juan Carvajal, had organised, and whom John Hunyadi led. [ ] The first stage of the victory was the five-hour fight on the Danube (July 14) when the crusaders forced their way through the Turks into the city and the citadel. Just a week later the sultan ordered a general assault. The Turks persisted for two days, and then they retired, in great confusion. Mohammed brought off his army indeed, but his losses were extremely heavy.

Hopes ran high at Rome, when the splendid news came in, and the pope, to commemorate for ever a victory which he regarded as a patent answer to his crusade of prayer, founded the new feast of the Transfiguration of Our Lord (August 6). Elsewhere the great victory was readily interpreted as a proof that no further effort was needed. In Servia itself the very worst happened. Hunyadi died -- of the plague -- only three weeks after the rout, and St. John also died, a few weeks later (October 23). And next, when the weakling Habsburg King of Hungary -- who had fled to Vienna as Mohammed's armies neared Belgrade -- arrived with reinforcements (November), there was so violent a quarrel between Germans and Hungarians that the crusade broke up.

So much had the energy and faith of Calixtus III accomplished in one short year, and to so little had it all been brought. But the failure did not break the pope's spirit, nor halt his effort. A new Christian champion -- Skanderbeg -- now appeared in Albania, [ ] and in August 1457 the little papal fleet won a battle off Mitylene, when twenty-five enemy ships were captured.

But the catastrophe which followed the relief of Belgrade was really the end of anything that Calixtus, at his great age, could expect to accomplish. Two years later he died, on the very feast he had founded, August 6, 1458.

As in 1455, and 1447, the vacant see was soon filled. On August 19 the Cardinal of Siena was elected, Aeneas Sylvius Piccolomini. He chose to be called Pius II, from devotion it may be thought to Virgil, rather than to the distant memory of that Pius I who was almost Virgil's contemporary. For Aeneas Sylvius, fifty-three years of age at his election, had been for a good thirty years and more one of the brightest figures in the revival of classical letters. He was not so learned as Nicholas V, nor had he that pope's natural affection for the sacred sciences. But much more than that enthusiastic collector of manuscripts, he had been throughout his life a most distinguished practitioner of the new literary arts. He had written poems in the classical metres, histories, romances even, and as a practical professional diplomatist he had shown himself a finished master of the new, highly-stylised oratory. His whole career had been rather that of a cultivated man of the world than of a priest, and in fact it was not until he was past forty that Aeneas Sylvius took the great step of receiving Holy Orders. What had delayed him for years he himself set down, with stark directness, in a letter to a friend: "Timeo continentiam. " His life as a layman had, indeed, been habitually marked by the gravest moral irregularities, and it was partly due to his way of life that at fifty-three he was prematurely old and broken, white-haired and crippled with gout. But the mind was as keen as ever, the enthusiasm for letters burned no less brightly, and the whole man, like another St. Augustine, was now devoted to the interests of religion.

The contrast between Pius II and his predecessor could not have been greater, save for one thing, his resolute will to free Christendom from the menace of Islam. With Pius II, too, this was the primary task before the Holy See. In a speech made on the very day of his election, the pope had made this clear. Given the many successes of his long diplomatic career, it was not strange that the pope should begin his reign by yet another effort to achieve the needed European unity, nor that the means he proposed was a congress of the sovereign princes. On October 12, 1458, he announced to the cardinals that he proposed to call this congress to meet at Mantua in the June of 1459, and that he would himself preside at it. On January 22 -- in the face of much criticism -- he set out from Rome. Travelling by slow stages, halting at Perugia, Siena, Florence, Bologna and Ferrara, he at length came to Mantua, on May 27.

The seven months of the pope's stay at Mantua [ ] were an all but unrelieved disappointment. Of all the princes invited not one had even troubled to send an envoy. The very cardinals had secretly worked to dissuade the princes, and now they did their best to persuade the pope to abandon the scheme. Scarampo especially, the late admiral of the papal fleet, showed himself hostile and contemptuous, and presently returned to Rome. The emperor, whose interests Pius II had served magnificently when he was his secretary, chose this moment to proclaim himself King of Hungary, and thereby to begin a civil war in "this kingdom which is the shield of all Christendom, under cover of which we have hitherto been safe. " [ ] The King of France, with whom the emperor was plotting to force a transfer of the congress to some imperial city, made it clear that he would not co-operate in the war unless the pope acknowledged the claims of the House of Anjou to the kingdom of Naples, and he underlined his hostility by scarcely veiled threats to renew the anti-papal agitation and feuds of Basel and Constance. The Venetians were so indifferent that the pope told them plainly they were thought to hold more with the Turks than with the Christians, and to be more interested in their trade than in their religion. [ ]

It was not until September 26, four months after the pope's arrival at Mantua, that enough envoys had appeared for the congress to hold a meeting. And though the pope, and various envoys, remained on for another four months it never met again. The pope thought it more practical to deal with the various ambassadors individually.

The delegates from France did at last arrive, in November 1459, but their real business was to bully the pope and to coerce him into a change of policy in Naples. [ ] But Pius II was resolute, and so far from cowed by the king's hostility that he took the offensive, and demanded a revocation of the Pragmatic Sanction of 1438. The Bishop of Rome, he said, was only allowed in France such jurisdiction as it pleased the Parlement to grant him. Were this to continue, the Church would become a monster, a creature with many heads. And to clinch the matter he published, from Mantua, the famous bull Exsecrabilis, [ ] condemning as a novel and hitherto unheard-of abuse, the practice of appealing from the pope to some future General Council.

The congress formally ended with a bull proclaiming a three-years' crusade and announcing new grants of Church revenues for its support. On January 19, 1460, the pope left Mantua. It was not until October 6 that he was back in Rome, after an absence of nearly two years.

The response of Europe to the new appeal was as poor as ever. Eleven months after the return of the pope to Rome the news came, in September 1461, that Mohammed had overrun the last Christian state in Asia Minor, the empire of Trebizond, and that he was master of the Black Sea port of Sinope. Then it was once more the turn of the Balkan states and Greece. Lesbos was captured in 1462, and Bosnia was conquered in 1463. The Venetian admiral had looked on unmoved while the Turks too k Lesbos, but their attack, later that same year, on the republic's colonies at Lepanto and in Argolis brought the war party in Venice into power. Pius II, though under no illusions about the nature of the new Venetian zeal for a crusade, [ ] thought the moment had arrived to publish the resolution to which he had come in March 1462 -- the resolution of a brave man indeed, but of one who has all but despaired of his generation, and who will all but demand that Providence shall save it by a miracle. Venice, at last, had been persuaded by events that the only way of salvation for a Christian state was to defeat and destroy for ever the Turkish forces. Hungary, whence alone could come the military complement to the maritime power of Venice, was at last delivered from the war with Frederick III. [ ] The French still resolutely held themselves aloof; Florence thought that Venice and the Turks should be left to fight each other until neither was strong enough to be dangerous to anyone else. But on September 12, 1463, the Venetians signed an offensive alliance with Hungary, and on September 23 the pope announced his resolve. To kill for ever the often-heard gibe that pope and cardinals would do anything except expose themselves to suffer in the Holy War, Pius II would personally lead the crusade, and all the cardinals would go with him, save only the sick and those needed for the vital administration of the Church.

"Whatever we do, " said the pope, "people take it ill. They say we live for pleasure only, pile up riches, bear ourselves arrogantly, ride on fat mules and handsome palfreys, trail the fringes of our cloaks and show plump faces from beneath the red hat and the white hood, keep hounds for the chase, spend much on actors and parasites, and nothing in defence of the Faith. And there is some truth in their words: many among the cardinals and other officials of our court do lead this kind of life. If the truth be told, the luxury and pomp of our court is too great. And this is why we are so detested by the people that they will not listen to us, even when what we say is just and reasonable. . . . Our cry [ ] 'Go forth' has resounded in vain. If instead, the word is ' Come, with me, ' there will be some response. . . . Should this effort also fail, we know of no other means. . . . We are too weak to fight sword in hand; and this is not indeed the priest's duty. But we shall imitate Moses, and pray upon the height while the people of Israel do battle below. "

So did the pope speak to his cardinals, and although there were political realists among them who only sneered, the majority caught something of his devoted spirit. To the princes who looked on unmoved at the last preparations, at the strenuous efforts to raise funds, the sale of vestments, chalices, and other plate, the renewed appeals to Florence, to Milan, and to Siena, and to the rest, at the slow labour of turning into an ordered force the thousands of poor men who came in from France, Germany, the Low Countries, from Spain and Scotland too, to seek victory and salvation with the pope, Pius II spoke his last word on October 22, 1463. "Think of your hopeless brethren groaning in captivity amongst the Turks or living in daily dread of it. As you are men, let humanity prompt you. . . . As you are Christians, obey the Gospel and love your neighbour as yourself. . . . The like fate is hanging over yourselves; if you will not help those who live between you and the enemy, those still further away will forsake you when your own hour arrives. . . . The ruin of the emperors of Constantinople and Trebizond, of the Kings of Bosnia and Rascia and the others, all overpowered the one after the other, prove how disastrous it is to stand still and do nothing. " The time was indeed to come when some of those who heard this would see the Turks masters of Hungary as far as Buda, masters, too, of the whole Mediterranean marine.

All through that winter, 1463-1464, the work of preparation continued, and the pope remained fixed in his resolve, though even his own subjects had to be constrained to subscribe to the war fund, though there were cardinals who used every chance to hinder and to destroy the great work, and though the French king, Louis XI, threatened an alliance with the Hussites and a new council once the pope was out of Rome.

On the day fixed, June 18, 1464, after a great ceremony in St. Peter's, Pius II left the city for Ancona, the port of assembly. He was already an old man, broken with years of gout and stone. The intense heat tried him further. It took him a month to reach Ancona, and by this time he was seriously ill. In the port all was confusion, crowded with Spanish and French crusaders -- all of the poorest class -- unorganised, leaderless and at daggers drawn. As August came in, and the temperature mounted, the plague broke out. The papal fleet had been delayed in its voyage from Pisa, and of course there was not a sign of any vessel from Venice. A new siege of the pope now began, to persuade him to abandon the expedition and to return to Rome. But the onetime elegant aesthete was long beyond the power of arguments addressed to his material happiness. He held firm to his resolve to sacrifice himself utterly, and tortured now by new anxieties as to the loyalty of Venice as well as by his fiendish bodily pain, Pius II slowly came to his end, with the disgusted among his cardinals occupied only with chances and prospects in the conclave that could not now be far off. At Ancona, in the night before the feast of Our Lady's Assumption, the pope died. He had had his last view of the world he had so loved, the antique world and the new, two days earlier, when carried to the window of his sickroom he saw the first of the Venetian galleys round the mole that runs outs beyond the triumphal arch of Trajan.

The body of the dead pope was taken back to Rome, and the cardinals hastened to follow it, for the funeral service and the conclave. The crusade had died with the pope. The doge used the opportunity of his presence at Ancona to make clear to the cardinals how ill-advised he thought the whole affair; and the cardinals, anxious above all else to get the expedition off their hands, made over the crusade fleet to him -- to be restored should the pope whom they were about to elect require it for a crusade. They also paid to the doge -- for transmission to the King of Hungary -- what remained of the treasure collected, 40,000 ducats. The doge returned to Venice on August 18, and gave orders immediately that the great fleet should be dismantled.

The cardinals were all back in Rome by August 25, and on the 28th they went into conclave. [ ] The election was soon over, for on the very first ballot they chose as pope a rich Venetian noble, forty-eight years of age, Cardinal Pietro Barbo, a nephew of Eugene IV. He took the name of Paul II. Personal leadership of the crusade was never any part of his policy. But Paul II was far from sympathising with the selfish policy of the great

.

city whence he came. He gave what aid he could to Hungary in the crisis of 1465, and to Skanderbeg when hard pressed at Croja two years later. But Albania fell to the Turks in 1468, and the important Venetian possession, Negrepont, in 1470. Here, for the moment, the tale of Moslem success ended. After twenty years of conquest the effort of Mohammed II was coming to a halt, and his death in 1481 gave relief to the West for a generation.

The last events in the drama of Mohammed's reign were first the naval expedition, organised by Sixtus IV in 1473, which took and sacked the Turkish ports of Attalia (whereupon dissensions, and the return home of the Neapolitan contingent) and of Smyrna (after which the Venetians deserted); and finally, in 1480, a Turkish invasion of Italy and the temporary occupation of Otranto (August 11). [ ] Had Mohammed's successor been such another as himself, nothing could now have saved Rome and Italy. The pope prepared to flee; Avignon was got ready for his court; [ ] a an immense effort was made to raise an army and equip a fleet, and then, on June 2, 1481, the welcome news came that Mohammed II was dead. Special services of thanksgiving were held, and it was in a wholly new spirit of confidence that the fleet sailed to besiege Otranto. After ten weeks of vigorous resistance the Turks surrendered. And then, as always, the coalition broke up. The pope's scheme of an attack on Valona, in preparation for an attempt to free Albania, came to nought. Plague broke out in the papal ships, the men refused to serve any longer, winter was at hand, and so, despite the pope's energy, all the advantage was lost. The Turks were no longer attacking -- when next a soldier of genius appeared among them it was Syria and Egypt that would attract him -- and the Christian states were only too willing to leave them undisturbed in their new empire.

## 3. THE RETURN OF THE ANCIENT WORLD

The fifty years that followed the Council of Constance saw a remarkable revival in the fortunes of the papacy; in that time the popes managed to reassert everywhere the idea and the practice of their traditional primacy of jurisdiction over the universal Church. In that same half century, despite the continuous endeavours of the same popes, Christendom, as a political association, refused to league itself against the new militant Mohammedanism of the Ottomans; and at the very moment when Islam was about to be expelled from the last remnant of its ancient hold on Spain, it was yet able to gain in the south-east a greater hold on Christian Europeans than had ever been its fortune in the whole eight hundred years of its existence. But what is more generally associated with the history of these first two generations of the fifteenth century is that first rapid new flowering in Italy of literature and the arts, which, universally, is called the Renaissance. The effect of this on the fortunes of Catholicism was speedy, it was profound, and it has lasted.

There is scarcely any need nowadays to labour the point that there were painters and sculptors of lasting significance before, let us say, Botticelli and Donatello, or that the Gothic is not sterile and barbarous; nor, on the other hand, is it necessary to insist how barren in creative literature was this new revival in its most enthusiastically classical stage. Nor, again, will it be any longer contended that the most splendid achievement of the thought of Greece was a closed book for the West until, in the fifteenth century, Chrysoloras and Gemistes Plethon began to teach the Greek grammar to the enthusiastic patricians of Florence. But although the nature of the change which then began was for long misunderstood, the scale of its effect has never been exaggerated. It brought about, ultimately, a change in the educated man's whole outlook upon life, a revolutionary change, which disturbed all his standards of judgment -- a change after which the Christian world was never to be, anywhere, quite the same kind of thing as before.

It all began with a new interest in the Latin literature of the golden age, in Cicero above all and in Virgil; and this interest became a permanent enthusiasm, and indeed a main purpose of life, in the world of the cultured as, during the late fourteenth and early fifteenth centuries, long forgotten works of these Latin poets, rhetoricians, philosophers and historians began to be "discovered" in the various monastic libraries of Italy, France and southern Germany. The second stage was the introduction to the West, now all aglow with the novelty of an artistic appreciation of literary form, of the still finer literature of the Greeks. It was in translations, first of all, that these masterpieces were read, translations made by the occasional Latin humanist of the new type who knew Greek. But presently the desire to read the actual texts bred a very passion to learn the language; and ability to read the Greeks themselves, once this became at all general, wrought such a revolution in the mind of the West that, for the next five hundred years, Greek studies would be everywhere considered not only the first foundation of all scholarship, but a vital necessity in the intellectual formation of the generally educated European.

It has been urged that the Renaissance had no importance, in the fifteenth century, for the ordinary man, that it passed by the people of its own time. This is no doubt true; but it by no means passed by the ruling classes of the time, whether rulers in the Church or in the State, and it actually created a new class, destined to be as powerful as either of these, the independent thinkers, with no official attachments, who wrote for the general public of men who could read. Also, this new ruling class came into existence almost simultaneously with that new art of printing, one of whose main results was precisely this, that now, for the first time, the ordinary man could really make a contact with all the great literature of the world. And the invention permanently established the public influence of this new ruling class, making it forever impossible to set barriers to the spread and development of new ideas, whether these were good or bad, whether to popes and kings they were found convenient or inconvenient.

Is it too much to say that the discovery of printing was the most important event of this century? Books had already been made, at the end of the fourteenth century, where each page was printed from a single block -- an adaptation of a Chinese invention already some hundreds of years old. But the all important idea was that of making separate types for each letter and to print by combining them in a frame. To whom was this due? The question is still much controverted. But, at a time when the idea was "in the air", it was the German, John Gutenberg (1398-1468) who first, successfully, began to print, at Mainz. The first piece we possess of his craftsmanship is an indulgence, dated 1454, and among his books are two magnificent bibles. Two of Gutenberg's associates, Fust and Schoeffer developed the new art. Bamberg, Strasburg, Augsburg and Nuremberg all had presses by 1470, and it was a printer at Cologne who taught the craft to the Englishman William Caxton, who set up his press at Westminster in 1476. The first Italian press was set up in 1464, very appropriately in the Benedictine abbey of Subiaco. Soon there was an abundance of printers in Italy, thirty-eight in Rome alone by the end of the century, and as many as a hundred in Venice. Printing came to France in 1470, where its first patrons were the king, Louis XI, and the theologians of the Sorbonne.

Everywhere, indeed, the ecclesiastics welcomed the new invention, patronised the craftsmen and protected them against the strong opposition of the calligraphers, and of the booksellers too. The bishops in Germany, for example, considering the craft as a work of piety, granted indulgences to the printers and to those who sold the new books. Naturally enough, among the first to set up presses were the Brothers of the Common Life. Canons Regular, Benedictines, Premonstratensians, did the same. The first printer at Leipzig was a professor of theology in the university, and it was a Franciscan lector in theology who set up the first press in the university town of Tubingen.

Such is the tale everywhere, cardinals, bishops, religious and clergy united in an immense practical enthusiasm to employ and develop the art. At Rome the pope who saw its beginnings -- Paul II (1464-1471) -- put at the disposal of the first printers the manuscripts collected by his predecessors. The generous zeal of Nicholas V now began to reap a harvest far beyond anything he could have hoped. Bessarion did as much for the presses of Venice, lending the printers his Greek manuscripts. The printers were held in high honour. Popes employed them as ambassadors, ennobled them. It was an art that the clergy were proud to exercise, and among these earliest printers there were, at Venice, even nuns. And when the navigators revealed to Europe the existence of the new lands beyond the Atlantic, it was the missionaries who took the printing press across the seas.

The question must indeed rise immediately to the mind, how such a humanist movement as this -- the humanist movement par excellence, in popular impression -- affected the religion to which, for many centuries now, Western humanity had brought its mind in captivity; how did it affect, that is to say, not so much Catholicism as a body of truths, but as an association of human beings who accepted those truths? The Renaissance came upon this Catholic world at a moment when the Church was labouring under serious disintegrating strains, effects of the schism, of the long disputes about the papal primacy, and of the long decay of thought; in an age characterised by a general scepticism about the usefulness, or the possibility, of philosophy, an age when prelates who were the leaders of Catholic thought managed, in simple unawareness, to hold simultaneously the Catholic faith and philosophical positions incompatible with it, and this without interference, amid the time's general unawareness; and while, since Ockham, this practical scepticism had been slowly rotting the Christian mind, considerations of quite another order had been shaping the religious outlook of the new capitalist bourgeoisie, chafing at a morality which would limit its opportunities of profit. It was upon a Christendom "ready for anything" that there now came this movement which, inevitably, would not stop at any mere artistic appreciation of literary form. Almost from the beginning the movement effected important -- if as yet concealed -- apostasies from the Christian standard of morals.

It was the greatest movement of the century, the greatest movement of the human spirit indeed, since that which began in the days of Abelard and John of Salisbury, and -- one of its most singular features -- among the chief patrons of the movement, and even among its leaders, were the popes. Not all of them, indeed, were enthusiasts, but hardly one was indifferent to it, and none of them set himself in direct opposition to it.

What, it may be asked, had the popes to do with a movement that was not religious in its nature, nor yet in its immediate objective? where was their place in this new world of poets and painters and sculptors, of men of letters and artists generally? Here, surely, is the very antithesis to that conception of Christian perfection which inspired the contemporary Devotio Moderna? Rarely, indeed, in history has the papacy placed itself at the head of any contemporary new development, whether in thought or life; rarely has its role been that of the pioneer. In the earlier, medieval, renaissance -- a renaissance not of a particular way of writing, of thinking, or of life, but a rebirth of life itself, of the activity of the human mind after the quasi-death of the terrible Dark Ages -- the popes had scarcely initiated at all. They had been sometimes helpful, always watchful, and more often than not extremely suspicious. There are no philosopher popes in the formative stage of the century of St. Thomas and St. Bonaventure and Siger. But now, in the fifteenth century, popes are themselves among the most famous exponents of the new culture. The contrast could not be greater than between the attitude of Gregory IX to the Aristotelian revival in the first half of the century of St. Thomas, and that of Nicholas V in the morning of the Renaissance. The earlier pope, theologian and canonist, saw only the dangers -- really latent -- in the new rising cult of the Greek, but not the immense value of what was true in his thought, nor how the dangers it presented could be met. His successor, two hundred years later, saw only the glorious promise of a new age of Christian culture and wisdom; in an age already more superficial than any for five hundred years, it is not surprising that he mistook the signs, already evident, of an essential antagonism of ideals for the personal indecencies of a handful of looseliving men of letters.

The earliest of the medieval popes whom we know as an interested and discerning patron of the fine arts on the grand scale, was Boniface VIII, and this was made a count against him in Philip the Fair's endeavour to bring about his posthumous condemnation as a heretic and a false pope. Boniface had, indeed, done much to assist the Roman art of his time, employing such masters as Pietro Cavallini and the Cosimati; and he had also brought to Rome, from Florence, Arnolfo di Cambio and Giotto. The record survives of the mass of precious church and altar furnishings, of vestments, episcopal jewellery, reliquaries, statues, work in metal and in ivory, tapestries and embroideries, made to the order of this pope by artists and craftsmen from every country in Europe. Boniface, in the last months before the fatal crisis of Anagni, also completed the organisation of the Roman university, by adding a faculty of arts to the existing faculties of the sacred sciences and law. He founded a second university at Fermo; he founded anew the archives of the Apostolic See, which had disappeared during the troubled years of the wars between his predecessors and Frederick II. Finally Boniface VIII collected what remained of the ancient library of the popes, works for the most part of theology, liturgy and canon law; and by his care to extend this collection he has a real claim to be a principal founder of the Vatican Library. Boniface VIII could find but a handful of manuscripts that had survived the storms and the years of chaos. He left behind no fewer than 1,300. Most of these were religious works, many of them newly transcribed for the pope, and illuminated by the staff of copyists he had formed. There were bibles and theology and philosophy, liturgy and law and church history; there were the Latin fathers and some of the Greeks too -- Origen at any rate, St. Athanasius and St. John Chrysostom. But there were also -- and it is this which interests this chapter -- manuscripts of Cicero and Seneca, Virgil and Ovid, Lucan, Suetonius and Pliny, the grammatical treatises of Donatus and thirty-three works in Greek, the earliest collection of Greek texts we know of in any medieval library, and works, all of them, of a scientific kind, Euclid, Ptolemy, Archimedes.

Boniface VIII died in 1303, his immediate successor reigned only a short nine months, and Clement V who next succeeded, the first of the Avignon popes, had not ever, until the close of his reign, any settled place of residence. Not until the coming of John XXII (1316-1334) were the popes again in a position to interest themselves in literature and the arts. It was this pope, and his successor, Benedict XII (1334-1342), the main organisers of the Avignon papacy as a system of government, who provided so magnificently for its housing in the great Palais des Papes that still dominates the ancient city by the Rhone. From this time Avignon became a centre to which architects, painters and sculptors and the whole world of craftsmen and artificers, flowed steadily in search of patronage; and with them came the men of letters, the most notable of all being Francesco Petrarch. While Rome, intellectually and materially, fell back into a very barbarism, Avignon, in these central years, of the fourteenth century, bade fair to become what Florence was a hundred years later.

The papal library was developed anew, and yet again there figured among its treasures what Latin classics the medieval world possessed -- no Horace as yet, nor anything of Tacitus -- and new translations from the Greek, of Aristotle, for example, and Aesop and Porphyry. But there is no Homer, no Demosthenes, no Thucydides, and no Greek tragedy. Yet although the Greek influence is still exercised in so limited a way, and through translations only, the fourteenth century is a time when contact with the Greek-speaking world is being steadily extended. The rapidly developing crisis of the Christian East, as the Ottomans advance, brings more and more Greeks to the West, in search of assistance or simply as refugees, and with both kinds of necessitous Greeks the papal court, in all these years, is very familiar. Gradually a practical knowledge of fourteenth-century Greek becomes more common at the curia and, through the curia, elsewhere too. The new religious discussions between Latins and Greeks also, inevitably, turn the mind of the West not only to the less familiar of the Greek fathers but to the original texts of all of them. In this new interest the pioneers are the Dominicans and the Franciscans -- the Franciscans especially -- whom, for more than a hundred years now, the popes have been employing as missionaries and agents in the islands of the Greek sea, in Asia Minor, in the very lands of central Asia as far as China itself. [ ] As the diplomacy rises and falls between the popes and these Eastern princes, presents are exchanged, and among the presents from the East there are manuscripts of the Greek classics.

It is this world into which Petrarch was introduced, a young man in his twenties, about the year 1330. Here, at the papal court, he found patrons, protection, books, and the stimulus of new opportunities, rewards, a career, the means to form his own famous library, and his first Greek. And after this, a first practical fruit of the ancient literature's hold on him, came his interest in the other remains of the ancient culture, the beginnings of all that practical historical and artistic interest in the sculpture and architecture of Greece and Rome. Petrarch, it was said long ago, is "the first modern man." Others have also been put forward for the distinction, but there is much in Petrarch which is new, and which since Petrarch has become characteristic and typical. We can see in him all the main elements of the promise which the Renaissance seemed to offer to the Christian future, and something also of what it was that blighted that promise. Recalling his career, and the development of his spirit, we can better understand the unmisgiving way in which such an admirable Christian as Nicholas V welcomed the movement with open arms and without any reservations. Petrarch is the "modern man" in his violent reaction against the cultural achievement of the medieval world. Here he is a pioneer and, given his genius, his effect is weighty indeed. He has, for example, nothing but scorn for the unclassical latinity of the Middle Ages. He mocks the time for its dependence on translations; Aristotle would not recognise himself in his thirteenth-century Latin disguise. And he mocks at the cult of Aristotle himself. He is impatient with the superstition that entangles the learning of the Middle Ages, the bogus sciences of astrology and alchemy, the charlatanry that often passes for medicine; and he is impatient with the new lawyers' religion of the civil law, which they so eagerly develop, with a jargon of its own and distinctions for the sake of distinguishing, into a new and profitable pedantic superstition.

In Petrarch we also note, for the first time in a personage of international importance, the study of ancient history passing into such a love of the ancient world therein portrayed that the restoration of that world is urged as a practical solution for present discontents. Here is a first crusader driven by that nostalgie du passe which has afflicted so many others ever since. Rome, the Rome of Cicero, is the golden age; all since is usurpation and decay. So fourteen hundred years of history must, somehow, be undone. Whence the crazy-seeming alliance of Petrarch with Rienzi; whence the new Ghibellinism in which Petrarch tries, with all the power of flattery at his command, to enlist the realist princes to restore the Roman State; whence also the new anti-papal spirit, for the fact and presence of the papacy in Rome is the great obstacle to any real restoration of the republic. Here are ideas and ideals which, once given to the world, will not die. They inspire very many of the humanists -- and conspirators -- of the next generation, and Machiavelli will give them a still greater vitality, and thence they come down to our own age. Who will be so bold as to say we have yet heard the last of them?

Petrarch was a poet and a man of letters, and only incidentally was he a thinker or politician -- these activities were but the overbrimming of his literary contemplation. But in one respect he makes an interesting contact of accord with the world of some contemporaries whom he never met, and with whom doubtless he would not have recognised that he had anything in common. For Petrarch was not anti-Aristotelian simply because, on crucial questions, he preferred the teaching of other philosophers, but because, fundamentally, he thought all such speculative philosophy a vain waste of time. Happiness is the object of life, thought cannot guide man to it, for in thought there is no certainty, and if a man wants to know how to be happy, let him read the Gospels -- or Cicero. Not, indeed, because Cicero is a thinker-another Aristotle -- but because Cicero is himself an apostle. Aristotle is cold, but Cicero is on fire with love of virtue and will enflame all those who read him. Not thought then but eloquence, not the philosopher but the artist, is the safe guide. Petrarch is yet another man who, sceptical about the power of reason, seeks elsewhere than in his reason the assurance he needs. And, as often happens when good men shrink from the labour of thought about their religious life, he assembles a strangely assorted company to aid him, and finds a curiously unchristian ratio for their union, and offers us Cicero and the divine Gospel as joint warranty for a Christian life, twin guardian angels for man cast into a world of temptation.

Petrarch, of course, knew that world as well as any other man. His sensitive spirit had been tried there as only such can be tried, and he had suffered defeats and perhaps routs. But the religious foundation remained secure. One day Petrarch was converted, and thenceforward he did battle manfully and continuously and, one may say, systematically with the tempter. Two traits, however, very notably, survived that conversion, to be a main source of anxiety with him to the end. They need to be mentioned explicitly, for they are to be the outstanding characteristics of almost all the great men of the Renaissance, though with these they are not defects, but rather the main end of life and the natural, hardly to be regarded, effect of their pursuit of it. Those traits are the desire for fame, and vanity. In Petrarch we find the earliest signs of that mania to be famous which is the leading note in the life of public men of all sorts during the last fifty years of which this book treats. No cult could be less compatible with the Christian ideal.

Petrarch, although he is hardly more than a precursor of the Renaissance as the term is generally used, is yet, as poet and man of letters, and as a man, a far greater personage than any of those who follow him in the more brilliant Italy of the next [ ]. century. Before we speak of these lesser men -- who by the accident of their special scholarship were necessarily the artificers of the greatest change of all -- and as a kind of preface to the statement

of the effect of their lives on the last generations of medieval
Catholicism, we need to note that Petrarch was not by any means
the only Italian whose genius these French popes fostered at their
court of Avignon. It is at Avignon that the popes first begin to
employ the new humanists as their secretaries. The new age is
not yet arrived when to write Ciceronian prose is the best of titles
to a prince's favour, and a rapid highroad to wealth; but it is fast
approaching. The last three of the Avignon popes -- Innocent VI,
B. Urban V, Gregory XI -- were all men of culture, all university
types, the first two indeed one-time professors. Innocent VI and
Urban V brought to the service of the chancery the famous
Coluccio Salutati, who later was to pass into the service of
Florence as its chancellor and there to sponsor the entry into life
and letters of "the heavenly twins" of the new age, Leonardo
Bruni (called Aretino) and Poggio Bracciolini, and to bring to
Florence the most active cultural force of all this time, the
Byzantine Manuel Chrysolorus from whom Poggio, and Cenci,
Filelfo himself, Ambrogio Traversari, and Thomas of Sarzana
who was to become Pope Nicholas V, all learned their Greek.
And it was Gregory XI's employment of Francesco Bruni that led
to the appearance of his nephew Aretino in the papal chancery,
and so to the beginning of all that development which made the
corps of papal secretaries one of the first and most important
centres of the classical revival in fifteenth-century Italy, a centre
from which almost everything else was to come.

This is not a history of that revival, but the story cannot be told
of the effect of the revival upon the papacy, and upon the
papacy's government of the universal Church, without some
mention of the famous humanists whom, from about this time,
the popes began to call into their service, nor without some
reminder of what that scholarship was which made these "civil
servants" so famous. The chief of them, Poggio Bracciolini,
entered the service of the popes, as a young man in his early
twenties, about 1403. He served them for fifty years, rising to be
the chief official of the chancery and amassing a huge fortune. In

1414 Poggio made one of the suite of John XXIII at the Council of Constance. For the debates there was presently great want of theological and patristic texts, and it was Poggio's task to organise the collection of needed manuscripts from the libraries of the monasteries of Switzerland and southern Germany. Along with the fathers he found in these libraries much else; a host of minor writers of the silver age of Latin letters, the histories of Ammianus Marcellinus, for example, Quintilian's Institutes and several long-forgotten speeches of Cicero. From this moment Poggio was a celebrity. Martin V was glad to retain him in the chancery as he reorganised it in 1418. Some few years later it was Poggio's good fortune to discover Petronius and Pliny and Tacitus. This man of letters was no less interested in what we have come to call antiques, and he was one of the first collectors of medals, coins, marbles, statues and other relics of the art of the ancient world. His museum was indeed celebrated, and the missionaries in the East were encouraged to contribute to it, for presents of this kind were the surest passport to Poggio's influence in the curia.

Among Poggio's colleagues in the offices of the chancery there were three other scholars of note, who shared in the hunt after the lost classics and who were also poets, Bartholomew Aragazzi, Agapito Cenci and Antonio Loschi. All three were already in the service of the curia by the time of Martin V's election (1417), and they remained in it for the rest of their lives. They are the first editors and commentators of the Latin classics, practitioners of the new art of writing Ciceronian prose, and they were brought into the papal service so that the state-papers -- bulls and the like -- might be drafted in a style worthy of the Roman See. Never did this somewhat pedantic occupation seem so marvellous an accomplishment; and never, before or since, was it so munificently rewarded. [ ]

The leading cardinals of the time followed the example set by the popes. It was Louis Aleman -- whom we have seen in set

449

opposition to the papacy at Basel -- who was even able, when legate at Bologna, to win to the papal service, for a few brief months, the most famous of all Italian teachers of Greek, Filelfo. The Bishop of Bologna at that same time, the Carthusian cardinal Nicholas Albergati, was also a generous and interested patron of the new fashions. In his palace Filelfo was welcomed and he found there, among those eager to learn from him, the two future popes, Thomas of Sarzana, now beginning as the master of the cardinal's household a twenty years' apprenticeship to the business of effectively patronising art and letters, and Aeneas Sylvius Piccolomini. A third patron in the Sacred College who, like Albergati, was known universally for the piety and austerity of his life, was the youthful Domenico Capranica. A fourth, very notable, figure was the wealthy Girolamo Orsini, who gave all his energies and his money to gather a great library which, like the papal collection, should be at the disposal of all who loved studies. It was due to the combination of Poggio and Girolamo Orsini that the long-lost comedies of Plautus were given back to the world, and another effect of the revival is to be seen in the cardinal's no less momentous recovery of the works of St. Cyprian.

What first brought the popes of the fifteenth century into contact with the Renaissance was the most practical reason of all. The immediate task before these popes was to reorganise the machinery of government, and to rebuild the ruined churches and palaces and offices of their capital. They needed Latinists, and they needed architects, and painters and sculptors; and in each department they strove to gain the services of the best With Martin V bringing to Rome Gentili and Masaccio and Ghiberti, that historic association of popes and artists begins that is, in the minds of all, one of the most permanent memories of the next hundred and fifty years; the association that reaches its peak in the collaboration of the two gigantic figures of Julius II and Michelangelo. Eugene IV's long reign was too broken for him to bring to a finish Martin V's great work of restoration. Of the work done by Eugene's orders in St. Peter's, only Filarete's great doors remain. The chapel in the Vatican, to decorate which this pope brought Fra Angelico from Florence, has disappeared, and there disappeared too, in the time of Paul III, (1534-1549), the frescoes painted for Eugene IV by Benozzo Gozzoli.

Eugene IV was, to the end of his days, a most observant religious, [ ] but neither by temperament nor training was he a man of letters or an artist. Nevertheless he too had learned Greek, and he was a great reader and student, especially of histories. His real interest in the new scholarship is shown unmistakably in his active patronage of one of the most winning figures of the time, the Camaldolese monk Ambrogio Traversari. This truly saintly man had learnt his Greek, when prior of his monastery in Florence, from Filelfo; and from his cell in that austere cloister, through conversations, and through a most extensive correspondence, he exercised a very real influence on the movement, proposing and executing translations from the Greek and joining in the quest for still more manuscripts. Eugene IV made Traversari, in 1431, General of his order. In 1435 he sent him to Basel as legate, in a critical moment of the council's proceedings, and the combination of learning, letters and perfect charity that was Ambrogio Traversari worked wonders with the touchy assembly. It was Traversari, again, whom the same pope sent as his legate to Venice in 1438 to receive the Greek emperor and the delegation that had come for the reunion council. In the council he played the chief part on the Latin side, and living long enough to see the reunion a fact, he died just a few weeks later felix opportunitate mortis (October 20, 1439). But none of these public employments really interrupted the main interest of Traversari's life. He translated, at Eugene's request, the lives of the Greek Fathers, the Greek acts of the Council of Chalcedon, and he undertook also a new translation of the Bible.

Another evidence of this same pope's interest in the new scholarship, for the services this might be expected to render to the study of Sacred Scripture, is Eugene IV's lifelong patronage of Cyriac of Ancona, [ ] a great traveller in the Greek East, a scholar and a practical archaeologist also. Eugene had first met Cyriac when, Cardinal Legate of the Marches, he had employed him to remodel the harbour of Ancona. From the East Cyriac brought back to the pope new manuscripts of the Greek Testament, and he was commissioned to compare these texts with the Vulgate translation; one of the first instances of the application of the new methods to scriptural studies. Cyriac was also a pioneer when he compiled the first collection of classical inscriptions.

Cyriac of Ancona is thus one of the earliest of archaeological writers. But still more celebrated, the very "Father of Archaeology," was Flavio Biondo of Forli (1388-1463), yet another of the college of papal secretaries, recruited for the service of the Holy See by Eugene himself in 1434. For the remaining twenty-nine years of his life Biondo remained in that service, studying actualities and composing the works which, after five hundred years, have by no means lost their value, and continue in daily use; namely the history of his own time, and the two great works Roma Instaurata and Italia Illustrata which are a skilled and detailed inventory of what still remained of the architecture and sculpture of the ancient world. No writings had a more speedy, or more lasting, effect in extending the general interest of that century in all the aims of the Renaissance.

The name of Tommaso Parentucelli -- more generally styled Thomas of Sarzana -- has already come into this story as a papal diplomatist and as one of the innermost circle of the leaders of the new movement. So late as 1444 he was still no more than the majordomo of the Cardinal Albergati. But when that saintly Carthusian -- for such he assuredly was -- died in that year, Eugene IV named Parentucelli to succeed him as Bishop of Bologna. In December 1446 the same pope gave him the red hat, and then, only ten weeks later, Tommaso was elected pope.

There seemed something all but miraculous about such a speedy exaltation of a man, still on the young side of fifty, from the utmost obscurity in the ecclesiastical world to the very summit In memory of his old master, the new pope took the name Nicholas, and in Nicholas V, so all historians have agreed to say, the Renaissance in all its unspoiled freshness was truly enthroned as pope. Here were combined, in fact, high technical competence, impeccable taste, limitless enthusiasm, magnanimity and magnificence in their only true sense, religious scholarship, deep sincere piety and humility of soul, and a disinterestedness from all thought of self not to be seen again in that chair for seventy years, [ ] and never again to be seen there allied with such a splendour of natural gifts.

But how far did Nicholas V, as pope, understand the realities of his time? the real condition of religion, the real nature of its weaknesses where it was weak, the causes of the weaknesses, and which weaknesses were heaviest with menace and even with mortality? To his immediate successor, the Aragonese crusader-pope Calixtus III, much of Nicholas V's programme was, apparently, little better than aesthetic trifling; and the next humanist pope, Aeneas Sylvius himself, made little secret of his belief, barely three years after Nicholas' death, that there were more urgent tasks before the papacy than the advancement of scholarship and belles lettres and the arts, even for what service these might bring to religion. We can, of course, hardly dismiss from our minds, as we regard the splendid schemes of Nicholas V, our knowledge of what the years that followed his reign were to bring, but if it is with a kind of reservation that we con the tale of his magnificent ideals, and of those vast achievements of his all too short and prematurely ended reign, we must remember also that to nothing were the later disasters due more, than to papal and episcopal neglect to foster ecclesiastical learning, and to make this truly effective by marrying it to all that was best in the intellectual life of the time. What the next fifty years needed was a succession of popes in whom the spirit of Nicholas V was active.

It has been a commonplace with the historians since the very reign of Nicholas V that, in him, the Renaissance itself was enthroned as pope. But true though this is, in one respect he was not a Renaissance type at all, as the term has come to be understood. For to Tommaso Parentucelli the central ultimate purpose of the passionately desired perfection in letters and the arts had never been the perfection of man, but the clearer manifestation of the glory of man's Creator. And this continued to be, no less certainly, the guiding principle of his immense humanistic activities as Pope Nicholas V.

To his brilliant constructive genius the chronic civil disorder of the Papal State was a challenge not to be ignored. A whole scheme, or rather series of schemes, sprang from his mind for the restoration of decayed towns, of bridges, of roads, of schools and universities, and for the establishment of permanent harmony between the fierce local patriotisms and the central Roman authority, between the patricians and the bourgeoisie, between the nobles and their papal ruler. And a most unlikely number of the schemes were carried through. No pope had ever built so much before. Nicholas did not indeed live to realise his dream of making the capital of the Christian religion the active chief centre and source of culture, too, for the whole Christian world; but it was he who finally swept away all the accumulated debris and patchwork restoration that remained from the disastrous Avignon century, and who crowned the tentative endeavours of the previous twenty-five years with an effective restoration on the grand scale. The walls of Rome in their whole circuit were rebuilt and strengthened, the great aqueduct of the Acqua Vergine was repaired and a beginning made thereby of a new era in the health of the city. Four of the bridges on the main roads out of Rome -- the Ponte Milvio, Ponte Nomentano, Ponte Salario, and Ponte Lucano -- were restored and fortified. The

Capitol, too, rose up again from its ruins, and a good dozen of the ruined churches were rebuilt, while great works of restoration were carried through at the basilicas of St. Mary Major, St. Paul-without-the-walls, the Twelve Apostles and St. Lorenzo. It is again to Nicholas V that the oldest part of the Vatican as modern times know it goes back; it is, indeed, from this pope's time that the palace begins to have that importance in the story of the popes which has ended in its name being almost synonymous with the papacy itself. In the plans of Nicholas V for the rebuilding of the Leonine city we see his creative genius at its greatest. [ ] These plans involved the most sacred shrine in Rome, the great basilica built by Constantine over the tomb of St. Peter. After a thousand years of wear and tear the fabric was, indeed, in a parlous state, the main south wall leaning outwards from the perpendicular as much as five feet, and the north wall pulled inward to the same degree. At first the pope thought only of rebuilding the choir, and the walls of the new choir had gone up as high as fifty feet when the views of the Leonardo of the day, Leon Battista Alberti, [ ] induced Nicholas to consent to the extremely drastic remedy of pulling the great church down and building something entirely new in its place. But the pope died before anything more had been achieved than a little preliminary destruction, and it was not until the time of Julius II, fifty years later, that the transformation was really put in hand.

Rome was, indeed, during the eight years reign of Nicholas V, one huge building yard, a workshop, a studio. But outside the capital city the pope was no less active. At Orvieto, Spoleto, Viterbo, Fabriano, Assisi, Civita Castellana, Civita Vecchia, Narni, Gualdo and Castelnuovo, public buildings of all kinds, and public works, were planned on a generous scale and undertaken and carried through. The pope's great aim was to end the misery of the long baronial wars which made central Italy one of the least safe places in Christendom. His diplomacy, and his frequent visits to the provincial cities, did much to end these feuds, and his "Bloodless restoration of peace and order to the

State of the Church", is indeed one of his chief glories. Particularly important was his reduction of the chronic insubordination of Bologna, in many ways the most important city in the pope's domains. Nicholas V is perhaps the most celebrated of the many great men who have passed from the spiritual rule of Bologna to the Roman See. [ ] He had spent twenty-five years of his life there as priest and bishop, and he now won the city over by a kindliness, and a willingness to concede, that were new in the history of Bologna's papal rulers.

The details of the history of the popes as rulers of their Italian principality are perhaps no great concern of the history of the Church, except in so far as their political activity and its attendant cares influenced the general fortunes of religion. But Nicholas V's policies were of such rare generosity, his achievements were on such a scale and so characteristic, both of his own constructive genius and of the new vitality of the great movement with which he is associated, that they could not go unmentioned. Nevertheless, all this activity of what we would call town-planning, of restoration and new building, this extensive employment of architects and builders, of sculptors and painters, of goldsmiths and jewellers and weavers of precious stuffs, was the less important part of the pope's great and lasting influence on the development of the European mind.

Nicholas was primarily a scholar -- an erudit, to be still more precise; the great passion of his life was books and the multiplication of other book lovers. The essential verse in the epitaph which Aeneas Sylvius wrote for him [ ] is surely Excoluit doctos doctior ipse viros. His mission was that of Albert the Great two hundred years earlier: "To make all these things understandable to the Latins"; "these things" being, now, not the ideas of Aristotle but the beauty and strength of Greek literature. "The Renaissance until now had been Latin, henceforward it was Greek," a modern scholar has said, with pardonably warm exaggeration. But to no scholars, indeed, was Nicholas V so liberal -- and his liberality to all of them knew scarcely any bounds -- as to those who knew Greek. As he planned a new cite vaticane where popes and cardinals and ambassadors and scholars and monks should live, and the central activity of the Church turn for ever in a setting worthy of its sublime ends, so the pope also planned a new Latin literature, the translation of the literature of Greece wrought by the masters of the new Latin prose and verse.

For Nicholas V, then, Valla translated Thucydides and Herodotus; Poggio and Lapo di Castiglione undertook Xenophon; the corpus of Aristotle was divided among a half-dozen "best wits", Bessarion doing the Metaphysics, and George of Trebizond (alas ! for he was more interested in pay than in accuracy, or indeed in good work at all), the Rhetoric and the Ethics; Plato's Republic too, was in the list and the Laws, and Philo Judaeus also. Polybius, one of the pope's favourite authors, went to Perotti, who also produced a wonderful version of Strabo that for a hundred years or more obscured the original. But the greatest desire of Nicholas was never to be realised, the translation of Homer into Latin hexameters. For this he was prepared to pay no less than 10,000 gold pieces. First of all he prevailed on Carlo Marsuppini -- then acting as secretary to the Florentine Republic -- to undertake it; and when he died, in 1453, Filelfo took up the task. But Nicholas was dead before Filelfo had really begun his work. These were but literature and philosophy. Nicholas also arranged for translations of the Greek Fathers, of St. Basil, of the two Gregories, of Nazianzen and Nyssa, of St. Cyril and St. John Chrysostom and also of Eusebius of Cesarea. Finally, he commissioned Gianozzo Manetti, the pupil of Ambrogio Traversari, and a leading personage in the great world of Florence for years until he fell foul of the rising Medici, to re-translate the Bible. Manetti [ ] knew Hebrew as well as Greek, and his Old Testament was to appear in three parallel columns, his own translation, the Septuagint and the Latin of St. Jerome's Vulgate.

But Nicholas V's time was short -- far shorter than the rejoicing humanists could have guessed when their fellow, at forty-nine years of age, was elected pope in 1447. In 1450 he was already so ill that his life was despaired of; in the first months of 1451 he was ill again, and from this time indeed, never really well, and alas, utterly changed in disposition, nervous and apprehensive and reserved, where he had been all his life the friend of all the world. He was ill again in 1453, and for the last eighteen months of his life (he died on March 25, 1455), he scarcely ever left his bed. "Thomas of Sarzana saw more friends in a day," he said to his Carthusian friends who were preparing him for death, "than Nicholas V sees in a year." It was a sad ending to such bright promise, and yet it was said of his saintly passing, "No pope in the memory of man has died like this." Not all the detail was realised of what the great pope had planned, but the fundamental things remained, and above all the great fact that the papacy -- an infinitely greater force than all the cultural courts and coteries of the day -- had taken up and blessed the new movement and, as it were, made it for a moment its own work. This certainly lasted, and it was the personal work of Nicholas V.

With the passing of this pope there comes a time of flatness in the Renaissance story. Not even Aeneas Sylvius -- Pope Pius II -- is his heir, nor the cultured Venetian, Paul II, who next succeeds, but, of all men the least likely, the Franciscan theologian Sixtus IV, elected pope in 1471. And by that date -- sixteen years after the death of Nicholas -- many tendencies had developed which in his time were but in germ. For there is another side to the story of all this splendour of scholarship and poetry and art. It is time to consider how the return of the ancient world affected other things in the artist besides his mastery of technique, to say something of those Renaissance ideas, which. from now on, acted most powerfully against what still remained of the medieval synthesis of natural and revealed knowledge, against what remained of medieval theology's prestige, against the educated man's appreciation of the prestige of Christianity itself, and against the traditional Christian scheme of virtuous living.

We should perhaps not be far wrong if, attempting the impossibility of summary description, we said that the Renaissance was the effect upon the men of the fifteenth century of their rediscovery of classical culture in all its fullness; and that what men found most novel and most characteristic in that culture, and most congenial, was its perfection of form. New respect and enthusiasm for the newly discovered perfection of form, and a new ambition to realise the like perfection, are perhaps what chiefly differentiates the men of the Renaissance from their medieval forerunners. Classical antiquity is, for them, the age of perfection; the golden age, of life no less than of art. Life, as that perfect thing the literature of the Greeks has revealed it, is for them the proper study of mankind; and it is now that there is born that prejudice of the superiority of the classical culture over the Christian which even yet, amongst educated men, is far from extinct. This new cult was all the more easily triumphant because it came upon the educated world in a moment when this lacked an object adequate to its needs. Not only, at the opening of the fifteenth century, was there no such figure as Dante, a spirit nourished by the philosophy and theology of the schools, but the philosophy of the schools had by now all but vanished from the ken of the liberally educated; it was now scarcely more than a preoccupation of the new scientists in their disputes with the professionals of the old university world. The influence of the characteristically medieval thought upon its own world had been steadily declining for years; the reappearance of Greece had, for the liberally educated world, the effect upon that thought of a coup de grace. All who know no Greek are now as nothing, and by Greek is meant the literature of the Greeks as literature and, above all, Plato.

Here again, in recent years, the specialists in the matter warn us that we must be ready to revise old judgments, as we endeavour to understand what kind of thing that re-appearance of the Greek texts of Plato is, in western Europe of the fifteenth century. Not only, they tell us, was Plato not unknown in the Middle Ages, but medieval Platonism was not mere neo-Platonism. There did exist in the Middle Ages an active direct tradition of Platonic doctrine. But what a wealth of difference there lies between devotion to such a tradition, and devotion fed with the newly-revealed texts of the master himself ! Once these were available the cultured world "went Platonic" in a generation or so -- and very consciously it went anti-Aristotelian -- and Platonic it has remained, consciously and unconsciously, almost ever since. How should this be important to Catholicism? Very evidently, in this way at least, that the official theology of the Church, for now nearly two centuries, had been bound up with many of Aristotle's logical and philosophical doctrines and with his methods. And now, for Aristotle, already defeated in the field of physics, and his supremacy threatened by the Nominalist denial of the possibility of metaphysics, there was to be substituted, as the ideal, his own vastly more attractive master. If Plato reigned instead of Aristotle, what would become of the old theology's hold -- none too secure already -- upon the mind of the educated? True enough, St. Thomas Aquinas, who had somewhat tamed Aristotle to the Christian yoke, was not the first in time of Catholic theologians. Stretching back for a thousand years before St. Thomas there was the long line of the Fathers, and these were Platonists all. And the greatest of the Latin Fathers, St. Augustine, was not only Platonist, but was indeed the main channel through which -- down to the discoveries of the fifteenth century -- knowledge of Plato had come to western Europe. Whence the natural result of a reaction towards the Fathers, producing theologians who would like to ignore the Scholastic Theology, about which, also, (to the new sensitiveness of this literary generation) there clung something of Aristotle's own grimness of speech.

But damaging as this new indifference, and even hostility, of the new theologian was to the hold of Scholastic Theology, the new cult of Plato wrought also a harm that was positive. For thinkers who were Christians, Plato had always had this first attractiveness that here was philosophic recognition of the existence of a nonmaterial order of reality, and of its superiority to the material order; there was recognition that there existed an order of reality accessible only to the intelligence, and superior to that other order of reality with which the senses are occupied, the model indeed and the archetype of this lower order. In practice, here was a philosophy teaching that the things of earth are inferior, and that man's only happiness lies elsewhere, in his contact with that superior world and with the divine; here were theories to explain the divine nature, the kind of thing man's soul is and his mind, the way man's mind works, and the way man can attain to wisdom which is the condition sine qua non of his true happiness. Plato's temperament, it has been said, is essentially religious and ethical, and the religious (and specifically the theistic) interpretation of the universe is the chief historical legacy of his philosophy to subsequent ages. And it was as "a fusion of the rational-mathematical, the aesthetic and the religious elements in the contemplation of the universe. . . [a] glorification of the cosmos" that Plato appeared to the men who so eagerly gave themselves to him in the fifteenth century. [ ]

How would these new disciples of the philosopher whom all styled " the divine ", accommodate their discovery with the Catholic faith in which they had been bred? Would that faith remain as the guide of life, or could not a man find all that he needed in Plato? It was, all over again, the trouble that had tormented the Christian mind when, two hundred years before, the corpus of Aristotle's thought had first been laid before it. In Plato, so Marsiglio Ficino, one of the finest flowers of the new age, was to say "there are set forth all the directives for life, all the principles of nature, all the holy mysteries of things divine." [ ] And again, "Plato. . . shows himself everywhere as much a

461

religious man as a philosopher, a subtle disputant, and a holy priest, a fecund orator. For which reasons, if you will continue as you have begun, to follow further in the footsteps of the divine Plato, you will -- God guiding you -- find happiness, and this especially because Plato, along with the philosophy of the Pythagoreans and Socrates, follows the law of Moses and is a precursor of the law of Christ." [ ]

Marsiglio Ficino was the protege of Cosimo de' Medici, and the very foundation of that Academy of Florence which was the chief shrine of the new Platonic studies. When his old patron lay dying, in 1464, Marsiglio (not yet a priest) came to his assistance. Cosimo had earlier written bidding him bring his promised translation of Plato, " For I desire nothing more ardently than to learn that way which most easily leads man to happiness." As Cosimo lay in his last illness he made his confession and received the last sacraments. With Marsiglio he spoke much of Plato, and Plato was read to the dying man. He spoke too of the miseries of earthly life and of the contempt for it which a man should have who aspired to higher happiness, and Marsiglio reminded him how "Xenocrates that holy man, the beloved disciple of Plato," had set forth these things in his treatise on death. The story is a curious melange of Catholicism and Platonism, with Catholicism, surely, already suffering from the alliance. [ ]

Nor did Plato come to the age unaccompanied. Only a pace behind, in his very shadow, and not always distinguished from him, came Plotinus and the religious cult of Neo-Platonism which had developed through Plotinus. [ ] Here was Platonism presented as a religion, where communion with the divine through ecstasy, for which lifelong asceticism prepared the soul, was presented as the supreme achievement of life. It was a "religion" where there was no place for real freedom, nor for personal responsibility, nor prayer, and where sin had no meaning. The world, for the Neo-Platonist was not created by the free act of a loving creator, but was the necessary expression of the nature of the first principle of all. Providence was but the kind of universal sympathy that links all things together in a fixed necessitated movement, all being moved by the single soul of the world. Here, in ultimate logic, is Pantheism and all its horrors; religion without a personal God, without any possibility of the Incarnation, mystical life without any need of grace and -- since there is no such distinction as between creator and created -- communion without subordination, and the idea that mystical experience is the basis and the test of truth.

Many things in Platonism and in Neo-Platonism can no doubt be given a Christian interpretation, but of themselves they are not Christian; for Christians with intelligences less than very well trained in Christian teaching, they are obviously dangerous.

But it was not only Platonism -- in its purer and in its baser forms -- that came to life again in the West as a force in men's lives. Stoicism also revived; and Epicureanism. Once more man is invited to the belief in the perfectibility of his nature, and to accept the doctrine of his own goodness. To the Christian doctrine of the fall and its effects on human nature, of all men's need of healing grace, there is opposed the new, more elegantly stated, cult of man as he is, meditations on a way of life unfettered by sobering thoughts of man as he ought to be. The new man is to be made perfect by the full freedom to indulge his every impulse, to satisfy his every desire; for this alone is life. Man is simply an animal endowed with the power to think, master of his fate indeed, sole captain of his soul, to whom all that is possible is lawful. Never before was the " natural " so attractively portrayed to the Christian world as good and perfectible. [ ]

And the artists re-echoed the philosophic teaching. "Such a feeling for nature in spring time," says a French critic of Lippo Lippi's "Adoration of the Shepherds," (painted about 1430) "as veracious in representation as it is intense in perception, had never before charmed the eye." Here, too, the primacy of nature begins to triumph, as the mysteries of the beauty of the human form are more and more lovingly explored. "Men had discovered that, outside Christianity altogether, there existed a culture, an art that was not only infinite in its riches, but which was also essentially natural, the spontaneous fruit of man's own faculties wherein was no element of dogma or revelation. And it SO happened that these products had, as things of beauty, an overwhelming superiority over all others. . . . The Christian centuries, from this point of view, seemed, -- indeed, a time of repression and of barbarism." [ ] Beauty -- it had, indeed, never been lacking to medieval man; but for the first time there was now revealed to his meditative gaze, and in what formidable competition with Christianity, the long lost beauty of that pagan world over which Christianity had once -- and it seemed finally -- been triumphant. Here, again, there was a system and a formula that were complete, a whole philosophy of nature and of life: here was most potent matter for the revolt of revolts against the authority of Christianity, and that in an age already in revolt against the personnel of the Christian Church. The revival of interest in classical letters was showing itself, by the middle of the fifteenth century, as but a step in the quest for other ideals of thought and life.

And with the new cult of the natural, following upon the new proclamation of the primacy of Nature, there began the new attack on what chiefly stood between it and success, the spiritual and moral teaching of the Church. It was now that there began, not attacks upon the clergy for their vices, but attacks upon the monks for the "folly" of their ascetic ideals, and -- another new feature -- the literary glorification of vice. Morals begin, in every city and court of Italy, their gadarene descent, and among the most notorious of these ill-living antagonists of Christian ideals are the humanists of the Curia Romana. Nowhere did the new worship of antiquity produce greater contempt and hatred for the culture and the religion inspired by other sources, than in this circle. Poggio made the sins of priests and religious the butt of his filthy Facetiae and in his work on Avarice he mocked the very spiritual ideals that should have prevented sin. Valla, author of the De Voluptate, made an open attack on the ideal of chastity declaring that prostitutes were more useful to mankind than nuns. Aretino wrote the Oratio Heliogaboli ad meretrices. Alberti, correct it would seem in his personal conduct, did not scruple to accept the dedication of Beccadelli's infamous Hermaphrodite [ ] There is scarcely one of the band whose work is free from sexual dirt, and their lives were as their writings. It has been said -- no doubt truly -- that public opinion by this time, looked upon the artist and the man of letters as a special kind of creatures, [ ] in whom laxity of life was no longer shocking. Familiarity with the spectacle of such wickedness, and a general toleration of whatever was well expressed, slowly corrupted the judgment of those ill authority also, and after the spectacle of popes who were good men giving employment to such active agents of moral dissolution we come, in the next generation, to popes who, themselves good-living men, begin to promote badliving men even into the Sacred College. Finally, there come popes whose own lives are an open scandal.

It is a curious thing that the two popes who, above all others, were by temperament in sympathy with the Renaissance, and who lavished honours and wealth upon the new humanist scholars -- Nicholas V and Paul II -- were taught by practical experience how real was the determination of some of these to restore the Rome of antiquity, even at the expense of the papacy. In the time of Nicholas V Stefano Porcaro and his associates had planned to capture the pope and his cardinals, if necessary to kill them, and to set up the republic. This was in January 1453. The plot was, however, discovered on the eve of the day appointed and the conspirators taken and executed.

Ten years went by -- the years when Calixtus III and Pius II were too engrossed with the urgencies of the crusade to be able to spare time or money for the patronage of poets and the arts. Then, in 1464, the newly-elected Paul II, re-arranging the curia, dismissed a number of the humanists appointed by Pius II. First they petitioned and then they threatened, prepared, they told the pope, to bring about a General Council before which he would have to justify his action. Their leader, Bartholomew Sacchi, called Platina, was arrested, put to the torture, and imprisoned in Sant' Angelo. After a time he was released, and presently, in revenge, he organised a new conspiracy.

The centre of this was Julius Pomponius Laetus, the most extreme -- not to say eccentric -- of all the humanists of Rome, a scholar who to the best of his ability and knowledge lived the life of Latin antiquity, refusing to learn Greek lest it injure the perfection of his Latin pronunciation, worshipping the Spirit of Rome, the leader of a band of like-minded semi-heathen freethinkers. Their aim was to re-establish the Republic of classical time and to drive out the pope and the whole body of clergy. In February 1468 the papal police suddenly rounded up the chiefs of the party. Again Platina was taken, again he was arrested and tortured. The plot, so the pope declared, [ ] was twofold -- to set up paganism once again in Rome and to murder himself. Presently Pomponius Laetus was arrested in Venice, and handed over to the pope. He too, like Platina, now confessed himself a most repentant Christian and, terror-stricken, begged for mercy. Their lives were spared, and presently they were released. Pomponius lived to become the principal tutor of three future popes, Leo X, Clement VII and Paul III; Platina to rise to great favour in the reign of Sixtus IV, the successor of the pope against whom he had plotted. He now became Vatican librarian, and was able to revenge himself on Paul II for all time by writing his life.

Return to Index

# CHAPTER 5: 'FACILIS DESCENSUS. . .' 1471-1517

## 1. A PAPACY OF PRINCES

THE title of this chapter is melodramatic; it is exaggerated; and, as a summary description of the life of the Church during the next forty years, too inexact, of course, to be true. But the Virgilian line summarises fairly correctly the impression which the reader usually retains from his study of the period; from one, quite understandable, point of view, it may even be said to describe the period very well.

The history of the Church, if history indeed describes the flowing stream of time, bears no relation to that tapestry of the ' full fed river winding slow mid herds upon an endless plain"; it is rather, and it must ever be, a stream in flood, driving over a hard bed and through a resisting channel, where the rapids are frequent, and where, once in a while, there comes a sudden gigantic alteration of the level over which the waters pour in a very Niagara. It is so, and it must be so, because the Church is not just humanity socially ordered for ends that are natural, and to be attained very largely by a harmony of action that need be no more than external. The Church is a divine creation, imposing an order whose ends are supernatural, where the needed harmony is utterly unattainable except by action that is rooted in personal conviction, and based on assents that are, of their nature, internal. Herein lies all the promise of the Church to labouring and expectant humanity; and herein lies the whole tragedy of its long history. For assents such as these lie wholly within the uncontrollable power of the individual; the Church, whose good fortune largely depends on these internal assents, cannot compel them. The Church continues through time, and must face its task, whatever the generosity, or the rarity, at any given period of these needed internal assents to its teaching and direction; and in all ages it never ceases, and can never cease, to demand such assents, and to demand that all else be subordinated to them. Temporal rulers, kings and princes -- the State -- are no doubt bound, in their function, by the same moral law that binds the spiritual ruler; but the spiritual ruler does not only need to keep the moral law, it is the primary function of his office continually to profess and to proclaim it. Kingdoms do not suffer, except accidentally, from the scandal of the ruler's bad life, but when the spiritual ruler falls it is, necessarily, the very institution and notion of the spiritual that the scandal harms. His wrong doing compromises immediately the very raison d'etre of the institution. It is, in a way, contrary to the very nature of his office and of the institution. It is disintegration in what only exists in order to promote integrity; in order to preach that integrity as the inescapable condition of human happiness, and to minister the divinely devised means of achieving integrity. Disintegration here must, always, have about it the air of catastrophe -- no matter how slight the degree in which it is allowed. And in this sense it is true to say that, over the history of the fortunes of the supernatural moving visibly among mankind, there ever hangs something of this dark possibility. "The gates of hell" shall never, indeed, prevail -- but where was it ever promised that they should cease to trouble? and was it not also mysteriously said " When the Son of Man cometh think you shall He find faith on earth?" The temporal kingdom can not only survive the sins of its rulers, it can even, for a time, profit from them; the wicked, here too, flourishing like a green bay tree. But in the spiritual kingdom sin tolerated, fostered, made an instrument of power, is fatal, instantaneously, to all that it touches. Sin in the actual ruling of that kingdom is necessarily not only blacker to the sight but more mischievous in fact; and so too, are all the personal sins of the rulers, whether these be such surrenders to the material as sexual licence, worldliness and avarice, or the still more grievous " spiritual" sins of ambition, libido dominandi, [ ] mental sloth, indifference to the development and spread of truth.

SIXTUS IV

With the advent of Sixtus IV, in 1471, the flood does, indeed, seem to pour over the edge of the abyss; the failures and the surrenders are suddenly more grossly material -- and, being this, they are more evidently shocking, shocking now to the least reflective, and perhaps, to these, the most shocking of all. The age of the della Rovere, Borgia, and Medici popes has become, in popular repute, the most scandalous age of all. But sinfulness of this kind -- whether, in the manner of old-fashioned Protestant controversy, we gloat over it as a final proof that the papacy is the Scarlet Woman of the Apocalypse, or whether, horror stricken, we strive to minimise it in a new apologetic -- was chiefly important in its distraction of the ruler from activities that would have made Protestantism impossible, from the devising of ways, for example, through which good bishops would have filled the sees of Christendom, a true philosophy and a live theology informed its universities, and a clergy, spiritually trained and equipped with professional knowledge been provided for all its parishes. It is a very easy mistake, and a fairly fatal mistake, to concentrate on the dramatic details of these personal sins of la papaute princiere [ ] while their graver, if more humdrum, faults of omission go by unconsidered. Such concentration -- as common as it is natural -- wrecks the real proportions of the event.

When Paul II died, so suddenly, July 26, 1471, there was not any obvious successor to him among the cardinals. They were fairly evenly divided into two rival parties and it was only after a certain amount of manoeuvring that, on August 10, they managed to agree on Cardinal Francesco della Rovere. The conclave had begun on the feast of St. Sixtus II, the pope who was the patron of the great Roman martyr St. Lawrence, and the new pope, appropriately, called himself Sixtus IV. He was now fifty-seven years of age, a Friar Minor (but not one of the new Observants) from the Genoese town of Savona, and sprung from so poor a family that it had not even a surname. In his order the friar had had a great career, as lecturer in theology in various

Italian universities, as a preacher and administrator. Bessarion had followed the lectures he gave at the university of Pavia and had brought him to the notice of Paul II. In 1464 the Franciscans had chosen him for their minister-general, and in 1467 he had been created cardinal. As minister-general of the Friars Minor, Francesco della Rovere had shown himself a reformer, and in the great theological dispute of the day -- the question of the Immaculate Conception -- he had risen high above the ordinary level of the controversy with his thesis that the views of Duns Scotus and St. Thomas were complementary rather than antagonistic.

It was a curious combination of forces that had secured his election as pope. Bessarion's high opinion of him as a scholar and a religious had done much. The wishes of the Duke of Milan -- Galeazzo Maria Sforza -- had been no less effective. And of a like nature with this political influence was the support of the cardinal vice-chancellor, Rodrigo Borgia, who now, forty-one years of age, after fifteen years of comparative seclusion in the routine of his office, makes his first steps in the public policies of the Holy See. A further element was the skill as negotiator of Francesco's young Franciscan nephew, Piero Riario, whom he had taken into the conclave as a kind of secretaryattendant. It was this young friar who, at the critical moments, did the actual work of binding together and keeping together the heterogeneous majority that made his uncle pope.

Francesco della Rovere, whose strong, intelligent face the genius of Melozzo and Pollaiuolo have made familiar to us, had immense energy; as pope he was to show himself strongwilled, and even imperious, but to be betrayed, time and again, by his lack of knowledge about the political world in which, almost exclusively, he now chose to be active. The one-time reformer of the Friars Minor was determined to make the Papal State secure, once and for all, against the princes who threatened its life, by developing its political resources to the full, and by making the papal sovereignty a reality everywhere within it. But over and over again he blundered, and after thirteen years of rule he left the papacy hated as a power, where before it had merely been mistrusted, and saddled with a new and most disastrous precedent of nepotism, aggressive war and even crime, to say nothing of unconcealed luxurious living and moral laxity. No charge against the pope's own morals -- in the narrow sense of that word -- has ever been seriously sustained. He was regular and attentive to his priestly duties, and noted indeed for his deep devotion to all that affected the cult of the Mother of God. But banquets of a crazy extravagance, hunting parties, gambling bouts, nightly revels began, in his time, and without any interference from him, to be part of the common order of high ecclesiastical life in Rome; and in all this departure of new unseemliness and wickedness the pioneers were the pope's own near relatives, young friars for the chief part, upon whom throughout his pontificate, he heaped one undeserved promotion after another. Never had pope such a horde of needy, insignificant, and incompetent kinsfolk for whom to provide; and never was any pope so lavish in the provision.

Sixtus IV was one of five children, and it was his eleven nephews and two nieces who were the main instruments through which whatever ideals he began with were brought to nought, and through whom a new poison was injected into the none too healthy system of the Renaissance papacy. Of the eleven nephews six were clerics -- it was a simple matter to make five of them cardinals, while the sixth became Bishop of Ferrara and Patriarch of Antioch. Two of his lay nephews the pope married to daughters of the King of Naples, a third to the heiress of the reigning Duke of Urbino, and a fourth to a daughter of the Duke of Milan. A sixth red hat went to one of his niece's sons.

The ablest of this small army -- the only one in fact who proved ultimately to have any real ability at all -- was Giuliano della Rovere, but far more influential in the policies of the reign were the two brothers, Girolamo and Piero Riario. To Piero, the manager of the conclave, a young friar of twenty-five, the pope gave the see of Treviso within a month of his election (September 4, 1471); on December 15 he made him a cardinal; in September 1472 next he gave him the see of Valence, and in 1473 the archbishoprics of Spoleto (April 28), Seville (June 25), and Florence (July 20), with the wealthy French see of Mende (November 3) -- all of which sees the young cardinal was allowed to hold simultaneously. [ ] He was, by now, as nearly the equivalent of a millionaire in the life of the time as it is possible to conceive. The story of his extravagances, and his profligacy, is writ large in all the diaries and diplomatic correspondence of the time, a subject of cynical mirth, where it does not provoke disgust. But Cardinal Piero did not last long. The pace soon killed him, and he died, "while he gave promise of still better things," said his uncle, in the first days of 1474. But in the two short years or so of his course he had been the pope's most confidential adviser and agent. This place was now taken by his brother Girolamo, one of the worst men of all this bad time, a typical Renaissance bravo and bully, for whom the moral law can scarcely be said to have held any meaning at all. For Girolamo, his uncle, when he married him to Caterina Sforza, had established a little principality in the north of the Papal State, centring round the episcopal city of Imola. The territory was small, but it was meant to extend, and its strategic importance was already considerable.

The Papal State [ ] could hardly have been less conveniently designed for popes who meant to be effective rulers. It may be described as made up of two roughly rectangular territories, one to the south based on the Mediterranean coast of Italy, and the other to the north based on the Adriatic. From the southern tip of the southern rectangle where it touched the kingdom of Naples, to the northernmost point of the state is, in a direct line, 260 miles. The Apennines, in their steepest and least easily traversable masses, are a prohibitive natural barrier between the rectangles in the central part of the state where, for seventy miles, these overlap. During the whole of the Middle Ages, down to the time when the Avignon residence began, the popes were never really masters of much beyond the southern rectangle, the district whose natural centre is Rome and that runs from, say Orvieto to the neighbourhood of Gaeta. By the time of Sixtus IV they were also, fairly securely, masters of the district beyond the Apennines called the Marches, the southern half of the northern rectangle, a region whose chief cities were Fermo Camerino and the port of Ancona. But the richest part of the State, and the wealthiest cities, were in the district to the north of the Marches, the territory called Romagna, the lands to the south of the Po, the ancient Roman Aemilia. Here was Bologna, the most important city of the whole State after Rome -- always violently anti-papal -- and Ferrara, and Ravenna. All this valuable territory was parcelled out into half a score of city states, some republican in their form of government, others ruled by families descended from the successful condottieri. The most important of these states was the Duchy of Ferrara, held by the d'Este family, who were also lords of Modena and Reggio, territories that formed a buffer state between the pope's territory and the Duchy of Milan. Imola lay twenty-five miles to the south-east of Bologna, and almost midway in the narrow part [ ] of the long neck that joined the Romagna to the half of the Papal State where the popes were really masters. Imola in strong, trustworthy hands would be a check to Ferrara, a good starting point if ever the pope planned to reduce Bologna, and an excellent centre from which to conduct the lengthy business of destroying the petty tyrants of the Romagna, at Faenza for instance, or Forli, Cesena, and Rimini. [ ] Hence the determination of Sixtus to plant his nephew at Imola as its lord, his insistence that Milan (in whose power it then lay) should restore it, and his willingness to pay the Milanese the heavy price asked, 100,000 ducats. And as the pope thus secured -- or hoped to secure -- this key city at the northern end of the " neck," so, by marrying another nephew, Giovanni della Rovere, brother of Cardinal Giuliano, to the heiress of the Montefeltre, he meant to make sure of the entrance to the " neck " from the south, their ducal city of Urbino. Giovanni's son did, in fact, live to inherit Urbino; he is the duke, Francesco Maria, who plays a part in the history of the second della Rovere pope, his uncle, Julius II. And Girolamo, the Count of Imola, lived to make himself master of Forli, and Cesena, and Rimini, and even of Sinigaglia, before, in 1488, some of his subjects found the courage to avenge a hundred crimes by assassinating him.

The other princes of Italy were not slow to realise that a new spirit was influencing the policy of the ruler of the Papal State. At the death of Paul II, Naples, Florence and Milan had stood leagued together against Rome. Now, by his marriage alliances, the pope had detached Naples and was, seemingly, about to make himself master of the all-important lands in the north. It was Florence -- the Florence of Lorenzo de' Medici -- that first grew definitely uneasy about this unmistakable threat on her north-eastern border; there was a succession of " incidents " between Lorenzo and the pope and then a great crime, a terrible repression, and war (1478). Florence was still, in name, a republic where the Medici family were no more than private citizens, but in fact they had now, for half a century, been its all-powerful rulers, through their immense wealth and their skilfully exercised technique for the secret management of public affairs. Lorenzo was much more truly the ruler of Florence, than the pope was ruler of Rome. When the reign of Sixtus IV opened, relations had been friendly, and presently the pope made the Medici the Holy See's banking agents. But he would not consent to make Lorenzo's younger brother Giuliano a cardinal, and then Lorenzo made difficulties about advancing the money that Sixtus needed to buy Imola from Milan for Count Girolamo; he even did his best to prevent the sale, not at all wanting to see the pope's nephew strategically installed on his flank. Then Sixtus changed his financial policy. The Medici were dismissed, and the papal business was given to their rivals, the Pazzi. Next, in 1474, there came a vacancy in the see of Florence. The pope named one of his own kinsmen, Francesco Salviati, but the Medici protested so strongly that he had to give way. When, some months later, he named the disappointed candidate to the vacant see of Pisa, the Medici again protested. This time, however, the pope held firm; but the Medici kept the new bishop out. Now came the conspiracy, a plot to overthrow the Medici regime in Florence in which Count Girolamo, the Pazzi, and the Archbishop of Pisa were the ringleaders. They also proposed to murder Lorenzo and his brother Giuliano. And, such was the pitch to which six years of the political game had brought the Roman mind, the conspirators, as a matter of course, laid the whole matter before the pope for his approval.

Sixtus was not at war with Florence, but he had only one objection to make to the plot -- there must be no murder of the two Medici. The count, the banker, the archbishop, and the assassin whom they had hired, laboured long to convince the pope that their death was unavoidable in the kind of thing that a revolution is, and argued that, since the Medici were bound to die, it could not much matter how exactly this happened. But Sixtus would have none of it. He did not indeed countermand the plot, but he explicitly commanded that the princes should not be murdered; it is, nevertheless, hard to believe that, after the interview as we have it recorded, he can have been under any illusion about what the conspirators were determined to do.

The visit to Florence of Count Girolamo's nephew, the newly-created Cardinal Raffaelle Sansoni (a lad of seventeen) provided the opportunity. The cardinal, brought to Florence by his desire to see the wonders of the Medici palaces, was to preside at a High Mass in the cathedral on Sunday, April 26, 1478, and afterwards be entertained by the Medici. The mass seemed to offer a most suitable moment for the murder; the two victims and all the notables of the city would be safely contained and held by the confusion in the great church while, outside, the main body of the conspirators would seize the seat of government and all the controls. At the last moment the bravo hired to do some of the killing -- Montesecco -- did indeed object, some scruple about the place and time of the deed was, it seems, troubling him. But a couple of priests, "patriotic" enemies of the Medici tyrants, were found to take his place. The cardinal entered and the mass began. Then -- at the elevation, or the priest's communion -- the signal was given and the murderers made for their victims. Giuliano de Medici, was killed with a dozen wounds or so in his body, but Lorenzo, only slightly wounded by the clerical enthusiasts who had undertaken to despatch him, managed to gain the sacristy and to barricade himself. Meanwhile in the church there was the expected pandemonium, but the fury was all against the assassins, and the young cardinal -- thought to be in the plot -- came so near to death that, in all the forty years of life that remained to him his face never lost the pallor which came into it that day. While, in the cathedral, the murderers were taken, the chiefs of the conspiracy outside had also failed. Something in the manner of the archbishop as he essayed to bluff the Gonfaloniere into surrender put that officer on his guard. He arrested the archbishop and those with him, and when, presently, the mob came streaming by, mad with the news, he acted very promptly, putting ropes round the necks of the prisoners and thrusting them out from the windows of the palace. When the ropes were cut the mob amused itself with the corpses, [ ] as we have seen happen again in that same land within these last few years. All that day, and the next, the vengeance continued. Whoever was thought a supporter of the Pazzi was mercilessly slain. Scores were thus hanged out of hand and thrown to the mob. The cardinal, meanwhile, was kept under close arrest.

The conspiracy then had failed, and except Count Girolamo, who all this time had not stirred from Rome, the conspirators had all of them been taken and executed. When the news reached him the count was beside himself, and the Florentines in Rome were for a time in great danger. The pope took no immediate public action. He regretted the crime of Giuliano's murder and wrote to

Florence a letter, which has disappeared, to say so. He also demanded the release of the unoffending cardinal. The Florentine envoy in Rome wrote to support the pope's demand, and Naples and Venice gave their advice that Florence should not add fuel to the fire by keeping the prelate in prison. On May 24 an envoy from Sixtus appeared in Florence with a formal written demand and the threat that, unless the cardinal were released, the pope would punish the republic. The Florentines were, however, not to be moved, and eight days later the bull appeared excommunicating Lorenzo and all who adhered to him, and threatening the republic with an interdict if, within three weeks, it had not obeyed the pope's commands. The pope's case is set out fully: all the political grievances of the years before the conspiracy, the excessive vengeance for the conspiracy itself, the hanging of an archbishop and other ecclesiastics, the imprisonment of the cardinal; the republic must accept the pope's sentence that neither Lorenzo nor anyone who supported him should be capable of ever holding any office in Church or State, or of performing any legal acts; their property must be confiscated, their houses torn down, and Lorenzo handed over to the pope; all this within a month. Again the Florentines refused to be moved, and on June 24 the interdict was declared.

The Pazzi Conspiracy, scandalous as is its history, is of course no more than one of a score of similar events in the complicated story of fifteenth-century Italian politics. It needs, however, to be told in some detail not only because, in this particular feud, the pope was one of the protagonists, but also because of the contrast between the high tone of the pope's demands before he knew he was going to be beaten, and his subsequent tacit surrender of all but the appearances of submission. Here is something which is, for a time, going to pass into the political habits of the papacy, and to be yet another potent cause of that alienation from the popes of their greatest natural resource, the sympathy of instructed Catholic opinion. No power has so rightly been expected to make war on the haughty and successful, to yield to none but the needy. With these political popes the Roman maxim began to be reversed, to the great hurt of their spiritual hold on their children everywhere.

Florence replied to these anathemas by skilfully-written manifestos which all Italy read. The clergy acknowledged that Sixtus was indeed helmsman of the barque of Peter, but complained that it was to Circe's island that he was steering it; while the republic broadcast the confession of Montesecco, in which that scrupulous assassin told the story of the ambiguous interview with the pope. The finished irony of the humanist is now, for the first time, set to mock the solemnities of the papal remonstrance and its awful sentence, and to call in question, by its reasoned moderation, the assumption that the pope is telling the truth. "Collect yourself, we pray you, Holy Father," say the Florentines, " and return to those sentiments which become the gravity of the Holy See."

In August the war began, Florence isolated and the pope leagued with Naples and Florence's eternal foe Siena. The Florentines turned for help to Louis XI of France, and not in vain. The king, already bitter because Sixtus had refused the red hat to the prelates he had nominated, was only too happy at the chance of harassing the pope into new concessions of jurisdiction in ecclesiastical affairs. He had already, in 1475, begun to proclaim himself the champion of the "liberties of the Gallican Church" and begun to speak of the need of a General Council to reform the Church and to elect a lawful pope in the place of the simonist Sixtus IV. [ ] Then, in March 1476, he had ordered all the French cardinals and prelates in Rome to return home for a great national council that would discuss the best way of bringing about the needed General Council. Now, upon the Florentine appeal, the French envoys to the Holy See were instructed to join with those of Florence, Milan, Venice, and Ferrara in a protest that the pope's conduct towards Florence and Lorenzo was a scandalous hindrance to the unity of Christendom. Since the pope would not listen to the ambassadors' petition for a removal of the interdict from Florence, a General Council must be summoned (July 11, 1478). [ ]

The pope did not find it hard to answer Louis XI, but the emperor -- Frederick III -- was no less pressing that Florence should be treated more mercifully, and most of the cardinals were anxious for peace. But Florence would not accept the only terms the pope offered and presently, her allies not venturing more against Sixtus than threats of a General Council, and her territories ravaged by the papal and Neapolitan armies, the situation of the republic grew desperate indeed. It was saved by the boldness and diplomatic skill of Lorenzo. In December 1479 he made his way uninvited, unannounced, to Naples and won over the king. The terms were hard, but Florence was delivered from the dilemma it faced of destruction or a humiliating submission to the pope. Some submission indeed there was to be, but it came now from the initiative of the republic, and at a time when all other questions were stilled by the recent descent of the Turks on the Italian mainland and their capture of Otranto. [ ] On Advent Sunday, 1480, [ ] twelve leading citizens of Florence knelt before the pope in the portico of St. Peter's, acknowledged the city's guilt, and humbly besought forgiveness. The pope lectured them, mildly enough, and absolved the city from all the spiritual censures laid upon it. As a penance Florence was to provide fifteen galleys for the war against the Turks. But not a word was said about the position of Lorenzo de' Medici, who, and not Florence, so Sixtus had repeatedly declared, was the real enemy and the reason for the war. Nor, of course, was Lorenzo among the twelve who knelt before the pope.

For a short eighteen months there was peace, but Count Girolamo, who had opposed the peace party in Rome in 1479, now made himself master of Forli on the death of the last of the Ordolaffi who had ruled it for a century or so (1481). And he planned to take Faenza also. In this he had the support of Venice;

and the great republic was willing to encourage also a much bolder design, nothing less in fact than that Girolamo should make himself King of Naples. Venice, as payment for its aid, was to be allowed to take Ferrara.

The King of Naples [ ] began the war, invading the Papal State (April 1482) when the pope's preparations had scarcely begun, and at a moment when a miniature civil war -- Orsini against Colonna -- was raging. Soon Rome itself was threatened with siege, and though the arrival of a Venetian general, Roberto Malatesta, to command the pope's troops, and his victory over the Neapolitans at Campo Morto (August 21, 1482), delivered the city, the general's death three weeks later, and the departure of the Venetian contingents, soon renewed the danger. For the next few months the Neapolitans ravaged the pope's lands with little hindrance, while in the north the pope's allies conquered Ferrara almost at their ease. To add to the papal misfortune a half-mad Dominican archbishop had re-inaugurated (if that be the word) the Council of Basel, and though, as yet, he was the only bishop present, Florence and Milan were beginning to wonder whether they had not here a useful weapon with which once more to beat the pope. It was Cardinal Giuliano della Rovere, seemingly, who finally decided the pope to break with Venice and make peace. On December 12, 1482, the treaty was signed between Sixtus and the King of Naples. All conquests were to be restored and the Duke of Ferrara was to be reinstated; also a pension was guaranteed to Count Girolamo. The Venetians -- with whom the war was going well -- had not been consulted about all this, but the pope now informed them of what had been done, and ordered them to ratify the treaty. Not very surprisingly they utterly refused, and warned the pope not to use spiritual weapons to coerce them, threatening, if he did so, to call in the Turks and plunge all Italy into war.

The pope's diplomacy had not brought him peace. Instead of fighting Naples as the ally of Venice, he was now to fight Venice as the ally of Naples. Immense sums had to be raised and a fleet equipped -- an essential condition for success against the great naval power, the pope declared. [ ] The 50,000 ducats needed were got by the creation of new posts, and the sale of the appointments. The immediate problem was to relieve Ferrara, and meanwhile (May 25, 1483) the Venetians were excommunicated, and their state placed under an interdict.

The war went very slowly. The Venetians used their sea power to capture towns on the Apulian coast of Naples, but they failed to take Ferrara. Soon, feeling the strain of their isolation, for the pope's diplomacy had momentarily leagued all Italy against them, they sued for peace (March 1484); but Count Girolamo succeeded in hardening the pope against them. Then the Colonna troubles burst out afresh in Rome, with greater violence than ever (April-June). The pope was successful against the great clan in Rome itself, but the incompetent Girolamo was baffled time and again in the fights for their various strongholds in the surrounding country. Sixtus IV was beginning to feel his age, the unlookedfor strength of the rebels depressed him, and then the great league began to break up -- after all, it had held together for nearly eighteen months. At what seemed the last hour for Venice, the Duke of Milan withdrew, and secretly came to the aid of the republic, and presently the Peace of Bagniolo was arranged (August 7, 1484). Once again all conquests were mutually restored; and this time without any gain at all to Count Girolamo. The news was brought to the pope as he lay dying, and the disappointment of such a peace finished him. On August 12, the feast of St. Clare, one of the two greatest saints of the order he had once governed, he passed away.

So died this first of the popes who showed what a difference the pope could make as a prince in this delicately balanced world of petty Italian states. Sixtus IV had indeed established his family among the reigning houses of Italy, but with all these years of war and of realist diplomatic practice he had not really developed the pope's hold on his own state, nor given that state any new security against the greedy and treacherous princes who surrounded it; while, in Rome itself, the habit of war and the sudden new insistence on the material aspects of the papal office, had given new life to the old habits of riot and feud and had indeed "revived a barbarous past." The cardinals' palaces were now strongholds where each lived surrounded by his own guards, centres of bloody tumult only too often, sanctuaries for bravoes and assassins. The degree of this sharp return to the ages of violence was shown very markedly during the interregnum that now followed the death of Sixtus IV, and the proceedings in the conclave are evidence how greatly he had secularised the college of cardinals.

No sooner was it known that the pope had died, than the mob rose, and with shouts of "Colonna for ever," stormed and sacked the palace of Count Girolamo, and the houses of all his hated Genoese compatriots. The count hastened back to Rome from his operations against the Colonna fortresses, and while he lay encamped outside the city, his wife, Caterina Sforza, the classic type Or the Renaissance virago, boldly installed herself as commandant of the all-important stronghold of Castel St. Angelo. Then, for a fortnight nearly, the rival bands of soldiery fought and plundered in the streets of the city. The Colonna had returned in force, and the different cardinals sent out in haste for reinforcements for their private armies. The funeral services of the dead pope began with hardly a cardinal present; few could have made their way to St. Peter's without fighting their way through the armed forces of their colleagues. Finally the strong statesmanship of one of the few cardinals whom all respected, the Venetian Marco Barbo, a nephew of Paul II, brought peace. He prevailed on the count to surrender St. Angelo, and to leave Rome; and he prevailed on his ally Virginio Orsini, the count being magnificently compensated in money and promises. The Colonna, the Savelli, and the Conti also agreed to march out from Rome. There was to be a truce, not to expire before two months from the day of the new pope's coronation. This was on August 22, and four days later the conclave began.

Sixtus IV had created cardinals lavishly, thirty-four in all, [ ] and in the conclave of 1484 no fewer than nineteen of the twenty-five present were of his naming. All but four of the twenty-five were Italians. [ ] The short-lived period of a more or less international college was over: [ ] even had the other seven cardinals then living [ ] been present, the Italians would have been twenty-two to ten. On the other hand, there was not between these Italians, subjects of half a dozen distinct and independent sovereign states, the modern bond of a common national feeling. The twenty-one were fairly evenly divided between the states only lately at war, and always mutually hostile. Venice had five cardinals, Milan four, Naples two; there were four Romans (Colonna, Orsini and Savelli), one from Siena, a Genoese and -- a new element -- four nephews of the late pope who formed a faction apart.

This is the first conclave of the type to be classic henceforward for a good three hundred years and more, where political considerations played a leading part, the first to which different princes sent instructions through their agents and at which, through cardinals who were their subjects, they even felt strong enough to declare to the Sacred College that there were certain cardinals who must not be elected. It was also a conclave in which bribery played a great part. The cardinals began by making a pact that whichever of them was elected would give the poorer cardinals -- those whose income from benefices was below 4,000 ducats -- an allowance of 100 ducats a month, and that he would compensate them for any benefice they lost through failing in their votes to oblige the various princes. The two leading figures in the conclave were Giuliano della Rovere and Rodrigo Borgia. The first wanted a pope he could control, and so maintain the influence on affairs he had begun to possess during his uncle's last years. The other wanted to be pope himself. All were agreed that the new pope must be acceptable to the league whose action had recently imposed the Peace of Bagniolo, and so a friend to Venice. Borgia was the leader of the cardinals who stood actively by the league, a small group that included such powerful personages as Ascanio Sforza, brother of the Duke of Milan, and Giovanni of Aragon, a son of the King of Naples. Borgia made certain he would be elected. But his actual following was small, and he was not trusted. The other leader was hardly more fortunate. In the first scrutiny a Venetian, Marco Barbo, came within five votes of election. Whereupon the skill of Giuliano della Rovere prevailed upon Borgia, and his associates, to abandon his candidature. The election of Barbo would mean an era of reform, and a restoration of ecclesiastical discipline. So Borgia and della Rovere combined forces, and through the night of August 27-28 they worked hard upon their colleagues, directing their minds towards the most complete nullity of them all, Giovanni Battista Cybo. They managed to secure for him eighteen votes in all, and on August 28, at nine in the morning, he was proclaimed as Innocent VIII. [ ]

INNOCENT VIII

The new pope was a Genoese, fifty-two years of age, a bishop since 1467, created cardinal by Sixtus IV in 1473. All contemporaries agreed to praise his kindly nature, his inability to refuse requests, but the different ambassadors noted also -- what events soon showed to be equally true of him -- that he had no judgment of his own, and little understanding of the problems that faced him. It was Giuliano della Rovere who would really reign, "the cardinal of St. Peter. . . pope and more than pope." Innocent VIII, it has also to be recorded, has the unfortunate distinction in the history of this time that he made no secret of the fact that he was the father of a family. [ ] "He was the first of the popes," says the grave Augustinian, Giles of Viterbo, [ ] " openly to make a show of sons and daughters, the first who openly arranged marriages for them, the first to keep up the weddings in his own palace. His predecessors had left him no such example. Would that he had not found successors to imitate him." As Sixtus IV had used the marriages of various nephews to assist his diplomacy, so Innocent VIII now made play with the marriage of his son and his granddaughters.

The pope was all but bankrupt as a result of the wars of his predecessor, the bitter Colonna-Orsini feud was still seething and yet, in the first twelve months of his reign, he, or his adviser-in-chief, drifted into yet another war. The enemy this time was Naples, and once again the papacy was almost without allies, while the rest of Italy stood by, neutral towards the pope and sympathetic to his foes. The cause of the war was the refusal of Naples to pay the annual tribute due to the pope as suzerain of the kingdom. It was another grievance that the king -- Ferrante -- was filling vacant sees without any reference to Rome. The war dragged on for nine months or so (October 1485-August 1486), each side helping the rebels in the territory of the other. Innocent appealed to one after another of the Catholic sovereigns for help, but all were deaf to him. Then Giuliano della Rovere revived the ancient remedy of calling in the French claimant to the Neapolitan kingdom. He went to Genoa to negotiate with the claimant -- Rene II of Anjou -- and to arrange a naval alliance with the republic. But by the time he returned Innocent, terrified by the disorders in Rome, and the damage done his territory by the marauding Neapolitans, scenting disapproval and treachery everywhere among his own commanders, had made peace. Ferrante too was alarmed, at the prospect of a Franco-Genoese invasion. He gladly made terms, giving way on all points to the pope -- it was merely a matter of making promises -- and then going home to glut his vengeance on the Neapolitan barons who had been the pope's allies.

For the next twelve months -- while Cardinal Giuliano sulked in his fortress at Ostia -- the papal diplomacy feebly plunged hither and thither, seeking allies, until it fell under the strong influence of Lorenzo de' Medici. The new alliance was sealed by the marriage of the pope's son Franceschetto to Lorenzo's daughter Maddalena -- a marriage where there was twenty years' difference between the age of bride and groom; and Innocent consented to give the red hat to Lorenzo's second son, Giovanni, a boy of thirteen. It was, however, provided that the young cardinal should not wear the insignia of his rank for another four years, nor be admitted to consistories. Meanwhile the disorders in the Papal State mounted higher and higher. In April 1488 at Forli, Count Girolamo, the once all-powerful bravo, was murdered, and a few weeks later the lord of Faenza met the same fate. At Perugia and Foligno, Ancona and Ascoli there were like troubles, and everywhere the King of Naples was busy aiding the rebels.

The one gleam of success that relieved the tale of ignoble drifting and its sorry fruit was the pope's securing, in the face of great competition, the person of the brother of the Sultan, Prince Djem. Here, it was felt, was a hostage possession of whom could be used to keep the Turks quiescent. The Turks, for their part, were willing to pay the pope handsomely [ ] to keep Djem under lock and key. He cost the pope a cardinal's hat to the grand-master of the Knights of St. John, and another to the French king's counsellor, the Archbishop of Bordeaux, and also a promise not to grant without delay the dispensation that would enable Alain d'Albret to marry the heiress or Brittany -- a bride desired for the boy king of France. The story of Djem's adventures, of his reception by the pope, his haughty, undisguised contempt for the whole paraphernalia of the Vatican etiquette, and the spectacle it all was for years to come, to Rome and all its visitors, makes pleasant reading after the petty, sordid chicanery to which the public activities of the papacy had now shrunk.

Towards 1488 a new kind of scandal was discovered, when high officials of the Chancery were arrested on a charge of forging papal bulls. The whole administration of justice had fallen into a bad way. It was a rare crime indeed that could not be atoned for by a money payment. The semi-bankruptcy in which Innocent had found the administration never really improved. Continually the pope created new posts to sell to the highest bidder, twenty-six new secretaryships in 1486, and fifty-two plumbatores whose duty was to affix the leaden seals to the bulls. These last paid, each, [ ],500 ducats on appointment: an immense sum which they would recoup from the fees paid by those for whose affairs the bulls were issued. There were obviously better ways still of compensating oneself, and in September 1489 two secretaries and four minor officials were arrested. In two years, they confessed, they had put out fifty bogus bulls, liberal grants and dispensations. For which the pope had them burned alive.

To the very end of the reign, the King of Naples continued to sap and mine the weak pope's authority. Innocent even spoke of leaving Rome, and taking refuge at Avignon. Then suddenly, in the last weeks of 1491, Ferrante veered round completely. Once more he made a treaty in which he accepted the pope's terms, and sealed it with an offer to marry his grandson Luigi of Aragon to the pope's granddaughter, Battistina.

The new year 1492 thus opened well, but in March, Innocent -- rarely free from illness -- began to fail. On April 18 Lorenzo de' Medici died, and all Italy waited in apprehension, for the son who succeeded him had none of his father's political genius. By the end of June it was known that Innocent was slowly dying, and the end came on July 25. [ ] Just nine days later one of his fellow countrymen set sail from Pelos on that voyage which was to discover the New World.

Innocent's reign left the papacy in worse case even than he had found it. He had been cautious in one respect, the creation of new cardinals, though in this he was yet again his own yielding, compliant self. For the existing cardinals had strongly objected to any substantial increase in their numbers. Innocent VIII had had

487

but one creation, March 9, 1489, and added only eight cardinals to the college. Thirteen cardinals had died during his reign, and at his death the total number was twenty-seven. Of these, twenty-three made up the conclave that was to elect his successor, all but two of them Italians; and of the total there were still twelve of the creation of Sixtus IV.

In this conclave of 1492 there was hardly any unity of national groups. There was no Cybo faction, and the four della Rovere cardinals were almost the only party when the election began (August 6, 1492). But there was a strong reaction against Giuliano della Rovere, held responsible for the disasters of the late reign. His rival of 1484, Rodrigo Borgia, so an ambassador hinted to his sovereign, might now achieve much, through the great array of wealthy benefices which h s election would cause to be vacant. The spoil, to a share in which his electors might look, would be tremendous. For four days the election hung fire, three scrutinies taking place without any sign which way the election would go. Then Ascanio Sforza, one of the undoubtedly bad men among the cardinals, doubting his own chances of election, went over to Borgia. Bargains were struck, the spoil apportioned out, and gradually -- counting Borgia's own vote -- he was only short of one vote to make the needed sixteen. Finally the confederates gained the promise of the ninety-six years old Patriarch of Venice, "hardly in possession of his faculties". [ ] Rodrigo Borgia was pope, at sixty years of age, Alexander VI. Such is the story as Pastor tells it, [ ] and it seems to be the true story.

## ALEXANDER VI

Alexander VI reigned for eleven years. He had won the name of a good administrator during the thirty-five years he had served the various popes, as cardinal and vice-chancellor. But no more than the weak Innocent VIII, or the technically inexperienced Sixtus IV, did this bureaucrat show himself a statesman in his handling of the grave political problems of the time. His solution, the same miserable superficial business of installing his own family and personal dependants in the chief posts, could, if it succeeded, only add to his successor's difficulties the presence within the curia and the state of yet another powerful faction of well-placed and experienced kinsmen of the last pope, determined to surrender as little as possible of the influence they had wielded. Alexander had to fight, as it were for his life, with the della Rovere. Was the next pope to have against him the Borgia as well? It was a policy that could only have succeeded had the papacy been hereditary, and even then it would have called for a higher degree of statesmanship than any of these papal families were ever able to boast.

The pope's own kin was numerous. In addition to various nephews, he had at least four children of his own who now came into prominence. The eldest son, Juan, betrothed to a cousin of the King of Spain, left Rome for his marriage and his Spanish duchy of Gandia in the first year of the reign. The second, Cesare, a lad of seventeen, was already, thanks to his father's influence, Bishop of Pampeluna. This see he now gave up, and was instead made Archbishop of Valencia, the see his father had held for thirty-six years, ever since the election to the papacy of Cesare's great-uncle, as Calixtus III, had vacated it. [ ] For the youngest son, Jofre, [ ] Alexander secured as a wife Sancia, a granddaughter of the King of Naples. The third of these children was a girl, that Lucrezia Borgia all too famous in the Borgia legend that was later developed by the innumerable enemies that the success of the family produced. Lucrezia, perhaps fourteen years old at the date of Alexander's election, was already engaged, but the marriage was immediately broken off, and a much more distinguished match arranged with a kinsman of the Duke of Milan, namely Giovanni Sforza, [ ] the Count of Cotignola and Lord of Pesaro.

The alliance of Alexander with Milan was far from welcome to Ferrante of Naples. Hostile to Alexander's candidature in the late conclave, and suspicious from the moment of his election, he now strove to avert the marriage. Once the contract was signed he began to work upon the hostility to Alexander of the disappointed Giuliano della Rovere. But the pope's diplomacy produced an anti-Naples combination, and yet another war seemed about to begin when Ferrante made the offer of a royal marriage for the boy Jofre. Upon which a general reconciliation took place, even between the pope and Cardinal Giuliano. Only a few weeks later the brittle peace was again all but broken when, in the first great creation of cardinals, Alexander gave hats to the nominees of almost all the princes of Europe except the King of Naples (September 20, 1493).

Ferrante did not live long enough again to trouble Alexander's peace. He died in the first weeks of 1494. [ ] The King of France, Charles VIII (1483-1498), immediately laid claim to the kingdom, and thereby not only brought to an end the first, easy part of Alexander's reign, but began the first chapter of the history of modern Europe, the long rivalry of France and Spain for the control of European affairs, that was to fill the next hundred and fifty years. The eleven years of Alexander's reign are thus a link between the older world when all the rivalries and wars of Europe are civil wars between small states which are, consciously, parts of a single Christian whole, and the modern age when princes and states strive for a position whence they may dominate the life of the whole world. The accident that Italy was the battle-ground of the first of these great national duels, and that it continued to be so for the next seventy years nearly, gave the popes of the new age a new kind of importance in international politics; they were, in all this game, extremely important figures, but they were not now important as the recognised spiritual chiefs of a christendom where a common religious faith produced a common public estimate of international right and wrong, but important principally as the rulers of a state centrally situated in the territories contended for, a state whose independence was one of the few indubitably fixed and stable elements of European life, and yet a state that might change sides at any moment, since its rulers were elected -- a state that might change sides often, since its rulers were rarely so young when elected as to be likely to reign for long. a

The French invasion of Italy in 1494 was a wholly new kind of thing, and this is the crucial year of Alexander's reign. He was now to meet the supreme test of the administrator promoted to rulership. Meanwhile, his first creation of cardinals was an indication that in his use of high ecclesiastical patronage he would follow faithfully the tradition of his last two predecessors. Unlike Innocent VIII, he was to be lavish in his creations, adding forty-seven in all to the Sacred College in the nine years of his reign, where Innocent had but added eight in almost the same length of time. Alexander's first cardinal, created five days after his coronation, [ ] was his nephew, Juan Borgia, who since 1483 had been Archbishop of Monreale. [ ] Now, in September 1493, the pope created another twelve, six of them from outside Italy. Seven were by favour to the different princes, namely the Roman ambassadors of the Kings of France and Spain, a confidential agent of the emperor, the Archbishop of Canterbury, [ ] the sons of the King of Poland, of the Doge of Venice and of the Duke of Ferrara. There was also a small family group, Cesare Borgia, Giuliano Cesarini (brother to a son-in-law of Alexander) and Alessandro Farnese, whose sister stood to Alexander in a relation that may most politely be described as equivocal. Cesarini and Farnese were both very young, Cesare Borgia was still in his teens and so too was the Ferrarese Ippolito d'Este. [ ]

The French king's claim to succeed Ferrante in Naples met with no support from the papal suzerain. Alexander recognised Ferrante's son Alfonso as king, and sent a papal legate to crown him. But the young Charles VIII was utterly carried away by the desire of military glory, and the opposition to him was welcome.

He began to prepare the mightiest army Italy had seen for hundreds of years, and meanwhile his diplomacy was busy "softening" the papal resistance. The threats now usual on the lips of princes determined to wring concessions from the pope were made, namely to withdraw the nation's obedience from him, and to confiscate all benefices held by his appointment. And, on the suggestion possibly of the Duke of Milan -- Charles's Italian partner in the coming expedition -- the services were enlisted of Cardinal Giuliano della Rovere. On April 24, 1494, Giuliano fled from Rome, first to his bishopric of Avignon, and then to the French camp. Soon Charles was proclaiming the need to call a General Council which should judge the pope, the Colonna -- worked upon by France -- began to move, and by the middle of June Alexander had passed from alarm almost to despair. He even turned to beg aid from the Turks. The pope's sole ally was his cruel, cowardly and treacherous vassal of Naples, Alfonso II.

In September Charles VIII crossed the French frontier. The Dukes of Milan and Ferrara joined him and so, publicly, did Cardinal Giuliano. By October 14 he had reached Pavia, whither Piero de' Medici journeyed from Florence, and surrendered to him -- whereupon the Florentines drove out the Medici and restored the old government of the republic. On November 17 Charles was at Florence, and presently moving against Rome. The French -- thanks to the Colonna -- were already in Ostia and their galleys menaced the mouth of the Tiber. Alexander began to send legates to the king. But Charles refused to treat with anyone but the pope. He had a vow to visit the Holy Places, he said, and must spend his Christmas at Rome. But the legates also reported to Alexander that, everywhere, the French were announcing their mission to reform the Church. And the advance continued, relentlessly. For a brief moment Alexander's hopes rose, for on December 10 the army of the King of Naples marched into Rome. But a closer view of all that his ally could do depressed him to the extreme of preparing for flight. By December 18 " everything in the Vatican down to the bedding and table service " had been packed. It was, however, too late. The very next day the French pickets made their appearance, and from the windows of his palace the pope could see them exercising their horses in the Prati. The Neapolitans retired, glad to be away before the army itself arrived. That same night -- December 25 -- Alexander made terms with the French king's commissioners, and on New Year's Eve his armies marched in.

Charles VIII remained in Rome almost for a month. He was fascinated by the wealth and the beauty and the luxury of the city -- as, indeed, he had been fascinated by all he had seen of Italy since the invasion began. He was also fascinated, and overcome, by the pleasant-mannered pope. No one has ever accused Alexander of haughtiness or awkwardness. His was, it would seem, a gay and gentlemanly spirit, good-humoured, witty, a kindly, talkative man of the world, and his charm worked wonders with the raw, awkward, misshapen little man who was the offspring of that oddest of kings, Louis XI.

Once king and pope had met informally, and Alexander, with no more than a graceful gesture of assent, had admitted two of his friends to the college of cardinals, the murders and rapes and plunderings of the troops in Rome ceased to matter. The army would soon be out of the city and on its way to Naples.

The pope managed to keep possession of St. Angelo, and he was not to be forced into any recognition of Charles as King of Naples. But he had to grant free passage to the French armies through his state, and to surrender his main port, Civita Vecchia; also he must appoint as legates and governors in all the chief cities prelates approved by Charles. He had, next, to surrender to Charles the invaluable brother of the Sultan, and also (as a hostage, though this was not expressly stated) his son Cesare. All the cardinals and barons who had supported Charles were to be forgiven, and especially Giuliano della Rovere. There was no more talk of reforming the Church. The eight cardinals who had gone over to Charles saw their leader become as papal as the pope himself. At the crucial moment of the audience, with Alexander in their toils, Charles had ruined it all by a sudden unconditional profession of obedience and homage, of recognition that Alexander was the true Vicar of Christ and successor of St. Peter. On January 28, 1495, the French marched out from Rome.

Charles had got no further than Marino, ten miles to the south, when the news came that Alfonso of Naples, terrified, had abdicated, leaving the chaos to the management of his young son Ferrantino. At the same time the French king received his first hint that even the cynical Europe of the Renaissance would not allow the papacy to become any one prince's tool, when the Spanish ambassadors brought him the strong protest of Ferdinand and Isabella against the invasion of the papal state and the occupation of Rome. And now Cardinal Cesare neatly gave him the slip. But, on February 22, Charles entered Naples, without opposition, the populace frantically enthusiastic for the novelty, more suo.

While the French gave themselves to the manifold pleasures of their new southern possession, the Italian diplomacy knit together a new league that would bar the king's return to France, the pope, Milan, and Venice joining with Spain and the emperor, the pope being pledged to use his spiritual powers for the objects of the alliance (March 31, 1495). Charles was mad with anger and alarm. He might make a parade of himself, crowned as King of Naples, in the cathedral of his new capital, but prudence bade him look to his communications, and only a week later (May 20), with half of his army, he began the return towards France. Alexander, this time, evaded, by a timely flight to Orvieto, the meeting Charles desired. Rome was stripped of its valuables in anticipation of a sack. But the French passed through without any delay. They got over the Apennines safely, and at Fornovo, on July 6, beat off the attack of the allied army without great difficulty. By October Charles VIII was back in France, and the great expedition was over, although it still remained for the allies to clear out the garrisons the king had left behind in the south, ten thousand men in all. It was not until July 1496 that the last of these surrendered, to the Spanish commander Gonsalvo of Cordova.

While the Spaniards were thus engaged, Alexander turned to punish the barons who had sided with the French. The chief of these were the Orsini. They were now excommunicated, and all their possessions declared confiscated. But the execution of the sentence was put into the hands of the pope's eldest son, the Duke of Gandia, and it proved a task beyond his powers. The main fortress, Bracciano, defied all his efforts, and sorties of the Orsini even descended as far as Rome, where the rebels joined forces with their supporters in the city. The fortress was still untaken when, on January 25, 1497, the Orsini completely routed the pope's army at Soriano. Alexander now had to make peace on their terms, and restore their castles. Then, for a moment, fortune smiled on the papal cause, and on March 9 the Spaniards drove the French from Ostia.

And now began a series of extraordinary events in the family life of the pope that kept Rome interested and alert for a year and a half. In Holy Week (March) 1497, Lucrezia's husband, Giovanni Sforza, suddenly disappeared from Rome. The question had been raised of declaring his marriage null, on the ground that he was impotent. Sforza had refused to let the case go against him undefended, and he now fled to his city of Pesaro to escape the anger of the pope. Lucrezia, it seems, stood by her husband. In May the pope created a third Borgia cardinal, another Juan Borgia, [ ] the son of one of his sisters and on June 7 he granted to the Duke of Gandia and his descendants for ever the Duchy of Benevento with Terracina and Pontecorvo; the next day Cesare was named legate for the coronation of the new King of Naples, Federigo. [ ] Then, on June 14, the Duke of Gandia mysteriously disappeared. For two days he was missing, and then his body, slashed with a score of wounds, the throat cut, was fished out of the Tiber. Was it the Orsini or some jealous lover or husband? The mystery has never been resolved, but the murder roused even the Rome of 1497, and it shook Alexander to the point that he solemnly promised to amend his life, and even named a commission to plan a complete reform of the curia and the Church.

It is after the murder of his elder brother that Cesare Borgia first comes into the public life of the reign. He returned from crowning the King of Naples meditating a dramatic change in his status. He now wished to break off his ecclesiastical career, and he thought an exchange might be arranged between himself and Jofre, his youngest brother. Cesare would be freed from all his obligations, and resign his archiepiscopal see of Valencia and his cardinal's hat; the marriage between Jofre and Sancia would be dissolved, on the ground that it had not been consummated; Cesare would marry Sancia and become a prince, while Jofre would succeed to his cardinalate and all his other benefices. Alexander was slow to agree, but by December he had got so far as to say that the change of status must be so arranged as not to give scandal. While the best way to do this was carefully considered, the other domestic problem, Lucrezia's marriage, was successfully solved. Her husband's long resistance ceased, and under pressure from his two kinsmen, the Duke of Milan and Cardinal Ascanio Sforza, Giovanni Sforza now swore that he had never consummated the marriage and that he was unable to do so, and on December 20, 1497, a decree of nullity was published. Lucrezia had broken with him in June, and in August negotiations were begun for her second marriage to a son of the Prince of Salerno. [ ]

Cesare's scheme still moved slowly, the first fantastic plan was abandoned, but a few months after the disgraceful tinkering with matrimonial justice on behalf of his sister, on April 7, 1498, the

King of France, Charles VIII, died. He left no son to succeed him, and the crown passed to his cousin the Duke of Orleans, Louis XII. This change in the succession was, in time, to make all the difference to Cesare's future. The new king had a claim on Milan, as a descendant of the ancient Visconti dukes; he was as eager to distinguish himself in the field as his predecessor had been; a second invasion of Italy was, then, to be looked for soon. Meanwhile, Louis sought the annulment of his own marriage with Jeanne de Valois, sister of Charles VIII, a poor invalid and a cripple, his wife for many years but who had not borne him any family; and he also sought a dispensation to marry Anne, the widow of his predecessor, and Duchess of Brittany in her own right (June 1498). The grounds on which the annulment of the marriage was sought were that Louis had married her through fear of his terrible father-in-law, Louis XI, and that the marriage could not be consummated. While a new chapter in French -- and indeed in papal history -- was thus beginning, the Borgia family's matrimonial history was also enlarged. Lucrezia was married on July 21 to Alfonso of Bisceglia, a son of the late King of Naples, [ ] and an effort was made to secure Carlotta, daughter of the reigning king, for Cesare, when his several resignations should have been allowed. But the lady refused, afraid, so she said, of the time it would take her to live down what her husband had been; she did not want to be known as the cardinal's wife. But on August 17, 1498, Cesare was at last free of his ecclesiastical rank, his orders [ ] and their obligations. The French king -- his nullity suit not yet terminated -- was granted the dispensation to wed the Duchess of Brittany, should his marriage to Jeanne be declared null, and he soon agreed to find a wife for Cesare, whom he created Duke of Valentinois, from among the women of his own family. On October 1 the new duke set out for France, with an outfit that cost his father 100,000 ducats, and a vulgar parvenu display that brought amused smiles to the face of the parsimonious French king. Louis offered him the choice between two ladies, and Cesare chose Charlotte d'Albret, the sister of the King of Navarre. In December Louis XII's marriage with Jeanne was declared null, he was free to marry Anne and rivet Britanny anew to the crown of France. The Colonna might once more rise against Alexander, and combine with Naples against him; the Spanish and Portuguese ambassadors might, to his face, reproach him for his evil worldliness, and utter threats; the King of France was now his fixed and most powerful ally, and even his kinsman. When next the French invaded Italy, they would come to conquer Alexander's enemies too. When the news reached Rome, on May 24, 1499, of Cesare's marriage, the pope's joy knew no bounds. His Italian policy was reversed, the full half circle, but this time to his certain profit. In July a French army again crossed the Alps.

The four years between the invasion of 1499, and Alexander's death, four years packed with incident, are wholly dominated by the pitiless craft and violence of Cesare Borgia. It had been agreed that Louis XII would aid his new cousin's campaign to subdue the Romagna. The pope issued a series of bulls declaring forfeited the fiefs of Rimini, Pesaro, Imola, Faenza, Forli, Urbino and Camerino, and in the autumn of this same year Imola and Forli fell to the Duke. In the spring of 1500 Louis' victory at Novara [ ] secured his hold on Milan and the North, and in the autumn Cesare opened his second campaign in the Romagna. The lords of Pesaro and Rimini did not await his attack; he took Faenza (April 1501) and had its lord and his heir murdered. The pope now created him Duke of Romagna; he and his descendants were to be lords of the finest province in the Papal State. Cesare next turned his power against the barons of the Campagna, and in June 1501 he forced the surrender of the Colonna fortresses and confiscated the possessions of the Savelli. When he threatened Florence the republic hastily bought him off with 36,000 ducats and an engagement not to hinder his attack on the maritime principality of Piombino. This, with its great fortress of Orbetello, fell to Cesare in September.

Alexander now divided the spoil. Piombino went to Cesare, and the Colonna lands were formed into two new duchies, Sermoneta, which went to Lucrezia's son Rodrigo, and Nepi, given to another tiny child of three or four, a Juan Borgia who may have been Cesare's son or perhaps Alexander's. [ ] Lucrezia herself was about to make a third marriage, [ ] to the heir to the Duchy of Ferrara, so that there also the future dukes would be Borgia. Practically the whole territory of the states of the Church had now been made hereditary in this family, and future popes, if all went well, would rule their states by grace of the descendants of Alexander VI.

Cesare's next objective was Tuscany, the republics of Siena and Florence, and the reduction of the great Romagna city of Bologna. In March 1502 he began his elaborate operations. But success, this time, was to be conditioned by the circumstance that the French king was no longer the sole great military power in Italy. Eighteen months before Cesare began his preparations for these new conquests Louis XII in November 1500, had had no alternative but to accept Ferdinand of Spain as a partner in the enterprise of conquering Naples. [ ] The two had agreed to partition the kingdom, and in the following June [ ] Alexander had ratified the treaty, and had obliged the partners by declaring the King of Naples, Federigo, deposed. Federigo, understanding perfectly that there was now no hope at all, abdicated in August. And now, six months later, the two robber powers were at issue over the spoil. In July 1502 war began between them, a momentous new war, the first of many, between France and Spain for the possession of Italy and fought on Italian soil.

By the time this war had begun, Cesare, drawing huge sums from the papal treasury for arms and munitions of war, had opened his own campaign in Central Italy. Such was the terror his cruelties inspired that, as his army advanced, the people fled, "as from a hydra". He was soon master of Spoleto, and of Urbino too, and of Camerino, and he began to plan the attack on Bologna. But now, October 1502, his captains conspired to put him out of the way, before he had murdered them. For a moment Cesare was in great danger. But the help of Louis XII, and his own craft and courage, saved him. He captured Sinigaglia, on the last day of the year, and massacred there those of the conspirators whom he had induced to desert. Then he made for Perugia to deal with the rest (January 1503).

In Rome, meanwhile, Alexander dealt with the Orsini. He had the Orsini cardinal arrested, and so many of the clan's supporters with him, that Rome was panic-stricken and the pope had to reassure the civil authorities personally that he meant to do no more. On February 22 the cardinal died; not improbably he was poisoned. In the country the Orsini, as always, made a good fight. They lost their fortress of Cere (April 4, 1503), but Bracciano held out once again. Alexander had to consent to an armistice. And while the pope and his son were thus striking down the last of their enemies, the Spaniards were beginning to defeat the pope's French ally in battle after battle. From the beginning Ferdinand's generals had profited from the traditional Aragonese command of the western Mediterranean. It was a great blow to Louis when, in March 1503, his fleet was destroyed in a great battle at sea. Then followed two more French defeats, at Seminara (April 20) and Cerignola (April 28), and on May 16 the Spaniards entered Naples, to be rulers there for the next two hundred years and more.

Cesare's fortune, built so far on the favour of the French, was gravely menaced. But he now planned to play off France against Spain. All he needed was a better army of his own and -- of course -- more money. One way to get the money was for Alexander to create, on March 29, eighty new court offices to be sold at 760 ducats apiece; another was to poison the extremely wealthy Venetian cardinal Giovanni Michele and seize his possessions (April 10); [ ] a third way was to repeat the iniquity of the consistory of 1500 [ ] and, by the creation of nine new cardinals for a consideration -- bring into the treasury some 120,000 ducats. Alexander began to negotiate, with the emperor, Cesare's nomination as sovereign of Pisa and Siena and Lucca, while the duke made himself master of Perugia. The future seemed once more secured. But though Alexander at seventy was, like Queen Elizabeth, just a hundred years later, active, gay and even frisky, his end was near. "Il papa sta benissimo, " a Mantuan correspondent told his sovereign in May. But ten weeks later he was dead (August 18, 1503) and Cesare, at the same time, so ill as to be in danger of death. For the circumstance of Alexander's death Cesare was prepared, and had, no doubt, his arrangements made. But, as he told Machiavelli later, [ ] the one contingency for which it had never crossed his mind he need prepare was, that when the pope died, he, too, would be at the point of death. This was surely the providence of God.

## JULIUS II

Four weeks and a day after Alexander's death thirty-seven cardinals went into conclave. Two were French, there was a block of eleven Spaniards, and twenty-two very divided Italians. Had Cesare Borgia been able to act, he might have imposed a pope of his own choice. But the cardinals, aided by the ambassadors of France, Spain and the emperor, were able to induce the sick man to make terms. His army was but one of three in the neighbourhood of Rome, and, the cardinals guaranteeing him his possessions and a free passage to them with his forces, and the French and Spanish ambassadors pledging that the armies of their sovereigns would not move nearer to Rome while the conclave debated, this most dangerous enemy of religion left Rome on September 2, still so ill that he was carried in a litter. Two days later the solemnities of the late pope's funeral began. On September 5 Giuliano della Rovere came back to Rome, after his long exile, and on the sixteenth the conclave began.

Giuliano made no secret that he meant to be pope himself. Two other powerful men were equally determined to be elected; Ascanio Sforza and the French king's chief minister, Georges d'Amboise, Archbishop of Rouen. For the cardinals, after the disgraceful history of the last thirty years, to elect another Italian or Spaniard and disregard the wishes of Louis XII would, so the French considered, be an unbearable insult. "Our generals, said this French Wolsey, "are aware of these intrigues, and they will not patiently endure such a slight to their king. "

For five days the conclave was hopelessly deadlocked, despite Giuliano's success in winning the Spanish cardinals to his side. Then d'Amboise and Ascanio joined forces to propose a quiet, neutral man against whom none had a word to say, the senior member of the college, Francesco Piccolomini, the nephew of Pius II. The whole college rallied to him, and on September 22 he was proclaimed as Pius III. He was indeed a colourless personage, though not a weakling of the type of Innocent VIII, and he was a man of unblemished life. [ ] Hopes of reform accordingly ran high, especially when he promptly announced that he would summon a General Council. But Pius III, sixty-five years of age, and like his uncle a lifelong martyr to gout, was indeed a very feeble old man. The long ceremonies that followed his election -- his ordination (for he was only a deacon), [ ] his consecration as bishop and his coronation -- and the first rush of routine business, were too much for him. He very soon fell ill, and in less than four weeks after his election he was dead. In October 1503 the competitors of September took up again their round of busy intrigue and, this time, of bribery and simony too. Cesare Borgia had now returned to Rome. On the eve of the conclave he made his bargain with Giuliano della Rovere. The cardinal was to have the votes of the Spaniards, and he was to confirm Cesare in his possessions, and in his post of commander-in-chief. A short conclave of a few hours' duration sufficed to elect Giuliano, and on November 1 he was proclaimed as Julius II.

The new pope had reached just to the end of his sixtieth year. He was notoriously violent and self-willed, restless, a politician who, when not in office, had always been a rebel; and during the greater part of the reign of Alexander VI he had been the pope's most dangerous enemy. What his contemporaries saw in the election was the emergence of a strong pope, and they looked forward to a time of order, good government and peace. This last hope was not to be fulfilled, and Giuliano della Rovere was to show himself in a new role as Pope Julius II, for his immense energy was to work itself out in military expeditions quite as much as in diplomatic manoeuvres. There was, of course, little that was lamblike in such of the pope's contemporaries as Ferdinand of Spain, Louis XII of France, our own Henry VII, the Emperor Maximilian or the Venetian Senate. It was a world of hard lying, of perfidy, of cruelty and violence that the pope had known, and worked in, during the thirty years since, at the invitation of his uncle, Sixtus IV, he had left his Franciscan cell to become a cardinal and man of affairs. He did not propose to retire from that world now, nor to shrink from using in defence of his rights the only argument whose force that world would appreciate.

Julius II found Cesare Borgia installed as the actual ruler of the greater part of his state, a vassal more powerful than his suzerain; and what cities of the Romagna were not in Cesare's power, Venice, in these late disturbed years, had laid hands on. But, in fact, Cesare Borgia's position was critical. His French patron's star had declined; and he was not himself well established, as yet, with the Spaniards. When the terrible condottiere betook himself to Naples, as a first step towards making himself once again a reality in Italian politics, his admiring friend the viceroy, Gonsalvo de Cordova, was nevertheless compelled, by Ferdinand's instructions, to arrest him. When the pope now suggested to the King of Spain that Italy would be a happier place for all its princes were Cesare out of it, Ferdinand readily agreed, and under a strong guard the most dangerous of the

Borgia returned in 1504 to his native land. Like many another of his kind he ceased to be terrible from the moment he came up against superior force and equal determination.

By this time Julius II had regained the most of the Romagna towns where Cesare Borgia had been lord. But the Venetians, with a polite kind of contempt, refused to take seriously the pope's repeated demands for a restoration of what they held, such great cities as Rimini, Faenza and Ravenna. And their intrigues to seduce from him the newly-acquired Romagna never ceased. The pope began to look round for allies; Venice was a power far beyond what his slight resources could hope to subdue. And the pope no longer looked to the other Italian states. Naples was now ruled by Spain, Milan by France. The new papal diplomacy must be international; the next war, if war there must be, would be a general European war. But while France and Spain were still at war about Naples, the pope's great schemes had to wait.

In the next two years (1504-1506) the pope secured from Venice a few small towns -- surrenders made in a manner that emphasised the Venetian determination to keep the main strongholds, and also the Venetian sense of the pope's helplessness -- and he took back the papal fiefs in the Campagna which Alexander VI had granted to the Borgia. Then, by three diplomatic marriages, he sought to bind to the Holy See the most turbulent of his own barons; one of his nieces married a Colonna, while, for a nephew and for one of his own daughters he arranged marriages with the Orsini. In October 1505 France and Spain finally came to an accord about Naples, [ ] the pope's diplomacy completed his alliances with the Italian states, [ ] his last preparations were made, and in the summer of 1506 he announced his plan. It was to reduce his own two cities of Perugia and Bologna, neither of which had ever been more than nominally subject to the popes. Despite the opposition of Venice, and of France, the expedition started, August 26, 1506, and Julius II led it in person. It was almost three years since his election. The remaining six years of his reign were to see almost continuous war.

The pope was absent from Rome for just seven months, and the event justified his courage. As had more than once happened in the days of the ruthless Cesare Borgia, the tyrants did not wait to try a fall with fate. While Julius halted at Orvieto (September 5-9), the Baglioni came in from Perugia to surrender at discretion. The pope took possession of the town four days later. He reached Imola by October 20, and while he planned there his last moves against Bologna, the news came that the tyrant -- Bentivoglio -- had fled. On November 10 Julius entered the city, the first pope to be really its lord. He remained at Bologna, reorganising the government, until after the New Year and returned to Rome on March 27, 1507. It was the eve of Palm Sunday, and the next day Julius made his ceremonial entry in the most magnificent procession known for years, under triumphal arches, and amid showers of flowers, with choirs singing in his honour the hymns from the day's great liturgy -- to the unconcealed scandal of the pope's master of ceremonies, who said openly to Julius that this was a scandalous way for a pope to begin Holy Week. [ ]

The next objective of the victorious pope was Venice. But a new obstacle now blocked the plan of a grand alliance. Ferdinand of Spain was introducing into his new kingdom of Naples that system of royal control over Church affairs which was one of the characteristics of his rule in Spain, where the king was all-powerful in appointments to sees, and where without his leave none dared, under pain of death, bring in any bulls or other documents from the Holy See. And while this trouble was yet unsettled Ferdinand, to the pope's chagrin, not only made his peace with Louis XII in a personal interview at Savona (June 1507), but refused to meet the pope. However, by the end of the next year, 1508, the needs of the Emperor Maximilian had brought about the long desired league against Venice. On December 10, 1508, the emperor and the King of France signed a pact of alliance at Cambrai -- a peace-treaty between the two powers and a league against the Turks. But secretly they had come to an agreement to attack Venice and to partition the republic's possessions on the European mainland, offering an appropriate share of the spoil to all interested. If the pope joined the league -- he was not represented at Cambrai -- he was to bring against Venice his spiritual powers also, and he would receive at the peace his own Romagna cities that Venice still detained. It was not until nearly four months later that Julius joined the league, until after the Venetians had repeatedly, and with their usual scorn, refused his new demands for the return of his territories. When the news came that the pope had joined the alliance they offered restitution. But Julius now stood by the pact, and on April 27 he laid an interdict on the republic.

The first act of the long war which followed was soon over. On May 14, 1509, the Venetian army was scattered like chaff at the battle of Agnadello. Venice was, for the moment, at the mercy of the league, and evacuating immediately the papal cities of Ravenna, Cervia, Rimini, and Faenza, the republic appealed to the pope for mercy. The envoys had a grim reception (July 1509), for almost the last act of Venice before the disastrous battle was to appeal against the pope to a future General Council. Before the pope would discuss the desired absolution from excommunication and interdict, the Venetians must accept his terms, promise to abandon their habit of installing bishops without the pope's consent, for example, or of levying taxes on the clergy. Moreover, the Venetians must restore. all their Italian conquests of the last eight years and more. While the pope held out, the fortunes of war suddenly changed; Venice, within a few weeks, had regained Padua and captured the pope's chief general. Julius, at the news, went off into one of his rages, throwing his biretta to the ground, cursing and swearing violently. The republic broke off the negotiations. And then the pope set them going once more. What brought the pope to approach Venice was a new fear of France, not only dominant now in northern Italy, but showing itself unpleasantly able to force from the pope new concessions in jurisdiction. On February 15, 1510, the pope made peace with Venice, and so deserted the league. The Venetians gave way on all points, and Julius reduced the humiliating ceremony of the reconciliation to a thin formality. But, in their hearts, the Venetians still held out. Nine days before the act of submission, the Council of Ten had drawn up a secret declaration that they would not hold themselves bound by what, so they declared, they only signed under compulsion. The gains of the war would be the pope's only so long as he had strength to keep them; and meanwhile he had mortally offended his allies, especially the French.

To Julius II this last particular was welcome rather than otherwise, for the pope now proposed to crown his career by driving the French out of Italy once and for all. If he did not actually utter the famous words "Out with the barbarians, " the sentiment was, from now, for ever on his lips. The year 1510 opened with the certainty of a speedy new war between the pope and France. He could not eat nor drink, nor sleep, he said, for the thought of the French. It was obviously the will of God that he should punish their ally, the Duke of Ferrara, and free Italy from their power. The first stage in the business was for the pope to destroy this powerful vassal, the Duke of Ferrara, who had disregarded the papal command to desert his French ally, and who was still harassing the Venetians. On August 9, 1510, Julius II excommunicated him, in a bull of staggering severity, and declared his fief forfeited. Then, at the end of the month, the pope once more left Rome at the head of an army marching north.

The French king had not passively awaited the pope's assault, but he was gravely handicapped by the loss of the shrewdest of his advisers, the cardinal Georges d'Amboise, [ ] whom a personal hatred of the pope stimulated to brave any extremity, and who was the one force that could keep the king's own vacillating will fixed and true to its purpose. And while the pope made an alliance that secured him the invaluable Swiss -- rightly reputed the finest soldiers of the day -- Louis XII fell into the abysmal mistake of attacking the pope through the spiritual arm. It was perhaps a natural kind of reprisal for Julius II's lavish use of excommunications to forward his plans. But all history was there to show how, in the hands of a Catholic prince, this weapon breaks sooner or later. To such contests there is but one end, submission and retraction on the part of the prince -- unless the prince turns heretic and leaves the Church, in which case all hope of dominating the Church is at an end.

But Louis XII was ill-advised, and Julius knew it. While the pope watched the French cardinals narrowly, imprisoning one of them and threatening to behead him, Louis, so Machiavelli, now Florence's ambassador in France, wrote home, was resolved to renounce obedience to the pope "and to hang a council round his neck. " Julius II was to be annihilated, in spirituals as well as in temporals, and another set in his place. This was on July 21, 1510, and nine days later the French king sent out to the bishops of France a summons to meet and arrange the preliminaries of the council. The technique for dealing with awkward popes invented by Philip the Fair, and by now a tradition with the French kings, was beginning to function. On August 16 a royal edict forbade French subjects to visit Rome, and in September, at a great meeting at Tours, the bishops gave Louis their support, and voted a generous subsidy to help the expedition that was to invade Italy once more and, this time, depose the pope.

By now Julius II was nearing Bologna, and there misfortunes crowded upon him. On October 17 he heard that five of his cardinals had gone over to Louis, and the next day the sickness, under which he had been labouring for some time, took a sudden turn for the worse. He fell into a delirium and raved that rather than fall into the hands of the French he would kill himself. The cardinals expected his death, and began to think of the conclave.

Meanwhile the French were within ten miles of the city, and Cardinal Alidosi, the pope's favourite, was treasonably negotiating with them.

But the old pope recovered as speedily as he had collapsed. He managed to keep the French away by a feint of negotiations and then, as the Venetians and Spaniards arrived, the French fell back. By the end of the year 1510 the initiative had once again passed to the pope, his armies were besieging the fortresses of Concordia and Mirandola that were the keys to Ferrara, and, scorning the doctors, he pressed on to take his place in the front of the attack (January 2, 1511). Never was the fiery spirit of Julius II so satisfied as in these weeks. Since his dangerous illness the pope had grown a great beard, and wearing his armour he stamped through the deep snow before the walls of Mirandola, delighting the soldiers with his familiarity as he mixed with them round the camp fires, and by the blunt, coarse language in which, from time to time, he raged at the incompetence and over-cautiousness of his generals. Men were killed at his side and the roof of the farmhouse where he lodged was shot away as he sat there. But the pope hung on, promising the soldiers the sack of the city once they had taken it. On January 20 Mirandola fell, and Julius made his way in with the troops up the scaling ladders and through the newly-opened breach.

But soon the Duke of Ferrara had beaten the papal army in open battle (February 28), the French were once more masters in Bologna, and the pope only just got away in time to Ravenna. Here there were violent scenes between Julius and his nephew, the Duke of Urbino, whom the pope blamed for the loss of Bologna, and who in turn blamed the favourite Alidosi. On May 27 the duke and cardinal met in the streets and, as the cardinal smiled contemptuously at him, the passionate young man cut him down and finished him off with a dozen wounds. The pope had, however, no time to indulge his sorrow, or his rage, nor to repress the unconcealed delight of all his court and cardinals at the disappearance of the wretched traitor. He had now to fly to Rimini, and there he found, fixed to the doors of the church with due formality, a summons from the rebellious cardinals citing him to a council which would meet at Pisa in the coming September; and not only the King of France, but the emperor too, supported them. The glories of Mirandola were ended indeed, and with all possible speed the pope made his way back to Rome. [ ] It was a dark hour in his life; Julius II was isolated, and the coming council would no doubt "depose" him.

But the religious situation was not so bad as it seemed. Although, in France, the University of Paris was once again stirred up to popularise that theory of the pope's subordination to General Councils which had already done the French kings such service, and although, along with this, a campaign was organised, in the press and on the stage, of anti-papal calumny and ridicule, the scheme for a great council at Pisa died almost at birth. The emperor found it impossible to persuade Hungary and Poland to join him; the English held aloof, and so did Spain. But it was the reply which the pope made to the rebels that killed the movement. For, on July 25, 1511, just a month after his return to Rome, Julius II made the plan of the rebels his own, and summoned a General Council which should meet at Rome on April 19, 1512. And during the summer his diplomacy managed to knit a new combination against France -- the Holy League, for the protection and defence of the pope. This was signed on October 4. On November 17 the new young King of England, Henry VIII, joined it and in the first week of the New Year the war began again.

Meanwhile, on November 1, 1511, the four rebel cardinals arrived at Pisa, with a dozen or so French bishops in support, to find that no one in the town would lodge them and that the canons had locked up the cathedral. In the next fortnight they managed to hold three pretentious sessions, where, with a wealth of declamation, they reaffirmed the ideals of the famous fifth session of Constance, and then, all but chased out by the townsfolk, they declared the council transferred to Milan, where Louis XII still reigned as duke.

The new anti-French offensive opened well. The Venetians took Brescia (February 2, 1512) and the Spanish and papal army laid siege to Bologna (January 26). But there now appeared one of the greatest military geniuses of all time, Gaston de Foix, a kinsman of Louis XII, twenty-three years of age, and in a few brief weeks he all but destroyed the league. He managed to make his way into Bologna (February 5) and forced a raising of the siege. On February 18 he retook Brescia, and on April 11 -- Easter Sunday -- he inflicted on the Venetians and Spaniards the terrible defeat of Ravenna. It was the bloodiest battle fought in Italy for a thousand years. The vanquished lost 10,000 killed, and a vast horde of prisoners, among them the Papal Legate Cardinal de' Medici. But the victor was himself slain in the battle.

When the news of the defeat reached Rome there was universal panic. Even the pope' for a moment, gave way. The French were masters of the key' province of his state. How long would it be before Julius was in their hands? And at Milan the rebel cardinals, on April 21, declared him suspended from his office, that all his acts henceforth were void in law, his appointments also; and they explicitly forbade him to create any new cardinals.

The ultimately decisive event, however, was not the victory at Ravenna, but the death of Gaston de Foix. This the Cardinal Legate shrewdly foresaw, and he managed to send his cousin, Giulio de' Medici [ ] to the pope to impress upon him the difference this must make. While the emperor recalled the troops he had sent to serve under Gaston -- the German professional mercenaries who had been a main element in the victory -- the Swiss now descended on Verona. The French, utterly disordered, led now by a weak and incompetent commander, and beyond the reach of reinforcements, were forced to retreat or see their line of communications cut. The pope now looked on at the most amazing spectacle of a victorious army in full retreat. Like mist before the sun the great threat disappeared. The Romagna, Bologna, Pavia, Milan itself, were abandoned, and in ten weeks after the victory of Ravenna the victors were back in France, a broken remnant. Somewhere in the rout were the cardinals and bishops of the rebel council. " Papa Bernadin" [ ] was finished. Meanwhile, on May 3, only a fortnight after the appointed date, the General Council which the pope had summoned, assembled in the basilica of the Lateran.

In August the allies met at Mantua to regulate the future of Italy. Milan, now recovered from the French, was given back to the Sforza, and Florence to the Medici. But from Milan were detached Parma and Piacenza, handed over to the pope, who also received Reggio. One awkward question defied settlement, the claim of the emperor on Venice for Verona and Vicenza. The pope was most anxious to win Maximilian's support for the council and he now, for the third time in his short reign, reversed his policy. On November 19, 1512, he made a treaty with Maximilian against Venice, his late ally. The emperor was to support the council, and to hand over Modena to the pope -- whose new territories were thus linked to the old -- while Julius was to join in compelling Venice to give up the fiefs which the emperor claimed, and to use on behalf of his new ally spiritual weapons too. This treaty was made public on November 25. Its effect, of course, was to drive Venice to seek help from France, and in March 1513 a new alliance was negotiated between them and a new war began. But by that time Julius II was no more.

Towards the end of 1512 the pope -- he was close on seventy -- began to fail rapidly, and he was apparently the first to realise that, this time, it was the end. His last days were harassed by the realisation that while he had destroyed the hold of the French on Italy, the Spaniards had very effectively taken their place. "If God grants me life, " he had been heard to say, "I will free the

Neapolitans from the yoke which is now upon their necks. "
Whether such feats were a proper occupation for popes, whether
indeed, Julius seriously meditated such a war, death found him
still restless and anxious about the menace of Spain. One thing
he impressed on the cardinals who stood round his bed, that they
should observe the new law he had just made about simony in
the conclave. In the night of February 20-21, 1513, he passed
away.

Julius II had died at a critical moment in the complicated
international life of which the pope was now a principal figure.
There was no certitude that his successor, even if faithful to his
ideals, would choose the same alliances through which to realise
them. All Europe would watch the conclave with even more
interest than usual. The dead pope was sincerely mourned by his
subjects, a new feature of papal obsequies, and it was a testimony
to his administration that, for the first time in fifty years, the
cardinals assembled in a city of unbroken calm.

There were twenty-five of them, in all, to go into conclave on
March 4, 1513. Those lately in active rebellion against the pope
were excluded. There were no outstanding personalities among
the cardinals, no intriguers of genius, and no well-defined
groups. In a leisurely way they first drew up the usual pact to
secure from the new pope what they thought their due share of
money and offices and privileges. On March 7 the impatient
guardians of the conclave reduced their rations of food, to hasten
their deliberations, and reduced them still further three days later.
The only line of conflict in the college was, seemingly, that of
age, the older cardinals against the younger men, Riario Sansoni,
a cousin of the late pope, against Giovanni de' Medici. It was
evident that no Venetian could be chosen, still less a Frenchman.
At the first ballot -- March 10 the votes were well scattered. Then
Sansoni and Medici met, the son of the all-but-murdered Lorenzo
de' Medici and the cardinal whom the murderers had used as a
decoy and in whose presence the crime had been committed. The

older man had too many personal enemies for his own election to be possible. He agreed that his friends should support Medici. A second scrutiny, pro forma, confirmed the pact, and on March 11 Medici was proclaimed as Pope Leo X, to the surprise of Rome and of the whole Christian world.

## LEO X

The new pope was only thirty-seven, but a chronic invalid, operated on in the very conclave for a fistula, popular for his easy-going ways and his generosity, likely to strengthen the international position of the papacy for the next few years since he was virtually the ruler of Florence. Pomponius Laetus, Poliziano, and Marsilio Ficino had been his tutors, and in the wealthy cultural palaces of Lorenzo de' Medici he had been fashioned after all the literary and artistic ideals of the age. Though he was not yet a priest he had been a churchman from babyhood. At eight he had been given an archbishopric, [ ] at thirteen he was a cardinal. Then, when he was barely nineteen, the revolution of 1494 had driven his family from Florence, and the cardinal for some years wandered about France and Germany. Alexander VI's court he had only known in the last two or three years of the reign. To Julius II he had been of great political importance, once the Florence dominated by his family's enemies had supported the schismatical Council of Pisa. It was Julius II who had restored the Medici rule in Florence, and now Giovanni, the eldest surviving son of Lorenzo, was pope.

Only twelve days after the election the threatened alliance between France and Venice (against the new Papal-Imperial pact made by Julius II) was published. How would Leo X react? Muratori has well described his general line of conduct, saying that he always steered by two compasses. A more recent Italian scholar, more familiarly, sees him as an eel slippery beyond belief, ever writhing and twisting to escape the hand that would grasp it. Hardly ever, in fact, was Leo X to make an agreement with any power without simultaneously coming to an understanding with its rivals. He realised fully how weak in resources his state really was, and even at the last extremity he shrank from definitely committing himself to political action. Even in the last agonies of a crisis, he would decide and reverse his decision, and reverse yet again. Secretive, bland, affable, every one's friend, he strove to maintain himself by smiling in silence as the inevitable awkward questions were put.

So now, when Henry VIII and Maximilian formed a new league that would check the Franco-Venetian alliance, the pope did not join it at once, although he approved, and sent subsidies. Whichever side won he proposed to have claims on its gratitude. On June 6, 1513, the French were heavily defeated on that field where so many armies met, at Novara, and their armies were once more driven out of Italy. Leo exerted himself to prevent their foes from being too completely victorious. But the English also had invaded France. They had taken Terouanne and Tournai, and they had won the battle of Spurs, and also, against the French king's Scots allies, the bloody fight of Flodden. Then in the autumn, Louis XII made his peace with the pope, repudiated the schism and acknowledged the council in session at the Lateran (December 19, 1513).

But when Louis, exhausted now, proceeded to make with Spain a peace that was definitive, and to offer Ferdinand, as dowry with one of his daughters, the French claims on Milan and Genoa, and to renounce in his favour the French claim on Naples, the shock to the pope was paralysing. The sole result for him would be King Stork in place of King Log. The Spaniards would be masters of Italy in the North as well as in the South. Hence the eagerness of the pope, now, to see peace made between Louis and Henry VIII, his despatch to England and to France of the most experienced diplomatist in his service, [ ] and his joy at the treaty that followed, the peace sealed by the marriage of Henry's youngest sister to the French king. Louis was now tied to the

English instead of to Spain (October 1514). But by this treaty of London the English king acknowledged his brother-in-law's rights in Italy ! So, once again, a new anxiety for the pope. Would Louis XII plan yet another invasion of Italy, with the security, this time, that the English would not attack his rear? However, on New Year's day, 1515, Louis XII died, killed by his endeavours to live up to the gaiety of a wife thirty years his junior; and it is on record that the superficial, short-sighted politician in the Vatican rejoiced. In the nature of things no relief could be more than momentary to so folly-ridden a ruler. Louis XII had no son, and so it was that, instead of that elderly broken man, Leo X had now to face a young king of twenty, valorous, ambitious, and capable, Francis I.

There is not space here to set out in detail all the sinuous writhings of the pontifical diplomacy in these years. The pope's chief confidant was Bernardo Dovizzi, called the Cardinal Bibbiena, his one-time tutor and secretary, a humanist of distinction, but utterly inexperienced in affairs of state, and as cocksure as he was incompetent. While Francis I was preparing a greater army than ever for the conquest of Italy the cardinal laughed at the news as mere gossip, and spoke of the lesson which his new league would soon be teaching the king. But when Francis moved, in July 1515, the pope, whose squandermania had already in two years exhausted the treasure Julius II had left behind, was soon at his wits' end. As to the league, Leo had at last brought himself to sign the pact, but would not have it published, in a desperate hope that he might still, somehow, charm away the advancing French. On August 12, however, by the victory of Villa Franca, they drove a wedge between the Swiss armies that were Italy's only hope. Ten days later Alessandria fell to them; and still the pope, while writing urgent commands to advance, to Bibbiena's twin in incompetence, the Cardinal Giulio de' Medici -- legate with the army -- was sending secret apologies to the French. First he sent an envoy to Francis, and then he hoped the legate would detain the envoy; and then the envoy, and his papers, fell into the hands of the pope's allies. Never was there such incompetent tergiversation since first priests set themselves to play the politician and the soldier.

But on September 8 the crushing victory of Francis I in the bloody two days' battle of Marignano tore these preposterous activities to shreds. All the north and centre of Italy lay at the mercy of the French, and the pope knew it. The king's terms were hard, but Leo had no choice. In December the two met at Bologna. What passed between them in their several long interviews has never transpired. But the pope lost all the conquests of Julius II, Piacenza, Parma, Reggio, and Modena. He had to forbid the Swiss to molest the king in his duchy of Milan, and he even offered the king a hope of the succession to Naples -- Ferdinand of Aragon lay dying at this moment [ ] -- Francis pledging himself to maintain the Medici in Florence; and the pope came to that arrangement about French ecclesiastical affairs, the Concordat of 1516, which practically placed at the king's mercy the whole system of appointments to abbeys and sees; that the pope also gave the king the right to tax the clergy -- a crusade tithe ! -- to the tune of 400,000 livres in two years is, beside this, a detail. To such disaster had the Medici finesse brought the Church in three short years. [ ]

Leo's own war was not yet over, however. His vassal the Duke of Urbino had failed to support him against the French, being in secret communication with Francis. At Bologna the victorious king had to leave him to the mercy of the pope. Leo -- despite the debt his family owed the duke, who had given them shelter in the days of their exile from Florence -- determined to destroy him, and to give the duchy to his nephew Lorenzo. The duke, Francesco Maria della Rovere, did not wait to be defeated by the combined forces of the pope and Florence, but fled to Mantua, where the duke his father-in-law took him in. By the end of June 1516, the Medici were lords of Urbino and Pesaro and Sinigaglia. The King of France had been too caught up with other affairs to be able to prevent it, but he warned Leo not to make any attempt on the other great papal vassal at Ferrara, reminding him that Reggio and Modena were to be surrendered to Ferrara. Then, in January, 1517 the dispossessed Duke of Urbino returned, with a force of Spanish and German mercenaries, unemployed since the recent general peace. Everyone helped him who hated the Medici, the French viceroy in Milan, the Gonzaga in Mantua, the Duke of Ferrara too. The pope was by now all but bankrupt, his army mutinous for lack of pay, and he had no real generals. Nor did Cardinal Bibbiena avail greatly as a peacemaker among the papal mercenaries. And at this moment, at Rome, a plot was discovered to murder the pope, and the chief plotters were cardinals.

Leo X had been pope now (April 1517) for a little more than four years; he was half-way through his reign. The whole spirit of the papal court had already, in that short time, been transformed. Under Julius II, if it had not been religious and spiritual, it had at least become decorous. The wild scandals of the previous twenty years had been checked, and the pope's understanding of the gravity of the tasks before him effected a certain seriousness everywhere. With the election of Giovanni de' Medici there was a rapid return to the days of Alexander VI, and the young pope led the rout. He had indeed been born, and he now showed it, one of the spoiled darlings of fortune. The years of wandering and exile that had followed upon his brilliant introduction to the high places of life, were now to find their compensation. "Everything unpleasant was removed as far as possible from him, for an insatiable thirst for pleasure was his leading characteristic." [ ] His chosen friends were the young cardinals who had brought about his election. Hardly one of them led a life that was not disreputable, and of the friends whom later he himself promoted to the Sacred College the greater part were, like himself, worldly triflers, wealth-devouring amusement hunters. [ ] Leo was passionately fond of music, and he loved equally that newest of cultural amusements, the theatre. In the Vatican the revels were indeed more seemly than in the heyday of the Borgia -- sexual irregularity was not among Leo's vices -- but the comedies performed before the pope could include such indecencies as the Mandragola of Machiavelli and the Calandria of Leo's bosom friend Cardinal Bibbiena. In the summer the pope would leave Rome for the country, and sport was now the all-absorbing occupation. To give, to scatter money indiscriminately to all who asked for it, was one of his greatest pleasures. Merit, well-studied needs, played little part in the directing of this largesse. Buffoons, comedians, the chance passer-by, the beggar who happened to move his sympathy, the servant who attracted his notice, all these were welcome to whatever the pope had in his pocket. And others too, with real claims upon the money, if they happened to be there at the lucky moment.

This was the setting against which the new papal game of false and double-dealing diplomacy was played which, to the great world of Christendom, was now the papacy in action. The pope, says Pastor, "was not a man of deep interior religion." This would seem likely. But he fasted three days each week, and if he said mass more rarely than, for generations now, has been the normal practice of all priests, he was careful to hear mass every day, and whenever he did celebrate he prepared himself by first making his confession.

The Petrucci conspiracy of 1517 is a violent reminder of the truth that morality is a single whole, and that to tamper with one particular precept is to risk bringing down the whole arch. . .One of the many mischievous novelties in papal practice since the election of Sixtus IV was the way in which the kinsmen of reigning princes were made cardinals simply as an act of favour to the prince. At the death of Alexander VI, in 1503, there was hardly a state in Italy whose ruler had not a son or brother who was a cardinal. Siena was one of the few states to lack such a court cardinal, and Julius II brought Siena into the system when, in 1512, he gave the red hat to Alfonso Petrucci, twenty years of age, the brother of the lord of Siena. Petrucci, a few months later, played a great part in the election of Leo X and he was soon one of the new pope's intimates. But Leo, who was nothing if not false, was soon intriguing to displace Petrucci's brother in Siena, and to instal in his place another member of the family, who would be less of a hindrance to the Medici ambitions. [ ] The revolution succeeded, and the cardinal turned against the pope (1516).

He began to intrigue with the dispossessed Duke of Urbino, and to express his mind to other cardinals already discontented with Leo X. In 1516 he left Rome for the country, but continued to keep his party together, it would seem, through his steward in Rome, Marco Nino. Suddenly the steward was arrested, suspected of being a link in intrigues with the Duke of Urbino. A letter in cipher was found on him, and when put to the torture the steward surrendered the key. Cardinal Petrucci, so it was alleged the cipher made known, was arranging with a physician to poison the pope. This doctor was, or claimed to be an expert in the treatment of fistula. He was to be introduced to the pope as a specialist and then make away with him. By a trick the pope now induced Petrucci to come back to Rome. He was immediately arrested and with him another cardinal, his friend Sauli, also young, and a one-time intimate of Leo. This was on May 19, 1517, and that same day the pope explained to the consistory what had happened and appointed three cardinals to study and report on the findings of the enquiry that would now open. The enquiry itself was in the hands of the pope's law officers.

Meanwhile Florence had obligingly arrested the physician and handed him over to the pope. He was speedily put to the torture, and so, it would seem, were the two cardinals. On May 29 there was a second consistory, to hear the interim report of the three cardinals; and now a third cardinal was arrested and thrown into St. Angelo. This was Riario Sansoni, that great-nephew of Sixtus IV whose life had already been so tragically interwoven with that of Leo X. Petrucci and Sauli had confessed that he was in the business too. Ten days later still, there was a third consistory. The pope had now before him fresh admissions from the prisoners, and the names of two more cardinals. He did not immediately announce these, but craftily tried by promises and threats and a general accusation -- "Some of you sitting here were in it too, and I know who," was the line he took -- to gain yet more information. None was forthcoming, however, and the names of the two new accused had to be read out. They were Soderini and Adriano de Castello, two cardinals of Alexander VI's last promotion in 1503. Soderini, with tears, confessed his guilt and asked for mercy. The other admitted that Petrucci had spoken to him of his wish to see the pope put out of the way, but said that from the way the young man spoke he had not taken it seriously. The three cardinals of the commission decided that these two should be fined, each of them, 12,500 ducats; and on their pledging themselves to pay this, and not to leave Rome until they had done so, the pope forgave them.

This seems an extraordinary way for a sovereign to deal with accessories in a plot to murder him. But still stranger was the fact that, when the cardinals paid the enormous fines, they were told that the pope now wanted as much again from each of them. This was on June 18, and two days later the two cardinals, no doubt unable to raise the new fines, fled from Rome.

On June 22, in a fourth consistory, the result was announced of the trial [ ] of the three cardinals imprisoned in St. Angelo. The pope declared that they had been found guilty of treason: for plotting during a pope's lifetime to make one of their number pope, for plotting the pope's murder, and for their dealings with the Duke of Urbino. The debates in the consistory were very long and stormy. For nine or ten hours pope and cardinals remained together, the sound of their voices, as they shouted and interrupted one another, heard by the attendants in the anticamera without. Finally the cardinals [ ] voted that the guilt of the three accused had been proved, and asked the pope to show them mercy. But Leo was inexorable, and confirmed the sentence demanded by the prosecution. Their goods were to be confiscated, they were to be degraded, and to be put to death.

Five days after this scene the lesser fry of the plot, the physician and the steward, were put to death, their flesh torn from their bones with red hot pincers at intervals during the procession to the place of execution, where finally they were hanged, drawn and quartered. On July 4 Petrucci was secretly put to death in St. Angelo, a Moor being employed for the purpose.

Now came another strange circumstance. The other two cardinals who lay under the same sentence were pardoned, and even restored to their dignities, and all in a generous, even lighthearted way, confessing their guilt and that they were even more guilty than they had told already, but agreeing to pay enormous fines cash down. Sauli paid 25,000 ducats; but Riario, one of the wealthiest of the cardinals -- as he was one of the most venerated -- entered into a bond to pay really staggering sums. There was a fine of 150,000 ducats [ ] -- 50,000 of it to be paid immediately and the rest within six months -- and a bail of like amount to be found that he would not leave Rome without the pope's permission. These bonds [ ] were signed on July 17 and in a consistory seven days later Riario was restored, Leo receiving him almost affectionately. But Riario was finished. He lingered on in a kind of chronic melancholia until he died, July 7, 1521. Five months later Leo also died, so deeply in debt, so well and truly plundered in the short interval between death and burial, that the only lights they could find to burn round his coffin were the remains of the candles that had served for Riario. [ ]

The conspiracy, and the judicial proceedings at Rome, extremely scandalous surely, have also this interest that they fall between the closing scenes of the General Council and the appearance of Luther. [ ] They are, indeed, almost the last thing to occupy the pope's attention before the Reformation came to force purely religious questions violently upon it. But one last political problem there was. It coincided with the beginnings of Luther's demonstration, and such was its importance that the politically-minded pope hoped, by solving it, to settle also the little matter of Luther. The problem was who should be emperor when Maximilian, old beyond his years and now obviously breaking up, should come to die. In many respects the high office had, for centuries now, been little more than a great ceremonial distinction. An emperor was effective just to the extent that he could persuade the myriad princes of Germany to support him. The dignity was not hereditary, but for the last eighty years it had remained in the family of Habsburg, which as yet was not of any great territorial importance. It was indeed so poor a family that the contrast between Maximilian's pretentions and his resources had been one of the jokes of Europe during all the time he reigned (1493-1519). His only son had died in 1506 and the old emperor greatly desired, and was actively working for, the election of his eldest grandson Charles. This was the young man of eighteen who, since 1506, had been Duke of Burgundy, ruler that is of the Low Countries and of Franche Comte, and since 1516 King of Spain and of Naples. Upon Maximilian's death he would inherit the German domains of the Habsburgs, not only Austria proper but provinces which, for a hundred miles or more, had a common frontier with Venice. Were a prince so splendidly dowered with hereditary possessions to become emperor, who could say what new reality might not be infused into the ancient title? And how could the future of Italy not lie entirely in his hands? No pope could be indifferent to such a possible menace, nor could the Medici pope be indifferent to the effect upon his family's precarious hold on Florence of the appearance of an emperor who was already such a power in Italy.

It was, then, inevitable that Leo X should work against the candidature of the young King of Spain. The event was a striking demonstration how weak was the pope's political influence.

Maximilian died on January 20, 1519, there followed six months packed with diplomatic manoeuvre, and on June 28 Charles was unanimously elected. As the emperor Charles V he was to reign for thirty-seven momentous years.

In these manoeuvres Leo played his wonted part. The new King of France, Francis I, was also a candidate for the succession, and when, in April 1518, it became evident that there was some opposition in Germany to the election of the King of Spain, the pope began to negotiate with Francis and to persuade him to offer himself in opposition to Charles. On January 20, 1519, he made a treaty with Francis that was really a pledge of support; and, characteristically, he made a secret treaty, of the same kind, at the same time, with Charles. But from the moment when Maximilian's death made the matter urgent, Leo gave up his pretence and began strongly to oppose the King of Spain. He still, however, had a double game to play. The pope did not in reality wish to see the imperial prestige in the hands of France. This would have been as dangerous a combination as the other. The pope had a candidate of his own, the Elector of Saxony, Frederick the Wise, ever since, in September 1518, this prince had declared himself opposed to the election of Charles. And since that date Leo had been secretly working for him. He still, in the spring of 1519, worked for Francis, offering the cardinalate to two of the electors should the King of France be chosen, and a legateship for life to the third archbishop-elector -- the Archbishop of Mainz -- who was already a cardinal. He even went so far as to say that if they alone should vote for Francis -- three out of the seven electors -- he would recognise the election as valid. But he only received snubs from these ecclesiastical princes, who denied his power to interfere with the procedure of the election.

By the end of May the pope realised that there was no chance for Francis I. By now it was hardly safe for a Frenchman to show himself in Germany, and the pope's nuncio had to flee for his life from Mainz. Leo turned to work for his own candidate. On June 7 he wrote declaring that if the Elector of Saxony could persuade two others to vote for him, and would add to these his own vote, the pope would recognise him as emperor. The Elector was Luther's sovereign, and nine months before this he had firmly refused the pope's request to arrest Luther and send him to Rome. The imperial dignity was now to be his through the pope's intervention -- such was Leo's really childish plan -- and Frederick, in gratitude, would hand over the heresiarch. And to keep Frederick in good humour all these nine critical months, the pope had, to all seeming, let the business of Luther fall into the limbo of forgotten cases.

Nevertheless Frederick was not to be caught. By June 17 Leo understood how powerless he was. He would not, he said, run his head against a stone wall. He removed the long-standing papal prohibition -- it went back to Clement IV and the now far-off days of Charles of Anjou -- that his vassal the King of Naples should accept the imperial crown, and when the news of the election reached him, he offered the accustomed words of approbation and good will. What had he effected, except to root in the young king's mind an idea which he would never lose that popes were politicians, to be treated as such? and in the minds of Catholics in Germany a suspicion that religion, for the pope, was secondary to the needs of politics? Nor was this, even yet, the end of Leo's duplicity. In September (1519) he made yet another secret treaty with France, pledging himself not to recognise Charles as King of Naples so long as he retained the imperial crown. Then, relations with Francis -- youthful, arrogant, bullying, and as crafty as the pope -- growing steadily worse, the pope again negotiated simultaneously contradictory treaties with him and with the emperor (January-April 1521). The problem of Luther could not possibly be solved without the emperor's cooperation. The Spanish ambassador in Rome explained to Charles how useful the pope's fear of "a certain monk known as Brother Martin" might be to extort concessions; and, indeed, for the last eighteen months of the pope's life, anxiety about the new heretic wholly filled his mind.

Leo's death found him again at war, despite all diplomacy, and the ally of Charles V against France. The war began in the summer of 1521, and after some setbacks and delays that greatly tried the pope's anxious soul, the French were driven from Milan, and Piacenza and Parma were reconquered. This was better news, said Leo, than even the news of his election as pope. Arrangements were in progress for a great thanksgiving service, when the pope fell ill (November 26). He had taken a chill as he sat watching the fireworks with which his Swiss were celebrating the victory. In the evening of December 1 he suddenly collapsed, and by midnight he was dead, at forty-six.

The pope's sudden death caused a financial panic. For nearly nine years he had lived with the utmost extravagance; there had been the expenses of the war of Urbino to meet; and now the still heavier expenses of the war against France. To cover the deficit every expedient had been used. Over 1,300 new offices and distinctions had been created, the sale of which brought in a sum equal to two years of the annual revenue. By 1521 the total number of these saleable offices was 2,150, their capital value 3,000,000 ducats -- seven times the annual revenue. [ ] Great sums had been raised at the creation of the numerous cardinals, there had been the astronomical fines of the cardinals involved in the conspiracy of 1517. Then the pope borrowed -- from his friends, his officials, his cardinals, and the banks, paying as high an interest as 26 per cent for six months. And he pawned whatever he could, plate from his table, jewels, the silver statues from his chapel. Meanwhile the troops went unpaid, the brilliant corps of scholars recruited for the pope's university, the artists, even Raphael and San Gallo. The pope died 850,000 ducats in debt, owing amongst others the Bini bank 200,000, and -- one is glad to know it -- his friend and kinsman, and evil genius, Cardinal Lorenzo Pucci [ ] 150,000.

## 2. CHRISTIAN LIFE AND THOUGHT, 1471-1517

Just one hundred years separate the beginning of Martin Luther's assault on the papacy from the election of Martin V at Constance, the first pope for forty years recognised as such by the whole Church. During the last fifty years of that century, of the major anxieties which, from the time of that pope, never ceased to menace the peace of religion, one in particular, the problem how to make the Papal State a real guarantee of papal freedom of action, had thrust the rest well into the background. But the preoccupation of all the five popes from Sixtus IV to Leo X with this undoubtedly critical matter is not, of course, the whole history of the Church in their time. It will perhaps make that history more intelligible as a unity if, as we pass from the story of the diplomatic and military activities of these popes, something is said of all this as it appears related to the general political life of the t; me. For impatient as we may be at the spectacle of the pope turned prince, and impatient that the pope yielded so much to the pressure of the time, to be aware of the spirit of the time, and of its reality as a compelling force, is a first condition for understanding the gravity of that papal surrender.

That spirit was not a papal creation; the papacy is victim, here, of something older than itself. In these last generations of the Middle Ages there had thrust into the life of Christendom a force very well aware of its own nature, very clear about its objective, and which now began to impose upon the whole of that life its own peculiar pace and rhythm. " The stubborn persevering progress of the State in its slow reconquest of its attribute of sovereignty is, as the sixteenth century rises above the horizon, the essential phenomenon of public life. This is the sign under which the Reformation is born." [ ]

The hold upon the human spirit of its ancient enemy, the absolute state, had been loosened and then shaken off, once the Catholic Church overcame the empire of the Caesars. From time to time there had been desperate attempts by one prince or another to restore that state and reimpose its yoke, but always, so far, those attempts had been foiled. Now, from the end of the fifteenth century, the attempt to renew it became a more serious menace than ever, because the attempt was made under conditions more than ever favourable; the atomised states of the Middle Ages were now coalescing into the great monarchies of modern times. Since the marriage of the King of Aragon to the Queen of Castile in 1479 there was a united kingdom of Spain, and since 1505 its ruler was also King of Naples; since Louis XI (1461-1483) the French king was really master of all France; since the battle of Bosworth in 1485 there was a new monarchy in England. There still remained in face of the new assault the three great obstacles on which the earlier assaults had broken, the fifteen hundred years-old Catholic habit of mind, more especially the peculiarly Christian ideal of the sacredness of human personality, and finally the organisation of Christianity in that Catholic Church whose sovereign independence all princes and states acknowledged. But in the new states, leaders of new boldness and of a new political capacity are about to appear -- Charles V and Henry VIII for example, and their counsellors of genius. The scale of the conflict is suddenly magnified. It is in the modern world that the duel will be fought out. And popes of a new boldness and a new political capacity will also appear, popes also of a new personal rectitude and with something of the purer spirit of St. Gregory VII. [ ]

This needed combination, of courage and capacity and otherworldliness, neither the Renaissance popes had possessed, nor the most part of their predecessors for two hundred years. It ought not to need proving that once the administrative system created by the medieval popes was permanently established, the presence of very great natural gifts in the popes was imperative for the well-being of religion. [ ] The pope is now very truly Dominus Ecclesiae, chef d'orchestre and composer too, since he has so centralised his administration and taken so much even of local affairs into his hands. Lacking a commanding intelligence in its chief, a machine so elaborate tends to become the sport of officials, its operation a matter of precedent merely and routine. In a state called into existence solely to promote the spiritual, such mechanisation means stagnation akin to death. Of the thirty-four popes whose reigns cover this period between St. Thomas and Luther, how many are there who rise above the mediocre? What has the office a right to demand of them? Holiness -- of course; then competent learning, in the sacred doctrine first of all, and next in the traditional lore of the religious ruler's art, the canon law; then judgment, and ability. Of all these thirty-four popes none has, so far, been canonised, [ ] but four have their place in the calendar as beatified. [ ] That almost all these popes are recruited from officials in the curia is but the continuance, in the closing centuries of the Middle Ages, of a most ancient, and very natural, tradition. The time had not yet come when the cardinalate was regularly conferred on resident diocesan bishops. It is only now, in the fifteenth century, that we see the beginning of this practice. The cardinal was still, in fact, the actual counsellor and trusted man of the pope, and the cardinal lived where the pope lived. [ ] And of course the overwhelming majority of the popes were chosen from among the cardinals. [ ] Of the first popes in our period, those who close the great century of Innocent III, four had risen to fame in the great world of Scholasticism. [ ] Boniface VIII, renewing the tradition of the first half of his century, is an eminent canonist; and so are almost all the French popes whose reigns make up the tale of Avignon. The great exception here is Benedict XII -- one of the most competent theological scholars of his generation; and he is the last constructive legislator among the popes, on the grand scale, until the Council of Trent. With the Schism the decline in personality is very marked. The only really outstanding figures of the century that follows it are the two humanist popes, Nicholas V and Pius II; and their reigns are too short, and their bodies too broken, for their personality to be really effective. Then comes the lamentable time at which the story has arrived, an age inaugurated indeed -- such is the incredible fact -- by a Franciscan [ ] who was also a theologian of real merit, to whom succeed in turn the weakling Giovanni Cybo, a competent bureaucrat -- Rodrigo Borgia, a lifelong political intriguer of no particular training -- Giuliano della Rovere, and the superficial dilettante Leo X, who closes the series.

Reviewing all this history the impression deepens that consistently, in one generation after another, the popes fail to read the signs of the times, and a study of the papal personalities helps to explain the failure. They do indeed discern a mortal foe of all they stand for in, for example, Marsiglio of Padua (though, so it would seem, they judge Ockham, as a speculative thinker that is to say, far too lightly). Repeatedly they do indeed point out to the faithful, with unmistakable clarity and vigour, how dangerous to faith Marsiglio's theories are; and to the best of their ability they prevent the circulation of his highly mischievous book. But never do they meet, with any constructive organisation of Catholic thought, the important fact which the Defensor Pacis and its sequel should surely have revealed to them, the fact namely that lay resentment at the cleric's desire to control the public life of Christendom is now beginning to crystallise into a system of "philosophy," a Weltanschauung even; and that Marsiglio speaks for a whole multitude of disgruntled, and educated, Catholic contemporaries. We are, in fact, here making early acquaintance with what is to become for centuries one of the permanent diseases of Christendom, the anti-clerical (and even anti-religious) spirit of the educated middle classes, burning somberly below deceptive ashes, its existence ignored, and implicitly denied, by a clerical regime that seems only aware of the surface of Catholic life.

Thinkers of Marsiglio's calibre have always been rare, in any generation. And among those who, in his own age and the succeeding century, fed their discontent on his theories, there were no doubt far more who bandied about the catchwords of his doctrine than had ever stud; ed the learned evangel itself -- as, in our own time, there are far more Marxists than there were ever actual students of Das Kapital. Such " Marsiglini " as these last would have disappeared speedily enough if the visible abuses in the ecclesiastical system which bred their discontent had really been corrected. Heresy, or a professed sympathy with the heretical reformer, is, in its early stages, only too often, no more than a readily-snatched-at chance to "rationalise" the concrete grievance against those in authority. It was the terrible, and lasting, misfortune of the Church that in these centuries, even when sincere reformers sat on the papal throne they merely tinkered with the trouble; reform rarely went beyond trite exhortations, and new decrees that re-enacted the old decrees; and never did it explore the roots of the abuses, consider the question whether the whole ecclesiastical machine did not stand in some need of re-designing. These popes, it is often said, had other things to do, they lived with a hundred crises crowding upon them. This is true; and it is the whole tragedy, that amid the welter of urgent daily business, with the danger of a real disruption of Christendom threatening for several generations, they had to make a choice where best to be active, and -- allowing them the best intentions and a real good will -- their choice too often relegated to the secondary what is the principal task of popes at all times.

In some respects, one is tempted to think, the medieval pope had an impossible task before him. Nothing could, of course, be further from reality than the picture of the Middle Ages as a golden time of universal peace and charity. The turbulence is chronic, and it is by the immense progress realised since the dark chaos of the ninth and tenth centuries that the achievement should be judged. Nor was the Holy See ever really able to exert all the needed control. The eleventh-century popes successfully drew closer the links that bound to Rome the local episcopate, as a first means of purifying it and of strengthening the local religious leader against the local tyrant. But communications --

the most material factor of all -- were never, in all these centuries, as good as they needed to be for the centralisation really to function steadily and regularly. What was accomplished is, indeed, more than remarkable. But it was not enough; and more was scarcely possible. So, for generations, the huge affair creaked and groaned, and it broke down continually. Nor did the episcopate, as a whole, ever come up to what Rome desired -- and indeed needed -- that it should be. It was never, as a whole, so able or so apostolic as its Roman chiefs. The popes were far indeed from having that freedom in appointing to sees the men of their choice which, to-day, we take for granted. Time and again vested interests were too strong for them, the will of the princes in Spain and France and England, the determination of the nobles in the chapters of Germany. All through the Middle Ages the popes are building a system -- and finding, all the time, opposition to their plans from vested interests, not infrequently the episcopate. Some popes are less able than others, than fifty sees were given to youths below the canonical age for consecration. These included the primatial sees of Poland, Hungary, and Scotland. Leo X gave Lisbon (and two other sees at the same time) to a child of eight, and Milan to another of eleven: both were children of reigning princes. [ ] Of the eighteen cardinals who elected Sixtus IV in 1471, four were non-resident diocesan bishops. At the next conclave (1484) the absentees were ten out of twenty-five, in 1492 they were eleven out of twenty-three, and in 1503 twenty-six out of thirty-seven. This grave abuse was, in the Sacred College, fast becoming the rule. Everywhere, by this time, there were powerful clerical vested interests to oppose reforms, not indeed by voting them down, but by systematically neglecting to put the decrees into execution. This is particularly true of the prince-bishops of Germany, of the episcopate in France, of the College of Cardinals and the Roman Curia, which last institution was to defy for years even the zeal of the reforming popes of the Counter Reformation. [ ]

Nothing could be more important than that there should be good bishops in all the seven hundred sees of the universal Church -- and that the popes should concern themselves with the quality of the men nominated would seem the most elementary duty of their universal administration. [ ] But the popes must first of all enjoy, in fact, a real freedom to appoint whom they chose. The sphere in which they were thus free was, all through the fifteenth century, steadily shrinking; and it shrank in part through the acts of the popes themselves. To free the future of the episcopate from the malign influence of such close corporations as the cathedral chapters had very often become, the popes built up the new system of appointment by papal provision. And now, as the rights of chapters to elect became a dim memory, the princes began to covet the power to name bishops which princes of the age before Hildebrand had enjoyed. At times the popes granted the right -- well limited -- as a favour or a privilege, and at times they did so in scarcely veiled surrender to threats. The period of the princely popes was naturally rich ill such surrenders.

Already, in England, by the middle of the fifteenth century, the Statute of Provisors had paved the way for a system where the popes always came to name as bishop the man whom the king recommended. And the emperor had gained from Eugene IV in the last days of the Council of Basel, and its anti-pope, extensive rights over half a dozen important sees. [ ] In France the Pragmatic Sanction of 1438, often condemned and ceaselessly reprobated, functioned nevertheless, and the popes had to put up with it, since to fight the king would have renewed all the chaos of the forty years' Schism, and possibly lost France to Catholic unity in the fifteenth century as so much of Germany was lost to it in the sixteenth.

Sixtus IV was then, once more, only typical of his decadent century when in 1473 he made over to the emperor the right to present to some three hundred benefices, and in 1478 increased the number of sees in his patronage. In 1476 the Dukes of

Saxony were similarly favoured and in 1479 the city of Zurich. Three years later, in 1482, the new Spanish monarchy also, after a fight in which the Catholic kings threatened to revive the Council scheme, was given new rights to name bishops. The next pope, Innocent VIII, although he fought off the claims of Portugal to hold up papal decisions and appointments, was defeated in his battle with Florence and other Italian states about the right to tax church revenues; and he further extended the rights of Spain when he gave to the crown rights to name bishops in the kingdom of Granada and in Sicily too, and indulged them in Sicily with that right to veto episcopal appointments which was to harass the popes in that kingdom down to our own time. [ ] Alexander VI has not to his charge, it would seem, any such surrenders; but Julius II, caught in the toils of political necessity, gave Spain extensive rights of patronage (in the West Indies) in 1508; and Portugal also profited from the mistaken liberality of Leo X, who gave the king various rights over the three military orders of the kingdom. The Lutheran crisis, in which Leo's reign ran out, was of course a golden opportunity for the princes of Germany to extort concessions.

The newest phase of this surrender of direct control over the life of the local church, the most mischievous of all, was the appointment of one of its bishops, a cardinal, as legate a latere for the whole country, with faculties so ample that he became a kind of vice-pope and a final court of appeal. So Georges d'Amboise, Archbishop of Rouen, was appointed for France by Julius II in 1503; and so Wolsey, Archbishop of York, was appointed for England by Leo X and re-appointed, for life, by Clement VII. And Albrecht of Brandenburg was offered a like appointment for Germany. This mischief was all the greater because these prelates were the principal ministers of their sovereigns; it was the king's prime minister who was made the vice-pope, and he received his powers at the king's request. The one man was, locally, supreme in Church [ ] and state, free to manage the whole as a unity, for the king's profit. And meanwhile the local church would grow accustomed to the Roman authority being no more than a distant splendour.

It was upon a papacy already slowly stripping itself -- under compulsion -- of its control of the distant provinces, that the new blow from Germany would presently fall. The most striking surrenders, however -- because not made to satisfy powerful prelates but creative of new institutions -- are those of Sixtus IV to Spain and of Leo X to France, the establishment in 1479 of the Spanish Inquisition, and the Concordat of 1516 with Francis I.

The story has already been told [ ] of the first establishment of the Inquisition, two hundred and fifty years before the time of Sixtus IV -- a special new tribunal set up, for the detection and punishment of concealed heretics, in a place and at a time when the doctrines propagated and the hidden organisation of believers were considered, and correctly, to be a real danger to civilised life, and a menace to be destroyed before it destroyed all that was good and natural and free. The Spain of 1470-1500 was, in some ways, such another land as the Languedoc of the Albigensian wars. Here, too, was a large body with non-Christian traditions, Jews and Mohammedans; and here, too, it was suspected, there were among the Catholic population, and amongst those highly placed, many who at heart were still, like their ancestors, Jews and Mohammedans. For centuries, a] most from the morrow of the Moorish conquest of Spain in the eighth century, the great effort of Christian Spain to throw out the infidels had never really ceased. Never had the various Christian races accepted the conquest as a permanent state of things to which they must now be resigned. For nearly seven hundred years, in that grim land, the fight had gone on, with very varying fortunes, of course, but with steady recovery of territory from the Moors. It was the great national achievement, the epic and the boast of a proud and military people. By the end of the fifteenth century only the Kingdom of Granada remained in Mohammedan hands, a strip of territory across the south-east corner of Spain, Granada its capital. In 1492 the armies of Ferdinand and Isabella conquered Granada too. For the first time since 711 the whole of Spain was under Christian rule.

The reorganisation of the Inquisition in Spain as a means to rid the country of crypto-Jews and crypto-Moors -- Marranos and Moriscos -- was the act of Sixtus IV, [ ] done at the request of Ferdinand and Isabella. The chief novelty was that it left the choice of the inquisitors to the sovereign. In September 1479 the new tribunal began its operations, and very soon appeals against the way it worked began to pour into Rome. Whereupon the pope protested [ ] to the Catholic Kings, and reminded them of their duty to be merciful. But he did not refuse their petition for the extension of the system to Castile and Leon, and he consented that, for the future, the appeals to his own tribunal should be heard and finally decided in Spain, by the Archbishop of Seville (1483). But any decisions given in Rome were to be valid in Spain. The next step was the appointment of a Grand Inquisitor, who should be the pope's representative, and hear the appeals made to Rome from the tribunals in Spain. On the presentation of Ferdinand, the pope named to the new office the Dominican Thomas Torquemada, whose name has since been, for many people, almost a synonym for the tribunal he directed. Then the kingdom of Aragon, also, was brought under its authority. The Inquisition was by now an ecclesiastical machine set up by the pope's authority, and manned by ecclesiastics -- but at the king's service and, in fact, very much what the king wanted it to be. The day would come when the king would use it for all purposes that seemed good to him.

Once the new tribunal got to work there was a steady exodus of Jews from Spain, to Portugal and to Rome, where the popes received them kindly enough, to the no small discontent of the Spanish sovereigns. In Spain there was for a time a state of war, the high peak of which was the skilfully planned murder of one of the inquisitors, a Canon Regular, Peter Arbues (September 15,

1485). [ ] Then, in 1492, it was determined to expel from Spain all the Jews who were not Catholics. They were given four months to choose between conversion and exile. Whereupon there was another exodus, and a certain number of conversions, whose sincerity no doubt varied from case to case.

The year that followed this edict saw the election of one of Ferdinand's own subjects as pope -- Alexander VI. For a time the spirit of Spain seemed about to take hold of Rome too. There were arrests of suspected crypto-Jews and trials. But all the accused cleared themselves, or recanted, and there were no severities save the imprisonment of a bishop and his son. Alexander VI was far from being a persecutor; the reason for this activity was political, the need to reassure Ferdinand of the pope's sympathy for Spain. But Alexander stands recorded as granting to the king for his Inquisition, privileges that went far beyond what a pope should have granted. [ ] His successor, Julius II, had to see Ferdinand introduce the new system into his kingdom of Sicily (1500). But when the king went a step further, and in 1510 brought Naples, too, under it, the people resisted violently and successfully, and the pope is thought secretly to have encouraged the resistance. So great a diminution of papal authority so near to Rome would hardly have been welcome to such a pope as Julius II. Leo X, however, returned to the policy of surrender to Spain, and after the election of the new king, Charles, to be emperor also, he withdrew (though very reluctantly) those briefs of his predecessors which hampered the king's use of the Inquisition in Aragon.

It was to matter enormously to the fortunes of the Catholic Church that, in the coming century of the Reformation, the monarch who ruled Spain and the Low Countries and a good half of Italy, and who was also emperor in Germany, remained true to the old religion. But it was a very real tragedy that, from the beginning of his reign, Charles V had reason to expect from popes, compliance, and, indeed, subservience on the grand scale.

And had Leo X -- for example -- persisted in his first refusal of concessions about the Inquisition, Charles could have pointed to the pope's recent surrender to France, the greatest surrender of direct control which the papacy has ever made, the Concordat of 1516.

The Concordat, a great papal surrender, it is true, but one that was balanced by an important royal renunciation, was a kind of sequel to the political revolution in northern Italy that followed on the great French victory of Marignano in 1515. The unlucky Leo X had been on the wrong side yet once again, as his cousin Clement VII was to be on the wrong side when, ten years late at Pavia, the French were beaten. The meeting with Francis I at Bologna in December 1515 was arranged, as Leo explicitly said, so that the pope could throw himself on the French king's mercy and remind him of the pope's claims on a victor who was yet a Catholic. But when, on December 11, Francis I suddenly asked the pope to confirm the Pragmatic Sanction of 1438, the scope of the negotiations, and their tone, was changed entirely. The great question that had divided one council after another -- the question of the relation of the papacy to the episcopate -- and which ever since the days of Peter de Luna had seethed and fermented in the churches of France especially, was now placed fairly and squarely before the pope. To confirm the act of Bourges was to acknowledge as good in law all those decrees of Basel which the popes had never confirmed and always repudiated, and it was to accept explicitly the theory that in the Church the General Council is the pope's master; it would also be an acknowledgment of the right of the king to regulate Church affairs -- without any authorisation from the pope. Not even Leo X could confirm such an usurpation, not even for Francis I after Marignano. The pope countered the embarrassing demand with the offer of a concordat -- a treaty about ecclesiastical matters. Francis accepted the idea, and soon the legal experts of both parties were busy discussing the bases of the pact, the king's chancellor, Antoine Duprat, one of the most celebrated jurists of the day [ ] and, for Leo, the two cardinals Lorenzo Pucci and Pietro Accolti.

By February 1516 the principles of the arrangement were mutually agreed; and no sooner were they known than opposition began to show, from all sides. The king was to abrogate the Pragmatic Sanction of 1438, and the pope was to grant him the full right to nominate to all the sees and abbeys of the kingdom; the whole system of rights to future appointments -- expectations, reservations -- was to be abolished entirely. From the French side came strong protests, the jurists objecting to the surrender of the position assumed in 1438, the university hostile to the implied repudiation of what it had achieved at Constance and Basel, the higher clergy opposed to the final disappearance of the system of elections. The pope had to face at Rome criticism that was just as strong, from the cardinals, who thought the scale of the concessions to the King of France extravagant and dangerous. For another six months both the principals laboured hard to persuade their own supporters, and the opposition from the other camp; and in the interval, the pope won the important concession that the Concordat would contain the king's explicit repudiation and annulment of the Pragmatic Sanction.

On August 18, 1516, the Concordat was signed: it regulated the religious life of France down to the Revolution. As finally agreed it gave the king the right to present to the pope for his confirmation the future bishops of the ninety-three sees of the kingdom and the abbots and priors of the 527 monasteries. Those presented for bishoprics were to be twenty-seven years of age and graduates in theology or law, those nominated for the monastic benefices were to be at least twenty-three and to belong to the religious order to which the abbey or priory belonged. If the nominee was a blood relation of the king, or a nobleman, he need not possess the stipulated qualifications. So there passed into the hands of the king, the all but absolute control of nomination to posts whose total income was almost equal to that of the state itself -- and to the French state this was, in 1516, the most important element in its victory. But it was not by virtue of any royal presentation that the bishop was bishop; the bishop's right still came through his appointment by the pope. If the pope, henceforward, placed his authority in this matter at the service of the king he did not, for all that, abdicate that authority; nor did the king deny that authority. Concession may have been pushed to the full extent of grave abuse, but there was never -- on the part of king or pope -- even a hint of the graver matter of a breach in the doctrinal trust. The difference between a system such as this and that which, twenty years later, the English king who saw the Concordat signed was to erect for his own realm, is one of kind, not of degree.

The system of expectations and reservations was abolished, and it was agreed that, save for causae maiores, all appeals from episcopal tribunals were to be heard in France. There were, however, two notable omissions in the text. Nothing was said about the proposed abolition of that papal tax on collations to benefices called annates; and there was no mention of the theory of the supremacy of the General Council, no explicit repudiation of it, and therefore every chance for those who later would wish to revive the theory.

At the end of the year, on December 19, 1516, the pope brought the Concordat before the General Council then sitting at Rome. It was now set out in the form of a bull -- Divina Disponente Clementia -- and the pope had the bull read in the council, meaning that it should go to the world as the council's act also. Even now, and in Leo's very presence, opposition showed itself. But a speech from the pope on the advantages that must come from the French king's surrender of such a weapon as the act of 1438, won general assent to the bull. And of no less effect was the fact that, in the same session of the council, immediately after the bull ratifying the Concordat, there was read a second bull --

Pastor Aeternus -- which condemned and utterly annulled the Pragmatic Sanction, repudiated the claim that a General Council (Basel) had sanctioned it, and took occasion to affirm with great energy that the pope's sole and supreme right to control General Councils was the age-long traditional belief of the Church. [ ]

These bulls were sent to Francis I together, and the king, in the next fourteen months, had to fight hard before he finally beat down the alliance of jurists, the university and the higher clergy -- the university of Paris even going so far as to demand an appeal to a future council, the infallible council now in session not being of the university's opinion. However, under the strongest pressure from the king, the Parlement of Paris finally gave way, and on March 22, 1518, registered the Concordat as law. Three weeks later, on April 14, the king by royal edict repealed the Pragmatic Sanction.

On balance, was the Concordat loss or gain for the cause of religion? We inevitably study the act through our knowledge of the way the French kings abused it -- and were by compliant, necessity-driven popes, allowed to abuse it. Had the scheme been fairly worked, by kings not necessarily saints like Louis IX but even faintly interested in the spiritual, or had the times been such that popes could have refused the impossible names presented to them, the new system might not have done more harm than the old arrangement under which, for a good hundred years and more, the elective regime in France had bred a rich progeny of feuds, riots and schisms. [ ] There was never again to be a St. Louis, few indeed were the kings who in the next two hundred years were even respectably religious, and for the first fifty years of the new system [ ] the kings were allowed to name whom they would, with disastrous results to more than one French see and with indescribable results to the life of the religious houses. These are results which concern rather the later history of the Church, and which cannot, of course, be laid to the charge of Leo X. One last remark may be allowed which also concerns that later history, namely that the story of the French opposition to the Concordat of 1516 reveals the strong, deep-rooted attachment of many powerful interests in France to the idea that the pope ought to be controlled and managed in his government of the Church. This is an idea that never disappears; it continues to be active, indeed to be a dominant force in French life, down to 1789, and beyond.

The tale of what these popes of the generation that bred Luther and Zwingli and Crammer and Henry VIII, as well as Fisher and More and Erasmus and Cajetan, did for the reform of abuses and the regeneration of the life of the Church is, alas, soon told. In the work of their classic historian the religious activities of Sixtus IV, Innocent VIII, Alexander VI, Julius II and Leo X fill but a few dozen pages out of thousands. The thirteen years' reign of Sixtus IV, whose chief achievement was the bull Quoniam regnantium cura that never got beyond the stage of being drafted, produced some half-dozen briefs to various monasteries bidding them amend their ways, "isolated decrees", and that was all. Under Innocent VIII there was no reform of ecclesiastical abuses.

Alexander VI, it may be thought, was hardly in a position to inspire belief that reform was necessary or that good living mattered. The great event of his reign, from this point of view, was the appointment in 1497, on the morrow of the murder of the Duke of Gandia, of a commission of cardinals to draft a scheme of general reforms. That scheme, worked out in detail through months of competent labour, was indeed never put into force, but it survives and, in the long train of curial weaknesses listed for correction, it is a terrible indictment. In the crucial business of episcopal appointments simony is to be put down, reservations abolished and also the bogus coadjutorships by which bishops secured, in their lifetime, that their see would pass to a relative; and bishops, it is laid down, are not to be translated against their will. The cardinals' way of life is to be altered; gaming and hunting are to cease, and none is to have a household of more than eighty, nor more than thirty of a mounted escort. Musicians, actors and youths are to be banished from their palaces, and there is to be no corruption in the conclave. Then the various curial offices are scrutinised, and in all of them, the bull insists, the opportunities for "graft" are to be abolished. Absentee bishops are to be punished and so are those who keep concubines. A new severity awaits "apostate" religious -- that is to say those who have abandoned their monasteries -- while, on the other hand, it is provided that monastic vows made by children are not binding. Princes are no longer to be granted tithes. Other evils noted are the granting of abbeys in commendam, the overriding of the rights of the patrons of livings, the changing of the destinations of pious legacies, and the alteration of conditions laid down in wills about pious foundations. So the list goes on, 127 headings in all, that cover every aspect of curial practice. The programme of things to be put right might have daunted St. Gregory VII himself. Alexander VI went no further than to read it.

Julius II is the author of one really great reform, the bull (1503) which declared that simony in the election of a pope invalidated the election. [ ] He, too, appointed a reform commission of six cardinals, in 1504; but it is not known whether they even got so far as to draft a scheme. And finally, Julius, who was originally a Friar Minor, gave some attention to the condition of the religious orders. He encouraged Cajetan in his efforts to reform the Dominicans, and he strove, unsuccessfully, to reunite the warring parties in his own order.

Leo X, it may well be, "never gave a thought to reform on the great scale which had become necessary." But like Sixtus IV and Julius II, he did give some attention to the state of the monasteries and convents. Nine of his briefs that treat of this most serious weakness are listed and many more await publication. [ ] And, successful where Julius II had failed, Leo X in 1517 brought to a final end the contentions about the rule which had divided the sons of St. Francis ever since the death of the founder. It has been told how John XXII cut the knot by measures which amounted almost to a new foundation of the order, a remodelling in which that attitude to ownership which was the speciality of St. Francis had no longer any official standing. But the spirit of St. Francis it was beyond the power of any regulation utterly to extinguish. Very soon a new movement for the primitive observance had begun within the remodelled order. It had the great advantage over the older " Spiritual" movement that it was not bound up with such unorthodox theories as the reveries of Joachim of Flora. Nor did those attached to it maintain that their special way of living the Franciscan life was the sole way of salvation. The new Observants -- as they were called -- were in nothing more truly the brethren of the first friars than in their charity. Their more rigorous interpretation of the ideal was never a stick with which pleasantly to belabour the rest of their brethren, and gradually the new movement gained a permanent hold in one convent after another. Whole convents were gained over to it, great saints appeared in its ranks, Bernadine of Siena, for example, and John of Capistrano, and James of the March, preachers and itinerant missionaries of immense power and wide influence. The friars who followed the Observance were gradually allowed to be organised, within the order, under a special vicar of their own, and the independence of their General was now carefully protected by one pope after another. By the end of the fifteenth century the majority of the Friars Minor were Observants, and the problem before the order now was rather the fate of the Conventuals, the official Franciscans -- one might say -- ever since the time of John XXII. Here was a paradoxical state of things indeed. Leo X solved it by separating the two types of friars, and organising each in a separate religious order, both of which were to be called, and with equal right, Friars Minor. But it was to the General of the Observants that he ordered that the seal of the order should be made over, and the title "successor of St. Francis" be given.

This reorganisation of the great order was perhaps the most beneficent act of Leo's reign. Two other laws that call for mention are his bull forbidding the Latins in the East to change or suppress or hinder the Greek ritual of the Catholics of the eastern churches, and the bull against the enslavement of the natives of the newly discovered Americas.

More spectacular than any of these, however, was the General Council held in the Lateran 1512-1517. Its most important act was a dogmatic definition, about the immortality of the human soul, which explicitly referred to the relations between natural knowledge and revealed, a vital topic with Christian thinkers for centuries now, and one on which St. Thomas had long ago -- all too unheeded -- said the decisive word. Of the plight that befell Catholic thought, once it went back on the great progress realised by the Dominican saint's theory of knowledge and his careful distinction of the spheres of reason and faith, something has already been said. And before we come to the Lateran definition, and to the other activities of the council, that account needs to be supplemented by some reference to the last phases of the philosophical and theological decline, in the century since the Council of Constance, and to a new birth of the thought of St. Thomas.

For the generation to which the fathers of Constance belonged, and to its successor, it was Gerson who, undoubtedly, stood out as the great religious thinker and preacher and writer. [ ] No other had anything like the prestige of this most attractive man who had been Chancellor of the university of Paris in the hour when the university really dominated the whole life of Christendom. He had played his part faithfully at Constance, he had shown himself a man of really pious life and marvellously void of ambition. All through the last twelve years of his life, when, an exile at Lyons, his chief occupation was the religious formation of the children he gathered round him from the streets, Gerson continued to influence the whole Church. As a thinker he must be classed, like Peter d'Ailly, among the Nominalists. But Gerson was not by nature a speculative. It was the practical aspect of religious truth that most attracted him, the rules of good Christian living, the itinerary of the soul's way to God. Hence in Gerson's sermons and in his writings there is a great deal of needed correction of current popular errors and superstitions, and a merciless exposure of bogus saints and mystics.

This practical direction was his greatest service to the spiritual life of his own time, and indeed of all the following century. The forty years of the Schism had been a very springtime of false visionaries and crazy doctrines about the mystical life -- about the inner life of the soul in communion with its Creator and its relation to ordinary conduct. The tide of false mysticism was, indeed, rising so high as to threaten to swamp the ideas of genuine Christian piety. And, usually, the danger was a development of that Beghard teaching which, through all the later Middle Ages, was at work, secretly and persistently, never really out of sight, a kind of caricature of the classic Christian idea of asceticism and prayer as the way to union with God.

What the Beghards were can be read in the great condemnation of their doctrines decreed at the General Council of Vienne in 1311. Man can in this life, they taught, attain to such a degree of perfection that he becomes unable to sin. When he reaches this stage, man is no longer bound to pray nor to fast, his sense nature being now so perfectly subjected to his spirit and his reason that he can freely grant his body all it desires. Again, once man has reached this stage he is not bound to obey any human authority, nor to keep any commandments of the Church. Where there is the spirit of God there is liberty, and the practice of the virtues is a mark of the imperfect man: the perfect soul emancipates itself from the virtues. From which seemingly remote abstractions the Beghard comes down to everyday life with a practical illustration and example, also condemned by the Council, to wit that whoever kisses a woman, unless led by sexual impulse, sins mortally, while no sexual act is sinful if it is done from a sexual impulse; such acts are especially free from blame if they are a yielding to temptation. [ ]

These are ideas that have never ceased to have a certain vogue in out-of-the-way places, giving life to a host of cults that might be called "curious". In Gerson's time, and for long after, they were much more than that. The early years of the Reformation were to see such theories the inspiration of armed hordes and carrying all before them, the basis of the new Jerusalem, established in concrete fact in the lands beyond the Rhine.

Gerson [ ] has left behind a mass of writing about this urgent matter. There are works of instruction and direction for those who feel called to set all else aside but the life of prayer, and there are treatises which criticise and attack the false mysticism and explain by what signs the tendencies towards it are to be recognised. To the exaggeration of those who declare "We can know nothing about God", he opposes the fact that the Faith teaches us much about Him. He will not allow that the contemplative life is meant for all; the divinely created differences of temperament are facts that must be reckoned with and allowed for, and differences also of duties. He notes acutely, as a matter that can be observed every day, the contemplative's temptation to be his own guide. Everyone knows, he says, how obstinately they hold to their own ideas, to false and absurd ideas at times; and how much more easily than others they fall victims to such ideas. The great examples here are the Beghards. Another pitfall is sentimentality. There are many who tend to imagine themselves devot, and called to the life of contemplation by experiences that are nothing else than their own emotional upheavals; if such is the basis of their spiritual life the end is certain, and Gerson notes how often false mysticism and a certain looseness about sex-morality go together. At the other extreme are those interested with a merely intellectual interest in the activities of the spiritual life, in prayer, and devotion; and contemplation as human activities and for their own sake, experts in the art of conversing on these topics, hard, proud, insubordinate amid all their spiritual learning. There are the quietists who neglect everything to drift in their spiritual day dreams, and those who assert that the last thing there is any need to be anxious about is one's own salvation.

Against all these chronic maladies -- now for the first time studied, as it were systematically, on the grand scale, and therapeutically, Gerson's remedies are simple. The first need of the contemplative is knowledge; true knowledge, to be got from the approved doctors and the teaching of the Church. As for the credentials of the new prophets, the moral standard of the disciples is one good test of the master's orthodoxy. But the only real judge whether the mystic's ideas are orthodox is the theologian. Finally, Gerson constructs a whole theology of practical spiritual direction, basing himself largely on St. Bonaventure [ ] -- whom he so closely resembles -- and on the writer still held to be Denis the Areopagite.

Nothing could be wiser, more orthodox, than this practical apostolate of Jean Gerson. He was by nature practical -- not a speculative. His speculative ideas he took from his age, and, like his age, in one fundamental matter Gerson was seriously in error. The essence of morality, for him as for others of the family of Ockham, was in the divine will. Actions that are good are only good because God has so decreed. Gerson was not the only theologian to be saying this in the early years of the fifteenth century, but no other had anything like his prestige, and none, for generations, had his influence as a moralist and spiritual guide. It is very rare that active minds who turn their back on speculative thought -- who, for one reason or another, refuse to think things out, or to have things thought out for them -- escape serious blunders; and these, only too often, vitiate all that their generous practical activity produces. Gerson was not alone in his error of enthroning the practical reason above the speculative, and in every age since there have been hundreds to imitate him. In his case this mistaken line of conduct made it impossible for the greatest spiritual force of the time really to be certain about the bases of his own action (and of the action he urged upon others); and it helped on, very considerably, the attitude to speculative theology now becoming fashionable among men who proposed to lead a holy life.

Jean Gerson died in 1429, living just long enough to hear of the marvellous events that centred round St. Joan of Arc and to express his belief in the reality of her visions. Four years later, at the Council of Basel, the new genius appeared who was to carry on his work as an apostle, a reformer and a Catholic thinker. This was the Rhinelander, Nicholas of Cusa, and here was another to whom the best traditions of scientific theology had not spoken, or had spoken in vain. Of the work of reform which this great ecclesiastic accomplished, some account has been given already. What of his role as a teacher and guide of the Christian intelligence?

Nicholas of Cusa is the first complete species of the Renaissance man born and bred north of the Alps. Though his first formation, his professional equipment, is juristic, there is no learning that he has not sampled and delighted in. He sympathises with all the anxieties of his age, and willingly slaves to remove them. He possesses the new cult for the ancient literatures, and he has distinguished himself beyond measure by discovering twelve lost comedies of Plautus. He is a scientist also, and perhaps the first to put out the complete hypothesis of the revolution of the earth round the sun. In his writings all the elements of the varied intellectual life of the time find their place.

The two leading, original, ideas in what -- yet once again -- is a practical doctrine, a programme to be followed, a methodology rather than a philosophy, are the docta ignorantia as the beginning of wisdom and the vision of the " coincidence of contradictories " as its peak. The intelligence -- the reasoning reason -- is the lowest of man's powers of knowledge, and it is not able to grasp reality. Knowledge of its own powerlessness is the highest knowledge it can achieve -- this is docta ignorantia. Why this powerlessness? Such is the nature, in the first place, of truth, and next, of knowledge. All knowledge can but be approximation and conjecture. But in God all can be known, and in Him can be seen the ultimate coincidence of contradictories. The great good for man, then, is to come to the point where he will see this coincidence, and thus really know; and man arrives at this by rising above the reasoning intelligence, and by knowing through his higher faculty of intuition. How is all this to be? Nicholas does not know; but he continues to "speculate," to gather views, to try out ideas; and, in a matter where words are of so little service, he makes use of symbols, and especially of geometrical symbols. All things are in God, and what is implicit in God becomes explicit in His creation. Every thing is a reflection of every other thing, all is contained in all. Of no creature is this so true as of man; and man, if ever he comes to a full understanding of himself, will know and possess all else. There are many ideas suggested here that will have a famous history in later centuries, but it will be a history well outside the tradition of thought that is Christian. From Nicholas of Cusa as a thinker the cause of the classic synthesis of Faith and Reason, labouring now all these years in adversity, had not much to hope.

Nicholas of Cusa is the last great "original" of the Middle Ages. Next, in order of time, there appear those Florentine Platonists [ ] who have been noted in their more fundamental character as men of letters. And the century closes with Gabriel Biel, [ ] who would be a celebrity for this, if for nothing else, that he is the one scholastic for whom Luther seems to have had a good word, the master indeed of Luther's own masters. It cannot be said that there is anything strikingly new about Master Gabriel, but he is beyond all doubt an Ockhamist; and, a teacher of great personality, he imposed the via moderna upon the new university of Tubingen when, in 1484, a very old man, he was appointed its rector and began to teach theology there.

Gabriel Biel, in whose commentary on the Sentences Ockham's theology yet once again makes its appearance, "so openly, so systematised, and so completed," [ ] the chief theological luminary of the last half of the fifteenth century, is, however, the last Catholic theologian of his school; and this is perhaps his real significance for whoever studies the history of Catholic thought. The revolution was indeed already preparing, in the very years when Biel so successfully "Ockhamised" the theological teaching at Tubingen, that was to destroy the via moderna once and for all, so that it sank from Catholic theology with scarcely a trace. What was, in fact, imminent was the return of St. Thomas, and the first sign of the coming event was the substitution of the Summa Theologica for Peter Lombard, as the basic text of all theological teaching, by the Dominican masters in the University of Pavia in 1480, and the sanction given to this by the Dominican Chapter-General at Cologne in 1483. [ ]

Meanwhile the via moderna continued in the enjoyment of its primacy, and for a long time yet such all-important principles as, for example, what has been called Voluntarism, continued to dominate fashionable theological thought. As we are about to see this principle developed in quite a new way, by another professor of theology, in yet another new German university, Brother Martin Luther, and fashioned into an evangel that really is something new in Christian experience, the mention of Gabriel Biel is an opportunity to recall how the principle appeared in the last years before it was associated with the great heresiarch and his new kind of religion. And lest these controversies seem to be about abstractions, and remote from human life, the reminder may be allowed that they in fact concern the very basis of religious life, and that theology, however speculative, is in fact the science of salvation. [ ]

We can take as a fair statement of the essence of the Voluntarist's view of God and man's relation with Him, the proposition of Duns Scotus, Omne aliud a Deo est bonum quia a Deo volitum. [ ] In all the Divine Life where This is directed towards created reality, it is the Divine Will which gives character and colour to the Divine Activity. And it is by means of his own will -- rather than by means of his intelligence -- that man will enjoy, once he is saved, the happiness of the absolute good that God is. Ockham -- in as full revolt against Scotus as the arch-Nominalist can be against such a realist -- maintains, however, and develops, this adherence to the general theory of "will rather than intelligence"; and he sums up in a marvellously concise phrase the relation of God as Creator to the goodness of created reality, eo ipso quod ipse vult bene et iuste factum est. [ ] The attention of the theologians all through the next hundred and fifty years after Ockham is more and more directed to the role of the Divine Will (and, indeed, of the human will, too) as against the intelligence. It becomes a general state of mind; another aspect of which is the revival of the ancient notion -- long ago condemned -- that, in the matter of salvation there is nothing beyond the power of man's will to accomplish. Man, say the theologians -- Gabriel Biel notably in this generation -- has a natural capacity for loving God above all else; for to love God thus is what reason rightly instructed bids man do; and to all the commands of reason rightly instructed the will, by its own natural forces, is able to conform itself. Against this point of contemporary teaching -- and the state of mind that goes with it -- and against Master Gabriel by name as an eminent promoter of it, Luther will now, very soon, violently revolt. It will be, for him, one reason to reject "the scholastic theology" outright.

If the tendencies of fashionable theological teaching in the latest and newest schools -- developments indeed of ideas now nearly two centuries old -- were thus to aid the coming age of heresy, the erroneous philosophical doctrines held by many orthodox theologians, and their superficial grasp of the relation between theology and philosophy, were to prove a serious weakness in another way. Again we approach a vital doctrine, and again we need to go back some centuries and to see first a false view of it; then the error corrected thanks to a mind philosophically well formed; and finally, as this last philosophical position is abandoned, a chronic malaise in the mind of the theologian who, believe he never so sincerely, yet must continue, being a man, to think.

The point at issue is the extent of man's share in the business of his salvation, of man's responsibility -- should he lose his soul -- for his own damnation; it is one of the topics on which Luther's divergence from Catholicism will be most evident and most far-reaching. Peter Lombard had taught, in the twelfth century, that the all-important grace which makes man pleasing to God, which "justifies" man as later theologians were to say, was charity dwelling in the soul, and that this divinely given, supernatural, charity was nothing else than God Himself, the Holy Ghost. [ ] "So highly," says St. Thomas, about to criticise the theory, "did the Master [ ] esteem charity." St. Thomas would have none of this theory. It was an impossibility. It could not ever be true. And for this reason, that man's love for God if it proceeded from such a Source and in such a way would be in no way spontaneous, his voluntary act; and therefore it would be devoid of merit. The act of any nature, says the saint, is perfect in so far as it proceeds from within that nature. Were the act of loving God, man's supreme activity, not to proceed from that free will which is at the heart of all that is human in man, it would be less perfect than man's other acts. Here, it is evident, the criticism of the Lombard and the solution of the difficulty that is offered, are wrapped up in a philosophy.

From that solution subsequent theologians did not move away. But they moved far indeed, the most of them, in the next two centuries, both from the philosophy and from St. Thomas's conception of the relation between philosophy and theology.

While they maintained the solution as true, because it was of faith, they nevertheless declared that, philosophically speaking, it was no more than probable. God had acted this way; he might have acted otherwise; that he had not acted otherwise was at any rate probable; and no more than probable. There is no need to labour the point that sooner or later such a division in the mind of the thinker must end either in the destruction of his belief, or the sterilisation of his power of thought. What is more nearly our business is to note that here is one of those philosophical speculations about what God might have done which we see taken, in Luther's mind, as what God actually did. What theologians of this type were doing was to fill the mind of the time with a host of such "probabilities," accompanying and associated with the certitudes of faith. It was only a matter of time before, in the mind of one or another of their hearers, the probability gained over what was only certain because taught authoritatively by the Church -- victory not for the probability which coincided with the faith as taught, but for its contrary which philosophically, was always probable so long as, in the mind of the thinker, the doctrine of faith was less than certain philosophically too.

On this most important point -- where Luther's divergence was to create the key doctrine of all Protestantism -- the Catholic theologians, of all schools, continued to teach that it is a nature that God has saved, and that it is saved not through a grace which works outside it, but through an activity of grace in which it has a real share. Charity is a virtue, through which man's salvation is operated by man's action too. Sanctifying grace -- the grace which, making man pleasing to God, justifies man -- is a real vital principle, whence acts proceed that really are man's acts; man's merit before God is a reality, as man's freedom to posit these acts is a reality, and as the supernatural efficacy of those acts when posited is real. And all the theologians defend too the great principle Naturalia manent integra: [ ] sin does not destroy human nature, because nothing can destroy a nature but God who called it into being by creation. Nothing could be more striking than this theological agreement, or than the general movement of theologians away from the immense authority of Peter Lombard when once he had gone wrong on this point. Nothing could be more directly opposed to all that was about to come in the wake of Luther. But it was a great misfortune that, for so long, so many theologians had testified to their faith, and to the traditional teaching, in an atmosphere vitiated by their enslavement to the probable.

In the early years of that dead time which followed the disappearance from the scene of Nicholas of Cusa and Pius II, and within a short two years of one another, five very remarkable men were born. At Gouda in Holland in 1467 Desiderius Erasmus was born; at Rome in 1468 Alessandro Farnese, who, as Pope Paul III, was one day to sanction the Jesuits and to assemble the Council of Trent; in 1469 Machiavelli was born at Florence, Thomas de Vio -- Cardinal Cajetan -- at Gaeta, and at Beverley, in Yorkshire, St. John Fisher, the solitary bishop in the hundred years that lay between St. Antoninus of Florence and St. Thomas of Villanueva to attain canonisation. Nine years later, in London, St. Thomas More was born. From four of these men, in the last few years before Luther's entry into world history, came the most characteristic work of their genius, four books which have influenced all subsequent thought: Cajetan's commentary on the Summa Theologica of St. Thomas began to appear in 1507, Machiavelli's The Prince was composed in 1513, Thomas More's Utopia was printed in 1516, and Erasmus's edition of the Greek Testament that same year. With these works of these great men the tableau is complete of Christian thought as Luther's revolt found it. Erasmus and Cajetan are priests and religious; More and Machiavelli laymen. Erasmus and Cajetan are ecclesiastically learned, though after a very different manner; More and Machiavelli are directly interested in the common life of men, in the Commonwealth. Let us begin with the laymen.

The Utopia and The Prince are classics too well-known to need much description. Some study of them has been part of the general culture of western Europeans for centuries. The authors are finished humanists, both of them; More is the English character at its very best, Machiavelli the Italian almost at its basest. The Italian is already, however, a figure in the public life of the time, a diplomatist who knows by long experience the great world of princes that is the subject of his meditations: More is but on the threshold of his career.

At this moment the future martyr is thirty-eight years of age, by profession a lawyer and one of the most successful advocates in the English capital. He is a scholar of the new type, a wit, a family man, and a man of deeply religious life, about whose ways with God there has clung something of the Carthusian spirit ever since the years when, as a young man, he lived as a guest in their London cloister. More fasts regularly, he has regular hours for prayer, he wears a hair shirt, he spends the midday hours of every Friday in meditation on the Passion of Our Lord, he not only hears mass daily but very frequently receives Holy Communion. Such is the man who in the Utopia uses brilliant and kindly satire to criticise the very foundations of his world. This he sees as a place where wickedness and greed flourish unchecked, and where the poor are more and more oppressed, despite the fact that rich and poor alike profess themselves believers in the doctrine that they are brothers in Christ, and that this fraternity is the one thing that matters. What a mess Christians are making of this Christian world, he seems to say. Even from pagans who knew only of God that He existed, more than this might be rightly expected. The book appeared in Latin, at Louvain in 1516, and it had from the beginning a great popularity. [ ] Thomas More was already known to humanists everywhere through the praise of his friend Erasmus; henceforward he was known, and as among the foremost of the humanists, in his own right.

Few books have suffered more from serious misunderstanding. This has been due, in part, to lack of knowledge about its author, and also to the prejudgment with which the critics -- friendly for the most part to More -- have begun their study of it. It is not a visionary book, nor an unpractical scheme of real living, but a philosophical satire upon the contemporary abuses of Catholic Europe, written by a passionately sincere Catholic. It does not discuss Catholicism, but it attacks the neglect of Catholics really to put into practice the faith which is their boast. As for the religion -- the natural religion -- of these Utopians, the remarkable thing is how closely, in some important points, it resembles Catholicism. Against two contemporary fashionable aberrations on the part of thinkers who are Catholics the Utopia is in violent reaction -- against Pomponazi's philosophical trifling with the doctrine that man's soul is immortal, and against the a-moralism whose representative figure is Machiavelli. " Parts of Utopia read like a commentary on The Prince". [ ] More is all against the new emancipation from fundamental dogma, against the new statesmanship, against the autocratic prince, and against the idea of "nations as totally independent, gladiators in the European arena." He is filled with horror at such ideas, and at their practical consequence that there are now Christian states that will look on as spectators, with complacency and even with satisfaction, while the Turks destroy the power of their own Christian neighbours.

The author of the Utopia is not blind to the acute general problem of religious disorder. But he is no destructive revolutionary. What he desiderates when, for example, considering the vexed business of the clergy's immunity from the law of the state, is not the abolition of the system -- which is a check on the tendency of the state to absorb the whole life of its people -- but a better clergy, " of exceeding holiness" indeed, and more carefully recruited and trained, who shall not need so frequently to shelter behind such immunities. As to another clerical matter, generally regarded as one of the great sores of the time, the condition of the monasteries, once again More is conservative. Monasteries -- good ones, of course -- are necessary; Monasticism is, indeed, the one European institution that the Utopians approve of.

There is hardly a single aspect of contemporary life -- even to the matter of colonising the newly discovered Americas -- that More's keen, kindly, humorous eye does not light upon. For each he has the appropriate comment, and for the innumerable victims of the social system, the new landless, rightless, proletariat, infinite pity. In Utopia there are no class distinctions, [ ] no slaves, no serfs, all men are free men, are workers, are students; and all at need are soldiers. By comparison with what is there pictured -- and with what could be, in this Catholic Christendom, were all really Catholic -- the commonwealths of the day are indeed "a conspiracy of rich men". [ ]

The Prince, written three years earlier than More's Utopia, [ ] 8 and addressed to Leo X's nephew, Lorenzo de' Medici, lately become the ruler of Florence, was the work of a man whose political career had just come to an end, at the age of forty-four. In that career of nearly twenty years in the service of Florence, his native state, Niccolo Machiavelli had risen to be the head of a leading branch in what we might call the Ministry of the Interior, and he had also been employed in half a dozen most important diplomatic missions. He had been sent to Cesare Borgia in the duke's great hour when he was all but King of the Romagna; he was at Rome when disaster came to the duke with the death of Alexander VI; he was with Julius II in the famous march on Perugia and Bologna in 1507, and three years later he was with Louis XII of France, fanning the king's hatred of Julius and advising him to stir up the Roman barons against the pope. With the restoration of the Medici at Florence, in 1513, Machiavelli fell. He was for a time imprisoned and tortured, but his life was spared. No public man is resigned, at forty-four, to the idea that his life is over, and The Prince, the first of Machiavelli's works, is in intention a first move to capture the good will of the Medici " tyrant" and gain a place in his counsels -- employment and money. For Machiavelli was not one of those philosophers who live only for thought. He was the Italian humanist at its best and worst, all the literary scholarship and skill, all the brilliance, all the scepticism, and all the vices, the deceit, the extravagance, the profligacy, and the cult of personal glory to the point of mania; the very antithesis in character of Thomas More.

The Prince is a slight pamphlet written in a new classical Italian prose, to be read in an hour or two, and meditated on for the rest of a lifetime. Its main theme is the way a prince ought to act who has lately become the master of a state which has previously been under the rule of another. The model for such a prince's imitation is, Machiavelli declares, Cesare Borgia; and the book is, substantially, an analytical account of the rise and fall of tyrants, with special reference to this hero, and with the moral always carefully drawn. The style is simple, unimpassioned, and for its power of irony beneath ordinary language and unimpeachable sentiments, the forerunner of Swift and Voltaire. Here is the political practice of contemporary rulers -- the state of things that provoked some of the most telling passages in the Utopia -- not now condemned for the bad thing it is, nor for the menace it holds for coming ages, but built into a doctrine, a kind of political religion, with villainy analysed and classified, its practice set out in appropriate maxims and precepts, and with warnings against using the right villainy at the wrong time. Well, indeed, may it be said that the little tract "marks the culminating point of the pagan renaissance." Here is the new gospel that, since the world is full of bad men, it is useless for the good to waste time considering what men ought to be, and dangerous to treat the wicked as only the good deserve to be treated. Bad men cannot be governed except by descending to their own level. Treachery, bad faith, cruelty, the careful affectation of the appropriate goodness, all these are called for, and must be studiously employed by the ruler who, in a wicked world, wishes to survive. And Machiavelli calmly debates the comparative usefulness of these vices, and explicitly enjoins his prince to make use of them.

States need, too, a religion: there is no instrument more useful to the ruler than the religion accepted by his subjects. Whether the ruler himself believes in that religion or not, and even if he knows it not to be true, it is an elementary duty to his welfare to foster it. This ideal national religion, whose importance -- from the ruler's point of view -- lies in its power to unify the nation and serve as a means through which to govern it, could hardly be Catholicism. Nor does Machiavelli mean that it shall be. Catholicism, as the religion not of the hated popes merely but of Jesus Christ, a religion that teaches mankind to look elsewhere than in the state for the abiding city, can never serve the ends of the prince. Moreover its doctrines of love, of self-denial, of pity and of compassion tend to form a type of character than which nothing could be more hostile, nay fatal, to the state he has in mind. The ideal religion is that of pagan antiquity and Machiavelli explicitly says this. [ ] Paganism alone will, by deifying the state, crown the achievement of the good prince.

A later generation of Catholics was to see the by then notorious treatise placed upon the Index of books forbidden to be read. But addressed to the nephew of Leo X it brought no immediate reprobation on its author, and in 1515 the pope was asking him for advice in the dilemma caused by the schemes of the new King of France and the shifting papal diplomacy. The pope's cousin -- the Cardinal Giulio who was afterwards to be Pope Clement VII -- still stood between Machiavelli and a new employment at Florence, but in 1519 he too was consulting him, asking for a statement on the best way of governing the state, and in 1520 he obtained for him, from Leo X, the commission which produced the great History of Florence.

The Prince is, evidently, in every line and turn of phrase a Renaissance product, and the worst feature of the book, the final pessimism about human nature, [ ] is no doubt the effect upon a well-placed observer of the sight of such universal cynical indifference to the elements of morality in the conduct of public affairs. Even the popes, as rulers, had now descended to the level of the condottieri princes. But there is another, and more enduring reason, for the pessimism. It is a reflection in the political writer of the contemporary revival of Aristotle according to Averroes, of the movement which at Padua, under the influence of Pietro Pomponazzi, was now carrying all before it with the youth of the university. Here, rooted in stern and compelling logic, was the old curse of the theory that man is wholly at the mercy of an impersonal world force, held in the grip of a fixed, unchanging, eternal cosmos. Everything has always been the same; it will always be so. Since this is the truth about life, and man's destiny, it is best to arrange life accordingly, and to crush out all talk of ideals and betterment and what we should call "progress," for beliefs of this kind can only cause activities in the state that are futile, fated to futility indeed, and a necessary cause of mischievous instability. Averroism, indeed, had never died despite St. Albert and St. Thomas, and Duns Scotus. And now, in the general disintegration, it was again in the forefront of life, threatening as always the very fundamentals of Christian belief. Its most evident assault was against the belief that the human soul is destined for a separate, personal immortality. [ ]

A French scholar of our own time has linked Erasmus, with Machiavelli and Thomas More, as a pioneer in political philosophy, for Erasmus also wrote his Prince. [ ] But, without demurring for a moment to the great Dutchman's right to figure prominently in such a history, his main importance in Catholic history lies elsewhere. In 1516 Erasmus was close on fifty, and he had reached that position as an influence in European life which no man of letters before, and none since -- not even

Voltaire -- has ever attained. [ ] For what was he known, in these last hours before the Lutheran controversies began? and whither did his influence upon educated Christians tend?

He had begun as an eager, and unusually gifted, student of classical Latin literature, in that monastery of Steyn where, in a kind of despair, this unwanted child of a long-dead priest had been over-persuaded, by guardians only too anxious to get him off their hands, to vow himself for life as an Austin Canon-Regular. The monastery was one of that congregation of Windesheim whose ideals and outlook have been described; its spirit for good, and for the less than good, was that of the Devotio Moderna. Erasmus was continuing here in the way of his early schooling under the Brothers of the Common Life, and there is no reason to doubt that he simply set down the facts when, in later days, he said of his brethren that among them "the least inclination for literature was then looked upon as little better than a crime." However, Erasmus was professed, in the way then general, solemn vows after a novitiate of twelve months, at the age of nineteen or twenty.

It cannot have been long before he realised the scale of the mistake he had made. The patronage of the Bishop of Cambrai provided a first way out, and after serving some time in his household, Erasmus presently found himself in the schools of Paris. Then came the momentous first visit to England, in 1498, the meeting with Colet and Thomas More, and the realisation of what must henceforth be his life's work, the restoration of a religious spirit in the clergy through their better education; and to better their education the preparation of improved editions of the classic Christian literature. This was, in the end, to be the main work of his most industrious life, and it is by what he achieved here, and by the spirit that directed his efforts, that Erasmus must be judged. One of the great ideals of Nicholas V -- the new humanism perfected by religion, religion still more splendidly set out and defended by the new humanism, the application of the new scholarship to Christian literature -- was to be realised at last, in the face of a thousand difficulties and anxieties, by the genius and enthusiasm of this obscure religious.

Those difficulties left a permanent searing mark upon his spirit. Penury, first of all; dependence on patronage for the very freedom which the task called for; the utter inability to understand, on the part of those in whose power it lay to arrest the work at any moment -- to understand not only his own competence for it, but religion's need that the work should be done; and hanging over him, through all these years, the possibility of a recall to the unsuitable monastic life and its sterility, where his talent must run to seed for lack of intelligent employment by superiors, and his mind turn in on itself; of a recall which would leave, as the only alternative, disobedience and disgrace, the terrible fate which then awaited the apostate religious, a life of concealment and an ultimate return to the religious life via the monastic prison. Erasmus knew his age thoroughly. Not Machiavelli, nor Thomas More, was more familiar with the spectacle of clerical disorder in the high places, the spectacle of church revenues squandered on worldliness, and neither was so well placed for the contrasts to be such a torment. [ ] That it was the friendship of Thomas More which made all the difference to this refined and much-tried spirit, no one will doubt. The meeting of 1498 was a turning point for Erasmus in more respects than one.

The first of Erasmus's books, the Adagia, appeared in 1500. It was a new kind of introduction to Latin studies, and an important factor in the development of a better method of teaching the classical language. Then, in 1502, studying Valla, the idea came to him of preparing a critical edition of the New Testament text, and Erasmus set himself to the study of Greek. It was not, however, until 1516 that the long awaited work appeared, dedicated not to his friend, the Bishop of Rochester, St. John Fisher, as Erasmus first intended, but to Leo X, who willingly accepted the dedication and wrote the famous enthusiastic praise of it which prefaces the third edition. Here was a critical edition of the text, with notes and a new Latin translation, and in the twenty years between its first appearance and the death of Erasmus, the bulky folio was reprinted sixty-nine times. And now, in succession, there appeared a series of new editions of the Fathers, St. Jerome, St. Athanasius, St. Basil and St. Cyprian (1516-1520), Arnobius, St. Hilary, Prudentius, St. John Chrysostom, St. Irenaeus, St. Ambrose and Origen, St. Augustine, Lactantius and St. Gregory of Nazianzen (1520-1531). And, of course, wherever he was, Erasmus formed others in the same way of scholarship.

But long before the tale of this gigantic work was completed, Luther had appeared, and Erasmus had become involved in the controversies about the new doctrines. In these controversies he satisfied neither side; and he won for himself the reputation as a doubtful kind of Catholic which he has, perhaps even yet, not lost. That reputation, which has too long over-shadowed his immense services, is also bound up with his strong, published criticisms of the abuses in the practice of Catholicism in his time. The most famous of the books in which these chiefly appear was The Praise of Folly dedicated to More, and published long before Luther had been heard of: but the other, a book designed to teach boys Latin conversation, the Colloquies, though also written in early life was only published, as a manual, in 1522. Here, in places, there is set out with biting satire the seamy side of ecclesiastical life in all its unpleasantness; here are all the scandals about which reforming councils, and outspoken popular preachers, have been occupying themselves for generations, unworthy clerics, ignorant clerics, sinful clerics -- and monks, the debasing popular superstitions, the mechanical unintelligent use of religion; here it all is, in words of one syllable, set out in condemnation, and in warning; abuses smiled at, sometimes politely, sometimes ironically, sometimes with the bitterness of a good man not a saint who has come nigh to despair of the only human force that can correct it all; and the moral is continuously pointed out that true religion is far different from all this, that what now obtains needs to be purified and simplified, and that what a man needs is to know Christ as the Bible speaks of Him and to follow His way. On its positive side [ ] the spiritual direction is that of the Devotio Moderna; but, allied now with the hostile critique of so many Catholic practices and institutions, and lacking the needed reference to man's need of sacraments and of Church-taught doctrine, and with the seeming theory that private study of the Bible is all-sufficient, and given to the world under the author's name barely two years after Luther's condemnation and with all northern Europe now in convulsion, the book, henceforward, lined up Erasmus as Luther's ally in the minds of a host of the Catholic partisans. Erasmus crying "Back to Christ in the Bible" was too like Luther crying "The Bible only "

But the most fatal weaknesses of all arose from the total absence in the great scholar's own formation of anything at all of the classic theology of the schools. To Scholasticism, indeed, Erasmus was as much opposed as Luther himself, and with perhaps less understanding of what it was that he was opposing. It would be a waste of time to belabour Erasmus for this lack of knowledge, of time better spent in enquiring where a religious of his antecedents could have got the kind of knowledge of scholastic theology that would really have informed his mind. What kind of a spectacle, in fact, did the world of Scholasticism present to a young Austin Canon in a Dutch priory of the Windesheim group, in the closing years of the fifteenth century? or to the student in the grim College de Montaigu of the Nominalist-rotted university of Paris? In a sense there was too much Scholasticism, Thomists, Scotists, Ockhamists of a score of schools, all disputing against each other. Which was in the right? And with what else were the most of them busy but with sterile inter-scholastic disputation? A young Friar Minor studying in the convents of his order with an unusually good master might be made into a useful Scotist thinker; or a young Dominican, if so lucky as to be taught by some Cajetan, might prove an effective Thomist. But outside these rare cases?

The life had, in fact, gone out of the business, and almost everywhere the philosophers and theologians of the via antiqua did little more than repeat their predecessors. A new world of literature and imagination had developed, and they ignored its existence. Their own technical Latin had actually declined in quality, and taken on a new barbarity, in the very age when nothing was so characteristic of the educated man as a carefully polished, classical Latinity. And the scholastics made no use at all of the new literary forms of the vernacular languages. The new humanism had brought to the West, not only new texts of Plato and Aristotle, but the means whereby all might read the masters in their own tongue. But the scholastics were too indifferent to their own origins to seize the great opportunity. And despite the fourteenth and fifteenth century critics who had already demonstrated the inadequacy of the Aristotelian physics, the universities clung to them with a truly stupid determination, refusing utterly to consider the new sciences, deliberately ignoring the way of experiment. The once great movement was now, by its own choice, cut off from all that was alive in the world of thought; and the needed systematisation, the constant relating of the old knowledge to the new which is the real life of the mind, had long since ceased.

Erasmus was by nature anything rather than a metaphysician, but in an age of more reasonable Scholasticism he could have been taught enough of this first of the sciences to understand why it is the first, and how all else depends on it, and that, without it, the theologian soon finds himself in difficulties once he is beyond wading-depth in his speculation. For Erasmus the consequences were disastrous. He had too great a mind not to suffer cruelly wherever he was deficient, and his role was too high for his mistakes to be small matters. For his theological insufficiency, and his own unawareness of it, he paid again and again. Luther's theories of the will as enslaved, for example, filled him with horror. Erasmus attacked the German unsparingly, but with what weapons? Here was a philosophical question, and the humanist had done nothing about philosophy, all his life, but ridicule the miserable philosophers of his experience.

"Caught unprovided with any such technical formation," says a theological historian, [ ] of the controversy about Free Will, " [these humanists] had only their personal tastes to trust to, and their own powers of initiative, seeking shelter, for good or ill, behind such Greek writers as Origen and St. John Chrysostom, whose scattered views had never been formed into a systematic theory about these problems, nor enjoyed any appreciable prestige in the Church. The intervention of such improvised theologians had the effect of creating, inside the theological system of Catholicism, a new antithesis whose consequences were to be far reaching indeed. . . ." And Mandonnet instances Erasmus [ ] who; "without any study of the classical theology of the Church, improvises solutions, and despite his circumspection he comes to affirm such enormities as this ' That nothing comes about without the will of God, I readily allow; but, generally, the will of God depends on our will'." [ ]

These controversies were however, in 1516, hidden in the unknown future. The pope had blessed the new work on Scripture and enthusiastically recommended it, and the only critics Erasmus had had to face, as yet, were obscurantist Catholics. But what these now were muttering, others, once the Lutheran storm broke, would soon be proclaiming loudly, and declaring that Erasmus, by his teaching about the role of Scripture, and his criticism of monastic life and devotional practices, was no better than Luther himself.

Under all the varied activity of this most industrious scholar, the single persisting aim is always evident, namely to bring men back to Christ; and this, Erasmus is persuaded, can best be done by setting before men Christianity as it first existed. His method is that of the humanist who would reconstruct Cicero's Rome or Plato's Athens, namely the critical use of the oldest literary monuments of the time that have survived. The one way back to Christ, in fact, is through study of the New Testament, and if our idea of Christ's doctrine gains in simplicity the more we read, this is a sure indication that we are on the right way. Here, in this craving for simplification, in a violent impatience with whatever is not grammatically self-evident, we have one leading motif of Erasmus's theological activity. He posits, in fact, of the inexhaustible content of revelation, the simplicity which belongs to the assent of faith through which the content is made accessible. This simplicity of statement for which Erasmus yearns, he does not find in the theologians. What has destroyed it there, so he thinks, is the theologians' use of philosophy, of metaphysics, in their task of exposition. With the theologians as they face their eternal problem -- the need to determine what doctrines actually mean, to solve the apparent contradictions, to resolve the seeming opposition between them and what is reasonably known -- Erasmus has no sympathy at all. From such problems he shrinks; and he has a marked antipathy for those who face them, and immense scorn for their barbarous, unclassical Latinity, their carefully devised technical terminology, and their methods of logical analysis, and of strict definition.

His own method will not give any doctrinal precision, and he does not desire it from any other method. Doctrinal precision is, in fact, not necessary; zeal for it is a mark of Christian decadence, not of progress in knowledge of God. In the hands of Erasmus, Catholic dogma thins out until it vanishes to nothing; and he would meet the problem of the real need, of even the most ordinary of mankind, for knowledge of the mysteries appropriate to the level of their intelligence, by scrapping technical language on all sides. Precision in these matters, he thought, was not worth what it cost; and even, for example, such a vitally necessary tool as the term homoousion ought to go, ought never to have been devised. It is not surprising if, in his theology, there are mistakes, inexactitudes, contradictions, and this especially in the matters then so violently controverted, doctrines about marriage, confession, the monastic life, the Roman primacy. [ ] Nor is it surprising if the next generation, its theological mind formed by the greatest of scholastic revivals, and its adherence to the scholastic method intensified by the Church's life and death struggle with the Reformation divines, should come to hold in abhorrence the great mind which, in these important matters, seemed stricken so perversely. Upon Catholic theology Erasmus, then, left no lasting mark; nor did his failure to appreciate its importance do any damage or lessen its prestige. Here the contemptuous blows he struck fell upon the air. For one thing the revival had begun; and next, theology had already become what it has since remained, a technique that only interested theologians and clerics. The sole effect of his excursions into theology was to discredit Erasmus with the theologians for ever. But the effect of Erasmus on the future of philosophy was very different. Philosophy had once been the occupation of all the educated, and it would in time become that again. Here, the scornful mockery of Erasmus for the Scholastics as he had known them, barbarous in diction, futile and sterile in act, came as a last blow from humanism in its classical age; and Erasmus, in this, helped enormously among educated men everywhere the prejudice from which, only in our own time, is the philosophy of the schools recovering. [ ]

As we review the personalities and the effective work, of Machiavelli and Erasmus and St. Thomas More, we seem to have parted company entirely from the medievals and to have rejoined our own contemporaries. Cajetan, their contemporary, was undoubtedly a medieval; [ ] and yet, in him also, we make a contact with later times, with our own time indeed in the strictest sense, for the spirit we encounter in Cajetan is the Catholic intellectualism of this mid-twentieth century, the age of Maritain and Gilson, of Leo XIII and Pius XII. Here, in Cajetan, is a rebirth of St. Thomas; here are the beginnings of his effective primacy in the Catholic schools as doctor communis.

Cajetan is, by birth, James de Vio -- Thomas in religion; and, born at Gaeta, made a Dominican at Gaeta, Bishop of Gaeta, Cajetanus inevitably for all time. He entered the Friars Preachers at the age of sixteen, in that very year when the Chapter-General made the momentous decision that the lectors should use St. Thomas as the basis of their teaching instead of Peter Lombard. In 1488 he was sent to Bologna, still a student; and after his ordination in 1491, to Padua, then exceedingly alive not only with the contention between the Dominicans and the great Scotist, Antonio Trombetta, but with the controversies that centred round the revival of Averroism and the graceful culture of its high priest Pietro Pomponazzi.

It was at Padua that Cajetan began his career as a teacher, and that he finally received that form of the complete metaphysician which was henceforth to be the vital principle of all his intellectual activity. [ ] In 1494 he made a brief appearance before a greater world when, in the theological tourney which, in those days, enlivened the meetings of the General Chapter, he met and brilliantly jousted with Pico della Mirandola, the hero, it will be recalled, of the early manhood of St. Thomas More. Cajetan was given the chair of Theology at Pavia in 1497; he went thence in 1499 to Milan, and in 1501 he was named Procurator-General of the order, its representative at the Roman Curia. Although, along with this, he obtained a chair in the Roman university, his career as a teacher was over, he was more important now as one of the order's superiors. [ ] In 1508, at the age of thirty-nine, he was elected Master-General of his order.

Cajetan held this office for nearly ten years, and showed himself in it as a reformer of great constructive power. Two things above all, he told his brethren, must be attended to, the restoration of a life that was genuinely a life in common -- a restoration, therefore, of monastic poverty -- and, at the same time, [ ] the raising of the level of Dominican studies. For other orders, he said, studies might be an ornament: for the Friars Preachers, they were life itself. "Once we cease to carry weight as teachers of theology," he said grimly, "our order's day is over"; and every novice has heard that other reported dictum that the Dominican who fails to study four hours a day is in a state of mortal sin.

But the Master-General was not kept exclusively to the service of his order. Julius II made all possible use of his genius in the theological controversy with the pseudo-council of Pisa, [ ] and Cajetan was a leading figure in the General Council of the Lateran, and not only as a theologian but also, once again, as a man who saw the rotten state of the spiritual city and how urgently drastic reform was needed. [ ]

At the end of the council Leo X made him a cardinal. [ ] and in May 1518 sent him to Germany as Papal Legate. One of his tasks was to unite the princes into an effective opposition to the new Turkish offensive; after a respite of thirty years a great soldier had again arisen among the Ottomans, and Christendom was once more in danger. An equally important commission was sent on to him some four months later. [ ] It concerned Luther, by this time cited to answer at Rome a charge of heresy. Luther's sovereign -- Frederick III of Saxony -- had persuaded Leo X to allow the enquiry to be held in Germany, and Cajetan was now put in charge of it, with power to give a definitive sentence, and to absolve Luther should he retract; with orders to have him arrested and sent on to Rome did he prove obstinate.

The two met at Augsburg, October 12, 1518, Dominican and Augustinian, Thomist and Ockhamist, the Papal Legate and the rebel. Much has been written about that celebrated interview, amongst others by Luther himself. Nothing came of it in the way of reconciliation. No reconciliation was possible; and Cajetan did not succeed in having the heresiarch arrested. But at the interview he spoke to Luther as one scholar to another, as one religious to another, laying aside his high rank and treating Luther -- we have the Augustinian's word for it -- with marked kindliness. But at Rome the legate seems, henceforward, to have been, for his superficial superiors, the man who had failed. One of his brethren of our own day has surely judged his action truly. "From the outset [Cajetan] realised, what many Catholics even after four hundred years have not grasped, that this was not just any kind of a revolt, but a revolt of the mind; that these demands of Luther were not a mere claim that the flesh should be emancipated, but demands in the domain of the spiritual, and, more particularly, demands in the domain of the theological. Cajetan was taken advantage of, and he was beaten; how could he possibly not have been? But this much at least must be said, that he did not touch the already gaping wounds of Christendom with hands that were not respectful and clean." [ ]

But it is Cajetan's influence as a thinker that is our subject, his permanent influence on his own and later ages. [ ] Cajetan's chief importance to Catholic history lies not only in this that he was the first to publish a commentary [ ] on the Summa Theologica of St. Thomas Aquinas, the classic masterpiece of Catholic theology, but in the spirit which informed that great commentary, still the classic commentary after four hundred years. Cajetan, considered in his own right, is the greatest theologian of his own time, and one of the greatest the Church has known. [ ] It was also his great merit that he understood the needs of his age, and that old methods must be adapted accordingly. His commentary on the Summa is the work of an original mind and it proved, from the first, a great originating work. What it first of all accomplished was the long needed reconciliation of the scholastic learning and the new culture of the humanists. The commentator understood his own time, realised fully the gross error of only too many theologians, to wit their indifference to the new critical scholarship and to the new positive sciences, and, so much a metaphysician himself that he was scarcely anything more, he yet brought the new learning to the assistance of the old. In this he is indeed a second Aquinas, bringing into synthesis humanism and Aristotelianism as the thirteenth-century doctor had brought together Aristotelianism and the theology of St. Augustine.

It is in the long series of Scripture commentaries to which the last years of his life were given that the flexibility of Cajetan's genius is most evident, his readiness to use the new learning and his skill in its use. But this spirit is already to be seen, fully at work, in the great commentary on the Summa. Like the best of the humanists he makes a critical use of the Scriptures in his argumentation, keeping rigorously to the literal sense, and observing scrupulously his own critical rule of not mixing the literal and spiritual senses indiscriminately -- a fault to which the classic theologians of the Middle Ages often tended, [ ] and which was never more evident than in the works of the great encyclopaedist of the generation before Cajetan -- Denis the Carthusian. [ ] And wherever he can do so he makes it his business to study the whole work in which his opponents' views are expressed, by no means content to judge them on the mere opposition of a text. Cajetan again shows himself of the new age in his scrupulous re-thinking of the author he is explaining. Nothing, not even unanimity among other theologians, will dispense him from this. And in nothing else does he separate himself more from his contemporaries, and his immediate predecessors, than in his violent repudiation of their formalist treatment of St. Thomas. [ ] This, and his candour, make Cajetan a singularly attractive author. There is about him an independence and an objectivity that is new. Here is the wisdom of St. Thomas given new life, and speaking to the Renaissance in an idiom it can understand. Here at last among the scholastic theologians was a great thinker, sensitive to all the life of his time, his work free from all those faults which drew upon his profession the wrath of Erasmus and the mockery of Rabelais. It is something to know that Erasmus was not only aware of Cajetan's existence, but of the different kind of thing his great work was, that he praised it highly -- and disinterestedly -- only wishing that books of this sort could be written by the score. [ ]

Cajetan was not an isolated figure in his own order. The Renaissance of St. Thomas's doctrine had begun about the time he entered the order, he was one of its earliest fruits. But almost his contemporary was the gifted Francis de Sylvestris of Ferrara (1474-1528) who published in 1525 the first, and greatest, commentary on the Contra Gentiles; and only ten years younger than Cajetan was Francis of Vittoria (1480-1546), [ ] the Spaniard whose lectures on the State and on the moral aspects of political life are a main foundation of the modern science of International Law. [ ] It is Cajetan's work, however, which is the real foundation of all the later achievement; it is due to him above all others that there was a new living theology in the university world of the later sixteenth century, ready when the great opportunity came to serve those two great inventions of that time which have especially formed the modern Church, the diocesan seminary and the Society of Jesus. [ ] And if Cajetan is the progenitor of the theological scholarship of modern Catholicism, Erasmus too has his Catholic progeny, no less distinguished, no less necessary to the fullness of Catholic life, the critical scholars and historical theologians and the exegetes, the Benedictines of St. Maur for example and the Bollandists, Petavius, Mabillon and Papebroch.

The General Council summoned by Julius II (in what circumstances has already been described) [ ] to meet in the Lateran Basilica of Rome, came together on May 3, 1512, and it was not dissolved until almost five years later, March 12, 1517. Many things in its history make the Fifth Lateran a thing apart among General Councils. It met very rarely -- seven times only in the last four years; its activities are recorded not in the usual list of canons and decrees but in a series of papal bulls; the attendance was never large, and the eighty or ninety bishops present were almost all Italians, from the Papal State and the kingdom of Naples; and, finally, the reform decrees it enacted were often openly ignored, sedente concilio, by the pope himself. "Au total rien de serieux" says a French scholar, truly enough; and it is hard to see what more could have been expected of such a character as Leo X, upon whom the conduct of the council fell from March 1513.

The most immediate practical effect of the council was that it broke the nascent schism fostered by the King of France and the, emperor; it reaffirmed the declaration of earlier popes that General Councils are instruments of government subordinate to the pope, primate and ruler of the whole Church of Christ; and it secured the assent of the French king to the condemnation of the Pragmatic Sanction as unlawful, null and void. [ ] And the council did a great service to the cause of the faith, and of right thinking, by its condemnation of the new Averroism of Pomponazzi, "pernicious errors concerning the nature of the rational soul, namely, that it is mortal and that it is the same [soul] in all men, and that this is true at least in philosophy." [ ] The bull goes on to say, " Since truth does not contradict truth, we declare that every assertion contrary to truth illuminated by faith is absolutely false," and it orders that those who lecture on these subjects in universities shall set themselves to refute the arguments of these philosophers, all of which will yield to reasoning. No cleric in holy orders shall, for the future, give himself in his first five years at the university to the exclusive study of philosophy or the poets; after that time, he may, as it were, specialise in them, provided always that, at the same time, he continues his study of theology and canon law.

There are two other acts of the council which show concern for the welfare of the Catholic mind, the bull on censorship [ ] and that on preaching. [ ] The first begins with a paean of thanksgiving to God for the recent marvellous invention of printing, and a recital of the new prospects thereby opened out to learning and to religion. The new art, however, is lending itself also to less worthy causes. Books are appearing filled with mistakes about the faith, and with all manner of harmful teaching, the very opposite of Christianity; and also books filled with slander, even of eminent personages. Whence this new law that, for the future, no one is to print anything before it has been sanctioned by ecclesiastical authority -- by the pope's officials in Rome, by the bishop or his diocesan officials elsewhere. Those who ignore this law risk a heavy complexity of penalties; the book will be confiscated, publicly burned, the printer fined 100 ducats, suspended from printing for a year and excommunicated.

The decree about preachers is interesting for what it reveals of current practices in the all-important office. It is indeed almost wholly taken up with them. Preachers are not to put their own personal interpretations on Sacred Scripture; they are expressly forbidden to predict future calamities in any definite way, or the coming of anti-Christ, or the end of the world. Those who have done this already are liars, and their wickedness is one reason for the contempt that has come upon preachers in general. Let no one, for the future, preach that any particular future event is foretold in Holy Scripture, nor say that he has a revelation from the Holy Ghost to state this, or any other like inane divination. Preachers must keep to the Gospel, teach a hatred of vice and a love of virtue. They must be a source of peace, not sowers of dissension. Especially must they abstain from scandalous denunciation of the faults of bishops and other superiors, "whom not only imprudently, but intemperately, they lecture and worry in sermons before the common people and laity"; and they must abstain from open declarations of the wrongdoing of superiors, even mentioning their names. It is, of course, always possible that a preacher may really have a special revelation, and a divine commission to make it known. But it belongs to the pope's authority to judge whether this really is so, and before anything of this kind is publicly preached it must be submitted either to the pope or, if there is no time to consult the pope, to the local bishop, who, along with three or four theologians, will carefully examine the matter. For those who ignore the law there awaits the penalty of an excommunication from which only the pope can release them.

Three decrees treat of reform. The lengthy bull Supernae dispositionis arbitrio [ ] recalls and renews all the old legislation, going back to 1179, designed to ensure good bishops in all the sees of Christendom. The pope's responsibility is stressed, and the bull explicitly reminds him that at the last day he will answer to God for his appointments. All the vices which, at this moment, disfigure the system are listed, and it is announced that the law that bans from the episcopate minors and the ignorant, and that forbids favouritism, the use of commendams, appointments of administrators -- and, in fact, everything that Leo X was at the moment doing and would continue to do to the end of his reign -- is henceforward to be enforced. The decree makes no difficulty about saying that the failure to observe these ancient laws has brought the papacy into disrepute throughout the Church; and it also renews all the laws designed to prevent monasteries from being made a means to give prelates and cardinals an income, while the monks starve and religious life dries up. The cardinals are then mildly admonished, in stereotyped language that merely repeats what was said at Constance and after Constance, about their duty to live pious and sober lives, and a vast amount of space is given to regulations about their dress and that of their households, and to set a limit to the expenses of their funerals -- 1,500 florins. There is a new law to punish blasphemy in clergy and laity, the obstinate sinner going to the galleys if he is a commoner, losing his nobility if he is a noble and, if a cleric, losing all his benefices. Concubinage, yet once again, figures as a custom that still flourishes, and bishops are warned not to let offenders off lightly on the plea that the custom is after all so general. There is a renewal of the old laws against simony, against encroachment on the rights and property of the Church, and against violation of the privilege of clerics. All this is, once again, little more than repetition. The legislation merely forbids and enacts penalties; the way has not yet been found to secure that the law will actually be put into force. [ ] And there is a special clause denouncing witchcraft and punishing those who resort to it, clerics and laity; and another clause calling for strict application of the heresy laws against pseudo-Christians.

A second bull [ ] strengthens the bishop's hand against the chapters and canons who resist his endeavours to correct them, on the plea that they are exempt from his authority; and it strengthens the prestige of the episcopal courts. Finally, the bishops are bidden to observe the law, which has long been a dead letter over four-fifths of the Church, that a provincial council should be held every three years.

The law that the bishops of every ecclesiastical province should meet in provincial council every three years was first made at the Fourth General Council of the Lateran -- the greatest of all the medieval councils -- by Innocent III ill 1215. In the period 1270-1517 there were held, for the 74 provinces then effectively existing, 235 provincial councils: had the law been observed everywhere, throughout that time, there would have been more than 6,000 councils held. The purpose of the provincial council -- it must be remembered -- was not merely to make laws: it was designed by Innocent III as the instrument by which episcopal slackness and shortcomings were to be corrected by the bishops of the province. Herein lay the chief usefulness of Innocent III's invention; and in the utter inability of the popes to enforce this law lay, undoubtedly, one of the chief reasons for the steady decline of religion and the ultimate corruption of such masses. It is not without interest to note that never were fewer councils held than in the years of the so-called conciliar movement -- 63 councils in 30 provinces. In many provinces no council was ever held. So, notably in Italy, where there were 29 provinces, councils were never held at all in 22 of them; in the rest there was one council in Benevento in 1378, one in Palermo in 1388, the fourth and last of Aquileia (i.e. held during these 247 years) took place in 1339, of Ravenna in 1317, of Grado in 1320, of Spoleto in 1344, of Padua in 1350. Of the 16 metropolitan provinces of France, most held councils, many of them at least once in an average man's lifetime; though at Arles, Embrun and Aix there was none after 1365, nor at Auch after 1387, though at Bordeaux the series ended in 1327, and at Toulouse in 1368, though Lyons (the primatial see) had but one council (after 1300) in 1376, and Reims only one in 111 years (1344-1455), and Rouen none in 140 years (1304-1445). The tale is much the same in Spain, although, at Toledo and Tarragona, councils were really frequent (six at Toledo and fourteen at Tarragona). In Germany, where there were seven provinces, councils were only regularly held at Prague and Magdeburg; Cologne had none from 1324 to 1423, Salzburg none from 1310 to 1409; Bremen had none at all after 1292, and Treves none after 1310. In Poland between 1285 and 1420 there was but one council, held in 1375; and there was but one in Portugal, held in 1436, in all the period 1270-1464. In Scotland, too, the law was a dead letter; a council was held in 1280 and the next was in 1436. Sweden went for 120 years without any provincial council (1275-1396), and Hungary for 130 years (1318-1449). Norway did not fare so badly until half-way through the fourteenth century, the council of 1351 being the last until 1436. In Denmark the series ends in 1389. In Ireland (where there were 4 provinces) there are only the two councils of Dublin in 1348 and 1351.

The third bull, [ ] of December 19, 1516, brings to an end the latest, and most clamorous, of all the struggles between the bishops and the mendicant orders, a quarrel so violent that the pope had to put off the next session of the council for months. "We are in the heart of a terrific storm," the general cf. the Augustinians [ ] wrote, " the attack upon us and upon all the mendicant orders by the bishops has now raged furiously for

three years in the very council." The cause was the old, old cause
-- the privilege which the Mendicants enjoyed of exemption from
all authority but that of the pope. The bishops charged the friars
with using the privilege to make money out of the laity at the
expense of the parish and diocese, and charged them also with an
abundance of wicked living; let them be brought under the
common law of the Church. The regulars riposted by a
staggering catalogue of episcopal sins. "Before you call upon us
to observe the common law of the Church," they said, "why not
begin to observe it yourselves?" If it were not for the regulars,
they boldly declared to the pope, the very name of Christ would
be forgotten in Italy. Who else but the friars ever preached? The
bishops pressed for the abolition at least of the privileges lately
showered on the Mendicants by the Franciscan pope Sixtus IV,
the bull called Mare magnum.

It was only the personal action of Leo X that saved the friars. [ ]
He arranged a compromise, and the bull Dum intra mentis arcana
of the eleventh session sets it out. Bishops were to have the right
to make visitations in parish churches held by the friars and to
enquire into all that concerned their parochial activity. Friars
would need the bishop's approval before they could hear the
confessions of his subjects. Friars were not to absolve from
episcopal excommunications or other censures, nor were they,
without leave of the parish priest, to administer Extreme Unction
to the dying or give them Holy Viaticum. Laymen who wished to
be buried in the habit of a religious order could be buried in the
order's churches and cemeteries if they so desired. Bishops had
the right to examine a friar's suitableness before they gave him
Holy Orders; and it is the bishop of the diocese who must be
asked to give this sacrament, and also to consecrate the friars'
churches, bless their bells, and perform all other episcopal
functions they may need. Friars are not to marry any of the
faithful without the leave of the parish priest; they are to be
careful to remind those who come to confession to them of their
duty to pay tithes to the parish priest; and, if the priest asks it of

them, they are to make a point of this in their sermons. Members of the Third Orders who live in their own houses have no right to receive from the friars of their order the so-called parochial sacraments (that is Easter Communion, Extreme Unction, and Holy Viaticum), though they may confess to the friars, and be buried with them, and by them, should they choose. Such tertiaries are bound by the same obligations as other layfolk, and they are not free from the jurisdiction of lay judges. Nor can they, in times of interdict, hear mass in the churches of the order to which they belong. But if the members of the Third Order live a common life, in a convent, they enjoy all the rights and privileges of the order.

The recital of the details of the compromise shows how the life of the orders had, by now, penetrated minutely into every nook and cranny of the Christian republic. At every turn there was room for friction between the two systems of jurisdiction, the episcopal and the exempt. And even the roughest survey of the lives of the saints and holy people of the century between Constance and this act of Leo X, shows the mendicant orders as the great active source of almost all the sanctity of the time -- so far as sanctity is known to us.

A biographical catalogue of saints [ ] gives a total of 150 saints and beati/ae who "flourished" between the beginning of the Schism and the end of the reign of Leo X (1378-1521). The "causes" of the great majority have so far not proceeded beyond the stage called beatification: only 26 out of the 150 have been canonised. Of these 150, the mendicant orders can claim as many as 115. Four of these were bishops, 35 nuns, 9 lay men and women members of the various Third Orders, and the rest priests and lay brothers; Franciscans and Dominicans account for over two-thirds of them. [ ] This huge lead the mendicant orders maintain to the end of the period. In the fifty years which this last chapter covers, this age of Sixtus IV and Alexander VI and Leo X, 76 saints and beati/ae "flourished", and 55 of them belonged to the mendicant orders, 19 women and 36 men. This ultimate glory of so many of their subjects -- their Italian subjects [ ] -- was hidden indeed from the generals of the orders- at that time, but how history has justified their reply to the bishops' assault made in the Fifth General Council of the Lateran !

There is yet another decision given by Leo X in the council which is of interest, not only in itself, but as the most important sign so far of the Church's recognition that the world has reached a new age in social and economic organisation; this is the bull Inter Multiplices [ ] which declares the new charitable pawnshops to be lawful, and protects them against the critics who had been denouncing the system as nothing else than usury. No crime, throughout the whole of the Middle Ages had been more continuously denounced by the Church than usury, and no sinners more severely punished. Nor did Leo X's sanction, given to pawnshops so organised that, while no interest was asked for the loan, a small charge was made to cover administration costs, alter in any way the definition of usury or moderate the condemnation of the crime. But while reviewing once again the nature of the reprobated "contract of usury", the pope explicitly reproved old-fashioned theologians who declared that whatever accrued to those who lent money must, in all circumstances, be usury.

Great changes, in progress by this time for a hundred years and more, had brought it about that money now had another use beyond that which all thinkers so far had considered could be its only use, namely, to be a means of making payments. In an economic system where, if money was not used to make a payment it was not, and could not, be used at all, all loans of money were necessarily unproductive loans. The money lent was as truly consumed in the borrower's use of it, as was ever a loaf of bread or a bottle of wine. Any charge made for any loan of money was, then, necessarily a usurious charge, the charge being inevitably a gain accruing directly from the mere act of loaning, and claimed as such.

But once industries began to be specialised and commerce to spread over a wider field, to pass from the transactions confined to one village, or town, and to take in first a whole country, then a continent and finally other lands at the very extremities of the world as known, a new use for money gradually developed. Any man could lend his money to these industrial and commercial pioneers, and legitimately qualify for a share in their profits -- as he also incurred a share in their risks. What such a man received from those to whom he lent his money was a share in what their use of the total moneys they controlled brought in; it was a fruit of industry and business capacity, not any longer a payment exacted simply for the loan of what could not be productive. To profits accruing from money used in this new way that the growth of commerce had made possible, the criticisms directed against usury could not apply. And it became necessary, in such a system as the Catholic religion, that those whose business it was -- whether by private or public direction of men's consciences -- to keep a clear idea of moral obligations before mankind, should take note of the new institutions which the changing circumstances of life were calling into existence.

The fourteenth century, which produced so much activity of a scientific kind -- and minds that, by preference, studied facts (and here, of course, Ockham's insistence on the importance of the fact told very favourably indeed) -- saw the first reflections of these new developments in what has come to be called Moral Theology. Durandus of Saint-Pourcain, for example, studied the nascent credit system and raised the question, which increasingly agitates our minds to-day, whether the state should not organise so important an element of man's well being. Francois de Mayronnes pointed out how money was beginning to have more than one use, and asked the great question if interest could not therefore sometimes be lawful. Jean Buridan sketched a theory of value, of exchange, and of money. Nicholas of Oresme, whose place in the history of other sciences has been referred to already, wrote his book on Money, its origin, nature, rights and exchange in which Gresham's Law makes its first appearance. All these men were clerics, and their first interest was the ultimate end of their fellows. They did not study Political Economy for the mere interest of the subject, but to clarify doubts whether certain commercial activities were lawful or sinful. It is not surprising that these questions, from now on hotly debated in the country that was the centre of the new finance, Italy, attracted the attention of the missionaries of the new Franciscan reform movement -- the Observants -- who, for the moment, were there carrying all before them as reformers of Christian moral life. In their sermons, and notably in those of St. Bernadine of Siena, there is a new precision in what is said on these questions which so vitally affect man's chances of salvation: questions of usury, of interest, of mortgages. But the crown of all this new movement was the work of a Dominican, St. Antonino, Archbishop of Florence from 1446-1459, in the very height of the career of Cosimo de' Medici.

St. Antonino [ ] was a disciple of Bl. Giovanni de Dominici, the Dominican who organised the great reform in his order that produced the famous Congregation of Lombardy, and who as a cardinal stood by Gregory XII, almost alone, in the dark days of the Council of Pisa. The saint grew up in the new, reformed monasteries of Fiesole and St. Marco; he had served as a missionary, as prior and as the head of his group of houses, and he had won a great name as a canonist, when Eugene IV gave him the see of Florence in 1446. It was one of those rare appointments where the man was ideally right for the place and the time, thinker, ruler, saint, and understanding his age from life-long contact with all its actuality.

The great work for which St. Antonino is chiefly known, the four volumes of the Summa Moralis, was written while he was archbishop, and it was meant, of course, for the use of his clergy. It is a new kind of work in two respects. First it treats exclusively of theology as this relates to conduct -- it is the pioneer work of the science that has come to be called Moral Theology. And next, it is specially devoted to these new anxieties about commercial morality and the use of money, and the ultimate moral import of what we should call economic doctrines. Here is to be found dispassionate analysis and discussion of all manner of problems that are still with us; poverty in itself is an evil, though it may be an occasion for good; possessions are good and ordained by God for the service of man; to serve God as God wills He shall be served, man needs a certain freedom from anxiety, a certain leisure -- and possessions secure this for him. The saint considers wealth in its production, distribution, and consumption, and discusses the comparative importance of labour and capital in the production of wealth. There is a careful detailed study of various methods of commercial fraud, of the question of usury, of interest on bills of exchange, of the distinction between money as coin and money as capital, and of the lawfulness of taking interest for money lent to the state. There is an attempt to state a principle whereby to determine the just price of goods, just to the seller and to the buyer; an examination of monopolies, and trusts; of the duties of the state to its citizens, its duty to provide for the poor, the aged, the sick -- and even its duty to provide, for the poor, doctors paid by the state; of the duty of employers to pay a just wage.

Florence, in St. Antonino's time, was as much the financial capital of the world as New York or London has been in our own. The evils which he analyses and deplores are the product of the last two hundred years or so before the Reformation; and already, in the Low Countries as in Italy, and in western Germany too, "there was sometimes a capitalism as inhuman as anything which the world has seen, and from time to time ferocious class wars between artisans and merchants." [ ] It was not the least of scandals to the poor as Catholics that, among their oppressors, were highly-placed clerics. St. Thomas More, in the Utopia, notes, for example, that monasteries too are prominent in that wicked development that is turning farms into sheep runs and thereby increasing the horde of wretched proletarians and vagabonds in the towns.

And it was another scandal that the popes had, for generations, made such use of the bankers. [ ] It was the skill of the French pope Urban IV, negotiating an agreement with the bankers of Siena in 1263, that had made possible the expedition of Charles of Anjou and the final defeat of the Hohenstaufen. Bankers played a great part in the supreme days of la fiscalite pontificale, during the Avignon regime. "In the first half of the fifteenth century the Medici or their representatives were always in attendance on the popes." [ ] John XXIII had Cosimo with him when he made the fatal journey to Constance in 1414, and he raised 15,750 florins from the firm on a magnificent mitre. Twenty-five years later Eugene IV, during the Council of Florence, raised a further 25,000 from the Medici on pledges of plate and jewels. Under Nicholas V the bank received the 100,000 gold florins which the pilgrims contributed at the Jubilee of 1450. By this time the great Florentine firm had branches everywhere, at Rome, Venice, Pisa and Milan in Italy; at Antwerp and Bruges; at London, Lyons, Avignon, Geneva, Valencia and Barcelona, and at Lubeck; and thereby it offered the pope a means to gather in revenues that was no doubt lawful enough in itself, but a means that lent itself easily to scandal. For example, " Fees had to be paid by any nominee to a bishopric or an archbishopric. The Roman house accepted the bull of nomination, dispatched it to that branch of the business which had, or was likely to have, business connexions with the new bishop, and this branch then delivered the bull on payment of the dues. If the dues were not paid, the bull was sent back." [ ]

The bankers were also used to collect the money offered by those who sought to gain some of the indulgences, [ ] and the classic example of scandal here is the indulgence of Leo X as it was preached in Germany in 1516, the indulgence which gave Luther his opportunity to secure for the new theology its first notoriety outside the universities of Wittenberg and Erfurt.

The movement called the Reformation, when it came, was but one of several revolutions simultaneously active, and the latest of them in time. This attempt to picture the setting in which the first events of the Reformation took place needs, in order to complete it, some mention of the new importance of the middle classes, and for this I should like to borrow the words of a recent French writer. The only "class to make any progress" -- he is speaking of the fifteenth century -- "is the middle class. The development of banking and industry, all that blossoming of capitalism which characterises the fifteenth and sixteenth centuries makes for the advantage of this class alone. On a par with this economic strength, is the hold which the middle class gains, little by little, on political life, the municipal authority and the parliaments. Well-established families dominate the municipal councils; in the Low Countries they take an ever-increasing part in public affairs, in Italy more than one of them rises to be ruler of the state. The other side of the picture is that, in all the large towns, a wretched proletariat already exists with no means to express itself in the national life; and this section of the community the great social and religious changes will toss about mercilessly. There is thus in formation, within the great industrial cities, a powerful commercial aristocracy, independent, critical of authority, with a tincture of literary tastes, of interest in law and theology, ambitious to exert its strength, to enforce its claims, a middle class seeking power and privileged status -- and there is a considerable mass of poor people, raw material for any revolutionary movement, just as ready to support the ambition of the middle classes, or the king's authority, or a peasant rebellion; to turn and sack the possessions of the clergy to-day or, to-morrow, to change sides and become a church-enthusiastic mob."
[ ]

Here the veil is lifted that still hangs over too much of medieval history, and something shows of the life and thought of the ordinary man, not only of him at whose expense history is so largely made, but of him whose scarcely recorded reaction to the direction of his betters often, at the turning points, makes history. It was to help this class that the Franciscan Observants had come with their invention of the Monts de Piete, protected now by Leo X in the General Council of the Lateran. What of the religious life of the ordinary man at this moment?

The movement of theology away from philosophy, more and more marked as the fourteenth century drew to an end, was more closely followed by a movement of devotional life away from theology -- though not, as yet, of devotional life away from the faith. It was not to the depths of the mysteries that men now turned for food for their souls, but to the mysteries as they had been shown to the senses. There is, from now on, an increasing familiarity in the tone of men's commerce with the supernatural world, and they make greater use of their imagination in their effort to make a contact with that world. Their meditation on it is more colourful, the emotions play a greater part in their spiritual life than ever before. The change is reflected in a new development in religious art; there are new subjects for the painters and sculptors and a new treatment of the old subjects. It matters much now that the representation shall be picturesque. And the great catastrophe which came half way through the fourteenth century, the Black Death, gave a sudden impulse, more powerful than all the new philosophical developments, to man's new preoccupation with emotions and imagination, to the attainment of a new stage in his devotional life, and to hasten the coming age of Pathos. On the one hand new luxury and new lusts, and on the other a new deep-rooted melancholy. Then came the terrible trials of the Schism and of the long-drawn-out uncertainties of the duel of the popes with the councils. Here are catastrophes and crises that remind men violently how brittle a thing is worldly glory, how short-lived man's happiness and how far from Christian perfection most Christians are, even the most highly-placed. The new age is much preoccupied with the thought of sin and its consequences, and with death as the moment when merited punishment will begin. As well as being the age that created the new moving iconography of the Passion, such devotions as the Stations of the Cross and the Five Wounds, and such touching images as that of Our Lord awaiting the last torture of the cross or of the Pieta, this is also the age of the Danses Macabres. "It is only Death who dances, in the procession; the rest follow unresisting, drawn along wherever the fatal cortege goes. The buffoon who zig-zags at its head is more than man can bear to look upon closely, with his strips and scraps of rotting flesh, his mockery of likeness to a man, and the irreverent display of ' what should be covered up in the earth'. " Here are the extremes of the new plane in which the popular religion lives and moves, skirting too often the fringes of the morbid, through the hundred and fifty years between the Schism and Luther.

Meanwhile the Third Orders flourished, and in the towns the guilds continued to build their corporate life around the means of grace -- prayer, the sacraments, almsgiving, and works of charity. New monastic foundations were extremely rare -- how could more be needed, all possible wants were surely long ago supplied? The charity of the munificent went now to colleges rather, to schools and to hospitals and to "homes" for the unfortunate; " homes " for orphans and foundlings and nursing mothers, for repentant street walkers; for old sailors, for pilgrims and for the poor of every sort. [ ] The poor are indeed not lacking. It is an age of "commercial expansion" and the tale of the ruined victims is considerable.

Another sign of spiritual vitality is the vast number of religious books, of all kinds, in the vernacular languages, diffused now through the new invention of printing, Soul's Guides, Ways to Heaven, Christian Missions and the rest. More important still are the Catechisms and handbooks of doctrine, such for example as the Libretto della doctrina christiana, Kalendrier des Bergers, Espeio de bien vivre, Instructions for Parish Priests. [ ] It is an age of preachers, in every country; and pious Christians make provision in their wills for the preaching of sermons and the maintenance of the preachers, "to assure them the leisure for the study they need." [ ] Sermons begin to be collected and printed. In Germany we know of a hundred such. But of all books (everywhere but in England) it is the Bible that is the most popular. It was translated into Italian by a Camaldolese monk Nicholas Malermi, and in Germany, by 1517, nineteen editions of German translations had appeared. " All Christians," say the editors of a Cologne edition, "should read it with devotion and reverence and in union with God."

An account of Christian life during these years when ideals were so gravely compromised by the bad example given in high places, would be singularly misleading did it say nothing of the violent reaction, open, at times defiant, when good men protested against the scandals of ecclesiastical life. In Italy "the upper and middle classes were in a ferment of hostility" [ ] to this papacy of princes. The " racket " was evident and bitterly resented. One who for years lived at its centre, and upon it, the servant of both the Medici popes, Leo X and Clement VII, has expressed in bitter words that resentment which, in all ages, is the most dangerous product of the ecclesiastic's unwillingness to allow that his administration can need criticism or reform -- namely that whatever the layman's loyalty to the Catholic faith, his impatience with clerical incapacity and self-sufficiency may lead him to welcome any movement which promises to shake up the clergy. Guicciardini -- for it is the great historian's words we are about to quote -- was no doubt an embittered man when he put together his Reminiscences and, like many another educated Italian of his time, not too sure of his religion. But here he only says more forcibly what, in all such times and circumstances, men naturally say. After speaking of the clerical wickedness he had witnessed -- ambition, covetousness, excesses -- and the scandal it must give, he says that his relations with various popes made him prefer their greatness to his own interests. "Had it not been for this consideration" -- he is writing now in 1529, after the event -- "I would have loved Martin Luther as myself; not that I might set myself free from the laws imposed on us by Christianity, as it is commonly interpreted and understood, but that I might see this scoundrelly rabble (questa caterva di scelerati) confined within due limits, so that they might be forced to choose between a life without crime or a life without power." [ ]

Guicciardini did not stand alone. Others of his contemporaries, who explicitly declare their attachment to the papacy, do not hesitate to complain about the scandal given by the contrast between what the office demands and the way those who hold the office conduct themselves. [ ] In England there are the profound criticisms scattered through the works of St. Thomas More; and St. John Fisher, the Bishop of Rochester, made his protest too. If the pope did not presently reform his court, said the future martyr, God would find a means to reform it for him. [ ]

But by far the most striking protestation was that of the Dominican Jerome Savonarola, a very great figure indeed, and still the centre of lively controversy among Catholic scholars. [ ] Savonarola was born at Ferrara in 1452 and after a good humanist education in that centre of the Italian renaissance, sickened by the renascent paganism of life, and somewhat morbidly preoccupied already with the sinfulness of human nature, he offered himself to the Dominicans in 1475, joining, at Bologna, the austere reformed congregation of Lombardy. Fifteen years later, as the newly-appointed prior of San Marco at Florence, he broke into the Italian scene with the force of a thunderbolt. Yet once again the combination of a passionate austerity of life, of utter and absolute disinterestedness to all but the salvation of the hearer, of clear and exact theological understanding, and of the very perfection of the oratorical temperament and gifts, proved irresistible. Savonarola was, after St. Bernadine of Siena, the greatest preacher of the Italian middle ages; and he was a pioneer in the new apologetic, the apologetic now beginning to be urgently necessary if the educated Catholics exposed to the seduction of the newly discovered pagan ideals were to be kept true to their belief. Within a couple of years the Dominican had conquered Florence. The gay, licentious capital had become a convent, said its cynical neighbours.

In no matter had Savonarola showed himself more outspoken and independent than in his condemnation of the Medici -- the founders and patrons of the very monastery he ruled, but, for the prior, the primary source of the city's sins, and the tyrannical oppressors of its liberties. And it was when the revolution of 1494 drove them out and Savonarola began, as the oracle of God, to be the inspiration of the new government of the republic, that there began also the stage in his career that could only end in tragedy. All Italy now -- save only Florence -- was combining to resist the French invader. The pope -- Alexander VI -- was naturally the leader in this combination, for Charles VIII not only menaced the Papal State, but, so it seemed, threatened immediately the pope's hold on the papacy itself. The king was urged on all sides to call a General Council, whose main business would be to depose the pope as a simonist and a man of evil life. And Savonarola, who had before this already begun to denounce in his sermons the pope's heinous sins, now began to preach that it was God's will -- revealed to him, Savonarola -- that Florence should be the French king's ally.

Alexander now summoned him to Rome (July 25, 1495) and when the Dominican managed to evade the summons, the pope forbade him to preach (September 8 and October 16). He even offered to make him a cardinal. [ ] For a while Savonarola was quiet, but after four months of silence he returned to his pulpit and took up again his mission to rebuke the sins of the pope. On May 12, 1497, Alexander excommunicated him. Whereupon the sermons against Alexander took a new turn. "Whoever excommunicates me," said the friar, " excommunicates God." In a series of letters prepared for the princes of Europe, [ ] he invited them to correct the pope's life and to thrust him out, for he was no pope, being elected by simony, and indeed not even believing in God; and the friar repeated the claim that his own mission was divine and that the excommunication was, therefore, void in the sight of God. "If ever I ask absolution from this excommunication," he said, in sermons preached about this time, [ ] " may God cast me into the depths of hell, for I should, I believe, have committed thereby a mortal sin"; and again he declared that those who allowed that the excommunication had any force were heretics.

The illusion that had been the weakness of Savonarola's whole career was working out to the very fullness of its terrible possibilities. For, from the beginning, although his doctrine v. as always orthodox, Savonarola, in the whole of his preaching, gave himself out as a man directly inspired by God to say what he said and to direct the action of others. There must not ever be contradiction, or opposition, to what he proposed or ordered. He recounted in his sermons, as warrant for his assumption, his dreams and his visions, and he foretold in what events God would chastise this disobedient generation. Lorenzo de' Medici was shortly to die, and Innocent VIII also -- which came to pass. The French would come in and overthrow the sinful Medici tyranny; his own mission would last just eight years and he would then die at the stake and his ashes be cast into the Arno. This also came to pass. But the Turks were not converted in ten years, as he also had foretold, nor was Rome taken and sacked and filled with desolation.

This burning conviction of his divine call -- which no man must question -- had been the main force of all Savonarola's public action. It was the main secret of the amazing ascendancy over his own followers, which by 1497 had filled San Marco with a host of new Dominican recruits, [ ] and riveted upon Florence a kind of moral dictatorship, in which the prophet's followers were organised to observe and correct the vices of their neighbours, and children were trained to report the sins of their parents. All the exaggerations in Savonarola's views of human misconduct, and the crazy severity imposed indiscriminately for some years under his influence, bred of course an immense resentment. Under the surface Florence was seething with discontent. The Dominican's want of prudence, his wild, unmeasured denunciations, had been a source of anxiety to his own brethren - - and not merely to the relaxed monasteries of his order -- and his success had been extremely galling to the traditional rivals of his order, the Friars Minor. If ever his ascendancy were shaken, it would go hard with the Prior of San Marco. Long before the time when he was convoking the Christian princes, half the city was watching for the chance to dethrone him. One defeat, and he would have no friend save his immediate disciples. And at Rome the pope knew, now, that when he chose to strike he could, with impunity, make an end of the embarrassing prophet.

In March 1498 the government of Florence -- threatened with an interdict by the pope -- induced Savonarola to desist from preaching. Alexander was not too pleased; they should have given an order, to which the friar ought obediently to have submitted. It was the scandal of his flagrant, rebellious -- and successful -- disobedience which, to the pope's mind, was the real crime. But although the Dominican was now silent, the controversy in Florence still raged, the Franciscans keeping up the attack and the Dominicans replying. Out of this pulpit warfare the final crisis suddenly flared. A Friar Preacher declared himself ready to go through fire to prove, by his survival, that his master was the prophet of God. A Franciscan publicly took his words at their literal value. He too would go through the fire. He would, he knew, be burned, but so would the other, and it was worth a life to expose the impostor. And so, on April 7, 1498, the government arranged the ordeal. An immense crowd gathered to watch. There were disputes about the procedure -- the Franciscans alleging that Savonarola might put a spell upon his champion; the Dominican demanding that he be allowed to carry the Blessed Sacrament as he walked through the flames. Out of this a theological dispute developed, and then came a storm and rain. Finally, to the disappointment of the crowds, the whole affair was put off.

The following day -- Palm Sunday -- the disappointed faction stormed the Dominican priory of San Marco, the authorities intervened, and arrested the prior and his two chief supporters in the community. When they sent the news to the pope, Alexander demanded that the accused should be sent to him for trial. This the republic refused, but they allowed Alexander's demand that the final sentence should be left to him. The prisoners were tortured, and on the admissions thus obtained -- Savonarola, it was said, confessing that he was an impostor -- condemned them. Then the pope sent to Florence as his commissaries Francisco Remolini, a Spanish canonist, who was his own kinsman, and Jerome Torrigiani, the aged and vacillating Master-General of Savonarola's order. Once more -- May 19 -- the prisoners were tortured; once more there were admissions. The final scene took place on May 23, 1498. In the Piazza della Signoria, along with the scaffold, three platforms were erected. At the first Savonarola's fellow religious, the Bishop of Vaison, [ ] degraded the three [ ] from their priestly rank and religious status. Then the papal commissaries declared them proved guilty of schism and heresy -- and announced that the pope, in his mercy, offered them a plenary indulgence. Savonarola bowed his head in sign of acceptance. At the third platform were the civil authorities, to sentence the three to death. They were immediately hanged, their corpses burnt, and the ashes thrown into the Arno.

It was, of course, a terrible retribution for the wild, unmeasured language in which the Dominican had attacked the evil life of the monstrously bad man who then disgraced the chair of St. Peter, and for the endeavours he had made to dislodge him from it. But such were the ideas then, and for centuries yet to come, of the punishment appropriate to acts even less harmful socially than the calling in question of a ruler's right to the position he filled. Nevertheless, to choose the heresy process as the convenient instrument of the destruction of the friars was a scandalous perversion of justice -- it was the case of the Templars and of St. Joan all over again, but with the pope a leading agent in the wickedness.

There was no reaction to follow the death of the Prior of San Marco. A faithful few clung fast to all he had taught them, but the great commercial city continued on its even way, corrupted and contented, as did, for many years yet, the papal curia against whose scandals the great Dominican had witnessed.

The Church, in these opening years of the sixteenth century, is by no means a body devoid of spiritual life. In the seething Renaissance activity, spiritual forces are active, too; the supernatural finds a generous response. Abuses are extensive and no doubt a more potent cause of scandal in their actuality than can be realised by those who only know them in the two dimensions of the literary record -- but reform has definitely begun in more than one place; among the reformers there are serious men, high in authority? and the promise is good.

In Spain, for twenty years, there has been the great Franciscan primate Ximenes; in England St. John Fisher. If, in a monastery of the Austin Friars in Germany, Martin Luther is growing up to be the genius who will draw all the disease and discontent to a single blazing-point of revolt, in another house of the same order in Spain the young religious is maturing who, as St. Thomas of Villanueva, and Primate of Aragon, will atone for the long

Borgia oppression of that see. In other centres in Spain other saints too are being formed, who will presently come forth to astound the world by their spiritual achievement, heroes of the authentic Christian type, men of prayer, utterly careless of self-interest or self-comfort (even in religion), wholly devoted to God, infinite in charity as in zeal: St. Peter of Alcantara, who will renew in all its splendour the authentic ideal of the Franciscans; St. Luis Bertrand, who will do as much for the Order of Preachers; St. John of God, who will found a new order of charitable workers; Blessed John of Avila, whose life as an evangelist will put new heart into the parochial clergy of Spain; and the Basque soldier in the service of Spain, now approaching the great moment of his conversion, Inigo Loyola. In England, in these same years, there is growing to maturity the generation of bishops which will presently apostatise, but the generation also of More and of Fisher, of the heroic Carthusians and the Friars Minor of the Observance. The weakest places are France and Germany and Italy. But in Italy there are signs of better things -- other signs besides those of indignation at the continued presence of abuses. In various cities of the north the saints are maturing who, within the next ten years, will found the much-needed new religious orders to face the new problems and needs: St. Jerome Aemilian founding the Somaschi, St. Antony Maria Zaccaria the Barnabites, St. Cajetan of Thiene -- from the very court of Julius II -- the Order of Theatines, whence was to come a whole new episcopate to be the chief executant of the reform. And, associated with this last saint, there has begun, so quietly that its early history is hard to trace, the as yet all but unknown Oratory of Divine Love. It is a brotherhood of priests and laymen, pledged to works of charity, meeting regularly for prayer in common. It began in Genoa in 1497, and now, in 1519, it is at work in Rome, where -- the happiest augury of all -- it has gathered in leading members of the curia of Leo X. In what seems universally agreed is the chief centre of all the mischief, there is set a pledge of better days. With all this, and with Cajetan and Erasmus and More in full active maturity of mind, what prospects might not seem at last to be opening, after the dark days since Sixtus IV?

"Alors se leva Luther." [ ]

## 3. LUTHER

In no part of Europe was this flood of Christian life more turbulent than in Germany. Here indeed the waters were stormy, swirling over rocks scarcely hidden, and over deeps that no one suspected. Germany was tormented by its own special political problems: the fact of the hundreds of petty independent sovereigns who divided up the vast territories between the Meuse and the Vistula, and, its necessary consequence, the ceaseless ambitious rivalry of the half-dozen leading princely families to dominate the whole. In the countrysides there was the old social problem of an economy still based on serf labour; [ ] and in the towns the new social problem of a growing urban proletariat. In Germany, as in Italy and in the Low Countries, the new estate of the capitalist was rising rapidly to a place of first importance. [ ] Humanism was in its lusty springtide, a practical Humanism, impatient of old ways, eager -- with some -- to refashion the world by re-educating mankind after the model of the ancients, and in full emancipation from Christian restraints; while -- with others -- Humanism was going the way of Erasmus, planning a Christian revival in which the scandals that everywhere disfigured religious life should be made for ever impossible.

Nowhere, however -- so a practical man might have thought -- were the chances of religious revival more slender. Nowhere, for example, was there such anarchy in the lives of churchmen as in Germany. Here were two worlds of clerics, clearly marked off by a chasm hardly ever to be bridged: the bishops, abbots, prelates and beneficiaries of the innumerable chapters, princes and nobles always -- and the vast horde of the clerical proletariat. If we judged the lives of the generality of all these clerics by what, for hundreds of years now, has been the standard practice of the average cleric, we might feel it impossible to find words too black to describe its disorder. Certainly the situation was worse than in contemporary England or France, and even more dangerous than in Italy because it lacked the Italian levity about sacred things. In Germany all were in deadly earnest: the good men earnest against the wicked indifference of the ecclesiastical rulers, against their greed and their simony; the bad men earnest against the system which held them to obligations they had for years neglected and broken through. As to the German attitude towards the Holy See, the whole nation, for generations now, had been consumed with resentment at what, seemingly, was now almost Rome's sole interest in Germany, its possibilities as a source of revenue for curial dignitaries. And if the German effort to reform the Roman Curia by shaking off its hold on Church revenues and Church appointments had ended long ago, so, too, the papacy had had to abandon, for the time, its long effort to break the monopoly of the German princes over nominations to high ecclesiastical office -- a first and main obstacle to religious reform, and one never finally overcome until the armies of the French Revolution swept away for ever all the last decayed remnants of the old medieval world.

When, from the depths of such a world, Martin Luther in 1517 came forth to address the Church universal, he also brought a new strength to the growing movement of Germany's consciousness of itself as a nation with a unique destiny; to the princes he offered not only the chance of taking to themselves, once and for all, the vast properties of the Church and its many states, but all the opportunity that must come to the State when religion ceases to be universal and supra-national and becomes a local thing; most of all was his appearance appropriate to the condition of German politics in that he brought a new kind of support and propaganda for a theory about the place of the Church in the State that offered advantages to all -- except to the clergy -- and to none more than to the princes. No setting could have been more appropriate for the appearance of the great anarch; nor could any man living have better typified the most serious aspects of the general disorder and decadence of Catholicism at that time than this Austin Friar, professor of theology in a Catholic university, and now about to offer the Church as a solution for its troubles a version of Christian teaching that would empty it of all Christian significance, making man, not God, the real focus of religious activity, divorcing morality from piety, and present conduct from the prospects of future salvation. Luther as a Christian force was to prove sterile; there would not follow upon his activities any betterment of the moral lives of his disciples, any advance in learning, any new peace through social renewal. Here again, the heresiarch is true to the forces that bred him, and to his generation. [ ]

The occasion of the false prophet's appearance in the public life of his time was a scandal that derived directly from Rome and the curia of Leo X, the preaching of a plenary indulgence proclaimed in aid of the fund to rebuild the Roman basilica over St. Peter's tomb. The uproar about indulgences which now, by reason of Luther's act, suddenly filled all central Germany in the winter of 1517, was not due to any one single cause. Luther's fire fell upon a train long laid. With the bishops of Germany, for example, the preaching of Roman indulgences within their jurisdiction had long been a sore subject; more than once, during the previous hundred years, this matter had brought them into conflict with the Holy See. And the particular indulgence which now proved Luther's great opportunity, was one which bishops outside Germany too had opposed, even before the indulgence had been made available to Germany; the primate of Spain, for example, the great reforming Franciscan, Cardinal Ximenes, had forbidden it to be preached there.

Indulgences -- it perhaps needs to be said -- are not a forgiveness of sins, nor have they ever been understood to be such; it was not as though this was claimed for them that they were criticised by these bishops or attacked by Luther. Indulgences are a remission of punishment justly due to sin, punishment to which sinners may remain liable even when the mercy of God has forgiven the sin. According to Catholic teaching such punishment would in part be "worked off" by the sinner's willing performance of good actions that went beyond the goodness to which he was bound. In the indulgence system the Church associated herself officially and solemnly with a man's willingness to make such special and "unobliged" exertions; the Church made these good actions her own, and making over to the forgiven sinner, to supply for his own deficiency, some part of the treasure of the infinite merits of the Passion of our Lord and of the satisfaction made by the saints, [ ] declared him relieved, by the authority divinely committed to her, from some of the punishment due. Indulgences -- remissions only of temporal [ ] punishment due for sin, and never of eternal punishment -- are also "applicable" to the souls in Purgatory; that is to say, they can profit the dead who, preparatory to entering Heaven, are purging the imperfections in which they died. But the Church has only authority to remit guilt and punishment over those of its members who are still alive. Indulgences, therefore, are not applied to the dead by a judicial act of direct absolution from punishment; they are profitable to the dead as an official suffrage on the part of the Church, an intercession in which the Church offers for the dead the treasury of merits just described. Indulgences indeed -- so far as the dead are concerned -- are then, truly, no more than "a solemn form of prayer for the dead." [ ]

Now, although it is the whole point of the system that, by means of it, man profits from the infinite merits of Our Lord and the goodness of his brethren the saints, realising thereby (in the most literal sense) "the communion of saints," man does not so profit without an exertion that is also his own activity; and this exertion, in the nature of things, cannot be any merely material, or purely natural exertion. It must be the act of a man united and reconciled to God by repentance and forgiveness and his own determination to persevere as God's friend; an act informed and enlivened by the supernatural virtue of charity -- whence the condition generally laid down explicitly in grants of plenary indulgences that the good act to the performance of which the indulgence is attached shall be accompanied by a sacramental confession of sins and the receiving of Holy Communion.

That "good act," the work of super-erogation -- to give it its technical name -- varies with the indulgence. It may be the recitation of prescribed prayers, or a pilgrimage, or some act of penitential austerity such as fasting, or it may be -- what since the Council of Trent it has never been -- the giving of a money alms to some specified work of piety.

The Council of Trent, some forty-six years after the Lutheran explosion, [ ] reformed the practical working of the indulgence system. Had one, at least, of the practices then reprobated been abolished a century earlier, Luther would have lacked his great opportunity. For the scandal of the great indulgence of 1517 arose in part from its association with money, though also, in part, from a wrong theory about indulgences held and taught by the priest commissioned to preach that indulgence.

Wittenberg -- the little town in whose newly-founded university [ ] Luther was already, in 1517, a great figure -- lay in the diocese of Brandenburg and in the ecclesiastical province of Magdeburg. The Archbishop of Magdeburg was Albrecht of Hohenzollern, [ ] a young and dissolute prince of the reigning family of Brandenburg. He was, at the same time, Bishop of Halberstadt, and he had also managed to acquire the greatest Church dignity in Germany, the archiepiscopal see of Mainz, which made him not only the titular primate of Germany but one of the seven prince-electors of the empire.

The expenses cf. this last success had, however, been enormous. For his dispensation to hold the see of Mainz while retaining Magdeburg and Halberstadt, Albrecht had had to pay the Roman Curia 10,000 golden ducats, and for the appointment to Mainz another 14,000. For these immense sums [ ] the young archbishop turned to the great banking house of the Fugger. [ ] And when he then had to face the problem how to pay the banker, it was a simple expedient to come to terms with the Holy See about the indulgence for the rebuilding of St. Peter's. Albrecht had, so far, not allowed this to be preached in his jurisdiction. This, now, covered a good third of Germany, [ ] and when the archbishop offered to lift the ban, on condition that he received one half the alms offered -- which half should go to the Fugger in repayment of the money borrowed to settle Albrecht's account with the Roman Curia -- the pope, Leo X, agreed. Presently the new indulgence began to be preached throughout central Germany.

But it was not yet preached in Wittenberg. Here there stood in its way another vested interest, another complication of popular piety and revenues accruing by reason thereof. The ruler in Wittenberg was the Elector of Saxony, Frederick III called the Wise, and when the cavalcade of the indulgence preacher reached the frontiers of his state it found them barred against it. In the castle church at Wittenberg, which was also the university church, there was preserved one of the most famous of all collections of relics. The Elector -- like the Archbishop of Mainz -- was, in fact, a keen collector of relics and the church was a great centre of pilgrimages; for Frederick had secured for the relics rich indulgences, that amounted [ ] up to 127,000 years. For the Elector -- Luther's sovereign -- the new indulgence was simply a rival attraction against which local interests must be strongly protected. However, by the end of October 1517, the rival attraction was in the neighbourhood of Wittenberg, just across the frontier in fact; the indulgence was the burning topic of the hour, and the greatest feast in the Wittenberg calendar was fast approaching, All Saints' Day, the patronal feast of the castle-church, when the pilgrims would come in to the city in their thousands. This church served also, as has been said, as the church of the university; it was here that degrees were conferred and the great university sermons preached. When, therefore, on the eve of the feast, October 31, 1517, Luther, Professor of Theology in the university, nailed to the door of the church a sheet challenging all comers to dispute a series of ninety-five theses [ ] on the subject of indulgences, his routine professorial gesture -- an academic contribution to the morrow's festivities -- summed up and brought to a point, and symbolised, a whole complex of exciting events and interests, local, general, social, political, religious.

There were local circumstances about the preaching of this particular indulgence which might have shocked many at the time, which gave any critic of the system an obvious opportunity, and which certainly shock the Catholic of later days as he looks back upon them. Great indulgences [ ] were so preached -- at that time -- that the affair closely resembled what later times have called a "mission." The actual announcement of the indulgence was preceded by a series of sermons calling sinners to repentance, sermons on the moral evils of the time, on God as the reward of the good and the vindicator of unrepented sin, on hell and heaven, on prayer and the means of persevering in grace. Then came an explanation of the doctrine of indulgences, the details of the indulgence now offered and an invitation to make use of it. What was shocking about the indulgence of 1517 was that upon the preacher's platform, by the side of the great coffer into which the alms were placed, there was also placed the desk where sat the representative of the bank, noting down what went into the chest and the appropriate amount due to the Fugger. And also, the archbishop lent his authority to a theory of the day about indulgences which was false; and the official preacher of the indulgence, a Dominican John Tetzel, published this theory broadcast. If the indulgence was to be gained for one who was dead it was not necessary -- according to this theory -- that the person who gained it should be in a state of grace; [ ] again, it was said that nothing but an offering of money was required to gain the indulgence for the dead; and Tetzel also taught [ ] that indulgences gained by the living for the benefit of the dead were gained infallibly -- that is to say, once the specified indulgenceact was accomplished, the soul of the deceased profited from it to the full, infallibly and immediately. [ ]

Conditions could hardly have been more favourable for such a public onslaught on the indulgence-system as now began. But the famous ninety-five theses were not, by any means, the starting point of Lutheranism. They were little more than a kind of particular practical conclusion to propositions already advanced as true, and already the subject of violent discussion in the narrow world of two minor German universities. And to those fundamental propositions Luther had come, not by any activity of pure speculation, but as one driven to speculate by his own inner conflicts. The private lives of great men have scarcely any place in text books of general history, but exception needs to be made for the Augustinian Friar who now accomplished the revolution of the ages by producing a version of Christianity in which piety was divorced from morality. On that day of the memorable gesture, October 31, 1517, Luther was within eleven days of his thirty-fourth birthday; he had been a professed religious for something more than eleven years, a priest for something more than ten. How he came to enter the monastery, the way in which he lived the monastic life, the whole character and temperament of the man who gave himself to religion, the intellectual formation he had then -- at twenty-one years of age -- achieved, and the quality of that which followed: some knowledge of all these is vital to the understanding of what was now about to begin. For although Luther did not create the conditions [ ] that made possible the dramatic success of his great assault, that assault, like others before it, would have been no more than a great historical incident, had it not been that the rebel, this time, was one of the Titans of history. The question what manner of man the Titan was is all important; and for more than fifty years now a vast new literature has been endeavouring to answer it.

At the time of Luther's birth [ ] his father, Hans Luther, was only a poor copper miner; but long before the son had found his monastic vocation, the father had left poverty behind and was a flourishing mine-owner. Nevertheless, Martin Luther really knew poverty as a child, and hardship and, the greatest hardship of all, an over-severe parental discipline. Nowhere, it is believed, does he ever speak of his mother with affectionate reminiscence. He was sent to various schools, and at one time to the school kept by the Brothers of the Common Life at Eisenach, which gives him a certain kinship with Nicholas of Cusa and with Erasmus too. In 1501 he was entered at the university of Erfurt, his father resolute to make his son a lawyer. Here, for a while, he continued his education in polite letters, reading Ovid and Virgil and Horace, Juvenal and Terence and Plautus, but no Greek. And he now made his first acquaintance with Aristotle, studying the works on logic, the physics and the De Anima. In August 1502, Luther took his bachelor's degree; and then, in preparation for the master's degree, he spent a further two years in philosophical study, ethics now and politics, metaphysics, natural philosophy and general mathematics -- all according to the Via moderna, as might be expected in one of the new universities. Luther has come down to us reputed a good, hard-working student, moody, and something of a musician. In January 1505 he took his M.A. and entered the Law School.

Of Luther's studies in the Corpus Iuris Civilis we know nothing, except that they were to him uncongenial studies. They did not last long however, for in the July of that same year, to the dismay of his family and friends, and despite their strong opposition, Luther became a novice in the Erfurt house of the Austin Friars. It was, perhaps, the rashest act of his whole life, and certainly the most serious. There is not, so far as we know, anywhere, any hint of an inclination in Luther, either to the priesthood or to the monastic life, prior to July 2, 1505, on which day as this young law-scholar of twenty-one was riding back to Erfurt, after a visit to his home, now in Magdeburg, there was a sudden violent thunderstorm, and a bolt falling in a nearby field threw him to the ground. The moody, highly-strung Luther vowed to St. Anne in his terror that if he lived he would become a monk. The Augustinians, at that time, dominated the university of Erfurt. It was natural enough that Luther should offer himself to them, and -- incredible as the thing sounds to modern ears -- just fifteen days after the rash, and certainly invalid vow, they accepted the promising young man as a novice.

Luther, says the sympathetic and experienced religious who is one of the greatest of his biographers, [ ] was not made for the monastic life. He was, indeed, highly-gifted, he was generous, impulsive and his life as a student had been good and orderly and pious. But there was about him a permanent inclination to melancholy; he was fear-ridden, guilt-haunted, a natural depressive. It is the last temperament to find the monastic life congenial, let alone helpful; and what if the motive for embracing that life is the wholly mistaken motive of fear, and fear that is natural and temperamental only? How long would such a subject last in the novitiate of any order to-day? How long would any order be willing to retain him?

Luther entered the novitiate dominated by his recent terrible, psycho-physical experience. His life-long agitation did not cease; the terrors that afflicted him did not disappear; the friar's habit worked no miracle of changing the material fabric of the unfortunate man. The moody, highly-strung student was a moody, highly-strung novice, with the violent alternations of hope and despair, of joy and depression, which characterise the type; and, always, his anxieties about himself were the main activity of his inner life.

One year after his reception the novice took the solemn vows that bound him for life (July 1506); in the autumn following he received the subdiaconate, and, on April 3, 1507, he was ordained priest, nine months after his profession, and less than two years after his first reception as a novice. He then began his theological studies. [ ] They really lasted no longer than eighteen months, for in the autumn of 1508 Luther was sent to Wittenberg, where, only six years before, a university had been founded, to lecture on Aristotle's Ethics, continuing to study theology at the same time. He was, however, given his bachelor's degree in theology in March 1509; and in the autumn of that same year he began himself to lecture in theology, as an assistant to the professor. He thus lectured as a bachelor for twelve months (1509-1510), first at Erfurt and then at Wittenberg. In the winter of 1510-1511 he made his famous visit to Rome, and upon his return he took up once more his Wittenberg appointment. On October 19, 1512, he received his doctor's degree, and was given entire charge of the Wittenberg school of divinity: he was now twenty-nine.

We are approaching the decisive moment of Luther's life. He is about to lecture, as a doctor, not on the text of Peter Lombard in the spirit of the via moderna but, according to his commission and in imitation of his predecessor and fellow-religious -- Johann Staupitz -- upon the text of Holy Scripture. It is not Ockhamist theology that will occupy him now, but more practical matters. Luther had found law uncongenial and philosophy too, and also theology in the technical sense of the term -- sciences, all of them, which call for an activity that is intellectual. Luther, however, is the artist, the poet, the musician; he is the orator, the fascinating lecturer, the man of impulse and creative imagination. He has turned from the repugnant intellectualism, shirked the discipline by which alone man's mind can come to a knowledge of natures and essences, and of reasons why. And, like every other rational and sentient being, he has his difficulties and perplexities, fruit of his rational and sentient nature. Like many another Catholic thinker [ ] who is deaf to theology he is now about to look to a mysticism divorced from theology for the answers he stands in need of. His reading, henceforth, is the text of Holy Scriptures and the writings of the mystics, the one interpreted by the other, and the whole read, studied and understood by the light of the conflicting fires burning within his own breast; they are researches, also, where it is urgent for the student to have his answer quickly. The personal contrast with -- say -- St. Thomas could not be greater.

The way out, it seems to Luther, is through "mysticism", the "mystical" use of Holy Scripture. The amateur theologian -- for so, by any standard, Luther must surely be judged -- is about to use the mystics as a guide to life, and, inevitably, he is about to make a mess of the business. He will not use the only key, the theologian's explanation of the doctrines the mystics express in their own personal and more vivid fashion; and so, with the characteristic first vice of the imprudent man, he precipitates himself into Gerard Groote and the Theologia Germanica, [ ] into Tauler and pseudo-Denis. There will result a mysticism in which the cross has no place, a mysticism ordered to Luther's own most burning need, namely assurance and consolation felt and experienced in the heart; and ultimately -- the inevitable end of any such system -- he will fall victim to the spiritual fallacy called presumption, to the belief and even obsession that "I am called by a special way." It was with such an attention to "my special case" that the great and anxious research began. It is with this that it ends. But now what was at first an anxiety has been discovered to be, in reality, the foundation of God's system to save mankind; Luther's case is the case of all mankind, and the saved all pass through the same set of crises, viz., conviction of sin, temptation to despair, conviction and assurance: "I am saved".

By 1517, when the indulgence crisis arose, Luther's religious position was all but complete. It is gradually worked out in his

Wittenberg lectures of the previous five years, lectures on the Psalms, on the Epistle to the Romans and on the Epistle to the Galatians. Before we come to the great principles in which that position is summed up, it needs to be pointed out against what a background of active life they were developed. Always one of the most striking characteristics of Luther is his tireless energy, the way in which he throws himself into a host of simultaneous and often unrelated activities. It was so in these critical last years of his Catholic life. As a student of theology he can never be said to have enjoyed over-much leisure to reflect on what he was learning; as a commentator discovering the true meaning of some of the stiffest books of Holy Scripture he was in no better case. The letter in which Luther himself describes the multiplicity of occupations with which his witless Augustinian superiors allowed this popular figure to burden himself, may be quoted once more. " I really ought to have two secretaries or chancellors. I do hardly anything all day but write letters. . . . I am at the same time preacher to the monastery, have to preach in the refectory, and am even expected to preach daily in the parish church. I am regent of the house of studies and vicar, that is to say prior eleven times over; I have to provide for the delivery of the fish from the Leitzkau pond and to manage the litigation of the Herzberg friars at Torgau; I am lecturing on Paul, compiling lectures on the Psalter, and, as I said before, writing letters most of the time. . . . It is seldom that I have time for the recitation of the Divine Office or to celebrate Mass, and then, too, I have my peculiar temptations from the flesh, the world, and the devil." [ ]

Luther is not, here, writing a statement meant for the critical examination of a hostile court. It is a friendly letter to a friend, in which there is room for the exaggeration that will not deceive and that is not meant to deceive. Luther was, no doubt of it, as active as he was capable, but the groans are not, therefore, all to be taken at their full face-value. Nor need we fasten on the reference to the flesh, and, oversimplifying a very complex business, see in this the key that explains all. Luther was, later on, to coin the phrase Concupiscentia invincibilis and to say Pecca Fortiter, and to marry in despite of his monastic vow, and to speak with the most revolting coarseness of sex life in general and of his own relations with his wife. [ ] Nevertheless, in his life as an Austin Friar, it was not in his body [ ] that the trouble was seated which, at times, all but drove him crazy, nor in his intelligence, but rather in his intensely active imagination. What never ceased to haunt him, seemingly, was the thought of eternal punishment; and not so much the thought that he might in the end lose his soul, as that he was already marked out for hell by God. Here was the subject of the long, often-repeated, discussions with Staupitz, his friend and one-time master and present superior. And it is, once again, a measure of the theological decadence in certain university circles that this professor was not able to dispel the young monk's fears by an exposition of the traditional teaching that no man loses his soul except by his own free deliberate choice, that God is not and cannot be the cause of the sin that merits hell. All Staupitz could do was to remind Luther of the infinite mercy won for man by the merits of the passion of Christ. But to the mind which, unaware of the nature of the problem, was wrestling, unequipped, with the mystery of man's predestination to grace and to glory, these counsels availed little. To one whose mind held the notion of a divine reprobation -- that those who went to hell went there, in ultimate analysis, because God destined them to hell when He created them -- the very thought of the Passion was an additional torture, and Luther has told us how, at times, he could not look upon the crucifix.

Here too, no doubt, is the secret of those terrible scenes, the convulsive panics that seized on him from time to time as a friar: the attempted flight from his first mass; the horror and terror in which he said mass, or walked in procession beside the priest who carried the Blessed Sacrament. [ ] It became the great anxiety and need of Luther's life that he should know that he was among those predestined to be saved, be free from all doubt that he could not lose his soul.

Once again, we must beware of over-simplifying. The genesis of the specifically Lutheran doctrines is, no doubt, not wholly to be sought in this dominant characteristic. But Luther's own needs -- which he came to see as the common problem of all mankind -- went undoubtedly for much, as he studied and put together the lectures on such classic treatises about God's grace as the Epistles of St. Paul to the Romans and to the Galatians. And once he had found his doctrine, if it was as an emancipator of mankind that he published it, it was, at the same time, with his great cry of personal liberation that he gave it to the world.

Luther did not, of course, come to his study of St. Paul with a mind devoid of theological notions. His conception of God for example -- as a Being omnipotent and arbitrary -- he derived from his Ockhamist masters. [ ] And what they stated and discussed as ways through which God might have arranged the work of sanctification and salvation, Luther proposed as the ways God actually chose. " From the moment when Luther learnt Ockham's doctrine, he necessarily lost all definite notion of what the supernatural is, all understanding of the necessity, the essence and the efficaciousness of sanctifying grace and, in a general way, of the supernatural virtues." [ ] Nor could it have been otherwise. The whole of Ockham's influence is the history of the disappearance of certitude; of the end of all grasp of reality, and of clear, distinct thought. And it was from Ockham, also, that Luther derived one of the two main elements of his own peculiar system, the idea, namely, that the whole work of grace and of salvation is something altogether external to man -- in cause and in effect. It is, for Luther, wholly and purely the act of God. Man's action can have no share in it, except in so far as God accepts that action as meritorious. As things are, so Ockham declares, such human acts must be the acts of a personality united to God by supernatural charity, acts of a soul possessed by sanctifying grace; but only as things are. For God could, in His Omnipotence, just as well accept as meritorious acts done by his enemies, the acts of souls devoid of sanctifying grace, the acts of souls given over to unrepented mortal sin. From Ockham the tradition had come down through a succession of masters. Gregory of Rimini has the same teaching, so has Peter d'Ailly, so has Gabriel Biel. [ ] It is not inherently impossible for man -- so they all concur -- to be accepted by God as meriting, even though he does not possess charity. Man could, on the other hand, be God's enemy even though he does possess charity. And he could pass from the state of enmity to friendship without any change in himself -- for the whole basis of man's relations with God is God's arbitrary attitude of acceptance or non-acceptance of his acts.

All this -- said the Ockhamist tradition -- was possible; this could be the way in which all would happen. Luther, meditating the mystery, and his own problem, thought he saw that, if this possible way were indeed the actual way, his problem was solved. He first seized on the notion of sanctification as a thing external to the soul; it resolved the difficulty arising from his position that man, by original sin, was wholly and for ever corrupted in his essence, [ ] incapable therefore for ever of any works really good. How could fallen man -- if this were his state -- do aught towards his sanctification? But, were sanctification something external to man's action, the cloak of the infinite merits of Christ thrown in pity around man's infinite wretchedness, to cover over his truly hopeless state -- did this indeed suffice, then the problem of man's own condition under the cloak would cease to be. Man's own sinfulness, the necessary effect of the poison of original sin working in him, can have no effect upon his eternal destiny once, clad in the robe of Christ's merits, he is accepted by God as justified. No sin, committed by such a man, would give the devil any hold upon him.

The Lutheran theory is not yet complete -- the all-important element is lacking which shall give man assurance, from outside the theory, that it is something more than a theory that seems to solve the terrible problem. But, even so, the logical, practical consequences of the theory are evident. If this doctrine be true, then the whole elaborate fabric of the theory and practice of good works as necessary for salvation is but a sham. Works of penance, in particular, are not only useless but blasphemous; they are acts based on a false theory, they are a standing contradiction to the saving truth. There is no point in prayer as a petition, and the whole sacramental system goes -- except as a sign or gesture affirming belief in God as Saviour. With the sacramental system there must disappear too, the clerical body, as a priesthood; as propagandists and teachers they may yet survive individually, and be organised. The very Church ceases to have any raison d'etre as such.

Not all these consequences were immediately drawn out, either by Luther or by his opponents. The immediate discussion centred around the fundamental principles, and in the twelve months that preceded the appearance of Tetzel and the great indulgence drive, Wittenberg was filled with conflict. There was, for example, the disputation of September 1516, when a pupil of Luther officially defended theses to the effect that man's nature is utterly powerless to do good; there were the lectures on Galatians in which Luther developed his views, and more lectures on the Epistle to the Hebrews; there was, above all, the great disputation of September 4, 1517, on ninety-seven theses directed against Scholasticism, when " the bitterness of innumerable priests, monks, preachers and university professors that, for two centuries at least, had been accumulating against the Scholastic philosophy found at last its complete expression." [ ] Luther was carrying all before him; none could compete with him as a speaker, and the publication of the theses against Indulgences, only eight weeks later, is a measure of his success, no less than it is a testimony to his boldness; their publication also served, and it is the real importance of the event, to bring Luther's new version of the Christian dispensation before the whole Christian world. Long before Rome's solemn condemnation of it (June 15, 1520) [ ] Luther's theory was discussed and fought over in every university of Christendom.

And long before that -- within a few months, indeed, of the move against the doctrine of Indulgence -- Luther had found the last vital element for his teaching. How shall a man know whether he is accepted of God, predestined, and not marked for hell? This acceptation is something external to him; justification does not change him; he is not any better, once he has gained it. That he is no better is, indeed, no proof that he is not justified. But how can man know with certainty that he is justified, accepted? The test is simple; the touchstone is his possession of faith. For the just man lives by faith alone -- not by faith which is the assent of the intelligence to God revealing the sacred doctrines, but by faith which is a firm confident belief that God has predestined one to glory as one of the accepted. It is this faith alone, so Luther henceforth held, [ ] which makes man accepted by God. Possession of this faith is the proof that one is accepted. Possessed of this faith man lives. For those who so believe, salvation is certain. And all men who come to attain this belief come to it through a stage of anxious tormenting doubt and temptations to despair. Luther's case is the case of all mankind. The religious reflection of his almost congenital phobia is a stage in his understanding that he is saved. The "dark night" has not issued in any purification of sense, but in an assurance that impurities do not matter, in the certitude that whatever happens one is saved. The great discovery is complete. "Christianity is nothing but a perpetual exercise in feeling that you have no sin, although you committed sin, but that your sins are attached to Christ" -- Luther's own summary of the matter. [ ]

This is not an attempt to sketch even the outline of Protestantism, the religion of the churches that issued from the Reformation [ ] -

- still less, of course, is it meant as a critique of Protestants. It is no more than an endeavour to explain Luther's own personal doctrinal invention; [ ] the starting point of his career as a destroyer of Catholicism and as one of the founders of the later Reformed Churches, the source of his strength and confidence and courage. The history of what he accomplished, of the evolution of a new church, of its immediate and willing subordination to the state, of the development of Lutheranism into Protestantism, cannot be separated from the later story of Catholicism, the story of the Catholic revival, of the Council of Trent and of the movement that has been called -- not too happily -- the Counter-Reformation; nowhere does the seamless web of history suffer greater harm than when the story of Luther is separated from that of our own modern age. It must therefore find its place in the concluding volume of this work. But something also needs to be said about Luther as the last of the medievals -- none the less truly a medieval man for being a great heretic.

There has never been any disposition, whether among Luther's critics or his supporters, from the reformer's time down to our own, to deny that he did much more than change people's purely religious beliefs and practices. Never, in fact, has there been a more striking demonstration than the Reformation that religion is the central activity of all human life. There is a lyrical description of Luther's accomplishment in one of the greatest of modern German historians, [ ] that will serve as an example of this view. It will also serve to introduce what still needs to be said in order to explain the monstrosity which Lutheranism seemed to the Catholics of Luther's time. "A new world," says this historian, "has come into being. One of the twin peaks of Christendom has crumbled away. . . . The spiritual power has disappeared. . . . Never before did man see such an overturning of political and juridical ideas. . . . All those ideas from which the State of modern times derives -- autonomy of the State's law, final sovereignty of the lay authority, the State's recognised exclusive hold on public action -- find in the Lutheran reformation their religious foundation and, thereby, their power to spread. The Reformation was not only a renewal of religion: it was a rebirth of the world in every respect."

The final importance of Luther, indeed, did not lie in the new theological ideas he invented, but in the fact that by combining with them existing theologico-social ideas he gave to these last the authority proper to religious belief; they are as fatal to the full natural development of the human personality, as the theological invention was fatal to Christianity itself. The anti-Christian social ideas and ideals of the last two hundred years and more were now presented as Christianity itself, and were presently organised in a new Christian Church, which was the active rival and bitter foe of the traditional Church whose president was the Roman pope. To that new conception of Christianity first of all, and then to that new Church, Luther rallied the greater part of Germany and Scandinavia; in the next generation -- under other reformers of kindred spirit, attached to the same fundamental theological discovery -- Switzerland and Holland and Scotland and England were likewise "reborn," while a powerful attempt was made to secure France also for the new world.

What were the distinguishing principles of this world, what was the* relation to the essence of Lutheranism, and what was the first appeal of the system to the nation among which it was first published?

That appeal was something much more lasting than any implied mere general invitation to monks and nuns and priests to throw over their religious obligations, something much more fundamental than the prospect of unhindered moral licence; to such saturnalia -- and, of course, there followed in Germany an indescribable saturnalia [ ] -- there always succeeds a period of reaction; even the loosest of mankind is in the end too bored to keep it up. Nor was it by publishing broadcast his theological lectures on the Epistles of St. Paul, that Luther roused Germany to his support. He did it by attacking, with new skill, with humour, and new boldness, the pope's hold on Germany as a source of income; he satirised the pope's claim to be the Holy Father of Christendom while presiding over such an establishment as the Roman Curia and Court of those days could be made to seem, and in great part actually was; and he offered the ruling classes of Germany a practical programme that would make them supreme in German life, and that appealed explicitly to the notion that it is Germany's destiny to rule mankind for mankind's greater good and happiness. It was in half a dozen writings put out chiefly in the years 1520 and 1521, that Luther laid the foundation of all that construction which the historian just quoted sees to have been built by later times. In the Sermon on Good Works, for example, the pope is denounced as the real Turk, exploiting the simplicity of Germans and sucking the marrow out of the national life. The Church, Luther explained in another tract -- On the Roman Papacy -- cannot need a visible head, for it is itself an invisible thing. That "power of the keys," possession of which is the basis of the pope's position, is in reality the common possession of all true believers; nor is it at all a power of government, but the assurance which Christians give to one another that their sins are not held against them, and thereby administer to one another the consolation and encouragement that sinners need as they face the fact of the divine moral law which it is beyond man's power to observe. This tract, like almost everything that Luther was now writing, is salted with vigorous, crude invective. But the classic instruments of this first propaganda were three pamphlets which appeared in 1520, the Address to the Nobility of the German Nation, the Babylonian Captivity of the Church and the Liberty of the Christian Man. [ ]

The first of these [ ] sketches the main lines which the needed Reformation ought to follow. Annates are to be abolished and no more money sent out of Germany to Rome; no more foreigners

are to be named to German benefices, and all papal jurisdiction
in Germany, spiritual or temporal, is to be abolished; pilgrimages
to Rome are to be abolished also, along with religious guilds,
indulgences, dispensations, holidays that are feasts, and masses
for the dead. All believers are priests -- Scripture says so -- and
this principle is developed to show that the ecclesiastical
hierarchy, and the clerical state, are merely human inventions
and have no real place in the Christian Church.
Excommunication, therefore, is but a meaningless word. Again,
since the special institution of ecclesiastical authority has no
justification (is, indeed, contrary to Scripture), it is the prince
who must preside over the believers. It is the prince who will
protect the true interests of the Church, reforming and correcting
as is found necessary, and taking over the property held by the
usurped authority of the self-styled ecclesiastical power. For
centuries this ecclesiastical power, in the person of the popes, has
claimed certain rights over the emperors. The truth is that the
empire alone is a reality, and the pope ought to surrender to it
even Rome itself. If Christendom and the empire are, indeed,
one, it is the emperor who is supreme and the imperial power is
the heritage of the German race. The noble princes then must
regain by force those benefices which the popes have " unjustly "
taken to themselves; the monks must free themselves from their
vows; the priests must "steal from the pope" their right to marry
and live like laymen. Here we can see how Luther, the reformer
of abuses in religion, incidentally makes provision for "all those
immense, disorderly dreams which, for more than a hundred
years, have been troubling the German heart: reform of the
Church in head and members in the sense of a return to its
spiritual, purely evangelical principle; reform of the empire in
the sense of a State which shall be stronger, more organic, and
capable, if not of dominating Europe, at least of guaranteeing to
Germany full economic and cultural independence." [ ]

The Babylonian Captivity, subject of the second pamphlet
named, [ ] is the tyranny of the papacy over the Church of Christ.

Its origins lie in the long falsification of Christian doctrine; and Luther sets out, in systematic opposition, his own teaching on the meaning of the Sacraments and their place in a Christian's life. There are but three sacraments in the real sense of the word, Baptism, the Holy Eucharist, and Penance, and their effectiveness is wholly a matter of the faith of the recipient. There is no sacrifice in the second of these sacraments, and the Mass is simple devilish wickedness.

More important, however, than the detail either of the abuses which Luther recommends the nobles to sweep away, or of the traditional doctrines and practices he now repudiates, is the teaching of the third and shortest of these tracts, The Liberty of a Christian Man. [ ] This is an eloquent plea for the central Lutheran doctrine that one thing alone is needed for justification-faith; [ ] that without this faith nothing avails. Luther's first target had been good works done in a Pelagian spirit, done, that is to say, with the idea that the mere human mechanic of the action secures of itself deliverance from sin. No one had had more to say about the spiritual worthlessness of such works than Luther's own contemporary and adversary Cajetan, and what Cajetan had to say was no more than a commonplace with Catholic preachers and writers then as now, and indeed always. [ ] But Luther went far beyond this. Although the just man would do good works -- as a good tree brings forth good fruit [ ] -- there was not, and there could not be, any obligation on the justified believer to do good works. He did good works -- but freely, out of love for his neighbour, or to keep his body subject to his soul; he did them as the natural acts of a soul that was justified. To omit them -- a possibility which Luther, in this part of his theory, did not envisage -- would not have entailed sin: "It is solely by impiety and incredulity of heart that a man becomes guilty, and a slave of sin, deserving condemnation; not by any outward sin or work." [ ] This goes far beyond any mere reaction against such a false theory as that mechanical religious activities are sufficient to reconcile a sinner with God whom he has offended.

Here we touch again what one of Luther's German editors [ ] has called the divorce between piety and morality; for "Sin we must, while we remain here; this life is no dwelling place of justice. The new heavens and earth that shall be the dwelling place of righteousness we yet await, as St. Peter says. It is enough that we confess through the riches of God's glory the Lamb that taketh away the sins of the world; from Him sin will not tear us away, even if thousands and thousands of times a day we fornicate or murder." [ ] Here is a truly revolutionary mischief, and it has its reflection in the new theory which Luther came to put out -- in the name of religion and as a part of Christian teaching -- about the kind of thing the State is, about man's relation to the State and the obedience he owes it; for in this theory there is a divorce between law and morality.

Luther is impatient of the old distinction between the spheres of what is known naturally and what can be known only by a divine revelation, as he is impatient of the careful scholastic delimitation of the spheres of nature and grace. He would, indeed, abolish the philosophical study of natures and causes and ends; Aristotle, because the chief inspiration here of such thinkers as were Christians, was the greatest of all mischiefs, "an accursed, proud, knavish heathen. . . . God sent him as a plague for our sins." [ ] His ethics, and his metaphysics, ought to be everywhere destroyed. [ ] The Christian, for an answer to his questionings about these matters, should go to Sacred Scripture and to Sacred Scripture only. Thither now went Luther. [ ] Like every other Catholic who has committed the blunder of refusing the natural reason its proper place, and its rights within that place, he fell into the most egregious confusion between the natural and the supernatural and so, necessarily, proceeded to a catastrophic misunderstanding of the supernatural. Taking the Bible as a divinely meant source of knowledge about natural reality, and consulting it about that natural thing, the State Luther proceeded to apply what it had to say about the religious law of the ancient Hebrews to the civil affairs of Germany in his own time. He read in St. Paul that "The law is not made for the just man, but for the unjust and the wicked" [ ] and, combining what he thought to be the application of this text with his own theory about man becoming just by faith alone, he henceforth saw the state as made up of two kinds of men: the believers who were just, the good men, subject to no authority but that of the Holy Spirit -- and the unbelieving wicked. It was because of these last that there had to be princes and States and civil government. The good would always remain good, because justified. The wicked would never be anything else but wicked, and they would be in the majority always. Wickedness, in fact, is for Luther supreme in human life, and must be so; it is the very nature of things, mankind having by original sin become the possession of the devil and human nature wholly corrupt. States, then, there must be, not only for the protection of the good against the wicked, but for the conservation of some external moral order amongst the unbelieving wicked upon whom the Holy Spirit has no effect. The State is, in fact, God's agent -- His sole agent -- for the work of ruling mankind and keeping it from growing morally worse; [ ] it is the divinely founded guide of man in morals, and it is divinely authorised to punish man for his infractions of morality as the State proclaims it. If we look closer at this Lutheran State, it closely resembles the state of Marsiglio's ideal, in this at least that power is its very essence. The State is Authority; whatever it decrees is, by the fact, right and must not ever be resisted; and wherever there is power, there is authority. Authority is always right; the fact of punishment is a proof of guilt; and the prince has a duty to be habitually merciless, since his role is that of "God's executioner." The most fitting symbol of his authority is the naked sword: ". . . Christians are rare people on earth. Therefore stern, hard, civil rule is necessary in the world, lest the world become wild, peace vanish, and commerce and common interests be destroyed. . . . No one need think that the world can be ruled without blood. The civil sword shall and must be red and bloody." [ ] Here, in all its simplicity, is the theory of the State as essentially a policeman, [ ] with its whole activity concentrated between the courthouse and the gallows; it is a theory that will dominate the political thought of all the Reformers. [ ]

Let it be said that Luther did not work out this theory, which so exalts the State that its subjects must fall below the human level of responsible freedom, merely as so much compliment and flattery to the princes his protectors; any more than he worked it out as believing these princes to be men of personally holy, or even reputable, lives. It is all disinterested; it flows from the new truth; Luther is "sincere." And if the tiny minority of the just, almost lost among the wicked subjects for whom this monstrous power has been divinely devised, suffer from the severity of the prince -- it is always unjust in regard of the just -- they must be content to suffer, and reverently to see in it a manifestation of the just anger of God.

This is a barbarous notion of the State indeed; and what a regression it represents by comparison with the theories of Luther's contemporaries Erasmus and More. Its effect, in practice, must be the same as the effect of Machiavelli, but, in one highly important respect, Luther is more effective by far than the Italian atheist. For Luther is, in his own mind, and in the mind of the century that follows, a religious teacher. He does not so much devise political theories as present Christians with a new notion of their civic obligations as Christians, and present the princes with a new religious conception of their office as rulers. Once Luther saw all this as a main truth of religion, a truth closely related to and in part flowing from the doctrines he held to be central, he riveted it on all his people, as he won them over to the new conception of Christianity.

What will be the nature and office of law, in the Christian State as Luther conceives this? The new doctor will have nothing to do with the traditional Catholic conception of earthly justice as the reflection of -- and man's share in -- the objective eternal order of the Divine Intelligence, an order first communicated to man's intelligence through the natural law. The Lutheran doctrine that Original Sin has wholly corrupted man's nature makes any such sharing an impossibility: man is nothing but sin, enmity towards God and, moreover, his will is not a free will but a will definitely enslaved, and captive to the devil. For such a being, the law in the Divine Intelligence is something too perfect ever to be fulfilled.

The order of justice divinely established is not an objective reality, not an actual equilibrium of actions objectively considered, belonging ad esse rei. [ ] And because it is wholly a matter of divine acceptation, the centre of all morality is the arbitrary will of God directing as it pleases the passive human hand. This notion of the will of God, as no less arbitrary than supreme, is reflected in Luther's ideas about human positive law.

Law is not subject to any consideration of morals or of reason. What it commands cannot be wrong nor unreasonable. Law only needs to be stated to have, immediately, all its power to oblige. As justice is whatever God likes, so law is whatever the prince likes; and, because it is the prince's act as prince, law is always an expression of the divine action upon the world, and so, sacrosanct -- although it remains no more than "a power to command and to compel" [ ], and cannot ever oblige a man in conscience. It can never be wrong for the prince to command wrongdoing, and to his commands the subject must always render external obedience at any rate. There is -- in this system -- no means by which the human reason can relieve the human subject of his obligations to submit to whatever the State decrees. Ius divinum quod est ex gratia non tollit ius humanum quod est ex lege naturali -- so the great synthesis of St. Thomas had proclaimed. Luther denied that there was such a thing as natural law; there could not exist any human right deriving therefrom. And as for the role, in human affairs, of the divine, Luther roundly stated the very converse of St. Thomas's liberating concept, declaring that "the Gospel does nothing to lighten human law." [ ]

What we are now given, in fact, is a theory of the divine right of the fait accompli in public affairs, and of the duty of Christian man to put up with whatever is ordained for him. What an answer -- and a final one -- in the name of the newly-discovered evangelical Christianity, to the long claim of religion to fix a standard for princely conduct ! The ghosts of the Ghibelline legists must have rejoiced at the triumph of the new servitude, and smiled to see the State freed now from the control of Christian morality in the very name of Christian revelation ! The religious peculiarities of Luther's revolution would, in the course of the centuries, suffer more than a sea change. They would pass, and be accounted of no importance, even to those heirs of Luther who continued, gratefully, to reverence his work and even his personality. But this at least would endure, the notion namely that the State, a lay thing, is exclusively sovereign because it stands alone as an authority representing the social order. As such the State has a moral and religious character and role, rendering needless the Church as a public thing. Here is the Reformation's essential political idea, [ ] the sole positive idea to we that vast transformation any real unity.

Throughout the fifteenth century the demand for the reformation of the Church had, in Germany, gone hand in hand with desire for political change. It was, then, in keeping with the spirit of the time, that the prophet, when ultimately he appeared, should be also something of a political philosopher. Quite apart from the undoubted fact that Luther, brought face to face with the papacy as a force bound to work for his destruction, realised that in the State was the papacy's own born enemy, [ ] there was a kind of inevitability in this development.

The State also could serve -- and could alone serve -- as an agent for the reform of religion. Here is the last element that completes the Lutheran new world, the subjection of religion to the State, the transformation of the State, indeed, into a kind of Church. To understand it we need to recall a distinction which Luther made between the real Church which is invisible (and subject to none but God) and all that organisation which comes into existence from the moment when a score of believers meet for worship, and by the very fact of their meeting, if only for the time of their meeting.

So far, down to these opening years of the sixteenth century, religion, in spite of many defeats and the constant hostility of the princes, had successfully maintained its place as the rightful, ultimate inspiration of the whole social order -- And by religion is meant an institution whose rights and supremacy as an institution were acknowledged by all princes, in all states, the Catholic Church; an independent, sovereign thing, to which all belonged, by which all were effectively ruled. This independence of religion was bound up with the admitted real distinction between the two authorities, the temporal and the spiritual, both of them sovereign over mankind, each in its own domain; and although the conflicts between the two were frequent, even continuous along the frontier where they met, no State ever contested the principle that the Church, within its own sphere, was as truly sovereign as the State itself. In practice this meant that the State could never claim a sovereignty that was absolute; it must always take account of the rights of religion, and avoid action that would trespass on functions considered as indispensable to the Church's spiritual mission. [ ] It is this sovereign independence of religion as a visible public power, this place of the Church in the life of the community, that Luther attacks and, wherever his theories gain a hold, destroys. And he does this by denying the validity of the traditional distinction between the two authorities, and by his new theory that the State is absolute by right divine.

The real Church, for Luther, is an invisible thing and purely spiritual. It is subject to God alone and within it there is no law but only love. True enough, the Church is made up of men and women who are visible, and these come together and perform each his own appointed ritual part. But since all believers are priests, those who officiate are not clergy in the Catholic sense but only a corps of preachers and ministers of sacraments, chosen for convenience's sake to do for all what, in fact, each could do for himself. All believers are equal in their freedom to follow grace as they understand it, all are equal in control of their inner life. There is none who is the spiritual sovereign of his fellows, nor is the whole body a sovereign body. The Church -- as an external organisation -- does not possess authority; it cannot even make laws, still less enforce them. The control needed to keep it in being must come from some other source than the fact that the Church is thus organised; and this control is the business of the prince, part of his general duty to care for morality and good order. The Church -- in this new scheme of things -- really does quit this world, except as an indefinite number of individual believers. It has no existence as such, no authority of its own, no rights, no property. For all these matters it is the State which will now function; the great era of secularisation of Church property and usurpation of Church jurisdiction opens, the State lays hands on the monasteries, for example, and on all that relates to marriage. The State also controls worship and ritual, teaching and preaching; these are but external manifestations of the Spirit. What about heretics? can there be such? Undoubtedly there can be those who openly contradict the articles of faith. Such men are public criminals, and it is the duty of the prince to punish them. As to the standard of orthodoxy -- what is the meaning of the faith -- it is for the prince to say what accords with Scripture and what does not. Who else, indeed, can decide, what other public authority is there but the State which, in virtue of its temporal power, is the temporal guardian of the divine law. Also, it is explained -- this will be readily understood -- that the State does the Church a service in undertaking these cares, for all these charges are material things, attention to which is fatal to the spirit.

So much, then, for the role of the prince as prince. But the prince has also his place in religion as an individual believer. He too is, thereby, a priest with the rest; and as all are priests in the measure of their gifts, the prince -- who has the unique gift, to wit his divine charge of ruling the State -- is most of all a priest, and in all crises and unusual circumstances it is he who will take the lead. He is not, indeed, the head of the Church -- no human being can be that -- but he is its principal member. [ ] As such, yet once again, it is for him to inaugurate needed reforms, and to organise the external appearance of the Church. In practice, the ancient maxim of St. Ambrose that sums up the whole long Christian tradition is wholly reversed, imperator enim intra ecclesiam, non supra ecclesiam est, and the dream of countless Ghibellines and legists is realised at last, "The State is the only legitimate authority the world knows. The State is truly sovereign." [ ]

Below all the forces that make the Reformation a success is the powerful swell of the lay revolt against the cleric; it is wholly victorious wherever the Reformation triumphs, and in those other countries where, for yet another two centuries, the Catholic Church retains its precarious hold as a recognised sovereign power, the lay revolt is greatly heartened by that triumph. This hold of the State on the religious life of man is the most valuable conquest of all, and the last which any of these States will ever relinquish. [ ] The Reformation does bring freedom from the rule of the pope and his bishops and his clergy, from the sovereign spiritual state which the Catholic Church is. But, ultimately, the main freedom it establishes is the freedom of the State to do what it likes with man: and all in the name of God. In place of the Catholic dogmas man must now accept -- wherever the Reformers triumph -- the new reformed dogmas; even the morality of private life will be brought under public control. In his heart man is indeed free to function as priest and prophet and consciously chosen and elected, justified, the friend whom no sin can separate from his Saviour -- and he is free to be faithful in his heart while yet, in obedience to the divinely established prince, going the other way to all appearances. It is the only freedom he does enjoy. Everywhere man is soon grouped in new churches; his religious life is as much regimented as ever; [ ] and in his life as a citizen he is -- unless he be wealthy -- little more than a pawn, whether the sovereign be the absolute Lutheran prince or the absolute Calvinist oligarchy. Of all who benefit from the destruction inaugurated by Luther's explosive thought, it is the prince who benefits most, and most lastingly. "None since the Apostles," said the Reformer, speaking of himself, "has done so much to give the civil authority a conscience; none, whether teacher or writer, theologian or jurist, has spoken so clearly, or in so masterly a fashion." [ ] The brag is characteristic, and not least in the naive innocent simplicity apparently all unconscious that the speaker comes at the end of four hundred years of the most intense discussion of human rights and political theory. And in the very years while Luther's exegesis is thus riveting the absolute State on Protestant Germany as a part of divine revelation, the Dominican Vittoria, in the absolute Spain of Charles V, is freely lecturing on the limitations of princely power, a task to be just as freely continued, a generation later, in that same country, under the absolutist Philip II by the Jesuit Suarez. [ ] In the most unlikely places, and at the most unlikely seasons, the true Church of Christ never ceases to battle for the real independence of the Gospel from every human fetter.

Luther, undoubtedly, scored a great initial victory. Then he was, definitely, checked. But not before that victory had produced an effect that still endures -- still dividing western Europe, and into two kinds of men, [ ] whom for convenience's sake we may call Protestants and Catholics. The story of the fortunes of the Reformation must be told elsewhere, and nowhere will any such impossible task be undertaken as to compare these Protestants and Catholics, in their lives at least. But at the risk of digressing into a much controverted theological matter, something needs to be said of Lutheranism as being the very inversion of Christianity and of this as providing the main source of difference between Protestants and Catholics. The kind of difference this was must be stated, for it explains why henceforth they never really understood each other, and why with Luther all previous Christian history is brought up sharp; it explains how, to Catholics, Luther is most of all a revolutionary, and the new reformed religion not religion at all in the sense that Catholicism is a religion.

Briefly, what Luther did was to make man and not God the centre of those activities to the sum of which we give the term religion -- man's need of God and not God's glory. And the Scriptural paradox was once again fulfilled that he who would save his life must lose it. From the beginning of his own career as a friar at least, the human subject was to Luther of more concern than God -- not as a theory, but practically, that is to say in the order of mystical experience, in the conduct of what is called, in the special technical sense, the spiritual life. Luther's great achievement, from this point of view, was, in effect, the translation of his own, more or less native, " mystical egocentreism" into a foundation dogma of Christian belief.

His first mystical awakening was anxiety about the judicial wrath of the Almighty (as Luther misconceived Almighty God), a practical anxiety how, despite the invincible concupiscence that poisons -- wholly corrupts -- human nature itself and not merely Martin Luther, (again an enormous misconception of the effect of Original Sin) man can escape that wrath. The reformer's first pre-occupation is to work out a theological doctrine of salvation, and in the new scheme of things theological the main purpose of religion is precisely this, that it is the means by which man escapes from the devil. "Saving faith", and not charity, is now the first, principal, and characteristic virtue of the model

Christian. And this faith -- an instrument divinely provided, by which man takes hold of the imputed justice of Christ our Saviour -- is not presented as (and it cannot ever be) a real participation in the Divine Life such as is sanctifying grace. Man's life is not thus grafted on to the Divine Life, in the Lutheran scheme of things; it remains a thing apart, and man is forever locked within himself. Man cannot make God the centre of his life, if he cannot believe that his life is actually one with God's life. From all possibility of such a union man is also cut off by his own ineradicable sinfulness, that fatal, inevitable state of corruption, the effect of Original Sin, which not even divine grace can cure. And God being barred out from man's innermost self, who there is ruler and supreme if not man himself?

Of the resulting principle that a man's self is the ultimate standard by which all else must be judged, who better than Luther is the classic example? The exaltation of self bred in his contemporaries by that Renaissance of letters and the arts for which Luther had such bitter words, [ ] is as nothing to the exaltation of self bred by his own new theology. To the spirit of man justified by saving faith, found free as none was ever free before, all external constraint or law is an unendurable wrong. There is posited an essential opposition between the liberty newly revealed in Luther, between the interior life, between the " spirit" -- and all that comes to man from without himself. And so all those things which are in reality links between the inner man and the truth outside him, must henceforth be barriers -- or not realities, except with such reality as the inner man chooses to confer upon them. The Church and the sacraments, the hierarchy, the teaching papacy, the objective doctrine -- these are considered as so many barriers between the inner man and God. Faith and works are in opposition for Luther, the Gospel and the law, the inner spirit and the external authority. From without there is, then, no hope; and once the emotional alternations cease of spiritual terror and spiritual exaltation, or once they are seen for what they are, merely temperamental reactions, acts not wholly human, what remains? The intelligence was long ago expelled by the prophet from the garden of spirituality, with bitter curses indeed, and the most obscene revilings. Faith, true faith, the assent of the intelligence to truth divinely made known, has no place there.

And what when man is through with the tragi-comedy of the interior emotional gymnastic? It is the deepest criticism of Luther's famous theory -- and the explanation of the unending, ever-developing miseries that have come from it, and were bound to come from it -- that it goes against the nature of things, and against nothing more evidently than against the nature of the spiritual. The new religion introduced, or rather established as part of the permanent order of things, a whole series of vital antagonisms to perplex and hinder man already only too tried by his own freely chosen wrong-doing, to fill his soul with still blacker thoughts about the hopeless contradiction and futility of all existence, to set him striving for centuries at the hopeless task of bringing happiness and peace out of a philosophy essentially pessimistic and despairing. It cut him off from all belief in the possibility of external aids, and in the very generation when Christian man needed nothing so evidently as a delivery that was divine, it handed him over to his own corrupt self, endowed now, for the task of self correction, with an innate omniscience and infallibility such as no cleric or pontiff or church had ever devised. [ ]

For the many terrible evils from which Christian life was suffering, Luther brought not a single remedy. He could do no more than exhort and denounce and destroy. There was the problem of clerical worldliness: Luther, heir to the long line of faux mystiques for whom clerical ownership was sinful, abolished the cleric altogether. There was the problem of the scandal caused by rival philosophies and the effect of the rivalry on theology and mysticism: Luther, again the term of a long development, drove out all philosophy, and theology with it. The very purpose of the intelligence is knowledge, to enquire is its essential act: but in the sphere of all but the practical and the concrete and the individual, Luther bade the Christian stifle its promptings as a temptation and a snare; once again Luther is not a pioneer in the solution he offers. There was the problem of the Church itself; how it could best be kept unspotted, despite its contacts with the world: Luther's solution is to abolish the Church.

It is the surrender to despair -- in the name of greater simplicity, which "simplicity" is presented as the road back to primitive truth and the good life; to despair: as though true religion was incompatible with the two great natural necessities, the ownership of material goods and the activity of the speculative intelligence; as though material destitution and contented, uncritical ignorance were conditions sine quibus non for the preservation on earth of the work of that Incarnate Wisdom through Whom the Creator called the earth into being.

All those anti-intellectualist, anti-institutional forces that had plagued and hindered the medieval Church for centuries, whose chronic maleficent activity had, in fact, been the main cause why -- as we are often tempted to say -- so little was done effectively to maintain a generally higher standard of Christian life; all the forces that were the chronic distraction of the medieval papacy, were now stabilised, institutionalised in the new reformed Christian Church. Enthronement of the will as the supreme human faculty; hostility to the activity of the intelligence in spiritual matters and in doctrine; the ideal of a Christian perfection that is independent of sacraments and independent of the authoritative teaching of clerics; of sanctity attainable through one's own self-sufficing spiritual activities; denial of the truth that Christianity, like man, is a social thing; -- all the crude, backwoods, obscurantist theories bred of the degrading pride that comes with chosen ignorance, the pride of men ignorant because unable to be wise except through the wisdom of others, now have their fling. Luther's own special contribution -- over and above the key doctrines which set all this mischief loose -- is the notion of life as radically evil.

When all has been said that can be said in Luther's favour, (and admittedly there is an attractive side to the natural man) [ ] the least harmful of all his titanic public activities was his vast indignation roused by abuses -- and by the sins of others. He gave it full expression and he did so very courageously. But the time needed more than this from one who was to restore it to health and to holiness, to holiness indeed first of all, in order that it might have health.

Made in the USA
San Bernardino, CA
29 August 2015